Informatik aktuell

Herausgeber: W. Brauer
im Auftrag der Gesellschaft für Informatik (GI)

Karsten Berns
Tobias Luksch (Hrsg.)

Autonome Mobile Systeme 2007

20. Fachgespräch
Kaiserslautern, 18./19. Oktober 2007

Herausgeber

Karsten Berns
Tobias Luksch
Technische Universität Kaiserslautern
Fachbereich Informatik
Arbeitsgruppe Robotersysteme
Postfach 3049
67653 Kaiserslautern
http://agrosy.informatik.uni-kl.de

Bibliographische Information der Deutschen Bibliothek
Die Deutsche Bibliothek verzeichnet diese Publikation in der Deutschen Nationalbibliografie; detaillierte bibliografische Daten sind im Internet über http://dnb.ddb.de abrufbar.

CR Subject Classification (2001): I.2.9, I.2.10, I.2.11, I.4.7, I.4.8, J.7

ISSN 1431-472-X
ISBN 978-3-540-74763-5 Springer Berlin Heidelberg New York

Springer Berlin Heidelberg New York
Springer ist ein Unternehmen von Springer Science+Business Media

springer.de

Printed in Germany

Satz: Reproduktionsfertige Vorlage vom Autor/Herausgeber
Gedruckt auf säurefreiem Papier SPIN: 12118793 33/3180-543210

Vorwort

Das 20. Fachgespräch „Autonome Mobile Systeme (AMS)“ findet am 18. und 19. Oktober 2007 in Kaiserslautern statt und wird von der Arbeitsgruppe Robotersysteme des Fachbereich Informatik ausgerichtet. Diese Tagung, die zum ersten mal an der Technischen Universität Kaiserslautern durchgeführt wird, hat das Ziel, Wissenschaftlerinnen und Wissenschaftler aus Forschung und Industrie, die auf dem Gebiet der autonomen und teilautonomen mobilen Roboter forschen und entwickeln, zusammenzubringen. Vor allem Nachwuchswissenschaftlern soll die Möglichkeit gegeben werden, die Ergebnisse aktueller Forschungsarbeiten auf diesem Gebiet zu diskutieren. Da die Tagung traditionell auf den deutschsprachigen Raum ausgerichtet ist, wird vor allem der nationalen Robotikindustrie die Möglichkeit zum Dialog mit Wissenschaftlern gegeben.

Inhaltlich setzt das Fachgespräch den diesjährigen Schwerpunkt auf Arbeiten im Bereich der kognitiven Automobile und der Laufmaschinen. Zu diesen beiden Themenblöcken werden auch die eingeladenen Übersichtsvorträge stattfinden. Gerade im Gebiet der kognitiven Systeme werden in der Forschung zur Zeit sowohl vollständig autonome Fahrzeuge als auch PKW-Assistenzsysteme erforscht. An den diesjährigen Beiträgen zeigt sich, dass diese beiden Bereiche immer weiter zusammenwachsen und sich positive Synergieeffekte einstellen. Die Laufmaschinenforschung in Deutschland, die noch in den 90er Jahren zur internationalen Spitze gehörte, wurde aufgrund geänderter öffentlicher Förderschwerpunkte nur noch gering unterstützt. Vor allem in den letzten beiden Jahren haben unterschiedliche Forschungsgruppen über kleinere Projekte begonnen, sich intensiv mit Laufmaschinen zu beschäftigen. Deshalb sieht sich die AMS 2007 als ein Forum, diese Forschungsgruppen zum wissenschaftlichen Erfahrungsaustausch zusammenzuführen. Über die genannten Schwerpunkte hinaus sind Beiträge aus den Bereichen Kartierung und Lokalisation, Navigation, Lernverfahren, System- und Steuerungsarchitekturen sowie der Anwendung von autonomen mobilen Systemen vertreten.

In diesem Jahr wurden für die AMS Kurzfassungen für über 60 Beiträge eingereicht. Der Fachgesprächsbeirat hat aus diesen Arbeiten 53 ausgewählt, wobei 45 in einen Vortrag und 8 in einer Poster Session präsentiert werden. Zusätzlich zu den wissenschaftlichen Präsentationen werden in einer Ausstellung mehr als 20 Roboter vorgestellt, um den hohen Leistungsstand bei der Entwicklung dieser Systeme einem breiten Publikum zu demonstrieren.

Die Organisatoren der AMS 2007 möchten sich zunächst beim Fachgesprächsbeirat für die Begutachtung und Auswahl der Beiträge bedanken. Unser herzlicher Dank gilt auch den Autoren für die Einreichung der wissenschaftlichen Arbeiten, die wie in den letzten Jahren von hoher inhaltlicher Qualität sind. Weiterhin sei auch Prof. Dr. Dr. h.c. Brauer, dem Herausgeber der Buchreihe "Informatik Aktuell" sowie dem Springer-Verlag für die erneute Bereitschaft, das Buch herauszugeben, und Frau Glaunsinger für ihre Unterstützung bei der

Erstellung des Manuskripts gedankt. Auch für die Durchführung einer Konferenz mittlerer Größe ist ein enormer organisatorischer Aufwand notwendig. Ohne den unermüdlichen Einsatz der Mitarbeiter, der Studenten sowie des Sekretariats der Arbeitsgruppe Robotersysteme, denen wir hiermit herzlich danken wollen, wäre diese Veranstaltung nicht möglich gewesen. Wir wünschen allen Teilnehmerinnen und Teilnehmern eine Tagung mit interessanten wissenschaftlichen Beiträgen und Exponaten, neuen Anregungen durch intensive Diskussionen, und angenehme Tage in Kaiserslautern.

Kaiserslautern, im August 2007

Die Herausgeber:
Karsten Berns, Tobias Luksch

Inhaltsverzeichnis

Kartierung und Lokalisation

Navigation

System- und Steuerungsarchitektur

Lernverfahren

Mensch-Roboter Interaktion

Kognitives Automobil

Laufmaschinen

Anwendungen

SVMs for Vibration-Based Terrain Classification

Christian Weiss, Matthias Stark and Andreas Zell

University of Tübingen, Department of Computer Science, Sand 1, 72076 Tübingen

Abstract. When an outdoor mobile robot traverses different types of ground surfaces, different types of vibrations are induced in the body of the robot. These vibrations can be used to learn a discrimination between different surfaces and to classify the current terrain. Recently, we presented a method that uses Support Vector Machines for classification, and we showed results on data collected with a hand-pulled cart. In this paper, we show that our approach also works well on an outdoor robot. Furthermore, we more closely investigate in which direction the vibration should be measured. Finally, we present a simple but effective method to improve the classification by combining measurements taken in multiple directions.

1 Introduction

In outdoor environments, a mobile robot should be able to adapt its driving style to the ground surface. Some surfaces like asphalt are flat and not slippery, and thus the robot can safely traverse them at high speeds. Other surfaces, like sand or gravel, are dangerous because they are slippery and/or bumpy. To prevent accidents or damages to the hardware, the robot has to traverse these surfaces carefully at low speed. Such hazards that originate from the ground surface itself can be called *non-geometric hazards* [1]. A system which can determine the type of the current or forthcoming ground surface therefore greatly contributes to the safety of a robot.

Iagnemma and Dubowsky first suggested to detect non-geometric hazards by vibrations that are induced in the robot while traversing the terrain [2]. The vibrations are different for different terrain types, and characteristic vibration signals can be learned for each terrain type. Based on the learned model, the terrain class of a newly collected vibration signal is estimated. Such a method can be used as a stand-alone classifier or to supplement other sensors.

Commonly, accelerometers are used to measure vibrations. The accelerometers can be placed at the wheels or the axes of the robot, as well as on the robot's body. Mostly, the acceleration is measured in up-down (z) direction. However, this paper shows that it could be better to use the acceleration measured in front-back (x) or left-right (y) direction.

Brooks and Iagnemma presented vibration-based terrain classification for low-speed planetary rovers [3]. They use *Principal Component Analysis* (PCA) to reduce the dimensionality of the vibration data and *Linear Discriminant Analysis* (LDA) for classification. Sadhukhan and Moore proposed an approach that is based on *Probabilistic Neural Networks* [4,5]. They used an RWI ATRV-JR robot driving up to 0.8 m/s. In [6], we presented an approach that uses *Support Vector Machines* (SVM) for classification. Stavens *et al.* suggested a method for vehicles driving up to 35 mph [7]. However, they focus on determining the roughness of the terrain to adapt the speed of the vehicle, instead of grouping the terrain into classes.

In [6], we presented experiments on data collected by a hand-pulled cart. This cart has relatively hard rubber wheels which lead to clear vibration signals. The big, air-filled wheels of common outdoor robots, however, are likely to dampen the vibrations. Therefore, this paper presents experiments that use our method on vibration data collected by an RWI ATRV-JR outdoor robot. We also more closely investigate the influence of different robot velocities on the classification. Additionally, we evaluate in which direction the acceleration signals should be measured. Finally, we propose a simple method to improve classification if the robot is able to measure accelerations in multiple directions.

2 Terrain Classification Method

This section summarizes our terrain classification approach presented in [6] and suggests a simple way to improve classification by using multiple directions of vibrations.

2.1 Basic Method

Our terrain classification approach has two phases: training and classification. Training is computationally intensive and therefore an offline step. Classification is very fast and can be done online. In the training phase, we learn characteristic vibration signals for known terrain types. For this purpose, the robot traverses different surfaces and collects vibration signals. To collect the vibrations, we use an accelerometer that works at 100 Hz. In the next step, we split the acceleration signals into segments, where each segment corresponds to 1 s of robot travel. In our case, this leads to 1×100-sized vectors. We then label each vector with the terrain type it corresponds to. Fig. 1 shows example acceleration vectors for some terrain types. Except for grass, they appear very similar to a human.

Next, we transform the raw acceleration signals to the frequency domain. In [6], we compared different transformations. Despite the fact that a 128-point Fast Fourier Transform (FFT) led to worse results than other tranformations on the cart data, we found the FFT to work best for the ATRV-JR data. After applying the FFT to each vector, we normalize each feature (= frequency component) to mean 0 and standard deviation 1. The normalization prevents features with high magnitude from dominating the training.

Next, we train a Support Vector Machine (SVM) [8,9] on the feature vectors. As kernel function we use a Radial Basis Function (RBF) $k(x, y) = \exp(-\|x - y\|^2/2\sigma^2))$, where x and y are two feature vectors. We tune the width σ of the RBF kernel together with the soft margin parameter C (which regularizes

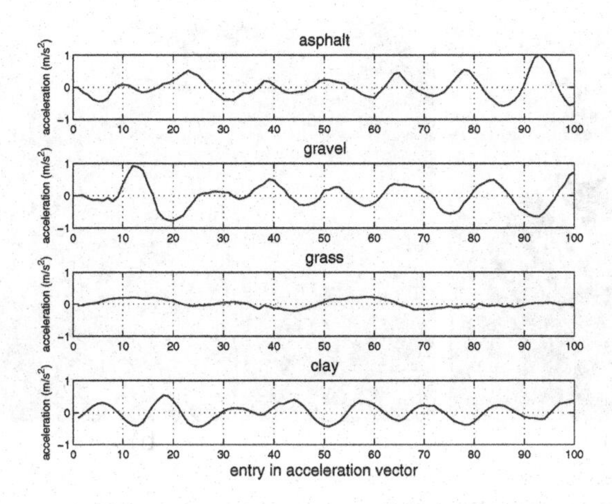

Fig. 1. Some example acceleration vectors for asphalt, gravel, grass and clay.

the trade-off between maximizing the margin between two classes and minimizing the training error) of the SVM by a grid search. The grid is defined by $\log_2 \sigma \in \{\hat{\sigma}/4, ..., 4\hat{\sigma}\}$ and $\log_2 C \in \{-2, .., 14\}$, were $\hat{\sigma}$ is set such that $\exp(-D/2\hat{\sigma}^2) = 0.1$. D denotes the length of the feature vectors. Each candidate parameter vector (σ, C) on the grid is evaluated by 5-fold cross-validation. The grid parameters are standard ones that are often used in other applications, too. As SVM implementation, we use LIBSVM [10].

In the classification phase, the robot traverses unknown terrain and collects vibration signals. Once per second, it creates a 1×100 test vector from the acceleration values taken during the last second and transforms the vector using the FFT. Additionally, the robot normalizes the feature vector using the same parameters used during training. Then, the trained SVM classifies the test vector and returns the estimated terrain type.

2.2 Combining Different Directions of Vibrations

In vibration-based terrain classification methods, vibration is commonly represented by the acceleration measured in up-down (z) direction. The reason is that bumps in the terrain are likely to have their major effect in up-down direction. However, the accelerations measured in other directions, e.g. front-back (x) or left-right (y), can also be used to capture the vibration. Our experiments presented in Section 3 show that these accelerations may even be more suitable for classification than the data measured in z direction.

In addition, many acceleration sensors are able to measure accelerations along three axes simultaneously. For robots equipped with such a sensor, we propose a simple but effective method to improve classification. For each terrain segment, we collect the acceleration signals along all three axes, in our case front-back (x), left-right (y), and up-down (z). Then, we transform the signals individually by

Fig. 2. a) Our RWI ATRV-JR outdoor robot "Arthur". b) The terrain types we used in our experiments: 1) indoor floor, 2) asphalt, 3) gravel, 4) grass, 5) paving, 6) clay.

the FFT. Next, we concatenate the transformed feature vectors and normalize the features. We then train the SVM on these feature vectors.

In the classification phase, we perform the same steps to get a test vector containing information about all three directions of accelerations. Finally, we classify the test vector using the SVM.

3 Experimental Results

To get experimental data, we used our RWI ATRV-JR outdoor robot (Fig. 2 a). We mounted an Xsens MTi sensor on an aluminium plate on top of the robot. The sensor measures the acceleration in x, y and z direction simultaneously at 100 Hz.

In total, we collected 10225 terrain vectors, some of them in mid-July and some in the beginning of December. Each terrain vector corresponds to 1 s of robot travel. The terrain vectors differ in the type of terrain and in the velocity of the robot. As terrain types, we used indoor floor, asphalt, gravel, grass, paving, clay (a boule court), and the situation in which the robot did not move (Fig. 2 b). The velocity of the robot was one of 0.2 m/s, 0.4 m/s or 0.6 m/s. Tab. 1 shows an overview of the dataset.

For evaluation, we used 10-fold cross validation, i.e. for each experiment, we split the data into 10 parts and evaluated 10 sub-experiments (= folds). In each fold, we used 9 parts for training and the 10th part for testing. The final result is the mean over the results of the individual folds.

Fig. 3 a) and Tab. 2 show the results of a first set of experiments, for which we used the three terrain classes grass, clay and gravel. We expected that higher speeds of the robot would lead to stronger vibrations and therefore to clearer vibration signals. However, the 3-class experiments did not confirm this expectation. Data collected at 0.2 and 0.6 m/s could be classified similarly well and

Table 1. Number of samples per class in our dataset

class	0.2 m/s	0.4 m/s	0.6 m/s	total
indoor floor	282	549	581	1412
asphalt	499	513	600	1612
gravel	311	323	392	1026
grass	482	572	631	1685
paving	314	573	567	1454
clay	423	579	605	1607
no motion	199	615	615	1429
total	2510	3724	3991	10225

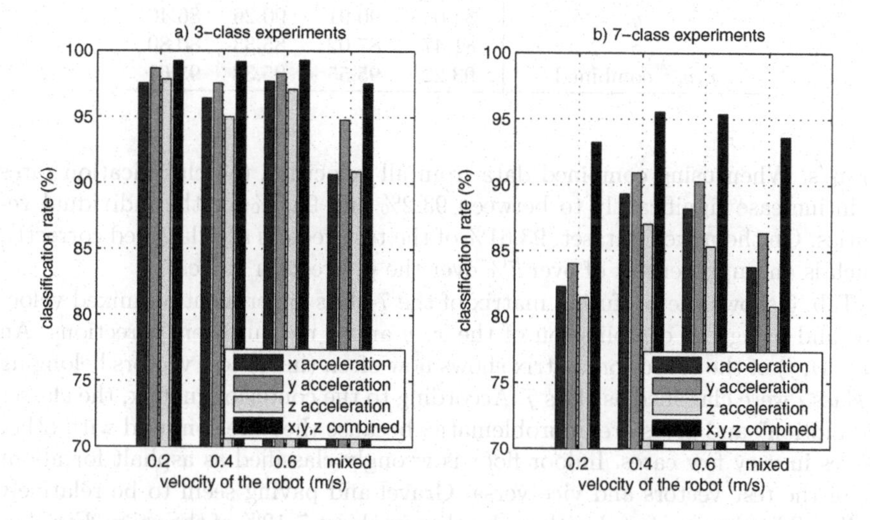

Fig. 3. Experimental results using a) 3 terrain classes, b) 7 terrain classes.

data collected at 0.4 m/s only slightly worse. However, in experiments on all velocities mixed together in one dataset, the classification rates decrease.

The experiments show that the vibration measured in y direction leads to better results than the vibration measured in x or z direction. The y data leads to classification rates of about 98.5% for robot speeds of 0.2 and 0.6 m/s, to 97.54% for 0.4 m/s and to 94.78% on mixed velocities. When combining the data from all three directions, the results get even better. For all individual velocities, the classification rate is higher than 99%. On the mixed dataset, 97.52% of the test vectors are classified correctly.

Fig. 3 b) and Tab. 3 present the results of experiments involving all seven terrain classes. In these experiments, the results for data collected at 0.2 m/s are significantly worse than for data collected at 0.4 or 0.6 m/s. Again, vibration data measured in y direction are classified better than data of the other directions. Additionally, x data yields to better results than z data. The classification rates for the y data are 84.04% at 0.2 m/s, 90.91% at 0.4 m/s and 90.26% at

Table 2. Classification rates (%) of the 3-class experiments

measurement direction	0.2 m/s	0.4 m/s	0.6 m/s	mixed
x	97.53	96.39	97.71	90.63
y	98.67	97.54	98.26	94.78
z	97.84	95.00	97.09	90.84
x, y, z combined	99.20	99.18	99.30	97.52

Table 3. Classification rates (%) of the 7-class experiments

measurement direction	0.2 m/s	0.4 m/s	0.6 m/s	mixed
x	82.28	89.31	88.19	83.78
y	84.04	90.91	90.26	86.40
z	81.47	87.02	85.33	80.80
x, y, z combined	93.22	95.55	95.38	93.61

0.6 m/s. When using combined data from all velocities, the classification rates again increase significantly to between 93.2% and 95.5% for the individual velocities. On the mixed dataset, 93.61% of the test vectors are classified correctly, which is an improvement of over 7% over the y direction alone.

Tab. 4 shows the confusion matrix of the 7-class experiment on mixed velocities and using the combination of the x, y and z measurement directions. An entry (i, j) of the confusion matrix shows how often (in %) test vectors belonging to class i were classified as class j. According to the confusion matrix, the classes "no motion" and grass are unproblematic, because they are confused with other classes in very few cases. Indoor floor is wrongly classified as asphalt for about 3% of the test vectors and vice versa. Gravel and paving seem to be relatively similar. They are confused with each other in about 7-12% of the cases. For clay, there is no clear trend towards misclassifiying it as a particular class.

On a 3 GHz Pentium 4 PC with 1 GB of RAM, classifying one terrain vector takes less than 1 ms. The time for training depends on the dataset. For example, training in the 3-class experiment on y data collected at 0.2 m/s takes about 7 min 4 s. This dataset contains 1216 feature vectors. Another example is the 7-class dataset with combined acceleration directions and mixed speeds. This dataset contains 10225 feature vectors, and training takes about 14 h 24 min.

4 Conclusion

This paper showed that our vibration-based terrain classification method presented in [6] works well on a common outdoor robot. Additionally, we presented a technique to improve the classification by using vibrations measured in different directions.

A comparison between data measured in front-back (x), left-right (y) and up-down (z) direction showed that the y data leads to significantly better classification rates than the z data. However, it is not clear if this result is specific for

Table 4. Confusion matrix (%) of the 7-class experiment with mixed velocities and combined measurement directions

	no motion	indoor	asphalt	gravel	grass	paving	clay
no motion	**99.79**	0	0	0	0.21	0	0
indoor	0	**94.05**	2.90	0.43	0.14	0.14	2.34
asphalt	0	3.29	**93.18**	0.37	0.19	1.12	1.86
gravel	0	0	0	**84.80**	3.12	11.89	0.20
grass	0	0	0	1.18	**98.34**	0.36	0.19
paving	0	0	0.96	6.88	0.21	**90.44**	1.51
clay	0	1.43	0.50	0.93	1.00	1.49	**94.65**

our robot or if this result can be generalized for robots of other types. Nevertheless, the result shows that it is worth trying some other measurement directions before relying on the up-down vibration. Our experiments showed that if the robot is able to measure the acceleration in multiple directions simultaneously, including all available information into the feature vector significantly improves the classification rate.

For future work, we plan online learning, where the new information of the test phase is integrated into the model. The robot should also be able to notice if it traverses some terrain that it has never traversed before.

References

1. Wilcox B. H.: Non-Geometric Hazard Detection for a Mars Microrover. Proc. AIAA Conf. on Intelligent Robots in Field, Factory, Service, Space. Houston, TX, pp. 675 - 684, 1994
2. Iagnemma K., Dubowsky S.: Terrain Estimation for High-Speed Rough-Terrain Autonomous Vehicle Navigation. Proc. SPIE Conf. on Unmanned Ground Vehicle Technology IV, 2002
3. Brooks C. A., Iagnemma K.: Vibration-Based Terrain Classification for Planetary Exploration Rovers. IEEE Trans. on Robotics, 21(6), pp. 1185 - 1191, 2005
4. Sadhukhan D., Moore C.: Online Terrain Estimation Using Internal Sensors. Proc. Florida Conf. on Recent Advances in Robotics, Boca Raton, FL, 2003
5. Sadhukhan D.: Autonomous Ground Vehicle Terrain Classification Using Internal Sensors. Masters Thesis, Dept. Mech. Eng., Florida State University, 2004
6. Weiss C., Fröhlich H., Zell, A.: Vibration-based Terrain Classification Using Support Vector Machines. Proc. IEEE/RSJ Int. Conf. on Intelligent Robots and Systems, Beijing, China, pp. 4429 - 4434, 2006
7. Stavens D., Hoffmann G., Thrun S.: Online Speed Adaptation Using Supervised Learning for High-Speed, Off-Road Autonomous Driving. Proc. Int. Joint Conf. on Artificial Intelligence, Hyderabad, India, 2007
8. Cortes C., Vapnik V.: Support Vector Networks. Machine Learning, 20, pp. 273 - 297, 1995
9. Schölkopf B., Smola A. J.: Learning with Kernels. MIT Press, Cambridge, MA, 2002
10. Chang C. C., Lin C. J.: LIBSVM: A Library for Support Vector Machines. Software available at http://www.csie.ntu.edu.tw/~cjlin/libsvm, 2001

Bearing-Only SLAM with an Omnicam

Robust Selection of SIFT Features for Service Robots

Siegfried Hochdorfer and Christian Schlegel

University of Applied Sciences
Fakultät Informatik, Prittwitzstr. 10, D-89075 Ulm
schlegel@hs-ulm.de

Abstract. SLAM mechanisms are a key component towards advanced service robotics applications. Currently, a major hurdle are the still high costs of suitable range measuring devices. A solution are bearing-only SLAM approaches since these can be used with cheap sensors like omnicams. The general approach of using an Extended Kalman Filter (EKF) for bearing-only SLAM based on artificial landmarks has been described and evaluated in [2][1]. Instead of artificial landmarks, we now use SIFT features [3] as natural landmarks.
This paper describes SIFT feature preselection and landmark identification mechanisms that are pivotal towards the robust application of SIFT features within a bearing-only SLAM approach based on the EKF. We exploit viewing areas to massively reduce ambiguities and mismatches in SIFT feature reobservations and thus significantly reduce false identifier assignments.
The approach has been successfully evaluated on a Pioneer-3DX platform in an unmodified indoor environment. The results show that bearing-only SLAM produces reliable results even with cheap vision sensors and natural landmarks.

1 Introduction

Many advanced applications for service robots require goal directed motions or systematic coverage of free space. This is best implemented based on pose knowledge. Of course, there is a large body of work available on pose estimation, pose tracking, relocalization or SLAM (simultaneous mapping and localization). However, one cannot neglect the specific demands on service robots. For instance, in most applications of service robots the consumer neither accepts modifications of the environment (like artificial landmarks) nor complex and time consuming deployment efforts. Thus, a SLAM component based on cheap sensors working without artificial landmarks is a key technology for many service robotic applications.

As long as no calibrated systems are needed, omnicams are cheap and small and thus suitable for service robots. Although omnicams provide feature rich information on the surrounding of the robot with high update rates, they do not provide range information. Thus a bearing-only SLAM approach is applied that only requires observation angles of landmarks.

Instead of articial landmarks, we now use SIFT features [3] as natural landmarks within the EKF based bearing-only SLAM framework presented in [1]. The SLAM state vector comprises the robot pose (x, y, ϕ) and 2d landmark poses (x_i, y_i). Depending on the parameter settings, a single omnicam image contains up to several hundred SIFT features. However, the EKF based approach shows two characteristics that need to be adressed. It does not scale well with increasing numbers of landmarks and it is very brittle with respect to false landmark identifications. Thus one needs a very robust mechanism to select a small but stable number of SIFT features in an image. These have to be distributed sparsely over the image and should also possess characteristic descriptor values to avoid false assignments.

2 Related Work

The bearing-only SLAM mechanism is explained in detail in [1]. This paper uses the exactly same approach but replaces the artifical landmarks (colored cylinders) by natural landmarks described by SIFT features. The *iterative SIFT* approach is based on a particle filter [5]. However, due to the particle filter, a much higher number of keypoints is needed compared to our approach. In our case, a small number of keypoints is even mandatory and we can set the SIFT parameters such that only very stable keypoints survive. Another particle filter based approach that estimates 3d landmark poses based on SIFT features is presented in [6]. A highly sophisticated monocular SLAM approach that extends beyond robotics is presented in [7].

3 Calculation of SIFT Features

The SIFT approach (scale invariant feature transforms) takes an image and transforms it into a „large collection of local feature vectors“ [3]. Each feature vector is invariant to scaling, rotation or translation of an image. SIFT features are also very resilient to the effects of noise in an image. Thus, SIFT features are means to describe natural landmarks. For instance, we do not have to rely on specific shape or color models.

SIFT features of an image are calculated by four steps executed consecutively. We apply the plain calculation scheme described in detail in [3]. The *first step* is named *scale-space extrema detection.* In our case, we use an omnicam image of size 480x480. The first octave consists of five images, that is the original image and another four images. The latter are obtained by repeatedly convolving the original image with Gaussians. We use a σ-value of 2.2. This parameter is very stable and can thus be determined empirically. A larger value increases the computational load without improving the re-recognition of SIFT features. It is set such that the output of the overall processing chain is a stable set of roughly 30 SIFT features. Now the four DOG (difference of gaussians) images are calculated. Finally, extrema are detected in the two inner DOG images by comparing a pixel to its 26-neighbors in 3x3 regions. We use a down-sampling factor of 2 where downsampling ends at an image of 4x4 pixels. Therefore, we consider 7 octaves. The *second step* is named *keypoint localization.* The contrast threshold is set to 0.15 (Lowe 0.03) and is again determined empirically. We first set it such that we obtain stable landmarks. Then we modify this threshold to reduce the number of obtained landmarks. Finally we modify it to reduce the computational load without further reducing the number of landmarks. The curvature threshold r is set to 10 (same as Lowe). The *third step* is named *orientation assignment.* Since we do not further exploit the orientation value, we omit this step. The *fourth step* is named *keypoint descriptor.* As described in [3], we use 4x4 sample regions with 8 gradients and perform a gaussian weighting with $\sigma = 1.5$. The result are SIFT feature vectors each of dimension 128 with 8 bit entries.

4 Bearing-Only SLAM with SIFT Features

The overall sequence of processing steps is shown in figure 1. It is important to note that we only use the observation angles of landmarks in the omnicam image. The observation angle of a landmark in the omnicam image is equivalent to the yaw-angle γ of the landmark in the 3d-environment when using polar-coordinates (pitch β, yaw γ, distance d). As can be seen in figure 2, the image distortion of the omnicam does not affect the observation angle. Of course, all landmarks with the same yaw-angle γ but different pitch-angles β possess the same observation angle. In case of distinct SIFT feature vectors, we just have different landmarks at the same observation angle. Otherwise, the same features occured at the same yaw-angle but at different pitch-angles and thus need not to be discriminated.

4.1 Processing of an Image

Each omnicam image is reduced to a 480x480 resolution. Now SIFT features are extracted based on the standard attributes (gaussian filter, contrast, curvature ratio). Since the omnicam image also comprises the robot and mountings of the cam, we finally remove all SIFT features in those areas by a simple masking operation. Then the current robot pose gets a unique index and is added to the EKF state vector as image acquisition pose to allow for delayed feature initialization as described in [1][2]. Each SIFT feature descriptor of the current image gets labeled by the above pose index.

4.2 Assigning Identifiers to SIFT-features

The decision tree behind the identifier assignment procedure is illustrated in figure 3. The SIFT feature descriptors of the current image are compared with all the SIFT feature descriptors of the previous images. However, we only consider those images where the euclidean distance to the image acquisition pose is less than two times the maximum viewing distance of the omnicam (in our case 15m).

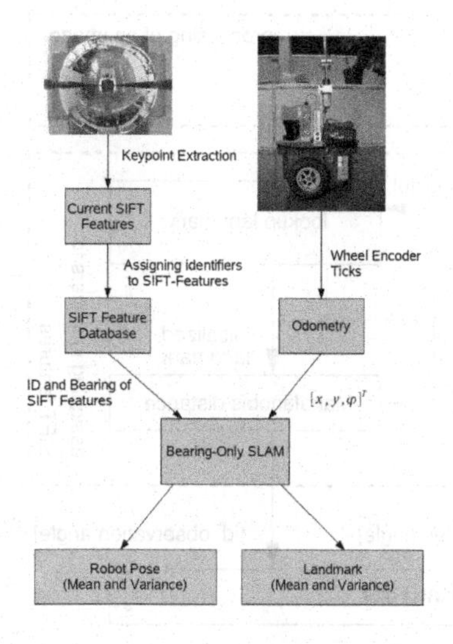

Fig. 1. The overall system.

Fig. 2. Identified SIFT features.

Next the euclidean distance between the current SIFT feature vectors and the remaining ones of the previous step are calculated.

A SIFT feature of the current image is considered as not matching an already known landmark (either initialized or not initialized landmark) if the ratio of the smallest and second smallest distance value is above a given threshold (value 0.6 [3]). In that case, this SIFT feature gets a new and unique identifier. This SIFT feature is the first observation of a potentially new landmark (first measurement of an uninitialized landmark).

Otherwise, the SIFT feature is considered as matching an already known landmark. In this case we have to check whether the SIFT feature matched an initialized or an uninitialized landmark. In the first case, the considered SIFT feature is just a reobservation of an already known landmark. This now is validated by a Mahalanobis distance based test [4]. In case this test is passed, the measurement is forwarded to the EKF as reobservation of the initialized landmark. Otherwise, the current measurement and its SIFT feature is the first observation of a potentially new landmark (first measurement of an uninitialized landmark).

In the second case, we solely have several observations (bearing-only measurements) of the same SIFT feature (uninitialized landmark) from different observation poses. Since in that case we cannot apply the Mahalanobis distance, we use geometrical reasoning for validating the reobservation. The new observation can belong to the uninitialized landmark only if its viewing direction intersects the visual cone given by the previous measurements of this uninitialized landmark. In that case this SIFT feature is considered as a new observation of this not yet initialized landmark. Otherwise this SIFT feature is the first observation of a potentially new landmark (first measurement of an uninitialized landmark).

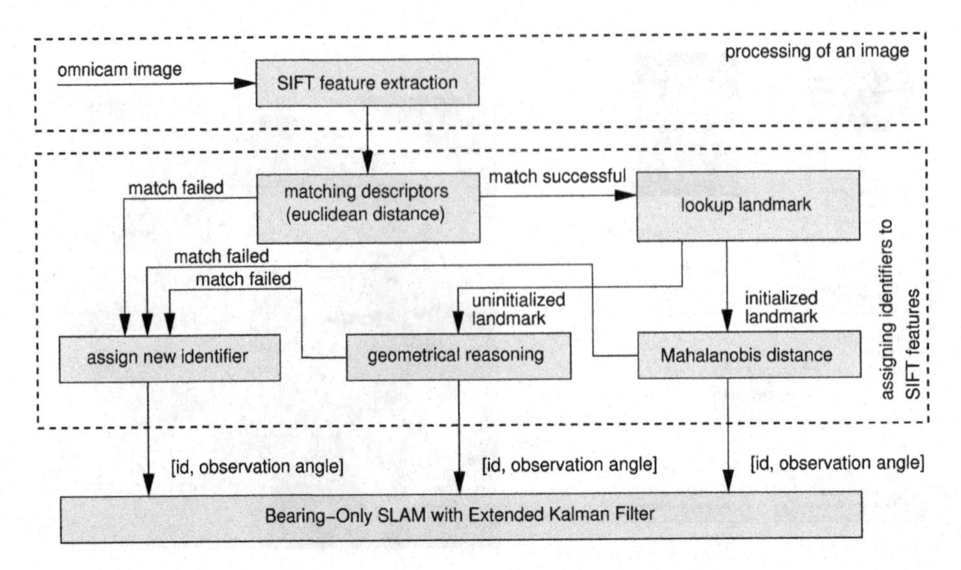

Fig. 3. Assignment of identifiers to SIFT-features.

4.3 Geometrical Reasoning

In case of an uninitialized landmark, covariances are not yet available. Thus, we cannot apply the Mahalanobis distance to validate the assignment. Therefore, we apply a simple geometrical validation scheme that reliably sorts out impossible matches. In figure 4, $P2$ denotes the current robot pose with a being the vector towards the previous robot pose $P1$ and $c2$ limiting the viewing range. At $P1$ a landmark L has been seen with heading b and a maximum distance as indicated by $c1$. Thus, L can only be seen from $P2$ in case its observation angle is in the range r.

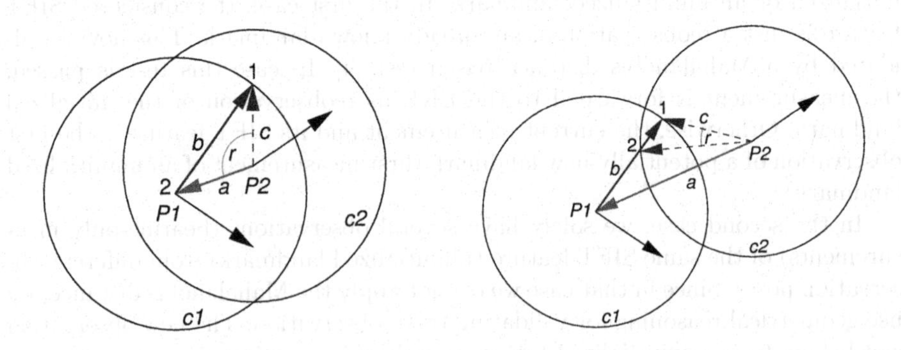

Fig. 4. Geometrical validation of matches.

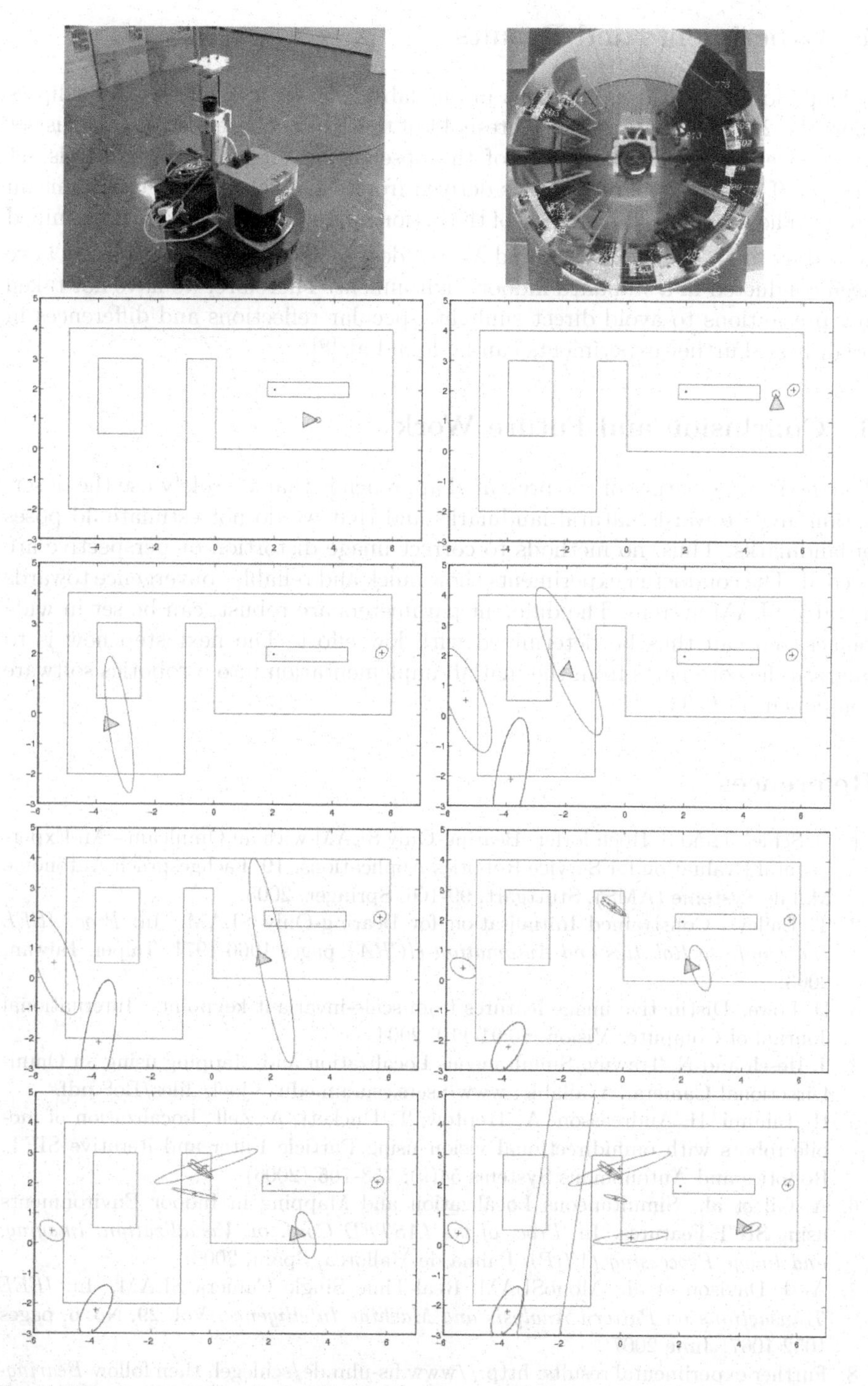

Fig. 5. The sensing steps 5, 9, 35, 40, 52, 53, 54 and 56 of a 75 step run with closing a loop.

5 Experiments and Results

A loop closure SLAM experiment in our lab is shown in figure 5. The ellipses show the 2-sigma contour. The threshold of the Kullback-Leibler distance is set to 12 (see [1]). The uncertainty of the observation angle measurement is set to $\sigma_\alpha^2 = 0.2727$ deg^2. This value is derived from a 1-pixel jitter in the omnicam image. The parameters σ_d^2 and σ_ϕ^2 of the action model of the robot are determined according to $\lambda_d = 0.001\ m^2/m$ and $\lambda_\phi = 4$ deg^2/360 deg. The experiments have been conducted in a standard indoor environment. Therefore, we have not taken any precautions to avoid direct sunlight, specular reflections and differences in brightness. Further experiments can be found at [8].

6 Conclusion and Future Work

The distinctive feature of the presented approach is that we solely use the observation angle towards natural landmarks and that we do not estimate 3d poses of landmarks. Thus, no methods to correct image distortion or perspective are needed. The conducted experiments show quick and reliable convergence towards a stable SLAM system. The different parameters are robust, can be set in wide ranges and can thus be determined with low effort. The next step now is to migrate the core parts from the matlab implementation into a robotics software component in C/C++.

References

1. C. Schlegel and S. Hochdorfer. Bearing-Only SLAM with an Omnicam - An Experimental Evaluation for Service Robotics Applications. 19. Fachgespräch Autonome Mobile Systeme (AMS), Stuttgart, 99-106, Springer, 2005.
2. T. Bailey. Constrained Initialisation for Bearing-Only SLAM. In: *Proc. IEEE Int. Conf. on Robotics and Automation (ICRA)*, pages 1966-1971, Taipei, Taiwan, 2003.
3. D. Lowe. Distinctive image features from scale-invariant keypoints. International Journal of Computer Vision, 60:91-110, 2004.
4. J. Hesch and N. Trawny. Simultaneous Localization and Mapping using an Omni-Directional Camera. Available: www-users.cs.umn.edu/~joel/_files/BoS.pdf.
5. H. Tamimi, H. Andreasson, A. Treptow, T. Duckett, A. Zell. Localization of mobile robots with omnidirectional vision using Particle Filter and iterative SIFT. Robotics and Autonomous Systems 54(9): 758-765 (2006)
6. A. Gil et al. Simultaneous Localization and Mapping in Indoor Environments using SIFT Features. In: *Proc. of the IASTED Conf. on Visualization, Imaging, and Image Processing (VIIP)*. Palma de Mallorca, Spain, 2006.
7. A. J. Davison et al. MonoSLAM: Real-Time Single Camera SLAM. In: *IEEE Transactions on Pattern Analysis and Machine Intelligence.* Vol. 29, No. 6, pages 1052-1067, June 2007.
8. Further experimental results: http://www.hs-ulm.de/schlegel, then follow *Bearing-Only SLAM*

Visual Bearing-Only Simultaneous Localization and Mapping with Improved Feature Matching

Hauke Strasdat, Cyrill Stachniss, Maren Bennewitz and Wolfram Burgard

Computer Science Institute, University of Freiburg, Germany

Abstract. In this this paper, we present a solution to the simultaneous localization and mapping (SLAM) problem for a robot equipped with a single perspective camera. We track extracted features over multiple frames to estimate the depth information. To represent the joint posterior about the trajectory of the robot and a map of the environment, we apply a Rao-Blackwellized particle filter. We present a novel method to match features using a cost function that takes into account differences between the feature descriptor vectors as well as spatial information. To find an optimal matching between observed features, we apply a global optimization algorithm. Experimental results obtained with a real robot show that our approach is robust and tolerant to noise in the odometry information of the robot. Furthermore, we present experiments that demonstrate the superior performance of our feature matching technique compared to other approaches.

1 Introduction

Mapping is one of the fundamental problems in mobile robotics since representations of the environment are needed for a series of high level applications. Without an appropriate model of the environment, for example, delivery tasks cannot be carried out efficiently. A large group of researchers investigated the so-called simultaneous localization and mapping (SLAM) problem. The majority of approaches focuses on proximity sensors to perceive the environment such as laser range finders, sonars, radars, or stereo vision cameras.

In this paper, we address the problem of learning maps using a mobile robot equipped with a single perspective camera only. Compared to a laser range finder, cameras have the advantage that they are cheap and lightweight. One of the problems, however, is the missing distance information to observed landmarks. This information is not provided by a perspective camera. We present a mapping system that can use this sensor setup to learn maps of the environment. Our approach applies a Rao-Blackwellized particle filter to maintain the joint posterior about the trajectory of the robot and the map of the environment. We furthermore present a novel method to establish the data association between features. It takes into account the individual feature descriptor vectors as well as spatial constraints. Our approach is able to compute the optimal matching between observed and already tracked features. To achieve this, we apply the Hungarian method which is an efficient global optimization algorithm. Experiments carried out with a real robot illustrate the advantages of our technique for learning maps with robots using a single perspective camera.

2 Related Work

Davison et al. [1,2] proposed a visual SLAM approach using a single camera that does not require odometry information. The system works reliable in room-size environments but is restricted in the number of landmarks it can handle. Landmarks are matched by looking back into the image at the expected region and by perfoming a local match. Sim et al. [3] use a stereo camera in combination with FastSLAM [4]. SIFT features [5] in both cameras are matched using their description vectors as well as the epipolar geometry of the stereo system. The matching between observations and landmarks is done using the SIFT descriptor only. In the bearing-only algorithm of Lemaire et al. [6], the feature depth is estimated using a mixture of Gaussians. The Gaussians are initialized along the first observation and they are pruned in the following frames.

3 Visual SLAM and Feature Matching

The joint posterior about the robot's trajectory and the map is represented by a Rao-Blackwellized Particle Filter (RBPF) similar to FastSLAM [4]. It allows the robot to efficiently model the joint posterior in a sampled fashion.

To obtain landmarks, we extract speeded-up visual features (SURF) [7] out of the camera images. These features are invariant to translation and scale. They can be extracted using a Fast-Hessian keypoint detector. The 64-dimensional feature descriptor vector d is computed using horizontal and vertical Haar wavelet responses. A rotational dependent version of SURF is used since the roll angle of the camera is fixed when it is attached to a wheeled robot.

In order to obtain spherical coordinates of a feature given its position in the image, we apply a standard camera model. In this way, pixel coordinates of detected keypoints are transformed into the azimuthal angle θ and the spherical angle ϕ. The distance ρ to the observed feature cannot be measured since we use only a monocular camera. The tuple (θ, ϕ) is referred to as bearing-only observation $\mathbf{z}$.

3.1 Observation Model

In this section, we assume that a map of 3D-landmark is given. Each landmark l is modeled by a 3D Gaussian (μ, Σ). Moreover, we assume data association problem between observed features and landmarks is solved. These assumption are relaxed in the subsequent sections.

For each particle k, each observation $\mathbf{z} = (\theta, \phi)^T$ perceived in the current frame is matched with a landmark $l \in M^{[k]}$, where $M^{[k]}$ is the map carried by particle k. For each complete assignment of the currently observed features to map features, an update of the Rao-Blackwellized particle filter is carried out.

In order to determine the likelihood of an observation $\mathbf{z}$ in the update step of the particle filter, we need to compute the predicted observation $\hat{\mathbf{z}}$ of landmark $l = (\mu, \Sigma)$ for particle k. To achieve this, we have to apply two transformations. First, we transform world coordinates $\mu = (\mu_1, \mu_2, \mu_3)^T$ into camera-centric coordinates $c = (c_1, c_2, c_3)^T$

using the function g. Afterwards, the camera-centric Cartesian point c is transformed into camera-centric spherical coordinates $\hat{\mathbf{z}} = (\hat{\rho}, \hat{\theta}, \hat{\phi})^T$ using the function h:

$$\hat{\mathbf{z}} = h(g(\mu_l, \mathbf{x}^{[k]})) \tag{1}$$

Here, $\mathbf{x}^{[k]}$ is the current pose of particle k. The corresponding measurement uncertainty Q is predicted using the Jacobean $G = h'(g'(\mu_l, x^{[k]}))$ as

$$Q = G \cdot \Sigma \cdot G^T + \mathrm{diag}(\sigma_\rho, \sigma_\theta, \sigma_\phi). \tag{2}$$

Here, Σ is the covariance matrix corresponding to landmark l, and σ_θ and σ_ϕ represent the uncertainty over the two spherical angles. The uncertainty over the depth σ_ρ is set to a high value in order to represent the bearing-only aspect of the update. The observation likelihood λ is based on a Gaussian model as

$$\lambda = |Q|^{-\frac{1}{2}} \exp\left(-\frac{1}{2} \begin{pmatrix} 0 \\ \theta - \hat{\theta} \\ \phi - \hat{\phi} \end{pmatrix}^T Q^{-1} \begin{pmatrix} 0 \\ \theta - \hat{\theta} \\ \phi - \hat{\phi} \end{pmatrix} \right). \tag{3}$$

Since the depth ρ to the observed feature is unknown, the pretended innovation $(\rho - \hat{\rho})$ is set to zero. We weight each particle k with respect to its observation likelihood λ.

Finally, the Kalman gain is calculated by $K = \Sigma \cdot G^T \cdot Q^{-1}$ so that the landmark (μ, Σ) can be updated using an *extended Kalman filter* (EKF) approach.

3.2 Depth Estimation and Landmark Initialization

Although it is possible to integrate bearing-only observations into the RBPF, the full 3D information is necessary in order to initialize landmarks in a 3D map. We track features over consecutive frames and estimate the depth ρ of the features using discrete probability distributions similar to [1] but in a bottom-up manner. When a feature f is initially observed, a 3D ray is cast from the camera origin o towards the observed feature. Equally weighted bins $b^{[j]}$ – representing different distances $\rho^{[j]}$ – are distributed uniformly along this ray within a certain interval. This reflects the fact that initially the distance to the feature is unknown. To get an estimate about the depth of the features, they are tracked over consecutive frames (the next subsection explains the feature matching process). In case the initial feature f is matched with a feature $\bar{f}$ in the consecutive frame, the bins are projected back into that frame. They lie on the so-called *epipolar line* [8], the projection of the 3D ray into the image. The depth hypotheses $\rho^{[j]}$ are weighted according to the distance to the pixel location of feature $\bar{f}$ using a Gaussian model. Figure 1 illustrates the estimation process for two features in consecutive frames. As soon as the variance of the histogram $Var(\rho^{[j]})$ falls below a certain threshold, the depth is estimated by the weighted average over the histogram $\rho = \sum_j h^{[j]} \cdot \rho^{[j]}$. If it is not possible to initialize a landmark within n frames, the corresponding feature is discarded (here n=5).

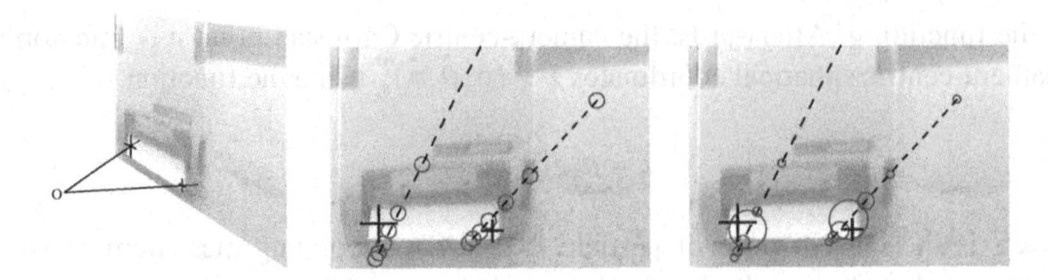

Fig. 1. This figure shows the depth estimation process for two features (crosses). Left: A ray is cast from the camera origin through the initial feature. Center: The ray is re-projected in the consecutive frame. This line (dashed) is called *epipolar line*. Depth hypotheses (circles) were distributed uniformly on the ray in the Cartesian space, which results in an irregular distribution in the image space. Right: Hypotheses are weighted according to their distance to the corresponding feature.

Depth Estimation as Preprocessing Step The robot's pose at the point in time, when the corresponding feature is observed initially, determines where the 3D ray is located in the world. Naïvely, for each particle a histogram of depth hypotheses has to be maintained so that the bins can be updated accordingly to the individual particle poses. However, this would lead to an overhead in computation time and memory. Fortunately, it is possible to maintain a depth histogram independently of the particles. The 3D ray is described by the angles θ, ϕ and an arbitrary origin o. Over the following n frames, the relative motion is added to o, so that the projection of the hypotheses' positions into the current frame can be calculated. Since the motion noise for wheeled robots is negligible within n frames, it can be omitted for the depth estimation process only.

Landmark Initialization Once a feature is reliably tracked and the depth of a feature is estimated, a landmark l is initialized. This has to be done for each particle k individually. Using the particle pose at the time t_f when feature f was observed for the first time, the global Cartesian landmark position μ can be calculated by

$$\mu_l := g^{-1}\left(h^{-1}\left(\rho_f, \theta_f, \phi_f\right), \mathbf{x}_{t_f}^{[k]}\right), \tag{4}$$

whereas the landmark uncertainty results from

$$\Sigma := G^{-T} \cdot H^{-1} \cdot R \cdot H^{-T} \cdot G^{-1}. \tag{5}$$

The uncertainty over the depth estimation process is reflected by the diagonal covariance matrix $R = \mathrm{diag}(Var(\rho_f^{[j]}), \sigma_\theta, \sigma_\phi)$.

3.3 Data Association

Finally, we describe how to match the current feature observations with landmarks in the map as well as with tracked features which are not yet contained in the map. This is done using the Hungarian method [9]. The Hungarian method is a general method to determine the optimal assignment under a given cost function. In our case, we use a cost function that takes into account differences of the feature descriptor vectors as well as well as spatial information to determine matches between observations and tracked features as well as between observations and landmarks.

Feature Matching Intuitively, features that are tracked to obtain the corresponding depth ρ can be matched based on their descriptor vectors using the Euclidean distance. However, this approach has a serious short-coming. Its performance is low on similar looking features since it completely ignores the feature positions. Thus, we instead use the distance of the descriptor vectors as a hard constraint. Only if the Euclidean distance falls below a certain threshold, a matching is considered. We define the cost function by means of the epipolar line introduced in Section 3.2. By setting the matching cost to the distance of the feature to this line in the image space (see Figure 2), not only the pixel locations of the comparing features are considered but also the relative movement of the robot between the corresponding frames is incorporated.

Landmark Matching Using Observation Likelihoods Similarly, during the matching process between landmarks and observations we use the distance of the descriptor vectors as a constraint. Landmarks are matched with observations using their positions. Since the observations are bearing-only, the distance to the landmark position cannot be computed directly. For this reason, the observation likelihood in Eq. (3) is used. It is high if and only if the distance between the observation and prediction is small. Thus, the cost is defined by the reciprocal of the observation likelihood $1/\lambda$. If the observation likelihood lies below a certain threshold, the cost are set to a maximum value. This refers to the fact that the features are regarded as different features with probability one.

4 Experimental Results

The first mapping experiment is performed on a wheeled robot equipped with a perspective camera and a laser range scanner (see Figure 3). The robot was steered through a 10m by 15m office environment for around 10 minutes. Two camera frames per second and odometry data was recorded. In addition, laser range data is stored in order to calculate a ground truth estimate of the robot's trajectory using scan matching on the laser data [10].

The results are illustrated in Figure 4. Following the presented approach, the average error of the robot path in terms of the Euclidean distance in the x/y-plane is 0.28m. The error in the orientation averages 3.9°. Using the odometry of the robot only, one obtains an average error of 1.69m in the x/y-plane and 22.8° in orientation.

We compared our feature matching approach using the Hungarian method on the distance to the projected line to other three techniques. Figure 5 shows a qualitative

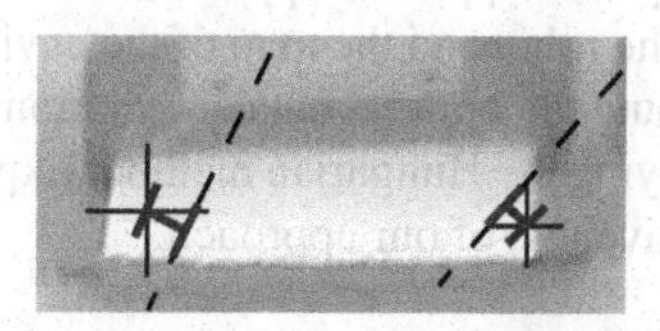

Fig. 2. Hungarian Matching: The cost function is set to the distance between the epipolar line and the feature location in the image space.

Fig. 3. Wheeled robot equipped with a perspective camera.

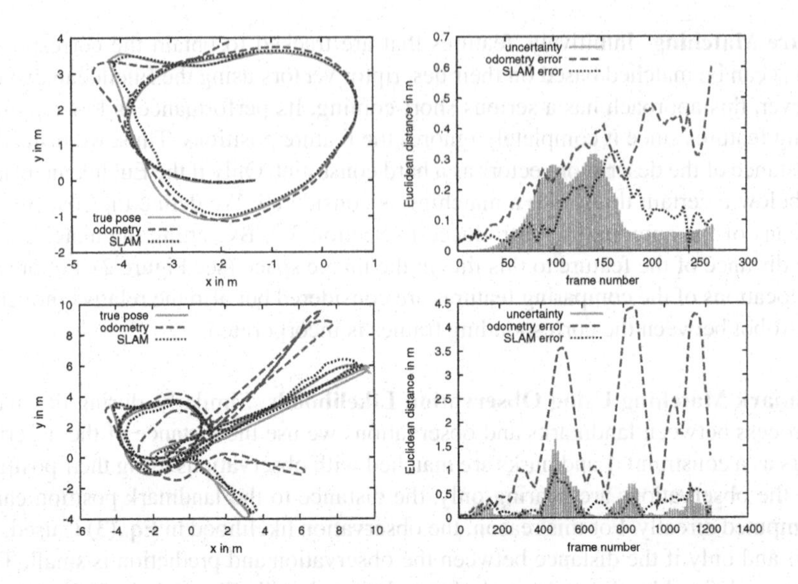

Fig. 4. The robot's trajectory is shown on the left, the corresponding error functions and uncertainty are shown on the right. Top: If the robot explores an unknown environment, the error values go up as well as the uncertainty. As soon as the loop is closed, the estimation error and uncertainty decreases, whereas the odometry error still goes up. Bottom: Complete trajectory.

evaluation of our approach on a difficult example – a heater which has a number of very similar looking features close to each other. Furthermore, we compare the Hungarian method quantitatively to the nearest neighbor approach, both using the distance to the epipolar line as cost function. If the Hungarian method is used, approximately 2% more landmarks are initialized. This number – obtained by four different sequences of 500 images each – can be explained by the fact that mismatches are likely to yield too high variances in the depth estimation. Landmarks, however, are initialized only if the depth can be estimated with low variance. By manual inspection, one can see that the data association has less errors than the nearest neighbor approach (see Figure 5).

5 Conclusions

In this paper, we presented a novel technique for learning maps with a mobile robot equipped with a single perspective camera only. Our approach applies a RBPF to maintain the joint posterior about the trajectory of the robot and the map of the environment. Using our approach, the robot is able to compute the optimal data association between observed and already mapped features by applying the Hungarian method. Experiments carried out with real a robot showed the effectiveness of our approach.

Acknowledgment

This work has partialy been supported by the German Research Foundation (DFG) under the contract numbers SFB/TR-8 and BE 2556/2-1. Special thanks to Dieter Fox,

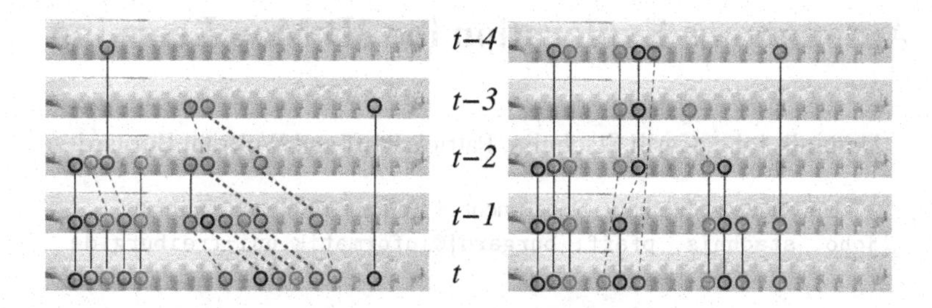

Fig. 5. Starting from the current frame at time t, we look back to evaluate how many features in the current frame were reliable tracked over the last four frames. The nearest neighbor assignment on SURF descriptors (left) results in 10 matches and 12 mismatches, whereas our approach results in 20 matches and 4 mismatches (right). Our approach also outperforms the two other combinations: nearest neighbor assignment using the projected line (14 matches, 7 mismatches) and the Hungarian method on the SURF descriptors (14 matches, 4 mismatches).

who supervised the first author in the early stages of developing the presented framework. We would like to thank Herbert Bay and Luc Van Gool for making the SURF binaries publicly available.

References

1. Davison A: Real-time simultaneous localization and mapping with a single camera. In Proc. of European Conf. on Computer Vision (ECCV), 2003.
2. Davision A, Reid I, Molton N, and Stasse O: MonoSLAM: Real-time single camera SLAM. IEEE Transaction on Pattern Analysis and Machine Intelligence 29(6), 2007.
3. Sim R, Elinas P, Griffin M, and Little J: Vision-based SLAM using a Rao-Blackwellized particle filter. In Proc. of IJCAI Workshop on Reasoning with Uncertainty in Robotics, 2005.
4. Montemerlo M, Thrun S, Koller D, and Wegbreit B: FastSLAM: A factored solution the to simultanieous localization and mapping problem. In Proc. of National Conference on Artificial Intelligence (AAAI), 2002.
5. Lowe D: Distinctive image feature from scale-invariant keypoints. In Proc. of International Journal of Computer Vision (IJCV), 2003.
6. Lemaire T, Lacroix S, and Sol J: A practical bearing-only SLAM algorithm. In Proc. of IEEE International Conf. on Intelligent Robots and Systems (IROS), 2005.
7. Bay H, Tuytelaars T, and Van Gool L: SURF: Speeded up robust features. In Proc. of European Conf. on Computer Vision (ECCV), 2006.
8. Hartley R and Zisserman A: Multiple View Geometry in Computer Vision. Cambirdige university press, second edition, 2003.
9. Kuhn H: The Hungarian method for the assigment problem. Naval Research Logistic Quaterly, 2:83-97, 1955.
10. Lu F and Milios E: Robot pose estimation in unkown environments by matching 2d range scans. In Proc. of IEEE Conference on Computer Vision and Pattern Recognition (CVPR), 935-938, 1994.

Autonomous Exploration for 3D Map Learning

Dominik Joho, Cyrill Stachniss, Patrick Pfaff and Wolfram Burgard

University of Freiburg, Department of Computer Science, Germany
{joho, stachnis, pfaff, burgard}@informatik.uni-freiburg.de

Abstract. Autonomous exploration is a frequently addressed problem in the robotics community. This paper presents an approach to mobile robot exploration that takes into account that the robot acts in the three-dimensional space. Our approach can build compact three-dimensional models autonomously and is able to deal with negative obstacles such as abysms. It applies a decision-theoretic framework which considers the uncertainty in the map to evaluate potential actions. Thereby, it trades off the cost of executing an action with the expected information gain taking into account possible sensor measurements. We present experimental results obtained with a real robot and in simulation.

1 Introduction

Robots that are able to acquire an accurate model of their environment are regarded as fulfilling a major precondition of truly autonomous mobile vehicles. So far, most approaches to mobile robot exploration assume that the robot lives in a plane. They typically focus on generating motion commands that minimize the time needed to cover the whole terrain [1,2]. A frequently used technique is to build an occupancy grid map since it can model unknown locations efficiently. The robot seeks to reduces the number of unobserved cells or the uncertainty in the grid map. In the three-dimensional space, however, such approaches are not directly applicable. The size of occupancy grid maps in 3D, for example, prevents the robot from exploring an environment larger than a few hundred square meters.

Whaite and Ferrie [3] presented an exploration approach in 3D that uses the entropy to measure the uncertainty in the geometric structure of objects that are scanned with a laser range sensor. In contrast to the work described here, they use a fully parametric representation of the objects and the size of the object to model is bounded by the range of the manipulator. Surmann et al. [4] extract horizontal planes from a 3D point cloud and construct a polygon with detected lines (obstacles) and unseen lines (free space connecting detected lines). They sample candidate viewpoints within this polygon and use 2D ray-casting to estimate the expected information gain. In contrast to this, our approach uses an extension of 3D elevation maps and 3D ray-casting to select the next viewpoint. González-Baños and Latombe [5] also build a polygonal map by merging safe regions. Similar to our approach, they sample candidate poses in the visibility range of frontiers to unknown area. But unlike in our approach, they build 2D maps and do not consider the uncertainty reduction in the known parts of the map.

The contribution of this paper is an exploration technique that extents known techniques from 2D into the three-dimensional space. Our approach selects actions that reduce the uncertainty of the robot about the world and constructs a full three-dimensional model using so-called multi-level surface maps. It reasons about the potential measurements when selecting an action. Our approach is able to deal with negative obstacles like, for example, abysms, which is a problem of robots exploring a three-dimensional world. Experiments carried out in simulation and on a real robot show the effectiveness of our technique.

2 3D Model of the Environment

Our exploration system uses multi-level surface maps (MLS maps) as proposed by Triebel et al. [6]. MLS maps use a two-dimensional grid structure that stores different elevation values. In particular, they store in each cell of a discrete grid the height of the surface in the corresponding area. In contrast to elevation maps, MLS maps allow us to store multiple surfaces in each cell. Each surface is represented by a Gaussian with the mean elevation and its uncertainty σ. In the remainder of this paper, these surfaces are referred to as patches. This representation enables a mobile robot to model environments with structures like bridges, underpasses, buildings, or mines. They also enable the robot to represent vertical structures by storing a vertical depth value for each patch.

2.1 Traversability Analysis

A grid based 2D traversability analysis usually only takes into account the occupancy probability of a grid cell – implicitly assuming an even environment with only positive obstacles. In the 3D case, especially in outdoor environments, we additionally have to take into account the slope and the roughness of the terrain, as well as negative obstacles such as abysms which are usually ignored in 2D representations.

Each patch p will be assigned a traversability value $\tau(p) \in [0,1]$. A value of zero corresponds to a non-traversable patch, a value greater zero to a traversable patch, and a value of one to a perfectly traversable patch. In order to determine $\tau(p)$, we fit a plane into its local 8-patch neighborhood by minimizing the z-distance of the plane to the elevation values of the neighboring patches. We then compute the slope and the roughness of the local terrain and detect obstacles. The slope is defined as the angle between the fitted plane and a horizontal plane and the roughness is computed as the average squared z-distances of the height values of the neighboring patch to the fitted plane. The slope and the roughness are turned into traversability values $\tau_s(p)$ and $\tau_r(p)$ by linear interpolation between zero and a maximum slope and roughness value respectively. In order to detect obstacles we set $\tau_o(p) \in \{0,1\}$ to zero, if the squared z-distance of a neighboring patch exceeds a threshold, thereby accounting for positive and negative obstacles, or if the patch has less than eight neighbors. The latter is important for avoiding abysms in the early stage of an exploration process, as some neighboring patches are below the edge of the abysm and therefore are not visible yet (see Fig. 1 (a)).

The combined traversability value is defined as $\tau(p) = \tau_s(p) \cdot \tau_r(p) \cdot \tau_o(p)$. Next, we iteratively propagate the values by convolving the traversability values of the patch and its eight neighboring patches with a Gaussian kernel. For non-existent neighbors, we assume a value of 0.5. The number of iterations depends on the used cell size and the robot's size. In order to enforce obstacle growing, we do not perform a convolution

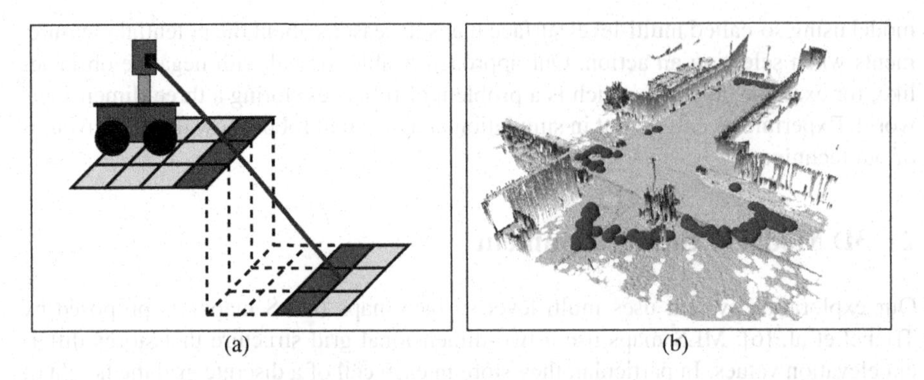

Fig. 1. (a) While scanning at an abysm, some of the lower patches will not be covered by a laser scan (dashed area). Since the patches at the edge of the abysm have less than eight neighbors, we can recognize them as an obstacle (red / dark gray area). **(b)** Outdoor map showing sampled candidate viewpoints as red (dark gray) spheres.

if one of the neighboring patches is non-traversable ($\tau = 0$), but rather set the patch's traversability directly to zero in this case.

3 Our Exploration Technique

An exploration strategy has to determine the next viewpoint the robot should move to in order to obtain more information about the environment. Identifying the best viewpoint is a two step procedure in our system. First, we define the set of possible viewpoints or candidate viewpoints. Second, we evaluate those candidates to find the best one.

3.1 Viewpoint Generation

One possible definition of the set of candidate viewpoints is that every reachable position in the map is a candidate viewpoint. However, this is only feasible if the evaluation of candidate viewpoints is computationally cheap. If the evaluation is costly, one has to settle for heuristics to determine a smaller set. A popular heuristic is the frontier approach [2] that defines candidate viewpoints as viewpoints that lie on the frontier between obstacle-free and unexplored areas. In our approach, a patch is considered as explored if it has eight neighbors and its uncertainty, measured by the entropy in the patch, is below a threshold. Additionally, we track the entropy as well as the number of neighbors of a patch. If the entropy or number of non-existing neighbors cannot be reduced as expected over several observations, we consider it to be explored nonetheless since further observations do not seem to change the state of the patch.

A frontier patch is defined as an unexplored patch with at least one explored neighboring patch. Most of these patches have less than eight neighbors and therefore are considered as non-traversable, since they might be at the edge of an abysm. Therefore, we cannot drive directly to a frontier patch. Instead, we use a 3D ray-casting technique to determine close-by candidate viewpoints. A patch is considered as a candidate viewpoint, if it is reachable and there is at least one frontier patch that is likely to be observable from that viewpoint. Instead of using ray-casting to track emitted beams from the sensor at every reachable position, we use a more efficient approach. We emit virtual beams from the frontier patch instead and then select admissible sensor locations along those beams. This will reduce the number of needed ray-casting operations as the number of frontier patches is much smaller than the number of reachable patches.

In practice, we found it useful to reject candidate viewpoints, from which the unseen area is below a threshold. We also cluster the frontier patches by the neighboring relation, and prevent patches from very small frontier clusters to generate candidate viewpoints. This will lead to a more reliable termination of the exploration process. Candidate viewpoints of an example map are shown in Fig. 1 (b).

3.2 Viewpoint Evaluation

The utility $u(v)$ of a candidate viewpoint v, is computed using the expected information gain $I(v)$ and the travel costs $t(v)$. As the evaluation involves a costly 3D ray-casting operation, we reduce the set of candidate viewpoints by sampling uniformly a fixed number of viewpoints from that set.

In order to simultaneously determine the shortest paths to all candidate viewpoints, we use a deterministic variant of the value iteration [7]. The costs

$$c(p,p') = \mathrm{dist}(p,p') + w(1-\tau(p')) \tag{1}$$

from patch p to a traversable neighboring patch p' considers the distance $\mathrm{dist}(p,p')$, as well as the traversability $\tau(p')$. A constant factor w is used to weight the penalization for traversing poorly traversable patches. The travel costs $t(v)$ of a viewpoint v is defined as the accumulated step costs of the shortest path to that viewpoint.

In order to evaluate the information gain of a viewpoint candidate, we perform a ray-cast operation to determine the patches that are likely to be hit by a laser measurement similar to [8]. We therefore determine the intersection points of the cell boundaries and the 3D ray projected onto the 2D grid. Next we determine for each cell the height interval covered by the ray and check for collisions with patches contained in that cell by considering their elevation and depth values. Using a standard notebook computer, our approach requires around 25 ms to evaluate one potential viewpoint including the 3D ray-cast operation. This allows us to run our algorithm with minimal delays only for typical environments.

For each casted ray that hits a patch, we temporary add a new measurement into the patch's grid cell with a corresponding mean and variance that depends on the distance of the laser ray. The mean and variance of the patch will then be updated using the Kalman update. As a patch is represented as a Gaussian, we can compute the entropy $H(p)$ of the patch as

$$H(p) = \frac{1}{2}\left(1+\log\left(2\pi\sigma^2\right)\right). \tag{2}$$

The information gain $I(p)$ of a ray-cast is then defined as the difference between the entropy $H(p)$ of the patch before and the entropy $H(p \mid m)$ after the temporary incorporation of the simulated measurement

$$I(p) = H(p) - H(p \mid m). \tag{3}$$

Additionally, we add a constant value for each empty cell traversed by the ray. In this way, we reward viewpoints from which unseen areas are likely to be visible, while we are still accounting for the reduction of existing uncertainties in the known map. Rays that do not hit any patch and do not traverse any empty cells, will result in an information gain of zero. The information gain $I(v)$ of a viewpoint v is then defined as the sum of the information gains of all casted rays. Finally, the utility $u(v)$ of each candidate viewpoint is computed by a relative information gain and travel costs as

$$u(v) = \alpha \frac{I(v)}{\max_x I(x)} + (1-\alpha) \frac{\max_x t(x) - t(v)}{\max_x t(x)}. \tag{4}$$

By varying the constant $\alpha \in [0,1]$ one can alter the exploration behavior by trading off the travel costs and the information gain.

3.3 Localization and Termination

The registration of newly acquired information involves a scan matching procedure with the previous local map. We therefore cannot drive directly to the next viewpoint, as the resulting overlap with the previous local map may be to small. Hence, we perform several 3D scans along the way, which has the benefit, that it allows us to optimize the localization of the robot with the pose returned by the scan matcher. We apply a 6D Monte Carlo localization proposed by Kümmerle et al. [9]. After each 3D scan, we replan the path to the selected viewpoint. If the viewpoint is unreachable, we choose a new one. The exploration terminates if the set of candidate viewpoints is empty.

4 Experiments

The experiments described here are designed to illustrate the benefit of our exploration technique which is able to build three-dimensional models of the environment and takes into account the travel costs and the expected change in the map uncertainty to evaluate possible actions. For the real-world experiments we used an ActivMedia Pioneer2-AT robot with a SICK laser range finder mounted on a pan-tilt unit to acquire three-dimensional range data. For a 3D scan we tilt the laser in a range of 40 degrees at four equally spaced horizontal angles while acquiring the laser data.

We tested our approach in simulation and in a real-world scenario. For the simulation experiments, we used a physical simulation environment that models our Pioneer robot with its pan-tilt unit. The simulated indoor environment consisted of four rooms, each connected to a corridor, and a foyer where the robot is located initially. The upper two rooms are connected directly through a door, while the lower ones are not. The robot efficiently covered the environment taking into account its constraints like travel cost, and information gain. The robot traveled 59 meters, visited eight viewpoints, and performed 15 scans (see Fig. 2 (a)-(c)). The final map, depicted in Fig. 2 (c) and (d), covers an area of $22m \times 17m$ and contains about 41,000 patches.

Real-world experiments have been carried out on the university campus. In the experiment shown in Fig. 2 (e)-(h) the robot traveled 84 meters, visited six viewpoints, and performed 23 scans. The map depicted in Fig. 2 (g) and (h) contains about 197,000

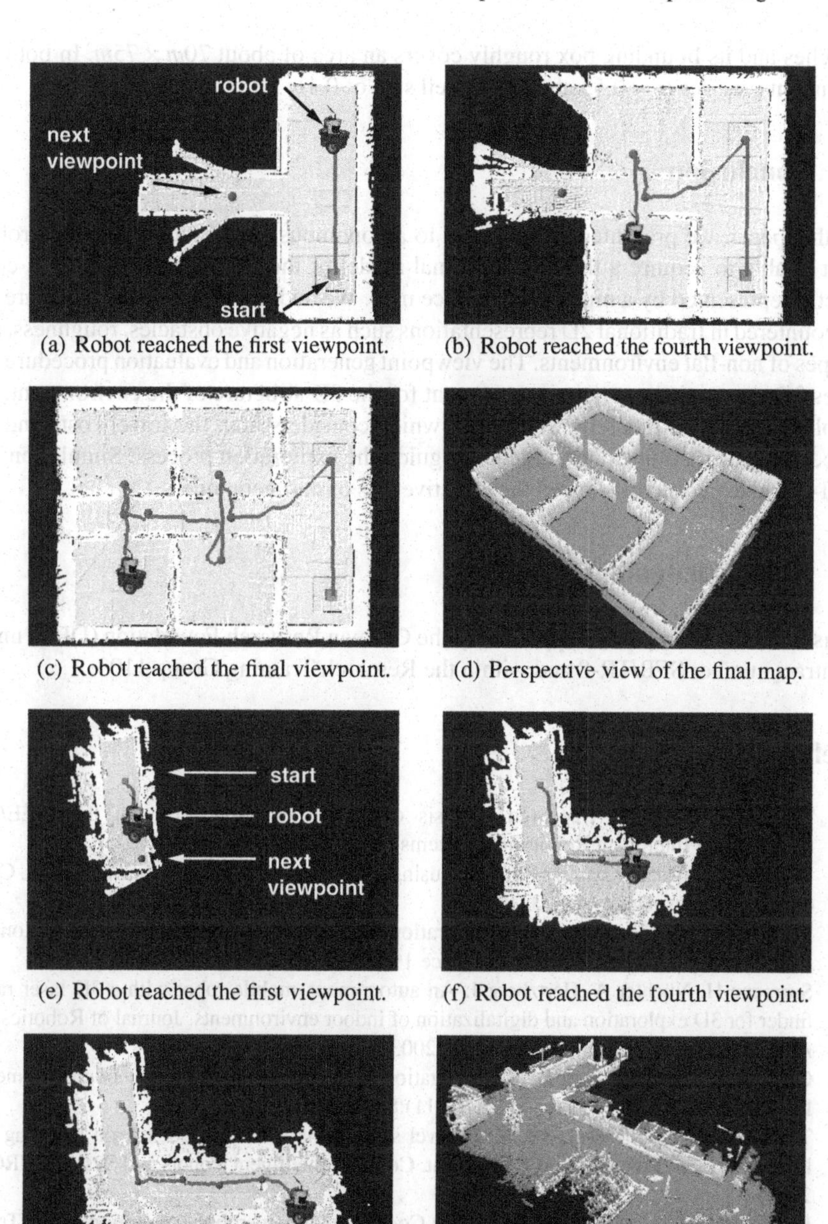

(a) Robot reached the first viewpoint. (b) Robot reached the fourth viewpoint.

(c) Robot reached the final viewpoint. (d) Perspective view of the final map.

(e) Robot reached the first viewpoint. (f) Robot reached the fourth viewpoint.

(g) Robot reached the sixth viewpoint. (h) Perspective view of the map.

Fig. 2. (a)-(d) Exploration in a simulated indoor environment. One can see four rooms, a corridor, and the foyer where the robot started the exploration. **(e)-(h)** Real-world exploration in an outdoor scenario. One can see the walls of three buildings, the pitched roof of a green house, and several street lamps and trees.

patches and its bounding box roughly covers an area of about $70m \times 75m$. In both experiments, we set $\alpha = 0.55$ and used a cell size of $0.1m \times 0.1m$.

5 Conclusion

In this paper, we presented an approach to autonomous exploration for mobile robots that is able to acquire a three-dimensional model of the environment, which is compactly represented by a multi-level surface map. We addressed problems which are not encountered in traditional 2D representations such as negative obstacles, roughness, and slopes of non-flat environments. The viewpoint generation and evaluation procedure utilizes 3D ray-casting operations to account for the 3D structure of the environment. We applied a decision-theoretic framework which considers both the travel costs and the expected information gain to efficiently guide the exploration process. Simulation and real-world experiments showed the effectiveness of our technique.

6 Acknowledgment

This work has been partly supported by the German Research Foundation (DFG) under contract number SFB/TR-8 and within the Research Training Group 1103.

References

1. Tovey C, Koenig S: Improved analysis of greedy mapping. Proc. of the IEEE/RSJ Int. Conf. on Intelligent Robots and Systems (IROS), 2003.
2. Yamauchi B: Frontier-based exploration using multiple robots. Proc. of the Second Int. Conf. on Autonomous Agents 47–53, 1998.
3. Whaite P, Ferrie FP: Autonomous exploration: Driven by uncertainty. IEEE Transactions on Pattern Analysis and Machine Intelligence 19(3):193–205, 1997.
4. Surmann H, Nüchter A, Hertzberg J: An autonomous mobile robot with a 3D laser range finder for 3D exploration and digitalization of indoor environments. Journal of Robotics and Autonomous Systems 45(3-4):181–198, 2003.
5. González-Baños HH, Latombe JC: Navigation strategies for exploring indoor environments. Int. Journal of Robotics Research 21(10-11):829–848, 2002.
6. Triebel R, Pfaff P, Burgard W: Multi-level surface maps for outdoor terrain mapping and loop closing. In Proc. of the IEEE/RSJ Int. Conf. on Intelligent Robots and Systems (IROS), 2006.
7. Burgard W, Moors M, Stachniss C, et al.: Coordinated multi-robot exploration. IEEE Transactions on Robotics 21(3):376–378, 2005.
8. Stachniss C, Grisetti G, Burgard W: Information gain-based exploration using rao-blackwellized particle filters. Proc. of Robotics: Science and Systems (RSS) 65–72, 2005.
9. Kümmerle R, Triebel R, Pfaff P, et al.: Monte carlo localization in outdoor terrains using multi-level surface maps. Proc. of the Int. Conf. on Field and Service Robotics (FSR), 2007.

Active Monte Carlo Localization in Outdoor Terrains Using Multi-level Surface Maps

Rainer Kümmerle[1], Patrick Pfaff[1], Rudolph Triebel[2] and Wolfram Burgard[1]

[1] Department of Computer Science, University of Freiburg, Germany,
{kuemmerl,pfaff,burgard}@informatik.uni-freiburg.de
[2] Autonomous Systems Lab, ETH Zurich, Switzerland,
rudolph.triebel@mavt.ethz.ch

Abstract. In this paper we consider the problem of active mobile robot localization with range sensors in outdoor environments. In contrast to passive approaches our approach actively selects the orientation of the laser range finder to improve the localization results. It applies a particle filter to estimate the full six-dimensional state of the robot. To represent the environment we utilize multi-level surface maps which allow the robot to represent vertical structures and multiple levels. To efficiently calculate the optimal orientation for the range scanner, we apply a clustering operation on the particles and only evaluate potential orientations based on these clusters. Experimental results obtained with a mobile robot in an outdoor environment indicate that the active control of the range sensor leads to more efficient localization results.

1 Introduction

The problem of mobile robot localization with range sensors in outdoor environments arises whenever GPS signals are missing due to occlusions caused by buildings, bridges, or trees. In such situations, a mobile robot typically has to estimate its position in the environment using its exteroceptive sensors and a map of the environment. However, when a robot attempts to perceive its environment to localize itself, the choice of the direction of the perception can substantially influence the accuracy of the position estimate. An example situation is shown in Figure 1. In the left image, the range sensor of the robot is oriented parallel to the floor plane as in most robot scenarios with a 2D sensor setup. This has the effect, that the vertical object shown in the image can not be sensed by the robot. However, this vertical object might be crucial for localization, because it might allow the robot to reduce its uncertainty. In contrast, the right image shows a robot with a slightly different sensor orientation so that the vertical object can be perceived. Accordingly, the robot can achieve a more accurate position estimate by actively orienting its sensor. This is why the technique is called *active localization*. In this paper, we consider the problem of active localization in outdoor environments by matching laser range measurements to a given map of the environment. In a former approach [1], we already applied multi-level surface (MLS) maps [2] to model the environment for passive localization with a fixed mounted laser range finder. The MLS maps can be regarded as an extension of the classical elevation maps [3,4,5,6] as they additionally represent intervals corresponding to vertical objects in the environment.

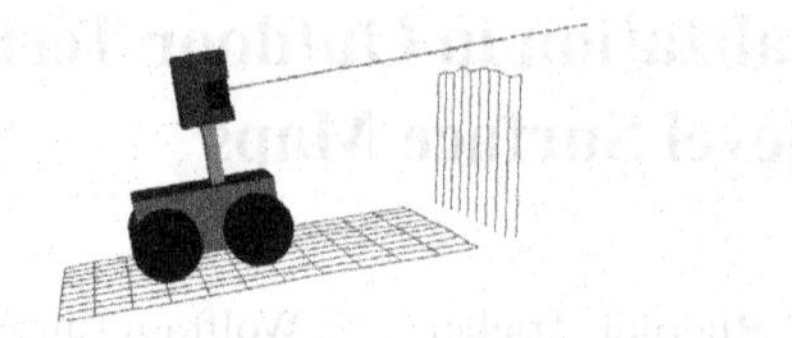
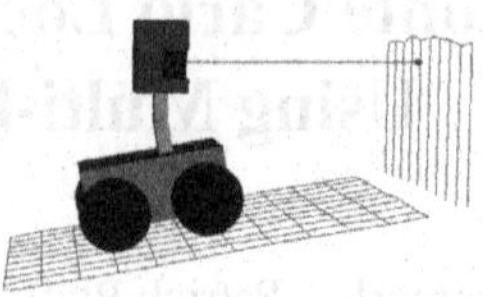

Fig. 1. Robot with the standard orientation of the range sensor where the robot is unable to sense the vertical object (left). In contrast to this the autonomously adapted sensor orientation allows the robot to sense the vertical object (right).

A further advantage of MLS maps is that they can represent multiple levels. This is important when mobile robots are deployed, e.g., in environments with bridges or underpasses.

The paper is organized as follows. After discussing related work in the next section, we briefly describe the general Monte Carlo localization technique in Section 3. The details of our active Monte Carlo localization are presented in Section 4. Finally, in Section 5, we present experimental results illustrating the advantages of applying active localization in outdoor environments.

2 Related Work

In general, the problem of active localization can be described as generating robot actions that particularly aim at improving its position estimate. In the past, this problem has been adressed by several authors. For example, Kaelbling et al. [7] and Koenig and Simmons [8] used a partially observable Markov decision process to model actions in the environment. The action selector chooses the action that minimizes the expected entropy after the next control action or maximizes the expected total reward, respectively. Jensfelt and Kristensen [9] applied multi-hypothesis localization to topological maps for active global localization. Davison and Kita [10] described a vision-based localization in which the robot actively senses the features based on visibiliy and information gain. Recently, Porta et al. [11] proposed an entropy-based criterion for action selection within a localization algorithm using a stereo vision system, which allows the robot to recover its location in the initial stages or within a failure recovery procedure more efficiently. To use fine-grained grid maps and laser range finders, Fox et al. [12] proposed an approach for active localization based on Markov localization. Whereas their approach is able to increase the efficiency of the localization by minimizing the expected entropy, Markov localization has high computational demands.

In contrast to the former approaches we focus on reducing the computational demands of the active localization. The goal of this paper is to develop an active localization method which is able to deal with large outdoor environments.

3 Monte Carlo Localization

To estimate the pose $\mathbf{x} = (x, y, z, \varphi, \vartheta, \psi)$ of the robot in its environment, we consider probabilistic localization, which follows the recursive Bayesian filtering scheme. The key idea of this approach is to maintain a probability density $p(\mathbf{x}_t \mid \mathbf{z}_{1:t}, \mathbf{u}_{0:t-1})$ of the robot's location $\mathbf{x}_t$ at time t given all observations $\mathbf{z}_{1:t}$ up to time t and all control inputs $\mathbf{u}_{0:t-1}$ up to time $t-1$. This probability is updated as follows:

$$bel(\mathbf{x}_t) = p(\mathbf{x}_t \mid \mathbf{z}_{1:t}, \mathbf{u}_{0:t-1}) = \alpha \cdot p(\mathbf{z}_t \mid \mathbf{x}_t) \cdot \int p(\mathbf{x}_t \mid \mathbf{u}_{t-1}, \mathbf{x}_{t-1}) \cdot p(\mathbf{x}_{t-1})\, d\mathbf{x}_{t-1}. \quad (1)$$

Here, α is a normalization constant ensuring that $p(\mathbf{x}_t \mid \mathbf{z}_{1:t}, \mathbf{u}_{0:t-1})$ sums up to one over all $\mathbf{x}_t$. The terms to be described in Eqn. (1) are the *prediction model* $p(\mathbf{x}_t \mid \mathbf{u}_{t-1}, \mathbf{x}_{t-1})$ and the *sensor model* $p(\mathbf{z}_t \mid \mathbf{x}_t)$. For the implementation of the described filtering scheme, we use a sample-based approach which is commonly known as *Monte Carlo localization* (MCL) [13]. Monte Carlo localization is a variant of particle filtering [14] where each particle $\mathbf{x}^{[i]}$ corresponds to a possible robot pose and has an assigned weight $w^{[i]}$. The *belief update* from Eqn. (1) is performed by the following two alternating steps:

1. In the **prediction step**, we draw for each particle with weight $w^{[i]}$ a new particle according to $w^{[i]}$ and to the prediction model $p(\mathbf{x}_t \mid \mathbf{u}_{t-1}, \mathbf{x}_{t-1})$.
2. In the **correction step**, a new observation $\mathbf{z}_t$ is integrated. This is done by assigning a new weight $w^{[i]}$ to each particle according to the sensor model $p(\mathbf{z}_t \mid \mathbf{x}_t)$.

The details of the particle filter implementation in combination with the MLS maps can be found in our previous work [1].

4 Active Monte Carlo Localization

The purpose of our active localization approach is to find the orientation of the laser range finder which reduces the uncertainty of the current pose estimate as much as possible. To achieve this, we apply the greedy approach of Fox et al. [12]. We assume that at a given time step t the robot is able to execute a discrete set of actions $\mathscr{A}$. The benefit of a sensing action $a \in \mathscr{A}$ can be determined by considering the uncertainty of the posterior $p(\mathbf{x}_{t+1} \mid a, \mathbf{z}_{t+1})$. The uncertainty of the pose estimate is represented by the entropy

$$h(\mathbf{x}_t) = -\int_{\mathbf{x}_t} bel(\mathbf{x}_t) \log bel(\mathbf{x}_t)\, d\mathbf{x}_t. \quad (2)$$

The ideal action would allow the robot to find out its position with a high certainty. In other words, the posterior would become a single peaked distribution with a very low entropy. Therefore the information gain $g_t(a)$ of an action a to change the orientation of the laser range finder is defined by:

$$g_t(a) = h(\mathbf{x}_t) - h(\mathbf{x}_{t+1} \mid a, \mathbf{z}_{t+1}), \quad (3)$$

where $h(\mathbf{x}_{t+1} \mid a, \mathbf{z}_{t+1})$ defines the entropy after the integration of a laser measurement according to the action a. In general we do not know which range measurement the robot will obtain after changing the sensor orientation according to the action a. Therefore, we instead consider the *expected entropy* by integrating over all possible measurements $\mathbf{z}_{t+1}$:

$$E[g_t(a)] = h(\mathbf{x}_t) - E[h(\mathbf{x}_{t+1} \mid a, \mathbf{z}_{t+1})], \quad (4)$$

where $E\left[h\left(\mathbf{x}_{t+1} \mid a, \mathbf{z}_{t+1}\right)\right]$ defines the expected entropy after the integration of a laser measurement obtained by executing action a. If we now take into account that changing the orientation of the range sensor does not change the location of the robot, then according to the reasoning by Fox et al. [12] the expected entropy is calculated as follows:

$$E\left[h\left(\mathbf{x}_{t+1} \mid a, \mathbf{z}_{t+1}\right)\right] = -\int_{\hat{\mathbf{z}}}\int_{\mathbf{x}_t} p(\hat{\mathbf{z}} \mid \mathbf{x}_t)\, bel(\mathbf{x}_t) \log \frac{p(\hat{\mathbf{z}} \mid \mathbf{x}_t) bel(\mathbf{x}_t)}{p(\hat{\mathbf{z}} \mid a)} \, d\mathbf{x}_t \, d\hat{\mathbf{z}} \quad (5)$$

Now the action $\hat{a}$ can be selected out of the action set $\mathscr{A}$ which maximizes the information gain as follows:

$$\hat{a} = \operatorname*{argmax}_{a \in \mathscr{A}} E\left[g_t(a)\right] = \operatorname*{argmax}_{a \in \mathscr{A}} h(\mathbf{x}_t) - E\left[h\left(\mathbf{x}_t \mid a, \mathbf{z}_{t+1}\right)\right]. \quad (6)$$

The calculation of the expected entropy $E\left[h\left(\mathbf{x}_t \mid a, \mathbf{z}_{t+1}\right)\right]$ can be achieved by performing ray casting operations in the given MLS map. The ray casting operation approximates a possible range measurement of the robot. So we do not have do consider all possible range measurements that our sensor may generate. Using ray casting operations seems to be a good approximation for a laser range finder, as we figured out in several experiments. The result of a ray casting operation depends on the position $\mathbf{x}$ and the action a. Furthermore this approximation allows us to compute the probability $p(\mathbf{z}_{t+1} \mid \mathbf{x}_t)$ which is required to calculate the expected entropy (5).

Performing a ray casting operation for each particle of our particle set would result in high computational demands. To reduce the required computation time, we only simulate the range beams on a subset calculated by a clustering operation. This is motivated by the fact that typically the particles are located in a small number of areas of high probability. Each cluster of particles represents such an area. To cluster the particle set into subsets, we apply a technique known as QT-Clustering [15]. This technique allows us to specify the maximal extent of a cluster beforehand and thus ensures that the centroid of each cluster represents the whole cluster well. In our current implementation the maximal diameter of a cluster is set to 1 m. The clustering algorithm yields a cluster set $\mathscr{K} = \bigcup_{j=1}^{J} (\mathbf{m}_j, \mathscr{I}_j)$, where $\mathbf{m}_j$ is the center of mass and $\mathscr{I}_j$ is an index set of the particles contained in cluster j. Each particle is a member of exactly one clustered subset. The range measurement generated for a subset is weighted according to the sum of the normalized weights of the particles contained in the subset. Following this approximation and also considering the underlying particle filter implementation, the expected entropy (5) is calculated as follows:

$$E\left[h\left(\mathbf{x}_{t+1} \mid a, \mathbf{z}_{t+1}\right)\right] = -\sum_{j=1}^{|\mathscr{K}|}\sum_{i=1}^{N} w(\mathscr{I}_j)\, p(\mathbf{z}^a_{\mathbf{m}_j} \mid \mathbf{x}^{[i]}) \cdot w^{[i]} \log \frac{p(\mathbf{z}^a_{\mathbf{m}_j} \mid \mathbf{x}^{[i]}) \cdot w^{[i]}}{p(\mathbf{z}^a_{\mathbf{m}_j} \mid a)}, \quad (7)$$

where $w(\mathscr{I}_j)$ refers to the sum of the normalized weights of the particles contained in cluster j and $\mathbf{z}^a_{\mathbf{m}_j}$ stands for a ray casting operation whose simulated laser beams originate from the center of mass $\mathbf{m}_j$ with a sensor orientation described by the sensing action a.

Eqn. (7) specifies how to compute the future expected entropy of a sensing action a based on our clustered subsets. Plugging this into Eqn. (6) we are able at any point in time to select the best action $\hat{a}$ to be executed next.

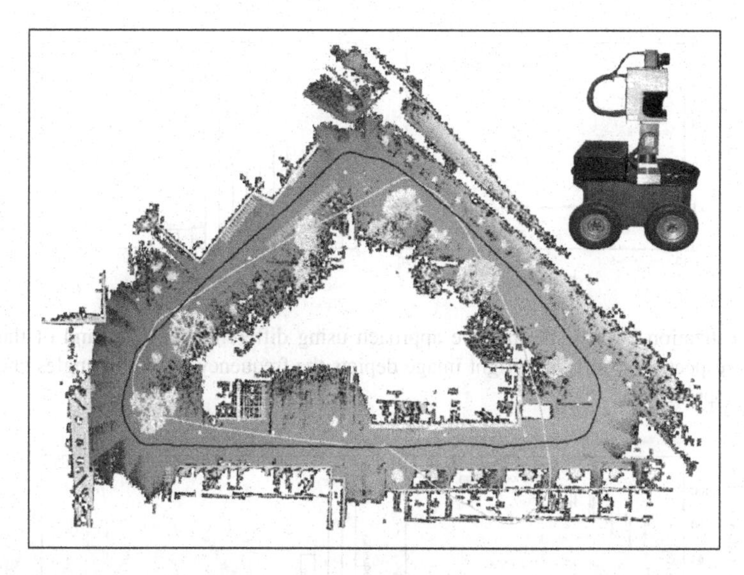

Fig. 2. MLS map and mobile robot used for the localization experiments. The area represented by this map spans approximately 195 by 146 meters. The blue / dark grey line shows the localized robot poses. The yellow / light grey line shows the pure odometry. The traversed trajectory has a length of 284 meters. The top right part depicts the robot Herbert used for the experiments.

5 Experiments

Our approach has been implemented and tested in real world experiments. The robot used for the experiments is a Pioneer II AT system equipped with a SICK LMS laser range scanner and an AMTEC wrist unit, which is used as a pan/tilt device for the laser (see Figure 2). The experiments are designed to investigate if the active localization approach facilitates mobile robot localization and whether it improves localization performance.

The first set of experiments is designed to evaluate the performance of the active localization approach during a position tracking task. To obtain the data, we steered along a 284 meter long loop in our campus environment. Figure 2 depicts a top view of the MLS Map. The blue / dark grey line shows the localized robot poses. The yellow / light grey line shows the pure odometry. The left image of Figure 3 depicts the average localization error for a tracking experiment with 1,000 particles. As can be seen from the figure, our active approach achieves the same performance as the passive approach as long as the laser range finder is not tilted more than 3° downwards. This is due to the fact that at higher tilt angles the robot perceives less vertical objects and therefore misses the map features that are important for a correct position estimate. The right image depicts the frequency of the tilt angles chosen by our active approach. As can be seen from the histogram our active approach prefers upwards to downwards orientations of the range sensors. Thus the active approach enables the robot to sense the important vertical features of the environment and avoids to obtain range measurements from the ground.

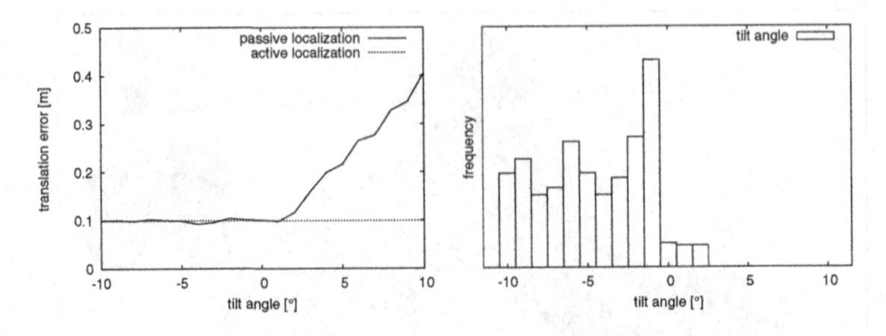

Fig. 3. Localization error of the passive approach using different tilt angles and of the active approach, respectively (left). The right image depicts the frequency of the tilt angles chosen by the active approach.

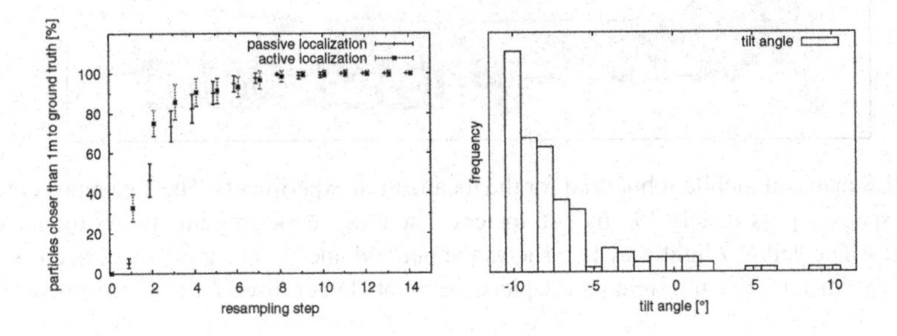

Fig. 4. The left image depicts the convergence of the particles to the true position of the robot with 500,000 particles. The right image depicts the frequency of the tilt angles chosen by the active approach during the global localization task.

Additionally we also carried out experiments, in which we evaluated the convergence of the active localization approach during global localization in a map that spans approximately 195 by 146 meters. Figure 4 depicts the convergence of the particles to the true position of the robot with 500,000 particles. Whereas the x-axis corresponds to the resampling step, the y-axis shows the number of particles in percent that are closer than 1 m to the true position. The figure shows the evolution of these numbers for the passive and active MCL. A t-test revealed that it is significantly better to apply the active approach than the passive one for the global localization task.

6 Conclusions

In this paper, we presented an approach to active Monte Carlo localization with a mobile robot using MLS maps. Our approach actively selects the orientation of the laser range finder to improve the localization results. To speed up the entire process, we apply a clustering operation on the particles and only evaluate potential orientations based on these clusters. In experiments obtained with a robot in a real outdoor environment we analyzed the active control of the range sensor and demonstrated that it leads to more efficient localization results.

Acknowledgment

This work has partly been supported by the German Research Foundation (DFG) within the Research Training Group 1103 and under contract number SFB/TR-8 and by the EC under contract number FP6-IST-027140-BACS.

References

1. R. Kümmerle, R. Triebel, P. Pfaff, and W. Burgard. Monte carlo localization in outdoor terrains using multi-level surface maps. In *Proc. of the International Conference on Field and Service Robotics (FSR)*, Chamonix, France, 2007.
2. R. Triebel, P. Pfaff, and W. Burgard. Multi level surface maps for outdoor terrain mapping and loop closing. In *Proc. of the IEEE/RSJ Int. Conf. on Intelligent Robots and Systems (IROS)*, 2006.
3. J. Bares, M. Hebert, T. Kanade, E. Krotkov, T. Mitchell, R. Simmons, and W. R. L. Whittaker. Ambler: An autonomous rover for planetary exploration. *IEEE Computer Society Press*, 22(6):18–22, 1989.
4. M. Hebert, C. Caillas, E. Krotkov, I.S. Kweon, and T. Kanade. Terrain mapping for a roving planetary explorer. In *Proc. of the IEEE Int. Conf. on Robotics & Automation (ICRA)*, pages 997–1002, 1989.
5. S. Lacroix, A. Mallet, D. Bonnafous, G. Bauzil, S. Fleury and; M. Herrb, and R. Chatila. Autonomous rover navigation on unknown terrains: Functions and integration. *International Journal of Robotics Research*, 21(10-11):917–942, 2002.
6. C. Parra, R. Murrieta-Cid, M. Devy, and M. Briot. 3-d modelling and robot localization from visual and range data in natural scenes. In *1st International Conference on Computer Vision Systems (ICVS)*, number 1542 in LNCS, pages 450–468, 1999.
7. L. P. Kaelbling, A. R. Cassandra, and J. A. Kurien. Acting under uncertainty: Discrete Bayesian models for mobile-robot navigation. In *Proc. of the IEEE/RSJ Int. Conf. on Intelligent Robots and Systems (IROS)*, Osaka, Japan, 1996.
8. S. Koenig and R. Simmons. Xavier: A robot navigation architecture based on partially observable markov decision process models. In D. Kortenkamp, R. Bonasso, and R. Murphy, editors, *Artificial Intelligence Based Mobile Robotics: Case Studies of Successful Robot Systems*, pages 91–122. MIT Press, 1998.
9. P. Jensfelt and S. Kristensen. Active global localisation for a mobile robot using multiple hypothesis tracking. *IEEE Transactions on Robotics and Automation*, 17(5):748–760, October 2001.
10. A Davison and N. Kita. 3d simultaneous localisation and map-building using active vision for a robot moving on undulating terrain. In *Proc. IEEE Conference on Computer Vision and Pattern Recognition, Kauai*. IEEE Computer Society Press, December 2001.
11. J. M. Porta, J. J. Verbeek, and B. J. A. Kröse. Active appearance-based robot localization using stereo vision. *Auton. Robots*, 18(1):59–80, 2005.
12. D. Fox, W. Burgard, and S. Thrun. Active markov localization for mobile robots. *Journal of Robotics & Autonomous Systems*, 25:195–207, 1998.
13. F. Dellaert, D. Fox, W. Burgard, and S. Thrun. Monte Carlo localization for mobile robots. In *Proc. of the IEEE Int. Conf. on Robotics & Automation (ICRA)*, 1999.
14. A. Doucet, N. de Freitas, and N. Gordan, editors. *Sequential Monte-Carlo Methods in Practice*. Springer Verlag, 2001.
15. L. J. Heyer, S. Kruglyak, and S. Yooseph. Exploring expression data: Identification and analysis of coexpressed genes. *Genome Res.*, 9(11):1106–1115, 1999.

Appearance-Based Robot Localization Using Wavelets-PCA

Hashem Tamimi[1], Christian Weiss[2] and Andreas Zell[2]

[1] College of Administrative Sciences and Informatics, Palestine Polythechnic University, P.O. Box 198, Hebron, Palestine
[2] Computer Science Dept.,University of Tübingen, Sand 1, 72076 Tübingen, Germany
{hashem.tamimi, christian.weiss, andreas.zell}@uni-tuebingen.de

Abstract. This paper presents an efficient image based feature extraction approach to solve the robot localization problem. The approach has two stages: in the first stage, the image is transformed to the wavelet domain using the fast wavelet transform. In the second stage, Principal Component Analysis (PCA) is applied to the wavelet coefficients in order to further reduce the feature dimension by selecting the significant feature elements. The experiments show that the proposed approach is superior to the PCA-based approach and the wavelet-based approach. The main advantages of wavelets-PCA are the efficiency in extracting the features and the robustness against illumination changes.

1 Introduction

In appearance-based localization, the robot environment is implicitly represented as a database of features derived from a set of images collected at known positions in a training phase. For localization, the features of the image observed by the robot are compared with the features stored in the database. The robot position is then considered as being the position of the most similar image in the database [1].

The main desirable properties of the features are: (1) They should be a compressed form of the original scenes so as to speed up the computation of the comparisons, but still, they should maintain distinguishing representations of the scenes. (2) They should exhibit invariance against different transformations on the scenes such as translation and scale. (3) They should also exhibit robustness against noise or illumination changes, which the robot encounters during its navigation.

In the literature, both global and local features are used to solve the robot localization problem. Global features are extracted from the image as a whole, such as histograms [2], PCA-based features [3] and integral invariants [4]. On the other hand, local features, such as the Scale Invariant Feature Transform (SIFT) [5] and kernel PCA-based features [6], are computed from areas of high relevance in the image. Since matching the local features is time consuming, global feature-based approaches are more preferable in real-time applications.

This paper is concerned with applying different global features extraction approaches to appearance-based robot localization in an indoor environment. The paper first reviews the PCA-based approach in Section 2. After that, the fast wavelet transform is reviewed in general in Section 3 and the idea of applying wavelet features for robot localization is investigated. Section 4 introduces the wavelets-PCA approach as an extension for the fast wavelet transform approach. The experimental work of this new approach is discussed in Section 5.

2 Feature Extraction Using PCA

The main steps to extract features using PCA are summarized by the following steps:

1. Each image I of size $N \times N$ is transformed to an $1 \times N \cdot N$ vector Γ_i. Here, we assume squared images for simplicity.
2. The average image Ψ is evaluated as $\Psi = \frac{1}{L}\sum_{i=1}^{L}\Gamma_i$, where L is the number of images in the training set.
3. The difference between each image I and Ψ is computed as $\Phi_i = \Gamma_i - \Psi$.
4. A covariance matrix is estimated as $C = \frac{1}{L}\sum_{i=1}^{L}\Phi_i\Phi_i^T$.
5. The eigenvectors u_i and corresponding eigenvalues λ_i of the covariance matrix C can be evaluated by using a Singular Value Decomposition (SVD) method: $Cu_i = \lambda_i u_i$.
6. To reduce dimensionality, only a small number K of eigenvectors corresponding to the largest eigenvalues are kept (where $K < L$).
7. A new image Γ, after subtracting the mean ($\Phi = \Gamma - \Psi$), can then be projected to the eigenspace by $\Phi = \sum_{i=1}^{K} w_i u_i$, where $w_i = u_i^T \Psi$ are coefficients of the projection and can be regarded as a new representation of the original image in the eigenspace.

3 Fast Wavelet Transform

For the two-dimensional images of size $N \times N$ used in the following descriptions, we assume $N = 2^M$ for clarity. The multi-resolution wavelet decomposition can be expressed as follows [7]:

$$S_{m+1,(n_1,n_2)} = \frac{1}{2}\sum_{k_1}\sum_{k_2} c_{k_1}c_{k_2}S_{m(2n_1+k_1,2n_2+k_2)} \quad (1)$$

$$T^h_{m+1,(n_1,n_2)} = \frac{1}{2}\sum_{k_1}\sum_{k_2} b_{k_1}c_{k_2}S_{m(2n_1+k_1,2n_2+k_2)} \quad (2)$$

$$T^v_{m+1,(n_1,n_2)} = \frac{1}{2}\sum_{k_1}\sum_{k_2} c_{k_1}b_{k_2}S_{m(2n_1+k_1,2n_2+k_2)} \quad (3)$$

$$T^d_{m+1,(n_1,n_2)} = \frac{1}{2}\sum_{k_1}\sum_{k_2} b_{k_1}b_{k_2}S_{m(2n_1+k_1,2n_2+k_2)} \quad (4)$$

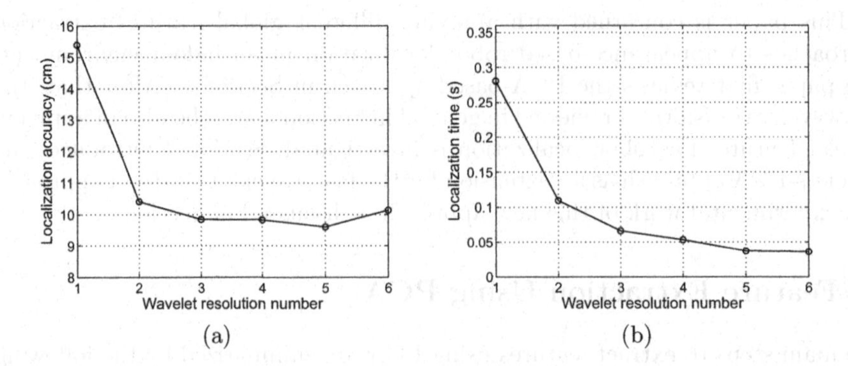

Fig. 1. Localization results using global wavelet features. (a) The average localization accuracy vs. the wavelet resolution number. (b) The corresponding localization time.

In Equations 1 to 4, k_1 and k_2 are the scaling coefficient indices, n_1 and n_2 are the location indices at scales $m+1$, and b_k and c_k are a high pass filter and a low pass filter, respectively.

The general idea of the two-dimensional wavelet decomposition is as follows: The original image is defined at scale index $m = 0$. Its components are input as the approximation coefficient at scale index 0, i.e. the matrix S_0. After the first wavelet decomposition, a decomposition array is formed at scale index 1, which is split into four distinct sub-matrices: the vertical detail components T_1^v, the horizontal detail components T_1^h, the diagonal detail components T_1^d and the remaining approximation components S_1. The decomposition array has the same size as the original array. The detail coefficients are subsequently left untouched and the next iteration further decomposes only the approximation components in the sub-matrix S_1. This results in detail coefficients contained within sub-matrices T_2^v, T_2^h and T_2^d at scale index 2 and approximation coefficients within sub-matrix S_2. This procedure may be repeated M times for a $2^M \times 2^M$ array to get a number of coefficient sub-matrices T_m^v, T_m^h and T_m^d of size $2^{M-m} \times 2^{M-m}$, where $m = 1, 2, .., M$.

In order to extract global features, we apply a multi-resolution decomposition to the image and maintain the information of the three approximation channels at a fixed scale. We maintain global features from only one resolution to keep the size of the features and the complexity of their data structure as small as possible.

To simulate the global localization of a mobile robot using wavelet features, we did the following experiments. The experiments consist of trying to match a set of indoor *benchmark* images[1] taken by a mobile robot during its localization phase to another set of images which represents the exploration phase. Each of the images is associated with ground truth information, namely the robot position in (x, y, θ) terms. An accurate localization is then evaluated to be one

[1] available at http://www.cs.ubc.ca/simra/lci/data/

which minimizes the distance between the positions of the images being compared from the two sets. We use the same image set as in [8], which consists of 121 indoor images. The images were taken in an 11×11 grid in a robot lab, 20 cm apart from each other. For testing, another 30 images distributed in the robot lab are used. The camera in all the experiments is always headed towards the same angle, which means that we only deal with (x, y) coordinates and can neglect the orientation θ.

In this experiment, the features were computed from only one of the wavelet resolutions. We use Haar mother wavelets because of their efficiency. The features are compared using the euclidean distance. The results are illustrated in Figure 1. Figure 1(a) shows that we can reach a good localization accuracy of less than 10 cm, which was obtained using the fifth wavelet resolution. Figure 1(b) shows the corresponding time required for localization. The time decreases as we use higher wavelet resolutions, because the feature vector size is reduced in each resolution. For example, in this experiment the fifth resolution has a feature vector of size 1×7200. From this figure we can see that this approach can be applied in real-time. Features from the fifth wavelet resolution can be extracted and compared to the features from the exploration phase in less than 0.05 seconds.

This result shows that we can perform fast and accurate localization using wavelet features. In the next section we further reduce the feature vector size by applying PCA to the wavelet features. This will not only reduce the feature vector size, but also inherit some advantages from the PCA approach. The proposed combination of wavelets and PCA is mainly applied here to address the illumination problem. This problem occurs when the robot builds the database under certain illumination conditions and then encounters images in the localization phase under different illumination conditions.

4 The Wavelets-PCA Approach

To further extend our approach, we combine the wavelet features with PCA. The first stage is to extract the wavelet coefficients from three different channels at a given resolution of the image. Each channel is investigated separately in order to decide which channels perform better than the others. Then, the wavelet coefficients are mapped to a different domain using the PCA approach. The stages of the wavelets-PCA approach are as follows:

1. For each image I, we transform the image into the wavelet domain and extract T_i^h, T_i^v and T_i^d, where i is a given wavelet resolution.
2. We map the information of each channel from a two-dimensional into a vector form, which is denoted $\overrightarrow{T^h}$, $\overrightarrow{T^v}$ and $\overrightarrow{T^d}$, respectively.
3. Each of these three vectors is mapped to a different compact space using PCA and the resulting three features $\overrightarrow{\overline{T^h}}$, $\overrightarrow{\overline{T^v}}$ and $\overrightarrow{\overline{T^d}}$ are investigated to see which of the features leads to the best localization rate.

Similar ideas of using wavelets-PCA have been proposed recently in other applications such as face recognition [9] and texture recognition [10].

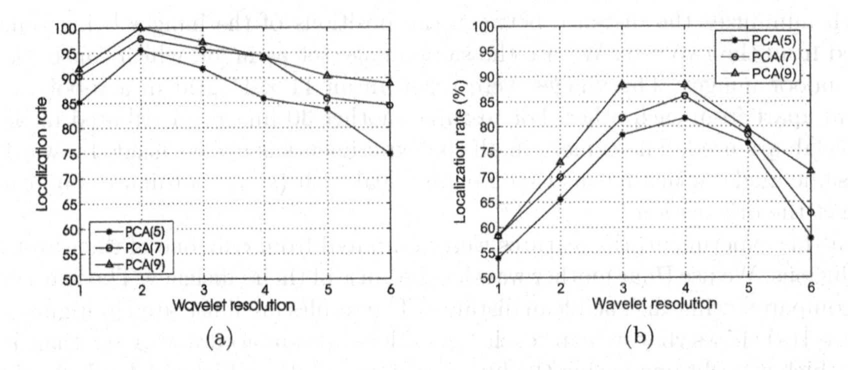

Fig. 2. Results of the wavelets-PCA approach when applied to robot localization (a) using images with illumination changes. (b) using images with translation and illumination changes.

5 Experimental Results

In this section, we demonstrate and discuss three different experiments that we performed. In the first experiment, we examine the illumination problem specifically. In the second experiment, we examine real robot localization cases, where both robot translation and illumination changes happen at the same time. Finally, in the third part, we compare the results of the wavelets-PCA approach to the PCA approach without the wavelet stage.

5.1 Varying Illumination

To investigate the performance of the wavelets-PCA approach for robot localization under illumination changes, we constructed a database of indoor images. We manually classified the images into four groups according to the degree of illumination. We use artificial illumination in these experiments. Each group consists of 45 different images. We did training with one group and testing with the other three groups. Thus, we considered four different training and testing combinations. The results of the localization are shown in Figure 2(a), where the number of eigenvalues K is assigned to 5, 7 and 9. The best results are obtained when using the second wavelet resolution, where the localization rate is 95%, 98% and 100% for K = 5, 7 and 9, respectively, while the localization rate of using PCA alone is 52%, 64% and 74%, respectively. This result shows the importance of the wavelet stage.

5.2 Varying Illumination and Translation

The previous experiments adressed the localization problem under illumination changes, given that the robot is in the same location as these illumination changes

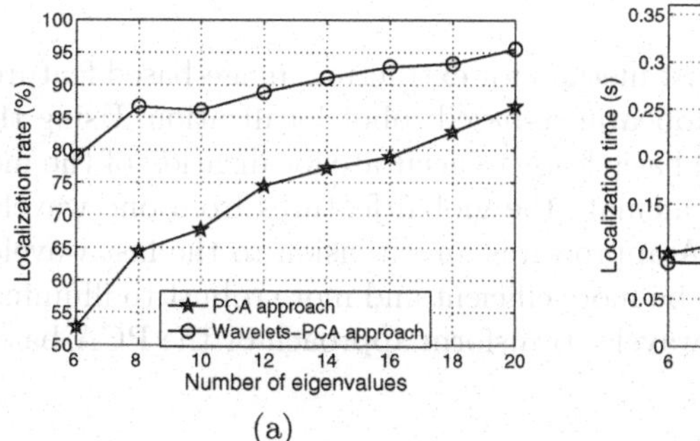

(a)

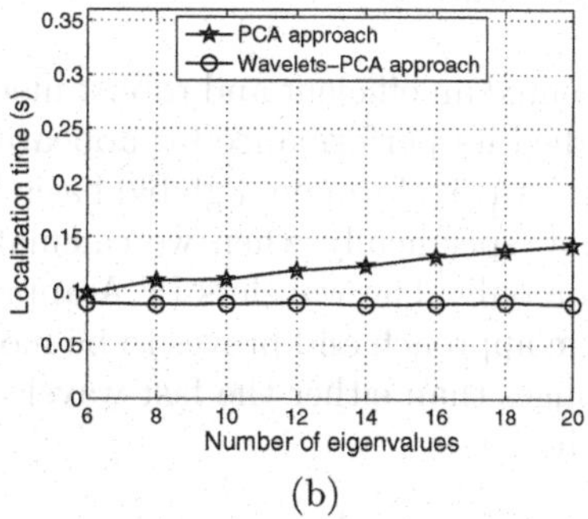

(b)

Fig. 3. (a) The average localization rate vs. the number of eigenvalues of the PCA features and the wavelets-PCA features. (b) The corresponding localization time using these features.

occur, but we should not solve the illumination problem apart from the translation problem. Figure 2(b) shows the results of repeating the approach used in experiment 1, this time considering images with illumination and translation changes. We can see that the best results are obtained using the third wavelet resolution and using K=9.

In both of the experiments shown above, it is important to mention that the three wavelet vectors $\overrightarrow{T^h}$, $\overrightarrow{T^v}$ and $\overrightarrow{T^d}$ have been investigated each by its own to find which combination of them will lead to the best performance. This also means that we have considered building three different PCA spaces, one for each of the three channels. The result of this investigation has shown that the best localization performance was obtained using only the horizontal channel. Considering other channels or applying combinations always led to lower localization rates.

5.3 Comparing Wavelets-PCA and PCA

We also compared the performance of the PCA-based approach and the proposed wavelets-PCA based approach. The comparison is performed in terms of the localization rate and the localization time for both approaches using different numbers of eigenvalues. Figure 3(a) shows the results for the localization rate. From these results we can see that the localization rate of the wavelets-PCA approach is always better than of the PCA approach under all different choices of eigenvalues. Figure 3(b) shows the results of comparing the localization time of both approaches under different numbers of eigenvalues, where we can clearly see that the wavelets-PCA approach is faster. This is because the input for the PCA stage in the case of the wavelets-PCA approach is the wavelet vector which has less dimensions than the whole image as in the case of PCA. This reduces the computation time of extracting the feature vector.

6 Conclusion

We presented an efficient and robust method for extracting image-based features and studied its performance for appearance-based robot localization. Using the fast wavelet transform on a global basis leads to accurate localization of the mobile robot, specifically when we calculate the global features from one wavelet resolution only. The wavelets-PCA approach is an extension to the fast wavelet transform approach and proves to be more efficient and more robust to illumination changes than either the fast wavelet transform approach or the PCA-based approach.

References

1. H. Tamimi. *Vision based-Features for Mobile Robot Localization.* PhD thesis, University of Tübingen, Tübingen, Germany, 2006.
2. C. Zhou, Y. Wei, and T. Tan. Mobile Robot Self-Localization Based on Global Visual Appearance Features. In *Proceedings of the IEEE International Conference on Robotics and Automation (ICRA)*, pages 1271–1276, Taipei, Taiwan, Sep. 14-19 2003.
3. D. Skocaj, H. Bischof, and A. Leonardis. A Robust PCA Algorithm for Building Representations from Panoramic Images. In *ECCV '02: Proceedings of the 7th European Conference on Computer Vision-Part IV*, pages 761–775, London, UK, 2002. Springer-Verlag.
4. J. Wolf, W. Burgard, and H. Burkhardt. Robust Vision-based Localization by Combining an Image Retrieval System with Monte Carlo Localization. *IEEE Transactions on Robotics*, 21(2):208–216, 2005.
5. D. Lowe. Distinctive Image Features from Scale-Invariant Keypoints. *International Journal on Computer Vision*, 60(2):91–110, 2004.
6. H. Tamimi and A. Zell. Vision based Localization of Mobile Robots using Kernel Approaches. In *Proceedings of the IEEE/RSJ International Conference on Intelligent Robots and Systems(IROS)*, pages 1896–1901, 2004.
7. P. Addison. *The Illustrated Wavelet Transform Handbook.* Taylor and Francis, London, UK, 2002.
8. R. Sim and G. Dudek. Learning Generative Models of Invariant Features. In *Proceedings of the IEEE/RSJ Conference on Intelligent Robots and Systems (IROS)*, pages 3481–3488, Sendai, Japan, 2004.
9. M. Safari, M. T. Harandi, and B. Araabi. A SVM-based Method for Face Recognition using a Wavelet PCA Representation of Faces. In *Proceedings of the IEEE International Conference on Image Processing*, pages 853–856, 2004.
10. H. Choi K. Kim, S. Oh. Facial Feature Extraction Using PCA and Wavelet Multi-Resolution Images. In *Sixth IEEE International Conference on Automatic Face and Gesture Recognition*, pages 439– 444, 17-19 May 2004.

Zur Selbstlokalisierung mobiler Systeme bei fehlenden absoluten Referenzen

Torsten Lilge[1], Wilfried Gerth[1] und Andreas Goronczy[2]

[1] Institut für Regelungstechnik, Leibniz Universität Hannover,
Appelstr. 11, 30167 Hannover, lilge/gerth@irt.uni-hannover.de
[2] Clausthaler Umwelttechnik-Institut GmbH, Clausthal-Zellerfeld,
andreas.goronczy@cutec.de

Zusammenfassung. Dieser Beitrag behandelt die Selbstlokalisierung einer Gruppe von autonomen mobilen Robotern ohne oder mit nur seltenen absoluten Positionsmessungen über GPS oder Landmarken. Es wird gezeigt, dass die Genauigkeit der Positionsbestimmung auch durch relative Positionsmessungen zwischen den Robotern im Vergleich zur Verwendung rein odometrischer Daten erheblich erhöht werden kann.

1 Einleitung

Basierend auf [1] und [2] wird ein Verfahren zur Verbesserung der Selbstlokalisierung einer Gruppe von Robotern ohne Möglichkeit zur Durchführung absoluter Positionsmessungen vorgestellt. Wie auch in [1] und [2] verfügt jeder Roboter der Gruppe über Sensoren zur Messung der eigenen translatorischen und rotatorischen Geschwindigkeit und misst den Abstand und die Richtung zu einem weiteren Roboter der Gruppe. Als Erweiterung wird hier ein Offset der Geschwindigkeitsmessungen berücksichtigt. Dieser entsteht z. B. bei konstanter Geschwindigkeit durch nicht exakt bekannte Raddurchmesser bei radgetriebenen Robotern oder durch Offset behaftete Drehratensensoren [3] zur Erfassung der rotatorischen Geschwindigkeit in autonomen Systemen wie Unterwasserfahrzeugen. Der letztgenannte Fall stellt insbesondere für die hier betrachteten Drehungen um die Hochachse ein Problem dar, da für diese Achse der Gravitationsvektor nicht als Referenz zur Verfügung steht. Eine Beobachtbarkeitsanalyse des Gesamtsystems zeigt die Möglichkeiten und Grenzen des Verfahrens. Eine dezentrale Berechnung des verwendeten EKF wie in [1] und [2] wird hier nicht betrachtet.

2 Das Systemmodell

2.1 Zeitkontinuierliche Modellierung

Im Folgenden wird eine Gruppe von $N > 2$ Robotern betrachtet. Der Zustand von Roboter i umfasst seine kartesischen Positionskoordinaten a_i und b_i sowie seine Orientierung ϕ_i. Die offsetbehaftet gemessenen Geschwindigkeiten v_i und

ω_i stellen die Eingangsgrößen des Systems dar. Die Berücksichtigung der Offsets erfolgt über zusätzliche, konstante Zustandsgrößen. Das kinematische Modell für Roboter i lautet somit

$$\begin{pmatrix} \dot{a}_i(t) \\ \dot{b}_i(t) \\ \dot{\phi}_i(t) \\ \dot{v}_{oi}(t) \\ \dot{\omega}_{oi}(t) \end{pmatrix} = \begin{pmatrix} (v_i(t) - v_{oi}(t)) \cos(\phi_i(t)) \\ (v_i(t) - v_{oi}(t)) \sin(\phi_i(t)) \\ \omega_i(t) - \omega_{oi}(t) \\ 0 \\ 0 \end{pmatrix} . \tag{1}$$

Messbare Ausgangsgrößen sind der relative Abstand und die Richtung von Roboter i zu Roboter j mit $j = (i \bmod N) + 1$, also

$$\boldsymbol{y}_i(t) = \begin{pmatrix} d_{ij} \\ \alpha_{ij} \end{pmatrix} = \begin{pmatrix} \sqrt{(a_i(t) - a_j(t))^2 + (b_i(t) - b_j(t))^2} \\ \arctan\left(\frac{b_j(t)-b_i(t)}{a_j(t)-a_i(t)}\right) - \phi_i(t) \end{pmatrix} . \tag{2}$$

Abb. 1 veranschaulicht die relativen Messungen zwischen zwei Robotern. Die

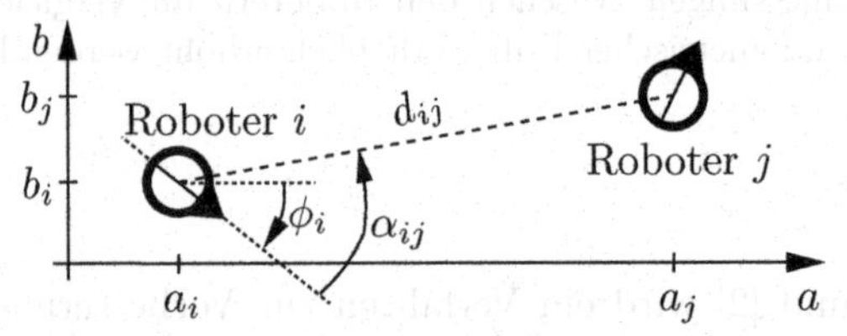

Abb. 1. Relative Messungen von Roboter i bezüglich Roboter j ($\phi_i < 0$)

Systemgleichungen für Roboter i mit dem Eingangsvektor $\boldsymbol{u}_i = \left(v_i \; \omega_i\right)^T$ und dem Zustandsvektor $\boldsymbol{x}_i = \left(a_i \; b_i \; \phi_i \; v_{oi} \; \omega_{oi}\right)^T$ können in der Form

$$\dot{\boldsymbol{x}}_i(t) = \boldsymbol{f}_i(\boldsymbol{x}_i(t), \boldsymbol{u}_i(t)), \quad \boldsymbol{y}_i(t) = \boldsymbol{h}_i(\boldsymbol{x}_i(t), \boldsymbol{x}_j(t)) \tag{3}$$

mit $i = 1, 2, \ldots, N$ und $j = (i \bmod N) + 1$ angegeben werden. Eine Kopplung zwischen den Robotern tritt somit nur in der Ausgangsgleichung auf.

2.2 Zeitdiskrete Modellierung

Zur Datenfusion wird ein Extended Kalman Filter (EKF) basierend auf einer Euler-Diskretisierung (Abtastzeit T) des aus den N Einzelsystemen (3) bestehenden Gesamtsystems verwendet. Den Messungen der Ausgangsgröße ist dabei das weiße Rauschen $\boldsymbol{\eta}(k)$ und den Geschwindigkeiten neben einem Offset noch das weiße Rauschen $\boldsymbol{\xi}_u(k)$ überlagert. Zur Berücksichtigung von Modellfehlern (z. B. durch die näherungsweise Diskretisierung) wird noch ein Prozessrauschen $\boldsymbol{\xi}_x(k)$ angenommen. Für das Gesamtsystem bestehend aus den N Zustandsvektoren $\boldsymbol{x}_i(k)$, $i = 1, 2, \ldots, N$ folgt somit

$$\boldsymbol{x}(k+1) = \boldsymbol{x}(k) + T\,\boldsymbol{f}\big(\boldsymbol{x}(k), \boldsymbol{u}(k) + \boldsymbol{\xi}_u(k)\big) + \boldsymbol{\xi}_x(k) \quad , \tag{4a}$$

$$\boldsymbol{y}(k) = \boldsymbol{h}(\boldsymbol{x}(k)) + \boldsymbol{\eta}(k). \tag{4b}$$

3 Beobachtbarkeitsanalyse

Wie bereits in [1] angegeben, kann ohne absolute Positionsmessungen offensichtlich schon für das Systemmodell ohne konstante Störgrößen keine vollständige Beobachtbarkeit vorliegen. Dieses gilt dann natürlich auch für das Modell mit modellierten Störgrößen, da hier Zustandsgrößen hinzugefügt werden, die nicht unmittelbar in den Ausgangsgleichungen erscheinen. Die nachfolgende Analyse erfolgt zunächst am zeitkontinuierlichen System. Eine entsprechende Untersuchung des zeitdiskreten Systems liefert gleiche Ergebnisse.

3.1 Beobachtbarkeit des linearisierten Systems

Für eine Beobachtbarkeitsanalyse bietet sich zunächst die Linearisierung des zeitkontinuierlichen Gesamtsystems an. Die dann mögliche Rangbestimmung der resultierenden Beobachtbarkeitsmatrix erlaubt zunächst eine allgemeine Aussage über die Beobachtbarkeit. Die sogenannte Kalmansche Beobachtbarkeitsmatrix linearer Systeme mit der Systemmatrix $\boldsymbol{A}$ und der Ausgangsmatrix $\boldsymbol{C}$ lautet

$$\boldsymbol{Q} = \begin{pmatrix} \boldsymbol{C} \\ \boldsymbol{C}\,\boldsymbol{A} \\ \vdots \\ \boldsymbol{C}\,\boldsymbol{A}^{n-1} \end{pmatrix}. \tag{5}$$

In einem weiteren Schritt erfolgt die Transformation des Systems in ein beobachtbares und in ein nicht beobachtbares Teilsystem. Diese Entkopplung ermöglicht dann eine genauere Analyse der Beobachtbarkeit einzelner Systemzustände.

System mit Störmodell Die Linearisierung des Systems mit konstanten Störgrößen v_{oi} und ω_{oi} mit N Robotern im allgemeinen Arbeitspunkt

$$\boldsymbol{x}_{i0} = \left(a_{i0}\; b_{i0}\; \phi_{i0}\; v_{oi0}\; \omega_{oi0}\right)^T, \quad \boldsymbol{u}_{i0} = \left(v_{i0}\; \omega_{i0}\right)^T, \qquad i = 1, 2, \ldots, N \tag{6}$$

liefert

$$\boldsymbol{A} = \begin{pmatrix} \boldsymbol{A}_1 & \boldsymbol{0} & \cdots & \boldsymbol{0} \\ \boldsymbol{0} & \boldsymbol{A}_2 & \cdots & \boldsymbol{0} \\ \vdots & \vdots & \ddots & \vdots \\ \boldsymbol{0} & \boldsymbol{0} & \cdots & \boldsymbol{A}_N \end{pmatrix}, \quad \boldsymbol{C} = \begin{pmatrix} \boldsymbol{C}_1 & \widetilde{\boldsymbol{C}}_1 & \boldsymbol{0} & \cdots & \boldsymbol{0} & \boldsymbol{0} \\ \boldsymbol{0} & \boldsymbol{C}_2 & \widetilde{\boldsymbol{C}}_2 & \cdots & \boldsymbol{0} & \boldsymbol{0} \\ \vdots & \vdots & \ddots & \ddots & & \vdots \\ \vdots & \vdots & & \ddots & \ddots & \vdots \\ \boldsymbol{0} & \boldsymbol{0} & \boldsymbol{0} & \cdots & \boldsymbol{C}_{N-1} & \widetilde{\boldsymbol{C}}_{N-1} \\ \widetilde{\boldsymbol{C}}_N & \boldsymbol{0} & \boldsymbol{0} & \cdots & \boldsymbol{0} & \boldsymbol{C}_N \end{pmatrix} \tag{7}$$

mit

$$\boldsymbol{A}_i = \begin{pmatrix} 0 & 0 & -(v_{i0} - v_{oi0})\sin(\phi_{i0}) & -\cos(\phi_{i0}) & 0 \\ 0 & 0 & (v_{i0} - v_{oi0})\cos(\phi_{i0}) & -\sin(\phi_{i0}) & 0 \\ 0 & 0 & 0 & 0 & -1 \\ 0 & 0 & 0 & 0 & 0 \\ 0 & 0 & 0 & 0 & 0 \end{pmatrix}, \tag{8}$$

$$\boldsymbol{C}_i = \begin{pmatrix} \frac{a_{i0}-a_{j0}}{d_{ij}} & \frac{b_{i0}-b_{j0}}{d_{ij}} & 0 & 0 & 0 \\ -\frac{b_{i0}-b_{j0}}{d_{ij}^2} & \frac{a_{i0}-a_{j0}}{d_{ij}^2} & -1 & 0 & 0 \end{pmatrix}, \quad \widetilde{\boldsymbol{C}}_i = \begin{pmatrix} -\frac{a_{i0}-a_{j0}}{d_{ij}} & -\frac{b_{i0}-b_{j0}}{d_{ij}} & 0 & 0 & 0 \\ \frac{b_{i0}-b_{j0}}{d_{ij}^2} & -\frac{a_{i0}-a_{j0}}{d_{ij}^2} & 0 & 0 & 0 \end{pmatrix} \tag{9}$$

und $d_{ij} = \sqrt{(a_{j0} - a_{i0})^2 + (b_{j0} - b_{i0})^2}$, $i = 1, 2, \ldots, N$, $j = (i \bmod N) + 1$.

Für das Gesamtsystem mit Modellierung konstanter Störgrößen ergibt sich für den Fall sich bewegender Roboter ($v_{i0} - v_{oi0} \neq 0$ für $i = 1, 2, \ldots, N$) für $\boldsymbol{Q}$ ein maximaler Rang von $n_o = 5\,N - 3$ und somit eine minimale Dimension des nicht beobachtbaren Unterraums von $n_u = 3$. Nach [4] lässt sich eine Transformation der Form

$$\widetilde{\boldsymbol{x}} = \begin{pmatrix} \widetilde{\boldsymbol{x}}_u \\ \widetilde{\boldsymbol{x}}_o \end{pmatrix} = \boldsymbol{T}^{-1}\boldsymbol{x} \quad \text{mit} \quad \boldsymbol{T} = \big(\ker\{\boldsymbol{Q}\} \mid \mathrm{Im}\{\boldsymbol{Q}\}\big) \tag{10}$$

angeben. Dabei ist $\widetilde{\boldsymbol{x}}_u \in \mathbb{R}^{n_u}$ der Zustandsvektor des nicht beobachtbaren und $\widetilde{\boldsymbol{x}}_o \in \mathbb{R}^{n_o}$ der Zustandsvektor des beobachtbaren Teilsystems. Aus $\boldsymbol{x} = \boldsymbol{T}\widetilde{\boldsymbol{x}}$ folgt unmittelbar

$$\boldsymbol{x} = \ker\{\boldsymbol{Q}\}\,\widetilde{\boldsymbol{x}}_u + \mathrm{Im}\{\boldsymbol{Q}\}\,\widetilde{\boldsymbol{x}}_o. \tag{11}$$

Für die hier vorliegende Beobachtbarkeitsmatrix eines Systems mit N Robotern weist $\ker\{\boldsymbol{Q}\}$ für Arbeitspunkte mit $v_{i0} - v_{oi0} \neq 0$ i. A. die Struktur

$$\ker\{\boldsymbol{Q}\} = \begin{pmatrix} \boldsymbol{k}_{\boldsymbol{Q},1} \\ \vdots \\ \boldsymbol{k}_{\boldsymbol{Q},N} \end{pmatrix} \quad \text{mit} \quad \boldsymbol{k}_{\boldsymbol{Q},i} = \begin{pmatrix} * & * & * \\ * & * & * \\ * & * & * \\ * & * & * \\ 0 & 0 & 0 \end{pmatrix} \tag{12}$$

auf, wobei jeweils die fünfte Zeile von $\boldsymbol{k}_{\boldsymbol{Q},i}$ lediglich Nullen enthält. Der fünfte Zustand eines Roboters, also der Drehratenoffset ω_{oi} hängt gemäß Gl. (11) somit nur von den beobachtbaren Zuständen $\widetilde{\boldsymbol{x}}_o$ ab. Dieser Offset erweist sich somit als beobachtbar. Seine Kenntnis lässt eine erhebliche Verringerung der Drift der geschätzten Orientierungen $\hat{\phi}_i(t)$ vermuten.

Die Forderung $v_{i0} - v_{oi0} \neq 0$ folgt aus der Struktur der Submatrizen $\boldsymbol{A}_i$. Neben verschwindenden translatorischen Geschwindigkeiten sind noch andere Szenarien möglich, die zu einer Reduzierung des Rangs der Beobachtbarkeitsmatrix führen. Beispiele hierfür sind:

- Alle Roboter bewegen sich mit der gleichen Geschwindigkeit in die gleiche Richtung.
- Der durch Geschwindigkeitsoffsets nicht erfasste Bewegungsanteil von Roboter j führt in den relativen Messungen von Roboter i zu Roboter j gerade genau zu einer Bestätigung der durch Geschwindigkeitsoffsets fälschlicherweise angenommenen Bewegung von Roboter i.

Im praktischen Einsatz ist i. A. nicht mit einem Auftreten dieser Szenarios über ein längeres Zeitintervall zu rechnen, so dass die Reduzierung des Rangs der Beobachtbarkeitsmatrix nur temporär auftritt.

System ohne Störmodell Das System ohne Störmodell weist für den Fall sich bewegender Roboter ($v_{i0} \neq 0$ für $i = 1, 2, \ldots, N$) einen maximalen Rang von $n_o = 3\,N - 2$ der Beobachtbarkeitsmatrix und somit einen nicht beobachtbaren Unterraum der minimalen Dimension $n_u = 2$ auf. Aus der Analyse des Nullraums der Beobachtbarkeitsmatrix folgt, dass die Orientierungen ϕ_i nur von den beobachtbaren Zuständen $\widetilde{\boldsymbol{x}}_o$ abhängen. Die Orientierung, die bei rein inertialer Messung aus oben genannten Gründen besonders schwer zu erfassen ist, erweist sich somit zumindest für das linearisierte System auch ohne absolute Messungen als beobachtbar. Die nicht im Beobachtungsmodell berücksichtigten Messoffsets führen dann aber zu einem (konstanten) Antrieb des Schätzfehlers.

3.2 Beobachtbarkeit des nichtlinearen System

Die Prüfung der lokalen Beobachtbarkeit eines nichtlinearen zeitkontinuierlichen Systems lässt sich nach [5] auf die Rangprüfung der Beobachtbarkeitsmatrix $\widetilde{\boldsymbol{Q}}(\boldsymbol{x}, \boldsymbol{u})$, die sich als Jakobimatrix der sogenannten Beobachtbarkeitsabbildung $\boldsymbol{q}(\boldsymbol{x}, \boldsymbol{u})$ ergibt, reduzieren. Diese hängt von der Eingangsgröße und für Systeme ohne Durchgangsanteil von max. $n-2$ zeitlichen Ableitungen der Eingangsgröße ab. Für eine möglichst einfache Darstellung soll hier von konstanten Eingangsgrößen $\boldsymbol{u} = \boldsymbol{u}_0$ ausgegangen werden. Dann ergibt sich

$$\widetilde{\boldsymbol{Q}}(\boldsymbol{x}, \boldsymbol{u}_0) = \frac{\partial \boldsymbol{q}(\boldsymbol{x}, \boldsymbol{u}_0)}{\partial \boldsymbol{x}} \quad \text{mit} \quad \boldsymbol{q}(\boldsymbol{x}, \boldsymbol{u}_0) = \begin{pmatrix} \boldsymbol{y}(t) \\ \dot{\boldsymbol{y}}(t) \\ \vdots \\ \boldsymbol{y}^{(n-1)}(t) \end{pmatrix} = \begin{pmatrix} \boldsymbol{h}(\boldsymbol{x}) \\ \boldsymbol{L_f h}(\boldsymbol{x}) \\ \vdots \\ \boldsymbol{L}_{\boldsymbol{f}}^{n-1} \boldsymbol{h}(\boldsymbol{x}) \end{pmatrix} \tag{13}$$

und der vektoriellen Form der Lie-Ableitung

$$\boldsymbol{L_f h}(\boldsymbol{x}) = \left(\boldsymbol{L_f h}_1(\boldsymbol{x})\; \boldsymbol{L_f h}_2(\boldsymbol{x}) \cdots \boldsymbol{L_f h}_m(\boldsymbol{x})\right)^T \tag{14a}$$

$$\text{mit} \quad \boldsymbol{L}_{\boldsymbol{f}}^0 \boldsymbol{h}(\boldsymbol{x}) = \boldsymbol{h}(\boldsymbol{x}), \quad \boldsymbol{L}_{\boldsymbol{f}}^k \boldsymbol{h}(\boldsymbol{x}) = \frac{\partial \boldsymbol{L}_{\boldsymbol{f}}^{k-1} \boldsymbol{h}(\boldsymbol{x})}{\partial \boldsymbol{x}} \boldsymbol{f}(\boldsymbol{x}, \boldsymbol{u}_0). \tag{14b}$$

System mit Störmodell Eine Analyse des Gesamtsystems mit Störmodell ergibt den gleichen Rang $n_o = 5\,N - 3$ ($n_u = 3$) wie bei der linearen Analyse. Allerdings ergibt die Untersuchung des Nullraums der nichtlinearen Beobachtbarkeitsmatrix, dass jetzt die letzten beiden Zeilen der Submatrix $\boldsymbol{k}_{\boldsymbol{Q},i}$ aus Gl. (12) nur mit Nullen besetzt sind. Somit hängen beide Offsets v_{oi} und ω_{oi} nur von den beobachtbaren Zuständen $\widetilde{\boldsymbol{x}}_o$ und nicht von $\widetilde{\boldsymbol{x}}_u$ ab.

System ohne Störmodell Die Untersuchung der nichtlinearen Beobachtbarkeitsmatrix des Systems ohne Störmodell liefert einen Rang $n_o = 3\,N - 3$ der Beobachtbarkeitsmatrix. Bemerkenswert ist die Tatsache, dass der Rang der nichtlinearen Beobachtbarkeitsmatrix damit geringer ist als der Rang der Beobachtbarkeitsmatrix des linearisierten Systems ($3\,N - 2$). Die Analyse des Nullraums von $\widetilde{\boldsymbol{Q}}$ führt außerdem zu dem Ergebnis, dass alle Systemzustände von den nicht beobachtbaren Zuständen $\widetilde{\boldsymbol{x}}_o$ der entkoppelten Darstellung abhängen.

Von der Linearisierung werden offenbar gerade die Terme höherer Ordnung in der Beobachtbarkeitsmatrix unterdrückt, die zu einer linearen Abhängigkeit zwischen den durch die zeitlichen Ableitungen der Ausgangsgröße und den durch die Ausgangsgröße selbst hervorgerufenen Zeilen in der Beobachtbarkeitsmatrix führt. Unter Vernachlässigung dieser höheren Terme erweist sich die Orientierungen der Roboter als beobachtbar, bei Berücksichtigung dieser Terme nicht. Dies legt die Vermutung nahe, dass sich die Orientierungen zumindest mit einer langsameren Drift schätzen lassen als die anderen Systemzustände.

4 Simulationsergebnisse

Für ein Szenario mit $N = 3$ Robotern wurde sowohl mit und ohne Berücksichtigung der Geschwindigkeitsoffsets ein EKF implementiert und die geschätzten Positionen mit der Integration der (fehlerbehafteten) Geschwindigkeitsinformationen verglichen. Neben den Geschwindigkeitsoffsets (translatorisch ± 0.001 m/s und rotatorisch ± 0.0015 rad/s (typisch für preiswerte Drehratensensoren)) wurde dabei zusätzlich noch ein falsch angenommener Radradius (2...5 % Fehler) vorausgesetzt. Die dem EKF zu Grunde liegenden Varianzmatrizen der Rauschsignale $\boldsymbol{\xi}_u(k)$ und $\boldsymbol{\eta}(k)$ weichen von denen der in der Simulation verwendeten Rauschsignale ab, was typischerweise einer realen Anwendung entspricht. Die Abtastzeit beträgt 0.5 s, die Anfangsfehler der Roboterzustände betragen ± 0.5 m bei der Position und ± 0.1 rad bei der Orientierung. Die Geschwindigkeitsoffsets sind anfänglich unbekannt. Abb. 2 zeigt die wahren Positionen der Roboter und deren Schätzungen (links, wahre Position und EKF mit Störmodell liegen nahezu aufeinander), die Schätzfehler der Oritentierung (rechts oben) sowie die Positionsfehler der untersuchten Schätzverfahren (rechts unten). Dabei ist deutlich die geringste Abweichung beim EKF mit Störmodell, also mit Berücksichtigung von Geschwindigkeitsoffsets im Beobachtungsmodell zu erkennen. Die sich ergebende langsame Drift der Orientierungen sowohl für das EKF mit und ohne Störmodell bestätigt die Ergebnisse der Beobachtbarkeitsanalysen.

Die in Abb. 2 dargestellten Verläufe zeigen besonders deutlich die möglichen Vorteile des vorgestellten Störmodells. Weitere Untersuchungen ergaben, dass bei sehr geringen Geschwindigkeitsoffsets eher das EKF ohne Störmodell im Vorteil ist. Insgesamt ergibt sich eine relativ hohe Abhängigkeit der Filtereigenschaften von der für das EKF angenommenen Varianz der Prozessstörung $\boldsymbol{\xi}_x(k)$, beim EKF mit Störmodell insbesondere bezüglich der erweiterten, konstanten Zustandsgrößen $\boldsymbol{v}_{oi}$ und $\boldsymbol{\omega}_{oi}$. Bei den in Abb. 2 dargestellten Verläufen wurden die Varianzen von $\boldsymbol{\xi}_x(k)$ als Kompromiss zwischen Schätzfehler und Rauschen der Schätzungen eingestellt.

Bei stets gleichen Varianzen $\boldsymbol{\xi}_x$ wurde in 1000 Simulationen mit zufällig gewählten Anfangswerten, Geschwindigkeitsoffsets und Varianzen der Störungen $\boldsymbol{\eta}$ und $\boldsymbol{\xi}_u$ über alle k und alle N Roboter die Summe des Abstandsquadrats $d_i(k)^2 = (\hat{a}_i(k) - a_i(k))^2 + (\hat{b}_i(k) - b_i(k))^2$ ermittelt. Dabei ergaben sich etwa 72 % Simulationen, bei denen das EKF mit Störmodell die geringere Fehlerquadratsumme aufwies als das EKF ohne Störmodell.

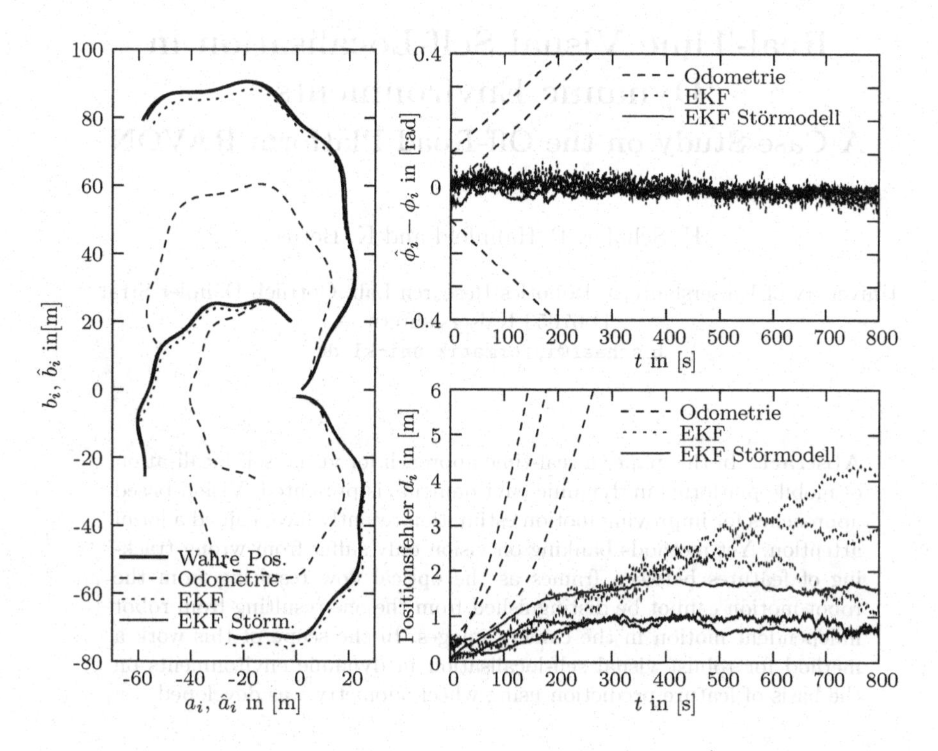

Abb. 2. Wahre und geschätzte Roboterposition(links); Fehler $\hat{\phi}_i - \phi_i$ der Orientierungsschätzung (rechts oben); Positionsfehler $d_i = |(\hat{a}_i\ \hat{b}_i) - (a_i\ b_i)|$ (rechts unten);

5 Zusammenfassung

In einer Gruppe von Robotern kann die Genauigkeit der Positionsbestimmung durch relative Messungen zwischen den Robotern deutlich erhöht werden. Die Orientierungen der Roboter erweisen sich dabei in einem Arbeitspunkt als beobachtbar. Die Modellierung konstanter Störgrößen erlaubt darüber hinaus die Erhöhung der Robustheit bei Fehlern der Geschwindigkeitsmessung.

Literaturverzeichnis

1. Roumeliotis, S. I. und G. A. Bekey: *Distributed multirobot localization.* Robotics and Automation, IEEE Trans., 18(5):781–795, Okt. 2002.
2. Mourikis, A.I. und S.I. Roumeliotis: *Performance analysis of multirobot Cooperative localization.* Robotics, IEEE Trans., 22(4):666–681, Aug. 2006.
3. Strasser, R.: *Untersuchung von Beobachterverfahren für eine inertiale Messeinheit.* Nr. 1072 der Reihe 8 der *VDI-Fortschrittberichte.* VDI, Düsseldorf, 2005.
4. Ludyk, G.: *Theor. Regelungstechnik,* Band 2. Springer, Berlin Heidelberg, 1995.
5. Rothfuß, Ralf und Michael Zeitz: *Einführung in die Analyse nichtlinearer Systeme.* In Engell, S. (Hrsg.): *Entwurf nichtlinearer Regelungen,* S. 3–22. Oldenbourg, München, 1995.

Real-Time Visual Self-Localisation in Dynamic Environments

A Case Study on the Off-Road Platform RAVON

H. Schäfer, P. Hahnfeld and K. Berns

University of Kaiserslautern, Robotics Research Lab, Gottlieb-Daimler-Straße, D-67653 Kaiserslautern
b_schaef@informatik.uni-kl.de

Abstract. In this paper a real-time approach for visual self-localisation of mobile platforms in dynamic environments is presented. Vision-based approaches for improving motion estimation recently have gained a lot of attention. Yet methods banking on vision only suffer from wrong tracking of features between frames as the optical flow resulting from the robot motion cannot be distinguished from the one resulting from robot independent motion in the camera images. In the scope of this work a method for robust visual self-localisation in dynamic environments on the basis of feature prediction using wheel odometry was developed.

1 Introduction

One of the key problems in mobile robotics is the localisation of a vehicle in unknown terrain. In recent years visual methods for pose estimation have become more and more interesting as they are now computationally feasible and do not suffer from the same sources of error as traditional approaches do. In fusion with other systems the robot pose estimation should become more stable in particular on the local level.

Fig. 1. RAVON, the Robust Autonomous Vehicle for Off-road Navigation.

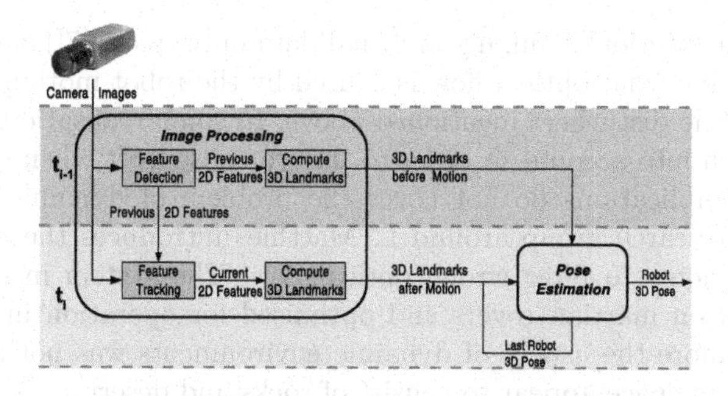

Fig. 2. Overview of Visual Odometry.

On the mobile off-road platform RAVON[1] – which is developed by the RRLab[2] at the University of Kaiserslautern – wheel odometry, a custom-built inertial measurement unit with integrated digital compass and a GPS receiver have been deployed so far. Now this suite of sensor systems shall be complemented with stereo ego motion in order to improve the local stability of the yielded pose information. Besides better results of the fused position information this extension opens the possibility to build up an absolute local obstacle map from stereo vision information in order to cover the blind angles of the camera system. In principle most visual odometry approaches follows the pattern outlined in Figure 2. The camera system captures a frame and a set of features that are suitable for tracking are selected in this image. After some time, another frame is taken. The features that have been detected in the previous frame are now tracked into the current frame. The vectors between these points contain the information about the change in orientation and translation of the robot between the two subsequent frames. The last step is an ego-motion estimation on the basis of the vectors to receive the robot pose according to a given starting point.

2 State of the Art

The idea of visual odometry was first developed by L. Matthies [2]. This approach was refined and deployed on several mars robots [3] and other researchers implemented different flavours of the original concept. The differences mostly lie in the camera system – monocular [4], omni-directional [5] or stereo [2] – used. The two first mentioned camera configurations are not an option in off-road terrain as a flat ground plane needs to be assumed in order to compute 3D coordinates from the image points. Therefore a stereo-ego-motion approach was chosen for implementation in this work.

In common outdoor scenarios a lot of dynamics come into play as people, other vehicles or tree branches and high grass affected by the wind cause vehicle motion independent movement in the camera images (See Figure 5 in Section 4).

1 RAVON → Robust Autonomous Vehicle for Off-road Navigation [1]
2 RRLab → Robotics Research Lab (`http://rrlab.informatik.uni-kl.de`)

Current implementations banking on visual data only (p.ex. [7]) suffer from the inability to decide what optical flow is caused by the robot motion and what is introduced by the disturbers mentioned above. In some realisations the vehicle velocity is taken into account in order to prevent pose drift when standing still [6], yet most publications do not cover the problem of dynamic sceneries at all. In [8] the research group around L. Matthies introduces the idea of using the wheel odometry to filter wrong optical flow. The system in question was to be deployed on martian rovers and optimised for operation in stop-and-go mode. Furthermore the aspect of dynamic environments was not addressed as the worlds out in space appear to consist of rocks and deserts.

3 Visual Self-Localisation in Dynamic Environments

Having introduced the concept of visual odometry in general and the problems which arise when dynamics come into play this section shall outline the approach implemented in the context of this work. The idea of incorporating wheel odometry into a filtering step for pose estimation was picked up and integrated into a real-time visual odometry system. The focus in this context was the development of a visual self-localisation system which would be robust against dynamic disturbers in order to obtain locally stable pose information. On this basis an absolute local map shall be built of obstacle detection output computed from the very same images as used for pose estimation.

The implemented system can be grouped into three modules (See Figure 3). Module *Image Processing* encapsulates feature detection and tracking as well as the 3D reconstruction of the landmarks. For `Feature Detection` the OpenCV[3] implementations of the Harris corner detector [9] is used. `Feature Tracking` and `Stereo Matching` steps are carried out with the Lucas-Kanade-tracker [10] also available in OpenCV. Given the 3D landmarks of two subsequent time steps (t_{i-1} and t_i in Figure 3) a *Feature Filtering* step is inserted using the `Pose Delta` computed from the correlated 2D poses of the robot from the wheel odometry. For

[3] OpenCV → Open Computer Vision Library `http://opencv.sourceforge.net`

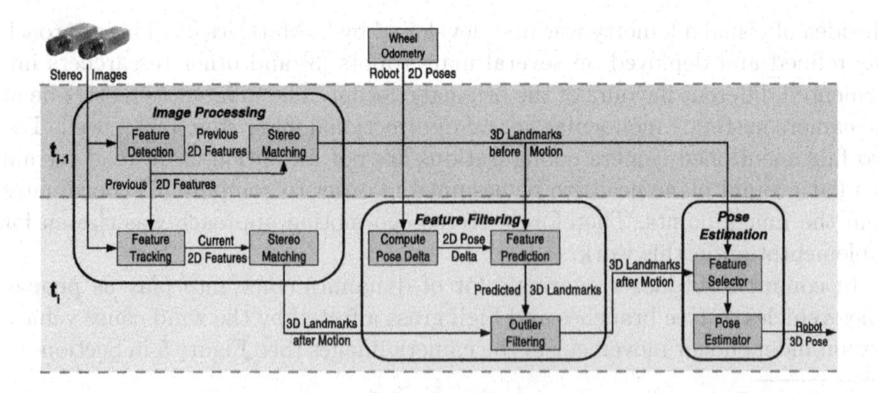

Fig. 3. Concept of the implemented Visual Self-localisation Facility.

Pose Estimation a suitable subset of the filtered 3D landmarks is computed using a preemptive RANSAC-based algorithm in combination with Singular Value Decomposition for computing the robot pose delta. The preemptive error function for RANSAC termination is computed from the reprojection of the transformed previous 3D landmarks into the image plane. Due to space limitations in this paper the reader shall be referred to [11] for the mathematical details. The attempt to fuse wheel odometry with visual odometry implies that both sources of information need to be synchronised. On the test platform RAVON stereo image processing runs on a dedicated computer system as it is computationally quite expensive. In order to correlate sensor data from different sources all computers are synchronised via the network time protocol which assures an accuracy of about 2-10 ms in a controlled network. This is given as RAVON features a switched network with only four computers connected. Furthermore traffic is limited by trying to compute as much as possible on the particular nodes owning the data source and only transmit filtered abstract representations over the network rather than raw sensor data [12]. The wheel odometry poses are computed from encoder data coming from a DSP attached with a time stamp. This time stamp is adapted to the system time and attached to the odometry pose. The same is done for the image data which come with internal time stamps from the cameras. That way both data sources are brought to the same time basis very early in the procedure. The odometry poses with the attached poses are placed into a ring buffer located in a shared memory. Every time new camera images are available the ring buffer is searched for the best timed odometry pose. In order to give the odometry pose collector facility enough time to place the current pose into the ring buffer and to transfer the data over the network the poses are fused with the images after an undistortion step which is necessary for precise stereo imagery.

4 Experimental Results

In this section some experiments carried out on the RAVON and in the simulation environment [13] developed at the RRLab shall be presented. First of all the parameters for optical flow computation were tuned in the simulation environment where no mechanical or optical inaccuracies are present (imprecise mounting of the cameras on the robot, defective position of the CCD's in the cameras, lens distortion, etc.). Furthermore no disturbers falsify the input images and therefore perfect conditions for optimising the optical flow component. As a benchmark for this procedure the track depicted in Figure 4 (a) of about 20 m was defined. Step by step the parameters were adjusted according to the best performance in comparison to ground truth which is naturally available in simulation. With the optimised system the endpoint deviation was about 1.75 % which corresponds to a distance of 0.38 m. In average the deviation of the estimated points compared to ground truth was about 0.15 m.

The parameters for optical flow computation set real experiments were carried out to test the influence of disturbers. Figure 5 shows the same images as

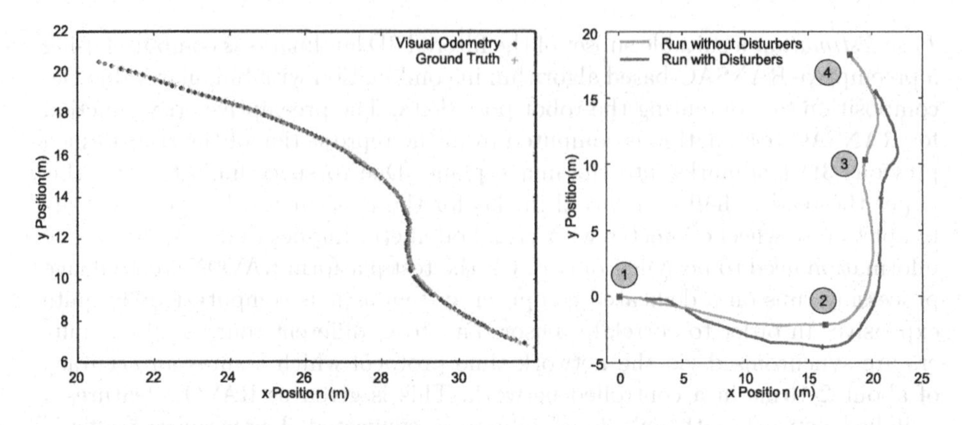

Fig. 4. Visual odometry compared to ground truth in simulation (left) and Visual odometry test runs on RAVON with and without disturbers (right).

introduced in Section 2 as examples for robot motion independent movements in the camera images. In these illustrations the reader can see that the optical flow introduced by the disturbers was classified as wrong optical flow which will not be taken into account. For clarity reasons the frames have been chosen such that the disturbing regions are not very large. In several test runs it was shown that external influences may occupy large regions without affecting the accuracy of the visual self-localisation.

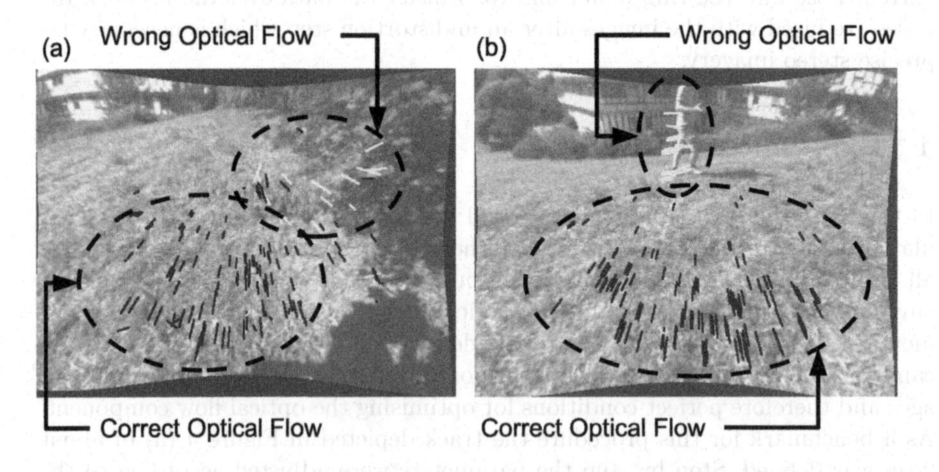

Fig. 5. Wrong optical flow correctly classified by the implemented system (yellow/light grey lines). Only the correct optical flow (blue/dark grey lines) is used.

In a first set of tests a course was marked on the test grounds of the RRLab. This course was covered twice, once without and once with disturbers. At the pre-

defined check points the position computed by the visual odometry was tagged in order to compare these spots later. Note that a quantitative conclusion on this type of test is difficult as repeatability of the very same run cannot be achieved. Nonetheless the plot in Figure 4 (b) shows that the computed poses with disturbers stay locally stable and the deviation of both runs is in a promising range. Over the whole run the deviation is about 10 % of the distance covered (15 m (checkpoint 2): 1.75 m, 30 m (checkpoint 3): 3,22, 40 m (checkpoint 3): 3.51 m) but this basically results from one minor orientation error in the very beginning which accumulated over time.
In order to get quantitative results ground truth comparisons using a powerful DGPS receiver as a reference would be necessary. As such a system was not available on RAVON until now these experiments are still pending. In the near future a StarFire2 GPS receiver which reaches a positioning accuracy of about 10 cm using the commercial satellite correction network Green Star will allow to carry out that kind of test. GPS receiver and Green Star license will kindly be provided by John Deere.

5 Conclusion and Future Work

In this paper a real-time stereo-ego-motion system for application in dynamic environments was presented. The idea of incorporating wheel odometry information to filter wrong optical flow was picked up from approaches approved in stop-and-go mode without dynamic sceneries in space robotics. In that context a method for careful correlation of stereo images and wheel odometry was introduced which results in a robust real-time stereo-ego-motion system. In particular the ability to distinguish ego-motion-born optical flow from the one introduced by disturbers makes the system suitable for dynamic environments. Experiments on the off-road platform RAVON showed that locally stable pose information can be achieved in dynamic environments.

In the future ground truth comparisons shall be carried out using a new high precision DGPS receiver. In that context the impact of further cascaded filtering mechanisms of the optical flow shall be evaluated. RAVON features an obstacle detection facility which uses the same stereo images as the pose estimation. In the future both systems shall be brought together in order to build an absolute local map to cover the blind angles of the camera system for obstacle avoidance. To assure optimal adjustment of the stereo camera head for obstacle detection an off-road-adapted pan/tilt unit was developed in recent months. Now that the mechanics are ready this active vision unit will be integrated into the existing framework. The camera head movement needs to be taken into account in pose estimation. Here again precise correlation is necessary to yield satisfactory results. The authors assume that the presented correlation approach already covers the problems that could arise with the new degree of freedom.

Acknowledgement

Research on the mobile robot RAVON is kindly supported by IK Elektronik, Mayser Polymer Electric, Hankook Tyres, Minitec, SICK, DSM Computer, Huebner Giessen and John Deere. The authors thank the sponsors for their support.

References

1. H. Schäfer, K. Berns RAVON – An autonomous Vehicle for Risky Intervention and Surveillance International Workshop on Robotics for risky intervention and environmental surveillance (RISE) 2006
2. Larry Matthies. Dynamic Stereo Vision (PhD. Thesis). Carnegie Mellon University October 1989.
3. Yang Cheng, Mark Maimore, Larry Matthies. Visual Odometry on the Mars Exploration Rovers. 2005.
4. Jason Cambpell, Rahul Sukthankar, Illah Nourbakhsh, Aroon Pahwa. A Robust Visual Odometry and Precipice Detection System Using Consumer-grade Monocular Vision. 2005.
5. Peter Corke, Dennis Strelow, Synjiv Singh. Omnidirectional Visual Odometry for a Planetary Rover. 2004.
6. David Nistér, Oleg Naroditsky, James Bergen. Visual Odometry. Sarnoff Corporation - Princeton
7. Niko Sünderhauf, Peter Protzel. Towards Using Sparse Bundle Adjustment for Robust Stereo Odometry in Outdoor Terrain. October 2006.
8. Daniel Helmick, Yang Cheng, Daniel Clouse, Larry Matthies. Path following using Visual Odometry for a Mars Rover in High-Slip Environments. 2004.
9. Konstantinos G. Derpanis. The Harris Corner Detector. October 2004.
10. Lucas, B., and Kanade, T. An Iterative Image Registration Technique with an Application to Stereo Vision Proc. of 7th International Joint Conference on Artificial Intelligence (IJCAI) 1981
11. P. Hahnfeld, H. Schäfer Vision-based Self-localization for Mobile Robots Project Thesis at Robotics Research Lab, University of Kaiserslautern http://rrlab.informatik.uni-kl.de 2007
12. H. Schäfer, M. Proetzsch, K. Berns Extension Approach for the Behaviour-Based Control System of the Outdoor Robot RAVON Autonome Mobile Systeme 2005
13. T. Braun, J. Wettach, K. Berns A Customizable, Multi-Host Simulation and Visualization Framework for Robot Applications 13th International Conference on Advanced Robotics (ICAR07) 2007

3D Reconstruction for Exploration of Indoor Environments

Jens Wettach and Karsten Berns

Robotics Research Lab, University of Kaiserslautern, Germany
{wettach,berns}@informatik.uni-kl.de

Abstract. Autonomous exploration of arbitrary indoor environments with a mobile robot depends on a reliable self-localization strategy. Existing approaches that use only 2D distance information from e.g. planar laser scanners may fail in highly cluttered areas due to the lack of stable landmark detection. This paper presents an approach for extracting room and furniture primitives from a 3D point cloud by matching shape primitives to the data samples. These basic building blocks can serve as landmarks for relocalization and give hints for interesting places during environmental exploration. Input data is acquired by a tiltable 2D laser scanner in reality and a realistic virtual sensor simulation. In the paper the complete process from sensor data acquisition, data filtering, RANSAC[1] based plane extraction and smoothing is described and tested in simulation and reality.

1 Introduction

Application scenario is an autonomous exploration of indoor environments with mobile robot MARVIN(see figure 1(b)). Its main sensors are a SICK S3000 laser scanner at its front side and a LMS200 scanner at its rear side which provide distances to nearest obstacles within a horizontal measurement plane about 10 cm above ground. Based on these sensors the robot is able to create a topological map of rooms and doors autonomously (see [4]). As this exploration relies on detection of room walls the strategy fails in cluttered areas where the two scanners do not "see" enough wall segments. Thus extraction of room primitives with an additional 3D scanner has come into focus to solve these problems.

The goal here is to create a sensor-based "robot view of the world" by approximating a 3D scene represented as point cloud of distance values with simple primitives as planes, cubes and cylinders (see [5] for a similar approach). These basis building blocks will help the robot to "understand" its environment sufficiently for localization and navigation tasks. Of course, for high-level tasks as fetching objects from a certain desk a matching of human understanding of things and these basic blocks has to be ascertained (long-term goal). By now only plane patches are extracted from the scene as this seems to be sufficient for getting a rough overview of a room and thus will serve as first step for solving the localization problem. The presented approach of plane extraction from an

[1] Random Sample Consensus (see[1])

arbitrary 3D point cloud is mainly based on the Grid-based Segmentation (GBS) algorithm presented in [2] and [3].

The remainder of this paper is organized as follows: the sensor data acquisition is decribed in section 2 and the feature extraction strategy in 3. Experimental results are given in 4, summary and outlook in 5.

2 Data Acquisition

Input for the feature extraction strategy is an arbitrary 3D point cloud as result of distance measurements which are either collected by a rotating 2D laser scanner or by a simulated sensor realized within the SIMVIS3D framework.

2.1 3D Scanner Device

The 3D scanner consists of a SICK LMS 200 laser range finder mounted on a tilt unit (see figure 1(b)) which enables an external rotation of the whole device around a horizontal axis from -45° to 45°. The scanner measures distances to nearest objects in sight using a pulsed laser beam that is deflected by a rotating mirror within the scanner case. The maximal scan area is 180° with a native angular resolution of 1°. Two consecutive scans are combined with an offset of 0.5° to get a resolution of 0.5°. Thus a complete scan consists of 361 distance values sent to the PC within one scan telegram (see figure 1(a)).

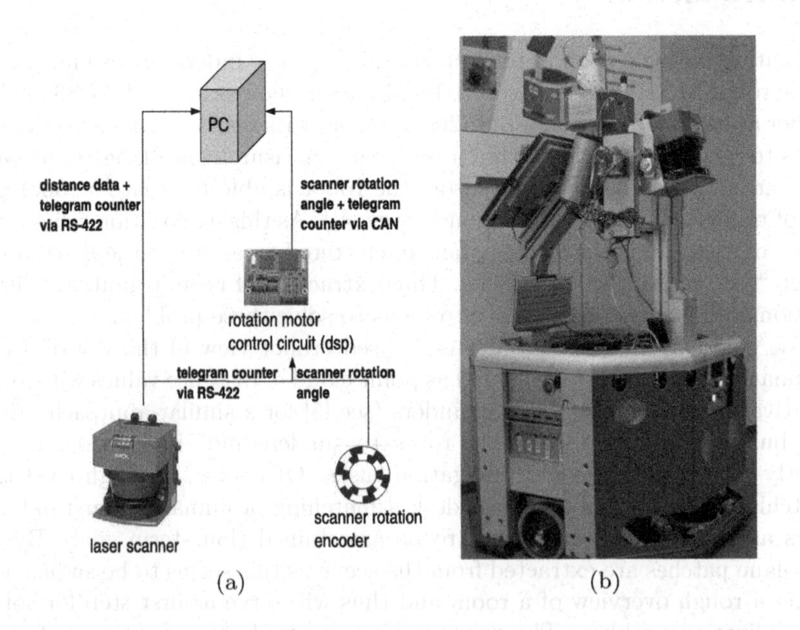

Fig. 1. (a) Fusion of distance data from laser scanner and external scanner tilt angle from DSP, (b) mobile robot MARVIN with mounted 3D scanner device

Each scan telegram is tagged with a counter value (modulo 256). The external rotation of the complete scanner device is controlled by a multi-purpose dsp control circuit (developed at RRLAB) which executes a speed and position control loop. This rotation is measured via an incremental encoder attached to the tilt axis with a resolution of 0.09°. For collecting a 3D point cloud the scanner is rotated continuously from start to end position. During this rotation the sensor collects distance data and sends scan telegrams to the PC via RS-422 link also in a continuous mode.

As the external sensor motion and the internal mirror rotation are independent of each other the problem is how to fuse distance and angular information consistently. As solution the motor control dsp also reads the scan telegrams from the RS-422 link. Whenever it has parsed a complete telegram it extracts the telegram counter and tags the corresponding scanner tilt angle with it. Here it takes into account that the device first collects data from two mirror rotations completely and afterwards sends the telegram. Thus the scanner tilt angle at the begin of each measurement is stored by the dsp program until the corresponding telegram counter has been retrieved and is then sent to the PC via CAN bus.

The data fusion software run in the PC receives scan telegrams from serial input and scanner tilt angles from CAN bus and brings them into correspondence via the telegram counter, using a local history queue. Furthermore, assuming a continuous scanner rotation, the tilt angles at the start and end of each measurement can be propagated to each distance value within one telegram. At this point it has to be taken into account that each measurement is composed of two scanner mirror rotations, that the distance values are retrieved during the first half of each rotation (when the laser beam leaves the device at its front side) and that the full scan angles belong to the first rotation and the half angles to the second.

This fusion strategy allows a complete independent internal (mirror) and external (scanner) rotation as long as the latter one is continuous. For that purpose the data evaluation is stopped at each turning point of the tilt motion which is signaled by the dsp via CAN bus. A dataset of distance values usually comprises measurements of one scan sweep (from start to end tilt angle or vice versa). As each distance value is affected by noise neighboring samples are smoothed locally within each scan using a windowing average filter.

2.2 Virtual 3D Scanner Within the SimVis3D Framework

For testing the feature extraction algorithm offline a virtual 3D scanner has been realized within the SIMVIS3D framework (see [6] for further information). As in reality the 3D sensor uses a tiltable (virtual) 2D scanner providing distance information from its mounting pose in the 3D scene to nearest objects in sight. It is realized as an additional sensor device like the existing camera sensor.

During implementation of the virtual scanner it has become obvious that a straight forward distance calculation based on ray tracing operations is too slow (about 2 s for 361 data points/180° range). Thus the simulation uses a virtual perspective scene camera whose image is rendered to an offscreen buffer. The depth values of this buffer are then evaluated taking the perspective distortion of the camera and the regular scan angle resolution of 0.5° into account. Naturally with one camera setting a viewing angle of 180° is not possible, so the camera image is rendered from two different positions (for scan angles 0°...90° and for 90.5°...180°). Hereby the camera viewport is adjusted so that its depth buffer resolution matches the distance value requirements optimally. This way also scanners with higher angular range (Hokuyo URG-04LX, SICK S300) can be simulated.

The camera-based distance value calculation strategy is fast enough to simulate a scanner at a rate of about 20 Hz. To make the measurements even more realistic a Gaussian noise is added to each data point. Thus the simulation allows to collect a 3D point cloud of distance measurements as the real device. Figure 3(a) shows a measurement within the virtual RRLAB.

3 Plane Extraction

The main goal of the plane extraction algorithm is to get reliable landmarks as floor, ceiling, walls, doors and big furniture objects like desks and cupboards from the collected 3D point cloud. These features are used for reliable robot localization in highly cluttered areas where the 2D scanners do not provide stable features.

As stated in section 1 the plane extraction procedure is realized according to the strategy presented in [3]. Goal is to approximate the input data by a set of plane patches such that each set of points is represented in a least square sense by its patch and that features represented by a huge amount of samples (e.g. corridor walls) are represented by one big patch. Of course using only planes as shape for 3D environmental approximation is invalid for many objects (e.g. dustbins would be better represented by a cylinder), but is suitable for finding the mentioned room primitives.

In the following a summary of the different steps of the extraction method is given. The complete strategy is described detailed in [7]. Algorithm 1 sketches the whole procedure.

The RANSAC algorithm in step 1 repeatedly calculates planes approximating the local set of points within one cell. In each iteration it randomly selects three (not aligned) points within the local set, calculates a plane through these points and computes the sum of the distances of all other points within the cell to this plane. This sum of distances is the minimization criterion: the calculated plane is used as best plane when its sum of distances is smaller than the one of the best plane calculated during the previous iterations. This procedure is motivated by the fact that the repeated random selection of points and plane approximation converges to a "good" fitting plane if such a plane exists at all (model valid) and the number of iterations is high enough.

Within this work not more than 100 RANSAC iterations are executed to save computation time. If the samples cannot be approximated well by a plane it will not be merged during region growing and thus filtered out in step 5.

Algorithm 1 RANSAC algorithm for plane extraction

Given: a set of 3D distance measurement samples (data points)
Return: a set of planes approximating disjunctive subsets of the input points
Step 1: split the whole 3D scene into a regular grid of cubic cells
Step 2: assign the input points to the corresponding cells
Step 3: calculate fitting plane for each cell:
for every cell **do**
  find approximating plane using RANSAC algorithm (output: best fitting plane after certain number of RANSAC iterations)
  remove outliers with respect to the best RANSAC plane
  calculate least-square fitting plane for inliers
end for
Step 4: region growing - fuse matching planes of neighboring cells:
for every cell **do**
  compare plane parameters with those of all neighboring cells
  if angle between plane normals below angular threshold and distance of center of gravity of points of neighboring cell to plane below distance threshold **then**
    mark both cells as belonging to same region
  end if
end for
for all regions **do**
  calculate best fitting plane for all points of cells belonging to the same region
end for
Step 5: remove small planes supported only by a small amount of cells

The outlier calculation regarding the best RANSAC plane uses an adjustable distance threshold. The plane fitting for all inliers within one cell as well as for all samples of one merged region is calculated via *principal component analysis*. A plane is described by its normal $\overrightarrow{n}$ and distance from origin d (eq. 1).

$$< \overrightarrow{n}, \overrightarrow{x} >= d \tag{1}$$

According to [3] the normal of the least-square fitting plane is the eigenvector of the smallest eigenvalue of covariance matrix A (eq. 2).

$$A = \begin{pmatrix} \sum_{i=0}^{N} w_i x_i^2 & \sum_{i=0}^{N} w_i x_i y_i & \sum_{i=0}^{N} w_i x_i z_i \\ \sum_{i=0}^{N} w_i x_i y_i & \sum_{i=0}^{N} w_i y_i^2 & \sum_{i=0}^{N} w_i y_i z_i \\ \sum_{i=0}^{N} w_i x_i z_i & \sum_{i=0}^{N} w_i y_i z_i & \sum_{i=0}^{N} w_i z_i^2 \end{pmatrix} \tag{2}$$

Here $x_i = x_i^{raw} - \overline{x}$, $y_i = y_i^{raw} - \overline{y}$ and $z_i = z_i^{raw} - \overline{z}$ are input points centered around mean and weights w_i represent measurement uncertainty of the samples (set to 1 as uncertainty is not yet taken into account). d is given by eq. 3

$$d =< \overrightarrow{cog}, \overrightarrow{n} > \tag{3}$$

where $\overrightarrow{cog} = (\overline{x}, \overline{y}, \overline{z})^T$ is the center of gravity of points belonging to the fitted plane. As A is a square symmetric matrix its eigenvalues can be computed efficiently via *singular value decomposition*. Table 1 lists all adjustable parameters used by the described algorithm.

step	parameter	value
1	cell size	200 mm
3	min. amount of points in a cell to start RANSAC algorithm	10
3	number of RANSAC iterations	50
3	max. point-to-plane distance for inliers	50 mm
4	angular threshold for normals of neighboring planes	15°
4	distance threshold for cog of one plane to neighboring plane	50 mm
5	min. amount of supporting cells for plane filtering	10

Table 1. parameters used for plane extraction

4 Experiments

The plane extraction algorithm has been tested successfully with real and simulated scanner data. Figure 2(a) shows a 3D scan of a typical scene at RRLAB and figure 2(b) shows the extracted planes. In figures 3(a), 3(b) a similar scenario is shown as simulation.

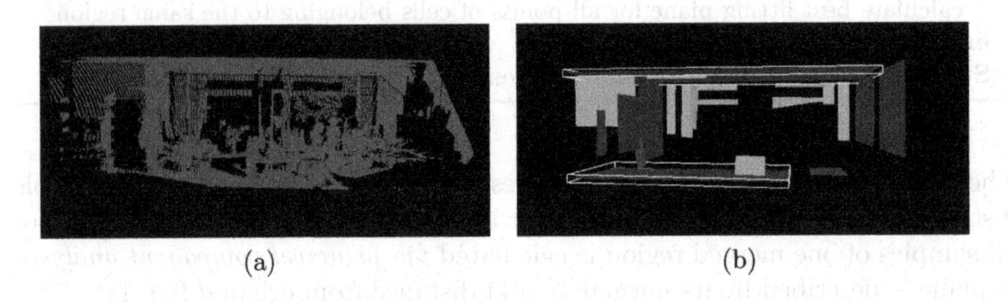

(a) (b)

Fig. 2. (a) Real 3D scan of RRLAB indoor scene, (b) extracted planes

The angular range of the tilt motion is -40° ... 40° with a resolution of about 0.3° per scan. The total number of samples is ~92000 in each case and the time for plane extraction is less than 2 s. In both figures floor and ceiling plane have been marked by their bounding boxes to get a better visual impression. As the minimum number of supporting cells is 10 (ref. table 1), only big planes representing room primitives as walls or large window frames (upper middle part in fig. 2(b)) have been extracted. The (a priori infinite) planes have been clipped by the bounding box of the supporting 3D points. Alternatively the planes can be clipped by the border lines of the supporting cells, but this leads to collections of small faces for diagonal planes which do not intersect a contiguous set of cells.

The simulation experiment within the virtual indoor scene yields similar results as in reality. As smaller objects like chairs, screens and dustbins are not yet included, the extracted planes are more regular and also table tops (middle part of fig. 3(b)) are extracted.

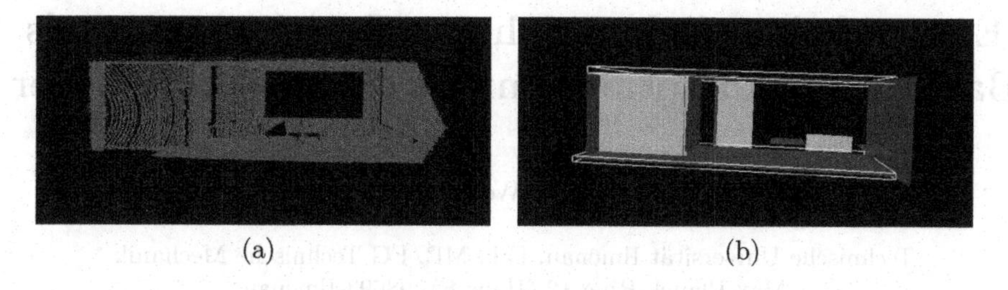

(a) (b)

Fig. 3. (a) Simulated 3D scan of virtual RRLAB scene, (b) extracted planes

5 Conclusion and Outlook

In this paper a strategy for extracting room primitives from 3D distance measurements has been presented. The applied sensor hardware and a corresponding simulation framework have been introduced and the RANSAC based feature extraction algorithm has been explained. The described test results give an impression how floor, walls and ceiling features are detected even in highly cluttered real-world scenarios. Thus these results can be used as reliable landmarks for robot localization during mapping and for navigation purposes.

Next steps comprise the extraction of additional shapes like cylinders and cuboids (composition of rectangular planes) to model the scene as collection of primitive building blocks. Besides the fusion of features from several consecutive 3D scans (i. e. matching of features from different viewpoints) has to be solved. As long-term goal also some semantic information has to be attached to the detected objects, e. g. a table as cuboid with horizontal top where often objects of daily use are placed. For then the extracted primitives can be matched with human scene understanding and thus help for managing higher level tasks as searching and fetching interesting objects.

References

1. M. A. Fischler and R. C. Bolles. *Random sample consensus: a paradigm for model fitting with applications to image analysis and automated cartography.* Commun. ACM 24, 1981.
2. J. Weingarten. *Feature-Based 3D SLAM.* PhD thesis, EPFL, September 2006.
3. J. Weingarten, G. Gruener, and R. Siegwart. A fast and robust 3d feature extraction algorithm for structured environment reconstruction. In *Proc. of ICAR 2003.*
4. D. Schmidt, T. Luksch, J. Wettach, and K. Berns. Autonomous behavior-based exploration of office environments. In *Proc. of ICINCO 2006.*
5. R. Schnabel, R. Wahl, and R. Klein. Shape detection in point clouds. Technical report, Computer Graphics Technical Report, 2006.
6. T. Braun, J. Wettach, and K. Berns. A customizable, multi-host simulation and visualization framework for robot applications. In *Proc. of ICAR 2007.*
7. X. Astigarraga. 3d reconstruction of structured indoor environments. Master's thesis, University of Kaiserslautern, March 2007.

Entwurf einer bahngeführten Positionierung als Basis der Lokomotion omnidirektionaler Roboter

K. Zimmermann, M. Jahn, M. Weiß, M. Braunschweig, T. Rieß

Technische Universität Ilmenau, Fak. MB, FG Technische Mechanik
Max-Planck-Ring 12 (Haus F), 98693 Ilmenau

Zusammenfassung. In diesem Beitrag wird beschrieben, welche Spurmuster omnidirektionale Roboter anwenden können, um ihr Beweglichkeitspotential bei der Bahnverfolgung und automatischen Positionierung auszuschöpfen. Konstruktive Eigenschaften vereinfachen die Verwendung schwingungstechnischer Grundlagen im Einsatz der frontalorientierten Kurvenfahrt.

1 Einleitung

Omnidirektionale Roboter sind auch ein Ergebnis stetiger Verbesserungen der Systeme im Bereich der Small- und Middle-Size-League des RoboCup- Wettbewerbes. Die enge Beziehung zwischen der konstruktiven Gestaltung der Teamroboter(speziell die Anordnung der Räder) und deren softwareseitigen Kontrollstruktur wird an diesem Projekt deutlich.

2 Zielstellung

Die durch Purwin et al. [1] und Rojas et. al. [2] vorgestellten Arbeitsprinzipen können stellvertretend für das schnelle, geschwindigkeitsgeregelte Ausführen von Bahnbewegungen stehen. Der Schwerpunkt unseres Ansatzes liegt im Gegensatz dazu auf der Minimierung der externen Datenrate. In der Struktur einer hybriden Verhaltensarchitektur werden geplante Pfade durch adaptive Bewegungsmuster ausgeführt. Analog zu Moore und Flann [3] stellen Abfolgen von Wegpunkten die geplanten Pfadlinien dar, wobei die entstehenden Segmente definierten Mustern zugeordnet werden. Nach dem Reglement der Small-Size-League ermöglicht ein PC-Masterprogramm mit implementiertem Bildverarbeitungssystem die zentrale Kontrolle und übernimmt für autonome Verhaltensaufgaben die Pfadplanung. Bei kontinuierlicher Planung ist für die übergelagerten Steuerungsebenen eine Entlastung von Regelungsarbeit zugunsten eines verminderten Datenflusses zum Roboter vorgesehen. Ohne Einbuße an Flexibilität kann ein Befehlssatz beschränkter Variablen die Umsetzung nichtlinearer Bewegung bestimmen. Roboterbeschleunigung und Spurtreue sind von den vorgegebenen Wegpunkten abhängig. Um den Roboter auch in Frontalorientierung frei zu positionieren, werden hier einige lagegeregelte Segmente nach dem Bahnverlauf von Lissajous-Kurven gefahren. Abschließend wird anhand von Kreis-Trajektorien die mit dem Roboter erreichte Reproduzierbarkeit und Bahnstabilität dargestellt.

3 Steuerstruktur des Roboters

3.1 Lagestabile Positionierung

Im Rahmen von 6-20 ms Latenzzeit gewährt die Funkverbindung zum Roboter der Mastersteuerung ein gutes Echtzeitverhalten. Das Prinzip der Kaskadenregelung ermöglicht die separate Sollwertvorgabe für Spannung, Drehzahl und Position, sowie kurze Berechnungszeiten des Regelzyklus.

Ohne die Berücksichtigung des dynamischen Modells ist durch konventionelle Steuerung nach kinematischer Berechnung der Radgeschwindigkeiten keine exakte, zeit-optimale Bahnführung möglich [1]. Bewegung durch Vorgabe von Geschwindigkeitsvektoren erfordert schnelle Bildwiederholraten (40-60Hz) zur Rückkopplung der permanenten globalen Spurkontrolle. Allein durch den PI-Regler der Radgeschwindigkeit ist eine Bahnkurve schwer zu stabilisieren, wenn sie Anteile von Querfahrt enthält. Mittels dynamischer Sollwertführung von Radwegen sowie der Odometrie kann aber hier alternativ auf die stabilisierende Wirkung des überlagerten Lagereglers ausgewichen werden.

In Abb. 1 ist eine Roboterkreisbahn in Frontalorientierung (ohne Eigenrotation) und die zugehörigen Funktionen der Mittelpunktkoordinaten und Radwinkelgeschwindigkeiten aufgezeigt. Die orthogonale Achslage in der Roboterkonstruktion bedingt, dass die Radgeschwindigkeiten mit den Sinusschwingungen der Mittelpunktkomponenten deckungsgleich verlaufen. Den Roboter selbst als Pendel eines ebenen harmonischen Schwingers zu betrachten, vereinfacht die Koordinierung frontalorientierter Bewegungskurven, weil der Schwinger keine Eigenrotation besitzt. Für die Realisierung von Bahnkurven ähnlich der vom ebenen Schwinger bekannten Lissajous-Figuren ist somit keine Lösung der kinematischen Bewegungsgleichung erforderlich [4]. Lissajous'sche Figuren enthalten ein breites Spektrum verwertbarer Bahnsegmente. Die Parameter der Schwingung (Frequenz, Amplitude, Phasenwinkel, Perioden, Offset) formen die resultierende Bahn, auf der sich der Roboter bewegt.

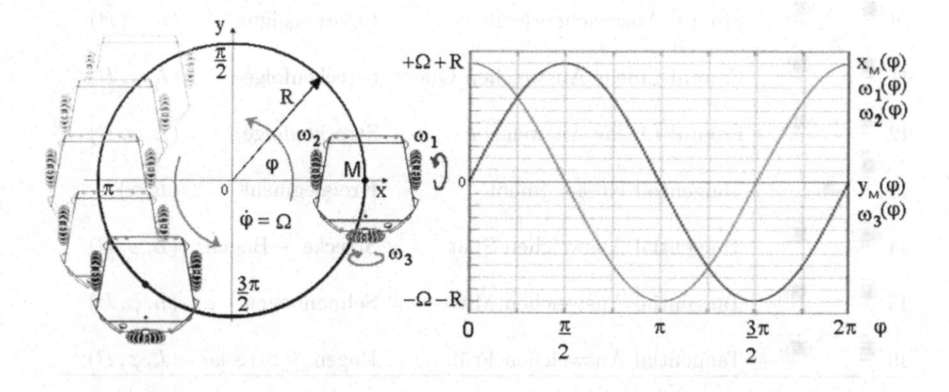

Abb. 1. Verlauf des Robotermittelpunktes bei frontaler Kreisfahrt

3.2 Roboterinterner Spurkatalog

Das Abrufen von spezifischen Spurformen erfordert im Roboter keine zeitkritischen Bahnberechnungen, obwohl sie im Toleranzrahmen durch Kombination und Parameterwahl zeittreu an beliebige Bahnkurven anzupassen sind. Jede Spur definiert den relativen Zielpunkt über die Vorgabe einer charakteristischen Form der Trajektorie. Ausweichende Bogenfahrten sind stellvertretend in drei typische Grundmuster 'Früh', 'Mitte' und 'Spät' für die zwei Hauptorientierungen 'Frontal' und 'Tangential' unterteilt worden (Tab. 1). In der Variation der drei Spurparameter (Länge, Winkel, Breite) verbleibt trotzdem noch genug Spielraum, um die geplanten Pfade den aufgegebenen Positionierungs- und Bewegungsaufgaben anzupassen. Mit der Wahl der Segmentlänge bis zum Zielpunkt (20.. 2000 mm) ist auch dessen gefahrene Durchschnittsgeschwindigkeit bestimmt. Die Spurmuster erweitern und integrieren die bis dahin vorhandenen Elementarbewegungen Translation, Rotation, Schrägfahrt, Drehstrecke, Drehbogen und Bahnsegmente schwingungsbasierter Vorsteuerung. Jeder Spuraufruf erfordert nur ein Datenpaket von 12 Byte und bestimmt über den Füllstand des roboterinternen Befehlpuffers, ob am Wegpunkt gehalten oder fließend weitergefahren wird.

Tabelle 1. Definition der charakteristischen Spuren

Code + Form	Bezeichnung	Zielpunktdef.	Parameter
25	Ball Antrippeln	Drehstrecke	(L, φ, α)
26	Ball Zielschuss	Drehstrecke	(L, φ, α)
33	FrontalEllipsensegment	Lissajousfigur	(R_f, γ, R_q)
34	Frontal Ausweichen Spät	Lissajousfigur	(L, φ, B)
35	Frontal Ausweichen Mitte	Lissajousfigur	(L, φ, B)
36	Frontal Ausweichen Früh	Lissajousfigur	(L, φ, B)
41	Frontal Linear Ausweichen Quer	Streckenfolge	(L, φ, B)
42	Frontal Linear Ausweichen	Streckenfolge	(L, φ, B)
43	Tangential Kreissegment	Kreissegment	(R, γ)
44	Tangential Ausweichen Spät	Strecke + Bogen	(L, φ, B)
45	Tangential Ausweichen Mitte	Sehnenbogen	(L, φ, B)
46	Tangential Ausweichen Früh	Bogen + Strecke	(L, φ, B)

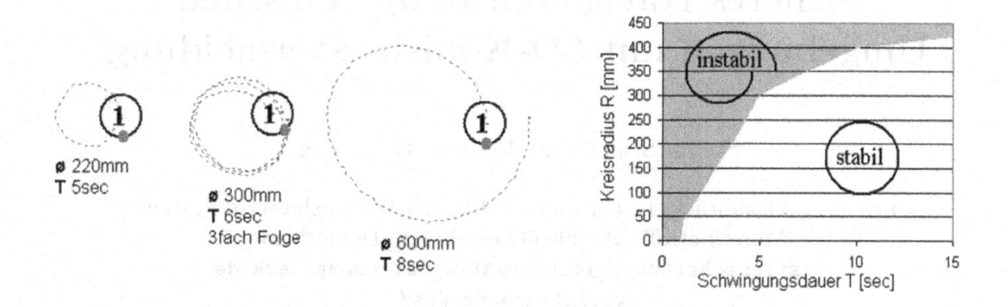

Abb. 2. Trajektorien der Spur 33 (Lissajous'sche Kreisfigur)

4 Anwendung und Ausblick

Obwohl der Roboter die Regelung in den Kurvenabschnitten selbst übernimmt, verliert die Reaktionsfähigkeit nicht an Flexibilität. Taktfrequenz und Art der Lagevorgaben bestimmen das gesamte Geschwindigkeitsprofils des Roboters und die Spurtreue zur Pfadplanung. Eine permanente Korrektur und Bahnverfolgung erfordert in diesem Fall nicht zwangsläufig eine stetige Befehlsübertragung. Der Roboter ist somit auch noch mit langsamerer Rückkopplung ohne stockenden Bewegungsfluss ortstreu steuerbar, auch wenn mit Bildwiederholfrequenzen unter 10Hz hierbei keine schnelle Reaktionsfähigkeit mehr vorhanden ist.

Die Anwendung des Spurkataloges soll schnell und präzise sein. Der Toleranzbereich stabiler Reproduzierbarkeit von Bahnen ist vor allem durch die Güte des Lagereglers, der Rad-Motor-Kopplung, der Räder und Laufoberfläche gegeben. Für größere Entfernungen sind die roboterinternen Spuren nicht konzipiert, weil hierfür die Positions-Bilderkennung des Feldes korrigierend genutzt werden kann. Am Beispiel der steigenden Kreisdrift in Abb. 2 ist die zunehmende Fehlersummierung durch Reibungs-, Masse- und Schlupfeinfluss zu sehen, mit der sich die Grenzen der Spurtreue und Bahnreproduzierbarkeit kennzeichnen lassen.

Das mit dem System erreichte Aktionsverhalten entspricht den Erwartungen. Die funktionalen Grundlagen sollen für den Ausbau der Taktiken im Formations- und Schwarmverhalten genutzt werden.

Literaturverzeichnis

1. Purwin O, D'Andrea R: Trajectory Generation and Control for Four Wheeled Omnidirectional Vehicles. Robotics and Autonomous Systems 54(1):13-22, 2006.
2. Rojas P, Förster AG: Holonomic Control of a Robot with an Omnidirectional Drive. Künstliche Intelligenz 20(2):12-17, 2006.
3. Moore KL, Flann NS: A Six-Wheeled Omnidirectional Autonomous Mobile Robot. IEEE Control Systems Magazine 20(6):53-66, 2000.
4. Grimsehl E: Lehrbuch der Physik. Teubner, Leipzig, 1991. 2000.

Sicheres Navigieren in dynamischen Umgebungen mit 3D-Kollisionsvermeidung

Stefan Stiene und Joachim Hertzberg

Universität Osnabrück, Inst. f. Informatik, AG Wissensbasierte Systeme,
Albrechtstraße 28, 49069 Osnabrück, Deutschland
{sstiene,hertzberg}@informatik.uni-osnabrueck.de
www.inf.uos.de/kbs/

Zusammenfassung. Diese Papier stellt eine neuartige Methode vor, die 3D-Hindernisvermeidung ermöglicht. Die Sensorkonfiguration beruht auf sechs Laserscannern, die die gesamte Roboteroberfläche abdecken. Die Daten der sechs Laserscanner werden zu einem virtuellen, zweidimensionalen, horizontal ausgerichteten 360°-Laserscanner kombiniert. Da der virtuelle Laserscanner die 3D-Umgebung in einem zweidimensionalen Datensatz repräsentiert, ermöglicht er in Kombination mit klassischen Hindernisvermeidungsalgorithmen wie der *Vector Field Histogram* Methode eine 3D-Hindernisvermeidung.

1 Problemstellung

Im Kontext des BMBF-Verbundprojekts LiSA (Assistenzroboter in Laboren von Life-Science-Untenehmen [1]) stellt sich das folgende Problem: Eine holonome Roboterplattform soll in einem in Betrieb befindlichen Laborgebäude auf Anforderung Arbeitsstationen anfahren und dort einfache Manipulationsaufgaben verrichten. Dazu ist Vermeidung der Kollision mit Laborpersonal zertifizierbar sicherzustellen. Weiterhin muss integrale, also den gesamten Roboterkörper betreffende Kollisionsvermeidung mit teilweise dynamischen Alltagsobjekten wie überkragenden Arbeitsplatten oder offen stehenden Schubladen in jeder Höhe gewährleistet sein. Pfadplanung und Lokalisierung sollen auf einer Umgebungskarte basieren, die zeitlich vor dem eigentlichen Robotereinsatz erstellt wird und die in größeren Zeitabständen änderbar sein sollte; diese Karte soll zudem als visuelles Element der Mensch-Roboter-Interaktion verfügbar sein.

Der vorliegende Aufsatz skizziert die Lösung dieses Problems. Sie beruht insbesondere auf Verwendung von Laserdaten zur Erfassung der 3D-Umgebungsgeometrie, die teils off-line (Kartierung), teils on-line (integrale Kollisionsvermeidung) eingesetzt wird. Da der reale Roboter erst zur Mitte der Projektlaufzeit fertiggestellt wird, wird die Simulationsumgebung USARSim [2] verwendet, um eine optimale Sensorkonfiguration zu bestimmen. Damit die Kontrollsoftware anschließend unverändert auf den realen Roboter angewendet werden kann, wird die Hardware Abstraktionssoftware Player [3] verwendet.

Häufig wird die Hindernisvermeidung bei autonomen, mobilen Robotern auf zwei Dimensionen beschränkt. Es existieren verschiedene Verfahren, kollisionsfreie zweidimensionale Bewegung in dynamischen Umgebungen zu realisieren [4].

Des Weiteren existieren dreidimensionale Pfadplanungsalgorithmen, die kollisionsfreie Bewegung in dreidimensionalen, jedoch statischen Umgebungen realisieren. Zur dreidimensionalen Hindernisvermeidung in dynamischen Umgebungen werden häufig Sonarsensoren über die Roboteroberfläche verteilt [5]. Diese Sensorkonfigurationen besitzen jedoch den Nachteil der Messungenauigkeit und des Übersprechens der Sonarsensoren.

Des Weiteren werden verschiedene Konfigurationen von rotierenden Laserscannern eingesetzt, um Hindernisvermeidung zu realisieren [6]. Gegenber diesen Konfigurationen hat die hier vorgeschlagene Sensorkonfiguration den Vorteil der permanenten Kollisionsvermeidung. Ferner wird in [6] sowie in [7] das Prinzip, 3D-Daten zu virtuellen Laserscans zu verarbeiten, angewandt, das in dieser Arbeit ebenfalls zum Einsatz kommt.

2 Navigationskarte aus 3D-Umgebungsaufnahmen

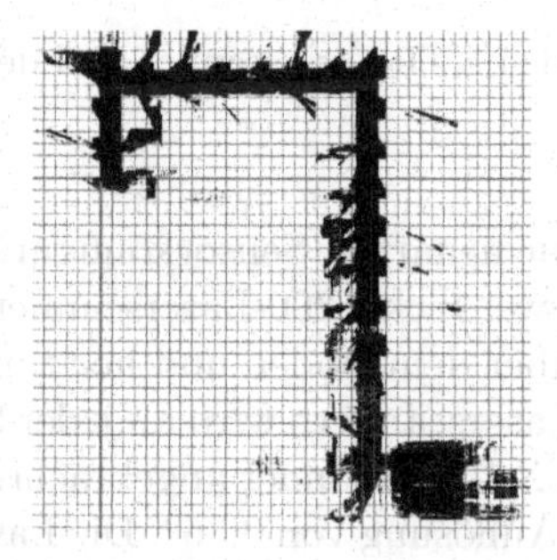

Abb. 1. Links: Der autonome mobile Roboter Kurt3D. Mitte: Aufsicht auf die dreidimensionale Punktwolke der Laborumgebung, wobei ein Kästchen die Seitenlänge 1m besitzt. Rechts: Perspektivische Sicht eines Ausschnitts der Punktwolke.

Da der LiSA-Roboter seine Umgebung nicht autonom explorieren soll, wird eine Karte der Umgebung benötigt, um eine für die Navigation notwendige Lokalisierung und Pfadplanung zu ermöglichen. Um diese Karte zu erstellen, wird die spätere Arbeitsumgebung mit Hilfe des autonomen Roboters Kurt3D (Abb. 1 links) dreidimensional vermessen. Dieser ist mit einem 3D-Laserscanner ausgerüstet, der es ihm ermöglicht, durch iteratives Scanmatching eine dreidimensionale Punktwolke der Umgebung zu erstellen (Abb. 1 mitte und rechts) [8]. Aus dieser Punktwolke wird halbautomatisch die zugrunde liegende Gebäudegeometrie extrahiert und in eine Karte für die Robotersimulationsumgebung USARSim umgewandelt. Aus dieser dreidimensionalen Simulationsumgebung wird die zweidimensionale Navigationskarte erstellt, indem in der Höhe der horizontalen Laserscanner des LiSA-Roboters eine Linienkarte als Schnitt durch die Simulationsumgebung erstellt wird. In die Navigationskarte wird zusätzlich manuell semantische Information der Umgebung (wie Türdurchfahrten, Arbeitsstationen,...) durch verschiedene Farben markiert. Die Navigationskarte sowie die Simulation dienen im LiSA-Projekt zusätzlich zur Visualisierung bei der Mensch-Roboter-Interaktion.

3 Sensorkonfiguration des LiSA-Roboters

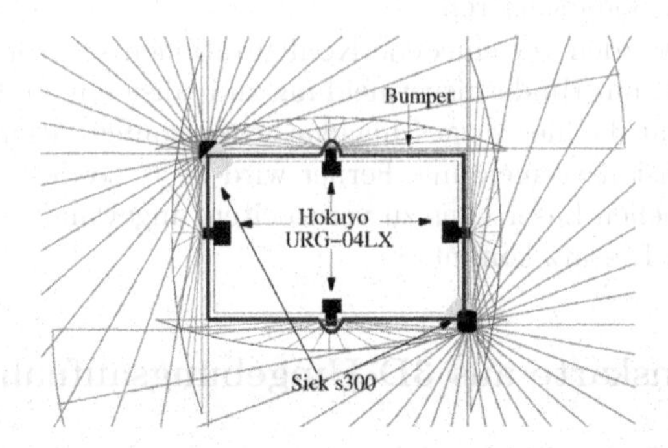

Abb. 2. Messbereiche der beiden S300-Laserscanner und der vier Hokuyo URG-04LX Laserscanner (Aufsicht)

Der LiSA-Roboter besitzt eine neuartige Sensorkonfiguration mit insgesamt sechs Laserscannern. So werden zwei Sick S300-Laserscanner an gegenüberliegenden Ecken des Roboters 10 cm über dem Boden und horizontal zu diesem ausgerichtet montiert. Neben diesen Laserscannern wird an jeder Seite des Roboters unten mittig ein Hokuyo URG-04LX Laserscanner angebracht. Sie besitzen eine Reichweite von etwa 4m und eine Auflösung von 0.36°. Die Laserscanner sind so ausgerichtet, dass ihre Scanebene mit dem Roboter einen Winkel von 40° einschließen, so dass die vier Scanebenen einen Trichter um den Roboter bilden (siehe Abb. 2 und 3 links). Neben den optischen Sensoren besitzt der Roboter Encodersensoren, die Daten über die Radwinkel und Radumdrehungen liefern, und eine IMU, die die Orientierung des Roboters im Raum bestimmt. Bekanntlich ist die Energieaufnahme ein potentielles Problem für einen Dauerbetrieb mobiler Roboter. Dieses Problem ist hier entschärft durch Verwendung neuer, relativ energieeffizienter Scanner-Modelle. Ein S300-Laserscanner braucht 8W, ein URG-04LX 2,5W - die Leistungsaufnahme der kompletten Scanner-Konfiguration beträgt also 26W. Zum Vergleich: die älteren Scanner LMS 200 haben eine Aufnahme von 20W.

4 Lokalisierung des Roboters

Zur Lokalisierung werden die beiden horizontalen Sick Laserscanner zu einem 360° Laserscanner kombiniert. Durch die Scanbereiche von jeweils 270° wird dadurch ein Sichtbereich von 360° realisiert, in dem sogar überlappende Einzeldatensätze existieren. Die Daten des Laserscanners sind in Abb. 3 rechts zu sehen. In Kombination mit der Odometrie und der IMU ermöglicht dieser kombinierte

Laser eine Bestimmung der aktuellen Pose des Roboters in der Navigationskarte mit dem *Monte-Carlo-Lokalisierungsverfahren* [9]. Der virtuelle, aus den Daten der beiden S300-Laserscanner kombinierte Laserscanner wird im Folgenden *Navigationslaserscanner* genannt.

5 Integrale Kollisionsvermeidung durch 3D-Laserdaten

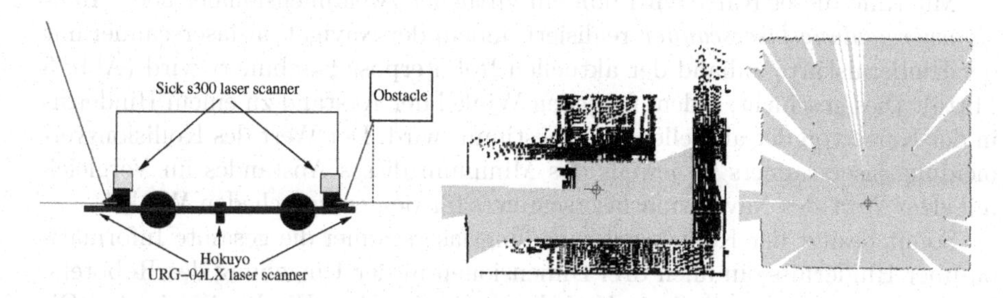

Abb. 3. Links: Schematische Seitenansicht des LiSA-Roboters. Mitte: Simulierter 360° Laserscanner (blau) unter Berücksichtigung der Hinderniskarte (schwarz). Rechts: Simulierter 360° Laserscanner ohne Hinderniskarte.

Da sich der Navigationslaserscanner aus zwei Sicherheitssensoren der Kategorie 4 bzw. SIL3 zusammensetzt und in etwa 10 cm über dem Boden scant, ist damit eine zertifizierbare Kollisionsvermeidung des Roboters mit Menschen in dessen Umgebung gegeben. Dies ist der Fall, da Beine bzw. liegende Menschen auf jeden Fall in den Daten der Laserscanner auftauchen und der Roboter eine softwareunabhängige Notstoppfunktion besitzt.

Den Navigationslaserscanner als einzigen Sensor zur Kollisionsvermeidung zu verwenden, ist jedoch unter dem Sicherheitsaspekt betrachtet zu riskant, da es für einen mobilen Roboter, der in einer dynamischen Umgebung arbeitet, nicht ausreicht, nur Hindernisse in einer Ebene zu erkennen.

Aus diesem Grund werden die vier Hokuyo-Laserscanner des LiSA-Roboters verwendet, um eine 3D-Kollisionsvermeidung zu realisieren, die die gesamte Roboteroberfläche abdeckt. Trifft ein Laserstrahl des aus den vier Hokuyo-Scannern gebildeten Trichters auf ein Hindernis, das im Kollisionsbereich des Roboters liegt (wie z.B. den Stuhl oder die Tischplatte in Abb. 4 rechts), wird dieses in die Ebene des Navigationslaserscanners projiziert (siehe Abb.3 links).

Es ist jedoch nicht ausreichend, dieses projizierte Hindernis in den Navigationslaserscanner zu übernehmen, um eine 3D-Hindernisvermeidung zu realisieren. Steht der Roboter z.B. direkt vor einem Hindernis wie einer Tischplatte, ist die Projektion der Tischplatte immer einen Wert größer Null vom Roboter entfernt, da der eingeschlossene Winkel zwischen Hokuyo-Scanner und dem Roboter größer Null ist (siehe Abb. 3 links). Ein Lösungsansatz wäre, den Roboter ausweichen zu lassen, sobald ein Hindernis in den Hokuyodaten auftaucht. Dies wrüde jedoch dazu führen, dass der eingeschlossene Winkel sehr klein zu wählen ist, um in der engen Laborumgebung die gesamte Roboteroberfläche abzudecken. Dies hätte wiederum zur Folge, dass der Roboter dementsprechend langsam fahren müsste, da Hindernisse erst spät in den Daten auftauchen.

Der in dieser Arbeit verfolgte Lösungsansatz trägt die projizierten Hindernisse in den Hokuyodaten anhand der aktuellen Roboterpose in eine Karte ein. Diese Karte besitzt durch die Bewegung des Roboters eine immer feinere Repräsentation der Hindernisse in der nahen Roboterumgebung, mit denen der Roboter kollidieren kann.

Mit Hilfe dieser Karte wird nun ein virtueller zweidimensionaler 360° *Kollisionsvermeidungslaserscanner* realisiert, indem der Navigationslaserscanner mit der Hinderniskarte anhand der aktuellen Roboterpose kombiniert wird (Abb. 3 Mitte). Dies geschieht, indem für jeden Winkel der Abstand zu einem Hindernis in der Karte von der aktuellen Pose bestimmt wird. Der Wert des Kollisionsvermeidungslaserscanners ist jeweils das Minimum dieses Abstandes im Vergleich mit dem Wert des Navigationslaserscanners für den entsprecheden Winkel.

Somit besitzt der Kollisionsvermeidungslaserscanner die gesamte Information über Hindernisse in allen drei Dimensionen in der Umgebung des Roboters. Der entscheidene Vorteil dieser Vorgehensweise ist, dass Hindernisse in drei Dimensionen in einem zweidimensionalen Datensatz repräsentiert werden. Somit können klassische Ansätze zur Kollisionsvermeidung wie der *Dynamic Window Approach*, *Nearness Diagrams* oder die *Vector Field Histogram Methode*, die ursprünglich zur zweidimensionalen Hindernisvermeidung enwickelt wurden, unverändert übernommen werden und ermöglichen in Kombination mit dem Kollisionsvermeidungslaserscanner dreidimensionale Hindernisvermeidung. Das kom-

Abb. 4. Der LiSA-Roboter in der Robotersimulationsumgebung USARSim. Links: Die Strahlen der vier Hokuyo Laserscanner (grün) bilden einen Trichter um den Roboter. Die Sick Laserscanner (blau) sind parallel zum Boden ausgerichtet. Rechts: Der Stuhl wird mit Hilfe der Hukoyo Laserscanner als Hindernis erkannt.

plette Robotersystem wird in der Roboter Simulationsumgebung USARSim [2] in Kombination mit der Roboter Steuerungssoftware Player/Stage [3] getestet. Player/Stage stellt ein Kollisionsvermeidungsmodul zur Verfügung, das nach der Vector Field Histogram Methode arbeitet. Unter Verwendung dieses Moduls in

Kombination mit dem Kollisionsvermeidungslaserscanner ist der Roboter in der Lage, alle Hindernisse, mit denen der Roboter potenziell kollidieren könnte, zu erkennen und ihnen auszuweichen. Abb. 5 zeigt den LiSA-Roboter (links) und seine Sensordaten (rechts). Es ist zu sehen, dass der geplante Pfad einen Tisch im Vordergrund kreuzt. Im rechten Bild sind zusätzlich die 3D-Umgebungsdatenpunkte eingetragen, die die vier Hokuyo-Scanner aufgenommen haben und mit dem Hüllquader des Roboters kollidieren könnten. Es ist zu sehen, dass der Kollisionsvermeidungslaserscanner bündig mit den auf den Boden projizierten 3D-Umgebungsdatenpunkten abschließt. Ferner ist zu sehen, dass der virtuelle Scanner nur die Beine der Bänke im Hintergrund als Hindernisse erkennt. Dies ist der Fall, da auf den Daten der Hinderniskarte einen Alterungsprozess laufen gelassen wird, damit temporäre Hindernisse, wie sich bewegende Menschen, einen Pfad nicht dauerhaft blockieren.

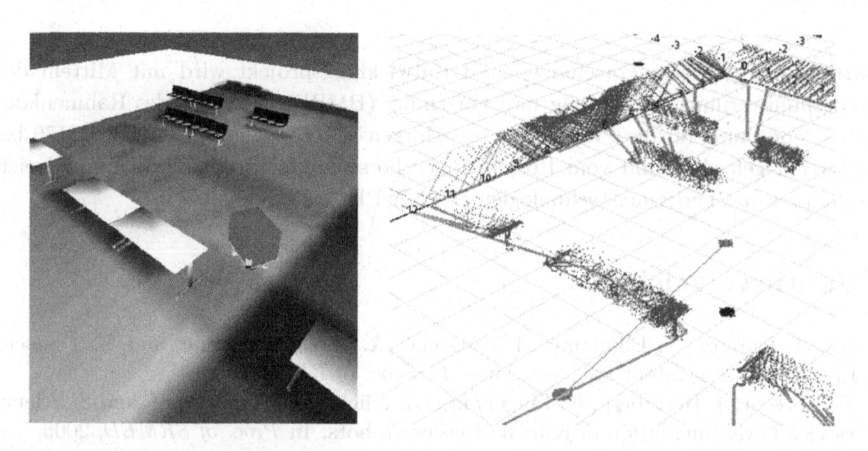

Abb. 5. Links: Der LiSA-Roboter in der Simulationsumgebung. Rechts: Sensordaten Visualisierung in Player. Die Verbindungslinie der beiden Kreise stellt den geplanten Pfad dar. Der schwarze Kreis markiert die aktuelle Roboterposition.

6 Zusammenfassung und nächste Schritte

In diesem Papier wurde eine neue Methode vorgestellt, die 3D-Hindernisvermeidung in dynamischen Umgebungen ermöglicht. Dazu werden die 3D-Umgebungsinformationen in einem virtuellen zweidimensionalen Laserscanner repräsentiert, so dass klassische Algorithmen zur 2D-Hindernisvermeidung unverändert 3D-Hindernisvermeidung ermöglichen.

Eine Alternative zu der hier vorgestellten Sensorkonfiguration wäre, die Hokuyo-Scanner mit Hilfe eines Servomotors zu montieren, so dass der eingeschlossene Winkel zwischen Roboter und Laserscanner dynamisch an die Fahrtrichtung und Geschwindigkeit angepasst werden kann. Diese Sensorkonfiguration kommt aufgrund des variablen Winkels ohne lokale Hinderniskarte aus.

Ein weiterer Schritt wäre, den ganzen Sichtbereich von 270° der vier Hokuyo-Scanner auszunutzen, da in der vorgestellten Sensorkonfiguration nur die nach oben gerichteten 180° verwendet werden. Die nicht verwendeten 45° auf jeder Seite könnten mit Hilfe einer Spiegelvorrichtung auf den vor dem Roboter liegenden Boden gerichtet werden. Dies würde dazu führen, dass selbst Hindernisse mit einer geringeren Höhe als 10 cm vom LiSA-Roboter erkannt werden.

Der Alterungsprozess der lokalen Hinderniskarte wird in Zukunft durch ein Verfahren ersetzt, das das jeweilige Raster der Karte erst wieder frei gibt, wenn es als frei gemessen wurde. Das Alterungsverfahren schließt nicht aus, dass ein Roboter, der sehr langsam an einen Tisch heranfährt, mit diesem kollidiert. Zusätzlich wird in dem neuen Verfahren bestimmt, ob ein Bereich nur temporär oder dauerhaft versperrt ist. Letzteres würde dazu führen, dass die dauerhaften Hindernisse in die globale Navigationskarte zur Pfadplanung und Lokalisierung eingetragen werden.

Danksagung Dieses Forschungs- und Entwicklungsprojekt wird mit Mitteln des Bundesministeriums für Bildung und Forschung (BMBF) innerhalb des Rahmenkonzeptes "Forschung für die Produktion von Morgen" (Förderkennzeichen 02PB2170 bis 02PB2177) gefördert und vom Projektträger Forschungszentrum Karlsruhe, Bereich Produktion und Fertigungstechnologien (PTKA-PFT), betreut.

Literaturverzeichnis

1. E. Schulenburg, N. Elkmann, M. Fritzsche, A. Girstl, S. Stiene, and C. Teutsch. Lisa: A robot assistent for life science. In *Proc. of KI*, 2007.
2. S. Albrecht, J. Hertzberg, K. Lingemann, A. Nüchter, J. Sprickerhof, and S. Stiene. Device Level Simulation of Kurt3D Rescue Robots. In *Proc. of SRMED*, 2006.
3. B. Gerkey, R. Vaughen, and A. Howard. The player/stage project: Tools for multi-robot and distributed sensor systems. In *Proc. of ICAR*, 2003.
4. R. Siegwart and I.R. Nourbakhsh. *Introduction to Autonomous Mobile Robots.* MIT Press, 2004.
5. W. Burgard, A. B. Cremers, D. Fox, D. Hähnel, G. Lakemeyer, D. Schulz, W. Steiner, and S. Thrun. The museum tour-guide robot RHINO. In *Proc. of AMS*, 1998.
6. D. Holz and C. Lörken. Continuous 3d environment sensing for autonomous robot navigation and mapping. In *Proc. of the 9. Fachwissenschaftlicher Informatik-Kongress, Lecture Notes in Informatics (LNI)*, 2007.
7. O. Wulf, K. O. Arras, H. I. Christensen, and B. A. Wagner. 2D Mapping of Cluttered Indoor Environments by Means of 3D Perception. In *Proc. of ICRA*, 2004.
8. H. Surmann, A. Nüchter, and J. Hertzberg. An autonomous mobile robot with a 3d laser range finder for 3d exploration and digitalization of indoor environments. *J. Robotics and Autonomous Systems*, 45:181 – 198, 2003.
9. D. Fox, W. Burgard, F. Dellaert, and S. Thrun. Monte carlo localization: Efficient position estimation for mobile robots. In *Proc. of AAAI*, 1999.

Bildbasierte Navigation eines mobilen Roboters mittels omnidirektionaler und schwenkbarer Kamera

Thomas Nierobisch, Frank Hoffmann, Johannes Krettek und Torsten Bertram

Universität Dortmund, Lehrstuhl für Regelungssystemtechnik,
thomas.nierobisch@uni-dortmund.de

Zusammenfassung. Dieser Beitrag präsentiert einen neuartigen Ansatz zur entkoppelten Regelung der Kamera-Blickrichtung und der Bewegung eines mobilen Roboters im Kontext der bildbasierten Navigation. Eine schwenkbare monokulare Kamera hält unabhängig von der Roboterbewegung die relevanten Merkmale für die Navigation im Sichtfeld. Die Entkopplung der Kamerablickrichtung von der eigentlichen Roboterbewegung wird durch die Projektion der Merkmale auf eine virtuelle Bildebene realisiert. In der virtuellen Bildebene hängt die Ausprägung der visuellen Merkmale für die bildbasierte Regelung nur von der Roboterposition ab und ist unabhängig gegenüber der tatsächlichen Blickrichtung der Kamera. Durch die Schwenkbarkeit der monokularen Kamera wird der Arbeitsbereich, über dem sich ein Referenzbild zur bildbasierten Regelung eignet, gegenüber einer statischen Kamera signifikant vergrößert. Dies ermöglicht die Navigation auch in texturarmen Umgebungen, die wenig verwertbare Textur- und Strukturmerkmale aufweisen.

1 Einleitung

Mobile Serviceroboter sollen in Zukunft dem Menschen monotone und körperlich anstrengende Aufgaben abnehmen, indem sie beispielsweise Hol- und Bringedienste ausüben. Hierzu sollen sich Roboter in unstrukturierten Umgebungen mittels visueller Rückkopplung autonom bewegen. Dieser Beitrag beschreibt einen neuen Ansatz zur entkoppelten Regelung der Kamera-Blickrichtung und der Bewegung eines mobilen Roboters im Kontext der bildbasierten Regelung [1]. Unsere Arbeiten stehen im Kontext der Forschungsaktivitäten [2,3], welche bildbasierte Regelungkonzepte anhand der Bildjakobimatrix sowie der Zerlegung der Homographie für die mobile Navigation von Robotern mit einer fest montierten Kamera verwenden. Um eine bildbasierte Weitbereichsregelung in texturarmen Umgebungen zu realisieren, wird der Arbeitsbereich auf Basis geeigneter Merkmale durch die Regelung der Kamera-Blickrichtung signifikant vergrößert. Im Gegensatz zu vielen in der Literatur vorgestellten Ansätzen wird keine Konnektivität der perspektivischen Referenzansichten benötigt, sondern lediglich die Konnektivität der Merkmale in den omnidirektionalen Ansichten. Diese Vorgehensweise ist flexibler und robuster einsetztbar, da die omnidirektionale Wahrnehmung die

Sichtbarkeit von Merkmalen über einen weiten Bereich des Arbeitsraumes garantiert. Abbildung 1 zeigt die der Navigation zugrundeliegende hybride Regelungsstruktur. Die Architektur folgt dem klassischen Dreischichtenmodell, einer unteren reaktiven Schicht, in welcher die Blickrichtungsregelung und das bildbasierte Navigationsverhalten angesiedelt sind, einer mittleren Koordinationsschicht zur kontextabhängigen Aktivierung einzelner Verhalten und einer Planungsschicht, die für die Lokalisation und Navigationsplanung verantwortlich zeichnet. Im Zentrum dieses Beitrags steht das entkoppelte bildbasierte Navigationsverhalten mit Blickrichtungsregelung, welches mittels bekannter Verfahren zur Verhaltenskoordination mit anderen reaktiven Verhalten beispielsweise zur Hindernisvermeidung und Korridorfolge kombiniert werden kann. So lässt sich das bildbasierte Navigationsverhalten nahtlos in die in [4] vorgestellte bildgestützte Navigation integrieren. Die Planungsschicht generiert aus den während der Demonstrationsfahrt erfassten omnidirektionalen Ansichten automatisch eine topologische Karte in Form eines gerichteten Graphen. Diese Karte dient nachträglich sowohl zur Lokalisation und Wegplanung als auch zur dynamischen Auswahl der momentan optimalen Referenzansicht zur bildbasierten Navigation des Roboters. Während der Navigation schaltet die bildbasierte Regelung bei hinreichender Sichtbarkeit von Merkmalen des laut Plan nachfolgenden Wegpunktes auf die nächste Referenzansicht um. Die bildbasierte Navigation und Lokalisation operieren mit eindeutig unterscheidbaren SIFT-Merkmalen [5]. Der im Rahmen der

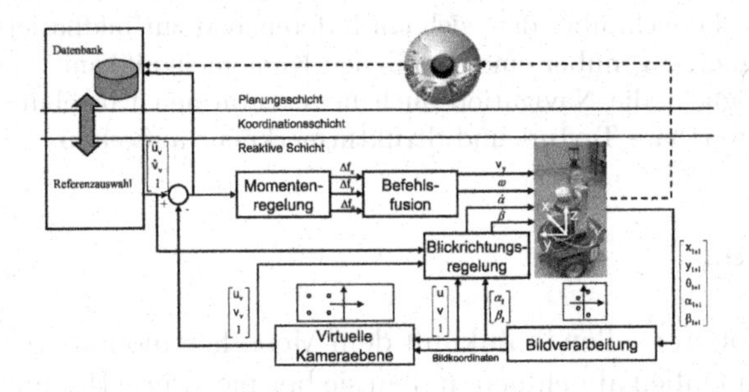

Abb. 1. Hybride Regelungsarchitektur für bildbasierte Navigation mobiler Roboter

Untersuchungen verwendete Roboter Pioneer 3DX ist mit einem schwenkbaren monokularem und einem omnidirektionalem Kamera-System ausgestattet. Der Differenzialantrieb erlaubt eine lokale nicht-holonome Bewegung des Roboters in Form einer Translation entlang seiner aktuellen Fahrtrichtung und einer Rotation um die vertikale Achse. Die Pose des Roboters in der Ebene und die Orientierung der Kamera sind durch den Zustandsvektor $[x, y, \theta, \alpha, \beta]^T$ beschrieben. Der Beitrag gliedert sich wie folgt: Im Abschnitt 2 wird das bildbasierte Navigationsverhalten detailliert beschrieben, insbesondere die virtuelle Bildebene und die bildbasierte Positionsregelung. Der Abschnitt 3 beschreibt die experimentelle Evaluierung des Gesamtsystems bei der Navigation zwischen zwei Landmarken in einer realen Umgebung. Der Beitrag schließt mit einer Zusammenfassung.

2 Bildbasiertes Navigationsverhalten

2.1 Virtuelle Bildebene und Blickrichtungsregelung

Die Merkmale werden auf eine virtuelle Bildebene projiziert und ermöglichen so eine von der Kamerablickrichtung unabhängige Zuordnung zwischen den Bildmerkmalen in der aktuellen Pose des Roboters und der Referenzpose. Eine Entkopplung der planaren Roboterbewegung von der Blickrichtungsregelung via Transformation der Bildpunkte auf eine vertikale virtuelle Bildebene wird in [6] vorgestellt. Nachteilig bei diesem Ansatz ist die Variation des Abstandes einzelner Merkmale zum Kameraursprung, weshalb sich eine deutliche Verbesserung durch die Definition einer horizontalen virtuellen Bildebene erzielen lässt. Die Transformation der Merkmale auf die horizontale virtuelle Bildebene ist schematisch in Abbildung 2 dargestellt. Unter der Annahme, dass die Kamera um

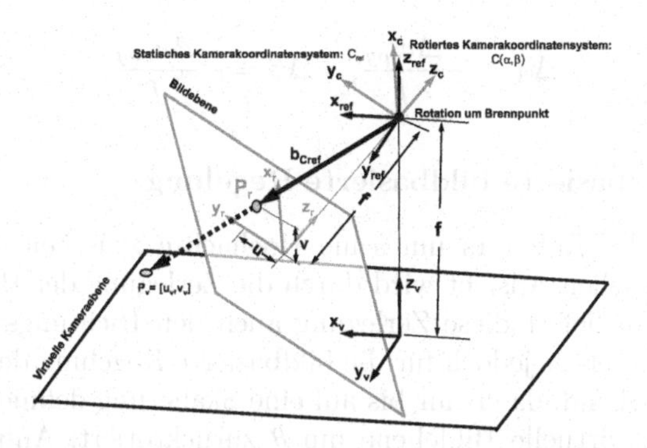

Abb. 2. Transformation der realen Kamerabilder auf die virtuelle Bildebene

ihren Brennpunkt rotiert, ist die Transformation der Merkmale von der aktuellen Ansicht u, v auf die virtuelle Bildebene u_V, v_V lediglich abhängig von der bekannten Orientierung der Kamera α, β sowie deren Brennweite f.

$$[u_V, v_V, 1]^T = \mathbf{T}_R^V(f, \alpha, \beta) \cdot [u, v, 1]^T \tag{1}$$

Die so transformierten Merkmalskoordinaten u_V, v_V fungieren als Regelgröße sowohl für die Regelung der Roboterbewegung als auch für die Blickrichtungsregelung. Die Blickrichtungsregelung richtet die Kamera unabhängig von der Position und Orientierung des Roboters aus, mit dem Ziel die zur Bewegungsregelung verwendeten Bildmerkmale über einen möglichst großen Arbeitsbereich im Blickfeld der Kamera zu halten. Die Regelung setzt sich zusammen aus einer Steuerung, die anhand der bekannten Geschwindigkeit des Roboters den optischen Fluss der Merkmale in der virtuellen Bildebene vorhersagt, und einem geschlossenen Regelkreis zur Kompensation von Störungen. Der geschlossene Regelkreis hält den mittels einer Homographie in die aktuelle Ansicht transformierten Schwerpunkt der Merkmale in der Referenzansicht im Bildmittelpunkt.

Die Homographie **H** beschreibt eine Punkt-zu-Punkt Transformation zwischen zwei perspektivischen Ansichten einer Ebene:

$$s\,[u_V, v_V, 1]^T = \mathbf{H}\,[\hat{u}_V, \hat{v}_V, 1]^T \text{ mit } \quad \mathbf{H} = \mathbf{R} + \frac{\boldsymbol{n}_g^T}{d_g}\boldsymbol{t}, \tag{2}$$

wobei **R** und $\boldsymbol{t}$ durch die Rotation und Translation zwischen den optischen Kamerazentren definiert ist. $\boldsymbol{n}$ beschreibt den Normalenvektor der Ebene und d_g den Abstand des optischen Zentrums der ersten Kamera zur Ebene. Durch Transformation des Schwerpunktes der Zielansicht $\hat{u}_{cog}, \hat{v}_{cog}$ in die aktuelle Ansicht u_{cog}, v_{cog}:

$$[u_{cog}, v_{cog}, 1]^T = \mathbf{T}_R^V(f, \alpha, \beta) \cdot \mathbf{H} \cdot \mathbf{T}_V^R(\hat{f}, \hat{\alpha}, \hat{\beta})\,[\hat{u}_{cog}, \hat{v}_{cog}, 1]^T \tag{3}$$

wird die benötigte Drehung der Kamera $\Delta\alpha$ und $\Delta\beta$ für die PTZ-Kamera wie folgt berechnet:

$$\Delta\alpha = -\frac{\Delta v_{cog}}{f}, \quad \Delta\beta = -\frac{\Delta u_{cog}}{f}, \tag{4}$$

2.2 Verhaltensbasierte bildbasierte Regelung

Die Rotation θ des Roboters um seine Hochachse zwischen der Referenzansicht und der aktuellen Ansicht wird durch die Zerlegung der Homographie bestimmt [7]. Zudem liefert diese Zerlegung auch den Richtungsvektor zwischen den Ansichten, dieser ist jedoch für die bildbasierte Regelung der Roboterbewegung nicht ausreichend, da er nur bis auf eine Skalierung definiert ist. Zunächst wird die aktuelle virtuelle Bildebene um θ zurückrotiert. Anhand der rotationsbereinigten Pixelkoordinaten wird der Schwerpunkt berechnet, welcher in einem direkten linearen Zusammenhang mit der longitudinalen und lateralen Verschiebung des Roboters relativ zur Zielkonfiguration steht. Die Komponenten des Schwerpunktes beschreiben die Bildmomente f_x und f_y. Die Bildfehler $\Delta f_\Theta, \Delta f_x, \Delta f_y$ sind wie folgt definiert:

$$\Delta f_\Theta = \theta,\ \Delta f_x = f_x - \hat{f}_x,\ \Delta f_y = f_y - \hat{f}_y,\ f_x = \frac{\sum_{i=1}^n u_V(i)}{n},\ f_y = \frac{\sum_{i=1}^n v_V(i)}{n} \tag{5}$$

Die aus korrespondierenden Merkmalen in der aktuellen und Referenzansicht berechneten entkoppelten Bildmomente und zugehörigen Bildfehler regeln die idealisierte freie Bewegung des Roboters in den drei Freiheitsgraden. In [2] wird eine Fusion der lateralen und der rotatorischen Geschwindigkeitskomponenten in eine Drehgeschwindigkeit vorgeschlagen, so dass initial die laterale Abweichung und erst nach deren Konvergenz die verbleibende Abweichung der Roboterorientierung ausgeregelt wird. Die Transformation der freien Bewegung auf die beiden lokalen Bewegungsfreiheitsgrade des Roboters erfolgt in diesem Beitrag durch eine Fusion der Stellgrößen über vier kontextabhängige Verhalten. Die Verhaltensrepräsentation sowie das aus dem Zusammenspiel der Einzelverhalten erwachsende Navigationsverhalten ist darauf ausgelegt, in Anlehnung an

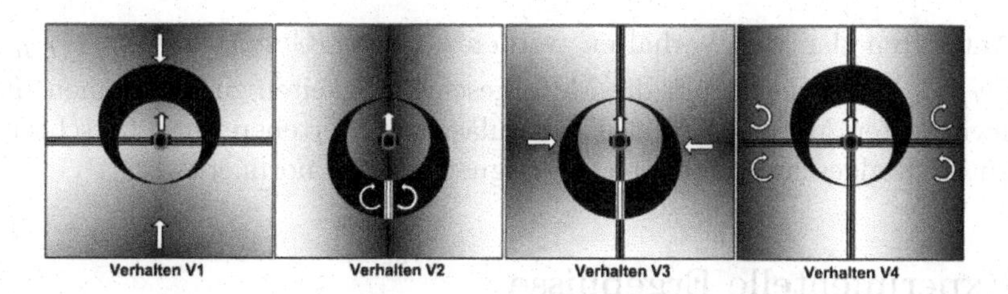

Abb. 3. Kontextabhängige Verhalten zur bildbasierten Regelung. Dunkle Bereiche beziehungsweise dicke Striche entsprechen Roboterkonfiguationen, in denen die Verhaltensaktivierung dominant ist. Die weißen Pfeile verdeutlichen die entsprechende Aktion, die von den Verhalten in der jeweiligen Konfiguration vorgeschlagen werden.

[2] zuerst den lateralen Positionsfehler zu eliminieren. Die Radgeschwindigkeiten v_L, v_R werden anhand der aggregierten Empfehlungen der Verhalten ermittelt. Die Abbildung 3 verdeutlicht die Wirkungsweise der vier Verhalten bei der bildbasierten Regelung des nicht-holonomen Roboters. Das Verhalten $V1$ regelt den longitudinalen Fehler aus, unter der Annahme, dass der laterale und der Winkelfehler zuvor kompensiert wurden. Hierbei wird der longidutinale Fehler Δf_y mit dem inversen Faktor $\Delta f_x \cdot \Delta f_\theta$ skaliert.

$$v_{L_{V1}} = v_{R_{V1}} = \Delta f_y \cdot \left| \frac{\Delta f_y}{\Delta f_x \cdot \Delta f_\theta} \right| \tag{6}$$

Für kleine Regelabweichungen in Δf_x und Δf_θ nähert sich der Roboter gradlinig der Zielkonfiguration, wie im oberen linken Teil der Abbildung 3 gezeigt. Das Verhalten $V1$ ermöglicht es dem Roboter prinzipiell den Zielpunkt auch rückwärts anzufahren. Die Aufgabe des Verhaltens $V2$ besteht in der Kompensation des Rotationsfehlers um die Hochachse als Funktion des lateralen und des Winkelfehlers.

$$v_{L_{V2}} = -\Delta f_\theta \cdot \left| \frac{\Delta f_\theta}{\Delta f_x \cdot \Delta f_x} \right|, \quad v_{R_{V2}} = -v_{L_{V2}} \tag{7}$$

Es korrigiert den Rotationsfehler, wenn der laterale Fehler bereits kompensiert ist. Die Verhalten $V3$ und $V4$ kompensieren den lateralen Fehler. Das dritte Verhalten ist im Fall eines lateralen Fehlers aktiviert und dominiert das Navigationsverhalten solange der longitudinale Fehler klein bleibt.

$$v_{L_{V3}} = v_{R_{V3}} = -\frac{\Delta f_x \cdot \Delta f_\theta}{|\Delta f_y \cdot \Delta f_y|} \tag{8}$$

Das Verhalten $V4$ dreht den Roboter, um den lateralen Fehler zu kompensieren. Dieses Verhalten ist essentiell, da der Roboter bei lateraler Auslenkung nicht zum Zielpunkt gelangt, solange die aktuelle Orientierung des Roboters identisch mit der gewünschten Orientierung in der Ziellage ist.

$$v_{L_{V4}} = -\text{sign}(f_y) \frac{\Delta f_x}{\Delta f_\theta} \cdot \left| \frac{\Delta f_x}{\Delta f_\theta} \right|, \quad v_{R_{V4}} = -v_{L_{V4}} \tag{9}$$

Die Antworten der vier Verhalten werden zu einer Gesamtantwort $v_{(L,R)} = \sum_{i=1}^{4} v_{(L,R)_{Vi}}$ aggregiert, um die Motorgeschwindigkeiten zu bestimmen. Falls die gewünschten Motorstellgrößen den zulässigen Wertebereiche überschreiten, werden die Radgeschwindigkeiten in geeigneter Weise normiert.

3 Experimentelle Ergebnisse

Die globale bildbasierte Navigation über weite Bereiche erfolgt anhand einer topologischen Karte, deren Knoten den Wegpunkten und ihren omnidirektionalen Ansichten entsprechen. Zusätzlich enthält ein Knoten monokulare Referenzansichten für die lokale Navigation. Dabei treten die gleichen Merkmale in verschiedenen zu benachbarten Knoten gehörenden Referenzansichten auf. Die Planungsschicht generiert eine Sequenz von Referenzansichten mit überlappenden Merkmalskombinationen, welche im Bild- und Arbeitsraum von der aktuellen zur Zielansicht führt. Das dynamische Aufschalten der jeweils nächsten sichtbaren Referenzansicht als Sollwert für die bildbasierte Regelung ermöglicht so die globale Navigation des Roboters. Die Abbildung 4 illustriert die Entwicklung der Merkmalsanzahl über mehrere Referenzansichten für einen lokalen Abschnitt des Navigationsgraphen. Die Güte einer Referenzansicht bestimmt sich sowohl aus der Anzahl der verfügbaren Merkmale als auch aus deren fortlaufender Sichtbarkeit über einen längeren Weg. Die dynamische Auswahl der in der aktuellen Situation günstigsten Referenzansicht zur lokalen bildbasierten Navigation erfolgt anhand der beiden benannten Kriterien. Abbildung 5 zeigt

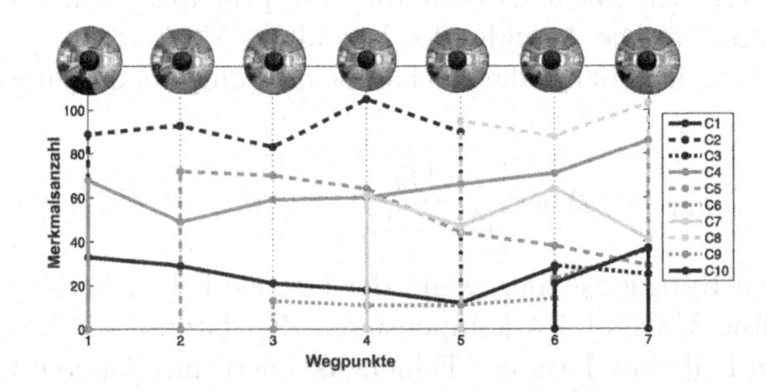

Abb. 4. Entwicklung ausgewählter Referenzansichten über mehrere Wegpunkte

den Verlauf der Bildmomente bei der bildbasierten Weitbereichsregelung über die Referenzansichten C3 und C8, die anhand der Merkmalsverteilung in Abbildung 4 extrahiert werden. Deutlich ist hierbei die initiale Kompensation des lateralen Fehlers und die anschließende Ausrichtung des Roboters anhand der kontextabhängigen Verhalten. Der Roboter ist initial relativ zur Zielposition um 50 cm lateral und 3 m longitudinal ausgelenkt. Nach 2 m wird anhand der omnidirektionalen Ansicht der nächste Merkmalssatz detektiert und auf das nächste

Referenzbild umgeschaltet. Der residuale Positionsfehler beträgt etwa 5 cm in beiden Raumrichtungen.

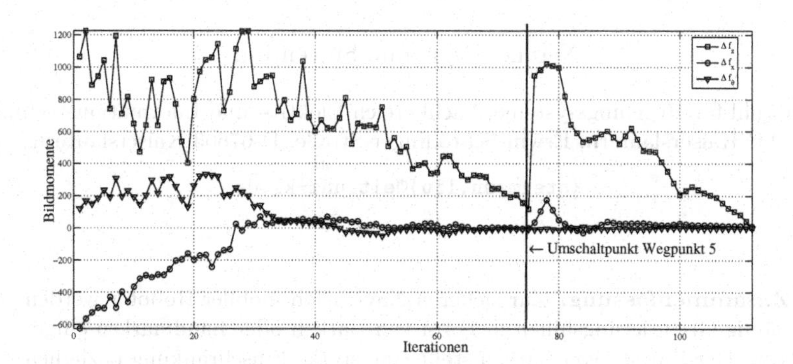

Abb. 5. Weitbereichsregelung über die Referenzansichten C3 und C8 aus Abb. 4.

4 Zusammenfassung

Das vorgestellte Verfahren ermöglicht die autonome bildbasierte Navigation eines mobilen Roboters in einer natürlichen Umgebung ohne zusätzliche Landmarken. Durch die Blickrichtungsregelung und die virtuelle Bildebene in Kombination mit der entwickelten verhaltensbasierten Geschwindigkeitsregelung erweitert sich der Arbeitsbereich für die lokale Navigation bezüglich einer einzelnen Referenzansicht erheblich. Diese Eigenschaft ermöglicht die globale bildbasierte Navigation auch über Bereiche hinweg in denen aufgrund geringer Textur geeignete visuelle Merkmale nur spärlich auftreten.

Literaturverzeichnis

1. S. Hutchinson, G. D. Hager, I. P. Corke, A Tutorial on Visual Servoing Control, IEEE Trans. on Robotics and Automation, vol.12, 1997.
2. G. Hager, D. Kriegman, A. Georghiades and O. Ben-Shahar, Toward domain-independent navigation: Dynamic vision and control, IEEE CDC'98, 1998.
3. Y. Fang et al., Homography-based visual servoing of wheeled mobile robots, IEEE Trans. on systems, man, and cybernetics-part B: Cybernetics, Vol. 35, No. 5, 2005.
4. T. Nierobisch, T. Schleginski, F. Hoffmann, Reactive behaviours for visual topological navigation of a mobile robot, OPTIM 2006, Vol.3, pp. 113-118.
5. D. G. Lowe, Distinctive image features from scale-invariant keypoints, International Journal of Computer Vision, 60, 2, 2004, pp. 91-110.
6. T. Nierobisch, W. Fischer, F. Hoffmann, Large View Visual Servoing of a Mobile Robot with a Pan-Tilt Camera, IEEE/RSJ IROS, Peking, 2006.
7. O. Faugeras, F. Lustmann, Motion and structure from motion in a piecewise planar environment, Int. J. of Pattern Recognition and AI, 2(3), 1988.

Eingangsgrößenrekonstruktion zur Trajektorienfolge mit elementarer Sensorik

Nadine Stegmann, Steven Liu

Lehrstuhl für Regelungssysteme, Fachbereich Elektro- und Informationstechnik,
TU Kaiserslautern, Erwin-Schrödinger-Straße, D-67663 Kaiserslautern

{stegmann,liu}@eit.uni-kl.de

Zusammenfassung. Zur sicheren Navigation mobiler Roboter werden häufig Orientierungshilfen in Form von Barken oder Landmarken eingesetzt. Der Einsatz von Barken stellt eine starke Einschränkung bezüglich des Einsatzgebietes des Roboters dar, die Navigation basierend auf Landmarken erfordert höhere Sensorik, die Datenauswertung und Aufbereitung sind mit hohem Rechenaufwand verbunden. Im vorliegenden Beitrag wird ein Ansatz zur regelungsbasierten Navigation vorgestellt. Dieser wird auf einem mobilen Manipulator mit elementarer Sensorik und eingeschränkter Rechenkapazität realisiert. Die Verfolgung einer a priori festgelegten Trajektorie wird durch Rekonstruktion der effektiven Aktuierung geregelt. Die Anwendung des Verfahrens ermöglicht die sichere Navigation trotz möglicher Aktorfehler oder äußerer Störungen.

1 Einleitung

Eine Grundvoraussetzung für das autonome Agieren mobiler Roboter ist die Bewältigung der sicheren Navigation. Dies beinhaltet sowohl die Verfolgung einer Trajektorie als auch die Vermeidung von Kollisionen mit unerwarteten Hindernissen und anschließender Rückkehr auf die Solltrajektorie. Dies kann, bei entsprechender Sensorausstattung, z.B. durch den Einsatz von GPS, lokaler Barken, Landmarken und Mapping-/Suchstragtegien geschehen. In grundsätzlich bekannter Umgebung besteht eine Alternative hierzu in der geregelten Verfolgung von Solltrajektorien. Die Navigation erfolgt dann durch Vorgabe und Einhaltung von Aktorsollwertfolgen. Hierzu werden keine höhere Sensorik und keine hohe Rechenleistung zur Auswertung der Sensordaten benötigt. Dieser Ansatz setzt die Kenntnis der tatsächlichen Systemaktuierung, bestehend aus Stellsignalen und Störungen, voraus. Diese kann entweder durch Messung oder durch Eingangsgrößenrekonstruktion erlangt werden. Bei letzterer werden auf das System wirkende äußere Störungen und Aktorfehler als zusätzliche Eingangsgrößen interpretiert, der Bedarf an Sensorik ist vermindert.

Ein in diesem Beitrag betrachtetes Anwendungsbeispiel für die Eingangsgrößenrekonstrution ist die Ermittlung des tätsächlichen Lenkwinkels einer autoähnlichen mobilen Plattform. Der betrachtete Roboter hat keine Sensoren, mit denen dieser gemessen werden kann. Die Einstellung des Lenkwinkels erfolgt

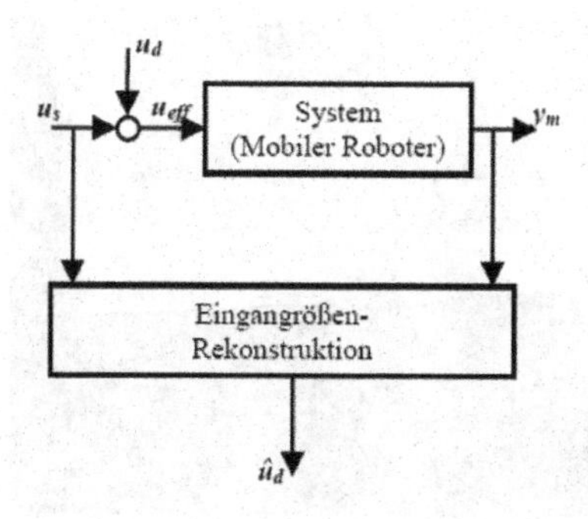

Abb. 1. Struktur der Eingangsgrößenrekonstruktion

über einen Schrittmotor. Insbesondere bei schnellen Änderungen des Lenkwinkelsollwertes können Schrittverluste und somit eine gestörte Aktuierung auftreten. Weitere Fehlerquellen liegen in äußeren Krafteinwirkungen auf die gelenkten Räder. Um dennoch eine sichere Navigation zu gewährleisten, wird der effektive Lenkwinkel mittels Eingangsgrößenrekonstruktion ermittelt und ein Regler zur Kompensation der Differenz zwischen Soll- und Istwert eingesetzt.

Die Rekonstruktion der Eingangsgrößen dynamischer Systeme findet hauptsächlich in der Systemdiagnose Anwendung. Hierbei werden die effektiv auf das System wirkenden Eingangsgrößen durch Systeminversion [1,2] oder durch den Einsatz eines Eingangsgrößenbeobachters [2,3] ermittelt. Die Entwicklung der benötigten Systemmodelle und Algorithmen zur Bestimmung der effektiven Eingangsgrößen eines mobilen Manipulators werden im Rahmen dieses Beitrags vorgestellt. Durch diese Rekonstruktion kann die Aktuierung des Roboters auch ohne direkte Sensoren zu jedem Zeitpunkt als bekannt angenommen werden. Im Folgenden wird eine neue Methode zur geregelten Bahnverfolgung mit Hilfe der Kenntnis dieser Aktuierung vorgestellt.

2 Eingangsgrößenrekonstruktion für den mobilen Manipulator CARMA

Abb. 1 zeigt eine schematische Übersicht der Eingangsgrößenrekonstruktion. Der Vektor der effektiven Eingangsgrößen u_{eff} beinhaltet alle auf das System einwirkenden äußeren Einflüsse, d.h. die realen Aktorgrößen und äußere Störungen wie z.B. Krafteinwirkungen. Die realen Aktorgrößen setzen sich additiv aus den Sollaktorgrößen u_s und auftretenden Störanteilen bedingt durch Aktorfehler, welche in u_d enthalten sind, zusammen. In Abhängigkeit von u_{eff} ändern sich der Systemzustand und folglich auch die Sensorwerte y_m. Auf Basis der Sensordaten und der Sollaktorwerte kann die effektive Aktuierung durch Berechnung von u_d ermittelt werden.

Bei dem betrachteten System handelt es sich um einen "**C**ar-like **A**utonomous **R**obot **MA**nipulator", bestehend aus einer autoähnlichen mobilen Plattform

Abb. 2. Mobiler Manipulator CARMA

und einem seriell-kinematischen Roboterarm (siehe Abb.2). Die Dynamik der Plattform kann durch ein Einspurmodell [4], siehe Gleichungen 1 bis 5, beschrieben werden, wobei x und y die Koordinaten des Manipulatorschwerpunktes in Bezug auf ein ortsfestes Koordinatensystem, ψ der Gierwinkel, β der Schwimmwinkel, v die Geschwindigkeit, δ der Lenkwinkel und A, B, C, D, E Konstanten, die von Masse, Reifeneigenschaften, usw. abhängen, sind.

$$\dot{x} = v\cos(\psi + \beta) \tag{1}$$

$$\dot{y} = v\sin(\psi + \beta) \tag{2}$$

$$\dot{\psi} = \dot{\psi} \tag{3}$$

$$\ddot{\psi} = -\frac{C}{v}\dot{\psi} + D\delta \tag{4}$$

$$\dot{\beta} = -\frac{A}{v}\beta + \frac{B}{v}\delta - \dot{\psi} \tag{5}$$

Der Manipulator hat zwei Aktoren, einen Gleichstrommotor zum Antrieb der Hinterachse und einen Schrittmotor zur Einstellung des Lenkwinkels der Vorderräder. Zur unterlagerten Regelung der Plattformgeschwindigkeit stehen als Sensoren ein Encoder für den Antriebsmotor und ein Beschleunigungssensor zur Verfügung. Zur Erfassung des Winkeleinschlags der Vorderräder stehen keine Sensoren zur Verfügung. Somit können die Geschindigkeit v als sichere Eingangsgröße u_{1p} und der Lenkwinkel δ als unsichere Eingangsgröße $u_{2p} + d$ betrachtet werden. Als Messsignale zur Rekonstruktion dieser Eingangsgröße werden die Geschwindigkeit des rechten und des linken Hinterrades, v_r und v_l, welche durch Inkrementalgeber bestimmt werden, genutzt. Als Ausgangsgrössen werden daher

$$y_{1,2} = v \pm vE\tan\delta \tag{6}$$

definiert. Das durch die Gleichungen 1 bis 6 beschriebene System ist nichtlinear und nicht eingangsaffin, die in [2,3] beschriebenen Vorgehensweisen sind somit nicht direkt anwendbar. Daher wird das System durch eine dynamische Kompensation der Form

$$\dot{u}_{1,2} = u_{p1,p2} \tag{7}$$

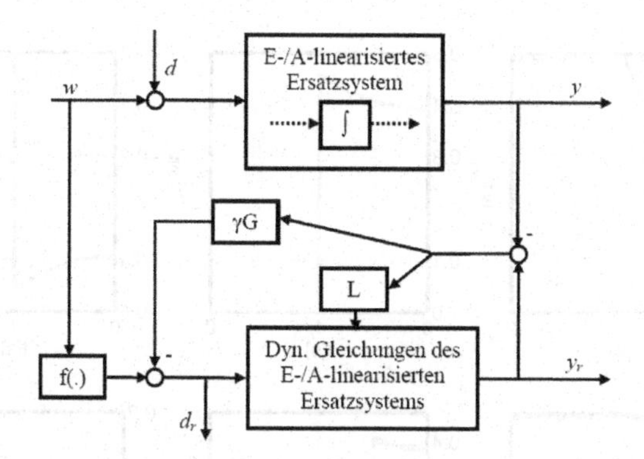

Abb. 3. Struktur des Eingangsgrößenbeobachters für das transformierte System

in ein eingangsaffines überführt. Das resultierende System ist beschrieben durch die Gleichungen 1 bis 6 und die zusätzlichen Zustandsgleichungen

$$\dot{v} = u_1, \tag{8}$$
$$\dot{\delta} = u_2. \tag{9}$$

Es hat einen totalen relativen Grad von 2, die Differentiation der beiden Ausgangsgrößen führt auf eine direkte Abhängigkeit von den Eingangsgrößen. Das System ist somit ein-/ausgangslinearisierbar [5]. Die Transformation

$$u = \mathbf{E}^{-1}\begin{pmatrix} w_1 \\ w_2 \end{pmatrix} = \begin{pmatrix} \frac{1}{2} & \frac{1}{2} \\ \frac{\cos^2\delta - E\cos^2\delta\tan\delta}{2vE} & \frac{-\cos^2\delta - E\cos^2\delta\tan\delta}{2vE} \end{pmatrix}\begin{pmatrix} w_1 \\ w_2 \end{pmatrix} \tag{10}$$

überführt das System in eine Integratorkette der Form

$$\begin{pmatrix} \dot{y}_1 \\ \dot{y}_2 \end{pmatrix} = \begin{pmatrix} 1 & 0 \\ 0 & 1 \end{pmatrix}\begin{pmatrix} w_1 \\ w_2 \end{pmatrix}. \tag{11}$$

Für diese wird nun ein Eingangs- und Zustandsbeobachter mit den Matrizen $\mathbf{L}$ und $\mathbf{G}$ und dem Tuningparameter γ nach der in [6] entwickelten Methode entworfen. Für die Durchführung des Entwurfs muss zunächst der Einfluss einer Störung auf die unsichere Eingangsgröße δ untersucht werden. Eine Verminderung des Lenkwinkels wirkt sich auf die Radgeschwindigkeiten v_r und v_l entgegengesetzt aus. Dies entspricht einer Verminderung der Eingangsgröße w_1 bei gleichzeitiger Erhöhung der Eingangsgröße w_2 und umgekehrt. Für den Entwurf des Beobachters wird die Systemdarstellung zu

$$\begin{pmatrix} \dot{y}_1 \\ \dot{y}_2 \end{pmatrix} = \begin{pmatrix} 1 & 0 \\ 0 & 1 \end{pmatrix}\begin{pmatrix} w_1 \\ w_2 \end{pmatrix} + \begin{pmatrix} 1 \\ -1 \end{pmatrix} d \tag{12}$$

erweitert. Der resultierende Beobachter hat die in Abb. 3 dargestellte Struktur. Die Beobachtergleichungen sind gegeben durch

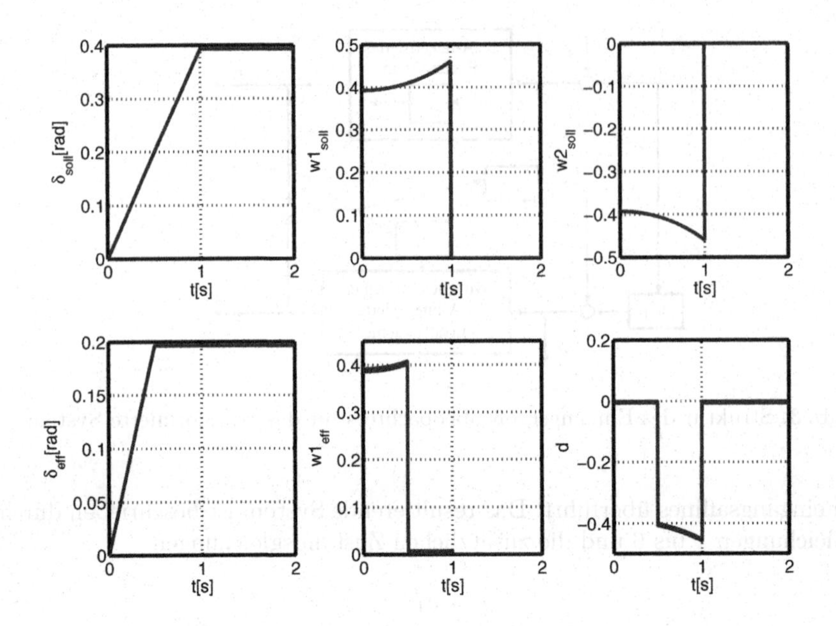

Abb. 4. Eingangsgrößenrekonstruktion bei Kreisfahrt und Blockieren des Schrittmotors

$$\dot{y}_r = \begin{pmatrix} 1 \\ 1 \end{pmatrix} f_r + \mathbf{L} \left[\begin{pmatrix} 1 & 0 \\ 0 & 1 \end{pmatrix} y_r - y \right], \tag{13}$$

$$f_r = \begin{pmatrix} 1 & 0 \\ 0 & 1 \\ 0 & 0 \end{pmatrix} \begin{pmatrix} w_1 \\ w_2 \end{pmatrix} - \gamma \mathbf{G} \left[\begin{pmatrix} 1 & 0 \\ 0 & 1 \end{pmatrix} y_r - y \right]. \tag{14}$$

In Abb. 4 sind exemplarisch die Ergebnisse der Eingangsgrößenrekonstruktion für ein Blockieren des Schrittmotors gezeigt. Der mobile Manipulator bewegt sich zu Simulationsbeginn mit konstanter Geschwindigkeit v_0 in x-Richtung. Zum Einleiten einer Kreisfahrt soll der Lenkwinkel δ_{soll} graduell von null auf $\frac{\pi}{8}$ erhöht werden, die dazu benötigten Eingangsgrössen $w_{1,2}$ sind oben mitte und oben rechts dargestellt. Zum Zeitpunkt $t = 0.5$ s blockiert der Schrittmotor und die vorgegebene Lenkwinkeländerung bleibt aus. Die vom Beobachter rekonstruierte Störgröße und die resultierende effektive Aktuierung w_1 sind unten rechts bzw. unten mitte dargestellt. Die Ergebnisse zeigen, dass die Störung d sicher rekonstruiert wird. Dies ist der Fall, obwohl für die Ein-/Ausgangslinearisierung die Sollgrößen von v und δ und nicht der effektive Lenkwinkel verwendet werden. Dies entspricht der Linearisierung entlang einer Solltrajektorie und kann somit als linearisierende Vorsteuerung interpretiert werden.

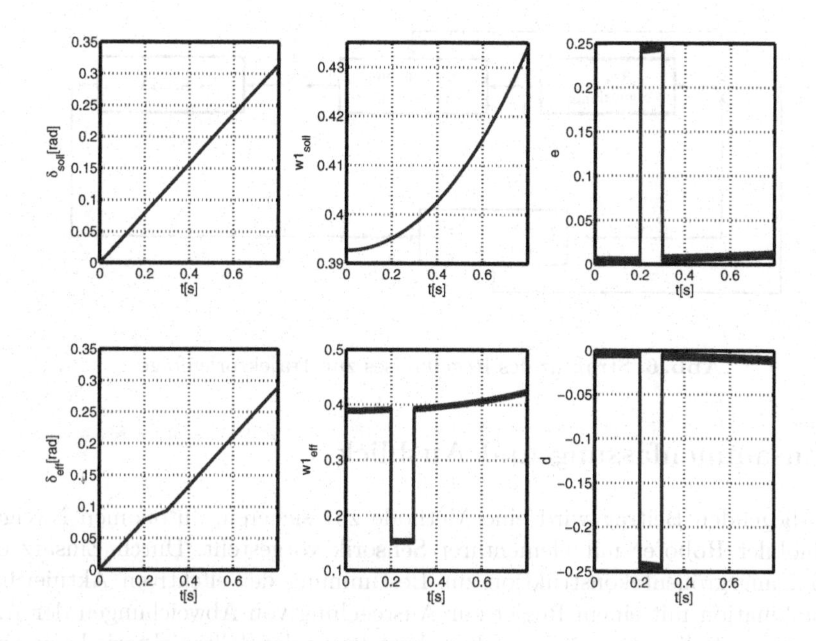

Abb. 5. Eingangsgrößenrekonstruktion und Regelfehler bei Verlust einzelner Schritte

3 Geregelte Trajektorienfolge unter Verwendung der Eingangsgrößenrekonstruktion

Die in Abschnitt 2 dargestellte Eingangsgrößenrekonstruktion wird zur geregelten Bahnverfolgung genutzt. Das gezeigte Beispiel des Blockierens des Schrittmotors stellt den ungünstigsten Fall einer Störung dar, da diese zwar durch die Eingangsgrößenrekonstruktion erkannt, aber nicht durch Einsatz einer Regelung kompensiert werden kann. Im Folgenden soll daher der Fall des Verlustes mehrerer Schritte des Schrittmotors zur Lenkwinkeleinstellung betrachtet werden. In Abb. 5 sind die Simulationsergebnisse der Eingangsgrößenrekonstruktion für dieses Szenario dargestellt. Der mobile Manipulator bewegt sich wie im zuvor betrachteten Fall zu Simulationsbeginn mit konstanter Geschwindigkeit v_0 in x-Richtung. Zum Einleiten einer Kreisfahrt soll der Lenkwinkel δ_{soll} wiederum graduell von null auf $\frac{\pi}{8}$ erhöht werden. Zum Zeitpunkt $t = 0.2$ s verliert der Schrittmotor nacheinander mehrere Schritte, dies resultiert in einer weniger starken Lenkwinkeländerung als erwünscht. Auch in diesem Fall wird die Störung des Lenkwinkels sicher rekonstruiert. Oben rechts ist exemplarisch der Fehler e zwischen Soll- und Istwert der Eingangsgröße w_1 dargestellt. Durch Einsatz jeweils eines Reglers mit integrierendem Anteil zur Ausregelung dieses Fehlers für beide Stellgrößen kann nun die Rückkehr auf die Solltrajektorie und die sichere Verfolgung dieser trotz auftretender Störungen gewährleistet werden. Die Struktur des resultierenden geschlossenen Regelkreises ist in Abb.6 dargestellt.

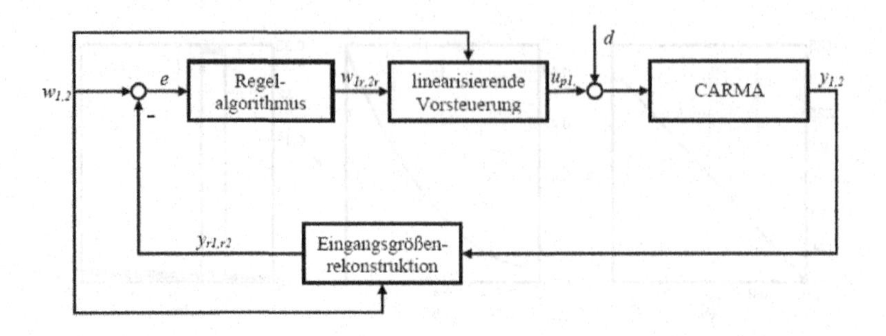

Abb. 6. Struktur des Regelkreises zur Trajektorienfolge

4 Zusammenfassung und Ausblick

Im vorliegenden Beitrag wird eine Methode zur sicheren, autonomen Navigation mobiler Roboter mit elementarer Sensorik vorgestellt. Durch Einsatz einer Eingangsgrößenrekonstruktion zur Bestimmung der effektiven Aktuierung in Kombination mit einem Regler zur Ausregelung von Abweichungen der Aktuierung vom Sollwert wird eine sichere Verfolgung der Solltrajektorie basierend auf der ausschließlichen Kenntnis innerer Systemgrößen gewährleistet. Sensoren zur Umgebungswahrnehmung werden nur für die Vermeidung von Kollisionen mit unerwarteten Hindernissen benötigt.

Die hier gewählte Vorgehensweise der Rekonstruktion der Eingagnsgrößen auf Basis des ein-/ausgangslinearisierten Systems resultiert in einer Beobachtervorschrift mit geringem Rechenaufwand. Alle rechenintensiveren Operationen werden offline ausgeführt. Eine Implementierung bei limitierter Rechenleistung ist somit möglich.

Die nächsten Schritte bestehen in der Erweiterung des Ansatzes zur Erkennung und Ausregelung weiterer Störeinflüsse und in der Untersuchung von Diskretisierungs- und Quantisierungseffekten.

Literaturverzeichnis

1. Moylan PJ: Stable inversion of linear systems. IEEE Trans Automat Control 22(1): 74-78, 1977.
2. Edelmayer A, Bokor J, Szabo Z, et al.: Input reconstruction by means of system inversion: a geometric approach to fault detection and isolation in nonlinear systems. Int J Appl Math Comput Sci 14(2): 189-199, 2004.
3. Hou M, Patton RJ: Input observability and input reconstruction. Automatica 34(6): 789-794, 1998.
4. Mitschke M, Wallentowitz H: Dynamik der Kraftfahrzeuge. Springer, 1998.
5. Slotine JJE, Li W: Applied Nonlinear Control. Prentice Hall, 1991.
6. Corless M, Tu J: State and Input Estimation for a Class of Uncertain Systems. Automatica 34(6): 757-764, 1998.

Modellierung von Anomalien in einer modularen Roboter-Steuerung

Kalle Kleinlützum, Werner Brockmann und Nils Rosemann

Universität Osnabrück, Institut für Informatik, AG Technische Informatik
kkleinlu@uos.de, wbrockma@uos.de, nroseman@uos.de

Zusammenfassung. Moderne Robotersysteme werden immer komplexer und dadurch schwieriger zu entwerfen. Außerdem steigt die Wahrscheinlichkeit von Fehlern. Organic Computing versucht durch Methoden organischer Systeme wie Emergenz und Selbstorganisation gleichzeitig das Entwurfsproblem zu lösen und das autonome Reagieren auf Fehler zu erreichen, ohne den Aufwand der klassischen Fehlertoleranz zu investieren. Um auf anormale Situationen reagieren zu können, muss quasi der „Gesundheitszustand" des Roboters erfasst werden. In diesem Beitrag wird beschrieben, wie dieser ausgehend von Sensorsignalen auf den verschiedenen Ebenen einer Steuerungshierarchie repräsentiert werden kann. Ein wesentlicher Mechanismus dazu sind „Health-Signale". Ihre Semantik und systematische Verknüpfung werden näher erläutert und an einem einfachen Beispiel demonstriert.

1 Einleitung

Autonome mobile Roboter werden zunehmend komplexer. Dadurch wächst das Engineering-Problem und die Wahrscheinlichkeit von Fehlern im Entwurf, in der Hardware und im laufenden Betrieb steigt. Mit den Methoden der klassischen Fehlertoleranz kann man diesem Problem nur unzureichend begegnen, da die Komplexität der benötigten Modelle ebenfalls steigt, was die Problematik, insbesondere im Entwurf, noch verstärkt. Deshalb werden Mechanismen benötigt, die ohne großen Engineering-Aufwand (wie z.B. explizite Fehlermodelle) und Realisierungsaufwand (wie z.B. Hardware-Redundanz) auskommen.

Komplexe Roboter besitzen meist auch komplexe Steuerungen, z.B. in Form von Three-Layer-Architekturen [1] oder Verhaltensnetzen [2]. Jedoch unterstützen die meisten Architekturen zur Zeit nicht explizit die Integration von Maßnahmen zur Erhöhung der Robustheit gegen die obengenannten Fehlerklassen. Ziel der ORCA-Architektur (Organic Robot Control Architecture [3], [4]) ist es, mit den Prinzipien des *Organic Computing* [5] Mechanismen in Steuerungen dieser Komplexität zu integrieren, die einerseits den Entwurf unterstützen und andererseits einen robusten Betrieb ermöglichen, selbst wenn Störungen auftreten. Eine Schlüsselrolle kommt dabei dem autonomen, aber sicheren Reagieren auf Anomalien zu. Unabhängig von der Ursache bewirken diese ein nicht mehr vertrauenswürdiges Verhalten des Roboters. Soll ein Roboter aber dennoch seine Mission fortsetzen, muss seine Steuerung robust reagieren und dazu seinen „Gesundheitszustand" kennen. Sogenannte *Health-Signale* [4] dienen dabei der vereinheitlichten internen Darstellung des „Gesundheitszustands", der durch Anomalien beeinflusst wird.

2 Stand der Technik

In der Entstehung der verhaltensbasierten Steuerung war es Brooks' formulierte Absicht, die Robotersteuerung durch bewussten Verzicht auf Modelle und Pläne robust zu machen [6],[7]. Nach Meinung von Lussier et al. [8] macht das Fehlen dieser symbolischen Repräsentationsform den effizienten Einsatz einer Brooks'schen Steuerung in einer komplexen Umgebung unmöglich. In ihrer dreischichtigen LAAS-Architektur findet die Behandlung von Fehlern daher auf symbolischer Ebene statt (durch regelbasiertes Checken von auszuführenden sequentialisierten Plänen).

In [9] beschreibt C. Ferrell eine der ersten und am weitest gehenden Arbeiten, die Fehlertoleranzmechanismen in eine Steuerung nach Brooks' Art integriert. Sie beschäftigt sich dabei hauptsächlich mit Hardwarefehlern und implementiert „robuste virtuelle Sensoren", die trotz Ausfall einzelner Sensoren verlässliche Werte liefern sollen. D.h. sie kapselt Sensorfehler auf niedriger Ebene und verbirgt sie vor nächst-höheren Steuerungsebenen. Ferrells Ansatz, der sich auf Hardwarefehler konzentriert, ist in der Semantik zu eingeschränkt, um die Vielzahl möglicher Anomalien zu monitoren. Zusätzlich ist durch das Verbergen erkannter Fehler die Qualität des Ausgangssignals der virtuellen Sensoren bezüglich seiner Vertrauenswürdigkeit für höhere Ebenen nicht nachvollziehbar. Damit ist ihr Ansatz für autonome mobile Roboter nur eingeschränkt sinnvoll. In der von uns verwendeten ORCA-Architektur werden daher Prinzipien von organischen Systemen übernommen, die diesen Einschränkungen nicht unterliegen und andererseits nicht den Aufwand für die Modellierung bzw. Implementierung der klassischen Fehlertoleranz aufweisen.

3 Die ORCA-Architektur

Die ORCA-Architektur (Organic Robot Control Architecture [4],[3]) ist eine modulare, hierarchisch strukturierte Kontrollarchitektur. Sie zeichnet sich durch ihren komplementären Aufbau aus funktionalen Einheiten, den BCUs (Basic Control Units) und überwachenden und ggf. korrigierend eingreifenden Kontrolleinheiten, den OCUs (Organic Control Units), aus. Abb. 1 zeigt exemplarisch die Umsetzung der ORCA-Architektur auf dem 4-beinigen Laufroboter WALTER (WALking TEst Robot). Die OCUs überwachen dabei den Zustand des Roboters, der ihnen u.a. in Form von Health-Signalen mitgeteilt wird, und reagieren auf Anomalien. Die propriozeptive Generierung von Health-Signalen wird in [4], [10] und [11] beschrieben.

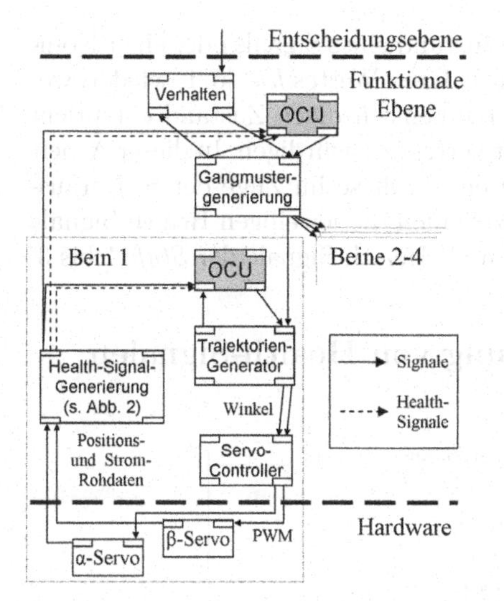

Abb. 1. Links: Hierarchische und modulare ORCA-Systemarchitektur des Laufroboters WALTER, rechts: Vierbeiniger Laufroboter WALTER.

4 Semantik der Health-Signale

Der „Gesundheitszustand" von Komponenten, oder genauer die Vertrauenswürdigkeit der von ihr generierten Signale, wird von verschiedenen Faktoren beeinflusst, einige davon sind Symptome von Anomalien vorgeschalteter Komponenten oder der Komponente selbst, andere resultieren aus dem Entwurf der Robotersteuerung oder dem Betrieb des Roboters. Die nachfolgende Klassifizierung zählt fünf solcher Faktoren auf, die per Health-Signal modelliert werden sollen. Unser Ansatz ist, alle fünf Faktoren graduell durch ein einheitliches, normiertes Health-Signal auszudrücken. Schließlich müssen nachfolgende Module Signale, denen sie nicht vertrauen können, grundsätzlich mit Vorsicht behandeln, unabhängig von deren Ursache.

1. **Signalqualität** Die Qualität eines Sensorsignals hängt z.B. vom Rauschen und der Auflösung des Sensors ab.
2. **Hardwarefehler** Ausfälle oder Störungen von elektronischen oder mechanischen Komponenten
3. **Interaktionsfehler** Eine Komponente oder der ganze Roboter interagiert nicht wie gewünscht/gewohnt mit der Umgebung.
4. **Spezifiziert/ unspezifiziert** Wenn eine Eingangs-Signal-Kombination in einem Modul beim Entwurf nicht spezifiziert wurde, ist seine Ausgabe nicht vertrauenswürdig.
5. **Gelernt/ungelernt** Ein im laufenden Betrieb lernendes Modul kann sich in einem Bereich befinden, für den eine Reaktion noch nicht oder nur unzureichend gelernt wurde.

Ein Health-Signal gibt den Gesundheitszustand eines Signals oder einer Komponente graduell in Form eines normierten skalaren Wertes $h \in [0,1]$ wieder, wobei ein Wert von 1 einem „gesunden", vertrauenswürdigen Zustand entspricht und ein Wert von 0 einem anormalen, nicht vertrauenswürdigen. In dieser Arbeit liegt der Fokus auf den ersten drei Kriterien, da diese im Zuge der Sensorauswertung zuerst behandelt werden. Wir bezeichnen die jeweiligen Health-Signale entsprechend ihrer Reihenfolge im Weiteren als Health-Signale der *Stufe* 1 bis 3.

5 Generierung und Verarbeitung von Health-Signalen

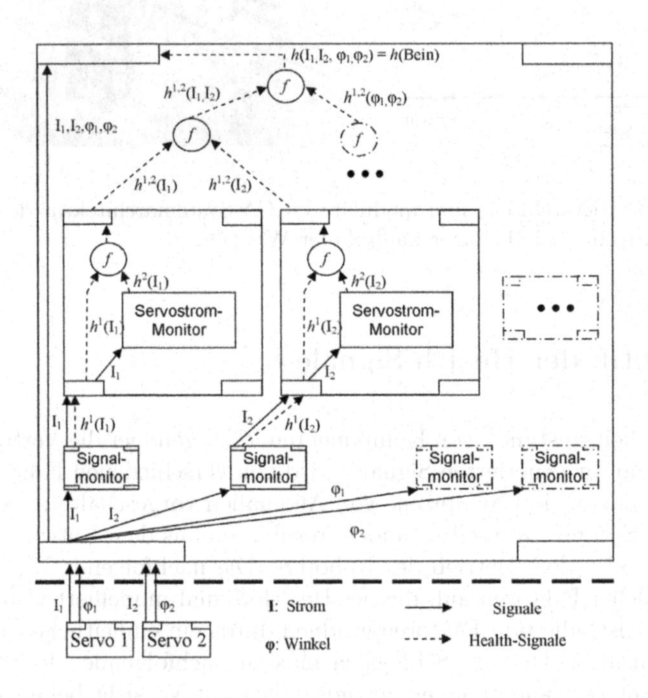

Abb. 2. Health-Signal-Generierung für ein Bein des Laufroboters WALTER.

5.1 Generierung von Health-Signalen

Bei der propriozeptiven Health-Signal-Generierung wird, ausgehend von den Sensorrohdaten, ein generisches Konzept zur Abstraktion und Verdichtung der Signale angewendet. In Abb. 2 ist die dreistufige Generierung einiger Health-Signale exemplarisch für ein Bein des Laufroboters WALTER dargestellt. In der untersten Verarbeitungsstufe wird dabei von *Signalmonitoren* zu jedem Sensorwert (in unserem Fall der Winkel ϕ_i und der Strom I_i eines Servos i) ein Health-Signal $h^1(I_i)$ generiert, das der Signalqualität des jeweiligen Sensors entspricht. Dazu kann A-Priori-Wissen über die Beschaffenheit der Sensoren verwendet werden. Diese Signalmonitore sind i.d.R. sehr einfach. Z.B. generieren sie hier bei

5 % Rauschen ein konstantes Health-Signal $h^1(I_i)$ von 0,95. In der zweiten Verarbeitungsstufe werden die Ströme I_i der einzelnen Servos auf Anomalien untersucht und Abweichungen vom erwarteten Verlauf in Health-Signalen $h^2(I_i)$ ausgedrückt. Die erwarteten Sensorwerte werden dabei entweder durch ein statisches Sensormodell oder durch aufgezeichnete Referenz-Stromverläufe festgelegt wie in [4], [10]. Die erzeugten Health-Signale $h^2(I_i)$ sind den Kriterien 2 oder 3 zugeordnet. Die Health-Signale $h^2(I_i)$ müssen jedoch vor der Weitergabe noch mit den eingehenden Health-Signalen $h^1(I_i)$ verknüpft werden (s. Abschnitt 5.2).

Die gleiche Verknüpfung von Health-Signalen findet in der in Abb. 2 dargestellten Struktur auf einer dritten Verarbeitungsebene noch einmal statt. Dort entsteht das neue Health-Signal $h^{1,2}(I_1, I_2)$ für die Stromaufnahme des Beins, jedoch ohne ein Monitor-Modul lediglich durch die Verknüpfung der zwei Health-Signale $h^{1,2}(I_1)$ und $h^{1,2}(I_2)$, die sich auf gleichartige Signale und Stufen beziehen. In einer vierten Verarbeitungsstufe werden danach die Health-Signale der Positionen und Ströme eines Beines verknüpft und repräsentieren so den Gesundheitszustand eines Beines als Ganzes. Eine fünfte Verarbeitungsstufe könnte die Signale aller vier Beine und des Ausgleichsgewichts zum Gesundheitszustand des gesamten Roboters zusammenführen.

Ein solches Health-Signal-Netzwerk kann einfach bottom-up entworfen werden bis alle benötigten Health-Signale generiert sind. Die skizzierte Verarbeitungsreihenfolge und der Signalfluss sind jedoch nicht zwingend, sondern applikationsabhängig. Es kann eine Vielzahl unterschiedlicher Health-Signale erzeugt werden, die sowohl einfachen Signalqualitäten entsprechen, als auch verdichteten abstrakten Gesundheitszuständen, die sich aus verschiedenen lokalen Verhaltensmodellen des Roboters zusammensetzen. Deshalb sind eine vereinheitlichende Semantik und Verknüpfung der Health-Signale wichtig.

5.2 Verknüpfung von Health-Signalen

Die Verknüpfung mehrerer Health-Signale ist ein zentraler Punkt bei der Health-Signal-Generierung und benötigt eine einheitliche und konsistente Methode. Die Verknüpfung kann sowohl innerhalb eines Moduls geschehen, als auch eigenständig außerhalb (vgl. Abb. 2). Außerdem müssen auch mehr als zwei Health-Signale verknüpft werden können, wobei das Ergebnis immer im definierten Wertebereich $h \in [0, 1]$ bleiben muss. Eine weitere sinnvolle Einschränkung ist, dass das Ergebnis der Verknüpfung mehrerer Health-Signale nicht „gesünder" bzw. vertrauenswürdiger sein darf als das schlechteste einzelne. Unser Ansatz ist deshalb, Health-Signale durch *t-Normen* zu verknüpfen, wobei die Wahl der t-Norm festlegt, wie kritisch der Gesundheitszustand bewertet wird. Das nachfolgende Zahlenbeispiel zeigt dies für das Minimum bzw. Produkt als t-Norm:

Beispiel 1: $h^0 = 0.6,\ h^1 = 0.75,\ h^2 = 0.85 \rightarrow \min(h^0, h^1, h^2) = 0.6,\quad h^0 \cdot h^1 \cdot h^2 = 0.38.$

Beispiel 2: $h^0 = \ldots = h^4 = 0.8 \rightarrow \min(h^0, h^1, h^2, h^3, h^4) = 0.8,\quad h^0 \cdot h^1 \cdot h^2 \cdot h^3 \cdot h^4 = 0.028.$

6 Anwendungsbeispiel

Der 4-beinige Laufroboter WALTER (WALking TEst Robot, Abb. 1), der als Demonstrator für die Health-Signal-Generierung dient, erfüllt zwei wichtige Eigenschaften: Er ist kinematisch verhältnismäßig einfach aufgebaut und doch komplex genug, um an ihm viele grundlegende Steuerungsprobleme eines Laufroboters untersuchen zu können. Er besitzt neun Servos als Aktuatoren (2 pro Bein + 1 Ausgleichsgewicht) und 18 Sensoren (Strom- und Positionsmessung der Servos). Für die Health-Signal-Untersuchungen wird ein einfaches starres Gangmuster verwendet, bei dem sich immer nur ein Bein in der Schwingphase befindet, während sich die übrigen drei Beine am Boden bleiben und das Ausgleichsgewicht für Stabilität sorgt.

Die Generierung der Health-Signale erfolgt analog zu Abb. 2. Die Ungenauigkeit der gemessenen Servoströme wird mit 5%, die der Winkel mit 0.5% modelliert. Die Interaktionsfehler werden in den Servostrom-Monitoren mittels Referenzsignal und Toleranzband bestimmt.

Abb. 3 (oben) zeigt den Stromverlauf für das obere Servo des linken Vorderbeins für den Fall, dass der Laufroboter vor einem flachen Hindernis steht, das er nicht überwinden kann, im Vergleich zum dem Referenzverlauf. Durch die in den Servos integrierte Positionsregelung ist der Effekt der Abweichungen bei den Servo-Positionen nicht so deutlich. Deshalb wird das Health-Signal $h(\text{Bein})$ wesentlich durch das Health-Signal $h^1(I_1)$ beeinflusst, wie in Abb. 3 (unten) zu sehen ist. Hier wird auch der Effekt des Minimums im Vergleich zum Produkt als t-Norm verdeutlicht. Der Verlauf beim Produkt als t-Norm ist deutlich pessimistischer und reflektiert auch die Einflüsse der anderen Sensorgrößen in den Phasen, in denen beim Minimum das Health-Signal konstant durch die Qualität der Strommessung $h^1(I_i)$ begrenzt wird.

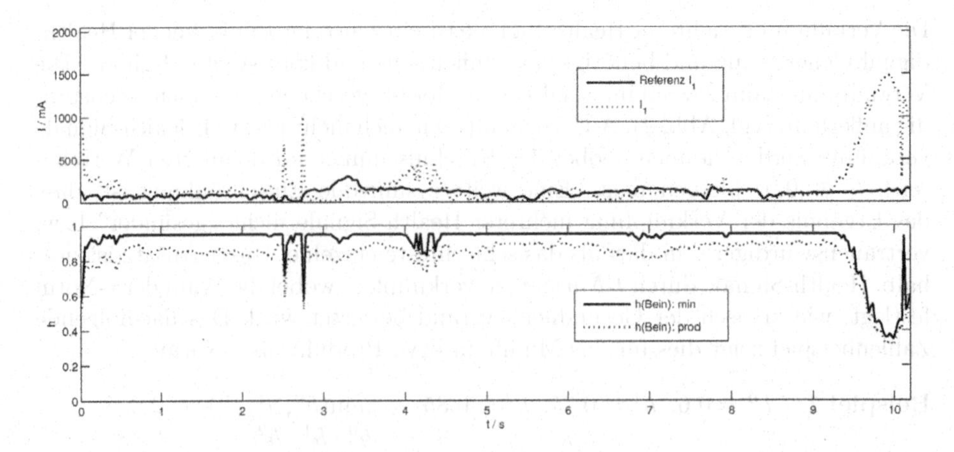

Abb. 3. Verlauf eines Servostroms und Health-Signal für ein Bein in dem Fall, dass der Laufroboter WALTER durch ein flaches Hindernis in der Forbewegung gehindert wird.

7 Abschluss

In dieser Arbeit wurde ein Ansatz zur schrittweisen Generierung zunehmend verdichteter Health-Signale vorgestellt. Diese sind zur Verarbeitung in den OCUs der ORCA-Architektur gedacht, stehen aber auch den BCUs zur Verfügung, sollten diese eine Information über den Gesundheitszustand, also die Vertrauenswürdigkeit, von Roboterkomponenten oder bestimmten Signalen benötigen. Zur Verknüpfung von Health-Signalen wurden t-Normen eingeführt, wobei die Wahl der t-Norm festlegt, wie sensibel die Robotersteuerung mit den zur Verfügung stehenden Health-Signalen umgeht. Eine empfindliche t-Norm wie das Produkt hat nämlich eine um so drastischere Auswirkung auf das fusionierte Health-Signal, je mehr Health-Signale verknüpft werden. Deshalb ist es wahrscheinlich sinnvoll, applikationsabhängig verschieden empfindliche t-Normen zu verwenden. In einer kinematischen Kette, wie einem Bein addieren sich mögliche Positionsfehler, daher könnte dort eine empfindlichere t-Norm nötig sein. Bei den gemessenen Strömen der Aktuatoren erscheint dagegen eine worst-case-orientierte Norm wie das Minimum angebracht. Neben der Frage der Verdichtung von Health-Signalen arbeiten wir an der Generierung von Health-Signalen der Kategorien 4 bzw. 5 und auch daran, den Wirkungskreis zu schließen, indem Reaktionen des Roboters von Health-Signalen abhängig gemacht werden.

Literaturverzeichnis

1. Gat E: On Three-Layer Architectures, Artificial Intelligence and Mobile Robots, MIT/AAAI Press: 195–210, 1997
2. Albiez J, Luksch T, Berns K, et. al: An activation based behaviour control architecture for walking machines 7th Int. Conf. on Sim. of Adapt. Beh., MIT Press: 118–126, 2002
3. Brockmann W, Maehle E., Mösch F: Organic Fault-Tolerant Control Architecture for Robotic Applications. 4th IARP/IEEE-RAS/EURON Workshop on Dep. Rob. in Hum. Env., 2005
4. Brockmann W, Großpietsch K, Kleinlützum K, et al.: Concept for a Fault-Tolerant Control Architecture for CLAWAR Machines. 9th CLAWAR: 643–650, 2006
5. http://www.organic-computing.de/SPP/
6. Brooks R, A robust layered control system for a mobile robot, IEEE Journal of Rob. and Aut. 2 (1): 14–23, 1986
7. Brooks R.A, Intelligence Without Reason, Proc. IJCAI-91:569–595, 1991
8. Lussier B, Chatila R, Ingrand F. et al.: On Fault Tolerance and Robustness in Autonomous Systems, 3rd IARP/IEEE-RAS/EURON Workshop on Dep. Rob. in Hum. Env., 2004
9. Ferrell C: Robust Agent Control of an Autonomous Robot with Many Sensors and Actuators. M.S. Thesis, MIT, 1993
10. Mösch F, Litza M, El Sayed Auf A, et al.: Organic Fault-Tolerant Controller for the Walking Robot OSCAR. Proc. of the Workshop on „Dependability and Fault Tolerance" at ARCS, VDI, 2007
11. Larionova S, Jakimovski B, El Sayed Auf A, et al.: Toward a Fault Tolerant Mobile Robot: Mutual Information for Monitoring of the Robot Health Status. IARP/IEEE-RAS/EURON Workshop on Dep. Rob. in Hum. Env., 2007

Schlüsselkomponenten für die Exploration mit teil-autonomen mobilen Robotern

Rainer Worst, Hartmut Surmann, Kai Pervölz und Marco Hartich

Fraunhofer-Institut für Intelligente Analyse- und Informationssysteme IAIS
Schloss Birlinghoven, 53754 Sankt Augustin
rainer.worst@iais.fraunhofer.de
http://www.iais.fraunhofer.de/

Zusammenfassung. Mobile Roboter finden immer weiteren Einsatz für verschiedenartige Erkundungsaufgaben. Diese Systeme werden meist von einem Bediener ferngesteuert. Auf der anderen Seite werden ständig bessere Verfahren entwickelt, um mobile Roboter autonom operieren zu lassen. Die am Fraunhofer IAIS entwickelten Schlüsselkomponenten 3D-Sensorik und Hybrid-Steuerung ermöglichen durch die Verbindung von Autonomie und Tele-Operation die Entwicklung von Erkundungsrobotern, die optimal an ihre Aufgaben angepasst werden können.

1 Einleitung

Mobile Roboter gewinnen weltweit zunehmend an Bedeutung, insbesondere bei einer Vielzahl anstehender Mess-, Erkundungs- und Bewachungsaufgaben. Ein typisches Anwendungsszenario stammt aus dem Bereich Urban Search And Rescue (USAR). Mobile Roboter sollen dabei helfen, eine unbekannte und unzugängliche Umgebung zu erkunden, z. B. Hohlräume in Gebäuden, die durch ein Erdbeben eingestürzt sind [1]. Dieses Szenario ist auch Grundlage des bekannten RoboCup Rescue Wettbewerbs. Das Ziel besteht hier darin, Opfer in den Gebäuden zu finden und ihre Position sowie ihre Befindlichkeit zu bestimmen.

Fraunhofer IAIS hat in den Jahren 2004 bis 2006, allein oder mit Partnern, an diesem Wettbewerb teilgenommen [2]. Die dabei gesammelten Erfahrungen sind in die Entwicklung von Komponenten eingeflossen, die für Explorationsroboter benötigt werden – unabhängig von deren konkretem Einsatzzweck. Derartige Roboter werden heute meistens ferngesteuert und nur selten autonom betrieben. Systeme, die beide Betriebsarten erlauben, bieten jedoch folgende Vorteile gegenüber reiner Tele-Operation:

1. Steuerung wird durch autonome Assistenzsysteme erleichtert.
2. Sicherheitsmechanismen aus dem autonomen Betrieb können auch bei Fernsteuerung aktiv sein.
3. Bediener werden von Routineaufgaben entlastet.
4. Betrieb mehrerer Roboter durch einen Bediener als Koordinator ist möglich.
5. Roboter kann bei Funkabbruch von Fernsteuerung auf Autonomie umschalten und dadurch selbstständig in einen sicheren Zustand übergehen.

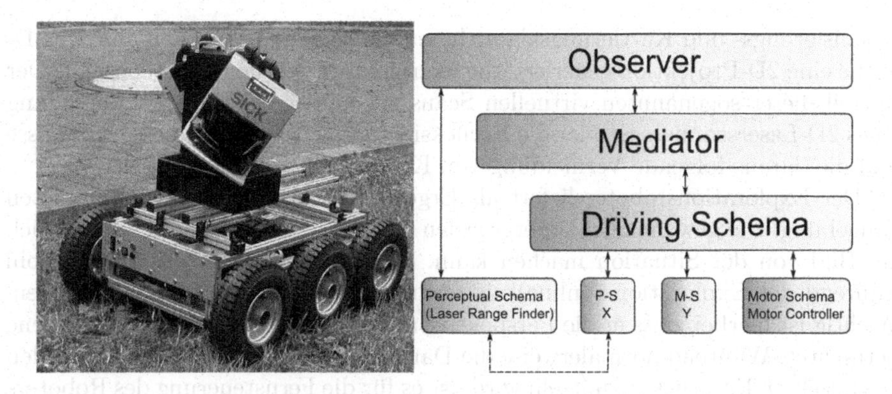

Abb. 1. Links: Explorationsroboter mit 2 kontinuierlich drehenden Laserscannern. Rechts: Schemabasierte Darstellung der Steuerungs-Software

Dieses Papier skizziert kurz die verschiedenen Schlüsselkomponenten mit den entsprechenden Verweisen auf die Literatur; es beschreibt keine Roboterarchitektur.

2 3D-Sensorik für Kartenbau und Navigation

3D-Kartierung mittels Robotern und 3D-Laserscannern findet zur Zeit das Interesse verschiedener Forschergruppen, weil diese Vorteile gegenüber den häufig eingesetzten 2D-Scannern bieten, z. B. beim Erkennen von überstehenden Objektkanten, wie sie an Tischen vorkommen.

Die am Fraunhofer IAIS entwickelten zwei Varianten (kontinuierlich drehend oder nickend) des 3D-Laserscanners 3DLS [3] erzeugen 3D-Punktwolken. Wird der Scanner auf einer mobilen Plattform (Volksbot oder KURT2) montiert, so generiert das System kontinuierlich bzw. von Fall zu Fall Punktwolken, die den mit dem Roboter abgefahrenen Bereich dreidimensional abbilden (Abb. 1). Die Punktwolken werden mit einer schnellen Variante des ICP-Algorithmus auf der Basis der Roboterposenschätzung registriert und so zu einer 3D-Karte der befahrenen Umgebung zusammengesetzt. In der zusammengesetzten Punktwolke können Linien und Flächen detektiert, sowie einzelne Bereiche, wie Boden, Wand oder Decke, klassifiziert werden. Es wird weiterhin versucht, diese klassifizierten Bereiche mit geometrischen Formen zur Deckung zu bringen [4,5].

Die Selbstortung des Roboters ist sowohl bei Tele-Operation als auch bei autonomem Betrieb von großer Bedeutung. Die oben erwähnte Registrierung einzelner Punktwolken ermöglicht eine verbesserte Selbstortung des Roboters durch SLAM-Algorithmen (Simultaneous Localization And Mapping) [6]. Sie erfolgt kontinuierlich und wird in gewissen Intervallen rekalibriert, z. B. immer dann, wenn der Roboter anhält, um eine neue 3D-Aufnahme zu erzeugen. Für den autonomen Betrieb lassen sich bekannte und bewährte 2D-Steuerungs-,

Lokalisierungs- und Kartierungsalgorithmen verwenden, wenn man aus der 3D-Szene eine 2D-Projektion generiert, die mehrere horizontale Ebenen enthält. Der Vorteil dieser sogenannten virtuellen Scans gegenüber der direkten Benutzung eines 2D-Laserscanners ist hier die Berücksichtigung überhängender Hindernisse und die daraus folgende Vermeidung von Kollisionen, etwa mit Tischen [2].

Der Explorationsroboter liefert als Ergebnis eine 3D-Karte der erkundeten Umgebung. Die gewonnenen Daten werden so dargestellt, dass der Bediener sich ein Bild von der Situation machen kann. Der Bediener kann das Bild sowohl während der Exploration (online) als auch im Nachhinein (offline) auswerten. Wichtig ist hierbei, dass er die Perspektive auswählen kann, aus der er die Szene betrachtet. Während normalerweise die Darstellung aus Sicht der Plattform den gewünschten Eindruck vermitteln wird, ist es für die Fernsteuerung des Roboters hilfreich, auch einmal die Perspektive eines externen Beobachters einzunehmen und so die Plattform in ihrer Umgebung zu sehen. Eine (zusätzliche) Grundrissdarstellung ist hier unter Umständen hilfreicher als eine reine 3D-Karte.

Bei der offline-Auswertung gibt es zusätzlich die Möglichkeit, bessere aber rechenzeit-intensivere Registrierungsverfahren zu verwenden und die Daten mittels einer speziellen Viewer-Software zu betrachten, mit der man die Szene beliebig drehen oder in sie hinein- und aus ihr herauszoomen kann. Auch das virtuelle Wandern oder Fliegen durch die Szene trägt zum besseren Begreifen der dargestellten Situation bei.

3 Grundlagen der Hybrid-Steuerung

Bediener, die Roboter steuern, sind oftmals schon nach kürzester Zeit erschöpft, wenn sie für die Steuerung des Roboters und die Überprüfung der gewonnenen Daten verantwortlich sind. Dies belegt eine Studie, die von Murphy nach dem Attentat vom 11. September durchgeführt wurde [7]. Die angegebenen Gründe sind zum einen primitive Benutzerschnittstellen und zum anderen unzureichende Funktionalitäten der Roboter. So wird es heute als sinnvoll angesehen, zwei Personen zur Steuerung heranzuziehen, und zwar einen Bediener, der steuert, und einen Supervisor, der die Daten auswertet und ggf. Befehle gibt. Deren Entlastung, die Reduktion auf nur einen Bediener oder aber technische Probleme wie Funkabbrüche erfordern weitere unterstützende Funktionen, wie beispielsweise das automatische Ausweichen vor Hindernissen. Diese verschiedenen Möglichkeiten der Robotersteuerung werden von Wegner [8] beschrieben. Er beleuchtet die Steuerungsproblematik speziell im Hinblick auf den Einsatz von Robotern im Bereich von USAR-Anwendungen und definiert dazu einen Schema-basierten Ansatz, der im Wesentlichen darauf beruht, dass durch die einzelnen Schemas ein gewichteter Vektor folgender Form generiert wird:

$$\bar{a} = \begin{bmatrix} \phi & 0 \\ 0 & 1 \end{bmatrix} \begin{bmatrix} M \\ \Theta \end{bmatrix} \tag{1}$$

wobei M der Amplitude, Θ der Ausrichtung und ϕ einer Gewichtung entspricht. Eine Priorisierung findet in der Form statt, dass jedes Motorschema seinen eigenen Vektor generiert. Der Parameter ϕ kann in einer Hybridsteuerung dazu genutzt werden, ein bestimmtes Verhalten zu priorisieren. Um die Autonomie und die Tele-Operation zu verschmelzen, stellt Wegner zwei Vorgehensweisen vor:

1. Eingriffs- und Bestätigungsverhalten (Intervention Recognition)
2. Vermittler (Mediator)

Steckt der Roboter fest, weiß er nicht mehr weiter oder hat einen Zielpunkt erreicht, so meldet er dies dem Bediener (Eingriffs- und Bestätigungsverhalten). Die Mischung aus Autonomie und Tele-Operation übernimmt der Mediator (Gewichtung durch ϕ). Dieser wägt ab, ob eine vom Operator veranlasste Aktion durchgeführt werden soll oder nicht, z. B. im Falle von drohender Gefahr für den Roboter (Fahrt auf eine Wand zu).

Große Verzögerungszeiten, Verbindungsabbrüche oder die Vernachlässigung der Kontrolle (z. B. bei multi agent navigation) müssen kompensiert werden. Je länger die Zeitverzögerung ist, desto mehr Autonomie muss der Roboter aufweisen. Im Experiment von Crandall und Goodrich [9] werden drei Verhalten verwendet: Zielgesteuertes Verhalten, Hindernissen ausweichen und ein widersprechendes Verhalten. Zudem definieren sie in ihrem Projekt drei Schemas:

1. Komplett teleoperiert
2. Vorgeben von Wegpunkten
3. Komplett autonom

Das Vorgeben von Wegpunkten stellt hierbei eine wichtige Verbindung zwischen der direkten Teleoperation und dem autonomen Fahren da. Im einfachsten Fall werden die Punkte durch den Bediener vorgegeben. Im Außenbereich können Wegepunkte automatisch durch ein Navigationssystem erzeugt und mittels GPS-Sensoren abgefahren werden. Im Innenbereich werden sogenannte Trajektorien mit Hilfe von Voronoi-Diagrammen basierend auf gegebenen Karten und Laserabstandsdaten erzeugt (Abb. 2). Für Verbindungsgeraden von Anfangs- und Endpunkten unterschiedlicher Linien wird auf der Hälfte eine Senkrechte konstruiert und mit den anderen Senkrechten verbunden. Die Schnittpunkte dieser Mittelsenkrechten schneiden sich an den Thiessen-Scheitelpunkten, deren Verbindung dann das Thiessen- bzw. Voronoi-Polygon ergibt. Der gesuchte Trajektorie läuft entlang der Scheitelpunkte. Im Laserscan wahrgenommene Hindernisse werden somit automatisch umfahren, wobei das Verfahren mit der GPS-Navigation im Außenbereich kombinierbar ist.

Eine weitere wichtige Komponente ist dann das Abfahren der Wegepunkte. De Wit et al. [10] aber auch Indiveri et al. [11] beschreiben geschlossene, zeitinvariante und global-stabile Regelungen, um durch Punkte vorgegebene Trajektorien abzufahren. Abb. 2 links zeigt ein abzufahrendes Dreieck und die tatsächlich gefahrene Strecke. Mit Hilfe eines Roboter- oder Fahrzeugmodells können die Fahrtrajektorien vorberechnet und dem Bediener zusätzlich zu den Solltrajektorien angezeigt werden.

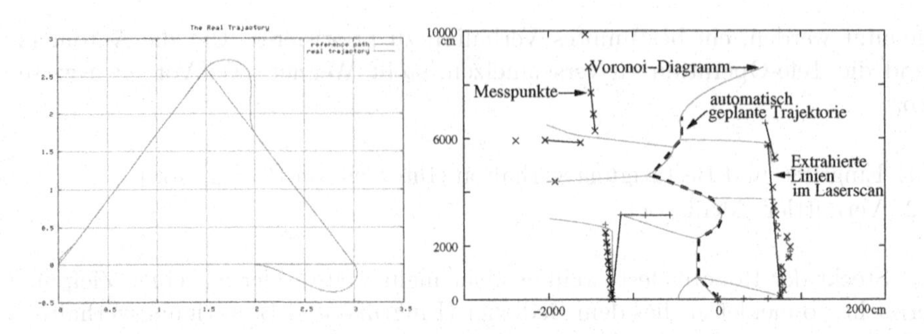

Abb. 2. Links: Fahrt nach Wegepunkten (Dreieck) mit dem Verfahren nach [11]. An den Eckpunkten fährt der Roboter auf einer Kurve zurück auf den Referenzweg. Rechts: Beipiel von selbständig geplanten Wegepunkten in einem Laserscan mit Hilfe eines Voronoi-Diagramms.

4 Verbindung von Autonomie und Tele-Operation

Mit der am Fraunhofer IAIS entwickelten grafischen Benutzerschnittstelle ist es möglich, einen einstellbaren Grad an Autonomie und Teleoperation zu realisieren. Die Berechnung des resultierenden Vektors wird ähnlich wie bei Wegner [8] mittels einer Vektoraddition ermittelt.

Für die grafische Benutzerschnittstelle (Abb. 3) wurde Java-Webstart verwendet. Dadurch ist es möglich, die Benutzerschnittstelle als Applikation von einem Webserver durch Anklicken eines Hyperlinks zu laden. Der Unterschied zu einem herkömmlichen Java-Applet ist, dass man zum einen nicht mehr auf den Browser angewiesen ist und zum anderen aus der Sandbox einer Applet-Applikation heraussteigen kann. Dies ist nötig, um z. B. auf dem Rechner des Bedieners einen Joystick nutzen zu können.

Um die Steuerung mittels der grafischen Benutzerschnittstelle so einfach wie möglich zu halten, wurde deren umfangreiche Funktionalität in Menüs verlagert. Bediener werden dadurch ausschließlich bei der Konfiguration des Roboters mit dessen Einstellungen konfrontiert. Während des Einsatzes können sie sich somit voll und ganz auf die Daten und die Steuerung selbst konzentrieren. Die grafische Benutzerschnittstelle wirkt damit nicht überladen. Bei Bedarf ist die Konfiguration des Roboters (Auswahl neuer Verhalten, Bearbeiten von Trajektorienpunkten, Gewichtung der einzelnen Parameter usw.) auch zur Laufzeit möglich.

Die Kommunikation zwischen grafischer Benutzerschnittstelle und Roboter wurde mittels SOAP umgesetzt. Ein Vorteil dieses Protokolls liegt in der einfachen Erweiterbarkeit. Funktionalitäten des Roboters können ohne Änderung des Protokolls zügig hinzugefügt oder entnommen werden. Weiter ist es bei der Verwendung von SOAP zusammen mit Java-Webstart, möglich eine Steuerung über das Internet zu realisieren, wobei natürlich die unterschiedlichen Laufzeiten im Internet berücksichtigt werden müssen.

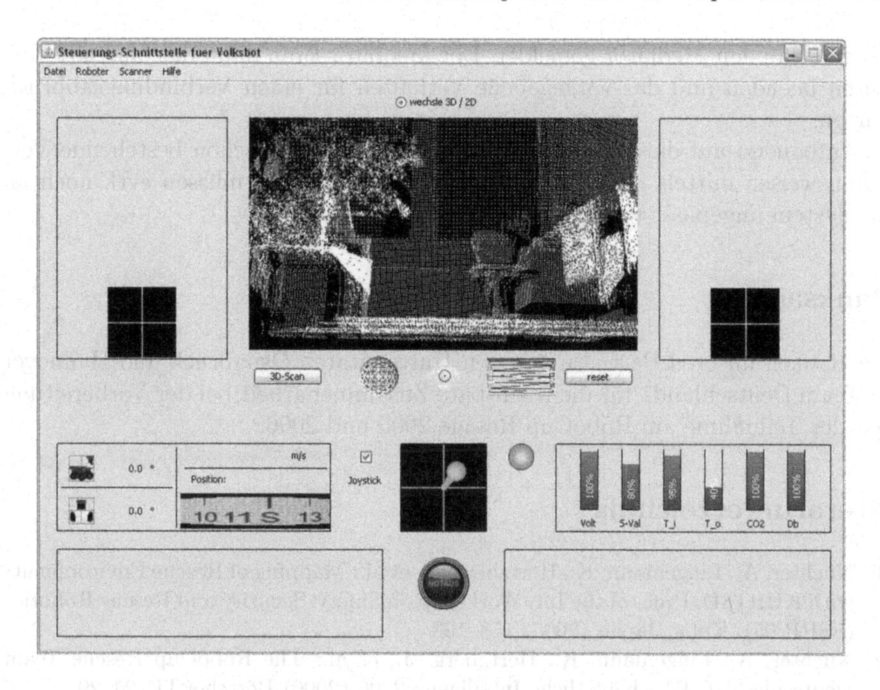

Abb. 3. Muster der grafischen Benutzerschnittstelle

Um eine Kommunikationsunterbrechung detektieren zu können, wurde ein Pollingverfahren implementiert. Der Client (grafische Benutzerschnittstelle) sendet, sofern keine anderen Daten – wie etwa Joystick-Kommandos – anstehen, ständig Polling-Informationen an den Server (Roboter). Das Verhalten bei Verbindungsabbruch wird im Voraus auf Seiten des Clients definiert. Das einfachste Verhalten ist z. B. ein Stopp-Kommando. Wurde die Verbindung wieder etabliert, so wird dem Client die Information des erkannten Verbindungsabbruchs gemeldet und der normale Betrieb wird nach Bestätigung durch den Client wieder eingerichtet. Das Bereitstellen dieses Dienstes erfolgt über den Observer (Abb. 1).

Der Mediator in Abb. 1 übernimmt die Auswahl der einzelnen Verhalten. Dazu liest dieser zu Beginn die Konfiguration des Roboters aus einer auf dem Roboter befindlichen Datenbank aus. In dieser Datenbank ist definiert, wie der Roboter gesteuert wird, mit welcher Gewichtung die einzelnen Verhaltensweisen in die Steuerung einfließen und was nach einem Verbindungsabbruch erfolgen soll. Mögliche Verhaltensweisen sind hier z. B. verschiedene Arten der Hindernisvermeidung oder ein zielgerichtetes Verhalten. Während der Laufzeit prüft der Mediator, ob eine Rekonfiguration seitens des Clients vorgenommen wurde. Ist dies der Fall, stoppt der Mediator alle laufenden Schemas, liest die neuen Konfigurationsdaten aus der Datenbank und übergibt diese dem Driving-Schema. Detektiert der Observer einen Verbindungsabbruch, so wird dieses Ereignis vom

Observer an den Mediator gemeldet. Der Mediator kann dann das laufende Verhalten beenden und das vorgegebene Verhalten für einen Verbindungsabbruch starten.

Aufbauend auf diesem neuen System ist es möglich, schon bestehende Verhaltensweisen mittels des Mediators zu verwalten. Diese müssen evtl. noch an das System angepasst werden.

Danksagung

Wir danken unseren Partnern von den Universitäten Osnabrück und Hannover im Team Deutschland1 für die fruchtbare Zusammenarbeit bei der Vorbereitung und der Teilnahme am RoboCup Rescue 2005 und 2006.

Literaturverzeichnis

1. Nüchter, A., Lingemann, K., Hertzberg, J., et al.: Mapping of Rescue Environments with KURT3D. Proc. of the Int. Workshop on Safety, Security and Rescue Robotics (SSRR'05), Kobe, Japan (2005) 158–163
2. Nüchter, A., Lingemann, K., Hertzberg, J., et al.: The RoboCup Rescue Team Deutschland 1. KI - Künstliche Intelligenz 2/06 (2006) Böttcher IT, 24–29
3. 3DLS: www.3d-scanner.net; Volksbot: www.volksbot.de; KURT2: www.kurt2.de
4. Nüchter, A., Surmann, H., Hertzberg, J.: Automatic Classification of Objects in 3D Laser Range Scans. Proc. of the 8th Conf. on Intelligent Autonomous Systems (IAS'04), IOS Press, Amsterdam, The Netherlands (2004) 963–970
5. Nüchter, A., Lingemann, K., Hertzberg, J., Surmann, H.: Heuristic-Based Laser Scan Matching for Outdoor 6D SLAM. Proc. of the Int. Workshop on Safety, Security and Rescue Robotics (SSRR'06), Gaithersburg, Maryland, USA (2006)
6. Surmann, H., Nüchter, A., Lingemann, K., Hertzberg, J.: 6D SLAM – Preliminary Report on closing the loop in Six Dimensions. Proc. of the 5th IFAC Symposium on Intelligent Autonomous Vehicles (IAV'04), Lisbon, Portugal (2004)
7. Murphy, R. R.: Human-Robot Interaction in Rescue Robotics. IEEE Transactions on Systems, Man and Cybernetics, Part C: Applications and Reviews 34 (2004) 138–153
8. Wegner, R.: Balancing Robotic Teleoperation and Autonomy in a Complex and Dynamic Environment. Master thesis, University of Manitoba (2003).
9. Crandall, J. W., Goodrich, M. A.: Experiments in Adjustable Autonomy. IEEE Int. Conference on Systems, Man and Cybernetics, Vol. 3 (2001) 1624–1629
10. de Wit, C. C., Khennouf, H., Samson, C., Sordalen, O. J.: Nonlinear Control Design for Mobile Robots. In Yuan F. Zheng, editor, Recent Trends in Mobile Robots, World Scientific Series in Robotics and Automated Systems (1993) 121–156
11. Indiveri, G., Corradini, M. L.: Switching linear path following for bounded curvature car-like vehicles. Proc. of the 5th IFAC Symposium on Intelligent Autonomous Vehicles (IAV'04), Lisbon, Portugal, (2004)

Entwurf einer semantischen Missionssteuerung für autonome Serviceroboter

K. Uhl, M. Ziegenmeyer, B. Gaßmann, J.M. Zöllner und R. Dillmann

FZI Forschungszentrum Informatik, Interaktive Diagnose- und Servicesysteme,
Haid-und-Neu-Str. 10–14, 76131 Karlsruhe
{uhl, ziegenmeyer, gassmann, zoellner}@fzi.de, dillmann@ira.uka.de

Zusammenfassung. In diesem Beitrag wird der Entwurf einer semantischen Missionssteuerung für autonome Serviceroboter mit dem Ziel der Inspektion von komplexen Umgebungen vorgestellt. Es werden die wesentlichen Komponenten der semantischen Missionssteuerung und ihr Zusammenwirken sowie der Aufbau der zentralen Wissensbasis beschrieben. Abschließend wird die Umsetzung der semantischen Missionssteuerung für die sechsbeinige Laufmaschine LAURON IV erläutert. Als konkretes Inspektionsziel wird das Auffinden von Müll in unstrukturiertem Gelände untersucht.

1 Einleitung

Die Missionssteuerung von autonomen Servicerobotern für die Inspektion von komplexen Umgebungen umfasst zwei Schwerpunkte: die Navigation des Roboters und die Inspektion der Umgebung an sich, d.h. das Auffinden und Untersuchen von *interessanten Entitäten* (Entities of Interest, EOI).

In diesem Beitrag wird der Entwurf einer semantischen Missionssteuerung vorgestellt, der sich sowohl für die Navigation als auch für die Inspektion an der menschlichen Vorgehensweise orientiert. Zur Navigation werden abstrakte räumliche Konzepte, wie z.B. „neben“ oder „vor“, herangezogen, um die *semantische Position* des Roboters zu definieren. Die Umgebung wird in einer semantischen Regionenkarte als Graph von hierarchisch angeordneten Regionen repräsentiert. Die Zusammenhänge zwischen den Regionen, ihren Attributen, den Aktionen, welche der Roboter ausführen kann, und seiner semantischen Position sind in einer Ontologie festgehalten. Bei der Untersuchung und Beurteilung von EOIs wird von Experten auf umfangreiches Hintergrundwissen und Erfahrung zurückgegriffen. Dieses Wissen wird dem System anhand eines semantischen Inspektionsmodells zur Verfügung gestellt, welches detaillierte Informationen über die einzelnen EOI-Klassen und Vorgehensweisen zur genaueren Untersuchung der EOIs enthält.

Die Vorteile des semantischen Ansatzes liegen zum einen in der einfachen Erweiterbarkeit des Systems, welche durch die explizite Trennung der Wissensrepräsentation und der Ablaufsteuerung erreicht wird. Zum anderen wird die Nachvollziehbarkeit der Entscheidungen des Systems wesentlich verbessert. Darüber hinaus wird dem Benutzer die Möglichkeit gegeben, mit dem System auf semantischer Ebene zu interagieren, wodurch sich eine deutlich einfachere Bedienbarkeit des Systems ergibt.

2 Stand der Technik

Traditionell unterscheidet man beim Aufbau von Steuerungsarchitekturen für autonome Roboter zwischen *deliberativen* [1], *reaktiven* [2] und *hybriden* [3,4] Architekturen. Aktuelle Steuerungsarchitekturen sind typischerweise hybrid. Sie enthalten einen reaktiven Teil, welcher für die Steuerung auf niedriger Ebene zuständig ist und über die Fähigkeit verfügt, schnell auf veränderte bzw. unvorhergesehene Ereignisse zu reagieren. Zusätzlich enthalten sie einen deliberativen Teil, der für die Planung und Überwachung der Mission des Roboters verantwortlich ist.

Die *Spatial Semantic Hierarchy* [5] verwendet erstmals eine semantische Beschreibung der Fähigkeiten eines Roboters und der Topologie der Umwelt. Diese umfasst jedoch nur das einfache Navigieren zwischen ausgezeichneten Orten. Für reale Inspektionsaufgaben müssen jedoch, wie in der Einleitung erläutert, zusätzliche Aspekte der Umwelt, der zu untersuchenden EOIs und des Missionsablaufs semantisch erfasst und somit für den Roboter verarbeitbar gemacht werden. Außerdem muss die Robotersteuerung um eine Komponente erweitert werden, die komplexe Missionen erfassen, in Teilziele zerlegen, koordinieren und überwachen kann.

3 Aufbau der semantischen Missionssteuerung

Die einzelnen Komponenten der semantischen Missionssteuerung sind in einer hierarchischen Architektur angeordnet. Die vier Ebenen der Architektur ergeben sich aus der Art der verarbeiteten Daten und sind in Abbildung 1 dargestellt. Im Folgenden werden die einzelnen Komponenten kurz vorgestellt.

Die *Basissteuerung* erhält von der Ausführungseinheit einzelne symbolische Aktionen. Diese übergibt sie in Form von subsymbolischen Kommandos an das Aktor- und das Sensorinterface des Trägersystems und überwacht deren Ausführung.

Die *Navigationsdatenauswertung* liest kontinuierlich die Daten der Navigationssensoren ein. Sie lokalisiert und klassifiziert die darin enthaltenen Regionen und bestimmt deren Parameter. Sie ist zustandslos und berücksichtigt immer nur die aktuelle Messung der Sensoren.

Die *Inspektionsdatenauswertung* verarbeitet kontinuierlich die Daten der Inspektionssensoren und überprüft sie auf EOIs. Wird eine EOI gefunden, wird der entsprechende Bereich in den Sensordaten segmentiert. Für den segmentierten Bereich werden anschließend geeignete Merkmale berechnet. Diese dienen als Eingangsvektor für einen Klassifikator. Die Inspektionsdatenauswertung ist wie die Navigationsdatenauswertung zustandslos und berücksichtigt jeweils nur die aktuellen Sensordaten.

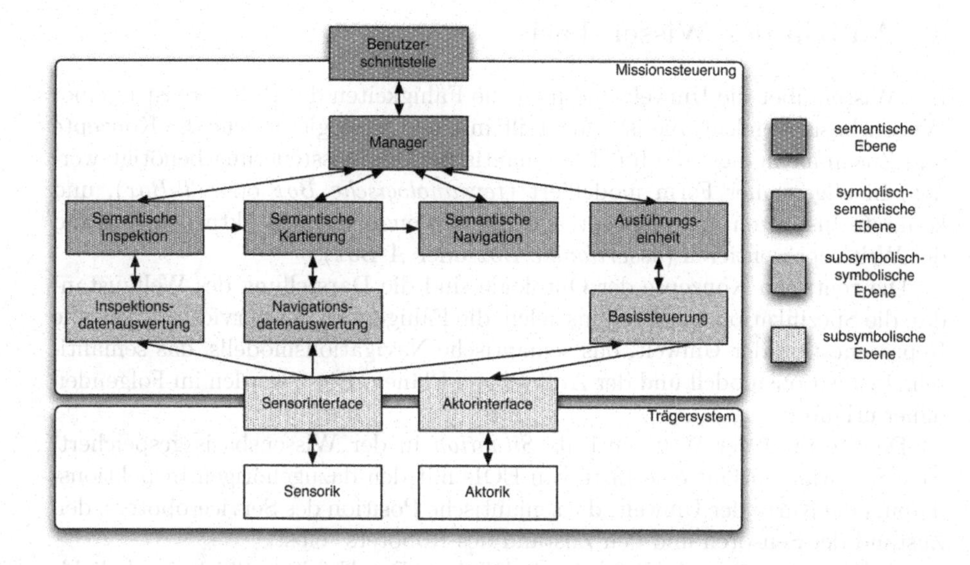

Abb. 1. Der Aufbau der semantischen Missionssteuerung.

Die *semantische Inspektion* führt die temporale Fusion der Einzelmessungen durch. In Abhängigkeit von den vorliegenden Inpsektionsergebnissen schlägt sie dem Manager anhand des semantischen Inspektionsmodells vor, ob und wie gefundene EOIs weiter untersucht werden sollten.

Die *semantische Kartierung* führt auf den Daten der Navigationsdatenauswertung eine temporale Fusion durch und berechnet bzw. aktualisiert die semantische Regionenkarte der Umgebung. Außerdem werden die von der semantischen Inspektion gefundenen EOIs in der semantischen Regionenkarte vermerkt.

Die *semantische Navigation* erhält vom Manager abstrakte Lokomotionsziele, berechnet mit Hilfe der semantischen Regionenkarte eine Aktionsfolge, mit der die Lokomotionsziele erreicht werden können, und gibt diese an den Manager zurück.

Die *Ausführungseinheit* erhält vom Manager einen Plan zur Ausführung des nächsten Teilziels einer Mission. Die Aufgabe der Ausführungeinheit ist es, die Aktionen des Plans nacheinander an die Basissteuerung weiterzugeben und deren Ausführung zu überwachen.

Der *Manager* ist die oberste Kontroll- und Entscheidungskomponente des Systems. Er zerlegt den ihm übergebenen Missionsplan in einzelne Teilpläne und koordiniert und überwacht deren Ausführung. Hierzu greift er auf die semantische Navigation, die semantische Inspektion und die Ausführungseinheit zurück.

Alle semantischen Komponenten verwenden eine gemeinsame *Wissensbasis*. Diese enthält die Ontologien zur Navigation und Inspektion sowie die semantische Regionenkarte.

4 Aufbau der Wissensbasis

Das Wissen über die Umwelt und über die Fähigkeiten des Roboters ist in einer Wissensbasis abgelegt. Sie ist aufgeteilt in eine Ontologie, welche die Konzepte und Zusammenhänge, die für die semantische Missionssteuerung benötigt werden, in allgemeiner Form modelliert (*terminologische Box* oder *T-Box*), und konkrete Instanzen von Konzepten und Relationen, die den aktuellen Zustand der Welt repräsentieren (*assertionale Box* oder *A-Box*).

Die zentralen Konzepte der Ontologie sind die Darstellung des Weltzustandes, die Spezifikation von Missionszielen, die Fähigkeiten des Serviceroboters, die Repräsentation der Umwelt, das semantische Navigationsmodells, das semantische Inspektionsmodell und der Aufbau von Plänen. Diese werden im Folgenden näher erläutert.

Der Zustand der Welt wird als *Situation* in der Wissensbasis gespeichert. Eine Situation enthält eine Liste von EOIs mit den dazugehörigen Inspektionsdaten, eine Karte der Umwelt, die semantische Position des Serviceroboters, den Zustand der Sensoren und den Zustand des Roboters selbst.

Ziele werden über ein Erfolgsmaß definiert. Das Erfolgsmaß ist eine beliebige Funktion mit Wertebereich $[0, 1]$, die auf die aktuelle Situation in der Wissensbasis zugreift um zu berechnen, zu welchem Grad ein Ziel erreicht ist. Um komplexe Ziele definieren zu können, kann ein Ziel aus mehreren Teilzielen zusammengesetzt sein. Das Erfolgsmaß des komplexen Ziels berechnet sich aus den Erfolgsmaßen der Teilziele über eine frei definierbare Gewichtungsfunktion.

Die Fähigkeiten des Serviceroboters werden in der Wissensbasis als *Aktionen* modelliert. Aktionen werden über eine *Bewertungsfunktion*, eine *Vorbedingung*, eine *Laufzeitbedingung*, eine *Endbedingung* und ein *Erfolgsmaß* definiert. Das Konzept der Aktionen ist untergliedert in *Inspektionsaktionen*, *Navigationsaktionen* und die elementaren *Roboteraktionen* des Trägersystems.

Das Basiselement der *semantischen Karte* stellt die *Region* dar. Eine Region ist eine abstrakte Repräsentation eines Ausschnitts aus der Umwelt. Regionen können in anderen Regionen enthalten sein und bilden somit eine hierarchische Repräsentation der Umwelt. Regionen auf gleicher Hierarchieebene dürfen sich nicht überlappen, können aber aneinanderstoßen. Aneinanderstoßende Regionen sind verbunden und bilden einen topologischen Graphen. Die semantische Karte stellt also eine hierarchisch-topologische Regionenkarte dar. Regionen sind in unterschiedliche Klassen unterteilt, welche die Semantik dieser Regionen repräsentieren. Es gibt eine grundlegende Unterteilung in *navigierbare Regionen*, *Hindernisse* und *Hotspots*. Die grundlegenden Regionenklassen sind abhängig von der konkreten Anwendung in weitere Klassen unterteilt. Zur Steuerung der semantischen Navigation ist jede Regionsklasse mit den erlaubten Aktionen annotiert. Hindernisse haben per Definition keine erlaubten Aktionen und werden somit bei der Navigationsplanung grundsätzlich gemieden.

Das *semantische Navigationsmodell* besteht aus der semantischen Karte, den Navigationsaktionen, den elementaren Roboteraktionen und der semantischen Position des Roboters. Navigationsaktionen sind komplexe Aktionen, die aus Roboteraktionen zusammengesetzt sind und als vorgefertigte Pläne in der Wissensbasis abgelegt sind. Die semantische Roboterposition wird definiert durch die Region, in der sich der Serviceroboter befindet, und durch abstrakte räumliche Relationen wie z.B. „neben“, „vor“ oder „in der Mitte von“ zu anderen Regionen in der Umgebung des Roboters. Bei der Berechnung von Plänen verwendet die semantische Navigation eine Diskretisierung der Umwelt. Diese ergibt sich aus den semantischen Positionen, welche durch die erlaubten Aktionen von der aktuellen Position aus erreicht werden können. Über diese Diskretisierung wird implizit ein Graph aufgespannt, auf dem der kürzeste Weg gesucht werden kann.

Das *semantische Inspektionsmodell* setzt sich aus den verfügbaren Inspektionsaktionen und den EOIs zusammen. Die Inspektionsaktionen stellen ein Unterkonzept der Aktionen dar und verfügen zursätzlich über einen Eingabe- und einen Ausgabedatentypen. Über diese Datentypen kann die semantische Inspektion entscheiden, welche Inspektionsaktionen miteinander verknüpft werden können. Die Inspektionsaktionen sind untergliedert in Aktionen zur Vorverarbeitung von Sensormessungen, zur Sensorfusion, zur Segmentierung von Messungen in interessante Bereiche, zur Merkmalsberechnung, zur Klassifikation und zur Fusion von Klassifikationsergebnissen. Die Inspektionsaktionen werden von der semantischen Inspektion dazu verwendet, EOIs zu finden und zu klassifizieren. Hierfür ist in der Wissensbasis für jede Klasse von EOIs gespeichert, welche Sensoren verwendet werden können und welche Inspektionsaktionen für die jeweilige Klasse geeignet sind. Dieses Hintergrundwissen wird von der semantischen Inspektion verwendet, um Pläne zu berechnen, mit denen die Konfidenz der Klassifikationsergebnisse einer EOI sukzessive erhöht werden kann. Die Pläne können auch Planungsknoten mit Navigationszielen enthalten. Mit diesen kann die semantische Navigation angewiesen werden, die Position des Roboters zu ändern oder Sensoren zu positionieren. Wird während der Inspektion eine EOI gefunden, so wird sie als Individuum in die Wissensbasis eingetragen und in der semantische Karte wird ein korrespondierender Hotspot eingefügt. Zur besseren Nachvollziehbarkeit der Beurteilung einer EOI werden die Messdaten und die Ergebnisse der einzelnen Inspektionsaktionen mit der EOI verknüpft.

Der Aufbau von *Plänen* ist an *Flexible Programme* [6] angelehnt. Ein Plan wird als Baum von *Knoten* dargestellt, der mittels einer Tiefensuchstrategie abgearbeitet wird. Es gibt drei Knotentypen: *Verzweigungsknoten*, *Aktionsknoten* und *Planungsknoten*. Jeder Knoten enthält eine *Bewertungsfunktion*, eine *Vorbedingung*, eine *Laufzeitbedingung*, eine *Endbedingung* und ein *Erfolgsmaß*. Diese werden zur Steuerung des Planablaufs benötigt. Alle inneren Knoten eines Plans sind Verzweigungsknoten. Sie haben die Aufgabe, den Planablauf in sequenzielle und parallele Teile zu gliedern. Hierfür enthalten sie parallel angeordnete *Gruppen*, die aus sequentiell angeordneten *Sitzen* bestehen. Für jeden Sitz gibt es mehrere Knoten als *Kandidaten*. Die Auswahl eines konkreten Knotens zur Laufzeit erfolgt durch Prüfen der Vorbedingungen und Auswertung der Bewertungsfunktionen der jeweiligen Kandidaten. Sowohl für die Auswertung der Vorbedingungen als auch für die Berechnung der Bewertungsfunktionen wird die aktuelle Situation aus der Wissensbasis verwendet. Die Blätter eines Plans sind entweder *Aktionsknoten* oder *Planungsknoten*. Aktionsknoten stoßen eine Aktion des Roboters an, die so lange ausgeführt wird, bis entweder die Endbedingung erfüllt ist oder die Laufzeitbedingung verletzt wird. Planungsknoten enthalten ein Unterziel. Wird ein Planungsknoten ausgeführt, wird das Unterziel an den Manager weitergegeben. Dieser erzeugt einen Plan für das Unterziel und ersetzt den Planungsknoten durch den neuen Plan. Die Planausführung wird daraufhin mit der Abarbeitung des neu hinzugefügten Unterbaumes fortgesetzt.

5 Realisierung

Für die Umsetzung der vorgestellten semantischen Missionssteuerung wird die sechsbeinige Laufmaschine LAURON IV (Abb. 2, links) verwendet. Als konkretes Inspektionsziel wird das Auffinden von Müll in unstrukturiertem Gelände untersucht. An Sensorik verfügt LAURON IV über ein Stereokamerasystem und einen 2D-Laserscanner auf einer Schwenk-Neige-Einheit, ein Inklinometer, welches Informationen über die absolute räumliche Orientierung des Roboters liefert, und über einen GPS-Empfänger zur Bestimmung der globalen Position.

Abb. 2. Links: Die sechsbeinige Laufmaschine LAURON IV. Mitte: Schwenk-Neige-Einheit mit Stereokamerasystem und 2D-Laserscanner. Rechts: Aufnahme eines herumliegenden Bechers mit einer Dragonfly-Kamera.

Die Basissteuerung von LAURON IV basiert auf einer verhaltensbasierten Architektur, die mit Hilfe des Rahmenwerks *MCA2* [7] realisiert wurde. Für die Lokomotion und die Navigation ist ein umfangreiches Verhaltensrepertoire vorhanden [8], auf dem die semantische Missionssteuerung aufsetzt.

Die Inspektionsdatenauswertung basiert auf den Bildern des Stereokamerasystems (Abb. 2, rechts) und verwendet statistische Texturmerkmale zur Klassifikation des vor dem Roboter liegenden Geländes. Als Klassifikator werden Support Vektor Maschinen mit Mehrklassen-Wahrscheinlichkeitsausgaben verwendet. Der Ansatz basiert auf einem Verfahren [9], das ursprünglich zur Klassifikation der Geländebeschaffenheit entwickelt wurde, und um Klassen für unterschiedliche Arten von Müll erweitert wurde. Die Ergebnisse der Inspektionsdatenauswertung werden von der semantischen Inspektion mit Hilfe eines wahrscheinlichkeitsbasierten Multihypothesenansatzes fusioniert.

Die Ontologie der Wissensbasis wurde mit Hilfe von *OWL-DL*[1] realisiert. Als Rahmenwerk zur Verwaltung der Wissensbasis und für Inferenzprozesse wird *KAON2*[2] verwendet.

6 Zusammenfassung und Ausblick

In diesem Beitrag wurde der Entwurf einer semantischen Missionssteuerung für autonome Serviceroboter mit dem Ziel der Inspektion von komplexen Anlagen vorgestellt. Es wurde ein Überblick über die Architektur der semantischen Missionsteuerung gegeben und das Zusammenwirken der einzelnen Komponenten erläutert. Darüber hinaus wurde das zentrale Element der semantischen Missionssteuerung – die in Form einer Ontologie realisierte Wissensbasis – detailliert beschrieben.

Abschließend wurde die Umsetzung der semantischen Missionssteuerung für die sechsbeinige Laufmaschine LAURON IV erläutert. Als konkretes Inspektionsziel wurde das Auffinden von Müll in unstrukturiertem Gelände untersucht.

Zukünftig ist geplant, die vorgestellte semantische Missionssteuerung auf weiteren autonomen Servicerobotern, wie etwa dem Kanalroboter Kairo-II, einzusetzen und damit weitere Inspektionsszenarien abzudecken.

Literaturverzeichnis

1. J. S. Albus. Outline for a theory of intelligence. *Systems, Man and Cybernetics, IEEE Transactions on*, 21(3):473–509, May/June 1991.
2. R. Brooks. A robust layered control system for a mobile robot. *IEEE Journal of Robotics and Automation*, 2(1):14–23, March 1986.
3. R. G. Simmons. Structured control for autonomous robots. *IEEE Transactions on Robotics and Automation*, 10(1):34–43, February 1994.
4. K. Konolige, K. L. Myers, E. H. Ruspini, and A. Saffiotti. The Saphira architecture: A design for autonomy. *Journal of experimental & theoretical artificial intelligence: JETAI*, 9(1):215–235, 1997.
5. Benjamin Kuipers. The spatial semantic hierarchy. *Artificial Intelligence*, 119(1-2):191–233, 2000.
6. R. Dillmann S. Knoop, S. R. Schmidt-Rohr. A flexible task knowledge representation for service robots. In *The 9th International Conference on Intelligent Autonomous Systems (IAS-9)*, Tokyo, Mar 07 2006.
7. Klaus Uhl and Marco Ziegenmeyer. MCA2 – an extensible modular framework for robot control applications. In *The 10th International Conference on Climbing and Walking Robots (CLAWAR 2007)*, 2007.
8. Bernd Gaßmann. *Modellbasierte, sensorgestützte Navigation von Laufmaschinen im Gelände*. PhD thesis, Fakultät für Informatik, Universität Karlsruhe (TH), 2007.
9. L. Ascari, M. Ziegenmeyer, P. Corradi, B. Gaßmann, J. M. Zöllner, R. Dillmann, and P. Dario. Can statistics help walking robots in assessing terrain roughness? Platform description and preliminary considerations. *The 9th ESA Workshop on Advanced Space Technologies for Robotics and Automation (ASTRA 2006)*, 2006.

---

[1] OWL http://www.w3.org/TR/owl-features/

[2] KAON2 http://kaon2.semanticweb.org/

An Architectural Framework for Cooperative Civil and Military Mission Scenarios

N. Oswald[1], S. Förster[1], H. Moser[2], T. Reichelt[3] and A. Windisch[1]

[1] EADS Military Air Systems
[2] University of Stuttgart - IPVS
[3] Chemnitz University of Technology

Abstract. Today's mission software requires ever more sophistication, being faced with the challenges of conducting Nnetwork-centric Operations (NCO) and exhibiting mission autonomy. Addressing these challenges, together with improving the engineering process in general, is the main output of the project described in this paper, accomplished at EADS Military Air Systems. The project comprises an architectural concept, a methodology, a development environment, a runtime environment and a simulation connector. The adequacy of the approach was demonstrated by means of a prototypical implementation of a NCO scenario.

1 Introduction

Complex scenarios like military operations, international peacekeeping missions, homeland security, or natural disaster relieve missions are more and more faced with the challenges of conducting network-centric operations and exhibiting mission autonomy. Although various conceptions exist of which capabilities are required for a system to be considered network-centric or autonomous, there are hardly any proposals or prototypes that describe concrete transformations for both capabilities into software. What has been missing so far is a holistic approach prescribing how disparate technologies can be adapted to fit together.

This paper reviews work accomplished at EADS Military Air Systems driven by the need to develop a holistic approach to combine established technologies with new methodologies for communication and autonomy in a proper architectural reference framework. The report presents the general architectural concept, the methodology as well as the development and runtime environment. The adequacy of the approach has been demonstrated by means of a prototypical implementation of a Network-Centric Operations (NCO) scenario.

A prerequisite for a fast, efficient and effective collaboration in highly-dynamic missions is the creation of a common understanding based on distributed situational information by means of an adequate IT infrastructure, comparable to the *Global Information Grid* (*GIG*) [1]. Participating systems in NCO do not necessarily form a homogeneous collective but are usually composed of a patchwork of disparate technologies: different communication protocols, transport medias (see

[2]), hardware-software architectures, or knowledge-based systems. The consolidation of these technologies demands a proper architectural concept for system interconnection and the availability of a corresponding framework implementation. This problem is acknowledged by the DoD Architecture Framework [3] but lacks an implementation.

The construction of such an architectural framework is a very complex task due to its interdisciplinary nature. Although plenty of applicable software standards (e.g., CORBA, FIPA, HLA, WSDL, ...) exist, their composition is difficult because standards usually were designed independently of each other but in this context have to work together. A further problem arises from the fact, that it is partly unclear how technologies will evolve. Up to now, only few correlation efforts have been made, e.g., JTA [4] and NC3TA [5], but those lack software engineering aspects. Projects which do provide an implementation, e.g., OASIS [6], COE [7] or JAUS [8], concentrate on particular aspects but lack a holistic and generic approach.

2 Architectural Approach

The conceptual development of the framework, called *Distributed Autonomy Reference Framework* (*DARF*) [9], is driven by the need to cover two fundamental principles, that are autonomy and NCO. In the following, the combination of both principles is modelled using a military analogy. However, the results can be easily mapped to the civil domain. While NCO serves in both domains to gain information superiority, autonomy in military systems is usually associated with unmanned vehicles or appears in command and control structures.

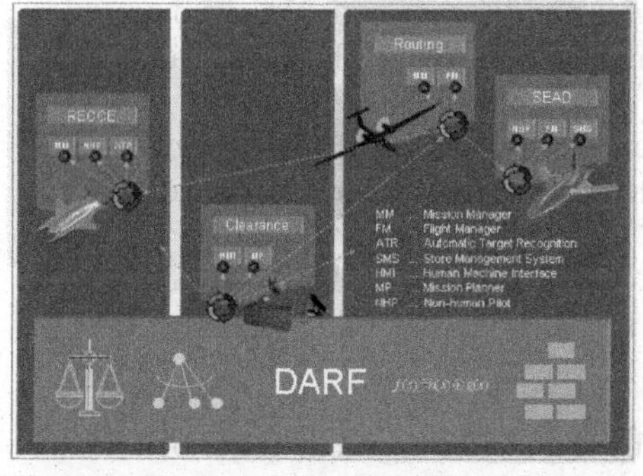

(a) Distributed Autonomy Reference Framework.

(b) Sensor-to-shooter scenario.

Fig. 1. The DARF alongside with the the scenario described in Section 3.

Key design principles of the DARF are its capabilities of constructing and assembling mission software sufficing the needs of manned or unmanned airborne, but also ground-based or maritime participants in collaborative missions.

Figure 1(a) illustrates the distributed framework, employed in a number of co-operating assets.

Through abstraction of hardware details, the DARF supports the building of flexible system architectures for different platforms, payloads and for various mission types. The DARF facilitates the integration of subsystems such as sensors, weapons and communications while minimising the impact of platform constraints. In addition, the DARF ensures interoperability between internal system components and external elements such as manned aircrafts, command and control centres, and space assets.

The general approach is to provide an infrastructure which enables the creation of a *Service-oriented Architecture* (*SOA*). All participating assets of a network-centric mission are publishing their capabilities as services. Capabilities include information provision (e.g., sensor data), basic algorithms (e.g., route planning) and concrete actions (e.g., target engagement) requestable by other assets. The way *how* services are internally structured and implemented (e.g., in form of an agent) and *where* they are located is transparent to the service consumer.

The DARF is based on the following core features:

Building Blocks: Providing service containers for functionality to ease development of new services or integration of existing code.

Situational Assessment: Providing means to build an operational picture composed of shared distributed information, complement the world view and to structure information using ontologies.

Decision Support: Providing means for the integration of reasoning and inference mechanisms, usage of declarative knowledge and to assist the decision making process.

Network Communication: Providing a middleware capable of communication in heterogeneous networking environments and platforms, adaptation of transport media by IPv6.

Simulation Connector: Integrate framework Building Blocks into complex simulation environments using High Level Architecture standard technology.

3 Experimental Platform

The approach was successfully validated by implementing an instance of a *sensor-to-shooter* scenario, as illustrated by Figure 1(b). The selected scenario is well understood but still poses a challenge in its implementation [10]. The central idea is the cooperation between two kinds of unmanned air vehicles, one acting as a reconnaissance unit (URAV[1]), essentially being the "sensor", and the other one acting as a combat unit (UCAV[2]), representing the "shooter." Figure 2 shows design- and run-time elements of the DARF.

[1] *Unmanned Reconnaissance Air Vehicle.*

[2] *Unmanned Combat Air Vehicle.*

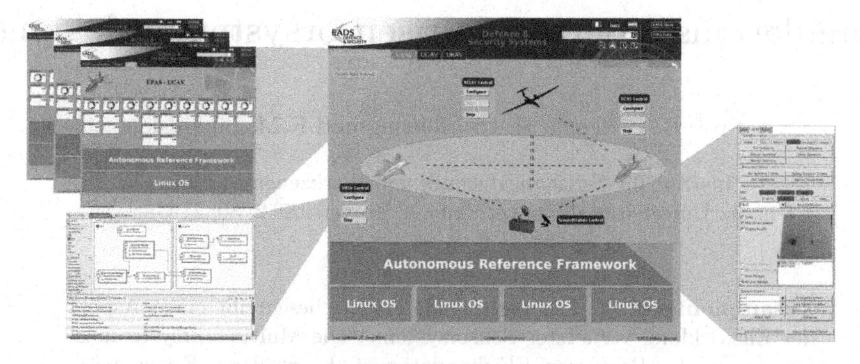

Fig. 2. Prototypical implementation with mission scenario, configuration and control.

4 Conclusions

Using DARF results in dramatically reduced integration efforts and shorter development cycles. The DARF infrastructure and methodology provides a number of facilities. It permits both, a simple construction of SOA solutions and the development distributed software systems. The infrastructure supports integration of third party code and even complex system of systems. The adaption of DAI tools eases the development of decision-support and -making algorithms and thus forms a reasonable basis for engineering systems requiring mission autonomy and collaborations in heterogeneous networks. Experiments with a prototype applied in a simulated sensor-to-shooter scenario exhibited a robust and predictable system behaviour and reached a significant technical readiness level.

References

1. David Alberts. Network centric warfare: Current status and way ahead. *Defence Science*, 8(3), September 2003.
2. Reichelt et al. IP Based Transport Abstraction for Middleware Technologies. In *3rd Int. Conf. on Networking and Services*, Athens, Greece, 2007. IEEE CS Press
3. DoD. *DoD Architecture Framework Version 1.0.* DoD Architecture Framework Group, August 2003.
4. DoD. Joint Technical Architecture. `http://www.acq.osd.mil/osjtf/pdf/jta-vol-I.pdf`, 2003.
5. NATO. C3 technical architecture. `http://194.7.80.153/website/home.asp`, 2005.
6. OASIS. Open advanced system for disaster and emergency management. `http://www.oasis-fp6.org/index.html`, 2006.
7. CMU SEI. Defense information infrastructure common operating environment. `http://www.sei.cmu.edu/str/descriptions/diicoe_body.html`, 1997.
8. JAUS. Joint architecture for unmanned systems. `http://www.jauswg.org`, 2006.
9. Oswald et al. A service-oriented framework for manned and unmanned systems to support network-centric operations. In *4th Int. Conf. on Informatics in Control, Automation and Robotics*, 284–291, Angers, France, May 2007. INSTICC Press.
10. William G. Chapman. Organizational concepts for sensor-to-shooter world. Master's thesis, School of Advanced Airpower Studies, Alabama, May 1997.

Simulationsbasierte Multisensorsystemauslegung

Prof. B. Denkena, H.-C. Möhring und K.M. Litwinski

Institut für Fertigungstechnik und Werkzeugmaschinen,
Leibniz Universität Hannover, An der Universität 2, 30823 Garbsen

Zusammenfassung. Die vorliegende Arbeit beschreibt einen Aspekt der Entwicklung vernetzter Sensorsysteme: Die Multisensorsystemauslegung auf der Basis von FE-Simulationen. Es wird ein Konzept beschrieben, welches optimale Sensorkonfigurationen bestehend aus Sensoren verschiedener Bauart zur Überwachung verschiedenartiger Größen bestimmt. Darge-stellt sind die Ergebnisse der Anwendung an einem Element eines Werk-stückspannbaukastens.

1 Einleitung

Die vorliegende Arbeit beschreibt die simulationsbasierte Auslegung von Multisensorsystemen als erste Phase der Entwicklung gentelligenter® Werkzeugmaschinenkomponenten, welche mittels vernetzter Sensorik und Nutzung von Erfahrungen sehr detailliert Maschinen und Prozesse überwachen können. Im Unterschied zur Auslegung von Sensorsystemen mit einzelnen Sensoren ist hier die Interaktion zwischen Sensoren zu berücksichtigen. So muss z.B. unterschieden werden, ob eine gemessene mechanische Spannung durch mechanische Belastung oder durch thermische Einflüsse hervorgerufen wird. Zur Identifikation optimaler Sensorkonfigurationen wird im Folgenden ein Algorithmus vorgestellt, welcher durch Minimierung der Störeinflüsse die Interaktion zwischen Sensoren berücksichtigt [1]. Anschließend sind Ergebnisse dargestellt, welche die Anwendung des Algorithmus demonstrieren.

2 Auslegung von Multisensorsystemen

Die Fusion von Sensoren in Multisensorsystemen ist auf der Signal-, Pixel-, Merkmal- und Symbolebene möglich. In Echtzeitanwendungen findet sie meist auf der Signalebene statt [2]. Eine Fusionierung auf dieser Ebene lässt sich durch Abbildung des Messsystems in die Sensorsystemauslegung einbeziehen. Hierfür ist die gesamte Messkette zu analysieren.

Signale werden selten direkt gemessen, sondern typischerweise durch indirekte Messungen ermittelt, welche mehrere Signalumwandlungen benötigen. Abb. 1 stellt den Signalpfad in einem indirekten Messsystem dar. Eingang ist ein Vektor $\boldsymbol{f}$, welcher sich aus den zu messenden Größen zusammensetzt. Der Schaltblock des physikalischen Messsystems beeinhaltet die Sensoren und alle Signalwandlungen, in welchen Interaktionen zwischen Sensoren berücksichtigt werden müssen. Der Block gibt den Vektor der theoretischen Messgrößen $\boldsymbol{x}$ zurück.

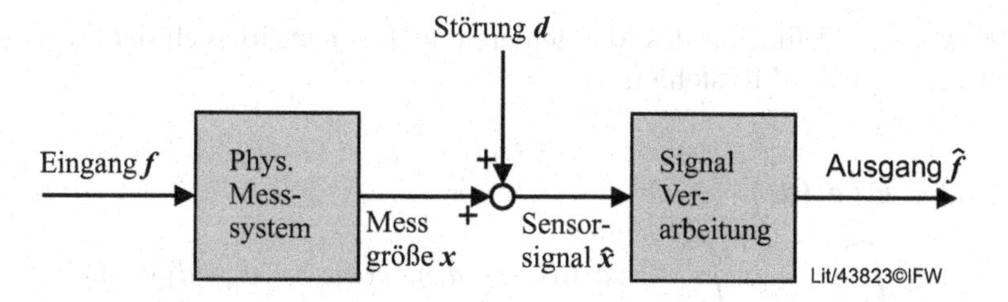

Abb. 1. Signalpfad eines indirekt messenden Systems

Für die Auslegung von Sensorsystemen ist es notwendig, Kenngrößen zur Bewertung von Sensorkonfigurationen im „physikalischen Messsystem" zu ermitteln. Eine wichtige Kenngröße ist die Sensitivität. Die Sensitivität des i-ten Sensorsignals im Ausgangsvektor $\boldsymbol{x}$ bezüglich des Eingangsvektors $\boldsymbol{f}$ ist definiert als

$$\boldsymbol{\nabla} x_i = \left(\frac{\partial x_i}{\partial f_1} \frac{\partial x_i}{\partial f_2} \cdots \frac{\partial x_i}{\partial f_n} \right)^T . \quad (1)$$

Bei Sensorsystemen mit einer minimalen Anzahl von Sensoren entspricht die Anzahl der Sensoren immer der Anzahl der zu messenden Größen. In Single Input Single Output (SISO) Systemen hat der Sensitivitätsvektor somit nur eine Komponente, die maximiert werden muss, um eine gute Signalqualität zu erreichen [3]. Im Gegensatz hierzu haben die Sensitivitätsvektoren in Multisensorsystemen mehr Komponenten. Zur Bewertung von Sensorsystemen muss eine weitere Eigenschaft berücksichtigt werden: Die Interaktion zwischen Sensoren. Eine Kennzahl aus der Literatur, welche diese Eigenschaft beschreibt, ist die Kollinearität zwischen Sensorsignalen

$$S_{i,j} = \frac{\boldsymbol{\nabla} x_i \cdot \boldsymbol{\nabla} x_j}{|\boldsymbol{\nabla} x_i| \cdot |\boldsymbol{\nabla} x_j|} \quad (2)$$

mit

$S_{i,j} = \pm 1$: Signale x_i und x_j sind kollinear und damit redundant
$S_{i,j} = 0$: Signale x_i und x_j sind orthogonal.

Kollineare Signale sind redundant und so für ein Messsystem mit einer minimalen Anzahl an Sensoren nicht geeignet. Cobb und Liebst verwendeten die Kollinearität und die Summe der Absolutwerte der Sensitivität zur Auslegung von Multisensorsystemen für die Überwachung der Strukturintegrität in der Luft- und Raumfahrttechnik [4]. Ihr Algorithmus teilt zunächst ähnliche Sensoren, durch Vergleich der Kollinearität mit einem Schwellwert, in Cluster auf. Anschließend wird aus jedem Cluster der Sensor mit der maximalen Summe der Absolutwerte des Sensitivitätsvektors für ein Sensorset ausgewählt.

In der vorliegenden Arbeit wird im Gegensatz zur Arbeit von Cobb und Liebst eine Zielfunktion abgeleitet, welche dem quadratischen Messfehler entspricht. Mit der Definition des Messfehlers $\boldsymbol{e} = \hat{\boldsymbol{f}} - \boldsymbol{f}$ ergibt sich der statistische Erwartungswert des Messfehlers zu

$$Q = E\left(\boldsymbol{e}^2(\boldsymbol{d})\right) \tag{3}$$

$$= \int_{d_1=-\infty}^{\infty} \cdots \int_{d_n=-\infty}^{\infty} \boldsymbol{e}^2(d_1, \cdots, d_n) \cdot p(d_1, \cdots, d_n) dd_1 \cdots dd_n. \tag{4}$$

Für eine große Anzahl an Sensoren ist die Anwendung dieser Zielfunktion im Wesentlichen zu komplex. Aus diesem Grund wird das Integral jeweils für zwei Sensoren gelöst, wobei angenommen wird, dass die Störungen der einzelnen Sensoren unabhängig voneinander sind und einer Gauß'schen Normalverteilung unterliegen. Es ergibt sich als Zielfunktion zur Bewertung einer Kombination zweier Sensoren

$$q_{i,j} = \frac{\left(\frac{\boldsymbol{\nabla x}_i}{\sigma_i}\right)^2 + \left(\frac{\boldsymbol{\nabla x}_j}{\sigma_j}\right)^2}{\left(\frac{\boldsymbol{\nabla x}_i}{\sigma_i}\right)^2 \left(\frac{\boldsymbol{\nabla x}_j}{\sigma_j}\right)^2 - \left(\frac{\boldsymbol{\nabla x}_i}{\sigma_i} \frac{\boldsymbol{\nabla x}_j}{\sigma_j}\right)^2} \tag{5}$$

mit

$q_{i,j}$: Kennzahl für die Qualität eines aus x_i und x_j kombinierten Signals
σ_i : Standardabweichung des Signals x_i.

Die Messsignale werden durch den Bezug auf ihre Standardabweichung normiert. Auf diese Weise lassen sich verschiedene Typen von Sensoren miteinander kombinieren. Die Güte einer Sensorkonfiguration ergibt sich als die Summe der Güten aller in der Konfiguration vorkommenden Sensorkombinationen

$$Q_{red} = \sum_{i=1}^{n-1} \sum_{j=i+1}^{n} q_{i,j}. \tag{6}$$

Für den Sonderfall, dass alle Sensitivitätsvektoren orthogonal zueinander stehen, lässt sich zeigen, dass diese Zielfunktion direkt proportional zum quadratischen Messfehler ist.

3 Anwendung in Simulationen

Für die Anwendung des beschriebenen Algorithmus' wurden verschiedene Baukastenspannelemente mittels FE-Modellierung abgebildet. Es können alle relevanten Größen der Sensorauslegung (thermische Lasten, Kräfte, definierte Verlagerungen) als Last angenommen und ihre Auswirkung auf virtuelle Sensoren in Simulationen untersucht werden. Eine implementierte Schnittstelle exportiert die Signale der virtuellen Sensoren in die Datenverarbeitungssoftware MATLAB™, in welcher durch Nutzung der oben beschriebenen Zielfunktion optimale Sensorkonfigurationen ermittelt werden.

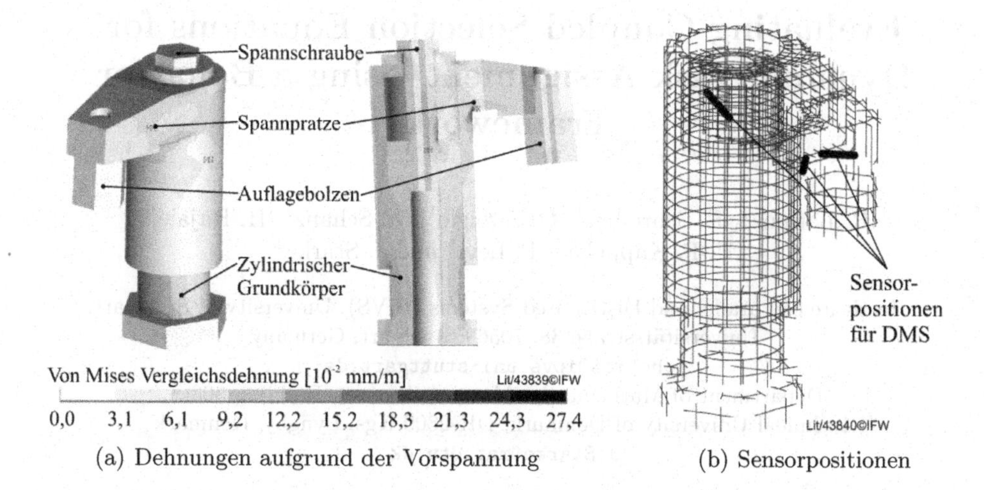

(a) Dehnungen aufgrund der Vorspannung (b) Sensorpositionen

Abb. 2. Simulationsbasierte Sensorplanung am Beispiel eines Aufsitzspanners

Beispielhaft ist hierfür in Abb. 2 (a) das Ergebnis einer Simulation an einem Element zur Aufbringung von Spannkräften dargestellt. Abgebildet ist die Verteilung der Von Mises Vergleichsdehnungen aufgrund der Belastung durch eine Vorspannkraft von 1 kN. Eine Herausforderung in dieser Simulation ist die korrekte Abbildung der Kontaktnichtlinearität zwischen der Spannpratze und dem zylindrischen Grund-körper. Die Ergebnisse dieser Simulationen wurden verwendet, um Dehnungsmessstreifen zu platzieren (siehe Abb. 2 b). Das System ist darauf ausgelegt, Kräfte in drei Raumrichtungen zu detektieren.

4 Zusammenfassung

In der vorliegenden Arbeit wird ein Algorithmus beschrieben, welcher Sensorkonfigurationen unter besonderer Berücksichtigung der Interaktion zwischen den Sensoren auslegt. Der Algorithmus ist in MATLAB™ implementiert und mit der Simulationssoftware ANSYS® gekoppelt. Beispielhaft sind die Ergebnisse einer Multisensorauslegung für ein Spannelement dargelegt.

Literaturverzeichnis

1. Denkena B, Möhring H-C, Litwinski KM: Design of Multi Sensor Systems for Gentelligent Process Monitoring, 2nd IC-EpsMsO, Athen, 2006
2. Luo RC, Yih C-C, Su KL: Multisensor Fusion and Integration: Approaches, Applications, and Future Research Directions, IEEE Sensors Journal, 2(2): 107–119, 2002
3. Lee JM, Choi DK, Chu CN: Real-Time Tool Breakage Monitoring for NC Turning. Annals of the CIRP 43(1): 81–84, 1994
4. Cobb RG, Liebst BS: Sensor Placement and Structural Damage Identification. AIAA Journal 35(2): 369–374, 1997

Evaluating Coupled Selection Equations for Dynamic Task Assignment Using a Behavior Framework

R. Lafrenz[1], F. Schreiber[1], O. Zweigle[1], M. Schanz[1], H. Rajaie[1], U.-P. Käppeler[1], P. Levi[1] and J. Starke[2]

[1] Institute of Parallel and Distributed Systems (IPVS), University of Stuttgart, Universitätsstraße 38, 70569 Stuttgart, Germany
robotics@ipvs.uni-stuttgart.de
[2] Department of Mathematics, Matematiktorvet, Building 303 S, Technical University of Denmark, DK-2800 Kgs. Lyngby, Denmark
J.Starke@mat.dtu.dk

Abstract. In this paper we focus on methods for a reliable and robust mechanism to distribute roles among a team of cooperating robots. In previous work, we showed the principal applicability of a novel approach based on self organization using coupled selection equations. To show the applicability in the robocup scenario we used a simple scenario to assign the roles attacker and defender. In this paper we present the application of the novel approach to more realistic and complex scenarios like kick-off or pass play. One of the critical parts in this method is the parameterization of utility and activation functions used to determine the additional parameters.

1 Introduction

One of the most critical parts in designing software concepts for multi-robot-teams is the assignment of robots to behaviors. Especially in a distributed system it is necessary to have a flexible mechanism for dynamic and situation-dependent re-assignment. In general, two principles are possible: First, the manual design of decision networks, and secondly the use of self-organized methods. While there is a lot of experience with the first, the latter is so far only used in research context.

Besides our successfully used XABSL [1] based role assignment mechanism we describe here experiments with the novel approach based on self organization using coupled selection equations. This concept relies on the work [2], and is inspired by self-organization principles [3,4] derived from natural systems. We consider the assignment of robot i to behavior j as a two-index optimization problem where the overall cost

$$c = \sum_{i,j} c_{ij} x_{ij}, \qquad x_{ij} \in \{0,1\} \tag{1}$$

has to be minimized such that in each row and in each column of the matrix (x_{ij}) there is at most one non-vanishing element. In case of equal numbers of robots and behaviors, x_{ij} is a permutation matrix.

One possible way to perform this minimization is to use a dynamical system consisting of coupled selection equations [2,5,6,7], where the x_{ij} are approximated by a matrix $\xi_{ij} \in [0,1]$. The temporal evolution of this matrix is given by the following differential equation:

$$\frac{d}{dt}\xi_{ij} = \xi_{ij}\left[1 + (2\beta - 1)\,\xi_{ij}^2 - \beta\left(\sum_{i'}\xi_{i'j}^2 + \sum_{j'}\xi_{ij'}^2\right)\right] \tag{2}$$

In case of a square matrix, it can be guaranteed that this system converges to a permutation matrix in the course of time. Usually, after a small number of time steps in the iteration process, the system tends to a clear assignment, which can be determined by using the maximum of a row or column. The temporal evolution of such a systems for three robots and seven possible behaviors is shown in Figure 1(a). At first, all behaviors show increasing assignment values, but after approx. 40 steps, all but one behavior is suppressed for each of the robots. Therefore, after another 30 time steps, the assignment is clear.

It could also be shown, that this method is applicable to more complex scenarios, where two robots are assigned to one cooperative task [8]. As an extension, the enhanced version uses situation dependent utility parameters $\alpha_{ij(t)}$ and activation parameters $\lambda_{ij}(t)$ to affect the dynamical behavior of the system [9]. The extended coupled selection equations are defined by:

$$\frac{d}{dt}\xi_{ij} = \kappa\xi_{ij}\left[\alpha_{ij}(t)\left(\lambda_{ij}(t) - \xi_{ij}^2\right) + 2\beta\xi_{ij}^2 - \beta\left(\sum_{i'}\xi_{i'j}^2 + \sum_{j'}\xi_{ij'}^2\right)\right] \tag{3}$$

The utility parameter $\alpha_{ij}(t)$ describes the benefit for robot i performing the behavior j in the current situation. As the situation may change frequently, the assignment is stabilized by the relatively slow evolution of the matrix ξ_{ij}, controlled by the parameter κ. Thus, oscillating is inhibited. On the other hand, too slow reaction of changes in the utility parameters can lead to inert system behavior, which must also be avoided. Determining the α_{ij} is a very critical part in the system design and subject to many tests. For the future, we plan to learn these values by reinforcement methods or neural networks.

The activation parameters $\lambda_{ij}(t)$ allow for switching groups of behaviors, which is useful for special situations, such as referee events like as kick-off or throw-in, which are triggered on referee program (the so-called RefBox) and communicated by wireless LAN. In these situations, special roles are needed instead of the usual ones used in the game-flow. For example, during a throw-in the opposing team has to keep a distance of $2m$ to the robot performing the throw-in. Therefore, the standard *GetBall* behavior is deactivated and the special behavior for throw-in defense is activated. As the situation is cleared, the activation parameters are set to the normal values.

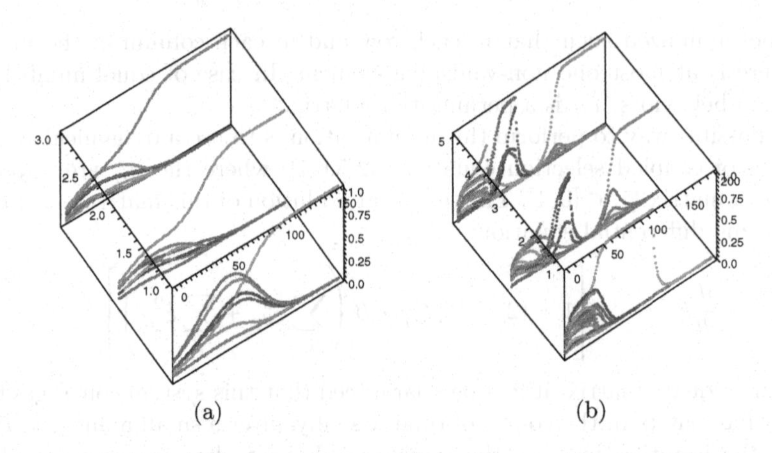

Fig. 1. Dynamics of assignment processes: (a) without changing activation. After approx. 30 time-steps, the assignment is clearly visible. In (b), the activation $\lambda_{ij}(t)$ changes twice, which leads to immediate reaction of the system

In Figure 1(b), the behavior of the system with changing activation parameters at two points in time is shown. One can see that the system responds immediately to the deactivation and a new assignment is established.

To show the applicability in the RoboCup, we used a simple scenario to assign the roles attacker and defender [10]. In this paper we present the application of this novel approach for more realistic and complex scenarios like kick-off or pass play. One of the critical parts in this method is the parameterization of utility functions used to determine the $\alpha_{ij}(t)$.

2 Test Scenarios and Results

In this section we describe several test scenarios in which self-organized methods are promising. These scenarios are intentionally kept simple, because we wanted to perform parameter studies and get a better understanding of the equations and their behavior during the use on our robocup robots.

2.1 Current Role Assignment Process

Basic Principle of Our Current Role Assignment Process As top instance of our behavior, we use the XPl (Player) module. This module is executed on each robot and manages the system status, initializes the system, communicates with the RefBox and is responsible to keep the distributed world model consistent among the robots. Also the player sets the necessary game state symbols for the XABSL based decision module.

When the game state is updated, the XABSL engine is executed, finds an appropriate behavior and executes this behavior. Team behaviors have to be coordinated with adequate flags.

The represented behaviors are structured in a hierarchical way, as the behavior of an agent is modeled in options and basic behaviors. A basic behavior consists of executable code and an option that consists of complex sub behaviors. In the current implementation we use no explicitly communication among the agents and we generally want to keep negotiation processes as short as possible because of the high dynamic in a robocup game.

Comparison – Disadvantages of the Old Assignment Variant

- In the current behavior assignment process only a local behavior decision on each robot is used. Due to the usage of complex hand made assignment rules of roles to individual robots it is not ensured that these roles are assigned correct, e.g. a role can be assigned twice. Therefore it is complicated to optimize the process to avoid such errors. Also in case of a variation in the team size during the game, a relatively complex new role coordination process has to be executed by the robots. Another problem is the oscillation of sub roles in some situation. This has to be managed also with relatively complex structures.

Comparison – Advantages of the New Assignment Variant The usage of the coupled selection equation gives us the following advancements in comparison to our previous assignment process:

- Each robot performs the same calculation of the coupled selection equation. Therefore, under the precondition of consistent environment data, each robot knows the role of any other robot in the team through the result of the calculations and we don't have to commit the chosen roles any longer.
- No special configuration treatment in case of defective robots, only an activation/deactivation is necessary to start the autonomously role assignment process. Even in complex role assignment scenarios a smooth change of the roles is possible if a defective robot has to be moved from the field or a replacement robot is inserted in game play (see also assignment of the keeper role 2.2. This only holds in our current implementation in case the robots are equally equipped.
- Our previous used role assignment rules can be simplified, because we don't need a fixed assignation of an individual robot to a default role any more. Therefore the robots find autonomously the best solution to approach their initial positions in case of a standard situation, like throw-in or goal-kick, etc. With our previous process, we planned these main role assignments before the game by hand.
- The dynamic activation/deactivation of objectives in the coupled selection equations allows us now easily to autonomously change the tactical behavior of the team, e.g. a second attacker role can be assigned autonomously during a special game situation to a robot to enforce a more aggressive game-play. These activation/deactivation processes can also be outsourced to independent intelligent game-play analyzation modules.

– A special quality of the coupled selection equations assignment process is the guaranty that a unique role is exclusively assigned to each robot. Therefore we don't need to check the consistency of the hand made role assignment rules any longer.

2.2 Dynamic Assignment of the Keeper Role

In the first scenario, the task is to nominate a new goalie, if the original one is defective. In our current behavior the goalie function is fixed to one individual robot for the whole game, this is seriously critical. This is enforced by the fact that a substitution of the goalie is currently not spread amongst the robots. This leads to some confusion in the goal area, where the goalie interacts sometimes with the defender. For this a dynamic behavior switching is very useful for us. One major point is that only the specially marked goalie is allowed to stay permanently in the goal area. If the system figures out, that the goalie is broken, a substitute is determined. But with the restriction that it has to leave the goal area every 10 seconds. By this, an uncovered goal can be avoided. If the rules change, even a fully autonomous role change is possible. In detail it is communicated regularly that there is an active goalie. If the robots detect in a decision cycle no active goalie signal, they activate their keeper-state in the assignment process, the coupled selection equation is evaluated and one robot becomes the new keeper according to his cost function in relation to the new keeper behavior. This new keeper communicates this information to other players.
We modeled this behavior in conformity to the ten seconds rule.
Tests showed that we need at most 200 ms to switch the behavior. As cost function we used with good results:

$$c = \sqrt{\frac{|P_{robot} - P_{goalieposition}| + d_{obstacle}}{d_{max}}} \tag{4}$$

There $|P_{robot} - P_{goalieposition}|$ is the euclidean distance between the robot and the goalie position before the goal, $d_{obstacle}$ a factor regarding the presence of obstacles and d_{max} is the maximum distance. Because we can drive relatively smooth around obstacles with the omnidrive it is enough to use an easy factor to represent the influence of them.

2.3 Kick-Off Situation

The previously used homing routine has fixed kick-off positions for all robots. This approach has two disadvantages: First, the ways can be long and the paths may cross, so that swichting e.g. a left defender and a right defender may be easier. Secondly, other factors like higher air pressure in the tank for the kicking device grade up the value of a robot, so this robot is best suited for kick-off. In this scenario, both variants were tested successfully. The different behavior of the system is shown in Fig. 2. The circles show the predefined kick-off positions with

their numbers, the boxes show the positions of the robots at the time the kick-off was ordered by the referee. The numbers in the boxes correspond to cost-terms. In Fig. (a), the cost-term is determinded by the distances to the target positons, in Fig. (b), the cost-term coresponds to the number of kicks already performed and the priority of the position to be occupied. In both cases, the is one positon more than robots exist, and this position (cricle with number 5) is not assigned. For use in a real game, both factors can be weighted to achieve good overall performance.
With this feature it is guaranteed that always a fully working robot positions himself at the most critical positions, this has to be seen in contrast with the old role assignment, there no autonomous role change depending on the robot status was possible.

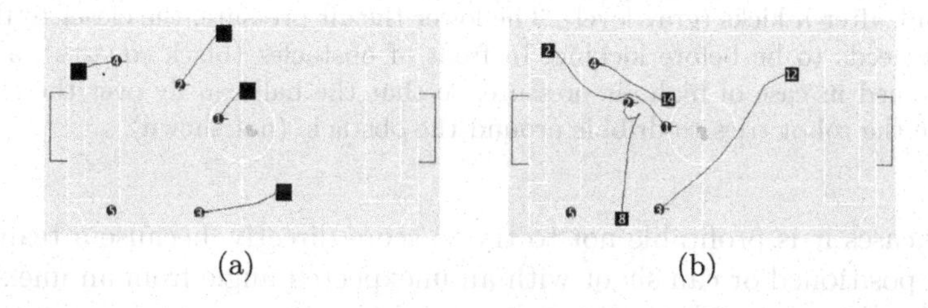

Fig. 2. Robots taking kick-off positions with cost-functions. TCircles show the predefined kick-off positions with their priorities, boxes show the positions of the robots at the time the kick-off was ordered by the referee. (a) cost-terms use only distances, (b) cost-terms use only the number of kicks already performed (numbers in boxes).

2.4 Attacker Behavior

In our standard player with decision nets, the behavior of an attacker is defined by three sub-behaviors: getBall, dribble, and shoot. In order to react on rapidly changing situations, all robots should have the possibility to change their role quickly. On the other hand, a competition between team-mates is unwanted. So the three sub-roles getBall, dribble, and shoot are active for every robot in the field, but with different cost functions. The cost function for getBall and dribble consider distance to the ball, angle to the opponent's goal, and the number of opponents on the way to it. The cost function for shoot Fig. 3 also considers the number of kicks already performed by the robot, because power and range decrease with every shot.

For the future, we also plan to include factors on a different level of abstraction, e.g., the remaining time of a game and the current score.

2.5 Pass-Play

There is another option for a player which has the ball besides dribbling and shooting directly to the opponent's goal, namely playing a pass to a team-mate.

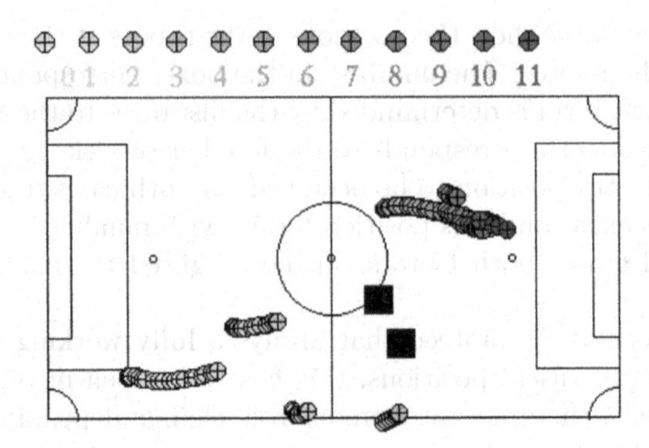

Fig. 3. Distance where the kick is activated in relation to the remaining pressure in the air tank after n kicks (gray level). The lower the air pressure, the closer to the goal the robot needs to be before kicking. In front of obstacles (black squares), a kick is only perfomed in case of high air pressure, so that the ball can fly over the obstacle. Otherwise the robot tries to dribble around the obstacle (not shown).

In many cases it is profitable not to try to score directly, because a team-mate is better positioned or can shoot with an unexpected angle from an unexpected position, and hence outflank the goalie.
To initiate a pass play, the dribbling robot analyzes which team mate is in a shorter distance to the goal, but not too near. When the robot has found possible pass partners it is checking the distances of the nearby obstacles to the considered pass line.

The implementation of this behavior was functional in the test scenario, see Fig. 4. As a result we found that it is very complex to find the best trade-off in ambiguous situations. Therefore we need to find more significant criteria to calculate if it is useful to pass or not, e.g. we can test a criteria like goal shoot estimation of the pass receiving robot's position.
Currently, we are not able to control the strength of a kick, but we are working on a kicking device with variable power to be able to perform a directed pass. With this kicker we want to test this behavior again on larger fields, because we expect better results from the trade-off rules if the distances between objects are larger.

3 Conclusion and Outlook

In this paper we have shown, that self-organized behavior is promising for multi-robot applications. The extension of the already successfully used coupled selection equations by utility and activation parameters leads to a very powerful framework for modeling self-organized behavior. For a first evaluation, we have modeled some typical situations in RoboCup. To achieve the full power of this concept, we plan to learn the utility functions instead of constructing them manually.

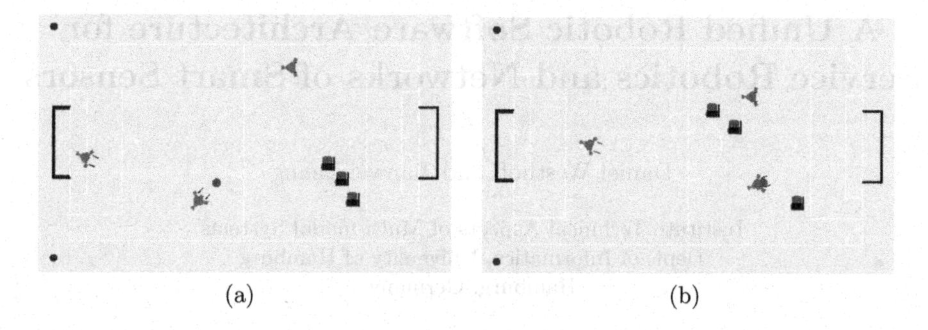

(a) (b)

Fig. 4. Situation dependent decision to shoot or play a pass: (a) the ball is passed, (b) the ball is directly kicked.

References

1. M. Lötzsch, J. Bach, H.-D. Burkhard, and M. Jüngel. Designing agent behavior with the extensible agent behavior specification language xabsl. In *7th International Workshop on RoboCup 2003 (Robot World Cup Soccer Games and Conferences*, 2003.
2. J. Starke. *Kombinatorische Optimierung auf der Basis gekoppelter Selektionsgleichungen.* PhD thesis, Universität Stuttgart, Verlag Shaker, Aachen, 1997.
3. G. Nicolis and I. Prigogine. *Self-Organization in Non-Equilibrium Systems.* Wiley, New York, 1977.
4. H. Haken. *Advanced Synergetics.* Springer Series in Synergetics. Springer-Verlag, Heidelberg, Berlin, New York, 1983.
5. J. Starke and M. Schanz. Dynamical system approaches to combinatorial optimization. In D.-Z. Du and P. Pardalos, editors, *Handbook of Combinatorial Optimization*, volume 2, pages 471 – 524. Kluwer Academic Publisher, Dordrecht, Boston, London, 1998.
6. P. Molnár and J. Starke. Control of distributed autonomous robotic systems using principles of pattern formation in nature and pedestrian behaviour. *IEEE Transaction on Systems, Men and Cybernetics: Part B*, 31(3):433 – 436, 2001.
7. J. Starke. Dynamical assignments of distributed autonomous robotic systems to manufacturing targets considering environmental feedbacks. In *Proceedings of the 17th IEEE International Symposium on Intelligent Control (ISIC'02)*, pages 678 – 683, Vancouver, 2002.
8. M. Becht, T. Buchheim, P. Burger, G. Hetzel, G. Kindermann, R. Lafrenz, N. Oswald, M. Schanz, M. Schulé, P. Molnár, J. Starke, and P. Levi. Three-index assignment of robots to targets: An experimental verification. In *IAS-6*, 2000.
9. J. Starke, C. Ellsässer, and Fukuda. Self-organized control in cooperative robots using pattern formation principles. submitted, 2005.
10. M. Schanz, J. Starke, R. Lafrenz, O. Zweigle, M. Oubbati, H. Rajaie, F. Schreiber, T. Buchheim, U.-P. Käppeler, and P. Levi. Dynamic Task Assignment in a Team of Agents. In P. Levi et al., editor, *Autonome Mobile Systeme*, pages 11–18. Springer, 2005.

A Unified Robotic Software Architecture for Service Robotics and Networks of Smart Sensors

Daniel Westhoff and Jianwei Zhang

Institute Technical Aspects of Multi-modal Systems
Dept. of Informatics, University of Hamburg
Hamburg, Germany

Abstract. This paper proposes a novel architecture for the programming of multi-modal service robots and networked sensors. The presented software framework eases the development of high-level applications for distributed systems. The software architecture is based upon the Roblet-Technology, which is an exceptionally powerful medium in robotics. The possibility to develop, compile and execute an application on one workstation and distribute parts of a program based on the idea of mobile code is pointed out. Since the Roblet-Technology uses Java the development is independent of the operation system. The framework hides the network communication and therefore greatly improves the programming and testing of applications in service robotics. The concept is evaluated in the context of the service robot TASER of the TAMS Institute at the University of Hamburg. This robot consists of a mobile platform with two manipulators equipped with artificial hands. Several multimodal input and output devices for interaction round off the robot. Networked cameras in the working environment of TASER provide additional information to the robot. The integration of these smart sensors shows the extendability of the proposed concept to general distributed systems.

1 Introduction

Robotic systems are becomeing more and more complex. The number of constitutional parts that make up current robotic research platforms is increasing. A multitude of sensors can be found in these robots: tactile sensors from basic bumper switches to force and torque sensors, range measuring systems like infrared, ultra-sonic, radar and laser based sensors or vision systems including cameras as different as low-cost web-cams and high-dynamic-range cameras. On the actuator side one finds mobile robot platforms with a variety of drive systems, walking or climbing robots, robot arms with different degrees of freedom or complex multi-finger robotic hands. In service robotics all these are combined in autonomous mobile manipulators that accomplish tasks in a diversity of applications.

Over the last years, the research community has come to realize that the ambitious objectives of robotic research can only be reached based on solid software architectures. These architectures must support the requirements of the heterogeneous modern robot systems. Briefly summarized, the main requirements are:

hardware abstraction, extendability, scalability, limited run-time overhead, actuator control, modularization, support for networked computing, simplicity, consistency, completeness, support for multiple operating systems. [1] and [2] have conducted surveys and evaluations of existing software systems. They provide a good elaboration on the merits and demerits of these architectures.

In this paper we present our robotic software framework, which is based on Roblet-Technology [3] and thereby meets the above challenges while enabling a programmer to easily develop advanced applications for service robots. First, we discuss related software architectures which have been proposed for robotic applications in the last years. Second, a short introduction to our robot system TASER is given which points out the need for a unifying development platform for robotic systems. Then, the main features of our framework are presented. Most important is the framework's ability to integrate existing solutions to specific robotic problems, making it a component-oriented approach. It is specially designed for networked applications. The system features a layer that encapsulates network programming and hides it from its user. A variety of hardware devices can be integrated into an application using our technique. We give examples how we used the framework to develop complex applications using a variety of robot components. Thereby, a layer of abstraction generalizes access to similar devices. In the conclusion we discuss that developed applications can be transferred to other robotic systems without major changes.

2 Related Research

This section gives an overview of existing software architectures for service robots. Recently, a workshop during the 2004 conference on Intelligent Robots and Systems (IROS) tried to list the various research activities in the field of robotic middleware [4]. In the following, some of these activities are discussed. Besides, further related research projects are stated.

In 2004 the *Orca project* [5] emerged from the *OROCOS project* [6] and focused on mobile robot systems. It adopts a component-based software engineering approach using *Ice* for communication and the description of interfaces. The project's goals are to enable and to simplify software reuse and to provide a generic repository of components. The use of different middleware packages for inter-component communication is extensively discussed on the project's home page. Beside writing custom middleware, the use of CORBA and XML-based technologies is compared to Ice. Orca is available for various operating systems like Windows or Linux.

[7] introduces the *Player/Stage project*, a client-server framework to enable research on robot and sensor systems. It provides a network interface to a variety of robot and sensor hardware and to multi-robot simulators. Multiple concurrent client connections to the servers are allowed. Client applications connect over TCP sockets. The project's server software and the simulators are limited to Unix-like operating systems.

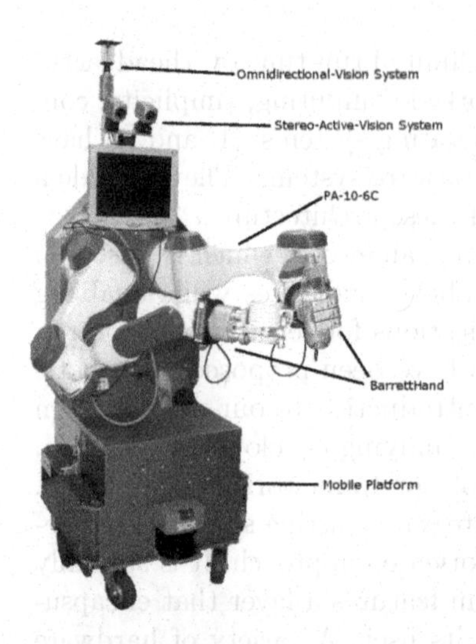

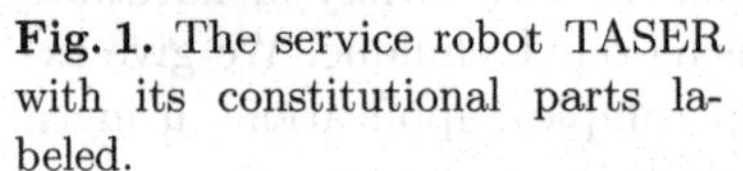
Fig. 1. The service robot TASER with its constitutional parts labeled.

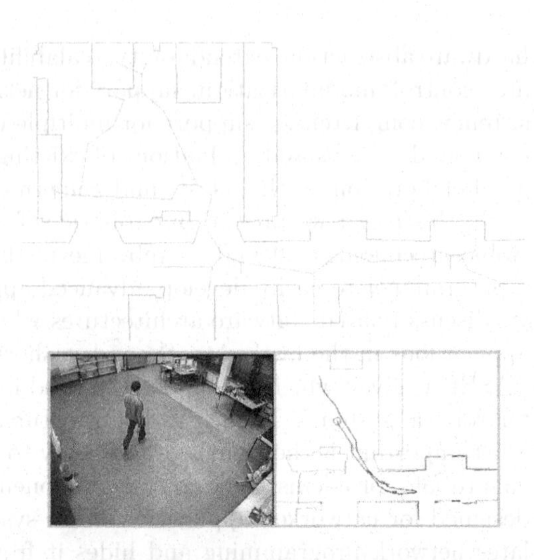
Fig. 2. Generalized motion trajectories within the laboratory of the TAMS institute (top) and a snapshot of the tracking process (bottom).

MARIE [8] is a design tool for mobile and autonomous robot applications. It is mainly implemented in C++ and it uses the *ADAPTIVE Communication Environment (ACE)* for communication and process management.

In 2002 *Evolution Robotics* introduced the commercial *Evolution Robotics Software Platform (ERSP)* for mobile robots [9]. It is a behavior-based, modular and extensible software available for Linux and Windows systems. The main components that are included are vision, navigation and interaction.

The ideas for the software framework explained in this paper emerged from previous work on a mobile robot working in a biotechnological laboratory [10]. An easy-to-use script language was proposed to define high-level work sequences. The scripts are parsed by the robot's control software and the robot fullfils the defined task. This encourages the idea of simplifying the programming of robots but lacks the flexibility of a widespread programming language including network programming for distributed systems.

3 Service Robot and Hardware Set-Up

The **TA**MS **Se**rvice **R**obot (TASER) is a mobile robot built from standard components. On top of the mobile basis, there are two manipulators with three-finger robotic hands and force sensors and a man-machine interface including a monitor for visual and loudspeakers for aural feedback. A stereo camera system for active vision and an omni-directional vision system provide visual input. Microphones are used as aural input sensors. Figure 1 shows TASER. The robot operates during normal workdays in our office environment.

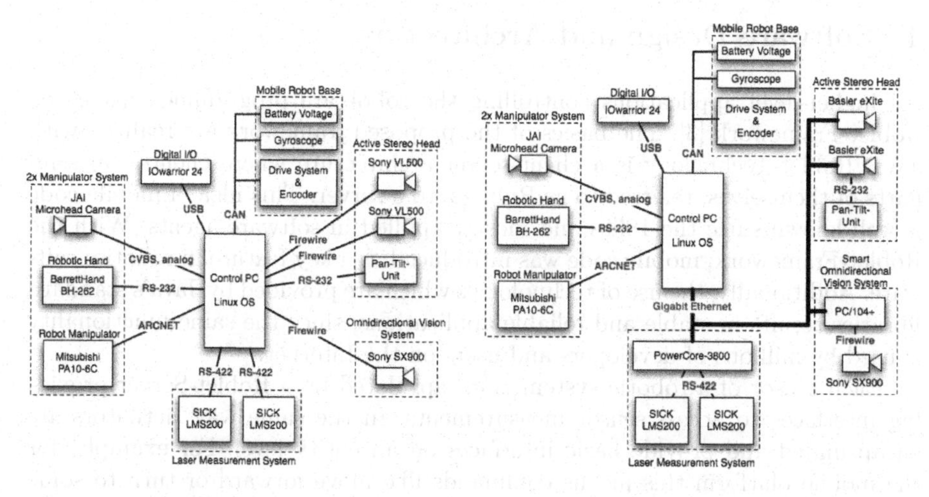

Fig. 3. The hardware set-up of TASER: The initial set-up with various bus systems (left) and the current refined set-up based on smart sensors (right). Both set-ups are connected to the stationary sensors and workstation computers via wireless LAN.

In addition to the on-board sensors of the robot, there are stationary cameras that monitor the environment. The data of the stationary cameras is available to the robot and to other networked applications. An exemplary application using both the robot's sensors and the stationary vision systems is a people tracking software [11]. This software tracks people, learns and generalizes motion trajectories of these people and provides predictions of trajectories to other applications. The service robot uses these predictions within its path-planning module to intercept people for interaction. Figure 2 shows the generalized trajectories for a part of the robot's working environment besides a snapshot of the camera tracking.

One fundamental idea we followed during the development of TASER was the integration of smart sensors and devices. Smart sensors are sensor devices that include additional computing power, which can be used for the pre-processing of sensor measurements before the data is made available to other system components. Pre-processing can be data compression, filtering or rudimental feature extraction. Smart sensors, actuators and control computers are connected via Ethernet. This has enabled us to unite and reduce bus systems used on the robot. Figure 3 points this out. Additionally, one-to-many connections can be implemented. For example, the laser range finders of the robot are used in parallel by the robot's low-level collision and obstacle avoidance system, the self-localization algorithm, both running on the control computer of the robot, and by the people tracking application running on a workstation computer in the laboratory [12].

These exemplary applications are strongly based on Roblets to combine the involved components. The following section explains the idea of Roblets and our robotic development environment.

4 Software Design and Architecture

All higher-level applications controlling the robot are programmed using the Roblet-Framework [3]. The basics of the proposed framework are realized with Java. Roblet-Technology is a client-server architecture where clients can send parts of themselves, referred to as Roblets, to a server. This idea of mobile code is well-known since the 1990s and mostly applied in software agents. With the Roblet-Framework, mobile code was introduced as a key feature in robotics software. Additionally, the use of technologies which are provided by Java's standard libraries results in stable and reliable applications, since the same functionality is used by millions of developers and users on the Internet.

Each sensor of a robotic system is encapsulated by a Roblet-Server providing interfaces to access sensor measurements. In the same way, actuators are encapsulated and provide basic interfaces on an entity level. For example, for the mobile platform this means commands like move forward or turn to some specific orientation can be executed.

Servers mostly wrap already existing lower-level software like the real-time control subsystems for the manipulators. Besides hardware encapsulation, existing software packages for robotic problems are available via Roblet-Servers. The path planning component of [10] is one such package and an example for the component-based reuse of software within our framework.

A basic Roblet-Server and a library for client applications are commercially available and supported by the *genRob GmbH.* It is freely available for research projects and extendable by self-programmed modules.

Modules are loaded when the Roblet-Server is started. These are meant to encapsulate a class of similar functionality. For the robot TASER we developed several modules. Figure 4 gives an overview of the current state of our system's implementation.

Client applications use units to query functionality. Units are provided and implemented by modules. They are specified as Java interfaces. In this way, different modules can implement the same units and therefore allow the use of similar hardware in a unified way. To point this out, a camera application is given as an example of a distributed application in figure 4. It uses a unit *camera* which is implemented by different modules. A directory service informs the client application about Roblet-Servers that are added or removed from the overall system during runtime.

Java classes, which implement the Roblet interface can be sent to a server from a client program and are executed on the remote side. Similar to Java applets this technique allows the sending of code over a network. Now, this enables the developer of a client application to decide were he wants the code to be run during runtime. Communication channels between servers and client applications can be created as needed by the Roblets. This leads to a novel flexibility for load distribution concerning computing power as well as the use of network bandwidth. Additionally, only one programming language is needed to develop higher-level applications.

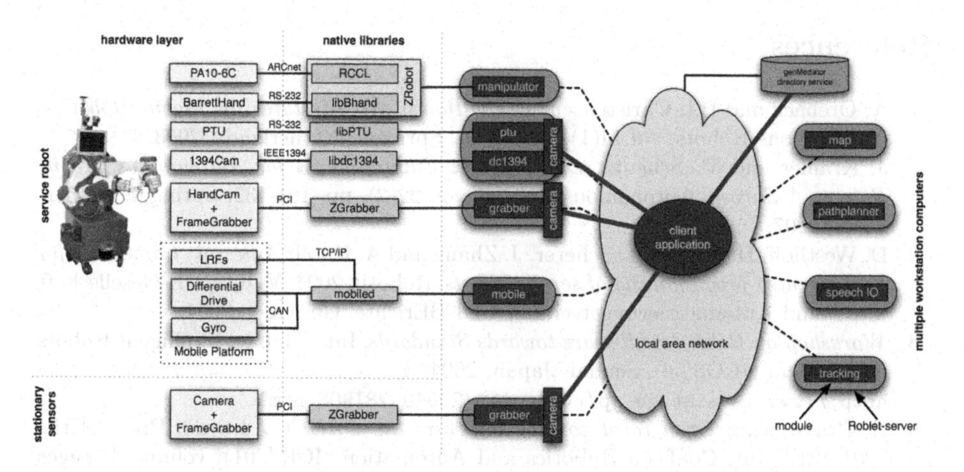

Fig. 4. The software architecture of the robot TASER. A client application uses the same unit *camera* implemented by the two different modules *grabber* and *dc1394* on three servers to display images. These images from the robot's cameras and the stationary cameras are transmitted and displayed synchronously.

In the camera example we execute compression and streaming algorithms within a Roblet before transmitting an image from a server to the client. This saves bandwith on the wireless network. During runtime the Roblet determines the quality of the wireless connection and adopts the compression level.

In the same way secure communication channels can be established. For a wireless connection the Roblet could decide to use stronger encryption algorithms if sensitive data is to be transmitted.

5 Conclusion

The presented software architecture enables the building of high-level applications for service robots using standard components for robots as well as specialized hard- or software. The software architechture of the robot based on the Roblet-Technologie is a powerful medium for robots. The feature of running client programs as a distributed software offers the possibility to run algorithms which need great computation power on different machines which provide this power. The type of communication, e.g. encrypted or compressed communication, can be changed during runtime. Each client application can use its individual and appropriate type of communication.

The next step will be to implement further software to improve the usability of the robot system and create a toolbox of reusable program parts. In this step the variety of the high-level functions like object grasping and multimodal interaction will be increased. Furthermore, the possibilities of autonomous navigation and map building will be extended.

References

1. A. Orebäck and H.I. Christensen: *Evaluation of Architectures for Mobile Robotics.* Autonomous Robots, vol.14(1), pp. 33-49, Springer, Netherlands, 2003.
2. J. Kramer and M. Scheutz: *Development Environments for Autonomous Mobile Robots: A Survey.* Autonomous Robots, vol. 22(2), pp. 101-132, Springer, Netherlands, 2007.
3. D. Westhoff, H. Stanek, T. Scherer, J. Zhang and A. Knoll: *A flexible framework for task-oriented programming of service robots.* Robotik 2004, VDI/ VDE-Gesellschaft Mess- und Automatisierungstechnik, VDI-BErichte, Germany, 2004.
4. *Workshop on Robot Middleware towards Standards*, Int. Conf. on Intelligent Robots and System (IROS'04), Sendai, Japan, 2004, `http://www.is.aist.go.jp/rt/events/20040928IROS.html`.
5. H. Bruyninckx: *Open robot control software: the OROCOS project*, Proc. of the 2001 IEEE Int. Conf. on Robotics and Automation (ICRA'01), volume 3, pages 2523–2528, Seoul, Korea, 2001.
6. A. Brooks, T. Kaupp, A. Makarenko, A. Orebäck, S. Williams: *Towards Comonent-Based Robotics*, Proc. of the 2005 IEEE/RSJ Int. Conf. on Intellegent Robots and Systems (IROS'05), Alberta, Canada, 2005.
7. B.P. Gerkey, R.T. Vaughn, K. Stoy, A. Howard, G.S. Sukhatme, M.J. Mataric: *Most Valuable Player: A Robot Device Server for Distributed Control*, Proc. of the IEEE/RSJ Int. Conf. on Intelligent Robots and Systems (IROS'01), pages 1226–1231, Wailea, Hawaii, 2001.
8. C. Cote, D. Letourneau, F. Michaud, J.-M. Valin, Y. Brousseau, C. Raievsky, M. Lemay, V. Tran: *Code Reusability Tools for Programming Mobile Robots*, Proc. of the 2004 IEEE/RSJ Int. Conf. on Intellige Robots and Systems (IROS'04), pages 1820–1825, Senda, Japan, 2004.
9. N. Karlsson, M.E. Munich, L. Goncalves, J. Ostrowski, E. Di Bernado, P. Pirjanian: *Core Tehnologies for service Robotics*, Proc. of the 2004 IEEE/RSJ Int. Conf. on Intelligent Robots and Systems (IROS'04), Senda, Japan, 2004.
10. T. Scherer: *A mobile service robot for automisation of sample taking and sample management in a biotechnological pilot laboratory*, University of Bielefeld, Ph.D Thesis, 2005, `http://bieson.ub.uni-bielefeld.de/volltexte/2005/775/`.
11. M. Weser, D. Westhoff, M. Hüser and J. Zhang: *Real-Time Fusion of Multimodal Tracking Data and Generalization of Motion Patterns for Trajectory Prediction.* Proc. of the 2006 IEEE Int. Conf. on Information Aquisition (ICIA'06), China, 2006.
12. H. Bistry, S. Phölsen, D. Westhoff, J. Zhang: *Development of a smart Laser Range Finder for an Autonomous Service Robot.* Proc. of the 2007 IEEE Int. Conf. on Integration Technology (ICIT'07), China, 2007.

Modulare Sicherheits- und Sensorsysteme für autonome mobile Roboter realisiert im Forschungsfahrzeug Marvin

Carsten Hillenbrand und Karsten Berns

Universität Kaiserslautern, AG Robotersysteme, D-67653 Kaiserslautern
{cahillen,berns}@informatik.uni-kl.de

Zusammenfassung. Fahrerlose Transportsysteme bzw. autonome mobile Roboter werden nicht nur in der Industrie, sondern vermehrt z.B. in Büros, Krankenhäusern und Museen eingesetzt um Transport-, Handlings- oder Überwachungsaufgaben zu übernehmen. Sie agieren nicht mehr in Sicherheitszellen, sondern immer stärker direkt in der menschlichen Umgebung. Somit muss es das oberste Ziel sein, durch kombinieren verschiedener Sensoren Gefahrenquellen sicher zu erkennen. In diesem Dokument wird eine Hardwarearchitektur vorgestellt, die es ermöglicht, zügig verschiedene Komponenten zusammen zu testen. Dabei wird immer eine sichere elektromechanische Abschaltung nach bisherigem Standart garantiert.

1 Einleitung

Die Automobilindustrie entwickelt kontinuierlich immer bessere Assistentssysteme um den Fahrer zu entlasten, jedoch bleibt die letzte Kontrolle beim Fahrer und diese Systeme sind noch weit davon entfernt, den Fahrer komplett zu ersetzen. Auf der anderen Seite wird in der Industrie der Herstellungsablauf mit Hilfe von Fließbändern, Robotern und Fahrerlosen Transportsystemen (FTS) immer weiter automatisiert. Am Anfang konnten die Systeme nur stupide Arbeiten erledigen und mussten vom Menschen durch Sicherheitsbereiche abgeschirmt werden. Auch gaben z.B. Fließbänder den Takt für den Arbeiter an, so dass sich der Mensch der Maschine unterordnen muss.

Dies zeigt, dass sich heutzutage und in Zukunft die Maschine immer mehr der menschlichen Umgebung anpassen und zurechtfinden muss. Sicherlich ist es schwierig für ein Assistentsystem im Auto alle Gefahrenquelle im Straßenverkehr zu erkennen und richtig einzuschätzen und es wir noch Jahrzehnte dauern bis es eine sichere Lösung gibt. Einfacher ist es hier für mobile Roboter, die in besser strukturierter Umgebung und mit geringerer Geschwindigkeit operieren. Jedoch um viele Gefahrenquelle zu vermeiden sind die unterschiedlichsten Sensoren notwendig. Wie kann man vermeiden, dass auf dem Boden stehende Hindernisse nicht umgefahren werden, eine Glastür als Hindernis erkannt wird, der Roboter nicht die Treppe herunter fährt oder mit Gegenständen kollidiert, die nicht bis auf den Boden reichen wie Tische oder von der Decke hängende Gegenstände. Es ist wichtig, dass unterschiedliche Sensoren miteinander kombiniert werden, um die verschiedenen Gefahren zu erkennen. Besonders in der Forschung stellt sich die Frage, wie Roboter mit neuen Eigenschaften schnell und einfach aufgebaut werden können. Dabei soll nicht auf eine reine Softwarelösung gebaut werden, da hier nur eine trügerische Sicherheit vorliegt. Auch ist es zu aufwändig alle Hard- und Softwarelösungen verifizieren zu lassen. In den folgenden Kapiteln wird ein Sicherheitskonzept bestehend aus einer Kombination von elektromechanischer Endabschaltung für den absoluten Notfall und einer softwaretechnischen Kollisionsvermeidung vorgestellt. Diese vereint die klassische Sicherheitstechnik mit einem Bussystem. Hiermit lassen sich Sensorkombinationen und Softwareansätze stets sicher testen.

2 Das modulare Sicherheitskonzept

Ein mobiler Roboter ist nicht nur durch eigene Energieversorgung, Rechnerarchitektur und einer Funkverbindung zu einer Zentrale charakterisiert. Auch sollte ein Sicherheitssystem existieren, welche folgende Anforderungen erfüllt:

- Notstopp des Antriebs durch mehrere Sicherheitseinrichtungen
- Keine Softwarelösung im Personalcomputer (Verifizierung unmöglich)
- Einfache und erweiterbare Verkabelung
- Erfassen des Störungsverursacher in der Software
- Bestätigung durch den Benutzer nach einem Störfall

Will man auf bestehende Teilkomponenten (Sensoren), meist von verschiedenen Herstellern, zurückgreifen, so ist der Aufbau eines Sicherheitssystems über einen sicheren Bus mit verifizierten Komponenten unmöglich. Eine gute Vermeidung dieses Problems ist es, auf die bekannte Verkabelung mit Relais zurückzugreifen.

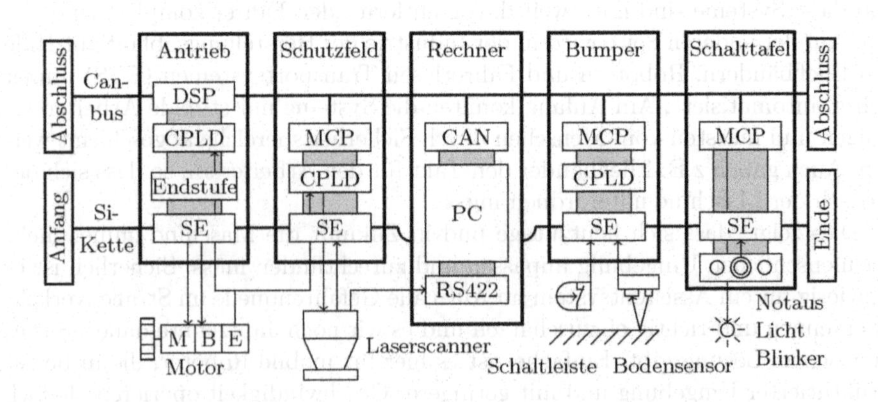

Abb. 1. Sicherheitskonzept bestehend aus Sicherheitskette kombiniert mit CanBus - Baugruppen mit Sicherheitseinrichtung (SE) sind dezentral im Roboter verteilt

Um jedoch obige Anforderung zu erfüllen ist es angebracht, ein Bus durch alle Sicherheitseinrichtungen zu legen, aufgeteilt in eine Sicherheitskette und einen

Kommunikationsbus (Abb.1). Somit kann ein Notstopp von allen Teilnehmern ausgelöst werden und die Antriebe bekommen den Zustand über diese Sicherheitskette zurück. Wer der Unterbrecher ist wird separat über einen I/O Erweiterungsbaustein (MCP 25050 von Microchip) über den CanBus übermittelt. Zum Lösen der Bremsen wurde ein Schiebemodus oder Handbetrieb integriert, der über die Schalttafel eingeschaltet werden kann. Aufgrund des modularen Aufbaus, ist das System durch beliebig viele Sicherheitseinrichtungen (egal ob Sensoren und Aktoren) erweiterbar.

3 Die Hard- und Softwarearchitektur

Die standardmäßige Hardwarearchitektur der Arbeitsgruppe besteht aus Digitalen Signalprozessoren (DSP - Freescale 56F803) in deren Speicherbereich ein Logikprogrammierbarer Baustein (CPLD - Altera EPM7256AE) eingeblendet ist. Diese Kombination ermöglicht es Funktionen des DSP's oder eigenen Implementierungen im CPLD flexibel an Stecker bzw. externen Bausteine zu legen. Der mit Hilfe dieser Architektur realisierte Antriebsregler steuert die SPI Schnittstelle eines D/A Wandlers an, der wiederum eine Endstufe bedient. Damit eine Regelung erfolgen kann, werden die Encoderwerte vom Motor in den DSP gespeist und gleichzeitig an eine Schutzfeldbaugruppe für den Scanner weitergegeben. Weiterhin kann der DSP aktiv die Sicherheitskette unterbrechen, Bremsen lösen und den Zustand der Kette abfragen. Der DSP wird über den CanBus mit dem Rechner verbunden und wird durch das Softwareframework MCA [1] angesteuert. Es ist möglich während des Betriebs Parameter im DSP zu ändern oder Debuggnachrichten vom DSP zu bekommen.

In diese vorhandene Architektur gliedern sich die einfachen Canbusknoten von Micochip ein. Mit deren Hilfe können die Zustände der einfacheren Sicherheitskomponenten abgefragt werden. Weiterhin werden Lichter und Blinker geschaltet und gedimmt bzw. der Benutzer wird über eine Lampe aufgefordert den Roboter zu aktivieren. Das Softwareframework wurde so erweitert, dass alle Canbusknoten beim Start nach deren Funktion gefragt werden, um automatisch Verknüpfungen zu höher liegenden Softwaremodulen herzustellen. Somit passt sich die Software beim Start neu integrierten Komponenten an.

4 Marvin ein autonomer Roboter fürs Gebäude

Der autonome mobile Roboter Marvin (Mobile Autonomous Robotic Vehicle for Indoor Navigation) der Arbeitsgruppe wurde als Basissystem zum Fahren im Gebäude konzipiert um Transport-, Handlings- Informations- und Überwachungsaufgaben in z.B. Büros, Museen oder Firmen zu übernehmen. Um den universell einsetzbaren Roboter an die verschiedenen Aufgaben anzupassen, können angepasste Sensoren und Aktoren ergänzt werden.

Die Mechanik gleicht über einen federlosen Kippmechanismus Bodenunebenheiten aus (Abb.2a), wobei die Antriebsräder bei unterschiedlichen Nutzlasten immer genügend Gripp haben. Eine Besonderheit sind die vorne und hinten

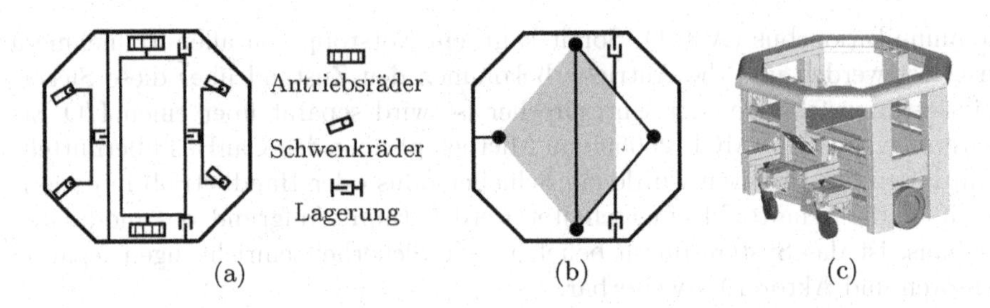

Abb. 2. (a) Kippmechanismus (b) Virtuelle Aufsetzpunkte zur Stabilitäsbetrachtung (c) Konstruktion aus Aluminiumprofilen der im Gebäude fahrenden Plattform

doppelten Schwenkräder, die über einen gelagerten Querbalken verbunden sind. Der sich ergebende Platz ist für einen in der Mitte und knapp über dem Boden liegenden Laserscanner (Laserstrahl auf einer Höhe von $12cm$) vorgesehen. Hierdurch konnte ein günstiger Differentialantrieb kombiniert mit kompakten Roboterabmaßen von $72cm$ in Breite und Länge umgesetzt werden. Für die Stabilitätsbetrachtung (Abb.2b) können die Schwenkräder durch einen virtuellen Stützpunkt ersetzt werden und es zeigt sich, dass die Stabilitätsfläche (grau im Bild) genügend groß ist. Dies hat sich auch in der Praxis bewahrheitet, da der Roboter bei einem Notstopp eher zum Rutschen als zum Kippen, nur möglich bis zu einem Anschlag, neigt. Realisiert wurde Marvin aus leichten Aluminiumprofilen (Abb.2c), die schnell zu montieren und erweiterbar sind. Der Antrieb besteht aus zwei Motoren die jeweils $59N$ auf den Boden übertragen und beschleunigt die $80kg$ Plattform auf max. $4,7\frac{km}{h}$ $(1,3\frac{m}{s})$. Hierzu liefern zwei $12V$ Blei-Batterien mit $60Ah$, die zusätzlich mit Ihrem hohen Gewicht direkt auf die Antriebsräder drücken, die notwendige Energie.

5 Sicherheitseinrichtungen

Die Verwendung eines Differentialantriebs ist zwar kostengünstig, aber aus sicherheitstechnischer Sicht problematisch. Denn die Steuerung kann abrupt die Fahrtrichtung ändern, weswegen normalerweise nur gelenkte Antriebsräder verwendet werden. Bei dem Forschungsroboter wurden deswegen die Encoder der Antriebsmotoren in der Schutzfeldbaugruppe vier Geschwindigkeitsklassen und fünf Kurvenfahrten zugeteilt und hieraus acht Schutzfelder im Laserscanner geschaltet. Sollten diese verletzt werden wird ein Notstopp ausgelöst. Bei Schleichfahrt ist der Scanner nicht mehr aktiv und ein Notstopp ist nur noch über Schaltleiste usw. möglich. Dies ermöglicht leichtere Türdurchfahrten. Für das freie Fahren wurden an dem Roboter acht IR Distanzsensoren angebracht um festzustellen ob der Boden nicht zu nah oder zu weit weg ist. Damit können Treppenstufen erkannt werden, die weder vom Laserscanner noch anderen Sensoren detektiert werden. Ein Ultraschallgürtel [3] wurde zwar nicht in die Sicherheitskette integriert (wäre aber möglich), aber wird von der Software ausgewertet um höher liegende Gegenstände, die nicht auf den Boden reichen, wie z.B. Tische, zu erkennen. Dabei sind jeweils zehn Sensoren vorne und hinten montiert. Um die Effektivität zu steigern, empfangen fünf nebeneinander liegende Sensoren gleichzeitig das reflektierte Akustiksignal, das vom mittleren Sensor ausgesandt wurde. Somit können schrägliegende Objekte und vor allem Tischkanten besser erkannt werden.

Abb. 3. (a) Sicherheitseinrichtungen (b) Hannovermesse 2007

6 Marvin in menschlichen Umfeld

Das Konzept vom AG Roboter ist zweistufig. Zum einen kann man sich auf die Notfallabschaltung, wie oben beschrieben verlassen. Zum anderen werden die Sensoren (außer Schaltleiste und Notaus) in der Software dazu genutzt Gefahren zu meiden, bevor die Notabschaltung anschlägt. Durch eine so genannte Verhaltensbasierte Steuerung [2] versucht der Roboter ständig alle Hindernisse zu umfahren. Ziel ist es, dass immer bessere Softwarealgorithmen implementiert werden, damit er sich souverän in Menschenumgebung bewegt. Dies wurde erfolgreich auf der Hannovermesse 2007 (Abb.3b) getestet. Dabei hat er ohne Aufsicht Personen mit Hilfe des Laserscanner [4] gesucht, sie angesprochen und diese konnten Informationen interaktiv über die Arbeitsgruppe abfragen.

Literaturverzeichnis

1. K.-U. Scholl, V. Kepplin, J. Albiez and R. Dillmann. *Developing Robot Prototypes with an Expandable Modular Controller Architecture.* Proc. of International Conference on Intelligent.
2. M. Proetzsch, T. Luksch and K. Berns. *The Behaviour-Based Control Architecture iB2C for Complex Robotic Systems.* KI 2007.
3. D. Schmidt *Entwicklung eines Ultraschallsensorgürtels zur Kollisionsvermeidung von mobilen Robotern.* Projektarbeit 2005 - University Kaiserslautern.
4. T. Braun, K. Szentpetery and K. Berns. *Detecting and Following Humans with a Mobile Robot.* Proc. of Conference On Industrial Imaging and Machine Vision 2005.

Towards Machine Learning of Motor Skills

Jan Peters[1,2], Stefan Schaal[2] and Bernhard Schölkopf[1]

[1] Max-Planck Institute for Biological Cybernetics, Spemannstr. 32, 72074 Tübingen
[2] University of Southern California, 3641 Watt Way, Los Angeles, CA 90802

Abstract. Autonomous robots that can adapt to novel situations has been a long standing vision of robotics, artificial intelligence, and cognitive sciences. Early approaches to this goal during the heydays of artificial intelligence research in the late 1980s, however, made it clear that an approach purely based on reasoning or human insights would not be able to model all the perceptuomotor tasks that a robot should fulfill. Instead, new hope was put in the growing wake of machine learning that promised fully adaptive control algorithms which learn both by observation and trial-and-error. However, to date, learning techniques have yet to fulfill this promise as only few methods manage to scale into the high-dimensional domains of manipulator robotics, or even the new upcoming trend of humanoid robotics, and usually scaling was only achieved in precisely pre-structured domains. In this paper, we investigate the ingredients for a general approach to motor skill learning in order to get one step closer towards human-like performance. For doing so, we study two major components for such an approach, i.e., firstly, a theoretically well-founded general approach to representing the required control structures for task representation and execution and, secondly, appropriate learning algorithms which can be applied in this setting.

1 Introduction

Despite an increasing number of motor skills exhibited by manipulator and humanoid robots, the general approach to the generation of such motor behaviors has changed little over the last decades [1,2]. The roboticist models the task as accurately as possible and uses human understanding of the required motor skills in order to create the desired robot behavior as well as to eliminate all uncertainties of the environment. In most cases, such a process boils down to recording a desired trajectory in a pre-structured environment with precisely placed objects. If inaccuracies remain, the engineer creates exceptions using human understanding of the task. While such highly engineered approaches are feasible in well-structured industrial or research environments, it is obvious that if robots should ever leave factory floors and research environments, we will need to reduce or eliminate the strong reliance on hand-crafted models of the environment and the robots exhibited to date. Instead, we need a general approach which allows us to use compliant robots designed for interaction with less structured and uncertain environments in order to reach domains outside industry. Such an approach cannot solely rely on human knowledge but instead has to be acquired and adapted from data generated both by human demonstrations of the skill as well as trial and error of the robot.

The tremendous progress in machine learning over the last decades offers us the promise of less human-driven approaches to motor skill acquisition. However, despite offering the most general way of thinking about data-driven acquisition of motor skills, generic machine learning techniques, which do not rely on an understanding of motor systems, often do not scale into the domain of manipulator or humanoid robotics due to the high domain dimensionality. Therefore, instead of attempting an unstructured, monolithic machine learning approach to motor skill aquisition, we need to develop approaches suitable for this particular domain with the inherent problems of task representation, learning and execution addressed separately in a coherent framework employing a combination of imitation, reinforcement and model learning in order to cope with the complexities involved in motor skill learning. The advantage of such a concerted approach is that it allows the separation of the main problems of motor skill acquisition, refinement and control. Instead of either having an unstructured, monolithic machine learning approach or creating hand-crafted approaches with pre-specified trajectories, we are capable of aquiring skills, represented as policies, from demonstrations and refine them using trial and error. Using learning-based approaches for control, we can achieve accurate control without needing accurate models of the complete system.

2 Foundations for Motor Skill Learning

The principal objective of this paper is to find the foundations for a general framework for representing, learning and executing motor skills for robotics. As can be observed from this question, the major goal of this paper requires three building blocks, i.e., (i) appropriate representations for movements, (ii) learning algorithms which can be applied to these representations and (iii) a transformation which allows the execution of the kinematic policies in the respective task space on robots.

2.1 Essential Components

We address the three essential components, i.e., representation, learning and execution. In this section, we briefly outline the underlying fundamental concepts.

Representation. For the representation of motor skills, we can rely on the insight that humans, while being capable of performing a large variety of complicated movements, restrict themselves to a smaller amount of primitive motions [3]. As suggested by Ijspeert et al. [4,5], such primitive movements can be represented by nonlinear dynamic systems. We can represent these in the differential constraint form given by

$$\boldsymbol{A}_{\boldsymbol{\theta}_i}(\boldsymbol{x}_i, \dot{\boldsymbol{x}}_i, t)\ddot{\boldsymbol{x}} = \boldsymbol{b}_{\boldsymbol{\theta}_i}(\boldsymbol{x}_i, \dot{\boldsymbol{x}}_i, t), \tag{1}$$

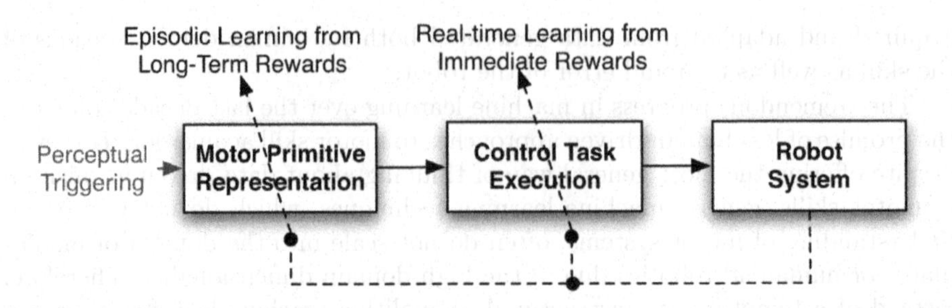

Fig. 1. This figure illustrates our general approach to motor skill learning by dividing it into motor primitive and a motor control component. For the task execution, fast policy learning methods based on observable error need to be employed while the task learning is based on slower episodic learning.

where $i \in \mathbb{N}$ is the index of the motor primitive in a library of movements, $\boldsymbol{\theta}_i \in \mathbb{R}^L$ denote the parameters of the primitive i, t denotes time and $\boldsymbol{x}_i$,$\dot{\boldsymbol{x}}_i$,$\ddot{\boldsymbol{x}}_i \in \mathbb{R}^n$ denote positions, velocities and accelerations of the dynamic system, respectively.

Learning. Learning basic motor skills[1] is achieved by adapting the parameters $\boldsymbol{\theta}_i$ of motor primitive i. The high dimensionality of our domain prohibits the exploration of the complete space of all admissible motor behaviors, rendering the application of machine learning techniques which require exhaustive exploration impossible. Instead, we have to rely on a combination of supervised and reinforcement learning in order to aquire motor skills where the supervised learning is used in order to obtain the initialization of the motor skill while reinforcement learning is used in order to improve it. Therefore, the aquisition of a novel motor task consists out of two phases,i.e., the 'learning robot' attempts to reproduce the skill acquired through supervised learning and improve the skill from experience by trial-and-error, i.e., through reinforcement learning.

Execution. The execution of motor skills adds another level of complexity. It requires that a mechanical system

$$\boldsymbol{u} = \boldsymbol{M}(\boldsymbol{q}, \dot{\boldsymbol{q}}, t)\ddot{\boldsymbol{q}} + \boldsymbol{F}(\boldsymbol{q}, \dot{\boldsymbol{q}}, t), \tag{2}$$

with a mapping $\boldsymbol{x}_i = \boldsymbol{f}_i(\boldsymbol{q}, \dot{\boldsymbol{q}}, t)$ can be forced to execute each motor primitive $\boldsymbol{A}_i\ddot{\boldsymbol{x}}_i = \boldsymbol{b}_i$ in order to fulfill the skill. The motor primitive can be viewed as a mechanical constraint acting upon the system, enforced through accurate computation of the required forces based on analytical models. However, in most cases it is very difficult to obtain accurate models of the mechanical system. Therefore it can be more suitable to find a policy learning approach which replaces the control law based on the hand-crafted rigid body model. In this paper,

[1] Learning by sequencing and parallelization of the motor primitives will be treated in future work.

we will follow this approach which forms the basis for understanding motor skill learning.

2.2 Resulting Approach

As we have outlined during the discussion of our objective and its essential components, we require an appropriate general motor skill framework which allows us to separate the desired task-space movement generation (represented by the motor primitives) from movement control in the respective actuator space. Based on the understanding of this transformation from an analytical point of view on robotics, we presente a learning framework for task execution in operational space. For doing so, we have to consider two components, i.e., we need to determine how to learn the desired behavior represented by the motor primitives as well as the execution represented by the transformation of the motor primitives into motor commands. We need to develop scalable learning algorithms which are both appropriate and efficient when used with the chosen general motor skill learning architecture. Furthermore, we require algorithms for fast immediate policy learning for movement control based on instantly observable rewards in order to enable the system to cope with real-time improvement during the execution. The learning of the task itself on the other hand requires the learning of policies which define the long-term evolution of the task, i.e., motor primitives, which are learned on a trial-by-trial basis with episodic improvement using a teacher for demonstration and reinforcement learning for self-improvement. The resulting general concept underlying this paper is illustrated in Figure 1.

2.3 Novel Learning Algorithms

As outlined before, we need two different styles of policy learning algorithms, i.e., methods for long-term reward optimization and methods for immediate improvement. Thus, we have developed two different classes of algorithms, i.e., the Natural Actor-Critic and the Reward-Weighted Regression.

Natural Actor-Critic. The Natural Actor-Critic algorithms [10,11] are the fastest policy gradient methods to date and “the current method of choice” [6]. They rely on the insight that we need to maximize the reward while keeping the loss of experience constant, i.e., we need to measure the distance between our current path distribution and the new path distribution created by the policy. This distance can be measured by the Kullback-Leibler divergence and approximated using the Fisher information metric resulting in a natural policy gradient approach. This natural policy gradient has a connection to the recently introduced compatible function approximation, which allows to obtain the Natural Actor-Critic. Interestingly, earlier Actor-Critic approaches can be derived from this new approach. In application to motor primitive learning, we can demonstrate that the Natural Actor-Critic outperforms both finite-difference gradients as well as ‘vanilla’ policy gradient methods with optimal baselines.

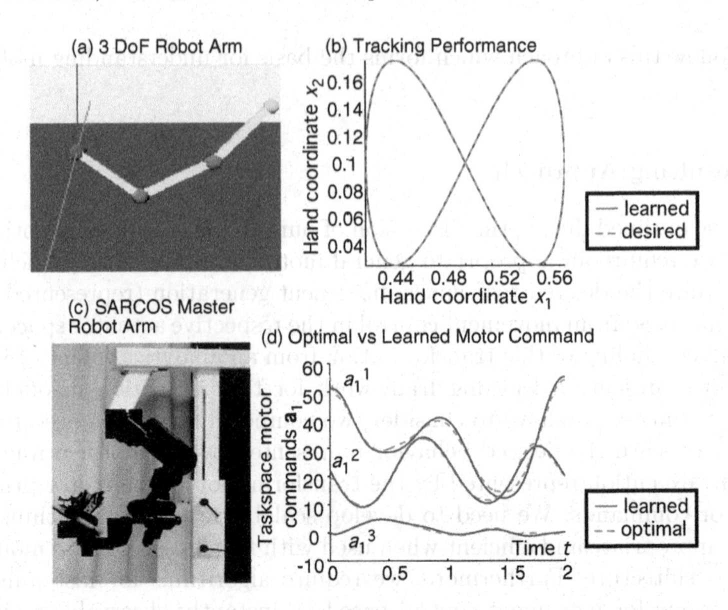

Fig. 2. Systems and results of evaluations for learning operational space control: (a) screen shot of the 3 DOF arm simulator, (c) Sarcos robot arm, used as simulated system and for actual robot evaluations in progress. (b) Tracking performance for a planar figure-8 pattern for the 3 DOF arm, and (d) comparison between the analytically obtained optimal control commands in comparison to the learned ones for one figure-8 cycle of the 3DOF arm.

Reward-Weighted Regression. In contrast to Natural Actor-Critic algorithms, the Reward-Weighted Regression algorithm [8,7,9] focuses on immediate reward improvement and employs an adaptation of the expectation maximization (EM) algorithm for reinforcement learning instead of a gradient based approach. The key difference here is that when using immediate rewards, we can learn from our actions directly, i.e., use them as training examples similar to a supervised learning problem with a higher priority for samples with a higher reward. Thus, this problem is a reward-weighted regression problem, i.e., it has a well-defined solution which can be obtained using established regression techniques. While we have given a more intuitive explanation of this algorithm, it corresponds to a properly derived maximization-maximization (MM) algorithm which maximizes a lower bound on the immediate reward similar to an EM algorithm. Our applications show that it scales to high dimensional domains and learns a good policy without any imitation of a human teacher.

3 Robot Application

The general setup presented in this paper can be applied in robotics using analytical models as well as the presented learning algorithms. The applications

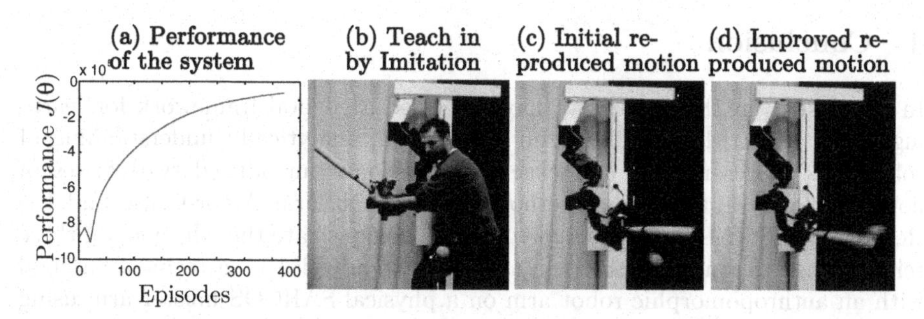

Fig. 3. This figure shows (a) the performance of a baseball swing task when using the motor primitives for learning. In (b), the learning system is initialized by imitation learning, in (c) it is initially failing at reproducing the motor behavior, and (d) after several hundred episodes exhibiting a nicely learned batting.

presented in this paper include motor primitive learning and operational space control.

3.1 Learning Operational Space Control

Operational space control is one of the most general frameworks for obtaining task-level control laws in robotics. In this paper, we present a learning framework for operational space control which is a result of a reformulation of operational space control as a general point-wise optimal control framework and our insights into immediate reward reinforcement learning. While the general learning of operational space controllers with redundant degrees of freedom is non-convex and thus global supervised learning techniques cannot be applied straightforwardly, we can gain two insights, i.e., that the problem is locally convex and that our point-wise cost function allows us to ensure global consistency among the local solutions. We show that this can yield the analytically determined optimal solution for simulated three degrees of freedom arms where we can sample the state-space sufficiently. Similarly, we can show the framework works well for simulations of the both three and seven degrees of freedom robot arms as presented in Figure 2.

3.2 Motor Primitive Improvement by Reinforcement Learning

The main application of our long-term improvement framework is the optimization of motor primitives. Here, we follow essentially the previously outlined idea of acquiring an initial solution by supervised learning and then using reinforcement learning for motor primitive improvement. For this, we demonstrate both comparisons of motor primitive learning with different policy gradient methods, i.e., finite difference methods, 'vanilla' policy gradient methods and the Natural Actor-Critic, as well as an application of the most successful method, the Natural Actor-Critic to T-Ball learning on a physical, anthropomorphic SARCOS Master Arm, see Figure 3.

4 Conclusion

In conclusion, in this paper, we have preseted a general framework for learning motor skills which is based on a thorough, analytically understanding of robot task representation and execution. We have introduced two classes of novel reinforcement learning methods, i.e., the Natural Actor-Critic and the Reward-Weighted Regression algorithm. We demonstrate the efficiency of these reinforcement learning methods in the application of learning to hit a baseball with an anthropomorphic robot arm on a physical SARCOS master arm using the Natural Actor-Critic, and in simulation for the learning of operational space with reward-weighted regression.

References

1. J.J. Craig. *Introduction to Robotics: Mechanics and Control.* Pearson Prentice Hall, Upper Saddle River, NJ, 2005.
2. L. Sciavicco and B. Siciliano. *Modeling and control of robot manipulators.* MacGraw-Hill, Heidelberg, Germany, 2007.
3. S. Schaal, A. Ijspeert, and A. Billard. Computational approaches to motor learning by imitation. In C. D. Frith and D. Wolpert, editors, *The Neuroscience of Social Interaction*, pages 199–218. Oxford University Press, Oxford, UK, 2004.
4. J. A. Ijspeert, J. Nakanishi, and S. Schaal. Movement imitation with nonlinear dynamical systems in humanoid robots. In *Proceedings of IEEE International Conference on Robotics and Automation (ICRA)*, Washinton, DC, May 11-15 2002.
5. A. Ijspeert, J. Nakanishi, and S. Schaal. Learning attractor landscapes for learning motor primitives. In S. Becker, S. Thrun, and K. Obermayer, editors, *Advances in Neural Information Processing Systems*, volume 15, pages 1547–1554, Cambridge, MA, 2003. MIT Press.
6. Douglas Aberdeen. POMDPs and policy gradients. In *Proceedings of the Machine Learning Summer School (MLSS)*, Canberra, Australia, 2006.
7. J. Peters and S. Schaal. Learning operational space control. In *Proceedings of Robotics: Science and Systems (RSS)*, Philadelphia, PA, 2006.
8. J. Peters and S. Schaal. Reinforcement learning by reward-weighted regression for operational space control. In *Proceedings of the International Conference on Machine Learning (ICML)*, 2007.
9. J. Peters and S. Schaal. Reinforcement learning for operational space. In *Proceedings of the International Conference on Robotics and Automation (ICRA)*, Rome, Italy, 2007.
10. J. Peters, S. Vijayakumar, and S. Schaal. Reinforcement learning for humanoid robotics. In *Proceedings of the IEEE-RAS International Conference on Humanoid Robots (HUMANOIDS)*, Karlsruhe, Germany, September 2003.
11. J. Peters, S. Vijayakumar, and S. Schaal. Natural actor-critic. In *Proceedings of the European Conference on Machine Learning (ECML)*, pages 280–291. springer, 2005.

Evolutionäre Algorithmen zur Topologieentwicklung von Neuronalen Netzen für die Roboter-Navigation im praktischen Einsatz

T. Köpsel, A. Noglik, J. Pauli

Universität Duisburg-Essen, Fachgebiet Intelligente Systeme

Zusammenfassung. Eine wichtige Frage in der mobilen Robotik ist die sichere Navigation in unbekannten Umgebungen unter der Anwendung preiswerter Sensorik. Solch eine Navigation kann ein künstliches Neuronales Netz (kNN) übernehmen, welches die Kopplung der Sensoren des Roboters mit dessen Antriebssystem herstellt. „Neuro Evolution of Augmenting Topologies" (NEAT) von Stanley und Miikkulainen [1] verwendet den Evolutionären Ansatz sowohl für die Topologieentwicklung, als auch für die Bestimmung der Gewichte eines kNN. NEAT hat sich als sehr gut, anpassungsfähig und relativ einfach in der Anwendung gezeigt. In diesem Beitrag wird NEAT in der Simulation angewendet, um ein kNN, das die Navigation des Roboters übernimmt, zu erhalten. Der Fokus liegt dabei auf der Erstellung der Fitnessfunktion und die Spezifikation und Durchführung einer realitätstreuen Simulation für den praktischen Einsatz. Die enge Verknüpfung von Realität und Simulationswelt hat entscheidend dazu beigetragen, dass der Umstieg aus der Simulation in die reale Welt ein Erfolg (höhere Anpassungsfähigkeit) wird. Dieser Artikel basiert auf der Diplomarbeit von T. Köpsel [2].

1 Einleitung

Die Arbeit von Thurun et al. in [3] über Probabilistische Robotik beschreibt aktuelle Ansätze zur Roboter-Eigenlokalisierung und Kartenerstellung der Umwelt basierend auf Partikel-Filter Methoden unter Verwendung von Modellen für die eingesetzten Sensoren und mobilen Roboter. Alternativ bzw. ergänzend dazu zeigt der vorliegende Beitrag wie algorithmisches evolutionäres Lernen während einer realitätsgetreuen Simulationsphase einbezogen werden kann um grobe Sensor-Motor Abbildungen offline zu erwerben. NEAT verwendet einen Evolutionären Ansatz um die Topologie sowie die Gewichte der kNN automatisch durch Evolution zu erlernen. NEAT konstruiert ein kNN, welches die Verhaltensweise von zum Beispiel mobilen Robotern repräsentiert und sucht nicht nach einer Value-Funktion. Die Suche nach kNN, die die Navigation der Roboter mit verrauschten Sensorwerten übernimmt, ist eine Reinforcement-Aufgabe. Für das gesuchte Netz gibt es keine expliziten Soll-Werte, sondern es kann die Leistung des Netzes ausgewertet werden. Es steht nur die Information zur Verfügung, wie gut das entwickelte kNN ist. Der Algorithmus ist zur Lösung von Reinforcement-Aufgaben geeignet. Der NEAT-Algorithmus ist schneller und effizienter als die Adaptive Heuristic Critic und das Q-Learning [4]. Die mit Hilfe der Evolution entstehenden Verhaltensweisen (repräsentiert jeweils durch ein kNN) sollen in der Lage sein den mobilen Roboter sicher in der Umwelt zu navigieren. In der Umwelt wurden Parcours in Form von Rundwegen aufgestellt. Der erhöhte Schwierigkeitsgrad stammt von den im Roboter verwendeten Infrarotsensoren, deren Signale nicht immer reproduzierbar und verrauscht sind.

Ein bedeutender Teil der Arbeit ist die Modellierung der realitätstreuen Simulation, um dem Roboter ein bestimmtes Verhalten beizubringen. Die realitätstreue Simulation ist entstanden durch die Anwendung der Messdaten der Sensoren in der realen Welt und die Fütterung der Robotermodelle mit diesen Daten. Diese nahe Verknüpfung der Realität und Simulationswelt hat entscheidend dazu beigetragen, dass das aus der Simulation entstandene kNN den Roboter ohne Schwierigkeiten und weitere Anpassungsschritte in der realen Welt sicher navigieren kann.

Für die Trainingsphase, die in der Simulation durchgeführt wird, werden unterschiedliche Parcours mit unterschiedlichem Schwierigkeitsgrad aufgestellt. Durch eine solche Vorgehensweise umgeht man das Problem die expliziten Ziele zu definieren, was selbst eine schwierige Aufgabe ist, und erhöht somit die Wahrscheinlichkeit, dass das kNN nach der Trainingsphase generalisierungsfähig ist.

Das Wesentliche für die Evolutionären Algorithmen ist eine richtig ausgewählte Fitnessfunktion. In der Arbeit werden drei Vorschläge für die Fitnessfunktion zur Lösung des gestellten Problems präsentiert.

2 Grundlagen von NEAT und der Fitnessfunktion

Die Hauptbestandteile eines *Evolutionären Algorithmus* (EA) sind *die Kodierung* des Individuums, die Suchoperatoren (*Crossover, Mutation und Selection*) und *die Fitnessfunktion*. Auf diese Bestandteile wird hier nur kurz im Hinblick auf das NEAT-System eingegangen. Die ausführliche Beschreibung des Systems ist in [1] dargestellt.

Bei NEAT ist jedes kNN ein Individuum. In dieser Arbeit übernimmt ein kNN die Navigation eines mobilen Roboters, der mit Infrarotsensoren ausgestattet ist. NEAT verwendet eine direkte *Kodierung*. Die Knoten und Kanten werden direkt im Genom in Form zweier Listen abgebildet. Da die Topologie, im Evolutionsprozess ebenfalls weiterentwickelt werden soll, haben beide Listen eine variable Länge. In dieser Arbeit wird das von Mat Buckland implementierte Paket Windows NEAT [5] verwendet.

2.1 Suchoperatoren für EA in Hinblick auf NEAT

Aufgrund der Eigenschaften der kNN kann der klassische *Crossover-Operator* nicht direkt übernommen werden, da das Wissen unvorhersehbar über das gesamte Netzwerk in den Knoten, Kanten und deren Gewichten verteilt ist. Für

NEAT wurde es so gelöst, dass nur ähnliche Bereiche zwischen zu kreuzenden Genomen ausgetauscht werden. Dabei behilft man sich der entwicklungshistorischen Ähnlichkeit.

Im NEAT wendet man drei verschiedenartige *Mutationen* an. Zuerst können sich durch Mutation mit einer einstellbaren Wahrscheinlichkeit die Gewichtungen der Kanten eines Individuums verändern. Zwei weitere mögliche Mutationen beeinflussen die Topologie eines vorhandenen kNN. Mit vorgegebener Wahrscheinlichkeit wird zu einem bestehenden kNN eine neue Kante zwischen zwei bestehenden Knoten addiert oder ein neuer Knoten auf einer bestehenden Verbindung eingefügt.

Relativ erfolgreiche kNN sind Grundlage für Nachkommen die von neuen kNN mit zusätzlichen Strukturen entstehen. Aber die neu eingefügten Strukturelemente besitzen die Tendenz, die Fitness zunächst negativ zu beeinflussen. NEAT verwendet deshalb einen Ansatz zum Schutz innovativer Strukturen, es werden Spezien gebildet. In einer Spezies sind ähnliche kNN zusammengefasst. Neu entstandene Individuen einer Spezies mit einer zunächst schlechteren Fitness werden durch einen Fitness-Payoff der Spezies vor dem Aussterben geschützt.

2.2 Fitnessfunktion

Das Wesentliche für EAs ist eine richtig ausgewählte *Fitnessfunktion*. Die Vergabe der Fitness muss dem gewünschten Lernziel möglichst gut entsprechen. Es wurden Versuche mit drei Varianten der Fitnessfunktion durchgeführt und untersucht.

Die Fitness-Funktion bewertet die Performance der kNN durch eine Punktvergabe in Testsituationen. Die Fitness bestimmt anschließend die Wahrscheinlichkeit für die Produktion der Nachkommen für die nächste Generation. Falls während der Episode eine Kollision stattgefunden hat, wird das Individuum gestoppt.

Der erste Vorschlag für die Fitnessfunktion wurde in [6] für ein ähnlich geartetes Teilproblem (der Autor hat nur Simulationen durchgeführt) angegeben:

$$F_{Kassahun}(t) = D(t) \cdot \exp^{-100(H(t)-H(t-1)^2)} \cdot S_{min}(t)$$

Wobei $D(t)$ die zurückgelegte Distanz in diesem Zyklus ist, $(H(t) - H(t-1))$ die Winkeldifferenz der Ausrichtung in diesem Zyklus zum letzten und $S_{min}(t)$ die minimale Sensordistanz zu einem Hindernis darstellt. So eine Fitnessfunktion begünstigt eine zügige, möglichst drehungsarme Navigation mit weitem Abstand zur Parcours-Begrenzung.

Eine andere Variante besteht darin, den Fortschritt innerhalb des Parcours zu belohnen. In Begriffen des Reinforcement Learning entspricht dies der Einsetzung von Zwischenzielen. Die am weitesten durch den Parcours in die vorgegebene Richtung gefahrenen Netze erhalten den besten Fitness-Wert. Da die Parcours jeweils einen Rundweg darstellen, liegt eine Möglichkeit darin, an den Parcours ausgehend von einem Mittelpunkt ein Winkelsystem anzulegen. Fitness-Punkte werden dann entsprechend der Winkelgeschwindigkeit vergeben, wenn der Parcours in der vorgegebenen Richtung durchfahren wird.

$$F_{AngleVelocity}(t) = \begin{cases} \left|\arccos(\frac{p_{best}^T \cdot p(t)}{||p_{best}|| \cdot ||p(t)||})\right| & : \left(\begin{pmatrix} 0 & -1 \\ 1 & 0 \end{pmatrix} \cdot p_{best}\right)^T \cdot p(t)\lambda \geq 0 \\ 0 & : \text{sonst} \end{cases}$$

Wobei p_{best} einen Vektor von den Zentrumskoordinaten bis zur besten bisher erreichten Position darstellt. $p(t)$ stellt einen Vektor vom Zentrum zur aktuellen Roboter-Position dar. Wenn die Bewegungsrichtung im Uhrzeigensinn angegeben wird, dann gilt $\lambda = 1$, sonst $\lambda = -1$.

Die dritte Möglichkeit für die Erstellung der Fitnessfunktion ist eine Kombination der ersten beiden Varianten:

$$F_{neu} = \alpha \cdot F_{Kassahun}(t) + \beta \cdot F_{AngleVelocity}(t), \text{ wobei } \alpha + \beta = 1;$$

Die $F_{Kassahun}(t)$-Funktion ist für eine sichere Fahrt verantwortlich. Die $F_{AngleVelocity}(t)$ -Funktion ist für eine schnelle Fahrt verantwortlich. α und β besagen wie ausgeprägt uns die beiden Eigenschaften interessieren.

3 Simulation

In der Simulation werden Parcours und Roboter in allen relevanten Eigenschaften nachgebildet. Die Evolutionäre Entwicklung findet nur in der Simulation statt.

3.1 Parcours in der Simulation

Ein Parcours wird durch eine Menge von Streckenabschnitten repräsentiert. Eine dieser Strecken entspricht einer Parcours-Wand der realen Umgebung. Zusätzlich zu diesem einfachen Modell besitzt ein Parcours einen Startpunkt und die Startausrichtung für den Roboter.

Jeder Parcours kann mit einer individuellen Fitness-Gewichtung ausgestattet werden. So ist es möglich, die erfolgreiche Bewältigung besonders komplexer Problemstellungen stärker zu belohnen als die leichterer Problemstellungen. Um eine Überanpassung an einen Parcours zu vermeiden, werden mehrere Parcours mit teilweise unterschiedlichen Zielsetzungen verwendet.

3.2 Roboter

Ein Individuum in der Population ist ein kNN, die Performance des kNN ist dann das Navigationsverhalten eines Roboters. Der Roboter ist ein Scorpion Roboter von der Firma Evolution und besitzt 13 Infrarotsensoren, 11 davon werden für das Navigationsproblem angewendet. Jeder Roboter besitzt für die Simulation ein eigenes Koordinatensystem für seine Sensorpositionen und die Position der eigenen Bounding-Box, die zur Kollisionserkennung mit der Parcours-Begrenzung verwendet wird. Die Kollisionserkennung erfolgt mittels einer Schnittpunktermittlung der Kanten der Bounding-Box mit allen Begrenzungen des Parcours.

Distanz	1	2	3	4	5	6	7	8	9	10
10	11,6	11,6	11,3	11,8	11,6	11,7	11,7	11,6	11,4	11,3
15	19,2	19,2	14,6	15,0	18,9	14,7	14,8	14,8	14,8	14,9
20	24,9	24,9	28,9	22,1	23,0	26,8	22,7	22,5	22,7	22,8
25	26,3	28,9	28,9	26,8	27,3	28,9	28,9	27,9	28,9	29,5
30	35,9	35,9	36,8	36,8	34,5	35,0	35,9	36,8	35,0	35,0
35	42,9	42,9	42,9	43,6	42,2	42,9	42,9	40,3	42,9	44,2
40	61,0	56,8	56,8	48,0	50,3	60,0	48,0	44,8	53,5	56,8
45	40,3	40,3	60,0		41,6		41,0	41,0	65,5	65,5
50					53,5		61,0	42,3		48,0
55				60,0			44,8			39,4
60	50,3	50,3		44,8				63,2		
65					48,0			42,3		
70		37,7							50,3	
75								64,3		
80										

Abb. 1. Ausschnitt aus der Referenztabelle

3.3 Verbindung der simulierten und realen Welten

Wie die Vorversuche gezeigt haben, sind die Sensorwerte, die geliefert werden, sehr verrauscht und nicht immer reproduzierbar. Um die Simulation so nah wie möglich an die Realität zu bringen, werden die Distanzen einer probabilistischen Verteilung der tatsächlich gemessenen Sensorwerte ermittelt. Diese werden in der Simulation zur Berechnung simulierter Werte aller real möglichen Distanzmessungen herangezogen.

Hierzu wurden im Vorfeld Messungen durchgeführt und die Ergebnisse gesichert. Die Messungen erfolgten separat für alle Infrarotsensoren im spezifizierten Messbereich der Infrarotsensoren von 10 cm bis 80 cm jeweils im Abstand von 5 cm (Diskretisierung). Um eine ausreichend gute Verteilung zu erhalten, wurden für jeden Sensor pro gemessener Entfernung 1000 Sensorwerte ermittelt und gespeichert[1].

Die Erstellung der stetigen probabilistischen Verteilung erfolgt in zwei Schritten. Zuerst wird ermittelt, ob für die in der Simulation ideal gemessenen Entfernung ein gültiger Sensorwert ermittelt werden muss[2].

Im nächsten Schritt wird zu der simulierten Entfernung eine gemessene Entfernung berechnet. Da die Diskretisierung relativ zu den zu erwartenden Messdaten ausreichend fein ist, kann die Ausfallwahrscheinlichkeit zwischen jeweils zwei aufgezeichneten Entfernungen linear interpoliert werden. Die Ausfallwahrscheinlichkeit P einer simulierten Entfernung d für den Sensor s berechnet sich wie folgt:

$$P(d,s) = \frac{P_r(i_{low},s)(i_{up} - d) + P_r(i_{up},s)(d - i_{low})}{5} \tag{1}$$

wobei gilt $i_{up}(d) = 5(\lfloor d/5 \rfloor + 1) : d \in [10, 80]$ und $i_{low}(d) = 5\lfloor d/5 \rfloor : d \in [10, 80]$. $P_r(i,s) \in [0,1]$ gibt den Ausfallanteil an der gesamten Messung für den Sensor

[1] Ein Auszug der Referenztabelle ist in Abbildung 1 dargestellt

[2] Die Infrarotsensoren liefern evtl. keinen gültigen Wert, die Wahrscheinlichkeit hierfür steigt mit wachsender Entfernung zum Objekt

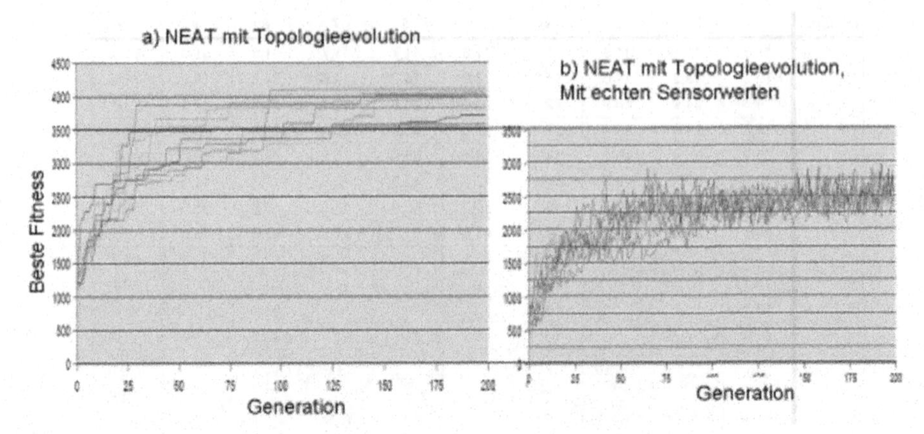

Abb. 2. Entwicklung der Fitness in der Simulation

s und die Entfernung i laut Referenztabelle an (siehe auch Abb. 1). Aufgrund der erstellten Referenztabellen wurde die Winkelabhängigkeit der Sensorwerte mitberücksichtigt.

Die erstellte probabilistische Verteilung bildet die Grundlage für die Input-Werte der kNN in der Simulation.

4 Ergebnisse

Es wurden mehrere Versuchsreihen durchgeführt um die aus den NEAT-Verfahren erhaltene autonome Steuerung des mobilen Roboters in einer unpräparierten Umgebung zu untersuchen. Dabei haben sich die entstandenen kNN als generalisierungsfähig und ausfallsicher gezeigt. Die Parcours, die in der Simulation modelliert wurden und die in der realen Welt verwendet werden sind sehr unterschiedlich. Dabei wurde die Mächtigkeit und Generalisierbarkeit der mit NEAT erzeugten Neuronalen Netze außerhalb der Simulationsumgebung bestätigt.

Für die Validierung des Lernerfolges in der Simulation wurden praktische Versuche am Roboter durchgeführt. Hierfür wurden verschieden trainierte Netze erzeugt und deren Lernerfolg in der Simulation mit deren Performance in der realen Versuchsanordnung verglichen. Für jede Versuchsreihe wurden jeweils zehn Simulationen durchgeführt. Anschließend wurden einige so trainierte kNN exemplarisch am mobilen Roboter evaluiert.

Die Versuchsreihen zeigten den Einfluss der Modellierung der Sensoren in der Simulation. Hierfür wurden Netze unter Verwendung von idealen Sensoren, einfach verrauschten Sensoren und verrauschten Sensoren mit Berücksichtigung der Winkelabhängigkeit der Infrarotrückstrahlung trainiert. In der Abb. 2 kann man beobachten, dass die Fitness nach der Evolution in der Simulation besser ist als für das mit *„realen“ Sensoren* trainierte Netz. Die Kurven sind nicht so zickzack-förmig und entwickeln sich für Evolutionäre Algorithmen gewöhnlich.

Aber wie man in Videos beobachten kann, haben sich die mit *„idealen" Sensoren* trainierten Netze als nicht so anpassungsfähig erwiesen (in manchen Situationen steuert das so trainierte Netz den Roboter gegen die Wand, siehe Video 1 [7]).

Weiterhin wurde der Einfluss der gewählten Fitness-Funktionen auf die Fitness-Entwicklung der Simulation und das praktische Fahrverhalten des Roboters untersucht. Hierzu werden drei unterschiedliche Ansätze verwendet und miteinander verglichen.

In einer weiteren Versuchsreihe zeigt sich der Einfluss der gewählten Parcours auf die Evolution, sowie die damit verbundene Gefahr einer Überanpassung an bestimmte Mengen von Parcours. Es werden zusätzliche Fitness-Werte von Parcours ermittelt, auf denen nicht trainiert wird. So lässt sich die Performance-Entwicklung von trainierten und nicht trainierten Parcours gegenüberstellen. Weitere Ergebnisse können in [2] nachgeschlagen werden.

5 Ausblick

Die enge Verknüpfung der Realität und Simulationswelt hat sich als ein mächtiger Mechanismus erwiesen. Der Übergang von der Simulation in die Realität mit dem oben genannten Mechanismus war überraschend problemlos. Ohne weitere Adaptionsschritte haben die evaluierten Netze in der Realität sehr gute Ergebnisse gezeigt. Die Navigation der Roboter war sicher und kollisionsfrei.

Ein interessantes Ergebnis ist auch, dass die minimalverbundenen Netze für das gestellte Navigationsproblem nicht schlechtere, in einigen Fällen sogar bessere, Ergebnisse liefern als Netze mit einer komplizierten Topologie. Die Erklärung dazu wurde aus dem Verhalten des Roboters ersichtlich, der gemerkt hat: Wenn ich die Wand entlang fahre, dann bekomme ich eine gute Fitness. Solch ein Verhaltensmodell benötigt tatsächlich weder ein Gedächtnis (rückgekoppelte Verbindungen) noch eine komplizierte Nichtlinearität durch verdeckte Schichten.

In weiterführenden Arbeiten werden Strategien für das algorithmische Nachlernen des neuronalen Netzes für komplexere Einsatzszenen im Online-Betrieb ermittelt.

Literaturverzeichnis

1. K. O. Stanley, R. Miikkulainen. Evolving Neural Networks through augmenting Topoplogies. Evolutionary Computation, 2002
2. T. Köpsel. Diplomarbeit: Evolutionäre Algorithmen zur Topologieentwicklung von Neuronalen Netzen für die Roboter-Navigation im praktischen Einsatz. Lehrstuhl für Intelligente Systeme, Universität Duisburg-Essen, 2007
3. S. Thrun, W. Burgard, D. Fox: Probabilistic Robotics. MIT Press, Cambridge, MA, 2005.
4. R. Sutton, A. Barto: Reinforcement Lernen, MIT Pries, Cambridge, MA, 1998.
5. M. Buckland: http://www.ai-junkie.com/ai-junkie.html.
6. Y. Kassahun. Evolution of Neural Networks through Incremental Acquisition of Neural Structures. Report 0508, 2005
7. Promotionsprojekt, http://www.uni-due.de/is/projekt_ emrobnav.php, 2007

Dynamische Satzgenerierung und Sprachausgabe für einen mobilen Serviceroboter

Christopher Parlitz, Bernd Amann und Martin Hägele

Fraunhofer IPA, Institut für Produktionstechnik und Automatisierung,
Nobelstraße 12, 70569 Stuttgart

Zusammenfassung. Die vorliegende Arbeit befasst sich mit der Entwicklung einer Sprachausgabe für ein mobiles Robotersystem. Dazu wurde zum einen ein auf die Anwendung zugeschittenes Text-To-Speech Verfahren und zum anderen eine Grammatik, die eine dynamische Satzgenerierung ermöglicht, implementiert. Die Verfahren arbeiten unabhängig voneinander und können daher auch gegen andere Komponenten ausgetauscht werden. Die Programme wurden als Client-Server Applikationen programmiert, um möglichst flexibel die Sprachausgabe einsetzen zu können.

1 Einleitung

Obwohl Sprache nur ein kleiner Teil der menschlichen Interaktion ist, wird eine zuverlässige und qualitativ hochwertige Sprachein- und -ausgabe bei einem Serviceroboter mit fortschreitender Entwicklung immer interessanter. Die natürlichsprachliche Kommunikation hat einige Vorteile. Zuerst einmal ist kein besonderes Training (des Benutzers) nötig, wie das beispielsweise bei einer Tastatur mit Bildschirm nötig wäre. Außerdem hat der Benutzer Augen und Hände frei und ist nicht an einen Ort gebunden.

Das Projekt wurde in zwei Teile aufgeteilt. Zuerst wurde eine Sprachausgabe entwickelt, anschließend ein Modul zur Satzgenerierung. Beide Module haben dokumentierte Schnittstellen und sind somit mit geringem Aufwand in eine Systemarchitektur integrierbar.

2 Sprachausgabe

In diesem Teil der Arbeit wurde eine Sprachausgabe für einen mobilen Serviceroboter entwickelt. Für die eigentliche „Text-to-Speech"-Synthese wurde ein „Unit selection"-Verfahren unter Verwendung des Sprachsynthesepakets Festival [1] genutzt. Ein „Text-to-Speech"-System (kurz: TTS) wird oft auch als Vorleseautomat bezeichnet. Die Eingabe ist eine Äußerung im Klartext, die (gesprochene) Ausgabe kann über Lautsprecher oder direkt in eine Audiodatei (z. B. *.wav) erfolgen. Das bei diesem Projekt verwendete Sprachsyntheseverfahren gehört zur Gruppe der konkatenativen Verfahren.

2.1 „Unit selection“

Die Idee der konkatenativen Synthese ist, aufgenommene natürlichsprachliche Äußerungen miteinander zu verketten und so zu einer natürlich klingenden Sprachausgabe zu kommen. Eines der wichtigsten Problemstellungen bei dieser Methode ist das Finden der sinnvollsten Einheitenlänge. Man muss in der Regel zwischen längeren und kürzeren Einheiten abwägen. Längere Einheiten erfordern wesentlich mehr Speicher und eine höhere Anzahl von Einheiten, haben dafür aber weniger Verkettungsstellen und eine natürlicher klingende Ausgabequalität. Kürzere Einheiten benötigen weniger Speicher, der Aufwand bei der Erzeugung der Stimme (Alignierung) ist allerdings höher.

Die meisten konkatenativen Synthesemethoden nutzen akustische Einheiten mit einer festen Länge (z. B. Diphone). Im Unterschied dazu hat die „Unit selection“-Synthese einen anderen Ansatz: die Länge der Einheiten ist variabel von einem Phonem bis hin zu einem ganzen Satz, was diese Methode sehr flexibel macht und die Qualität der Sprachausgabe in einem begrenzten Korpus erhöht. Im Durchschnitt ist die Einheitenlänge bei der „Unit selection“ höher als die Länge von Diphonen oder Halbsilben (nach [2]). Der Auswahlalgorithmus findet bei einer begrenzten Domäne meistens sogar ganze Wörter als Einheiten, was die Anzahl der Verkettungsstellen gering hält und gut für die Sprachqualität ist. Im idealen Fall wird die gesamte Äußerung als Einheit gefunden und die Sprachausgabe spielt diese lediglich ab.

Allerdings muss wie bei grundsätzlich jeder konkatenativen Synthesemethode der Sprachkorpus zuerst erzeugt werden, damit eine individuelle Stimme entsteht und auch der Korpus die zu sprechenden Sätze gut abbildet.

2.2 Algorithmen

Das in Festival [1] verwendete „Unit selection“-Verfahren wurde von Alan W. Black und Paul Taylor 1997 erstmals publiziert [3]. Es verbindet das Verfahren der kontextuellen Klassifikation (Cluster-Algorithmus, z. B. [4]) mit dem Einheiten-Auswahlverfahren nach Hunt und Black [5].

Bei der kontextuellen Klassifikation wird eine Menge von Merkmalen in Äquivalenzklassen (Cluster) eingeteilt. Die Einteilung erfolgt mit Hilfe von binären Entscheidungsbäumen. Die Knoten von Entscheidungsbäumen stellen kontextuelle Fragen dar, anhand derer die Klassifikation erfolgt. Das gesamte Klassifikationsverfahren wird im Voraus durchgeführt, dadurch muss während der Synthese nur noch die strukturierte Datenbank durchsucht werden, was erheblich Rechenzeit einspart. Um den Abstand zwischen Einheiten des gleichen Phonemtyps zu ermitteln, wird ein akustisches Distanzmaß verwendet. Realisiert wird das durch verschiedene akustische Vektoren. Mit dem akustischen Distanzmaß werden Mengen (Cluster) von Einheiten so erzeugt, dass die akustische Distanz („impurity“) der Einheiten innerhalb eines Clusters minimal ist.

Das Einheiten-Auswahlverfahren verwendet zwei Arten von Kosten, um die bestmöglichen Einheiten auszuwählen. Die Zielkosten und die Konkatenationskosten sollten beide jeweils minimiert werden. Je geringer die Zielkosten, desto besser passt eine Einheit aus der Datenbank auf das Anforderungsprofil. Wie gut sich aufeinanderfolgende Einheiten der Datenbank an der Konkatenationsstelle zusammenfügen lassen, wird durch die Konkatenationskosten dargestellt. Je höher die Kosten, desto schwieriger ist die Anpassung der Einheiten an der Verkettungsstelle. Da die zur Verfügung stehenden Einheiten meist nur geringe Unterschiede in den Eigenschaften aufweisen, werden die Konkatenationskosten durch einen Gewichtungsfaktor etwas höher gewichtet.

2.3 Umsetzung

Nach einer Analyse der Einsatzszenarien des Serviceroboters „Care-O-bot 3“ wurde der Sprachkorpus von einem professionellen Sprecher erzeugt. Bei der Definition des Korpus wurde darauf geachtet, dass alle 48 Phoneme des Deutschen enthalten sind. Damit können, obwohl der Korpus nur eine begrenzte Domäne abdeckt und lediglich 379 verschiedene, vom Roboter häufig gebrauchte Wörter umfasst, auch unbekannte Wörter synthetisiert werden.

Um zur einsetzbaren Stimme zu gelangen, wurden die Sprachdaten einer qualitativen Kontrolle unterzogen und danach aligniert. Mit Hilfe eines Aligners wurden die Audiodateien grob in drei Spuren aufgeteilt (Phonem, Silbe, Wort). Eine aufwändige manuelle Überprüfung ist auf Grund der mangelnden Genauigkeit und Fehlerfreiheit im Anschluss nötig.

Wenn die Sätze nur von Wörtern, die im Korpus enthalten sind, erzeugt werden, ist die Sprachqualität sehr hoch. Es treten gelegentliche minimale Schwankungen der Sprechgeschwindigkeit und kleinere Probleme mit der Prosodie (z. B. bei Fragesätzen) auf. Aufgrund des kleinen Sprachkorpus und der konkatenativen Synthesemethode sind Probleme dieser Art nicht völlig zu verhindern.

Die Qualität der Synthese fällt bei unbekannten Wörtern teilweise deutlich ab, das ist systembedingt und wäre nur durch ein wesentlich größeres Phoneminventar kompensierbar. Die Synthese eines durchschnittlichen Satzes von ca. 10 Wörtern benötigt auf aktuellen Computersystemen weniger als eine Sekunde Rechenzeit. Somit ist die Sprachausgabe schnell genug für einen natürlichen Dialog.

Die tatsächliche Realisation der Sprachausgabe findet innerhalb der Care-O-bot 3-Architektur mittels eines Client/Server-Prinzips statt. Dazu wird Festival [1] durch eine (in C++ geschriebene) Serveranwendung gestartet. Der Client, der via Sockets mit dem Server kommuniziert, ist in Python implementiert worden. Der Client kann Text, aber auch Steuerbefehle an den Server senden und ist somit flexibel einsetzbar.

3 Satzgenerierung

Da die gesprochenen Sätze des Roboters situationsabhängig sind, wurde ein Modul zur dynamischen Satzgenerierung entwickelt. Die in Python geschriebene Klasse lädt zuerst ein separates Lexikon, um dann entweder bei der Generierung von Sätzen zu helfen oder automatisch zufällige Sätze zu erzeugen.

Das Programm gibt immer einen String zurück, im Erfolgsfall enthält der String die Äußerung (den Satz), im Fehlerfall ist der String leer. Eine genauere Beschreibung des Fehlers kann dann mit der Methode „getError()“ ermittelt werden, die einen String zurückgibt.

3.1 „sentence()“-Methode

Diese Methode erzeugt aus einer Satzvorlage und übergebenen Variablen einen korrekt flektierten Satz. Beim Aufruf muss als erster Parameter ein String (die Satzvorlage) übergeben werden, die weiteren (optionalen) Parameter enthalten die Variablen. Diese enthalten die Grundformen der Wörter.

Anhand von Beispielen wird die Funktionsweise deutlicher (Ein- und Ausgabe in der Python-Kommandozeile):

```
sentence("Ich _pred011 in _obj01sa!",_pred011="fahren",
 _obj01sa="Zimmer gelb")

>>> 'Ich fahre in das gelbe Zimmer!'

sentence("_subj01p _pred014 auf _obj01ud.",_subj01p="Tasse",
 _pred014="stehen",_obj01ud="Tisch schwer")

>>> 'Die Tassen stehen auf einem schweren Tisch.'

sentence("Auf _obj01sd _pred014 _subj01o.",_subj01o="Flasche",
 _pred014="sein",_obj01sd="Regal")

>>> 'Auf dem Regal sind noch Flaschen.'
```

Um die Strings zu erzeugen wird folgendermaßen vorgegangen:

Zuerst wird der erste Parameter (die Satzvorlage) in einzelne Worte aufgesplittet und es werden etwaige Sonderzeichen (Kommas, Punkte, ...) entfernt. Die Variablennamen werden geparst (s. u.) und anschließend die jeweiligen Werte der Variablen mit Hilfe des am Anfang geladenen Lexikons flektiert und erweitert (z. B. Artikel hinzufügen). Dann werden die Variablennamen durch die soeben erzeugten Strings ersetzt und der fertige Satz zurückgegeben. Sollte ein Fehler aufgetreten sein, so ist ein leerer String der Rückgabewert.

3.2 Syntax

Die Variablen beginnen immer mit einem Unterstrich („_“) und müssen eindeutig sein. Die Reihenfolge der Variablen in der Satzvorlage und in der Parameterliste kann beliebig sein. Es gibt drei Variablentypen: „pred“ (Verben), „subj“ (Subjekte) und „obj“ (Objekte). Zur besseren Unterscheidung wurden die Nomen in Subjekte und Objekte aufgeteilt, die Adjektive sind nicht separat berücksichtigt worden, sondern werden dem Objekt angefügt. Die Syntax der Variablen ist wie folgt:

Auf den bereits erwähnten Unterstrich („_") folgt der Variablentyp (z. B. „pred"). Danach wird eine zweistellige ID eingefügt, die nur der eindeutigen Identifikation der Variablen dient. Anschließend folgt je nach Variablentyp (siehe folgende Tabelle) Numerus und/oder Kasus oder Person. Diese Schreibweise ist sehr kompakt und einfach zu parsen.

Im obigen Beispiel ist die erste Variable vom Typ „pred" mit der ID „01", das Verb ist 1. Person singular, also „1". Die zweite Variable ist ein Objekt (mit der ID „01"), welches im Singular („s") verwendet wird und im Akkusativ („a") steht. Eine tabellarische Übersicht aller möglichen Kombinationen:

Art	Typ (+ID)	Person	Numerus	Kasus
Verb	_pred(ID)	1, 2, 3, 4	-	-
Nomen	_subj(ID)	-	s, p, o, u	-
Nomen	_obj(ID)	-	s, p, o, u	a, d

Legende:	Person:	**1, 2, 3**	1., 2. und 3. Person singular
		4	Plural
	Numerus:	**s**	Singular
		p	Plural
		o	ohne Artikel
		u	unbestimmter Artikel
	Kasus:	**a**	Akkusativ
		d	Dativ

Aus der Tabelle erkennt man, dass die Syntax nicht ausreicht, um alle grammtatikalischen Möglichkteiten auszuschöpfen, was auch nicht der Anspruch war. Um ein möglichst einfaches System zu bekommen, wurde zum einen vereinfacht (z.B. Reduktion auf vier Personentypen), zum anderen wurde manches nicht für diese Anwendung benötigt (z.B. Genitiv) oder lässt durch andere Formulierungen ersetzen, die das Gleiche aussagen.

3.3 „rand_sentence()"-Methode

Mit Hilfe der obigen Methode lässt sich auch eine zufällige Generierung von grammatikalisch korrekten Sätzen implementieren. Die implementierte Methode „rand_sentence()" wird ohne Parameter aufgerufen und erzeugt aus intern abgespeicherten Satzvorlagen („templates") und den Wörtern des Lexikons einen Zufallssatz. Dazu wird zunächst eine Satzvorlage (ähnlich wie bei den obigen Beispielen) per Zufallszahl ausgewählt. Dann werden je nach Anzahl der Variablen weitere Zufallszahlen erzeugt, die als Arrayindex bei dem geladenen Lexikon dienen und je nach Variable somit ein Verb, Nomen oder Adjektiv heraussuchen. Mit diesen Informationen wird dann die Methode „sentence()" aufgerufen und der Satz(string) zurückgegeben. Diese Methode wird hauptsächlich für Tests und Demonstrationen verwendet.

4 Ausblick

Da bei der Robotersteuerung sehr allgemein Zustände (stehen, fahren) und Objekte (Schrank, Glas) verwendet werden, ist dieses Modul eine zentrale Schnittstelle, um eine abstrakte Repräsentation in einen natürlichsprachlichen Satz umzuwandeln. Das Lexikon enthält den gesamten Korpus des Serviceroboters Care-O-bot 3.

Bisher wurde das System nur in Simulationen getestet. Der Roboter, für den das Sprachsystem entworfen wurde, befindet sich gerade im Aufbau. Bisherige Erfahrungen haben aber gezeigt, dass eine Sprachausgabe an Servicerobotersystemen die Akzeptanz deutlich steigert. Für die Spracheingabe wird ein kommerzielles Produkt eingesetzt. Um den Einfluss von Umgebungsgeräuschen etc. zu minimieren, wird ein Headset verwendet.

Literaturverzeichnis

1. The Festival Speech Synthesis System (University of Edinburgh, CSTR), http://www.cstr.ed.ac.uk/projects/festival/ (Retr. Jun 2006)
2. Bernd Möbius. Sprachsynthesesysteme. In: Kai-Uwe Carstensen et al. (editors), Computerlinguistik und Sprachtechnologie: Eine Einführung, Spektrum, (Heidelberg, Germany), 2001.
3. Alan W. Black and Paul Taylor. Automatically clustering similar units for unit selection in speech synthesis. In: Proceedings of the European Conference on Speech Communication and Technology (Rhodos, Greece), volume 2, pages 601–604, 1997.
4. W. J. Wang et al. Tree-based unit selection for english speech synthesis. In: Proceedings of the International Conference on Acoustics, Speech, and Signal Processing (ICASSP)-93, (Minneapolis, MN, USA), volume 2, pages 191–194, 1993.
5. Andrew J. Hunt and Alan W. Black. Unit selection in a concatenative speech synthesis system using a large speech database. In: Proceedings of the International Conference on Acoustics, Speech, and Signal Processing (ICASSP)-96, (Munich, Germany) volume 1, pages 373–376, 1996.

Schlüsselkomponenten für Roboter in der Produktion

Roboterhaut und Sicherheitskonzept für die Mensch–Roboter Kooperation

B. Denkena, P. Hesse, J. Friederichs, A. Wedler

Institut für Fertigungstechnik und Werkzeugmaschinen (IFW),
Leibniz Universität Hannover, An der Universität 2, 30823 Garbsen
{denkena, hesse, friederichs, wedler}@ifw.uni-hannover.de, www.koSePro.de

Zusammenfassung. Vorgestellt wird der Aufbau einer aktiven Sensor-Matrix zur Abstands- und Kontaktdetektion in der Robotik. Diese besteht aus einem Sensornetzwerk zur Fusion und Überlagerung differenter physikalischer Wirkprinzipien. Die Sicherheit der I^2C-Bus Kommunikation, der Aufbau der Roboterhaut, Ergebnisse der Abstandsdetektion mit Infrarot-, und Ultraschallsensorik werden dargestellt. Ferner wurden Temperatur-, und Beschleunigungssensoren auf die Oberfläche der Roboterhaut aufgebracht um Informationen über die Umgebung sicher an ein übergeordnetes Leitsystem zu übertragen. Eine unterlagerte sichere Roboterhaut mit Kontaktdetektion zeigt als einfache Schlüsselkomponente ein analoges Ausschaltverhalten für geringe Latenzzeiten. Als Schluss wird auf den Einsatz an einem Industrieroboter in der Produktion ohne trennende Schutzeinrichtungen (OTS) eingegangen.

1 Einleitung

Die Forderungen nach standardisierten Architekturen in der Robotik [1], Verbesserung bestehender Strukturen bei gleichzeitiger Zielerfüllung, (z.B. Einfachheit in der Produktion als Nutzen für Komponentenhersteller) ergeben die Zielgröße effizienter Software- und Rechnerarchitekturen. Insbesondere gilt dies für die Schlüsselkomponenten, die universell an verschiedene Robotertypen angeschlossen werden. Ein Teil dieser sicheren Schlüsselkomponenten werden inhaltlich durch die Forschungstätigkeiten im BMBF Projekt koSePro der Leitinnovation Servicerobotik abgebildet. Dies gilt insbesondere für eine sichere Roboterhaut und die Mensch–Roboter Interaktion.

2 Roboterhaut für Industrieroboter

Die Roboterhaut wird um den Roboter als Freiformgeometrie um Kollisionen mit Menschen oder Gegenständen zu erkennen und bei Kollision ein sicheres Signals zu übertragen. Die Ausführung dieser Matte kann durch verschiedene physikalische Prinzipien erreicht und als passive oder aktive Struktur abgebildet werden [2]. Die hier dargestellte Haut wird durch einen schichtartigen Aufbau von unterschiedlichen Polymeren erstellt, welche einen möglichst großen Biegeradius erlauben und die Restenergie bei einer Kollision aufnehmen. Diese Grundfunktion kann erweitert werden, wobei besonders Oberfächensensorik mit abstandsbasierenden Verfahren zu nennen sind.

3 Anforderungen und Bildung einer Sensormatrix auf I²C- Basis

Ein besonderer Fokus liegt auf der Bildung einer Sensormatix durch Verschaltung und Fusion unterschiedlicher Sensorik zu einem Netzwerk, welches bei einem Roboter den Abstand erkennt und gleichzeitig die Position des Sensors geometrisch auf der Roboterkinematik festgelegt. Hierbei gilt es, auf bestehende Bus-Systeme wie dem verwendeten I²C- Bus zurückzugreifen, welcher wegen seiner Einfachheit sich für eine unzählige Anzahl von Sensoren nutzten lässt. Ferner gilt es insbesondere, die Fehlersicherheit des I²C- Bus zu verbessern um diesen für sicherheitsrelevante Applikationen nutzen zu können. Da hardwareseitige Prüfmöglichkeiten komplett fehlen, müssen diese mit anderen Mitteln nachträglich geschaffen werden. Möglich ist Überschneidung der Messbereiche mehrerer Sensoren, um so eine Kontrollmöglichkeit zu haben

4 Erweiterung einer taktilen Haut mit einem Sensornetzwerk

Ziel ist es, durch die Vernetzung von mehreren differenten Sensortypen eine genauere Objekterkennung und Positionsbestimmung zu erreichen und die physikalischen Messbereiche unterschiedlicher Sensoren miteinander zu kombinieren. Vorgestellt wird eine Kombination aus taktiler Roboterhaut, Infrarot- und Ultraschallsensoren, Temperatur-, und Beschleunigungssensorik sowie eine Erweiterung mit analogen Signalgebern wie in Abbildung 1 aufgezeigt wird. Das Netzwerk besteht aus einem Mikrokontroller als I²C- Master und fünf Ultraschallsensoren für den Fernbereich und vier Infrarotsensoren für den Nahbereich der Roboterhaut. Ebenso werden im Annäherungsbereich die Temperatur und die Beschleunigung bestimmt.

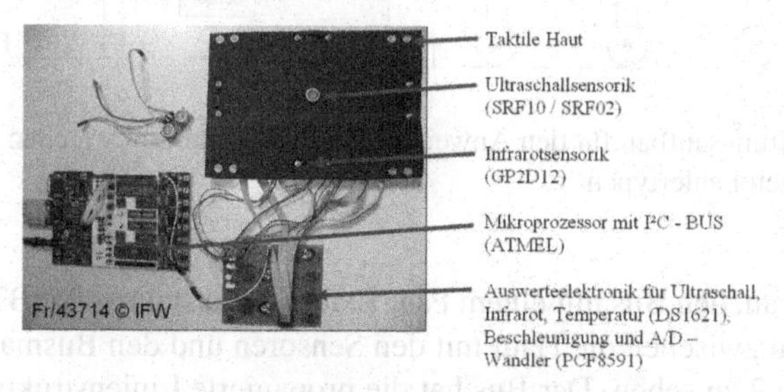

Abb. 1. Prototyp einer Abstandsdetektierenden Roboterhaut

5 Möglichkeiten zur softwareseitigen Absicherung des I²C- BUS

5.1 Erkennung und Maßnahmen bei dem Auftreten von Fehlern

Im Folgenden werden einige Überlegungen aufgezeigt, wie der I²C-Bus mit Hilfe von Erweiterungsbausteinen an spezielle Aufgabenstellungen angepasst werden kann.

- Der Baustein P82B715 ist ein Bus-Extender, das heißt dieser ermöglicht eine räumliche Trennung von zwei Bus-Abschnitten. Dazu wird ein Paar dieser Bausteine zwischen die zwei Bus-Segmente geschaltet. Zwischen den Extendern darf die Leitungslänge bis zu 50*m* betragen.

- Beim Baustein PCA9540B handelt es sich um einen Fünffach-I^2C-Hub. Dieser erlaubt es, fünf voneinander unabhängige Bus-Zweige parallel zu betreiben. Diese lassen sich durch Softwarebefehle beliebig aktivieren oder deaktivieren. Auf diese Weise ist es möglich Adressen mehrfach zu vergeben, solange sich die Teilnehmer nicht im selben Bus-Zweig befinden. Sollen mehrere Abschnitte gleichzeitig aktiv sein, dürfen sie allerdings die maximale Kapazität von $400pF$ nicht überschreiten.
- Mit dem Baustein PCA9515, einem sogenannten Repeater lässt sich der Bus in zwei Segmente teilen, die jeweils eine Kapazität von $400pF$ haben dürfen. So können die Anzahl der Bus-Teilnehmer und die Leitungslänge verdoppelt werden. Aus Sicht des Bus-Masters dürfen von diesen Bausteinen sogar mehrere parallel geschaltet werden.

5.2 Anwendungsbeispiel Roboterarm

Wenn die Sensor-Matrix als Teil einer Roboterhaut auf einem Roboter montiert werden soll, kann es von Vorteil sein, wenn der Bus-Master nicht mit auf der Maschine sitzen muss. Bei diesem Anwendungsfall wird eine mittelgroße (durch den Adressraum abgedeckte) Anzahl Sensoren benötigt, die alle relativ nah beieinander liegen.

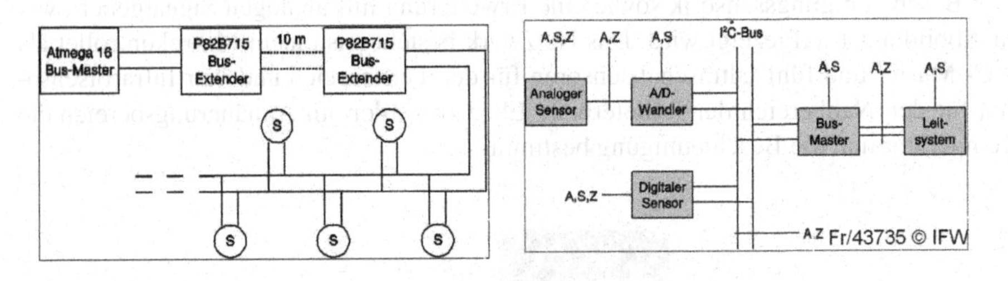

Abb. 2. links: Schaltungsaufbau für den Anwendungsfall „Roboterarm", rechts: Mögliche Fehler in der Messkette nach Fehlertypen

Es bietet sich an, den Bus mit einem Paar Extenderbausteinen P82B715 zu verlängern. Diese werden zwischen die Haut mit den Sensoren und den Busmaster geschaltet, wie in Abbildung 2 zu sehen. Der Bus hat die propagierte Linienstruktur mit Abzweigungen zu den Sensoren (im Bild mit „S" gekennzeichnet).

5.3 Sicherheit und Fehlerkontrolle bei dem I^2C-Bus

In diesem Abschnitt wird die Sicherheit bei der Datenübertragung innerhalb der Sensor-Matrix beleuchtet. Zunächst werden mögliche Fehlerursachen aufgezeigt. Im Anschluss wird diskutiert, wie diese Störungen erkannt und vermieden werden können.

5.4 Möglichkeiten der Fehlererkennung

Die oben genannten Fehler sind unterschiedlich schwer zu erfassen. Grundsätzlich gilt, dass ein Totalausfall meist sehr schnell festgestellt wird. Das I^2C-Protokoll sieht vor, dass jeder Teilnehmer den Empfang von Daten mit einem Bestätigungsbit quittieren muss. Bleibt diese Bestätigung mehrmals in Folge aus, liegt ein Totalausfall vor. Tabelle 1 gibt einen Überblick über den erforderlichen Aufwand um Fehler und Störungen aufzuspüren. Ein Strich in einem Tabellenfeld zeigt an, dass dieser Fehler an der betreffenden Stelle mit hoher Wahrscheinlichkeit nicht auftreten kann.

Tabelle 1. Benötigter Aufwand zum Erkennen verschiedener Fehler.

Ort des Auftretens	Ausfall	Systematischer Fehler	Zufälliger Fehler
Analoger Sensor	Referenzmessung	Referenzmessung	Redundanz
A/D-Wandler	Normalbetrieb	Referenzmessung	-
Digitaler Sensor	Normalbetrieb	Referenzmessung	Redundanz
Analogleitung	Referenzmessung	-	Redundanz
I^2C-Bus-Kabel	Normalbetrieb	-	Redundanz
Serielles Kabel	Normalbetrieb	-	Normalbetrieb
Mikrokontroller	Normalbetrieb	Referenzmessung	-
Leitsystem	Normalbetrieb	Referenzmessung	-

5.5 Messungen der Sensormatrix mit implementierter Fehlererkennung

Auf Grund ihres Messprinzips liefern die Infrarotsensoren als Ergebnis eine Spannung, die umso größer ist, je kürzer die Distanz zwischen Sensor und Objekt ist. Dabei handelt es sich dabei um eine umgekehrt proportionale Beziehung mit der Gleichung

$$d = \frac{A}{u - B}$$

u stellt dabei die gemessene Spannung, d den Abstand zum Objekt dar. Die Konstanten A und B müssen experimentell ermittelt werden.

Mit dieser Konfiguration kann nun eine Messreihe zur Bestimmung der Konstanten A und B aufgenommen werden. Für die Spannung u wird einfach die dimensionslose 8-Bit-Zahl eingesetzt. Zur Bestimmung der zwei Unbekannten werden zwei Paare aus Abstand und Wandlerergebnis benötigt. Die zugehörige Gleichung kann durch Umformen und Einsetzen gewonnen werden. Sie lauten

$$A = (u_2 - u_1) \cdot \frac{d_1 \cdot d_2}{d_1 - d_2}, B = \frac{d_2 \cdot u_2 - d_1 \cdot u_1}{d_2 - d_1} \quad (1)$$

Abbildung 3 zeigt den Verlauf des Messwertes in Abhängigkeit der Distanz (die blaue Kurve). Die rote Kurve ist eine rechnerische Annäherung der Werte mit den Parametern $A = 1100cm$ und $B = 0,6$. Da bei den Sensoren vom Typ SRF02 die Betriebsparameter nicht verändert werden können, lässt sich hier keine Variation durchführen. Im Gegenzug konnten Messungen für verschiedene Abstände durchgeführt werden. Neben den Messungen gegen eine Hallendecke und eine Wand wurde auch gegen eine große Metallplatte gemessen. Für diesen Sensor wurden ebenfalls jeweils 100 Messergebnisse gemittelt. Die ermittelten Abstände können Abbildung 3 entnommen werden.

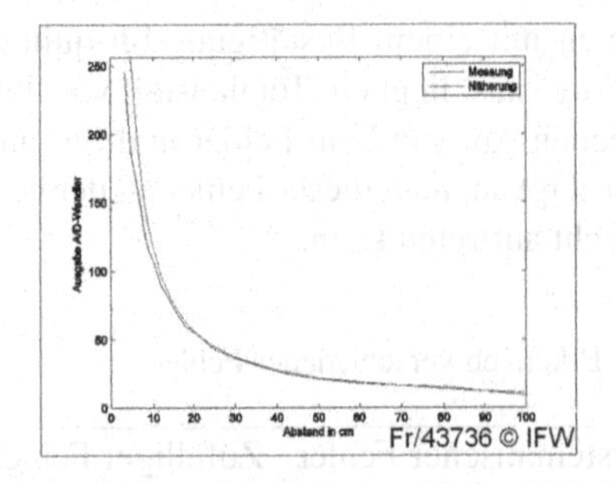

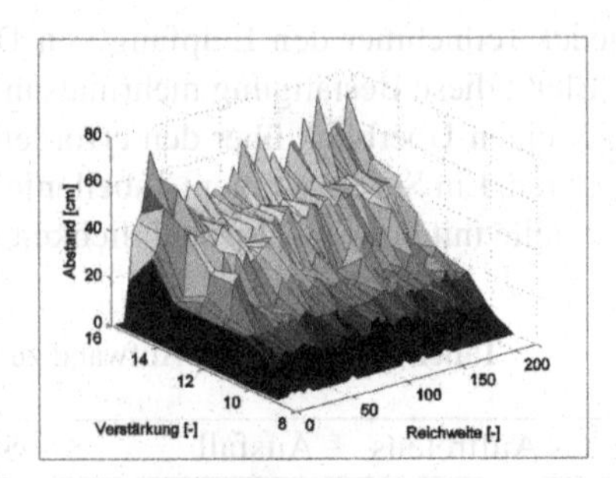

Abb. 3. links: Messreihe zur Kalibrierung der Infrarotsensoren sowie mit einer Näherungsfunktion berechnete Werte, rechts: Gemittelte Abstandsmessung mit vier Sensoren SRF10 gegen einen Probekörper bei $20ms$ Wartezeit.

6 Zweistufiges Sicherheitskonzept für Roboter

Ein weiterer Aspekt behandelt ein überlagertes zweistufiges Sicherheitskonzept durch Überwachung des Arbeitsraums ohne trennende Schutzeinrichtungen. Werden Menschen oder Gegenstände im Arbeitsraum des Roboters detektiert, wird dieser in den Modus „sicher reduzierte Geschwindigkeit" versetzt. Entsteht jetzt eine Kollision mit der Roboterhaut, wird der Roboter in den Modus „sicherer Halt" geschaltet. Der Weg, den der Roboter benötigt, um von der „sicher reduzierten Geschwindigkeit" zum Stillstand zu gelangen, wird in der Nachgiebigkeit der Roboterhaut aufgefangen.

7 Zusammenfassung und Ausblick

Es wird eine zweistufige Sicherheitstechnik entwickelt. Eine innovative Roboterhaut, die bei Kontakt mit dem Menschen den Roboter in den sicheren Zustand überführt, entsteht in diesem Projekt. Somit lässt sich eine Gefährdung des Menschen sicher reduzieren. Der I^2C-Bus ist ein einfaches Bus-System mit einem schlanken Protokoll. Dies birgt Vor- und Nachteile: Zum Einen ist die Ansteuerung von Bausteinen über den Bus unkompliziert. Der Bus ist leicht erweiterbar und die Komponenten wie Bus-Master und Sensoren sind vergleichsweise kostengünstig. Zum Anderen bietet das Protokoll des I^2C-Busses nahezu keine Funktionen zur Fehlererkennung und -vermeidung. Diese Funktionen müssen, soweit dies aufgezeigt wurde, als Software nachgebildet werden.

Danksagung

Das diesem Bericht zugrunde liegende Vorhaben wurde mit Mitteln des Bundesministeriums für Bildung und Forschung unter dem Förderkennzeichen 02PB2163 gefördert.

Literaturverzeichnis

1. Prassler, E.; Plöger P. et al.; DESIRE: Schlüsseltechnologien für alltagstaugliche Serviceroboter, BMBF Leitinnovation Servicerobotik, Berlin, 2006
2. Heiligensetzter, P.; Sichere Mensch-Roboter Kooperation durch Fusion haptischer und kapazitiver Sensorik, Dissertation, Karlsruhe, 2003

Intelligente Fahrzeuge
Technik, Chancen und Grenzen

Christoph Stiller

Institut für Mess- und Regelungstechnik, Universität Karlsruhe, 76131 Karlsruhe
stiller@mrt.uka.de

Zusammenfassung. Dieser Überblicksbeitrag wirft Schlaglichter auf den Stand, die Chancen und die Grenzen Intelligenter Fahrzeuge. Ausgehend von der Zielsetzung von Fahrerassistenzsystemen werden zunächst die bereits früh realisierten vollautonomen Fahrzeuge aus der Forschung den bisher im Markt realisierten Fahrerassistenzfunktionen gegenüber gestellt. Als eine treibende Kraft für dieses Forschungsfeld kristallisieren sich jüngst die sog. *Grand und Urban Challenge* Wettbewerbe in den USA heraus. Der Beitrag schließt mit einem Blick auf den Sonderforschungsbereich *Kognitive Automobile.*

1 Motivation

Obgleich in den vergangenen Jahrzehnten beachtliche Fortschritte in der Fahrzeugsicherheit erreicht wurden, sind die hohen mit Automobilen verbundenen Unfallzahlen nach wie vor aus wirtschaftlicher, gesellschaftlicher und nicht zuletzt ethischer Sicht gänzlich inakzeptabel. Während in Deutschland die Häufigkeit von durch Automobile verursachten Fatalitäten wenigstens allmählich sinkt, steigt die weltweite Rate kontinuierlich an und hat die Marke von 1 Million Tote pro Jahr bereits überschritten. Ehrgeizigen politischen Programmen - etwa der EU oder der NHTSA[1] - zum Trotz konnten keine signifikanten Verbesserungen oder gar eine Wende dieser Tendenz erreicht werden. Es gilt als sicher, dass ein großer Teil der Unfälle vermieden bzw. die Unfallschwere deutlich gemindert werden könnte, wenn es nur gelänge, geeignete Notmanöver rund eine Sekunde früher einzuleiten.

Diese Überlegungen begründen dir weltweit große Aufmerksamkeit für das Forschungsgebiet Intelligenter Fahrzeuge, dessen Ziel die sensorielle Erfassung von Umgebungsinformation und deren Nutzbarmachung in Fahrerassistenzsystemen ist. Die Bewertung erster im Markt befindlicher Fahrerassistenzfunktionen umfasst das gesamte Spektrum vom mitleidigen Belächeln unfähiger Technik bis hin zur euphorischen Prophezeiung des kurz bevorstehenden automatischen oder unfallfreien Fahrens. In diesem Zusammenhang ist es wichtig, sich der funktionellen Vielfalt von Fahrerassistenz und deren Wirkung bewusst zu sein. Funktionsgetrieben lassen sich Fahrerassistenzsysteme unterteilen in *autonome Systeme*,

[1] National Highway Traffic Safety Administration [1]

Komfortsysteme, *warnende Systeme*, *Informationssysteme* und *effizienzsteigernde Systeme*. Dabei ist der Übergang fließend und ein System nicht notwendig auf nur eine Kategorie beschränkt. Während Systeme der ersteren Kategorien vornehmlich in der Forschung konstruiert werden, befinden sich vielfältige Beispiele der letzteren Kategorien bereits im Markt oder in der Entwicklung [2].

2 Frühe Forschungserfolge autonomer Fahrzeuge

Die seit den 60er Jahren aufgenommenen Forschungsaktivitäten an autonomer Fahrzeugführung wurden durch das europäische PROMETHEUS Programm über einzelne Firmen und Institutionen hinweg gebündelt. Diesem Programm und seinen Nachfolgern stehen mit dem AHS und IVI Programm vergleichbare amerikanische und von der AHSRA initiierte japanische Programme gegenüber, die jeweils in erheblichem Maße öffentlich gefördert wurden. In den 90er Jahren gelang es einzelnen internationalen Gruppen erstmals auf Testgelände und in einfacher Umgebung wie Autobahnen oder gut ausgebauten Landstraßen die meisten Situationen unter Überwachung autonom zu bewältigen. In schwierigen Fahrtabschnitten musste allerdings immer wieder durch einen menschlichen Sicherheitsfahrer spontan übernommen werden [3,4,5,6].

In mehreren Vorführungen konnten Intelligente Fahrzeuge ihre Fähigkeiten öffentlich demonstrieren. Eine als Demo'97 bekannte entsprechende Veranstaltung auf der Interstate I-15 nahe San Diego zeigte verschiedene PKWs, Busse und Lastwagen. Dabei konnten im wesentlichen autonomes Spurfolgen mit gewöhnlichen sichtbaren oder Radar-reflektierenden Fahrbahnmarkierungen bzw. in die Fahrbahn eingelassenen Magneten sowie autonomes Fahrzeugfolgefahren mit Laser- oder Radarsensoren und teils mit Fahrzeug-Fahrzeug-Kommunikation demonstriert werden (s. z.B. [5,7]). Situationen und Fahrmanöver wurden mit festem rein zeitgesteuertem Ablauf, mit Hilfe von GPS und ortsgesteuertem Ablauf oder mit einfachsten situationsgetriggertem Verlauf realisiert. Eine vergleichbare Veranstaltung fand bereits 1996 in Japan statt. Später folgten weitere in Holland, Frankreich und den USA. Über die bloße Technologiedemonstration hinaus wurde die interessierte Öffentlichkeit über mögliche künftige Entwicklungen Intelligenter Fahrzeuge informiert.

3 Fahrerassistenzsysteme im Markt

Die aus den frühen Forschungserfolgen resultierenden Erwartungen an die Produktüberführung haben sich bisher vielfach als überhöht erwiesen. Bei den frühen Fahrerassistenzfunktionen, die bereits in den Markt gekommen sind, haben zunächst nicht informierende oder warnende Systeme, sondern erstaunlicherweise gerade aufgrund der Unvollkommenheit der Sensorik zunächst Komfortsysteme die Vorreiterrolle übernommen.

Beginnend mit einer bereits 1995 im Mitsubishi Diamant realisierten ACC Funktion[2] wurden zunächst Systeme innovationsfreundlicher japanischer Hersteller angeboten. Europäische Hersteller zogen ab 1999 mit Daimler-Benz/A.D.C. und Jaguar/Delphi nach. Im Nutzfahrzeugbereich wurde zusätzlich zu ACC im Mercedes Actros ein videobasierter Spurverlassenswarner angeboten. Nach Übernahme eines amerikanischen Anbieters von Spurverlassenswarnern „AssistWare" bot Visteon früh Spurverlassenswarner im Nutzfahrzeug- wie im PKW-Bereich an. Der Ausrüstungsgrad der angebotenen Fahrerassistenzsysteme im Nutzfahrzeugbereich ist noch niedrig.

Alle vorgenannten ACC Systeme werden ausschließlich als Komfortsystem angeboten und belassen die Verantwortung beim Fahrer. Ihr Arbeitsbereich ist deutlich eingeschränkt. So arbeiten die Systeme nur in einem vorgegebenen Geschwindigkeitsintervall und sind in Beschleunigung und Bremsverzögerung beschränkt. Natürliche Weiterentwicklungen zielen darauf ab, den Arbeitsbereich zu erweitern. So biten die meisten Hersteller bereits mit *ACC Stop & Go* ein System an, das auch im niedrigen Geschwindigkeitsbereich bis hinunter in den Stand arbeitet und zunehmend auch Sicherheitsfunktionen einschließt.

Seit Mitte 2003 wird von Honda der Accord mit HIDS auf dem japanischen Markt angeboten, einem Fahrerassistenzsystem, das die Längsführungsunterstützung von ACC um eine koordinierte Querführungsunterstützung erweitert. Das von GM angebotene Nightvision System stellt dem Fahrer das Bild eines FIR[3] Sensors dar, so dass Objekte mit thermischem Kontrast gegenüber ihrer Umgebung auch im Dunkeln sichtbar werden. Auch deutsche Fahrzeughersteller bieten inzwischen Nachtsichtsysteme an. Dabei muss sich noch zeigen, ob sich langfristig passives FIR oder aktives NIR[4] durchsetzt.

4 Grand und Urban Challenge

Um die Forschungsaktivitäten - vornehmlich in den USA - zu verstärken, hat die US DARPA seit 2004 verschiedene „Challenges" initiiert. Das „Grand Challenge" war ein offener Wettbewerb autonomer Landfahrzeuge, dessen Ziel das autonome Befahren einer den Teilnehmern bis zum Renntag unbekannten ca. 132 Meilen lange Strecke über Straßen, Wege und querfeldein durch die Mojave Wüste in Nevada war. Nachdem 2004 kein Fahrzeug über eine Entfernung von 7 Meilen vom Start hinaus kam, wurde der Wettbewerb im Oktober 2005 neu ausgerichtet. Aus rund 200 Teams, die sich mit einem Konzept um die Teilnahme bewarben, wurden in verschiedenen Ausscheidungsrunden, bis hin zu einem Halbfinale mit Barrieren, Tunneldurchfahrten, spiegelnden und nicht spiegelnden Hindernissen sowie weiteren Schikanen, schließlich 23 Finalisten ausgewählt,

[2] Adaptive Cruise Control; Tempomat, der mit mit Hilfe eines Abstandssensors den Sicherheitsabstand zum vorherfahrenden Fahrzeug regelt.

[3] Fernes Infrarot

[4] Nahes Infrarot. Der Sichtbereich wird zusätzlich durch für das menschliche Auge unsichtbares NIR Fernlicht ausgeleuchtet.

Abb. 1. Das Fahrzeug ION der Universitäten Ohio State und Karlsruhe

die am 8. Oktober 2005 in Primm, Nevada an den Start der ca. 132 Meilen langen Strecke des Finales durften. Die Strecke wurde den Teilnehmern erst drei Stunden vor dem Start in Form eines zulässigen Korridor mitgeteilt, der durch eine Folge Wegkoordinaten mit lateraler Toleranz definiert wurde [8].

Die Partner Ohio State University und die Universität Karlsruhe (TH) beteiligten sich mit dem in Abb. 1 dargestellten Fahrzeug. Dabei wurden weitestgehend für den Straßenverkehr entwickelte Verfahren der Fahrerassistenzgruppe an die zu erwartende Offroad-Umgebung der Mojave Wüste angepasst. Das Fahrzeug fuhr über eine Strecke von 47 km kollisionsfrei, bevor es liegen blieb und damit den 10. Platz belegte [9,10]. Abb. 2 und 3 zeigen Beispiele für in städtischer Umgebung bzw. der Mojave Wüste ermittelte Bahnen. Die Stanford University belegte den ersten Platz [11], gefolgt von zwei Fahrzeugen der Carnegie Mellon University.

Inzwischen hat die US Darpa den Urban Challenge Wettbewerb für November 2007 ausgeschrieben, der autonomes Fahren in gemischtem städtischen Verkehr zum Inhalt hat. Abb. 4 zeigt einen Schnappschuss aus dem Viertelfinale vom Fahrzeug *AnnieWay* der Universitäten Karlsruhe und München, nachdem das Fahrzeug unbemannt eine Kreuzungssituation vollautonom bewältigt hat.

5 Kognitive Automobile

Ein wesentliches Hemmnis für die breite Einführung kognitiver Funktionen in Fahrzeugen stellt – vor allem für sicherheitsrelevante Aufgaben – die noch fehlende Robustheit und Verlässlichkeit der Erkennungsleistungen dar: Unter normalen Bedingungen (Beleuchtung, Wetter, strukturierte Umgebung) arbeiten die Erkennungsalgorithmen weitgehend korrekt, aber bei schlechter Beleuchtung (Nacht, Nässe), bei ungünstigem Wetter (Regen, Nebel, Schnee, grelle Sonne) oder in komplexen Situationen (innerstädtische Umgebung) sind sie überfordert.

Abb. 2. Kamerabilder mit berechneter Bahn in Karlsruhe

Abb. 3. Kamerabilder mit berechneter Bahn in der Mojave Wüste

Diese Herausforderung an künftige Wahrnehmungssysteme bildet einen Schwerpunkt des Sonderforschungsbereichs Transregio 28 *Kognitive Automobile* der Partneruniversitäten in Karlsruhe und München ergänzt durch das Fraunhofer IITB und das Forschungszentrum Karlsruhe. Kognitive Automobile sollen in die Lage versetzt werden, nicht nur sich selbst und ihre Umgebung wahrzunehmen sondern ihr Wissen selbständig anzusammeln und zu strukturieren. Kognitive Automobile sollen dabei sowohl zu individuellem als auch zu kooperativem Wahrnehmen und Handeln fähig sein. Dafür verfolgt der SFB eine Reihe von im Diskursbereich Straßenverkehr neuartigen Ansätzen, von denen einige exemplarisch aufgeführt werden [12]:

Durch Nutzung von Diversität auf und zwischen unterschiedlichen Kognitionsebenen wird eine erhöhte Zuververlässigkeit in der Wahrnehmung erreicht. In [13] wurde erstmals eine aktive Kameraplattform vorgestellt, die sich fortlaufend durch Analyse der Disparitäten und Verschiebungen selbst kalibriert und dadurch eine 3D-Geometrieerfassung des Umfeldes in einem Blickbereich von bis nahezu 180° erlaubt. Abb. 5 zeigt die Kamera im Erprobungsfahrzeug. Abb. 6 zeigt die erzielten Ergebnisse einer 3D-Rekonstruktion während einer Kurvenfahrtfahrt.

Abb. 4. Das unbemannte Kognitive Automobil AnnieWay (links) nach verkehrsregelkonformer Bewältigung einer Kreuzung (Juni 2007, in Palo Alto, Kalifornien)

Zur formalen Modellierung und Beschreibung des aktuellen Lagebildes und des beabsichtigten Verhaltens eines Agenten reicht metrische Information alleine nicht aus. Vielmehr ist eine Kombination aus metrischer und symbolischer Information erforderlich. Rudimentäre symbolische Information kann implizit in Zustandsautomaten oder (Petri-) Netzen abgebildet werden. Für komplexere Vorgänge wurden Situationsgraphenbäume vorgeschlagen [14], die eine sprachnahe Beschreibung von Bildfolgen ermöglichen. Für die generische Repräsentation komplexer Informationsstrukturen wird die Eignung von probabilistischen *Ontologien* untersucht. Dies sind Domänenbeschreibungen, wie sie beispielsweise im *Semantic Web* oder durch OWL[5] genutzt und die um stochastisch modellierte Relationen erweitert werden. Dadurch lassen sich auch wahrscheinliches Verhalten oder seltene Regelverstöße explizit repräsentieren [12].

6 Schlussbemerkungen

Wenngleich der Stand der Forschung - und erst recht der Stand der im Markt befindlichen Technik - Intelligenter Fahrzeuge hinter der Leistungsfähigkeit menschlicher Fahrer und manch hehrer Erwartung zurückstehen, sind gerade in jüngster Zeit bemerkenswerte Fortschritte zu verzeichnen. Dabei zeigen sich für die praktische Realisierung und Erprobung die von der US DARPA veranstalteten „Challenges" als Treibkräfte, die besonders in den USA universitäre Forschung und industrielles Sponsoring auf dieses Thema lenkt. Als eines der Grundlagenforschungsprojekte wurde der SFB *Kognitive Automobile* beschrieben, der insbesondere die Methodenerforschung für eine hohe Zuverlässigkeit und zur probabilistischen Situationswahrnehmung zum Ziel hat.

[5] Web Ontology Language

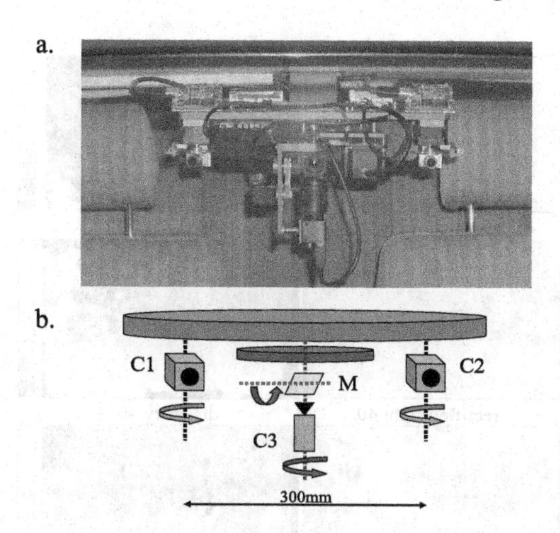

Abb. 5. a. Aktive Kamera Platform im Erprobungsfahrzeug. Die Plattform umfasst zwei (Stereo-) Kameras mit einem horizontalen Blickwinkel von 46° und eine Telekamera. Die Blickrichtungen der Kameras sind steuerbar. b. Konzeptskizze der aktiven Kamera Platform (C1, C2: Stereokameras, C3: Telekamera, M: Spiegel).

7 Danksagung

Ein Teil der berichteten Arbeiten wird durch die Deutsche Forschungsgemeinschaft in Rahmen des SFB Tr. 28 *Kognitive Automobile* unterstützt. Mein Dank gilt der DFG sowie den beteiligten Kollegen für die fruchtbare Zusammenarbeit.

Literaturverzeichnis

1. National Highway Traffic Safety Administration. NHTSA website. http://www.nhtsa.dot.gov/.
2. M. Maurer and C. Stiller, editors. *Fahrerassistenzsysteme mit maschineller Wahrnehmung.* Springer-Verlag, Heidelberg, 2005.
3. E. D. Dickmanns. Road vehicle eyes for high precision navigation. In Linkwitz et al., editor, *High Precision Navigation*, pages 329–336, Bonn, 1995. Dümmler Verlag.
4. H.-H. Nagel, W. Enkelmann, and G. Struck. FhG-Co-Driver: From map-guided automatic driving by machine vision to a cooperative driver support. *Mathematical and Computer Modelling*, 22:185–212, 1995.
5. C. Thorpe, T. Jochem, and D. Pomerleau. The 1997 automated highway free agent demonstration. In *Proc. IEEE Conf. on Intell. Transp. Systems*, pages 496–501, Boston, USA, 9–12 November 1997.
6. A. Broggi, M. Bertozzi, A. Fascioli, and G. Conte. Automatic vehicle guidance: The experience of the ARGO vehicle. *World Scientific*, April 1999.
7. K.A. Redmill, Ü Özguner, and al. The OSU Demo '97 Vehicle. In *IEEE Intelligent Transportation Systems Conference*, pages 502–507, October 1997.
8. Darpa. Grand Challenge '05. http://www.darpa.mil/grandchallenge/overview.html, October 2005.

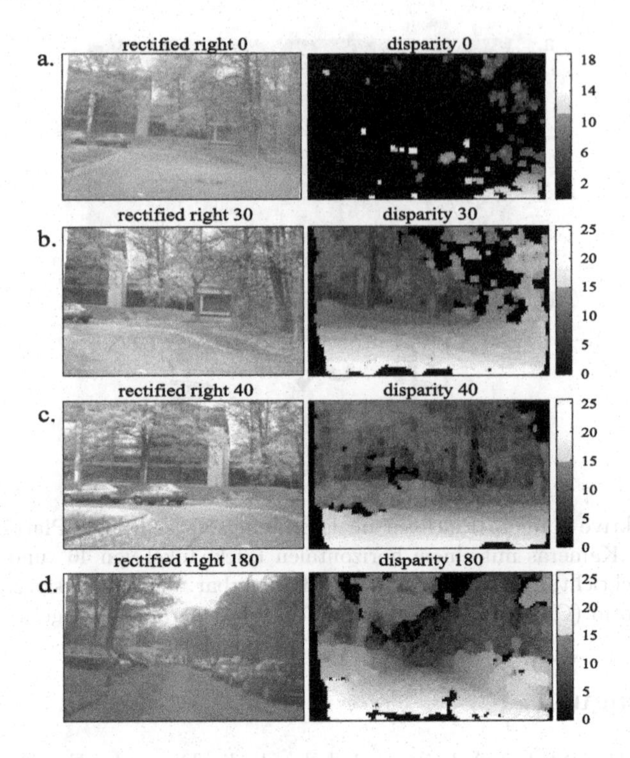

Abb. 6. Bild (links) und stereoskopische Tiefeninformation (rechts) der selbstkalibrierenden Kameraplattform. a: Unmittelbar nach dem Einschalten verfügt die Kamera nur über eine grobe Initialkalibrierung, die keine 3D-Rekonstruktion erlaubt. b: nach einer Sekunde (Bild 30) c und d: erstes Bild nach einem sakkadischen Kameraschwenk in bzw. nach der Kurve (Bild 40 bzw. Bild 180).

9. Ü. Özgüner, C. Stiller, and K. Redmill. Systems for safety and autonomous behavior in cars: The DARPA Grand Challenge experience. *IEEE Proceedings*, 95(2):1–16, February 2007.
10. C. Stiller, S. Kammel, T. Dang, C. Duchow, and B. Hummel. Autonome Fahrzeugführung durchs Gelände – ION im Grand Challenge. *at - Automatisierungstechnik*, 55(6):290–297, June 2007.
11. S. Thrun, M. Montemerlo, H. Dahlkamp, D. Stavens, A. Aron, J. Diebel, P. Fong, J. Gale, M. Halpenny, G. Hoffmann, K. Lau, C. Oakley, M. Palatucci, V. Pratt, P. Stang, S. Strohband, C. Dupont, L.-E. Jendrossek, C. Koelen, C. Markey, C. Rummel, J.v. Niekerk, E. Jensen, P. Alessandrini, G. Bradski, B. Davies, S. Ettinger, A. Kaehler, A. Nefian, and P. Mahoney. Stanley: The robot that won the DARPA Grand Challenge. *Journal of Field Robotics*, 23(9):661–692, 2006.
12. C. Stiller, G. Färber, and S. Kammel. Cooperative cognitive automobiles. In *Proc. IEEE Intelligent Vehicles Symposium*, pages 215–220, Istanbul, Turkey, June 2007.
13. T. Dang, C. Hoffmann, and C. Stiller. Self-calibration for active automotive stereo vision. In *Proc. IEEE Intelligent Vehicles Symposium*, pages 364–369, Tokyo, Japan, June 2006.
14. M. Arens and H.-H. Nagel. Quantitative movement prediction based on qualitative knowledge about behavior. *KI Künstliche Intelligenz*, (2/05):5–11, 2005.

Innovativer Speditionshof mit fahrerlosen Fahrzeugen

Operative Optimierungsansätze und simulativer Nachweis

Daniel Hillesheim

DaimlerChrysler AG, Truck Product Engineering (TPE/VES),
Mercedesstraße 137 (HPC T332), 70546 Stuttgart,
daniel.hillesheim@daimlerchrysler.com

Zusammenfassung. Dieser Artikel beschreibt die Idee des innovativen Speditionshofes und erklärt operativ, warum das System einen Mehrwert für den Betreiber mit sich bringt. Fahrerlose Fahrzeuge, automatisierte Einrichtungen des Speditionshofes und eine intelligente Leitsteuerung stellen die Basis des Systems dar. Ziel des zukunftweisenden Konzeptes ist, dem Betreiber durch optimierte Abläufe Kosten und Zeit zu sparen.

1 Einleitung

Um einen effizienteren Warenumschlag zu erreichen werden seit einigen Jahren fahrerlose Transportsysteme (FTS) eingesetzt. Häufig finden diese Systeme Anwendung in Containerterminals von großen Häfen [1], aber auch in der Produktion werden oft FTS zum Transport von Gütern eingesetzt. Die eingesetzten Fahrzeuge werden meistens speziell für ihre Verwendung entwickelt.

Nutzfahrzeuge für den Straßenverkehr werden nicht für den fahrerlosen Betrieb konzipiert, allerdings zeigen Entwicklungen der letzten Jahre, dass der Grad der Automatisierung auch in diesem Bereich stetig steigt. Der Abstandsregeltempomat (ART) übernimmt zum Beispiel die komplette Längsregelung des Fahrzeuges durch Motor- und Bremseingriff. Die Aufgabe des Fahrers reduziert sich damit auf die Querregelung (Lenkung) des Fahrzeugs.

Auch im Bereich der Lenkung wird an Assistenzsystemen gearbeitet. Mit der Aktivlenkung für PKW entstand ein System, das eine elektronisch geregelte Überlagerung eines Winkels zum Lenkradwinkel ermöglicht. In der ersten Entwicklungsstufe lag der Fokus auf Größen wie Komfort, Lenkaufwand, Lenkdynamik und Lenkeingriffe zur Verbesserung der Fahrzeugstabilisierung. Weiterentwicklungen werden in der Zukunft das elektronische Ansteuern der Lenkung für eine Sollbahnverfolgung ermöglichen, was bedeutet, dass fahrerloses Fahren mit Serienfahrzeugen technisch möglich wäre.

Verkehrsrechtliche Gründe verhindern jedoch bis dato das fahrerlose Fahren auf öffentlichen Straßen [2]. Welche Möglichkeiten sich aber eröffnen, wenn mit Serien-Nutzfahrzeugen auf abgesperrten Geländen fahrerlos gefahren werden kann, soll in diesem Artikel herausgestellt werden. Die Idee des fahrerlos geführten Speditionshofes soll dazu näher erläutert werden. Es wird ein Konzept vorgestellt, das dem Betreiber den Mehrwert des Systems verdeutlicht und die entscheidenden Verbesserungen gegenüber dem manuellen Betrieb herausstellt.

2 Systembeschreibung

Der Leitrechner spielt im fahrerlosen Betrieb des Speditionshofes eine zentrale Rolle. Er koordiniert und steuert die LKW selbstständig nach einem von ihm vorher berechneten Plan. Die steuernde Software auf dem Leitstand wird somit zum wichtigsten Element. Da sich im LKW kein Fahrer mehr befinden wird, muss der Leitstand für die intelligente Steuerung der Fahrzeuge sorgen. Er generiert die Fahrbefehle, die vom Fahrzeug ausgeführt werden. Dafür ist die Kenntnis über alle logistischen Bewegungen auf dem Hof die Basis. Der Leitstand muss über Prioritäten entscheiden, Zeitpläne einhalten, Wege planen und Kollisionen vermeiden. Eine interaktive Eingreifmöglichkeit für den Betreiber und eine 3D-Animation der Geschehnisse sind Bestandteil des Konzepts. Das Ziel ist ein sicherer und reibungsloser Ablauf auf dem Gelände. Die Software soll die Fähigkeit besitzen sowohl einen realen als auch einen simulierten Logistikhof darstellen zu können. Das Simulieren des autonomen Betriebes ermöglicht dem Spediteur eine Bewertung des Systems vor der eigentlichen Umsetzung. Auch Änderungen an der Software können so vor der Anwendung am realen Objekt getestet werden. Schnittstellen zu Intralogistiksystemen machen es zudem möglich, den kompletten Warenumschlag zu vernetzen und zu optimieren. So erkennt das System zum Beispiel, dass an einer bestimmten Rampe gerade die Ladung für einen bestimmten LKW zur Verfügung steht und generiert den entsprechenden Fahrauftrag. Nach Verladung der Ware wird ein elektronischer Ladungsschein generiert und über das System zur Verfügung gestellt. Dies garantiert dem Betreiber jederzeit Übersicht über die einzelnen LKW samt Ladung.

3 Optimierungsansätze

Verschiedene Ansätze zur Disposition fahrerloser Transportsysteme in Containerterminals beschreiben Natarajan et al. in [3]. Einem ähnlichen Anspruch haben fahrerlose LKW auf einem Speditionshof zu genügen.

Bei der operativen Ermittlung des Mehrwertes für den Anwender wird der Speditionshof in Standardkomponenten (Entitäten) zerlegt. Nach der Ermittlung der für die Optimierung des Hofes wichtigen Faktoren, werden diese mit Hilfe von Werkzeugen des Operations-Research bewertet. Ziel ist es, die Beschaffenheit eines beliebigen Speditionshofes anhand dieser Bewertungsvorschrift zu beschreiben und daraus Optimierungspotentiale abzuleiten.

3.1 Entitäten des Speditionshofes

Um die Komplexität zu reduzieren, wurde die Beschreibung des zugrunde liegenden Speditionshofes beschränkt auf folgende Standardkomponenten:

- Fahrwege
- Rampen
- Waschanlage
- Tankstelle
- Abstellplätze (Wartebereiche)
- Rangierplätze zum An- bzw. Abkuppeln von Anhänger/Auflieger
- Ein- bzw. Ausfahrt (Übergabebereiche)

Mit diesen Komponenten lässt sich ein Großteil der Extralogistik aller Speditionshöfe beschreiben. Der Fahrer übergibt den LKW an der Einfahrt an das System. Hierfür können auch bestimmte Übergabebereiche zur Verfügung stehen. Je nach Verfügbarkeit wird der LKW dann be- bzw. entladen, gewaschen, getankt und nach einer eventuellen Wartezeit an der Ausfahrt wieder an den Fahrer übergeben.

3.2 Optimierungsparameter

Um die Optimierung des Ablaufes auf dem Speditionshof über die Leitsteuerung zu realisieren, müssen zunächst die für den Betreiber wichtigen Kriterien ermittelt werden. Zeitliche Faktoren spielen dabei eine große Rolle, sei es die Rangierzeit, die Wartezeit oder die Abfertigungszeit an der Rampe. Die Anzahl der Fahrzeuge auf dem Gelände sowie die zur Verfügung stehenden Ressourcen wirken sich auch auf die Performance des Systems aus. Für die oben beschriebenen Entitäten des Speditionshofes werden Modelle erstellt, die unter Berücksichtigung der abzuleitenden Parameter eine Ablaufsimulation ermöglichen.

3.3 Modellierung der Entitäten

Am Beispiel der Rampe soll nun gezeigt werden, wie die Bewertung der Parameter sich auf die Performance des Systems auswirken. Der betrachtete Prozess an der Rampe besteht aus einem Rangiervorgang zum Andocken, dem eigentlichen Be- bzw. Entladevorgang und einer eventuellen Wartezeit nach dem Umschlag. Die eigentliche Dauer der Vorgänge ist dabei stark abhängig von verschiedenen Einflußfaktoren, welche wiederum abhängig sind von der Beschaffenheit des Speditionshofes. So beeinflussen zum Beispiel die Anzahl der Rampen, der zur Verfügung stehende Platz zum Rangieren und die Geometrie der Rampe maßgeblich die Rangierzeit. Vorrangig intralogistische Prozesse haben Auswirkung auf die Umschlagdauer. Hier spielen Faktoren wie bereits vorkommissionierte Ware und automatisierte Be- bzw. Entladung eine entscheidende Rolle. Die Dauer einer eventuellen Wartezeit ist wiederum abhängig von Ressourcenengpässen und der Einplanung von Folgeaufträgen. Die letztendlich benötigte Zeit für den kompletten Prozess auf einem beliebigen Speditionshof ergibt sich aus der Summe der gewichteten Vorgangszeiten:

$$t_{Rampe} = (Rangierzeit * E_1) + (Umschlagzeit * E_2) + (Wartezeit * E_3) \quad (1)$$

Rangier-, Umschlag- und Wartezeit sind definierte Standartgrößen, die als Erfahrungswerte von mehreren Speditionshöfen bekannt sind. Die Faktoren E_1 bis E_3 berücksichten die Einflüsse auf den Ablauf des Vorgangs. Für einen beliebigen Hof kann nun anhand einer Matrix der Wert für die Faktoren ermittelt werden. Dieser richtet sich nach den oben beschriebenen Einflußgrößen und wirkt sich direkt auf die resultierende Gesamtzeit t_{Rampe} aus, welche dann als Eingangsgröße für die Simulation des Speditionshofes verwendet werden kann.

4 Funktionsweise der Leitsteuerung

Zum Nachweis der ermittelten Mehrwertparameter wurde in Zusammenarbeit mit der Universität Koblenz-Landau (Fachbereich Informatik, Institut für Softwaretechnik, Arbeitsgruppe Echtzeitsysteme) ein Leitstandkonzept entwickelt. Der Leitstand dient zum einen als Optimierungswerkzeug, soll aber auch als Planungswerkzeug für neue Speditionshöfe eingesetzt werden. Eine 3D Visualisierung stellt die Ablaufszenarien dar, die über XML-Dateien generiert wurden. Ein Auswertungsmodul ermöglich die spätere Analyse der verwendeten Szenarien im Hinblick auf die Optimierungsparameter.

4.1 Komponenten der Leitsteuerung

Der Leitstand besteht im Groben aus zwei Komponenten, der Planung und der Überwachung. Nach Eingabe eines Auftrages (Fahrzeug kommt auf das Gelände), wird für alle Teilaufgaben dieses Fahrzeuges (z.B. Beladen, Waschen, Tanken...) ein Plan erstellt. Dabei werden für Fahraufträge alle Pläne im Voraus berechnet und mit den Plänen anderer Fahrzeuge abgeglichen. Der vom Planungsmodul berechnete Plan wird an das Überwachungs-modul gesendet. Dessen Aufgabe ist es nun, die berechneten Trajektorien an das Fahrzeug zu übermitteln, für die Einhaltung des Planes zu sorgen und die Sicherheit der Fahrzeuge zu gewährleisten.

Die *Auftragsverwaltung* hat die Aufgabe den Auftrag für ein ankommendes Fahrzeug zu bestimmen und ihn in Form einer speziellen Datenstruktur an die Terminplanung zu übergeben. Als Grundlage hierfür dient ein statischer Aufgabenbaum, der alle auf dem Gelände durchführbaren Fahraufgaben beinhaltet.

Die *Terminplanung* besitzt 2 Funktionen. Zum einen muss sie die Einplanung der Teilaufgaben für die Fahrzeuge koordinieren. Die zweite Aufgabe besteht darin, die Teilaufgaben zum richtigen Zeitpunkt zu starten.

Die Aufgabe der *Routenplanung* ist es, den optimalen Weg für eine Fahraufgabe zu finden. Um diese Berechnung durchzuführen, muss die Routenplanung auch mit anderen Komponenten des Planungsmoduls zusammenarbeiten. Zuerst berechnet die Routenplanung den schnellsten Weg zwischen Start- und Zielpunkt. Die Detailplanung versucht anschließend diese Route einzuplanen. Führt dies nicht zum Erfolg, wird bei der Routenplanung eine neue Route angefordert.

Die *Detailplanung* schließt den Planungsvorgang der Terminplanung und Routenplanung letztendlich ab und vereint deren Datenstrukturen. Die anfallenden Daten sind Flächen und Zeiten. Ziel ist es, einen Raum-Zeit Plan zu erstellen, der Auskunft darüber gibt, welche Bereiche auf dem Gelände zu einem bestimmten Zeitpunkt belegt sind und von welchem Objekt sie belegt sind. Der Raum-Zeit-Plan dient der Kollisionsvermeidung und der optimalen Ausnutzung des Raumes durch Vorausplanung.

Die *Fahrzeugkontrolle* analysiert in regelmäßigen Abständen die Situation auf dem Gelände und kontrolliert die Fahrzeuge dementsprechend. Sie verwaltet die Flächenbelegung auf dem Gelände und erkennt sowohl Flächen, die von statischen Hindernissen belegt sind, als auch Flächen die dynamisch von aktiven Fahrzeugen belegt werden. Die Fahrzeugkontrolle besteht aus folgenden Sub-Modulen, die für die Überwachungsfunktionen verantwortlich sind:

– Kollisionsverhinderung: Regelt die Geschwindigkeit der Fahrzeuge, um Kollisionen mit anderen Fahrzeugen oder Hindernissen zu vermeiden.
– Spurkontrolle: Die Aufgabe der Spurkontrolle ist die Überwachung des korrekten Fahrweges.
– Raum-Zeit-Überwachung: Kontrolliert und steuert die Einhaltung des Ausführungsplans der Fahrzeuge.
– Deadlock-Erkennung: Erkennt Deadlocks, die trotz Raum-Zeitplan aufgetreten sind
– Deadlock-Beseitigung: Berechnet für alle beteiligten Fahrzeuge neue Trajektorien um den Deadlock zu lösen

Das *Fahrzeugmanagement* hat die Aufgabe, Fahrzeuge und andere registrierte Objekte (wie zum Beispiel Wechselbrücken) zu verwalten und deren Daten anderen Leistand-Modulen zur Verfügung zu stellen. Enthaltene Daten sind zum Beispiel Abmessungen, Kinematik, Fahrzeugteile oder das Kennzeichen. Fahrzeuge müssen sich mit diesen Daten an der Fahrzeugverwaltung anmelden und beim Verlassen des Geländes auch wieder abmelden.

4.2 Simulationsumgebung

Das Konzept des Leitstandes umfasst nicht nur die Leitsteuerung selbst, sondern stellt zusätzlich Module zur Simulation des Speditionshofes zur Verfügung. Diese Module kommen im Normalbetrieb der Leitsteuerung nicht zum Einsatz. Sie sind notwendig, um im Simulationsmodus die Daten zu generieren, die im Normalfall von realen Fahrzeugen oder Entitäten auf dem Gelände kommen.

Zur Simulation der Fahrzeuge gehört neben der Übermittlung der dynamischen Fahrzeugdaten (Position, Ausrichtung und Lenkwinkel) auch das Übertragen der Fahrzeuginformationen (Fahrzeugtyp, Kennzeichen und Abmessungen). Der Leitstand übermittelt den (simulierten) Fahrzeugen die Sollgeschwindigkeit und alle abzufahrenden Trajektorien. Für die Entitäten findet eine Prozesssimulation statt. Diese sendet und empfängt Kontrollnachrichten der Entitäten und ahmt die eigentlichen Vorgänge durch Blockieren der Einheit für eine gewisse Zeit nach. Die Kommunikation erfolgt hierbei stets über die Schnittstellen, die auch im Realeinsatz verwendet werden, so dass für den Leitstand kein Unterschied zwischen realem und simuliertem Fahrzeug besteht. Die Abläufe sind konfigurierbar über XML-Dateien, was die Generierung von Szenarien für die Betriebshof-Simulation erleichtert. So können mit Hilfe der Simulation auch Stresstests durchgeführt, Probleme aufgezeigt und anschließend durch Anpassung der Module beseitigt werden. Das externe Modul der Visualisierung bietet dem User eine dreidimensionale Sicht auf das Gelände und gibt ihm die Möglichkeit, über ein graphisches Interface Manipulationen am Betriebsablauf vorzunehmen. Ein Beispiel hierfür ist die Veranlassung eines Nothalts. Die Visualisierung steht im Simulationsmodus wie auch bei realem Betrieb zur Verfügung und zeigt den aktuellen Zustand des Geländes.

4.3 Auswertungs- und Statistikmodul

Dieses Modul ermöglicht dem Nutzer eine Auswertung der Geschehnisse auf dem Speditionshof. Es empfängt Informationen vom Leitstand und schreibt sie laut der zugehörigen Mapping-Definition in eine Datenbank. Die Aufbereitung der Daten kann dann tabellarisch und graphisch erfolgen. Es ist unter anderem möglich die Auslastung des Geländes zu beobachten sowie Informationen über einzelne LKW oder Fahraufträge abzurufen. Der Nutzen des Moduls besteht darin, durch die erhobenen Daten Schwachstellen zu erkennen und somit die Leitsteuerung zu optimieren.

5 Zusammenfassung und Ausblick

Basis für die Entwicklung des innovativen Speditionshofes ist die Annahme, dass ein fahrerloser Betrieb von LKWs auf abgesperrten Geländen technisch und rechtlich möglich ist. Das vorgestellte Konzept stellt somit eine mögliche Anwendung des fahrerlosen Fahrens dar.

Mit der Entwicklung des Leitstandkonzeptes erfolgte der erste Schritt zur Realisierung des Projektes. In naher Zukunft ist geplant, mit Hilfe der Simulation die Wirtschaftlichkeit und somit den Mehrwert des Konzeptes nachzuweisen, sowie Akzeptanz in der Branche zu generieren. Dabei werden reale Szenarien in der Simulation nachempfunden und durch Auswertungen des Statistikmoduls mit der Simulation verglichen und bewertet.

Literaturverzeichnis

1. Steenken D., Voß S., Stahlbock R.: Container terminal operation and operations research - a classification and literature review. Container Terminals and Automated Transport Systems: 3–49. Springer, Berlin, 2005.
2. Bewersdorf C.: Zulassung und Haftung bei Fahrerassistenzsystemen im Straßenverkehr. Schriften zum Technikrecht Band 8, Duncker & Humblot, Berlin 2005
3. Natarajan K. et al.: Dispatching Automated Guided Vehicles in a Container Terminal. Applied Optimization Volume 98: 355–389, 2005.

Bildung kooperativer Gruppen kognitiver Automobile

Automatische Parameteroptimierung für einen verteilten Algorithmus zur dynamischen Gruppenbildung

Christian Frese[1] und Jürgen Beyerer[2,1]

[1] Lehrstuhl für Interaktive Echtzeitsysteme, Institut für Technische Informatik, Universität Karlsruhe (TH), frese@ies.uni-karlsruhe.de

[2] Fraunhofer Institut für Informations- und Datenverarbeitung IITB, Karlsruhe, Juergen.Beyerer@iitb.fraunhofer.de

Zusammenfassung. Durch Kooperation zwischen vernetzten Fahrzeugen kann die Verkehrssicherheit weiter erhöht werden. Im vorgeschlagenen Ansatz zur verteilten Kooperation spielt die Bildung *kooperativer Gruppen* eine zentrale Rolle. Dieser Artikel stellt ein Kriterium zur Gruppenbildung vor, das auf einer Bewertungsfunktion beruht. Die Parameter der Bewertungsfunktion werden mit Hilfe eines evolutionären Algorithmus optimiert. Ein Kommunikationsprotokoll für die verteilte Gruppeneinteilung wird beschrieben. In einem Simulationsexperiment wird die Robustheit des Verfahrens gezeigt.

1 Einleitung

Verschiedenste Sicherheitssysteme von Kraftfahrzeugen haben in den letzten Jahrzehnten zu einer deutlichen Verbesserung der Verkehrssicherheit beigetragen. Diese Systeme beschränken sich allerdings fast ausnahmslos auf die Betrachtung des eigenen Fahrzeugs. Im Zeitalter der drahtlosen Kommunikation ist jedoch ein zusätzlicher Sicherheitsgewinn durch neuartige Systeme realisierbar, die eine Fahrzeug-zu-Fahrzeug-Kommunikation zum Informationsaustausch und zum Aushandeln gemeinsamer Fahrmanöver nutzen. Während die Ad-Hoc-Vernetzung von Fahrzeugen und der Informationsaustausch zur Warnung vor Gefahrenstellen bereits in einigen Projekten untersucht wurden [1–3], ist das Potenzial kooperativer Fahrmanöver bisher noch nicht erschlossen.

Um optimale kooperative Verhaltensentscheidungen zu erzeugen, verfolgen wir einen *top-down*-Ansatz: Kognitive Fahrzeuge werden zunächst zu kooperativen Gruppen zusammengefasst. Für jede Gruppe wird ein gemeinsames Lagebild aufgebaut, das alle relevanten Informationen über die Fahrzeuge der Gruppe enthält. Auf der Basis dieses Lagebilds werden die anschließenden Schritte der Situationserkennung und der gemeinsamen Verhaltensentscheidung durchgeführt. Damit die Komplexität der nachgelagerten Verarbeitungsschritte beherrschbar bleibt, dürfen die kooperativen Gruppen nicht zu groß werden. Andererseits sollten alle Fahrzeuge, für die ein sicherheitsrelevantes gemeinsames Fahrmanöver

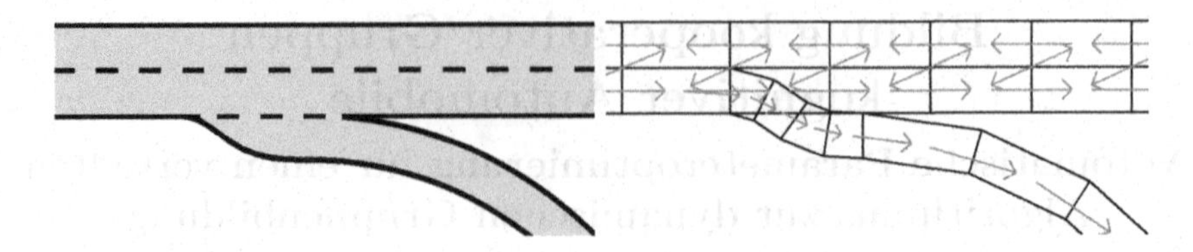

Abb. 1. *links:* Ausschnitt eines Straßennetzes. *rechts:* Partition des Straßennetzes und Kanten des Graphen $\mathcal{R}$

erforderlich sein könnte, der selben Gruppe angehören. Daher ist es wichtig, ein geeignetes Bildungskriterium für kooperative Gruppen zu definieren.

Ein erster Ansatz dazu, der bereits in [4] vorgestellt wurde, wird in Abschnitt 2 zusammengefasst. Er basiert auf einem graphentheoretischen Abstandsmaß und einer Bewertungsfunktion für kooperative Gruppen. Abschnitt 3 beschreibt die Optimierung der Parameter der Bewertungsfunktion. Ein robustes Kommunikationsprotokoll für die verteilte Gruppenbildung ist Gegenstand von Abschnitt 4. Die mit dem Bildungskriterium erzielten Simulationsergebnisse werden in Abschnitt 5 dargestellt.

2 Bildungskriterium für kooperative Gruppen

Die Grundlage für das vorgeschlagene Kriterium ist das Abstandsmaß d, das auf einer Diskretisierung des Straßennetzes in Form eines Graphen $\mathcal{R}$ beruht:

$$d(c_1, c_2) = \min_{v_\mathrm{m} \in \mathcal{R}} \max\{p_\mathcal{R}(c_1, v_\mathrm{m}), p_\mathcal{R}(c_2, v_\mathrm{m})\} \tag{1}$$

Dabei bezeichnet $p_\mathcal{R}(v_1, v_2)$ die Länge des kürzesten Weges in $\mathcal{R}$ zwischen den Knoten v_1 und v_2. Der Abstand zweier Fahrzeuge c_1, c_2 ist definiert als die Zeitspanne, in der beide Fahrzeuge ihren nächsten potenziellen Treffpunkt v_m im Straßennetz erreichen können. Unter Verwendung dieses Abstandsmaßes ist folgende Bewertungsfunktion definiert:

$$\begin{aligned} s(\mathcal{G}) &= \lambda_\mathrm{D} s_\mathrm{D}(\mathcal{G}) + \lambda_\mathrm{V} s_\mathrm{V}(\mathcal{G}) + \lambda_\mathrm{S} s_\mathrm{S}(\mathcal{G}) + \lambda_\mathrm{T} s_\mathrm{T}(\mathcal{G}) \qquad (2)\\ &= \lambda_\mathrm{D} \frac{1}{m(m-1)} \sum_{i=0}^{m-1} \sum_{j=i+1}^{m-1} d(c_i, c_j) \\ &\quad + \lambda_\mathrm{V} \frac{1}{m(m-1)} \sum_{i=0}^{m-1} \sum_{j=i+1}^{m-1} \frac{\partial}{\partial t} d(c_i, c_j) \\ &\quad + \lambda_\mathrm{S} \max\{0, m_0 - m\} \\ &\quad + \lambda_\mathrm{T} \frac{1}{m} \sum_{i=0}^{m-1} \begin{cases} t_i & \text{falls } 0 < t_i < t_\mathrm{T} \\ t_\mathrm{T} & \text{falls } t_i = 0 \text{ oder } t_i \geq t_\mathrm{T} \end{cases} \end{aligned}$$

Die Funktion bewertet eine Gruppe $\mathcal{G} = \{c_0, \ldots, c_{m-1}\}$ hinsichtlich ihrer räumlich-zeitlichen Ausdehnung, ihrer Expansions- bzw. Kompressionsgeschwindigkeit, ihrer Größe und ihrer zeitlichen Konstanz. Dabei bezeichnet m die Anzahl der Fahrzeuge und t_i die Zugehörigkeitsdauer von Fahrzeug c_i zu $\mathcal{G}$. Die optimale Partition P^* einer Fahrzeugmenge C erhält man nun durch Minimierung der Summe der Funktionswerte von s:

$$P^* = \arg \min_{P \in \mathcal{P}(C)} \sum_{\mathcal{G} \in P} s(\mathcal{G}) \tag{3}$$

3 Parameteroptimierung

Die subjektive Festlegung der freien Parameter λ_i ($i \in \{\mathrm{D, V, S, T}\}$), m_0 und t_T in der vorgeschlagenen Bewertungsfunktion (2) wäre willkürlich, und der Zusammenhang zwischen einer Parameteränderung und der resultierenden Gruppeneinteilung ist nicht unmittelbar ersichtlich. Aus diesem Grund verwenden wir ein Optimierungsverfahren, das die Parameter anhand eines Gütemaßes bestimmt. Da das Problem offensichtlich nicht analytisch lösbar ist, muss die Optimierung numerisch durchgeführt werden. Bei einem reinen Gradientenabstiegsverfahren beobachtet man eine starke Abhängigkeit von den Anfangswerten, was auf die Existenz lokaler Optima hindeutet. Um das globale Optimum zu finden, werden daher zusätzlich im Stile eines evolutionären Algorithmus zufällige Variationen der Parameter vorgenommen.

Die Gewichtungsfaktoren λ_i können durch Multiplikation mit einer beliebigen positiven Zahl skaliert werden, ohne dass sich die resultierende Gruppeneinteilung ändert. Daher kann einer der Faktoren bei Optimierung festgehalten werden. Der Parametervektor für den evolutionären Algorithmus wurde daher wie folgt gewählt:

$$\mathbf{v} = (v_j)_j = (\lambda_\mathrm{D}, \lambda_\mathrm{S}, \lambda_\mathrm{T}, m_0, t_\mathrm{T})^\mathrm{T} \tag{4}$$

Der evolutionäre Algorithmus besteht aus den drei Schritten Mutation, Rekombination und Selektion (siehe z. B. [5]). Bei einer Mutation wird zu einer Komponente v_j des Parametervektors eine normalverteilte Zufallsvariable addiert, die mit dem zulässigen Wertebereich des jeweiligen Parameters skaliert wurde. Der Rekombinationsschritt erfolgt durch gewichtete Addition der Komponenten zweier Parametervektoren $\mathbf{v}$, $\mathbf{w}$:

$$v_j^\mathrm{Rek} := a_j v_j + (1 - a_j) w_j \,, \quad (j = 1, \ldots, 5) \,, \tag{5}$$

wobei die a_j gleichverteilte Zufallszahlen aus dem Intervall $[0, 1]$ sind (intermediäre Rekombination). Bei der Selektion werden die besten Individuen in den nächsten Evolutionsschritt übernommen, es wird also eine reihenfolgebasierte Selektion durchgeführt.

Als Gütemaß für den Selektionsschritt wird derzeit die Übereinstimmung der mit Hilfe des Kriteriums berechneten Gruppeneinteilung mit einer manuell vorgegebenen ‚Grundwahrheit' verwendet. Dies kann insbesondere dazu genutzt

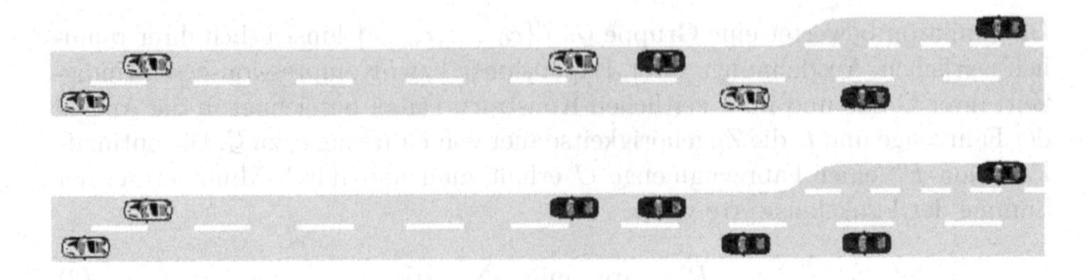

Abb. 2. *oben:* Gruppeneinteilung in einer Autobahnszene, visualisiert durch die Farben der Fahrzeuge. *unten:* Verbesserte Gruppeneinteilung nach der Parameteroptimierung

werden, um ausgehend von einer initialen, automatisch berechneten Gruppeneinteilung einzelne unbefriedigende Zuordnungen gezielt zu verbessern. Das Optimierungsverfahren ist aber flexibel genug, um auch mit anderen Gütemaßen arbeiten zu können. Sobald entsprechende Daten verfügbar sind, bietet sich hier insbesondere der Sicherheitsgewinn an, der mit der kooperativen Verhaltensentscheidung auf Grundlage der Gruppeneinteilung erreicht wird.

Formal lässt sich das derzeit verwendete Gütemaß J mit Hilfe des Kronecker-Symbols δ wie folgt ausdrücken:

$$J(g_{\mathbf{v}}) = \sum_t \sum_{i=0}^{n-1} \delta(g_{\mathbf{v}}(c_i, t), g_{\mathrm{GT}}(c_i, t)) \tag{6}$$

Dabei bezeichnet $g_{\mathbf{v}}(c_i, t)$ die Gruppe, in die Fahrzeug c_i zum diskreten Zeitschritt t bei Verwendung des Parametervektors $\mathbf{v}$ eingeteilt wird, und $g_{\mathrm{GT}}(c_i, t)$ die entsprechende Gruppeneinteilung in der Grundwahrheit. Für die Auswertung des Gütemaßes muss also die Gruppeneinteilung $g_{\mathbf{v}}$ mit dem Verfahren aus Abschnitt 2 auf Grundlage des Parametervektors $\mathbf{v}$ über das gesamte Szenario hinweg berechnet werden.

Mit Hilfe des beschriebenen Optimierungsverfahrens lässt sich die Gruppenzuordnung weiter verbessern. Insbesondere lassen sich unbefriedigende Situationen, die mit den initial gewählten Parametern vereinzelt auftreten, gezielt beseitigen (siehe Abb. 2).

4 Kommunikationsprotokoll zur verteilten Gruppenbildung

In diesem Abschnitt wird ein Protokoll für die Kommunikationsabläufe im Lebenszyklus kooperativer Gruppen beschrieben. Dabei ist zu unterscheiden zwischen der Kommunikation innerhalb einer Gruppe und der Inter-Gruppen-Kommunikation. In jeder Gruppe wird ein ausgezeichnetes Fahrzeug bestimmt, das die Kommunikation mit anderen Gruppen koordiniert. Alle Mitglieder einer Gruppe senden Nachrichten mit ihren eigenen Positionsdaten an diesen Gruppenkoordinator. Der Koordinator sendet periodische *broadcast*-Mitteilungen, um

Name	S → E	Quittung	Beschreibung
VehiclePositionMessage	F → K	nein	Positionsmeldung
GroupAnnouncementMessage	K → B	nein	Bekanntmachung der Gruppe
GroupPositionMessage	K → K	nein	Austausch von Positionsdaten zwischen Gruppenkoordinatoren
GroupAssignmentMessage	K → K	ja	Vorschlag neuer Gruppeneinteilung
GroupAssignmentResponse	K → K	ja	Akzeptieren oder Zurückweisen der vorgeschlagenen Gruppeneinteilung
GroupChangeMessage	K → F	ja	Wechsel der Gruppenzugehörigkeit

Tabelle 1. Nachrichtentypen im Kommunikationsprotokoll. In der zweiten Spalte sind **S**ender und **E**mpfänger der Nachricht aufgeführt (K = Koordinator, F = beliebiges Fahrzeug, B = Broadcast). Die dritte Spalte gibt an, ob für die Nachricht eine Quittung erwartet wird.

die Gruppe allen Fahrzeugen in Funkreichweite bekannt zu machen. Er prüft in Abstimmung mit benachbarten Gruppenkoordinatoren, ob durch eine andere Gruppenzuordnung der Fahrzeuge eine Verbesserung der Bewertungsfunktion erreicht werden kann. Zwei Gruppen $\mathcal{G}_1 = \{c_0, c_1, \ldots, c_{m-1}\}$ und $\mathcal{G}_2 = \{c_m, \ldots, c_{m+k-1}\}$ gelten dabei als benachbart, wenn für ihre Koordinatoren c_0 und c_m folgende Bedingung erfüllt ist:

$$\nexists c_z : d(c_0, c_m) > \max\{d(c_0, c_z), d(c_m, c_z)\}, \tag{7}$$

d. h. es gibt keinen weiteren Gruppenkoordinator c_z zwischen c_0 und c_m. Durch diese Einschränkung kann die Rechenlast auch dann gering gehalten werden, wenn viele Gruppen in Funkreichweite sind. Falls die Nachbarschaftsbedingung erfüllt ist, berechnet einer der beiden Gruppenkoordinatoren die optimale Gruppenzuordnung für die Fahrzeugmenge $C := \mathcal{G}_1 \cup \mathcal{G}_2 = \{c_0, \ldots, c_{m+k-1}\}$ gemäß Gleichung (3). Diese Berechnung wird von c_0 für alle benachbarten Gruppen und zusätzlich für $C := \mathcal{G}_1$ durchgeführt. Der letztere Fall behandelt eine mögliche Aufspaltung von $\mathcal{G}_1$ in mehrere Gruppen.

Wenn sich die resultierende Partition P^* von der bisherigen Gruppeneinteilung unterscheidet, wird dies dem zweiten beteiligten Koordinator c_m mitgeteilt. Dieser muss die neue Einteilung entweder akzeptieren oder zurückweisen. Eine Ablehnung erfolgt, falls c_m inzwischen bereits in Abstimmung mit einer anderen benachbarten Gruppe eine Neueinteilung vorgenommen hat und die Berechnung von P^* somit auf veralteten Daten beruht. Erst nach einer Bestätigung wird die neue Gruppeneinteilung allen betroffenen Fahrzeugen mitgeteilt. Diese Vorgehensweise ähnelt dem *two phase commit protocol*, das aus dem Bereich der verteilten Datenbanksysteme bekannt ist [6].

Es wird angenommen, dass jedes Fahrzeug eine eindeutige Identifikationsnummer hat (z. B. seine physikalische Netzwerkadresse). Die Identifikationsnummer kann nicht nur zur Adressierung von Nachrichten verwendet werden, sondern auch zur Auswahl des Gruppenkoordinators und zur Arbitrierung zwischen verschiedenen Koordinatoren. In der momentanen Implementierung erhält dabei stets das Fahrzeug mit der niedrigsten Identifikationsnummer den Zuschlag.

Damit das Protokoll robust gegenüber einer unsicheren Kommunikationsverbindung ist, müssen für die kritischen Abläufe bestätigte Nachrichten verwendet werden, bei denen vom Empfänger eine Quittung angefordert wird. Diese Nachrichten werden so lange wiederholt, bis die Quittung erhalten wurde. Um veraltete Nachrichten erkennen zu können, müssen außerdem synchrone Uhren in allen Fahrzeugen vorhanden sein. Diese Zeitsynchronisation könnte in der Realität beispielsweise über Satellitennavigationssysteme erreicht werden.

Tabelle 1 fasst die verwendeten Nachrichtentypen zusammen.

5 Ergebnisse

Die Anbindung an die Verkehrssimulationssoftware [7] ermöglicht einen umfassende Erprobung und Bewertung der vorgeschlagenen Verfahren in verschiedenen Szenarien. Der benötigte Straßengraph $\mathcal{R}$ kann automatisch aus den Daten des Simulators erzeugt werden (siehe Abb. 1). Die Positionsdaten der simulierten Fahrzeuge sind über eine Datenbank zugänglich [8].

Bezüglich des Kommunikationsprotokolls ist vor allem die Robustheit gegenüber Paketverlusten von Interesse. In der Simulation setzen wir Nachrichten und Pakete gleich, d. h. jede Nachricht besteht aus genau einem Paket. Diese Annahme ist angesichts des vergleichsweise geringen Umfangs der Nachrichten gerechtfertigt. Das einfachste Modell für Paketverluste besteht darin, dass eine Nachricht mit einer Wahrscheinlichkeit p_1 verloren geht, unabhängig vom Verlust anderer Nachrichten. Etwas realistischer ist die Annahme, dass die Verbindung zwischen einem bestimmten Sender-Empfänger-Paar für einen längeren Zeitraum gestört ist, dass die Paketverluste also in Bündeln auftreten. Dies kann dadurch modelliert werden, dass eine Nachricht mit einer höheren Wahrscheinlichkeit $p_2 > p_1$ verloren geht, wenn bereits die vorhergehende Nachricht auf der gleichen Sender-Empfänger-Verbindung nicht angekommen ist.

Der verteilte Gruppenbildungsalgorithmus wurde für verschiedene Werte von p_1 und p_2 simuliert. Die Bewertung erfolgt durch Vergleich des Ergebnisses g mit der Gruppeneinteilung g_0, die mit dem zentral ablaufenden Algorithmus aus [4] unter sonst gleichen Bedingungen berechnet wurde. In Tabelle 2 ist jeweils die relative Übereinstimmung unter dem Gütemaß aus Gleichung (6) angegeben.

Die Verschlechterung selbst bei ungestörter Kommunikation kommt durch den geringfügig verzögerten Gruppenwechsel infolge der Latenzzeiten zustande. Mit steigender Fehlerwahrscheinlichkeit nehmen auch diese Latenzen immer weiter zu. Dennoch bilden sich bei mäßig gestörter Kommunikation die gleichen Gruppen wie im ungestörten Fall, wenn auch entsprechend verzögert. Bei stark gestörter Kommunikation kommt es gelegentlich zur Bildung anderer Gruppen, die aber häufig nur unwesentlich schlechter sind und eine gute Approximation an die optimale Einteilung darstellen. Lediglich im letzten untersuchten Fall ($p_1 = 0.5, p_2 = 0.9$) ist die Kommunikationsqualität zu schlecht für eine sinnvolle Gruppenbildung.

Paketverlustwahrscheinlichkeit p_1	0.0	0.2	0.5	0.1	0.5
Wahrscheinlichkeit für Bündelfehler p_2	0.0	0.2	0.5	0.9	0.9
Gütemaß $J(g)/J(g_0)$	96.3%	93.7%	90.3%	81.3%	64.9%

Tabelle 2. Einfluss von Paketverlusten auf die Gruppeneinteilung

6 Zusammenfassung und Ausblick

In diesem Artikel wurde ein Kriterium zur verteilten Gruppenbildung vorgestellt. Die Parameter der verwendeten Bewertungsfunktion für kooperative Gruppen kognitiver Fahrzeuge wurden mit einem evolutionären Algorithmus optimiert. Es wurde ein Kommunikationsprotokoll für das Lebenszyklusmanagement kooperativer Gruppen entwickelt. Seine Robustheit gegenüber Paketverlusten wurde mit Hilfe eines Verkehrssimulators nachgewiesen. Somit stellt das beschriebene Verfahren eine gute Grundlage für die nachfolgenden Schritte der Situationsanalyse im gemeinsamen Lagebild und der kooperativen Verhaltensentscheidung dar.

Danksagung

Die vorliegende Arbeit wird von der Deutschen Forschungsgemeinschaft (DFG) im Rahmen des SFB/Tr 28 „Kognitive Automobile“ gefördert.

Wir danken unseren Partnern im SFB/Tr für die Bereitstellung der Simulationssoftware.

Literaturverzeichnis

1. Dirk Reichardt, Maurizio Miglietta, Lino Moretti, Peter Morsink und Wolfgang Schulz. CarTALK 2000 – safe and comfortable driving based upon inter-vehicle-communication. In *Proc. IEEE Intelligent Vehicles Symposium*, 2002.
2. Christian Adler und Markus Straßberger. Putting together the pieces – a comprehensive view on cooperative local danger warning. In *World Congress on Intelligent Transport Systems and Services*, 2006.
3. Marc Torrent-Moreno, Andreas Festag und Hannes Hartenstein. System design for information dissemination in VANETs. In *Proc. International Workshop on Intelligent Transportation*, 2006.
4. Christian Frese, Jürgen Beyerer und Peter Zimmer. Cooperation of cars and formation of cooperative groups. In *Proc. IEEE Intelligent Vehicles Symposium*, S. 227–232, 2007.
5. Hartmut Pohlheim. *Evolutionäre Algorithmen.* Springer, 2000.
6. Andrew S. Tanenbaum und Maarten van Steen. *Distributed Systems.* Prentice Hall, 2002.
7. Stefan Vacek, Robert Nagel, Thomas Batz, Frank Moosmann und Rüdiger Dillmann. An integrated simulation framework for cognitive automobiles. In *Proc. IEEE Intelligent Vehicles Symposium*, S. 221–226, 2007.
8. Matthias Goebl und Georg Färber. A real-time-capable hard- and software architecture for joint image and knowledge processing in cognitive automobiles. In *Proc. IEEE Intelligent Vehicles Symposium*, S. 734–740, 2007.

Ein Lasersensor-basiertes Navigationssystem für Nutzfahrzeuge

Roland Stahn[1,2] und Andreas Stopp[1]

[1] DaimlerChrysler AG, Group Research, Assistance and Safety Systems, Berlin
[2] Technische Universität Berlin, Computer Vision and Remote Sensing Group

Zusammenfassung. In diesem Beitrag wird ein Lasersensor-basiertes Navigationssystem zum automatisierten oder assistierten Manövrieren von Fahrzeugen und Fahrzeugkombinationen vorgestellt. Das System unterstützt positionsgenaue, kollisionsfreie Bewegungen relativ zu einem oder mehreren erkannten Zielobjekten. Eine gitterbasierte multidimensionale Bewegungsplanung berechnet den kostengünstigsten kollisionsfreien Anfahrtsweg für die jeweilige Fahrzeugkombination. Die Navigation und Bahnregelung entlang der geplanten Trajektorie erfolgt durch fortlaufende Auswertung von Laserentfernungsdaten. Im vorliegenden Artikel wird die Anwendung des Systems auf verschiedene praxisrelevante Szenarien erläutert.

1 Einleitung

Zu den Aufgaben von LKW-Fahrern gehört das präzise Manövrieren ihrer Fahrzeuge z.B. beim Einparken, beim Andocken an Laderampen oder beim Aufnehmen von Wechselbrücken. Oftmals muss dabei auf engem Raum rangiert werden. Dies ist insbesondere bei Gliederzügen selbst für erfahrene Fahrer schwierig und fehleranfällig, da die Abmessungen des Fahrzeuges sehr groß sind und die Sicht aus der Fahrerkabine stark eingeschränkt ist. Das nachfolgend vorgestellte Lasersensor-basierte Navigationssystem erlaubt es, diese Aufgaben zu automatisieren bzw. dem Fahrer zu assistieren. Vorgesehene Anwendungsfälle sind neben

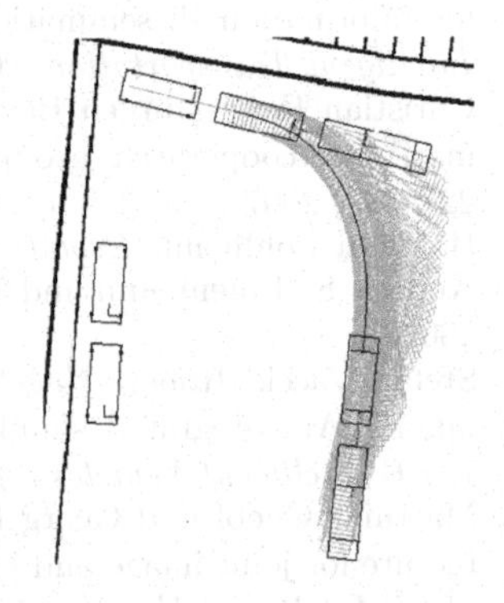

Abb. 1. Ausgangsposition und Wegplanung für eine 80 ° Anfahrt mit einem Gliederzug.

Abb. 2. Lasersensoren am Heck von LKW und Anhänger.

den bereits genannten auch der Wechsel des Anhängers beziehungsweise des Sattelaufliegers. In [1] wurde die Fähigkeiten des Systems anhand eines Container-Wechsel-Assistenten zum teil-automatisierten Unterfahren von Wechselbrücken beschrieben. Abb. 1 zeigt ein entsprechendes Beispielszenario.

2 Systemüberblick

Die Entwicklung und Erprobung des Systems erfolgte mit einem Gliederzug bestehend aus einem handelsüblichen LKW *Mercedes-Benz Actros* und einem 2-Achs-Anhänger mit gelenkter Vorderachse, auf denen jeweils ein Containerwechselrahmen montiert ist (Abb. 1). Lkw und Anhänger haben jeweils eine Länge von ca. 9,5 m und einen Radstand von 5 m. Das Versuchsfahrzeug besitzt eine elektronische Ansteuerung der Lenkung und der Fahrzeuggeschwindigkeit. Am Heck von LKW und Anhänger wurde jeweils ein scannender Lasersensor vom Typ *SICK LMS 200* montiert (Abb. 2). Beide liefern Entfernungsmessdaten für die Objekterkennung mit einer Reichweite von bis zu 80 m im Außenbereich, einem Sichtwinkel von 180 ° und einer Winkelauflösung von 0,25 °.

Eine typische Anwendung der Laserbasierten Navigation ist der Assistenzbetrieb. Der Nominalablauf umfasst dabei die folgende Schritte:

1. Der Fahrer positioniert das Fahrzeug bzw. den Gliederzug vor dem gewünschten Zielobjekt und aktiviert das System.
2. Es erfolgt eine Szenenanalyse. Das System erkennt alle anwendungsspezifischen Zielobjekte im Sichtbereich des Sensors und bietet sie dem Fahrer zur Auswahl an. Dabei wird vom System ein Zielobjekt vorausgewählt.
3. Der Fahrer bestätigt oder korrigiert die Zielauswahl. Das System plant einen Weg zur gewünschten Zielposition und signalisiert Bereitschaft.
4. Der Fahrer aktiviert die Anfahrt durch Gasgeben. Das Fahrzeug wird vom System bis in die Zielposition gesteuert und dort positionsgenau eingebremst. Außerdem überwacht das System den Fahrraum hinter LKW bzw. Anhänger und bremst bei auftretenden Hindernissen selbständig.

Darüber hinaus ist das System auch für autonome Anwendungsfälle ausgelegt, beispielsweise auf einem automatisierten Betriebshof oder Logistikzentrum. Die

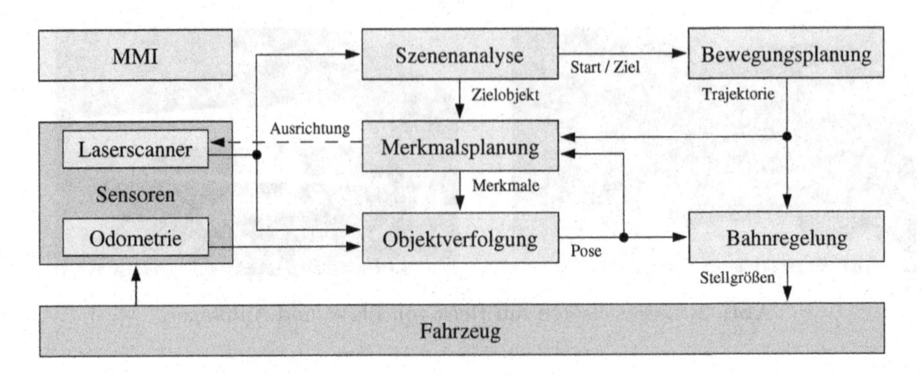

Abb. 3. Systemarchitektur

Vorgabe von Zielobjekten bzw. Stellpositionen erfolgt dabei typischerweise durch eine übergeordnete Missionssteuerung.

Das Gesamtsystem gliedert sich in mehrere Module (siehe Abb. 3). Der Initialablauf der Lasernavigation umfasst die *Szenenanalyse*, die *Zielauswahl* und die *Bewegungsplanung*. Der innere Regelkreis besteht aus den Modulen *Sensorik* (Laser und Odometrie), *Merkmalsplanung*, *Objektverfolgung* und *Bahnregelung*. Aus den Messdaten der Sensorik wird anhand prädizierter *Merkmale* fortlaufend die aktuelle *Pose* des Fahrzeuges berechnet. Diese wird mit der von der geplanten *Trajektorie* vorgegebenen Sollpose verglichen und aus der Abweichung werden die beiden *Stellgrößen* Geschwindigkeit und Lenkwinkel zur Ansteuerung des *Fahrzeugs* ermittelt. Im Falle eines Gliederzuges erfolgt die Stabilisierung von Hänger- und Deichselwinkel während der Rückwärtsfahrt durch einen zusätzlichen eingebetteten Regler der *Mercedes-Benz Nutzfahrzeugentwicklung*. Die Mensch-Maschine-Schnittstelle (*MMI*) stellt dem Benutzer Bedienelemente zur Aktivierung des Systems, zur Auswahl des gewünschten Zielobjektes, zur Unterbrechung einer Anfahrt sowie eine Statusanzeige zur Verfügung.

3 Objekterkennung

Die Navigation zu einer Zielposition erfordert die sensorielle Erfassung des Zielobjektes bzw. umliegender Landmarken. Abb. 4 zeigt einige typische Zielobjekte. Das vorgestellte System verwendet Laserentfernungsdaten, die sich durch eine hohe Präzision und Robustheit gegenüber Umwelteinflüssen auszeichnen. Für die Objekterkennung aus der Bewegung heraus ist gegenwärtig kein Lasersensor verfügbar, der dreidimensionale Daten mit einer ausreichenden Auflösung und Genauigkeit sowie mit einer hohen Aufnahmegeschwindigkeit liefern kann. Daher verwenden wir einen 2D-Laserscanner, der bei Bedarf für 3D-Aufnahmen aktuiert werden kann.

Die Objekterkennung gliedert sich grundsätzlich in zwei Stufen: Szenenanalyse und Objektverfolgung. Bei der Szenenanalyse werden alle potentiellen Zielobjekte im Sichtbereich des Sensors erfasst und identifiziert, während bei der

Abb. 4. Zielobjekte: Wechselbrücken, Anhänger, Halleneinfahrten, Laderampen.

Objektverfolgung nur noch die Pose des Fahrzeuges relativ zum ausgewählten Zielobjekt verfolgt wird. Die Szenenanalyse (Abb. 5) erfolgt vorzugsweise in 2D. Die zweidimensionale Analyse hat den Vorteil, dass sie nur einen einfachen Sensor benötigt und sehr schnell arbeitet. Unter Verwendung eines hierarchischen Objektmodells, werden einfache Merkmale (Sprungkanten, Liniensegmente) anhand räumlicher Abhängigkeiten schrittweise zu Merkmalsmustern und letztlich Objekten gruppiert. Das Vorgehen für Wechselbrücken wird in [1] detailiert beschrieben. Analog wurden mit diesem System bereits erste Versuche für Anhänger, Auflieger und Hallentore durchgeführt. Lassen sich Objekte nicht eindeutig in 2D unterscheiden, so wird durch Aktuierung des Sensors eine dreidimensionale Aufnahme und eine automatische Objektklassifizierung durchgeführt. Während der Anfahrt erfolgt die Lokalisation anhand von 2D-Entfernungsdaten. Derartige Algorithmen sind im Innenbereich bereits gut untersucht, im Außenbereich dagegen noch selten. In [2] und [3] werden Ansätze unter Nutzung künstlicher und natürlicher Landmarken vorgestellt, welche für eine präzise Lokalisation relativ zu einem Zielobjekt jedoch nur bedingt geeignet sind. In der vorliegenden Arbeit wurde ein Multi-Phasen Objektverfolgungsalgorithmus entwickelt, der aufbauend auf den Ergebnissen der Szenenanalyse in Abhängigkeit der Entfernung vom Zielobjekt unterschiedliche Objektmerkmale verfolgt [1]. Die Phasen können entweder je Objekt fest vorgegeben sein oder unter Nutzung eines 3D-Modells des Zielobjektes durch die Merkmalsplanung dynamisch während der Anfahrt ermittelt werden [4]. Im Nahbereich kommen bekannte Verfahren wie ICP zum Einsatz. Im Fernbereich (>10 m) wird die Auflösung der Laserdaten jedoch zunehmend geringer. Hier werden analog zur Szenenanalyse robuste Merkmale wie Sprungkanten und Liniensegmente genutzt. Durch die geringe Strukturiertheit von Außenszenarien reichen diese Merkmale als Kriterium jedoch oft nicht aus, um Objekte eindeutig zu identifizieren. Im Rahmen der vorliegenden Arbeit hat es sich als sehr effektiv erwiesen, zusätzlich Freiraum-Bereiche als zu einem Objekt gehörende Merkmale heranzuziehen. Dies betrifft beispielsweise den Freiraum einer Halleneinfahrt oder den Einfahrbereich unter einer Wechselbrücke (siehe Abb. 5). Aber auch Freiraumdefinitionen rund um typischerweise freistehende Zielobjekte tragen dazu bei, dass diese zuverlässig erkannt werden. Optional können auch zusätzliche künstliche Merkmale wie Reflektoren die Erkennung vereinfachen, sofern dies die jeweilige Anwendung erlaubt.

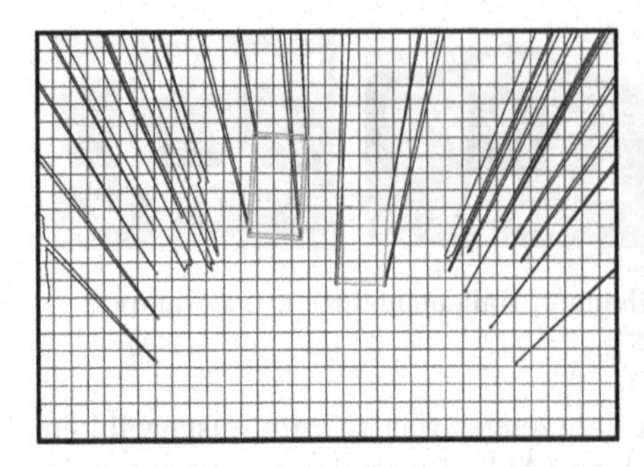
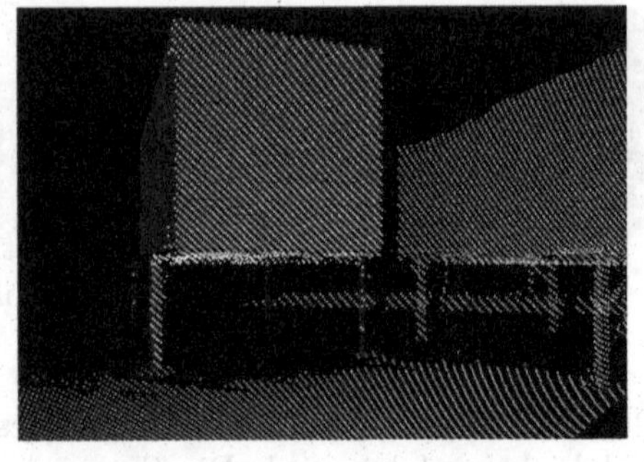

Abb. 5. Szenenanalyse anhand von Laserentfernungsdaten in 2D und 3D.

4 Bewegungsplanung

Ein wichtiger Aspekt für die präzise Navigation mit Fahrzeugen ist eine kollisionsfreie, kosten-optimierende Bewegungsplanung. Die grundlegenden Algorithmen dafür sind aus der mobilen Robotik bekannt [5]. Im Rahmen der vorliegenden Arbeit wurden diese für die Anforderungen eines praxisnahen Einsatzes der Lasersensor-basierten Navigation angepasst [6]. Wesentliche Bedingungen sind:

- Planung für nicht-holonome, kinematisch stark beschränkte Fahrzeuge und insbesondere Fahrzeugkombinationen, wie z.B. Sattelzüge, Gliederzüge und GigaLiner.
- Laufzeiten im Sekundenbereich, um eine Akzeptanz beim Benutzer im Assistenzbetrieb zu erreichen.
- Exakte Berücksichtigung der gegebenen Start- und Zielposition, da die geplante Trajektorie die Grundlage für die exakte Bahnregelung darstellt.

Es wurde ein gitterbasierter Ansatz verwendet, bei dem mit Hilfe eines A^*-Algorithmus fahrbare Trajektorien mit kurzer Laufzeit gefunden werden. Zum Ausgleich des systembedingten Gitterfehlers an der Zielposition erfolgt eine nachgeschaltete, schrittweise Korrektur auf die vorgegebene Zielposition. Die Suchalgorithmen und das Planungsgitter sind multidimensional ausgelegt: Fahrzeuge mit bis zu fünf Freiheitsgraden (Position, Ausrichtung, Anhängerwinkel, Deichselwinkel) werden so unterstützt. Die Planung selbst ist multimodal aufgebaut und unterscheidet die folgenden Anwendungsfälle:

Direkte Anfahrt: Zunächst versucht der Planer einen direkten Weg ohne Wendepunkte in die Zielposition zu bestimmen (Abb. 1). Ein direkter Weg stellt typischerweise die einfachste Lösung dar und kann im derart begrenzten Suchraum schnell gefunden werden.

Anfahrt mit Wendepunkten: Wird kein direkter Weg gefunden, so wird ein Weg mit möglichst wenigen Wendepunkten gesucht (Abb. 6). Die Suche dauert länger, deckt jedoch viele praxisrelevante Szenarien mit eingeschränktem Bewegungsraum oder komplexen Startpositionen ab.

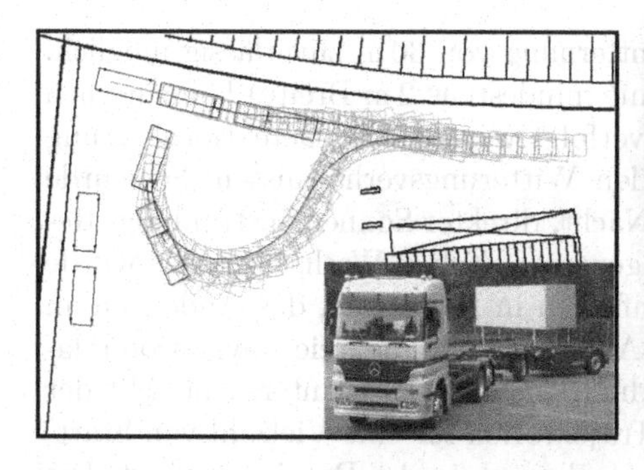

Abb. 6. Planung mit Wendepunkt auf detektierter Rangierfläche aus 3D Weltmodell.

Langstreckenplanung: Insbesondere im Autonomiefall können Start- und Zielposition weit voneinander entfernt sein. Für diese Aufgabe wird ein speziell für die Langstreckenplanung optimierter Modus verwendet, der die Suche zunächst in einem groben Gitter beginnt und dieses dann schrittweise verfeinert.

In jedem Fall erfolgt die Planung kollisionsfreier Wege basierend auf einer Karte mit statischen Hindernissen. Diese Polygon-basierte Karte wird vorgegeben oder aus Laserdaten erstellt bzw. dynamisch ergänzt. Abb. 6 zeigt ein Beispiel für eine automatisch aus 3D-Daten bestimmte Rangierfläche. Dynamische Hindernisse werden durch eine permanente Kollisionskontrolle während der Anfahrt erfasst. Erforderlichenfalls erfolgt ein Abbremsen oder Anhalten des Fahrzeuges – alternativ eine Neuplanung. Die Karte eignet sich darüberhinaus auch zur kooperativen Aktualisierung und Planung für Multi-Fahrzeug-Anwendungen.

5 Ergebnisse

Das System wurde am Anwendungsbeispiel des rückwärts gerichteten Unterfahrens von Wechselbrücken mit LKW und Gliederzug unter verschiedenen Umgebungs- und Wetterbedingungen erfolgreich erprobt. Eine assistierte Anfahrt war aus Startpositionen mit bis zu 100 ° Anfahrtswinkel und bis zu einer Entfernung von 30 m zwischen Fahrzeugheck und Zielobjekt zuverlässig möglich. Beim Einfahren wurde dabei eine Wiederholgenauigkeit von ±1 cm in Querrichtung, sowie an der Zielposition eine Abweichung von ±3 cm in Fahrtrichtung und ±0,2 ° bei der Orientierung gemessen. Damit wurden die strengen Genauigkeitsanforderungen dieser Anwendung erreicht. Ein typischer Andockvorgang aus ca. 20 m Entfernung dauert weniger als 60 Sekunden. Die Durchschnittsgeschwindigkeit über den dabei zurückgelegten Weg von 30 m beträgt 0.5 m/s. Die Maximalgeschwindigkeit des Fahrzeuges wird derzeit auf 1 m/s begrenzt. Darüber hinausgehend wurde in weiteren Experimenten die Sichtbarkeit und Genauigkeit verschiedener Basis-Merkmale in Abhängigkeit von der Entfernung untersucht [4]. Mit dem verwendeten SICK Laserscanner ist eine Detektion von schmalen

Objekten (10 cm Breite) bis zu einer Entfernung von 30 m zuverlässig möglich. Große Flächen (z.B. Kastenaufbauten mit mindestens 2 m Breite) können auch noch in Entfernungen von bis zu 80 m verfolgt werden. Die Detektionsleistung ist dabei weitgehend unabhängig von den Witterungsverhältnissen. So wurde die Funktionsfähigkeit des Systems bei Nacht, direkter Sonneneinstrahlung, Regen und leichtem Nebel erfolgreich nachgewiesen. Neben Wechselbrücken wurde das Ankoppeln von Anhängern, das Einfahren in Hallentore, das Andocken an Laderampen, sowie das Aufnehmen von Aufliegern und die freie Navigation relativ zu natürlichen und künstlichen Landmarken erfolgreich untersucht. Mit der Bewegungsplanung wurden erfolgreich Trajektorien für eine Vielzahl von Start- und Zielposition sowohl in der Simulation als auch in der Praxis generiert. Die typische Suchzeit der gitterbasierten Planung lag dabei bei unter 1 s für eine direkte Anfahrt, unter 10 s für Anfahrten mit Wendepunkten und unter 30 s für Langstreckenanfahrten über bis zu 100 m.

6 Zusammenfassung

Das hier vorgestellte System zur Lasersensor-basierten Navigation für LKW und Gliederzüge unterstützt eine Vielzahl autonomer oder teilautonomer Aufgaben auf Betriebshöfen und im öffentlichen Verkehr. Ziel ist das schadensfreie Manövrieren und damit die Entlastung von Fahrern bei schwierigen Aufgaben wie dem Einparken, Andocken, Aufnehmen oder Ankuppeln von Nutzfahrzeugen, insbesondere auch nachts. Das System leistet für alle Anwendungsfälle neben der hohen funktionalen Genauigkeit und einfacher Handhabbarkeit auch für ungeübte Fahrer vorteilhafterweise kontinuierlichen Kollisions- und Personenschutz. Darüberhinaus schafft es die technischen Voraussetzungen für zukünftiges autonomes Manövrieren mittels freier Navigation.

Literaturverzeichnis

1. Roland Stahn, Gerd Heiserich, Andreas Stopp: Laser scanner-based navigation for commercial vehicles. *IEEE Intelligent Vehicles Symposium*: 969–974, Istanbul, 2007.
2. Jose Guivant, Eduardo Nebot, Stephan Baiker: Autonomous navigation and map building using laser range sensors in outdoor applications. *Journal of Robotic Systems* **17**: 565–583, 2000.
3. Thorsten Weiss, Klaus Dietmayer: Robust host localization in skidding situations using laserscanner. *4th Workshop on Intelligent Transportation*, Hamburg, 2007.
4. Roland Stahn, Andreas Stopp: 3D model-based dynamic feature planning for laser scanner-based navigation of vehicles. *3rd European Conference on Mobile Robots*, Freiburg, 2007.
5. Howie Choset, Kevin M. Lynch, Seth Hutchinson, George Kantor, Wolfram Burgard, Lydia E. Kavraki, Sebastian Thrun: *Principles of Robot Motion - Theory, Algorithms, and Implementations.* MIT Press, Cambridge, 2005.
6. Roland Stahn, Tobias Stark, Andreas Stopp. Laser scanner-based navigation and motion planning for truck-trailer combinations. *IEEE/ASME International Conference on Advanced Intelligent Mechatronics*, Zürich, 2007.

Detektion von Fahrspuren und Kreuzungen auf nichtmarkierten Straßen zum autonomen Führen von Fahrzeugen

Stefan Vacek, Cornelius Bürkle, Joachim Schröder und Rüdiger Dillmann

Institut für Technische Informatik, Universität Karlsruhe (TH),
Haid-und-Neu-Straße 7, 76131 Karlsruhe
vacek@ira.uka.de

1 Einleitung

Das Wissen über Position und Verlauf der Straße ist eine der wichtigsten Informationen, die zum Führen autonomer Straßenfahrzeuge benötigt wird. Die meisten Arbeiten gehen davon aus, dass Markierungen auf der Straße vorhanden sind, die die Erkennung enorm erleichtern. Üblicherweise werden die Fahrbahnränder detektiert und die Fahrspur mit Hilfe eines Kalman-Filters geschätzt [1]. Andere Arbeiten verwenden zusätzlich die Straßenfarbe und kombinieren die verschiedenen Hinweise in einem Partikel-Filter [2]. Ein allgemeiner Überblick über Verfahren zur Fahrspurdetektion findet sich in [3].

In dieser Arbeit wird ein Ansatz vorgestellt, der in der Lage ist, auch auf nichtmarkierten Straßen den Fahrspurverlauf zu schätzen und Kreuzungen zu detektieren, um ein Fahrzeug autonom zu führen. Zur Fahrspurerkennung wird ein Partikel-Filter verwendet, das verschiedene Merkmale im Kamerabild auswertet und daraus die beste Schätzung ableitet. (Kapitel 2) Kreuzungen werden ebenfalls mit einem Partikelfilter vorsegmentiert. Anschließend werden die Begrenzungen der Einmündung durch Bézier-Kurven approximiert (Kapitel 3). Zur Evaluation des Verfahrens wurden Testfahrten mit dem autonomen Fahrzeug „Smart Roadster“ durchgeführt (Kapitel 4).

2 Fahrspurerkennung

Zur Fahrspurerkennung wird ein Partikel-Filter verwendet, welches die Parameter des Fahrspurmodells schätzt. Die Fahrspur wird durch ein gerades Straßenstück modelliert, das für kurze Distanzen genau genug ist. Das Modell ist durch zwei parallele Geraden gegeben, deren Lage durch vier Parameter beschrieben sind.

Gesucht ist die a-posteriori Verteilung des Zustandsmodells $\mathbf{X}_t = [x_0, \psi, w, \phi]^T$, mit der Verschiebung x_0 des Fahrzeug von der Fahrspurmitte, Gierwinkel ψ, Fahrspurbreite w und Kameranickwinkel ϕ. Jedes Partikel repräsentiert eine Parameterausprägung des Fahrspurmodells. Für jedes Partikel wird das Fahrspurmodell ins Bild projiziert und anhand von Hinweisen bewertet. Das beste Partikel repräsentiert die aktuelle Schätzung.

Da die zu erkennenden Straßen über keine eindeutige Markierung verfügen, reichen Kanten alleine zur Schätzung nicht aus. Vielmehr werden neben Kanten noch die Straßenfarbe sowie die Textur ausgewertet. Für jeden Hinweis erhält man ein Maß, das angibt, wie gut das Fahrspurmodell zu den Merkmalen passt, und die Gesamtbewertung ist das Produkt der Einzelbewertungen. In [4] ist das Verfahren auf markierte Straßen mit mehreren Fahrspuren angewendet worden.

Zur Bewertung Straßenrands wird das Bild zunächst mit einem Canny-Kantendetektor gefaltet. Für jeden Bildpunkt wird dann der minimale Abstand zur nächsten Kante berechnet und als Maß verwendet. Die Bewertung des Hinweises ergibt sich, indem die Punkte entlang des rechten und linken Rands des Fahrspurmodells aufsummiert und normiert werden.

Zur Bewertung der Straßenfarbe wird das Kamerabild in den HSV-Farbraum konvertiert und ein Farbmodell im HS-Raum gebildet. Für jeden Pixel innerhalb des Fahrspurmodells wird die Wahrscheinlichkeit bestimmt, mit der er zum Farbmodell gehört. Die Wahrscheinlichkeitswerte werden für alle Pixel aufsummiert und der normierte Wert ergibt die Bewertung des Hinweises. Da sich die Fahrbahnbeschaffenheit ändern kann, wird das Farbmodell kontinuierlich angepasst, indem die Farbverteilung der letzten Fahrspurschätzung mit dem aktuellen Farbmodell fusioniert wird.

Um ein Maß für die Textur zu erhalten, wird das Bild mit einem horizontalen Laplacian-of-Gaussian gefaltet. Um die charakteristische Textur der Fahrbahnoberfläche zu ermitteln, werden zwei Histogramme über die Kantenstärke gebildet. Das erste Histogramm repräsentiert alle Pixel im Bild, wohingegen das zweite nur die Pixel unmittelbar vor dem Fahrzeug auswertet. Daraus wird die erwartete Kantenstärke der Fahrspurregion bestimmt und die Pixel des Bildes entsprechend klassifiziert. Abbildung 1 zeigt die entstandenen Histogramme und den daraus resultierende Kantenstärke der Fahrbahnoberfläche.

Um die Straßenregion anhand der Textur abzuleiten, ist ein Nachbarbeitungsschritt nötig, der Bereiche außerhalb der Straße ausschließt. Dabei wird angenommen, dass der Bordstein keine starken horizontalen Kanten aufweist. Die Mitte der Fahrspur der letzten Schätzung wird benutzt, um mittels Regionenwachstum die Straßenregion zu segmentieren. Für jede Bildzeile wird die Region nach rechts und links erweitert, so lange die Pixel zum Texturmodell gehören, oder die Anzahl der aneinanderhängenden, nicht segmentierten Pixel unterhalb eines Schwellwerts ist. Abbildung 2 zeigt das Resultat.

3 Detektion von Kreuzungen

Die Detektion von Kreuzungen baut auf der Fahrspurdetektion auf. Es wird davon ausgegangen, dass keine digitale Karte vorliegt, anhand derer Hinweise auf Kreuzungen abgeleitet werden können. Die Erkennung erfolgt in zwei Phasen. In der ersten Phase werden mit Hilfe eines Partikel-Filters mögliche Kandidaten für Kreuzungen geschätzt und in der zweiten Phase werden die Hypothesen überprüft und die exakten Parameter der Einmündung bestimmt.

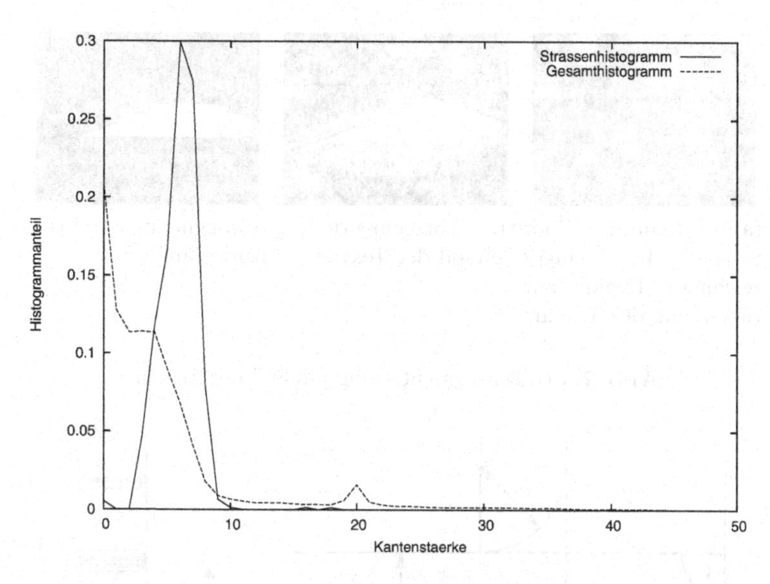

Abb. 1. Histogramme der Kantenstärken des Gesamtbildes und des Bereichs vor dem Fahrzeug.

Mit Hilfe eines Partikel-Filters werden die Parameter Abstand d zur Kreuzung, Radius r_o und Winkel β der Einmündung bestimmt (s. Abbildung 3 (a)). Da dieses Ergebnis noch sehr ungenau ist, wird die Schätzung in jedem Zeitschritt durchgeführt und aus diesen Schätzungen Cluster gebildet, die einzelne Hypothesen für mögliche Kreuzungen darstellen. Dazu werden die Mittelwerte über die geschätzte Entfernung d, den Radius r_o sowie die Bewertung p_k aus dem Partikel-Filter herangezogen. Insgesamt erhält man so u.U. mehrere Ballungen, wie es in Abbildung 3 (b) dargestellt ist.

Aus der Vorklassifikation sind der Abstand d zur Kreuzung, der Radius r_o sowie der Winkel β der Einmündung bekannt. In der zweiten Phase werden die Breite b der Einmündung und der Verlauf der unteren (d.h. dem Fahrzeug zugewandten Seite) Begrenzung bestimmt, indem das Textur- und das Kantenbild herangezogen werden. Zuerst werden mit Hilfe des Texturbildes Kandidaten für obere und untere Begrenzungspunkte der einmündenden Fahrspur bestimmt und anschließend über diese Punkte mit einem kleinste-Quadrate-Schätzer gemittelt, um die Begrenzung der Einmündung zu schätzen. In jedem Zeitschritt erhält man so eine Schätzung der Kreuzung im Fahrzeugkoordinatensystem und die Kreuzung wird als erkannt betrachtet, wenn sich die Lage der oberen und unteren Begrenzung in drei aufeinanderfolgenden Beobachtungen nicht signifikant ändert. Abschließend wird noch der Verlauf der unteren Begrenzung der Einmündung bestimmt. Dieser wird durch eine Bézierkurve 2. Grades repräsentiert und mit Hilfe des Kantenbildes berechnet. Dazu werden Kantenpunkte S_1 und S_3 aus dem Kantenbild auf den Geraden E und F (s. Abb. 3 (a)) bestimmt, die mögliche Stützpunkte für die Bézierkurve darstellen. Zusammen mit dem Schnittpunkt S_2

(a) Aufnahme einer Straße mit eingezeichneter Region zur Bewertung der Textur (b) Vorsegmentierung anhand der Textur (c) Segmentierter Straßenverlauf

Abb. 2. Straßensegmentierung anhand der Textur

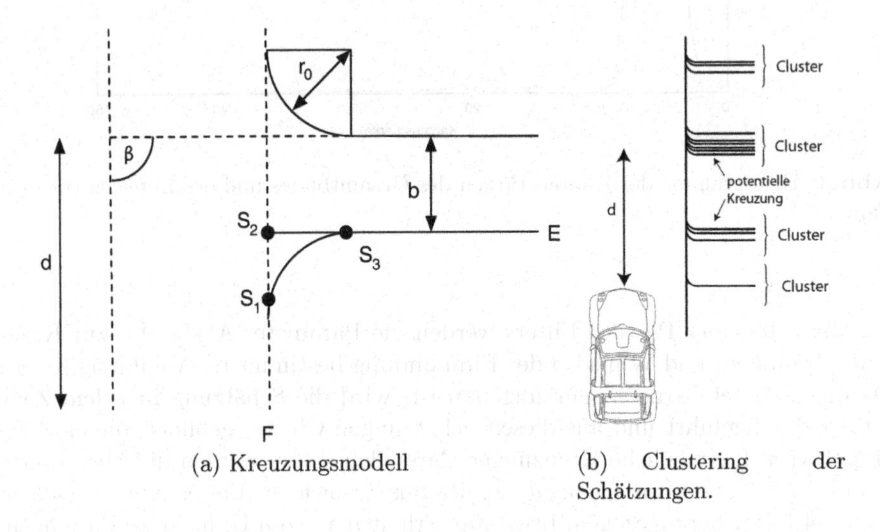

(a) Kreuzungsmodell (b) Clustering der Schätzungen.

Abb. 3. Modellierung der Kreuzungen und Hypothesenbildung durch Clustering der Schätzungen.

der beiden Geraden E und F werden Bézierkurven erzeugt, und anhand des Kantenbild wird bewertet, wie gut die Kurve den unteren Verlauf der Einmündung wiedergibt.

Abbildung 4 (a) zeigt die Bestimmung der Stützstellen zur Berechnung der Bézierkurven. In Abbildung 4 (b) ist die detektierte Fahrspur zusammen mit der geschätzten Kreuzung ins Originalbild eingezeichnet.

4 Ergebnisse

Mit dem autonomen Fahrzeug „Smart Roadster“ [5] wurden mehrere Fahrten durchgeführt. Im ersten Experiment wurde das Fahrzeug auf einer markierten, geraden Straße bewusst in Schlangenlinien gesteuert, um die Erkennung der

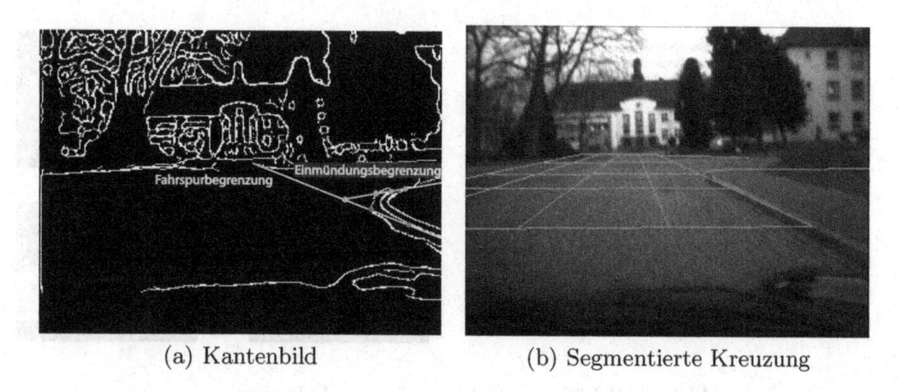

(a) Kantenbild (b) Segmentierte Kreuzung

Abb. 4. Kreuzungsmodell und segmentierte Kreuzung

Straßenränder zu demonstrieren. Der Graph im linken Teil der Abb. 5 zeigt die gefahrene Strecke des Fahrzeugs sowie die geschätzten linken und rechten Begrenzungen der Fahrspur.

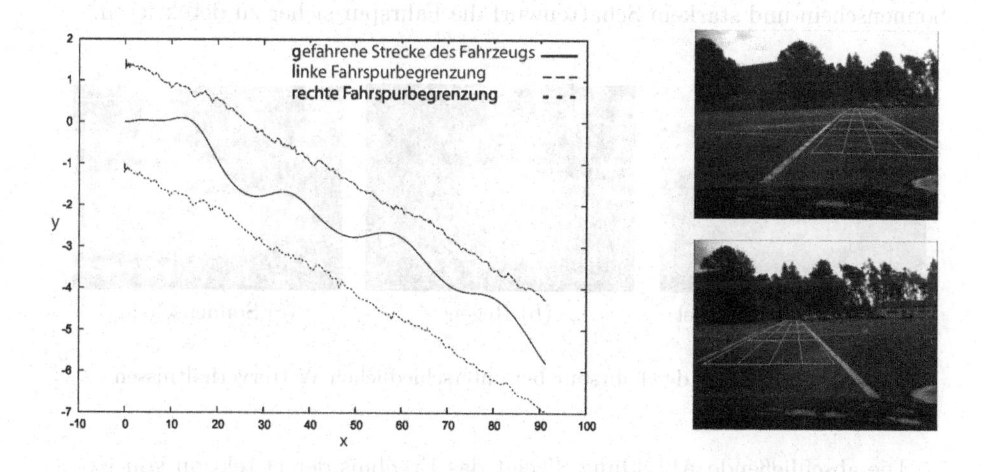

Abb. 5. Schätzung der markierten Fahrspur bei Schlangenlinienfahrt.

Im zweiten Experiment wurde das Fahrzeug auf einer Straße ohne Markierungen gesteuert. Im linken Teil der Abbildung 6 sieht man wiederum die gefahrene Strecke und den geschätzten Verlauf der Fahrspur. Die vier Einzelbild zeigen Ausschnitte der befahrenen Straße mit dem überlagerten geschätzten Fahrspurverlauf.

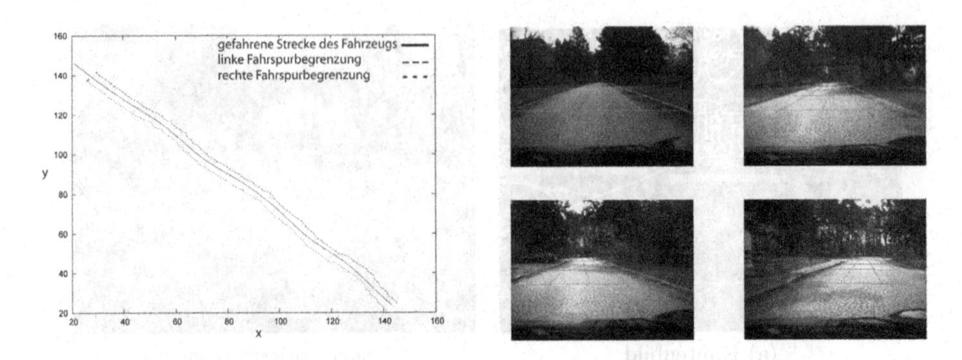

Abb. 6. Schätzung nicht-markierter Fahrspuren.

Die Zuverlässigkeit der Verfahrens zeigt sich bei ungünstigen Wetterverhältnissen. Wie die Beispiele in Abbildung 7 erkennen lassen, würde jedes Merkmal für sich alleine genommen die Fahrspur nicht schätzen können. Durch die Merkmalsfusion im Partikel-Filter ist es aber möglich sowohl bei Regen als auch bei Sonnenschein und starkem Schattenwurf die Fahrspur sicher zu detektieren.

(a) Bedeckter Himmel (b) Regen (c) Sonnenschein

Abb. 7. Detektion der Fahrspur bei unterschiedlichen Wetterverhältnissen.

Die abschließende Abbildung 8 zeigt das Ergebnis der Detektion von Kreuzungen. Der linke Teil (a) zeigt die rekonstruierte Kreuzung sowie den geschätzten Straßenverlauf. Im rechten Teil (b) ist das Kamerabild mit der geschätzten Kreuzung überlagert.

Literaturverzeichnis

1. E. D. Dickmanns and B. D. Mysliwetz. Recursive 3-D road and relative ego-state recognition. *IEEE Transactions on Pattern Analysis and Machine Intelligence*, 14(2):199–213, Februar 1992.
2. Nicholas Apostoloff. *Vision based lane tracking using multiple cues and particle filtering.* PhD thesis, Department of Systems Engineering, Research School of Information Science and Engineering, Australian National University, 2005.

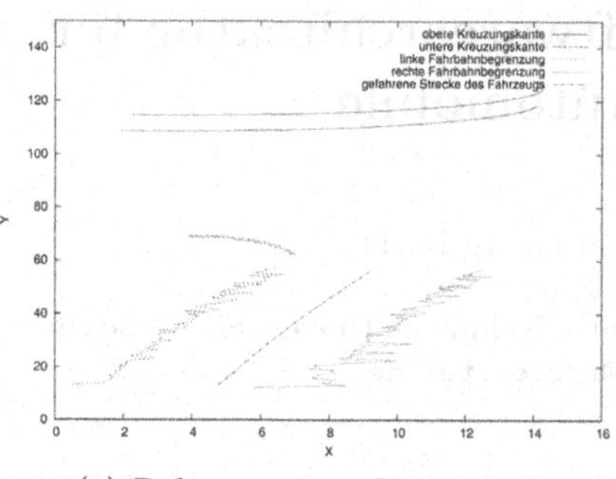

(a) Rekonstruierte Kreuzung.

(b) Szene mit überlagerter Kreuzungsschätzung.

Abb. 8. Detektion von Kreuzungen auf Straßen ohne Markierung.

3. Joel C. McCall and Mohan M. Trivedi. Video based lane estimation and tracking for driver assistance: Survey, system, and evaluation. *IEEE Transactions on Intelligent Transportation Systems*, 2005.
4. Stefan Vacek, Stephan Bergmann, Ulrich Mohr, and Rüdiger Dillmann. Rule-based tracking of multiple lanes using particle filters. In *2006 IEEE International Conference on Multisensor Fusion and Integration for Intelligent Systems (MFI 2006)*, Heidelberg, Germany, September, 3-6 2006.
5. Joachim Schröder, Udo Müller, and Rüdiger Dillmann. Smart roadster project: Setting up drive-by-wire or how to remote-control your car. In *The 9th International Conference on Intelligent Autonomous Systems*, pages 383–390, Tokyo, Japan, March 2006 2006.

Eine realzeitfähige Softwarearchitektur für kognitive Automobile

Matthias Goebl und Georg Färber

Lehrstuhl für Realzeit-Computersysteme, Technische Universität München
{goebl,faerber}@rcs.ei.tum.de

Zusammenfassung. Kognitive Automobile erfordern unterschiedlichste Algorithmen auf allen Wahrnehmungsebenen. Um diese zu verbinden und deren erfolgreiche Kooperation sicherzustellen werden flexible und leistungsfähige Schnittstellen benötigt. Für eine sichere Reaktion auf plötzliche Umwelteinflüsse muss zudem insbesondere auf den unteren Ebenen eine schritthaltende Verarbeitung gewährleistet sein. Die hier vorgestellte Architektur bietet Schnittstellen, die sowohl große Datenmengen effizient transportieren können, als auch Methoden zur blockierungsfreien zeitlichen Entkopplung. Eine besondere Stärke ist die nahtlose Integration von realzeit- und nicht-realzeitfähigen Wahrnehmungsprozessen.

1 Einleitung

Ein „Kognitives Automobil“ ist in der Lage seine Umgebung wahrzunehmen, zu verstehen und selbständig der Situation entsprechend zu handeln. Das Vorhaben des SFB/TR 28 [1,2], kognitive Fähigkeiten durch autonomes Fahren zu demonstrieren, ist die vollständige Automatisierung der Fahraufgabe. Das gewonnene Umfeldverständnis kann jedoch zwischenzeitlich bereits Anwendung in weniger eingriffsstarken aktiven Fahrerassistenzsystemen finden.

Damit sich das Fahrzeug in seiner Umgebung sicher bewegen kann, muss von der sensoriellen Wahrnehmung (Video, Radar, Lidar, GPS, Odometrie, usw.) bis zur Regelung des Fahrzeugs eine schritthaltende Datenverarbeitung garantiert werden. Dies erfordert zum einen schnelle und deterministische Algorithmen in einer effizienten Implementierung. Auf der anderen Seite muss eine Hard- und Softwareumgebung existieren, die diesen Algorithmen die notwendigen Ressourcen zur Verfügung stellt und den reibungslosen Datenaustausch ermöglicht.

Die softwaretechnische Integration der von den beteiligten Entwicklern des Forschungsbereichs beigesteuerten Softwaremodulen in verschiedenen Programmiersprachen stellt eine zusätzliche Herausforderung dar. Will man dabei auch die erwähnten Zeitanforderungen erfüllen, ist eine leistungsfähige Architektur unabdingbar.

2 Architektur

Die hier vorgestellte Softwarearchitektur setzt auf der bereits in [3] beschriebenen Hardwarearchitektur auf: Ein leistungsfähiges PC-System dient der Bild-

und Wissensverarbeitung, ein eingebettetes System (MPC) regelt die Kameraplattform, eine DSpace Autobox bindet die Fahrzeugsensorik und -aktorik an und dient der Sicherheitsüberwachung.

Das PC-System bildet ein schneller Dual-DualCore-Opteron-PC, der die gleichzeitige Ausführung mehrerer Module erlaubt und durch schnelle interne Bussysteme wie Hypertransport eine breitbandige Interprozesskommunikation mit niedrigen Latenzzeiten ermöglicht. Die gewählte Opteron-Architektur ermöglicht Designs mit weiteren Prozessoren, die sich durch Hypertransport zu einem einheitlichen System zusammenfügen. Die Leistungsaufnahme der energieeffizienten Prozessoren einschließlich Mainboard und Speicher beträgt ca. 160 Watt im Fahrzeug. Der Verzicht auf mehrere PCs erlaubt eine ganzheitliche Softwarearchitektur und verhindert das Entstehen von später nicht mehr zu vereinheitlichenden Software- und Hardwareinsellösungen.

2.1 Realzeitdatenbasis für kognitive Automobile (KogMo-RTDB)

Zentrales Element der Softwarearchitektur ist die entwickelte „Realzeitdatenbasis für kognitive Automobile“ (KogMo-RTDB) [4]. Sie dient als Framework zur Integration aller Softwaremodule und ist in der Lage, alle in der Verarbeitungskette anfallenden Daten zu speichern und wieder bereitzustellen.

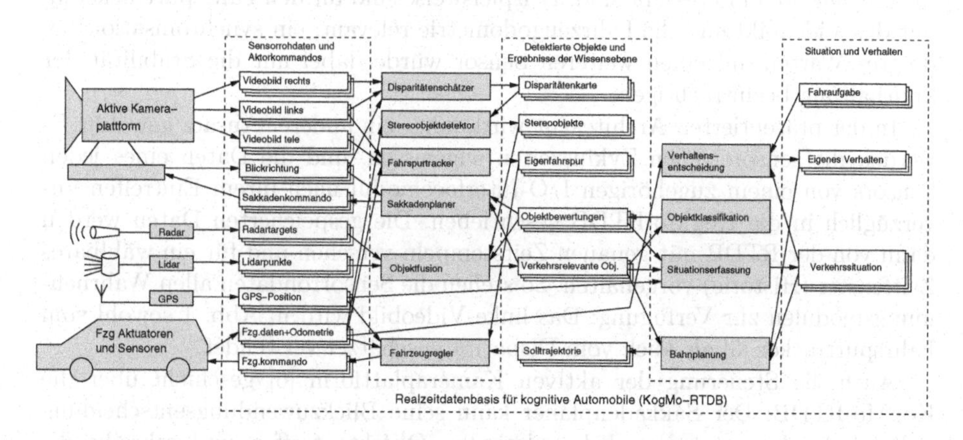

Abb. 1. Datenfluss ausgewählter Wahrnehmungsmodule über die KogMo-RTDB

Abbildung 1 zeigt einen Teil der Module des kognitiven Automobils und deren Verbindung über die KogMo-RTDB. Alle Module sind in der Lage, beliebige Daten in der KogMo-RTDB zu publizieren und auf alle veröffentlichten Daten anderer Module zuzugreifen. In obiger Darstellung ist die KogMo-RTDB zur Gliederung der Verarbeitungsebenen dreigeteilt dargestellt, die enthaltenen Daten (gestrichelter Bereich) bilden dennoch eine Einheit. Dies wirkt der Entstehung von Informationslücken zwischen der Bild- und der Wissensverarbeitung entgegen. So kann beispielsweise die Verhaltensentscheidung ihre Entscheidung abhängig machen von der aktuellen Fahrzeuggeschwindigkeit, die sie aus dem Objekt „Fahrzeugdaten" erhält.

Die Datenbasis ist aus Geschwindigkeitsgründen rein hauptspeicherbasiert. Da klassische Datenbankschnittstellen wie SQL zu langsam wären, geschieht der Zugriff über neu entwickelte Methoden, die aus verschiedenen Programmiersprachen (C,C++,..) genutzt werden können und einen einheitlichen Blick auf die Daten liefern.

2.2 Sensor- und Aktorschnittstellen

Das kognitive Automobil ist mit einer Vielzahl von Sensoren ausgestattet, die jeweils eine individuelle Zykluszeit besitzen. Zur Erleichterung der Datenfusion wäre es wünschenswert, die Sensoren zu synchronisieren. Bei gleichartigen Sensoren wie Videokameras ist das problemlos möglich. Für andere ist es aufwendig, gerade wenn Sensoren von verschiedenen Instituten beigesteuert werden. Aus physikalischen Gründen kann es sogar unmöglich sein: Der rotierende Laserscanner liefert kontinuierlich Daten, der Startzeitpunkt einer Umdrehung lässt sich nicht beliebig verschieben und synchronisieren, da er sich aufgrund seiner Masse nicht beliebig schnell beschleunigen lässt. Die Bestimmung eines taktgebenden Sensors ist ebenfalls problematisch, da es Module gibt, für die nur wenige Sensoren interessant sind. Beispielsweise sind für den Fahrspurtracker [5] nur das Videobild und die Fahrzeugodometrie relevant, ein synchronisationsbedingtes Warten auf einen weiteren Sensor würde dabei nur die Stabilität der Spurhaltung beeinträchtigen.

In der präsentierten Architektur wird daher ein anderer Ansatz gewählt: Es werden die sensoreigenen Zykluszeiten zugelassen, und die Daten eines jeden Sensors von einem zugehörigen I/O-Interfacemodul nach ihrem Eintreffen unverzüglich in die KogMo-RTDB geschrieben. Die gespeicherten Daten werden dann von der RTDB mit genauen Zeitstempeln versehen und für ein wählbares Zeitfenster (Historie) vorgehalten. So stehen die Sensorrohdaten allen Wahrnehmungsmodulen zur Verfügung: Das linke Videobild wird in Abb. 1 sowohl vom Fahrspurtracker [5] als auch vom Disparitätenschätzer verwendet.

Auch die Steuerung der aktiven Kameraplattform [6] geschieht über die KogMo-RTDB: Der Sakkadenplaner kann seine Blickzuwendungsentscheidung anhand der bewerteten verkehrsrelevanten Objekte treffen und schreibt die Sollposition in ein Objekt „Sakkadenkommando". Auf dieses reagiert das Kameraplattform-Interfacemodul und versendet eine CAN-Nachricht an die Plattformsteuerung [3]. Die jeweils aktuelle Kamerastellung wird von der Plattform periodisch zurückgemeldet und im Objekt „Blickrichtung" hinterlegt, wo sie für alle interessierten Module (z.B. o.g. Fahrspurtracker) verfügbar ist.

2.3 Zeitverwaltung

In der KogMo-RTDB werden durchgängig absolute 64–Bit Zeitstempel mit einer Auflösung von $1ns$ verwendet. Diese werden in der Realzeitkonfiguration der

RTDB aus dem Timestampcounter (TSC) der modernen x86 Prozessoren gewonnen. Die Synchronisation der TSCs der einzelnen Prozessoren untereinander geschieht über den Hypertransport-Bus mit einer Genauigkeit von $< 1\mu s$[1].

Allen Objekten wird bei jedem Schreiben automatisch der aktuelle Zeitstempel angehängt (Commit-Timestamp). Zusätzlich müssen die Module den Gültigkeitszeitpunkt der Daten mit angeben (Data-Timestamp). Sämtliche Abfragen von Objekten werden mit einem genauen Zeitpunkt parametrisiert. Dadurch wird sichergestellt, dass der anfragende Prozess genau die Daten aus den internen Ringpuffern bekommt, die zu den gegebenen Zeitpunkt aktuell sind bzw. waren. Dies liefert langsameren Prozessen ein konsistentes Abbild aller Daten und ist vor allem für die zeitlichen Entkopplung von Wahrnehmungsprozessen unterschiedlicher zeitlicher Auflösung relevant. In der Fusion kann die verfügbare Historie der Daten zur Interpolation verwendet werden um beispielsweise fehlende Sensorwerte zu berechnen.

2.4 Realzeitfähigkeit

Die Dynamik der Fahrzeugsituation setzt enge zeitliche Grenzen für alle Ebenen der Verarbeitung, bis hinunter zum Betriebssystem. Ein Standardbetriebssystem zeigt bei höherer Rechenlast leicht Latenzen in der Größenordnung von $10ms$. In dieser Zeit bewegt sich ein $200\frac{km}{h}$ schnelles Fahrzeug über $0.5m$. Ein „Kognitives Automobil" erfordert daher zwingend ein Realzeitbetriebssystem, das Zeiten im μs-Bereich garantiert.

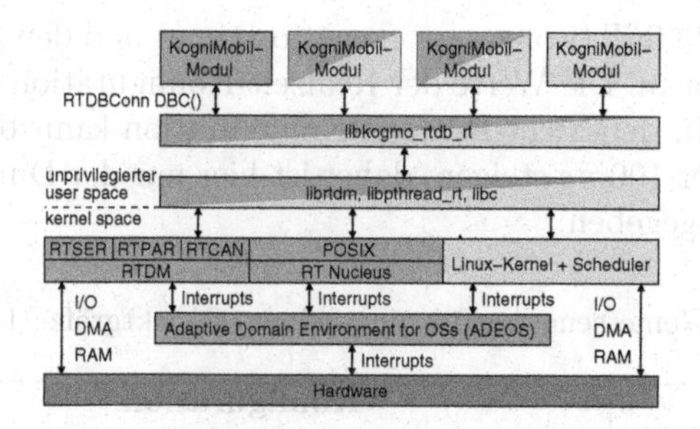

Abb. 2. Architektur der KogMo-RTDB in der Realzeit-Konfiguration

Abb. 2 zeigt die Realzeit-Konfiguration der KogMo-RTDB. Die Basis bildet das Open-Source-Betriebsystem Linux mit der Realzeiterweiterung Xenomai[2]. Das ADEOS-Layer leitet Realzeit-Interrupts ohne Beteiligung des Linux-Schedulers direkt an den Real-Time Nucleus weiter. Über den POSIX-Skin erreichen diese die KogniMobil-Module. Der Zugriff der KogniMobil-Module auf die

[1] Zeit für den Transfer einer Cacheline zwischen den CPUs durch einen einzelnen Speicherzugriff, $<= 330ns$ in [7]

[2] Die Weiterentwicklung von RTAI/fusion, http://www.xenomai.org

KogMo-RTDB geschieht über die dazugehörige Bibliothek `libkogmo_rtdb`. Diese kann sowohl von Realzeitmodulen (dunkelgrau), Nicht-Realzeitmodulen (hellgrau) und dazwischen alternierenden Modulen genutzt werden. Realzeitkritische Module wie z.B. der Fahrspurtracker werden als Xenomai-Tasks ausgeführt, andere Module wie z.B. die Visualisierung bleiben Linux-Tasks. Die KogMo-RTDB bietet die blockierungsfreie Kopplung beider Domänen: Alle Module können auf die veröffentlichten Daten der Realzeitmodule zugreifen ohne diese zu behindern. Die Realzeitmodule wiederum können die Daten der Nicht-Realzeitmodule durch realzeitfähige RTDB-Operation nutzen, ohne ihre eigene Deadline durch Interaktion mit Nicht-Realzeitmodulen zu gefährden.

Sollte ein Modul abstürzen, kommt ein weiterer Vorteil der Softwarearchitektur zum Tragen: Da alle wichtigen Daten wie z.B. Umfeldinformationen in der KogMo-RTDB hinterlegt sind, sind sie nach Ausscheiden des Moduls für den gewählten Historienzeitraum weiter verfügbar. So kann beispielsweise für eine Notbremsung der letzte bekannte Spurverlauf genutzt werden. Das Design der KogMo-RTDB sorgt dafür, dass dabei auf die gewünschten Daten blockierungsfrei aus dem Realzeitkontext eines Überwachungsmoduls zugegriffen werden kann.

Alle genannten Softwaremodule des Fahrzeugs werden zudem im sogenannten Userspace des Betriebsystems Linux ausgeführt. Sie stehen damit unter dem Speicherschutz des Betriebsystems, ein Modul kann nicht auf den Speicher eines anderen zugreifen und dieses zum Absturz bringen.

3 Experimentelle Ergebnisse

Tabelle 1 zeigt die WCET (worst case execution time) und den Durchsatz einzelner RTDB-Operationen. Die Werte der Realzeit-Konfiguration entstanden unter starker CPU-Last. In der Nicht-Realzeit-Konfiguration kann bei beliebig hoher Last die WCET über 100ms steigen, daher ist hier nur der Durchsatz des unbelasteten Systems angegeben.

Tabelle 1. Gemessene Ausführungszeiten (Objektgröße: 152 Bytes)

KogMo-RTDB Operation	**Konfiguration**		
	Realzeit	**Nicht-Realzeit**	
	WCET	**Operationen/Sek.**	**gemittelte Zeit**
Einfügen	75.6 μs	16528	60.5 μs
Löschen	18.5 μs	192307	5.2 μs
Lesen	16.8 μs	217391	4.6 μs
Schreiben	25.6 μs	120481	8.3 μs
Benachrichtigung	66.5 μs	33783	29.6 μs

Normalerweise werden beim Schreiben oder Lesen aus der KogMo-RTDB die Objekte vom/in den Speicher des anfragenden Prozesses kopiert. Daraus ergibt sich eine Abhängigkeit der Ausführungszeiten von der Objektgröße.

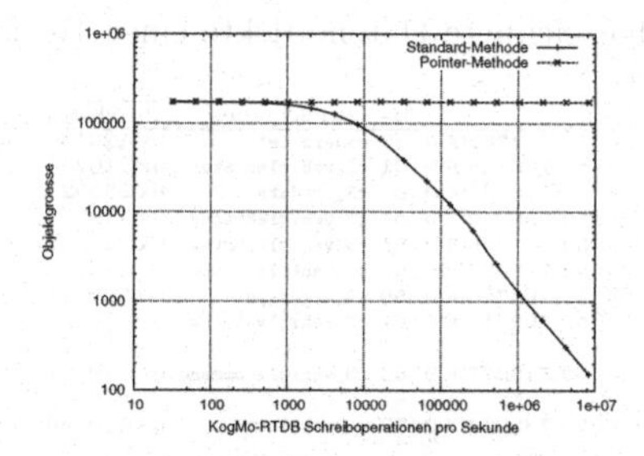

Abb. 3. Ausführungrate einer KogMo-RTDB Schreiboperation

Abbildung 3 zeigt, dass das nur bis zu einer Größe von ca. 10^4 Bytes vertretbar ist, für größere Objektblöcke sollten direkte Pointeroperationen verwendet werden. Diese bringen den Nachteil mit sich, dass bei einem zu kleinen Ringpuffer der Lesebereich von einem schreibenden Prozess wieder überschrieben wird. Lesende Prozesse müssen daher nach Abschluss der Verarbeitung alle Lesebereiche erneut auf Gültigkeit überprüfen. Die erlaubte WCET für einen solchen Prozess ergibt sich daher beim Zugriff auf eine Menge von $\mathcal{D}$ Objekten mit individueller Historienlänge $T_{history,D}$ zu $t_{WCET} < \min_{D \in \mathcal{D}}\{T_{history,D}\}$. Die Laufzeiten einzelner Module können vom jeweiligen Entwickler angegeben werden. Alternativ können sie auch über die RTDB gemessen werden. Dazu muss von einem Modul das Trigger-Objekt A und das Ergebnisobjekt B bekannt sein. Durch die Abfrage der Commit-Timestamps t_B und t_A kann die Laufzeit $t_{ET} = t_B - t_A$ berechnet werden. Dies kann auch im Labor anhand der folgenden Aufzeichnung geschehen.

3.1 Datenaufzeichnung zur Simulation und Analyse

Sämtliche in der KogMo-RTDB vorhanden Objekte können mit dem dazugehörigen RTDB-Recorder einschließlich ihres Verlaufs aufgezeichnet werden. Dazu wurde das AVI-Format so erweitert, dass dessen Videostreams (Kamerabilder) trotzdem auch mit einem normalen AVI-Videoplayer abgespielt werden können. Zur Nutzung aller Daten muss die Aufzeichnung wieder mit dem RTDB-Player in eine laufende RTDB eingespielt werden. Dann erscheinen wieder alle (bzw. ausgewählte) Objekte mit ihrer zeitlichen Entwicklung in der RTDB. So ist auch in der Wiedergabe zu jedem Videobild der aktuelle Kamerablickwinkel und die Fahrzeugodometrie verfügbar und kann im Labor ausgewertet werden. Außerdem können alle Entscheidungen der Wahrnehmung nachvollzogen und neue Wahrnehmungsmodule mit aufgezeichneten Verkehrsobjekten getestet werden.

Das Protokoll einer Aufzeichnung zeigt Abb. 2. Darin ist zu erkennen, dass die linke Kamera alle $33.3ms$ ein neues Bild liefert. Dieses wird ca. $4 - 5ms$ vom Fahrspurtracker bearbeitet, der dann ein Spur-Objekt schreibt. Die Autobox schickt mit $1kHz$ aktuelle Fahrzeugdaten. Der Fahrzeugregler arbeitet mit einer festen Periode von $40Hz$ und errechnet neue Sollwerte, die er in ein Objekt c3_vehiclecommand schreibt, dessen Daten an die Autobox versandt werden.

Tabelle 2. Aufgezeichnete Datenobjekte einer Testfahrt (Auszug)

Zeit	ID	Objektname	Objekttyp	Objektgröße
2007-01-31 20:00:52.704761000	57	camera_left	0xA20030	307248 bytes
2007-01-31 20:00:52.705145000	61	c3_vehiclestatus	0xC10201	88 bytes
2007-01-31 20:00:52.705749000	64	c3_gpsdata	0xC30021	124 bytes
2007-01-31 20:00:52.706050000	61	c3_vehiclestatus	0xC10201	88 bytes
2007-01-31 20:00:52.707036000	61	c3_vehiclestatus	0xC10201	88 bytes
2007-01-31 20:00:52.708024000	61	c3_vehiclestatus	0xC10201	88 bytes
2007-01-31 20:00:52.708723000	59	a2_eigenspur	0xA20101	184 bytes
2007-01-31 20:00:52.709012000	61	c3_vehiclestatus	0xC10201	88 bytes
⋮				
2007-01-31 20:00:52.713077000	62	c3_vehiclecommand	0xC10101	96 bytes
⋮				
2007-01-31 20:00:52.738004000	57	camera_left	0xA20030	307248 bytes
⋮				
2007-01-31 20:00:52.741996000	59	a2_eigenspur	0xA20101	184 bytes
⋮				
2007-01-31 20:00:52.753101000	62	c3_vehiclecommand	0xC10101	96 bytes

4 Zusammenfassung und Ausblick

Die vorgestellte Softwarearchitektur erfüllt die Anforderungen kognitiver Automobile und bietet mit der Realzeitdatenbasis KogMo-RTDB offene Schnittstellen und realzeitfähige Methoden für den Datenaustausch. Sie wird in den Fahrzeugen des Forschungsprojekts erfolgreich eingesetzt. Weitere Arbeiten beschäftigen sich mit dem Scheduling der Module anhand der in der RTDB enthaltenen Daten.

5 Danksagung

Die Autoren danken der Deutschen Forschungsgemeinschaft (DFG) für die Förderung des Sonderforschungsbereich/Transregio 28 „Kognitive Automobile“ und allen Projektpartnern für die gute Zusammenarbeit.

Literaturverzeichnis

1. Sonderforschungsbereich/Transregio 28. *http://www.kognimobil.org*
2. Christoph Stiller, Georg Färber und Sören Kammel. Cooperative Cognitive Automobiles. *IEEE Intelligent Vehicles Symposium*, pp. 215–220, 2007.
3. Matthias Goebl, Sebastian Drössler und Georg Färber. Systemplattform für videobasierte Fahrerassistenzsysteme. *Autonome Mobile Systeme 2005*, pp. 187–193. Springer-Verlag, 2006.
4. Matthias Goebl und Georg Färber. A Real-Time-capable Hard- and Software Architecture for Joint Image and Knowledge Processing in Cognitive Automobiles. *IEEE Intelligent Vehicles Symposium*, pp. 734–740, 2007.
5. Stephan Neumaier und Georg Färber. Videobasierte Fahrspurerkennung zur Umfelderfassung bei Straßenfahrzeugen. *Autonome Mobile Systeme 2005*, pp. 173–178. Springer-Verlag, 2005.
6. T. Dang, C. Hoffmann und C. Stiller. Self-calibration for Active Automotive Stereo Vision. *IEEE Intelligent Vehicles Symposium*, pp. 364–369, 2006.
7. Jürgen Stohr. Auswirkungen der Peripherieanbindung auf das Realzeitverhalten PC-basierter Multiprozessorsysteme. Diss., Lehrstuhl für Realzeit–Computersysteme, Technische Universität München, March 2006.

Semantic Road Maps for Autonomous Vehicles

Saman Kumpakeaw and Rüdiger Dillmann

ITEC, Universität Karlsruhe, Haid-und-Neu-Str. 7, 76131 Karlsruhe
{kumpakea, dillmann}@ira.uka.de

Abstract. The semantic informations extracted from traffic scenes are proposed to enhance the capacity of on-the-shelf navigation systems and made more suitable for autonomous vehicles. The additional classifications of essential traffic informations and estimation of the driving visibility are the basis for making decision to navigation tasks. Furthermore, the semantic structure can be also supporting to the behaviour-based networks and traffic scene interpretations.

1 Introduction

Car navigation systems are nowadays widely used in the everyday traffic. Their technology and visualization for better navigations are developed rapidly e.g. high accuracy GPS receivers, visualization technique in three dimensions from SiemensVDO [1] or Volkswagen and Google [2]. In the field of autonomous vehicles, there are also many researches about the outdoor navigational tasks [3]. The recent example is e.g. the Urban Challenge 2007 organized by DARPA [4].

It can not be contradicted that the car navigation systems are very useful for drivers. But for autonomous systems, it is not adequate to take a complete navigation using only the car navigation system. The machines have lack of some important current traffic informations to decide which way they should take further.

The navigation systems should also be made more easy for machines to notice, understand and record some essential traffic situations in everyday use like "experienced" drivers do in their routine driving: recognizing these conflict situations and reacting almost unconsciously [5].

The aim of this approach is the information abstraction from traffic scenes and evaluation of "driving experiences" working correctly together with informations from the navigation systems and how to organize them in database. Consequently, an autonomous vehicle should be shown or warned for danger sites or essential traffic events just in time, so that the self-planning of routes and traveling time with performance and safety is possible.

2 Driving Conditions for a Successful Navigational Task

Informations from the car navigator are only a guide for drivers. The optimal route planning, which is time-optimized and stress-free for drivers and passengers, still requires the man-like decisions for every traffic situations.

Proposed are essential driving experiences which are important for navigation tasks. When the machines can recognize such conditions of:

- visibility distances and optimal brightness for street lightning (with daylight or lanterns)
- good driving dynamic and control of vehicle
- rapid recognition of road conditions and road surfaces
- adequate traffic information supports about the traveling route before and during the planning phase

They can better decide and plan the route to destination.

2.1 Visibility Distances

Bad weathers like fog, rain or snow (fig. 1) cause the reduction of visibility distance. They can reduce driving safety and increase insecure-feeling for passengers

Fig. 1. Visibility distances by driving in foggy weather

The approaches from Hautière et.al [6], [7] and Murase et. al [8], [9] should be applied to estimate the visibility distance and safety driving velocity respectively. Recognizing the poor driving visibility in time can prevent accidents and help by route preparation and route decision for better traveling in the next time. Visibility with poor brightness and contrast on streets are also the main criteria for safety driving. The opimal and bad driving conditions can be classified with the evaluation of histogram from traffic scenes (see fig. 2). The histogram shows the difference between the optimal visibility (the histogram peak is in the middle) and the poor visilibity. (the histogram curve is almost not observable.) These can be warnings for arising alertness for the machines.

2.2 Driving Dynamic and Control of Vehicle

The platform vehicle is modified with the drive-by-x concept and controlled by the self-developed control framework named "MCA2" [10], so that the most

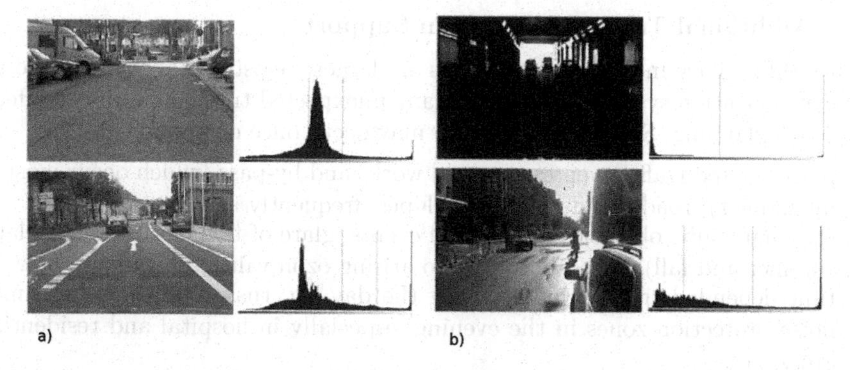

Fig. 2. Brightness and contrast proportion representing with hitrogram for a). the optimal light condition and b). the poor light condition

dynamical parameters of the vehicle can be simply observed and influenced from higher level such as a navigation level [11].

The observable critical values of some parameters e.g. *braking too hard, too much accelerating, or abrupt steering*, will be registered in the driving log book which synchronizes with the GPS coordinates. These informations will be remarked by the next travel on the same route. The handling performances of the machine should not exceed these critical values again.

2.3 Road Conditions and Road Surfaces

Recognizing various road surfaces (fig. 3) is very helpful for setting suitable driving velocity and therefore making the travel for passengers safety-feeling. The cognitive automobile should recognize different road surfaces e.g. dry, wet,

Fig. 3. Dry, wet, and snowed road surfaces

and snow covered. When the recognition is correct and in time, the machine can react properly. The semanic database is also updated for the next travel preparation. The navigation task in the next time will decide, wether the same path should be chosen again, if the road condition were bad.

2.4 Additional Traffic Information Supports

Many traffic signs and speed limit zones are largely registered and integrated in the car navigation systems. However, many unexpected traffic holdup can affect the route planning. Some traffic holdup may occur once or periodically e.g.

- place-related traffic events, e.g. road works and by-pass (which occur mostly in summer), road inclinations and slopes, frequently accident spots, etc.
- seasonal traffic obstacles e.g. annual events, glare of the sun (mostly in late summer and fall), speed limit due to arising ozon values in summer, etc.
- time-depended traffic events during the day e.g. rush hour, quitting time, noise protection zones in the evening, especially in hospital and residential areas, etc.
- other traffic rules which are not available from the navigation systems e.g. one-way road that bicylists can drive in the contrary direction (especially in Germany) [12].
- other driving experiences e.g. watching out for unclear junctions, suitable points for changing lane (remarked with GPS coordinates), etc.

These additional informations about time-depended and periodical events are certainly useful for route planning and route decision along the way to destination.

3 Semantic Maps and Geography Information Systems (GIS)

As a base component of semantic maps, the geographical and topological maps are helpful for developers to visualize and prove the correctness of semanic data in real time. The maps are usually available from the navigation system or from the land surveying office.

The topological map are extracted directly from the car navigation systems and kept in XML format with extensible attributes to every node and edge. Besides GPS coordinates, road forms, or distance to the next node as attribute elements, we can also add some other attributes mentioned in the previous section. All of the map data are not extracted to the MCA2 framework because of a huge amount of data and slow access time consequently, but just only the map from current GPS position and the circumference of about 5 km are concerned as shown in Figure 4

Sometimes, there are still no maps available from the navigation system or the land surveying office due to the private terrains. The self-measured maps are the alternative options (in this case: the test area for cognitive automobiles in Fig. 5).

From MCA2 program, the start and end point of route can be chosen. Paths between start and end point are firstly suggested from the navigation system. During the travel, the semantic information database are simultanously considered. The planned route from the navigation system maybe now changes depended on the current traffic situation and available semantic database at that point, so that the whole route planning is optimal.

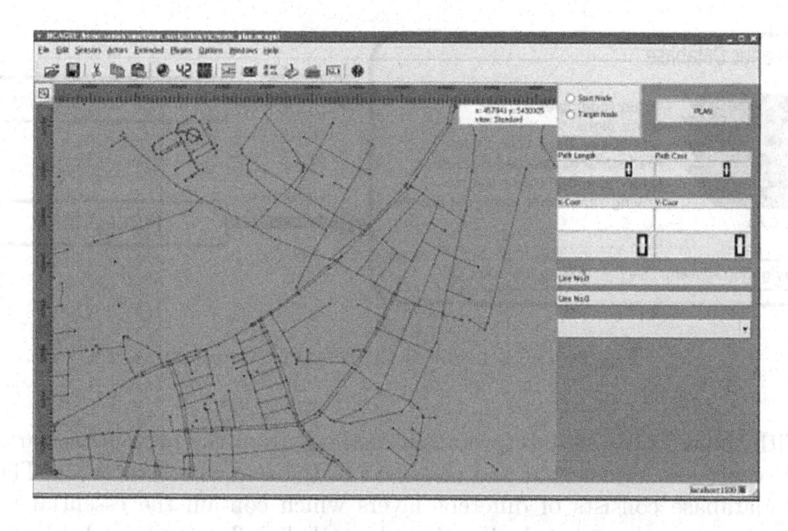

Fig. 4. GIS representation with MCA2-Framework

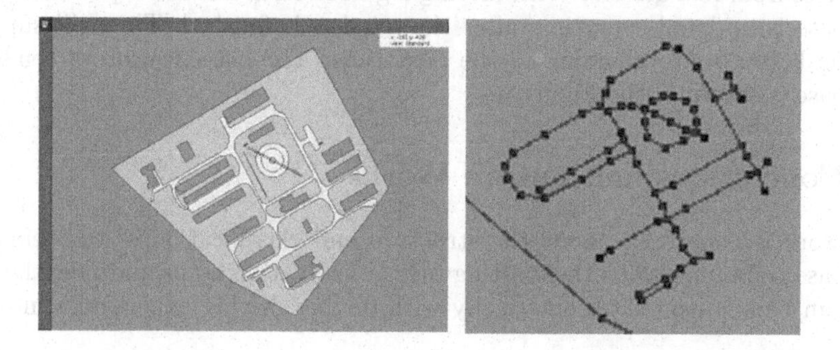

Fig. 5. The self-measured geometry and topology maps for the test area

4 Semantic Maps and Behaviour-Based Networks

The classified semantic database can be used to support the other parts of the "cognitive automobiles" (e.g. scene recognition, situation decision and behavior-based control).

The behaviour-based networks are inspired from biological creatures. They have instinctive ability to sense and avoid obstacles or danger [13]. This concept is implemented to control the cognitive platform. But the driving reactions are purely instinctive. The machine would react only when the obstacle or danger are near enough that the perception can detect.

The semantic map complements this instinctive capability with available early informations and warnings about roads ahead. These motivate the bahaviour-based networks early enough, so that the handling performance of autonomous vehicle is much alike the driving performance of human as possible.

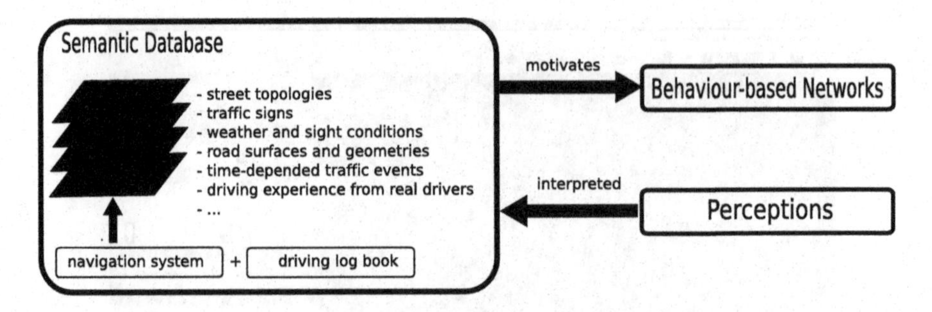

Fig. 6. The concept of the semantic database

With the aid of scene interpretation methods from the perception part, the traffic scenes can be selected and classified to the semantic structures. The semanic database consists of different layers which contain the essential traffic informations e.g. street topologies, time-depended traffic events and driving experiences from real drivers. With driving log book from last route plannings, the database is updated everytime after the mission is finished. This will support for the better route planning in the next time. The classification of semantic database is shown in the Figure 6

5 Conclusions and Future Works

The work is concerned about the structure and classification of the semantic database combining with the existing digital navigation maps and how the system can be augmented automatically with further driving experiences into the system.

The future work is concerned about support and cooperation with the behaviour-based networks. The behaviour-based networks control the vehicle directly. The directive instructions from navigation level give useful informations for lookahead driving patterns. The informations from behaviour-based level also help supplemently by route analysis for navigational task in the next time.

References

1. SiemensVDO, http://www.siemensvdo.com/
2. Volkswagen of America, Inc, http://www.vwerl.com
3. S. Vacek, S. Bergmann, U. Mohr and R. Dillmann, Fusing image features and navigation system data for augmenting guiding information displays, *In Proc. of IEEE International Conference on Multisensor Fusion and Integration for Intelligent Systems*, Heidelberg, Germany, 2006.
4. DARPA, Urban Challenge 2007, *http://www.darpa.mil/grandchallenge/*.
5. W. Fastenmeier, *Autofahrer und Verkehrssituation*, TÜV Rheinland, 1995.
6. N. Hautière, R. Labayrade and D. Aubert, Estimation of the Visibility Distance by Stereovision: a Generic Approach, *Conference on Machine Vision Applications*, Tsukuba, Japan, 2005.

7. N. Hautière, R. Labayrade and D. Aubert, Detection of Visibility Conditions through use of Onboard Cameras, *In Proc. of Intelligent Vehicles Symposium*, Las Vegas, USA, 2005.
8. H. Kurihata, T. Takahashi, I. Ide, Y. Mekada, H. Murase, Y. Tamatsu and T. Miyahara, Rainy Weather Recognition from In-Vehicle Camera Images for Driver Assistance, *In Proc. of Intelligent Vehicles Symposium*, Las Vegas, USA, 2005
9. K. Mori, T. Kato, T. Takahashi, I. Ide and H. Murase, Visibility Estimation in Foggy Conditions by In-vehicle Camera and Radar, *In the 1st International Conference on Innovative Computing, Information and Control*, Beijing, China, 2006.
10. Forschungszentrum Informatik Karlsruhe (IDS), Modular Controller Architecture Version 2 (MCA2), *http://www.mca2.org/*
11. J. Schröder, U. Müller and R. Dillmann, Smart Roadster Project: Setting up Drive-by-Wire or How to Remote-Control your Car, *In Proc. of the 9th International Conference on Intelligent Autonomous Systems*, Tokyo, Japan, 2006.
12. D. Alrutz, W. Angenendt, W. Draeger and D. Gündel, *Verkehrssicherheit in Einbahnstraßen mit gegengerichtetem Radverkehr*, Straßenverkehrstechnik, 2002.
13. R.C. Arkins, *Behavior-Based Robotics*, MIT Press, 1998

Kamera-basierte Erkennung von Geschwindigkeitsbeschränkungen auf deutschen Straßen

Dennis Nienhüser[1], Marco Ziegenmeyer[1], Thomas Gumpp[1], Kay-Ulrich Scholl[2], J. Marius Zöllner[1] und Rüdiger Dillmann[1]

[1] FZI Forschungszentrum Informatik, Interaktive Diagnose und Servicesysteme, Haid-und-Neu-Str. 10–14, 76131 Karlsruhe
{nienhues, ziegenmeyer, gumpp, zoellner}@fzi.de, dillmann@ira.uka.de
[2] Harman/Becker Automotive Systems GmbH, Becker-Göring-Str. 16, 76307 Karlsbad
kuscholl@harmanbecker.com

Zusammenfassung. An Fahrerassistenzsysteme im industriellen Einsatz werden hohe Anforderungen bezüglich Zuverlässigkeit und Robustheit gestellt. In dieser Arbeit wird die Kombination robuster Verfahren wie der Hough-Transformation und Support-Vektor-Maschinen zu einem Gesamtsystem zur Erkennung von Geschwindigkeitsbeschränkungen beschrieben. Es setzt eine Farbvideokamera als Sensorik ein. Die Evaluation auf Testdaten bestätigt durch die ermittelte hohe Korrektklassifikationsrate bei gleichzeitig geringer Zahl Fehlalarme die Zuverlässigkeit des Systems.

1 Einleitung

Nicht technische Mängel von Fahrzeugen oder schlechte Witterungsbedingungen sind die vorherrschenden Sicherheitsrisiken auf deutschen Straßen. Das Statistische Bundesamt ermittelte im Jahr 2005 einen Anteil von 86,4% von durch menschliches Fehlverhalten verursachten Unfällen mit Personenschaden oder Todesfolge [1], alleine 14,5% gehen auf das Konto nicht angepasster Geschwindigkeit. Ein erster Schritt, diesen Anteil zu reduzieren, ist die Warnung des Fahrers vor Überschreitung der erlaubten Höchstgeschwindigkeit. Ein Fahrerassistenzsystem, das diese Aufgabe übernimmt, muss u.a. die aktuell erlaubte Höchstgeschwindigkeit kennen. Statisches Kartenmaterial ist dafür nicht ausreichend, da es nicht die notwendige Aktualität bietet. So fehlen Informationen zu Baustellen und dynamische Anzeigen können gar nicht berücksichtigt werden. Abhilfe schafft die Erkennung von Geschwindigkeitsbeschränkungen mit Hilfe einer Farbvideokamera. Im Folgenden wird ein System beschrieben, das die in der Straßenverkehrs-Ordnung beschriebenen Verkehrszeichen "Zulässige Höchstgeschwindigkeit" und "Ende der zulässigen Höchstgeschwindigkeit" erkennt.

2 Stand der Technik

Ein System zur robusten Erkennung aller bekannten Verkehrszeichen in Echtzeit ist derzeit noch nicht realisierbar. Allein in Deutschland gibt es über 400 verschiedene Verkehrszeichen, die insbesondere im innerstädtischen Bereich leicht mit anderen Objekten wie z.B. Werbetafeln verwechselt werden können. Dennoch wurden Systeme entwickelt, die erfolgreich eine Untermenge von Verkehrszeichen unter geeigneten Bedingungen erkennen. Dazu wird oft ein zweistufiger Prozess verwendet, bei dem zunächst in einem Segmentierungsschritt interessante Regionen (ROIs) extrahiert werden. Diese Regionen werden anschließend mit einem geeigneten Verfahren aus dem Bereich des maschinellen Lernens klassifiziert. Die Segmentierung stützt sich meist auf Farbe und Form von Verkehrszeichen als Hauptmerkmale. Zusätzlich wird Hintergrundwissen in Form von Einschränkungen hinsichtlich Ort und Größe von Verkehrszeichen im Bild eingebracht. Beispielsweise schränken Piccioli et al. [2] die Segmentierung auf den rechten mittleren Bildrand ein.

Nachdem anfänglich recht komplexe Farbsegmentierungsverfahren wie CCC (color connected components, [3]) oder CSC (color structure code, [4]) entwickelt wurden, lässt sich in den vergangen Jahren eine Abkehr von der Farbe von Verkehrszeichen hin zur Form als wichtigstem Merkmal beobachten. Dies lässt sich in erster Linie dadurch erklären, dass aufgrund wechselnder, nicht vorhersehbarer Beleuchtungssitutationen die Farbinformation kein zuverlässiges Merkmal darstellt. Beliebte Verfahren zur Farbklassifikation sind einfache Pixelklassifikatoren in Form von neuronalen Netzen [5], Gauß-Verteilungsklassifikatoren [6] oder einfachen schwellwertbasierten Regeln [7] [8]. Hinsichtlich geeigneter Farbräume gibt es keinen Konsens. So finden sich Verweise auf RGB [7] [8] [9], Irg [10], HSV [11], HSI [5] und YUV [12].

Übliche Formen von Verkehrszeichen sind Dreiecke, Rechtecke, Achtecke und Kreise. Priese et al. [11] definieren Regeln, anhand derer die Ähnlichkeit der konvexen Hülle einer erkannten Form zu bekannten Formen berechnet wird. Andere Autoren benutzen Template Matching [7], Varianten der Hough-Transformation [6] [13] oder genetische Algorithmen [9] zur Erkennung von Kreisen.

Neben getrennter Analyse von Farbe und Form finden sich auch hybride Verfahren. Bahlmann et al. [8] präsentieren eine Variante des Viola-Jones Algorithmus mit Haar-Wavelet ähnlichen Merkmalen für Farbe und Form von Verkehrszeichen. Das von Torresen et al. [7] benutzte Verfahren basiert auf Template Matching und bezieht zusätzlich die Ergebnisse der vorangestellten Farbklassifikation mit ein.

Mit Hilfe von Nächster-Nachbar-Klassifikatoren [14], Template Matching [2] [12] [13], neuronalen Netzen [6] [7] oder Bayes-Klassifikatoren [8] werden Piktogramme von Verkehrszeichen klassifiziert.

Zur Verfolgung von Verkehrszeichen über mehrere Bilder hinweg werden Kalman-Filter [2] [5] verwendet. Andere Ansätze benutzen Korrelation und Entfernung von Objekten in aufeinanderfolgenden Bildern als Merkmale für die Verfolgung [6]. Ein ähnliches Vorgehen basierend auf einem einfachen Bewegungsmodell wird von Bahlmann et al. [8] beschrieben.

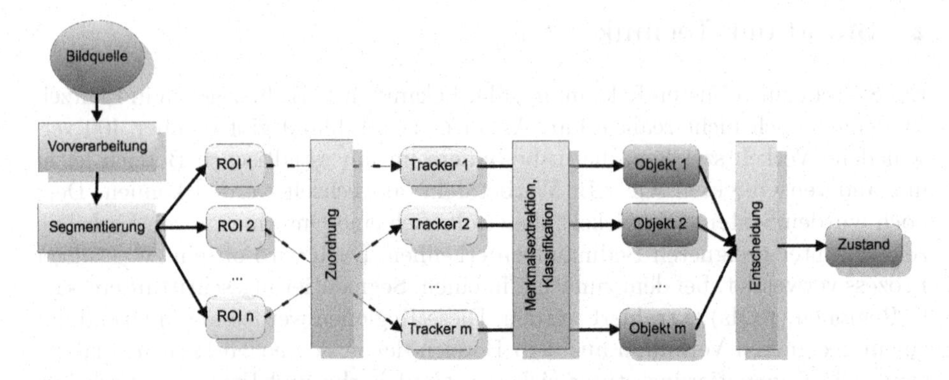

Abb. 1. Verarbeitungsschritte von der Bildaufnahme bis zur Entscheidung, ob und welche Verkehrszeichen im Bild zu beobachten sind.

3 Konzept

Wie im Bereich der Mustererkennung propagiert und in den meisten der vorgestellten verwandten Systeme ebenfalls umgesetzt, verfolgt das in dieser Arbeit vorgestellte System den merkmalbasierten Ansatz der Klassifikation segmentierter Bildbereiche. Ein zusätzlicher Tracker erhöht die Robustheit und die Verarbeitungsgeschwindigkeit des Systems (Abbildung 1).

Um eine optimale Sichtbarkeit von Verkehrszeichen zu gewährleisten, wird die Kamera in Fahrtrichtung blickend in der Nähe des Innenspiegels angebracht. Zur initialen Segmentierung, also der Bestimmung zusammenhängender Bereiche, die mit hoher Wahrscheinlichkeit Verkehrszeichen enthalten, werden mit Hilfe der generalisierten Hough-Transformation (SHT) [15] kreisähnliche Objekte im vorverarbeiteten Bild bestimmt. Als Vorverarbeitung wird eine Kontrasterhöhung und ggfs. eine Nachbelichtung durchgeführt. Um Laufzeiteinschränkungen durch die aufwendige SHT zu umgehen, wurden einige schnellere Varianten entwickelt [13] [15]. Höhere Geschwindigkeit wird jedoch meist durch geringere Genauigkeit erkauft. Um dies zu vermeiden und trotzdem die Onlineverarbeitung zu ermöglichen, wird die SHT auf alternierende Fenster (rechteckige Bildausschnitte wechselnder Größe und Position) eingeschränkt. Auf diese Weise ist die Onlineverarbeitung möglich, ohne Bildteile komplett ausschließen zu müssen. Durch die Fensterung erfolgt die erstmalige Erkennung eines kreisähnlichen Objekts im Allgemeinen später als bei Betrachtung des kompletten Bildes, was sich allerdings aufgrund der hohen Bildrate von typischerweise 25 oder 30 Bildern pro Sekunde kaum negativ auswirkt.

Wird ein rundes Objekt von der SHT im Bild erkannt, übernimmt ein Tracker weitere Verarbeitungsschritte wie Farb- und Piktogrammklassifikation. Ein vom Tracker dynamisch aufgebautes, einfaches Bewegungsmodell (Geschwindigkeit und Position des Fahrzeugs in Weltkoordinaten) wird zur Prädiktion benutzt. Zur Aktualisierung des Zustands des Trackers wird erneut die Hough-Transformation für Kreise benutzt. Um Rechenzeit zu sparen, wird die SHT nur in der Umgebung der prädizierten Position und für Radien ähnlich der prädizierten Größe durchgeführt. Das so ermittelte kreisähnliche Objekt mit minimaler Distanz zur prädizierten Position wird als neuer Zustand des Trackers übernommen.

Zur Verifikation des Kandidaten erfolgt eine Farbklassifikation, die Bildpunkten eine der Klassen *weiß*, *rot* oder *Hintergrund* zuweist. Dazu werden ein Schwellwertklassifikator im RGB-Raum (*weiß*) und ein Bayes-Klassifikator im HSV-Raum (*rot*) benutzt. Ist der Anteil von Bildpunkten der Klasse *rot* bzw. *weiß* ausreichend hoch, erfolgt eine abschließende Klassifikation durch eine Support-Vektor-Maschine (SVM) mit RBF-Kernel, um den Typ des Verkehrszeichens zu bestimmen. Als Vorverarbeitung erfolgt eine Grauwerttransformation, Kontrasterhöhung und Größennormalisierung auf 20×20 Bildpunkte mit Standardverfahren. Die Transformation in den Frequenzbereich zeigte experimentell keine Verbesserung der Klassifikationsrate.

Um die Robustheit weiter zu steigern, werden die Ergebnisse vorheriger Klassifikationen des gleichen Verkehrszeichens herangezogen. Die endgültige Konfidenz $P_{i,n}(\omega_k)$ im Bild G_i ergibt sich als altersgewichteter Durchschnittswert der einzelnen Konfidenzen $P_i(\omega_k)$ der letzten n ROIs:

$$P_{i,n}(\omega_k) = \sum_{j=0}^{n-1} \frac{j(j+1)}{2} P_{i-j}(\omega_k)$$

Per Maximum- und Differenzkriterium (1) erfolgt eine Rückweisung (Zuweisung der Klasse ω_0 “kein Verkehrszeichen”), um die Verwechslung ähnlicher Schilder bzw. die Erkennung unbekannter Objekte zu vermeiden:

$$G_i \rightarrow \omega_k$$

mit

$$\omega_k = \begin{cases} \omega_0, & \max_l P_{i,n}(\omega_l) < c_{\max} \\ \omega_0, & \max_l P_{i,n}(\omega_l) - \max_{m,m\neq l} P_{i,n}(\omega_m) < c_{\text{diff}} \\ \arg\max_l P_{i,n}(\omega_l), & \textit{sonst} \end{cases} \quad (1)$$

und geeigneten Konstanten $c_{\max}$ und c_{diff}.

Da häufig mehrere Verkehrszeichen in einem Bild vorkommen – beispielsweise durch die Kombination unterschiedlicher Geschwindigkeitsbeschränkungen für verschiedene Fahrzeugtypen oder durch das Aufstellen von Schildern am rechten und linken Fahrbahnrand – ist eine zusätzliche Konsistenzprüfung notwendig. Da bisher Zusatzsschilder nicht erkannt werden, wird die Klassifikation von Verkehrsschildern unterschiedlichen Typs innerhalb einer Zeitspanne von wenigen Bildern als nicht zulässig angesehen. Andernfalls wird das Verkehrszeichen inklusive der errechneten Konfidenz ausgegeben.

4 Evaluation

Zum Training und zur Evaluation des in Form eines C++ Programms umgesetzten Systems lagen mehrstündige Aufnahmen unterschiedlicher Verkehrsszenen in

Video	Kamera	Länge (Bilder)	# Verkehrszeichen
Langensteinbach	Sony, 720x576, 25 Hz	32380	14
Brochterbeck II	Dragonfly, 640x480, 30 Hz	73938	84

Tabelle 1. Testdaten zur Evaluation

Video	SRER	SFR	Falschpositivrate
Langensteinbach	0%	0%	0,000031
Brochterbeck II	7,14%	1,85%	0,000027

Tabelle 2. Ergebnisse der Auswertung

Form von Videos vor. Sie wurden mit einer Sony DCR-TRV22 und einer Point Grey Research Dragonfly Kamera aufgenommen. Auflösung und Bildrate dieser Kameras (siehe Tabelle 1) werden mittlerweile auch von kostengünstigen Kameras erreicht, die im industriellen Umfeld zu erwarten sind.

Aus etwa dreistündigem Videomaterial wurden Trainingsbeispiele für die Farbklassifikation und etwa 8000 ROIs für die Support-Vektor-Maschine entnommen, die sich auf die sieben trainierten Klassen 30, 50, 60, 70, 80, 100 und 120 km/h, eine Klasse für Aufhebungszeichen sowie eine Klasse für andere Objekte verteilen. Die Support-Vektor-Maschine erreichte auf einer disjunkten Menge von etwa 1000 Testbeispielen eine Korrektklassifikationsrate von 98%.

Zur Gesamtevaluation wurden die system recognition error rate (SRER) [8] und die Systemfehlerrate (SFR) für zwei Videos (Tabelle 1) berechnet. Die SRER bezeichnet den Anteil falsch erkannter Verkehrsschilder, die SFR den Anteil falsch erkannter Schildgruppen. Eine Schildgruppe wird von redundant aufgestellten Schildern gebildet, etwa rechts und links der Fahrbahn angebrachte Geschwindigkeitsbeschränkungen. Die SRER ist damit ein Bewertungsmaß aus Entwicklersicht, die SFR aus Benutzersicht. Tabelle 2 zeigt die Ergebnisse.

Fehler treten hauptsächlich dann auf, wenn Verkehrszeichen nur kurz sichtbar oder zu weit entfernt sind. Dies lässt sich gut an den unterschiedlichen Ergebnissen für SRER und SFR im Video Brochterbeck II beobachten: 6 der insgesamt 84 Verkehrszeichen wurden nicht erkannt, allerdings konnte bei 5 davon ein gleichartiges Verkehrszeichen auf der anderen Fahrbahnseite erkannt werden. Dieser Fall tritt typischerweise auf mehrspurigen Autobahnen und in Baustellen auf, wenn Verdeckungen durch andere Fahrzeuge auftreten.

Bei uneingeschränkter Sicht (vergleiche Abbildung 2.1, 2.2) werden Aufhebungszeichen früher als Geschwindigkeitsbeschränkungen erkannt. Das lässt sich dadurch erklären, dass Aufhebungszeichen für unterschiedliche Geschwindigkeiten zu einer Äquivalenzklasse zusammengefasst wurden. Die SVM muss dadurch nur zwischen den drei Klassen *Ende Geschwindigkeitsbeschränkung*, *Ende Überholverbot* und *anderes Objekt* unterscheiden, wofür eine niedrigere Auflösung ausreicht im Vergleich zur Erkennung der aufgedruckten Zahl bei Geschwindigkeitsbeschränkungen.

Abb. 2. Verkehrszeichenerkennung unter verschiedenen Umweltbedingungen. Rechts unten ist jeweils eine Ausschnittsvergrößerung der erkannten Verkehrszeichen eingezeichnet, im Bild (5) außerdem die vorverarbeite ROI. Die Verkehrszeichen in den Bildern (1) bis (5) wurden korrekt erkannt, im Bild (6) zurückgewiesen.

5 Ausblick

In Zukunft soll der Einsatz einer Kamera mit hohem Dynamikbereich untersucht werden. Insbesondere in Situationen mit seitlich einfallendem Sonnenlicht (Abbildung 2.3, 2.4) verspricht dies eine zuverlässigere Segmentierung. Weitere Optimierungen betreffen Nachtsituationen (Abbildung 2.5), die eine adaptive Anpassung der maximalen Belichtungszeit erfordern.

Das derzeitige System erkennt keine dynamischen Anzeigen, die Geschwindigkeitsbeschränkungen schwarz/weiß invertiert darstellen. Hier sollen die Erkennung und Invertierung sowie das Training der SVM mit solchen ROIs untersucht werden. Auch die Erkennung von Einschränkungen durch Zusatzzeichen soll integriert werden.

Literaturverzeichnis

1. *Das Statistische Jahrbuch 2006 für die Bundesrepublik Deutschland.* Statistisches Bundesamt Deutschland, 2007.
2. Piccioli, G., E. De Micheli, P. Parodi M. Campani: *Robust road sign detection and recognition from image sequences.* IEEE Intelligent Vehicles Symposium, 1994.
3. Ritter, W.: *Traffic sign recognition in color image sequences. IEEE Intelligent Vehicles Symposium*, 1992.
4. Priese, L., V. Rehrmann, R. Schian R. Lakmann: *Traffic Sign Recognition Based On Color Image Evaluation.* IEEE Intelligent Vehicles Symposium, 1993.
5. Chiung-Yao Fang, Sei-Wang Chen Chiou-Shann Fuh: *Road-sign detection and tracking.* IEEE Transactions on Vehicular Technology, 52, 2003.
6. Lindner, F., U. Kressel S. Kaelberer: *Robust recognition of traffic signals.* IEEE Intelligent Vehicles Symposium, 2004.
7. Torresen, J., J.W. Bakke L. Sekanina: *Efficient recognition of speed limit signs.* Intelligent Transportation Systems, 2004. Proceedings. The 7th International IEEE Conference on, 2004.
8. Bahlmann, Claus, Ying Zhu, Visvanathan Ramesh, Martin Pellkofer Thorsten Koehler: *A System for Traffic Sign Detection, Tracking, and Recognition Using Color, Shape, and Motion Information. IEEE Intelligent Vehicles Symposium*, 2004.
9. Liu, Han, Ding Liu Jing Xin: *Real-time recognition of road traffic sign in motion image based on genetic algorithm. International Conference on Machine Learning and Cybernetics, 2002*, 1, 2002.
10. Janssen, R., W. Ritter, F. Stein S. Ott: *Hybrid Approach For Traffic Sign Recognition.* IEEE Intelligent Vehicles Symposium, 1993.
11. Priese, L., J. Klieber, R. Lakmann, V. Rehrmann R. Schian: *New results on traffic sign recognition.* IEEE Intelligent Vehicles Symposium, 1994.
12. Miura, J., T. Kanda Y Shirai: *An active vision system for real-time traffic sign recognition.* Intelligent Transportation Systems, 2000. Proceedings. 2000 IEEE, 2000.
13. Barnes, N. A. Zelinsky: *Real-time radial symmetry for speed sign detection.* IEEE Intelligent Vehicles Symposium, 2004.
14. Yong-Jian Zheng, W. Ritter R Janssen: *An Adaptive System for Traffic Sign Recognition.* IEEE Intelligent Vehicles Symposium, 1994.
15. Yuen, H. K., J. Princen, J. Illingworth J. Kittler: *Comparative study of Hough transform methods for circle finding. Image and Vision Computing*, 8. Butterworth-Heinemann, 1990.

Hinderniserkennung und -verfolgung mit einer PMD-Kamera im Automobil

Thomas Schamm[1], Stefan Vacek[2], Koba Natroshvilli[3], J. Marius Zöllner[1] und Rüdiger Dillmann[2]

[1] FZI Forschungszentrum Informatik, Interaktive Diagnose und Servicesysteme, Haid-und-Neu-Str. 10–14, 76131 Karlsruhe
{schamm, zoellner}@fzi.de

[2] Universität Karlsruhe (TH), Institut für Technische Informatik, Technologiefabrik, Haid-und-Neu-Str. 7, 76131 Karlsruhe
{vacek, dillmann}@ira.uka.de

[3] Harman/Becker Automotive Systems GmbH, Becker-Göring-Str. 16, 76307 Karlsbad
KNatroshvili@harmanbecker.com

Zusammenfassung. Die Detektion von Hindernissen vor dem Automobil ist eine Hauptanforderung an moderne Fahrerassistenzsysteme (FAS). In dieser Arbeit wird ein System vorgestellt, das mit Hilfe einer PMD-Kamera (Photomischdetektor) Hindernisse auf der Fahrspur erkennt und deren relevante Parameter bestimmt. Durch die PMD-Kamera werden zunächst 3D-Tiefenbilder der Fahrzeugumwelt generiert. Nach einem initialen Filterprozess werden im Tiefenbild mit Hilfe eines Bereichswachstumsverfahrens Hindernisse gesucht. Zur Stabilisierung des Verfahrens und zur Parameterberechnung wird ein Kalman Filter eingesetzt. Das Ergebnis ist eine Liste aller Hindernisse im Fahrbereich des Automobils.

1 Einleitung

In dieser Arbeit wird ein System vorgestellt, mit dessen Hilfe Verkehrshindernisse rechtzeitig erkannt werden können, so dass die Folgen einer Kollision vermindert oder eine Kollision komplett verhindert werden kann. Klassische Systeme zur Hinderniserkennung basieren entweder auf Radar- oder Lidarsensorik, Monokular- oder Stereokameras oder auf einer Fusion beider Systeme. Viele Arbeiten beschäftigen sich dabei entweder mit der Erkennung anderer Automobile oder mit der Erkennung von Fußgängern [1,2].

In dieser Arbeit werden 3D-Tiefenbilder der aktuellen Verkehrssituation mit einer PMD-Kamera (Photomischdetektor) aufgenommen. Die Vorteile einer PMD-Kamera im Vergleich zu Radar- und Lidarsystemen liegen in der deutlich höheren lateralen Auflösung, mit der auch nahe beieinander stehende Hindernisse voneinander trennbar sind. Gegenüber Stereokamerasystemen ermöglicht die Lichtlaufzeitmessung der PMD-Kamera eine höhere longitudinale Genauigkeit. Da zur Messung der Lichtlaufzeit die Umgebung aktiv beleuchtet werden muss, hat die PMD-Kamera allerdings eine geringere Messreichweite, die mit derzeit üblichen Lichtquellen bei 40 Meter liegt. Frühere Arbeiten beschäftigten sich daher hauptsächlich mit einer Fußgängerdetektion in PMD-Bildern, in dem übliche Verfahren zur Personendetektion auf 3D-Tiefenbilder angewendet wurden [3,4].

Diese Arbeit beschreibt ein System zur Hinderniserkennung und -verfolgung, welches Hindernisse unabhängig von ihrer Form oder speziellen Merkmalen in 3D-Tiefenbildern erkennt. Im folgenden Abschnitt wird das grundlegende Konzept des Systems beschrieben. Daran anschließend werden Ergebnisse durchgeführter Experimente diskutiert, mit denen das entwickelte System getestet wurde.

2 Systembeschreibung

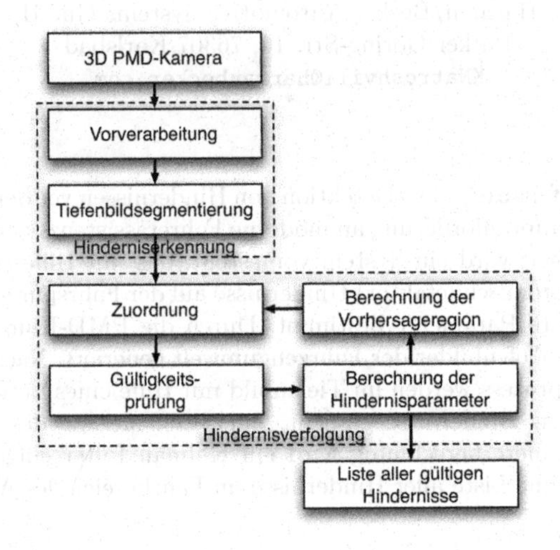

Abb. 1. Komponenten des aufgebauten Systems.

Abbildung 1 zeigt das Konzept des Systems zur Hinderniserkennung. Mit Hilfe von zwei LED-Beleuchtungseinheiten wird eine Szene mit amplitudenmoduliertem Infrarotlicht aktiv bestrahlt. Die Kamera empfängt das durch die Szene reflektierte Licht und misst dessen Laufzeit, d. h. die Zeit, die zwischen Aussenden und Empfangen des Lichts vergangen ist. Daraus lässt sich ein 3D-Tiefenbild erstellen. Diese Sensorik hat gegenüber herkömmlichen Sensoren zur Tiefenerfassung vor allem den Vorteil, dass eine sehr genaue Messung mit Hilfe eines günstig zu produzierenden CMOS-Chips durchgeführt werden kann. Abbildung 2 zeigt die zur Hinderniserkennung eingesetzte PMD-Kamera. Für die Detektion von Hindernissen in 3D-Tiefenbildern ist ein zweistufiges System notwendig. In der ersten Stufe wird eine Hinderniserkennung durchgeführt, die einzelne Pixel zu Objekten zusammenfasst. Daraufhin werden in der zweiten Systemstufe erkannte Hindernisse temporal verfolgt.

Abb. 2. Eingesetzte PMD-Kamera mit zwei Beleuchtungseinheiten.

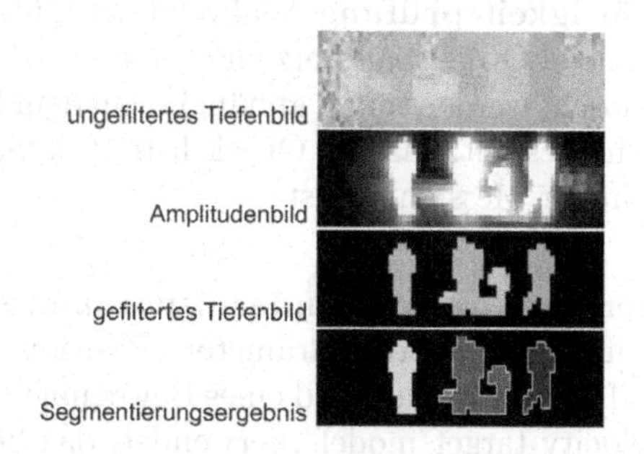

Abb. 3. Schritte der Hinderniserkennungsstufe (Tiefenbild in Falschfarbendarstellung).

2.1 Hinderniserkennung

Die Hinderniserkennung verlangt zuerst eine Gültigkeitsprüfung der aufgenommenen Tiefendaten. Für jedes PMD-Pixel wird gemessen, wie stark die Signalamplitude ist [4]. Wird das Pixel zu schwach beleuchtet, führt dies zu größeren Messvarianzen. Daher wird das Pixel herausgefiltert, falls dessen Messsignal zu schwach ist.

Daran anschließend müssen Bildbereiche identifiziert werden, die ein Hindernis darstellen könnten. Dazu werden in den Tiefendaten nahe beieinander liegende Pixel zu einem Objekt zusammengefügt. Für diese Segmentierung bietet sich das "Unseeded Region Growing"-Verfahren an, mit dessen Hilfe ohne Benutzereingriff ähnliche Punktemengen anhand eines Homogenitätskriteriums zu Regionen zusammengefasst werden können [5]. In Abbildung 3 sind Ergebnisse der Hinderniserkennungsphase gezeigt.

2.2 Hindernisverfolgung

Die temporale Verfolgung trägt wesentlich zur Robustheit des Hindernisdetektionssystems bei. Hindernisse, die während einem Messzyklus nicht detektiert werden konnten, müssen für mehrere Messzyklen als gültige Objekte bestehen bleiben, bis sichergestellt werden kann, dass die ausbleibende Detektion nicht durch Messfehler verursacht wurde. Der zeitliche Verlauf eines Hindernisses über mehrere Messungen wird als Objektbahn bezeichnet. Das Ergebnis der Hindernisverfolgung ist eine Objektliste, die alle gültigen Objekte und deren Parameter enthält. Zur temporalen Hindernisverfolgung wird ein System verwendet, welches aus vier Komponenten besteht [6]:

Zuordnung In der Zuordnungsphase wird für jedes gerade detektierte Hindernis entschieden, welcher Objektbahn die Messung zugewiesen wird. Dies erfolgt anhand einer Vorhersageregion, die für jede Objektbahn berechnet wird. Fällt eine Messung in eine Vorhersageregion, wird diese der Objektbahn zugewiesen.

Gültigkeitsprüfung Während der Gültigkeitsprüfung wird entschieden, ob eine neue Objektbahn erzeugt, eine Objektbahn bestätigt oder eine Objektbahn gelöscht werden muss, abhängig von dem Ergebnis der Zuordnung. Dadurch wird sichergestellt, dass die Objektliste ständig aktualisiert wird, aber auch robust gegenüber Messfehlern ist.

Berechnung der Hindernisparameter Im dritten Schritt erfolgt die Berechnung der Hindernisparameter (Position, Geschwindigkeit, etc.) mit Hilfe eines Kalman-Filters anhand eines Bewegungsmodelles. Als Modell wird das "constant velocity target model" verwendet, das bei Experimenten zu den besten Ergebnissen geführt hat [8]. Die Objektbahn wird einerseits durch die ihr zugeordnete Messung aktualisiert. Zum anderen wird überprüft, ob diese Aktualisierung dem angenommenen Bewegungsmodell entspricht. Große Abweichungen von dem erwarteten Modell führen dazu, dass die Messung schwächer in die Aktualisierung einfließt. Dadurch können Messvarianzen geglättet werden.

Berechnung der Vorhersageregion Der vierte Schritt beinhaltet die Berechnung der Vorhersageregion für die nächste Zuordnungsphase. Auf Grundlage der a posteriori Schätzung und der Schätzfehlerkovarianzmatrix der vorhergehenden Phase wird der a priori Zustand des Hindernisses berechnet. Die Vorhersageregion entspricht einer 3D-Ellipse um den a priori vorhergesagten Mittelpunkt des Objekts.

2.3 Versuchsträger

Als Versuchsplattform wird ein modifizierter Smart Roadster verwendet [9]. Die Plattform ist mit einer Drive-by-Wire Steuerung ausgestattet, so dass die Fahrzeugsteuerung per Computer erfolgen kann. Dadurch können auch autonome Fahrten mit dem Automobil durchgeführt werden. Die autonome Steuerung basiert auf einem Verhaltensnetzwerk, mit dessen Hilfe das Fahrzeug einen Fahrkorridor generiert, in dem unfallfrei navigiert werden kann [10].

3 Ergebnisse

Auf einem Gelände der Universität Karlsruhe (TH) wurde die Funktionsweise des Systems getestet. Da das Hindernisdetektionssystem sämtliche Objekte erfassen muss, die sich im Fahrkorridor des Fahrzeugs befinden, wurden Experimente verschiedener Art durchgeführt. Anhand der Experimente wurde untersucht, wie genau die Hindernisparameter ermittelt werden können. Dies erfolgt in Bezug auf eine Eignung des Systems für Precrash- bzw. Adaptive Cruise Control-Systeme.

3.1 Precrash-Eignung

Eine Kernanforderung an das System zur Hindernisdetektion ist die Erkennung von Fußgängern auf der Fahrbahn. In diesem Experiment wurde die Fahrbahn vor dem Versuchsträger von einem Fußgänger in verschiedenen Abständen zum Fahrzeug überquert. Dies wurde jeweils mehrere Male wiederholt, damit Aussagen über die Standardabweichung der Positionsmessung ermittelt werden konnten.

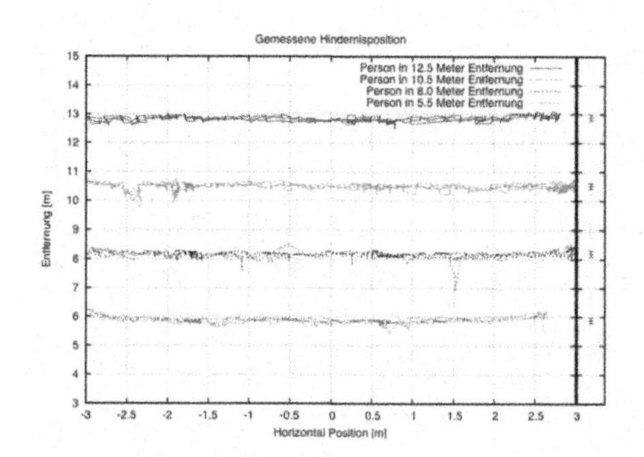

Abb. 4. Gemessene Position des Fußgängers und Standardabweichung der Messung.

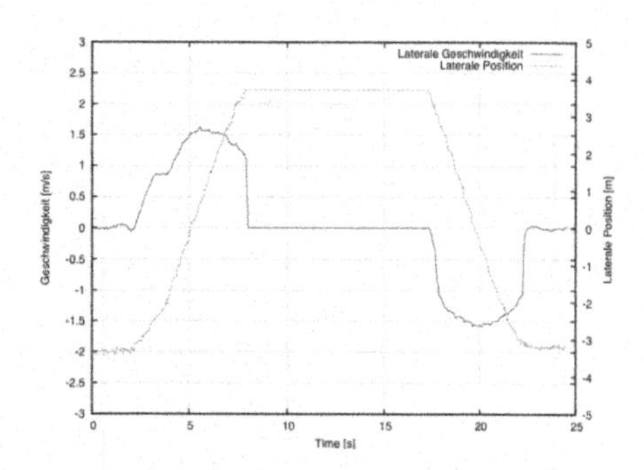

Abb. 5. Evaluation der lateralen Geschwindigkeitsmessung.

Abbildung 4 zeigt die Position des Fußgängers, die durch das Hindernisdetektionssystem ermittelt worden ist. In allen Messentfernungen kann die Trajektorie der Person korrekt gemessen werden. Die Standardabweichungen der Messungen sind am rechten Rand der Abbildung eingetragen. Die geringe Varianz von 0,1 Meter in 12,5 Meter Entfernung zur 3D-Kamera erlaubt genaue Aussagen über die Trajektorie der Person. Vereinzelt treten stärkere Messabweichungen auf. Dies lässt sich dadurch begründen, dass die ermittelte Entfernung dem minimalen Abstand des Hindernisses zur Kamera entspricht. Dieser Wert muss mit jeder Messung aktualisiert werden, da er zur Berechnung der minimalen Time-to-Collision notwendig ist. Somit unterliegt die Position keiner Glättung durch die temporale Verfolgung.

Weiter wurde evaluiert, welche Genauigkeit die Geschwindigkeitsschätzung der Hindernisverfolgung erreicht. Die Ermittlung der Bewegungsgeschwindigkeit eines Objekts ist zur Vorhersage einer möglichen Kollision bei Precrash-Systemen von großer Bedeutung. Im Experiment wurde eine Bahn von einem Fußgänger mit konstanter Geschwindigkeit von 1,2 m/s abgelaufen.

Die Ergebnisse der lateralen Geschwindigkeitsmessung belegen eine gute Bestimmung der gemessenen Geschwindigkeit. Die maximal berechnete Geschwindigkeit des Fußgängers beträgt 1,5 m/s. Dies ist ausreichend genau für eine Vorhersage der Hindernistrajektorie.

Ein weiterer wesentlicher Parameter ist die Ausdehnung eines Hindernisses. Diese Parameter können nur sehr ungenau von Radar- bzw. Lidarsensorik bestimmt werden. Zur Ermittlung einer möglichen Klassifikation des Hindernisses spielt die Ausdehnung eine große Bedeutung. Abbildung 6 zeigt die Ergebnisse der Evaluation. Der Fußgänger misst in der Breite 0,55 m. Man erkennt eine

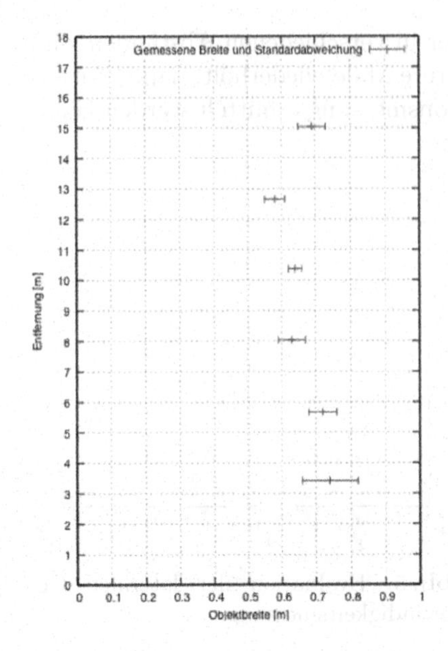

Abb. 6. Ermittelte Objektbreite und dessen Standardabweichung in verschiedenen Entfernungen.

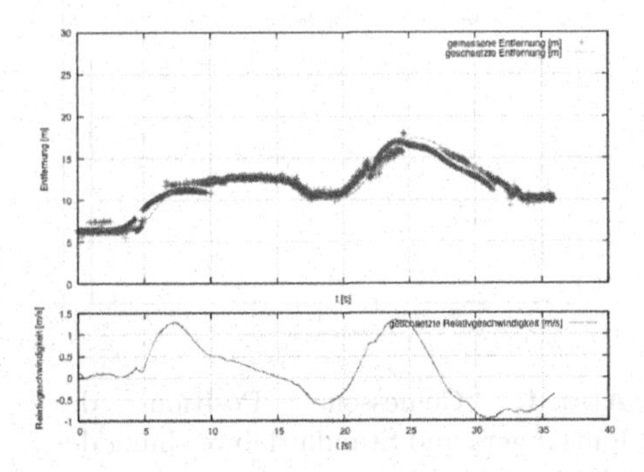

Abb. 7. Unten: Diagramm der gemessenen Relativgeschwindigkeit; oben: gemessener und geschätzter Abstand zum Hindernis.

systematische Abweichung von etwa 0,15 m. Dies lässt sich darauf zurückführen, dass das um den Fußgänger gelegte begrenzende Rechteck nicht der tatsächlichen Breite des Fußgängers entspricht.

3.2 Adaptive Cruise Control-Eignung

Für Fahrerassistenzsysteme wie Adaptive Cruise Control (ACC) ist besonders die Erkennung von Fahrzeugen und deren Geschwindigkeit relevant. Mit diesem Experiment soll gezeigt werden, dass die Hindernisdetektion auch für ein ACC-System verwendet werden kann. Die maximale Sensorreichweite von 40 Meter beschränkt das System allerdings auf einen Einsatz bis Fahrzeuggeschwindigkeiten von 30 km/h.

Im oberen Graph der Abbildung 7 ist der gemessene Abstand zu einem vorausfahrenden Fahrzeug eingetragen. Der untere Teil der Abbildung zeigt die durch die temporale Fusion geschätzte Relativgeschwindigkeit des Fahrzeugs. Während dem Verlauf des Experiments beschleunigt das vorausfahrende Fahrzeug bei Geradeausfahrt auf 3 m/s. Die Versuchsplattform folgt dem Fahrzeug mit einem Mindestabstand von 10 Meter.

4 Zusammenfassung

In dieser Arbeit wurde ein System zur Hindernisdetektion vorgestellt, das mit Hilfe einer PMD-Kamera Hindernisse auf der Fahrspur erkennt und deren relevante Parameter bestimmt. Das System ist robust gegenüber der spezifischen Form und Textur möglicher Hindernisse, da es zur Hinderniserfassung einzig die 3D-Tiefenwerte der Fahrzeugumgebung erfasst. Das 3D-Tiefenbild wird während eines Segmentierungsprozesses in relevante Bereiche zerlegt. Diese Messungen werden in einem weiteren Schritt den im System bekannten Hindernissen zugewiesen und über mehrere Zeitschritte verfolgt.

Die Ergebnisse belegen, dass das System sowohl als Precrash-System wie auch zur Vermeidung von Kollisionen mit anderen Fahrzeugen eingesetzt werden kann. Durch Experimente wurde gezeigt, dass die Hindernisdetektion alle relevanten Objektparameter ausreichend genau bestimmen kann, so dass in weiteren Arbeiten beispielsweise eine Klassifikation der Hindernisse anhand dieser Parameter erfolgen kann. Zukünftige Arbeiten befassen sich außerdem mit der Berechnung des optischen Flusses in 3D-Bildern wie auch mit der Fusion von Monokularbildern und 3D-Tiefendaten.

Literaturverzeichnis

1. Tons, M. and Doerfler, R. and Meinecke, M.-M. and Obojski, M.A. Radar sensors and sensor platform used for pedestrian protection in the EC-funded project SAVE-U. *Proc. of the IEEE Intelligent Vehicles Symposium (IV'04)* 2004.
2. A. Broggi and M. Bertozzi and A. Fascioli and M. Sechi. Shape-based pedestrian detection. *Proc. of the IEEE Intelligent Vehicles Symposium (IV2000)*, 2000.
3. Björn Elias and Petri Mähönen. Pedestrian Recognition Based on 3D Image Data. *Proc. of the International Symposium on Industrial Electronics*, 2007.
4. Basel Fardi, Jaroslav Dousa, Wanielik Gerd, Elias Björn, and Alexander Barke. Obstacle detection and pedestrian recognition using a 3D pmd camera. In *Proceedings of Intelligent Vehicles Symposium, 2006 IEEE*, pages 225–230, 2006.
5. Zheng Lin, Jesse Jin, and Hugues Talbot. Unseeded region growing for 3D image segmentation. In Peter Eades and Jesse Jin, editors, *Selected papers from Pan-Sydney Workshop on Visual Information Processing*, Sydney, Australia, 2001. ACS.
6. S.S. Blackman. Multiple hypothesis tracking for multiple target tracking. *Aerospace and Electronic Systems Magazine, IEEE*, 19(1):5–18, Jan 2004.
7. G. Welch and G. Bishop. An introduction to the Kalman filter, 2001.
8. Y. Bar-Shalom and T.E. Fortmann. Tracking and Data Association. *Academic Press*, San Diego, CA, 1988.
9. J. Schröder and U. Müller and R. Dillmann. Smart Roadster Project: Setting up Drive-by-Wire or How to Remote-Control your Car. *Proceedings of the 9th International Conference on Intelligent Autonomous Systems*, 383–390, 2006.
10. J. Schröder and M. Hoffmann and R. Dillmann. Behavior Decision and Path Planning for Cognitive Vehicles using Behavior Decision and Path Planning for Cognitive Vehicles using Behavior Networks. *Proceedings of the IEEE Intelligent Vehicles Symposium (IV'07)*, 2007.

PMD basierte Fahrspurerkennung und -verfolgung für Fahrerassistenzsysteme

T. Gumpp[1], T. Schamm[1], S. Bergmann[3], J.M. Zöllner[1] und R. Dillmann[2]

[1] FZI Forschungszentrum Informatik, Interaktive Diagnose und Servicesysteme,
Haid-und-Neu-Str. 10–14, 76131 Karlsruhe
{gumpp, schamm, zoellner}@fzi.de

[2] Universität Karlsruhe (TH), Institut für Technische Informatik, Technologiefabrik,
Haid-und-Neu-Str. 7, 76131 Karlsruhe
dillmann@ira.uka.de

[3] Harman/Becker Automotive Systems GmbH,
Becker-Göring-Str. 16, 76307 Karlsbad
SBergmann@harmanbecker.com

Zusammenfassung. In diesem Artikel wird ein System zur Verfolgung von Fahrspuren unter Verwendung von PMD-Kameras vorgestellt. Er gibt einen Überblick über die Auswertung der Intensitäts- und Tiefenbilder dieses Sensors in einem System zur fremdlichtunabhängigen Fahrspurverfolgung. Ein Kalman-Filter wird verwendet, um neben den Fahrspurparametern auch die Position und Orientierung des Fahrzeugs relativ zur Fahrspur zu schätzten.

1 Einleitung

Zur Steigerung von Sicherheit und Komfort im Fahrzeugverkehr werden zunehmend Fahrerassistenzsysteme eingesetzt. Eine Grundlage dieser Assistenzsysteme ist die zuverlässige Erkennung von Fahrspuren. Adaptive Cruise Control (ACC) Systeme erkennen beispielsweise anhand der Fahrspur das vor ihnen fahrende Fahrzeug, um gerade bei Kurvenfahrt auf mehrspurigen Straßen die Geschwindigkeit an das richtige Fahrzeug anzupassen. Auch Spurverlassenswarner nutzen die Fahrspurerkennung, um anhand des Abstands des Fahrzeugs von der Fahrspurmitte den Fahrer auf ein unbeabsichtigtes Verlassen der Spur hinweisen [1]. In diesem Artikel wird ein Spurverfolgungsansatz auf Basis der PMD Kamera vorgestellt.

2 Stand der Technik

Bildinterpretierende Systeme zur Fahrspurerkennung verwenden meist Grauwert- oder Farbkameras, aus deren Bildern Merkmale extrahiert werden. Verwendete Merkmale sind Fahrspurmarkierungen wie Mittelstreifen und Fahrbahnbegrenzung [2], [3], [4], [5]. Andere verwendete Merkmale sind Kanten, die am Übergang zwischen dem Fahrbahnbelag und dem Bankett entstehen [2]. Auch Straßenfarbe, welche mittels eines Histogramms [6] oder Klassifikationsverfahrens ermittelt werden kann, wird verwendet, um Fahrspuren zu extrahieren.

Die verwendeten Grauwert- und Farbkameras empfangen als passive Sensoren Umgebungslicht. Damit reagieren sie empfindlich auf Beleuchtungswechsel. Diese treten vor allem abends und in der Nacht, sowie bei Tunneleinfahrten und -ausfahrten und an Schlagschatten auf. Schwierige Lichtverhältnisse erhöhen bei Fahrspurverfolgungssystemen, die diese Sensoren verwenden, die Ungenauigkeit sowie die Gefahr, dass die Spurverfolgung fehlschlägt. Dies wirkt sich auf alle Fahrerassistenzsysteme aus, die auf den Ergebnissen der Spurverfolgung aufbauen, und könnte beispielsweise beim ACC zur Gefährdung der Fahrzeuginsassen führen.

Um auch in diesen Situationen zuverlässig die Fahrspur verfolgen zu können, wird ein neuartiges System vorgestellt, welches unabhängig vom Umgebungslicht auch in diesen Situationen die Verfolgung der Fahrspur gewährleisten kann. Dies wird durch Verwenden der PMD-Technologie (Photomischdetektor) [7] erreicht, die als aktiver Sensor den beschriebenen Einschränkungen nicht unterliegt. Der PMD-Sensor liefert ein Intensitätsbild, in dem die Fahrspurmarkierungen deutlich sichtbar sind.

Im Gegensatz zu Farbkameras kann der PMD-Sensor Entfernungen zu Objekten direkt messen, und so ein Tiefenbild der Umgebung aufbauen. Dies kann verwendet werden, um die Gültigkeit der Markierungsdetektion zu verifizieren, sowie den Nickwinkel des Fahrzeugs zu schätzen. Somit kann mit PMD-Kameras eine zuverlässige Fahrspurverfolgung realisiert werden, die nicht von Beleuchtungsänderungen der Umwelt negativ beeinflusst wird, und 3D-Informationen aus der Umgebung verwenden kann.

3 PMD Sensor zum Detektieren und Verfolgen von Straßenmarkierungen

Zur Detektion von Straßenmarkierungen wurde die in letzter Zeit verstärkt im automobilen Umfeld verwendete PMD Kamera als Sensor ausgewählt. PMD Kameras (Abb. 1) sind aktive Sensoren, die zudem gezielt Fremdlicht unterdrücken, um von den umgebenden Lichtverhältnissen möglichst ungestörte Messungen vornehmen zu können.

Ein PMD Sensorsystem besteht aus der Kamera sowie einer oder mehreren Lichtquellen, die moduliertes Infrarotlicht aussenden, um die zu vermessende Szene zu beleuchten. Das ausgesendete Licht wird von Objekten der Umgebung reflektiert, und trifft auf den Sensor der PMD Kamera. Diese steuert die Modulation der Lichtquellen und kann somit aus der Phasenverschiebung einen Entfernungswert berechnen. Diese Entfernungswerte ergeben ein Tiefenbild der beobachteten Szene.

Neben dem so erstellten Entfernungsbild liefert der Sensor je Bildelement einen Intensitätswert, welcher der Menge des empfangenen Infrarotlichts entspricht. In dem so erstellten Helligkeitsbild treten die Fahrspurmarkierungen

Abb. 1. PMD-Kamera eingebaut in ein Fahrzeug, sowie mit Beleuchtungseinheit.

gut sichtbar hervor, da sie das ausgesendete Infrarotlicht relativ stark reflektieren (Abb. 2).

4 Vorstellung des Tracking - Systems

Zum Detektieren und Verfolgen der Fahrspur wird ein modellbasierter Ansatz verwendet. Hierfür wurde ein Klothoidenmodell ausgewählt, welches bereits mit anderen Sensoren erfolgreich eingesetzt wurde [4]. Die Klothoide wird über ein Polynom dritter Ordnung approximiert.

Die zu schätzenden Parameter des Modells beinhalten die Breite und Krümmung der Fahrspur, sowie die seitliche Verschiebung und den Gierwinkel des Fahrzeugs relativ zur Fahrspur. Da die verwendete PMD-Kamera eine geringe Auflösung von 64x16 Bildpunkten aufweist, ist die Erkennung der Fahrspur auf den Nahbereich beschränkt. Auch die Stärke des reflektierten Infrarotlichts nimmt mit der Entfernung ab. Daher wurde die Länge des Fahrspurmodells auf 30 m beschränkt.

Abb. 2. Intensitätsbild der PMD Kamera

Abb. 3. Projektion der Fahrspur

In der ersten Stufe des Trackingsystems wird ein an die aktuelle Zustandsschätzung angepasstes Modell in das Intensitätsbild der PMD-Kamera projiziert (Abb. 3).

An den prädizierten Fahrspurmarkierungen des Fahrspurmodells wird entlang von horizontalen Linien ein Helligkeitsübergang von Dunkel-Hell-Dunkel detektiert. Hierfür wird eine Maske verwendet die entlang der Suchlinie mit dem Intensitätsbild gefaltet wird. Die Breite der Maske entspricht der dreifachen Breite der zu erkennenden Fahrspurmarkierung w_m im Intensitätsbild.

Die Breite w_m (in Pixeln) der zu erkennenden Fahrspurmarkierung wird durch die Projektionseigenschaften der Kamera festgelegt. I_m bezeichnet die Werte des Intensitätsbilds, an denen eine Markierung gesucht wird, und entspricht daher einem Bereich der Bildzeile der Länge w_m. Analog bezeichnet I_r die Bereiche mit Länge w_m der Zeile, die seitlich an diesem Bereich anliegen.

Die außenliegenden Bereiche der Maske multiplizieren die Intensitätswerte des Bildbereichs mit einem Faktor von $-\nu$, der innenliegende Bereich mit einem Faktor von 2ν. Faltet man die Maske mit einem homogenen Bildbereich, in dem die Intensitäten I_m der Bildelemente in der Mitte der Maske identisch sind mit den Intensitäten I_r der Bildelemente an den außenliegenden Bereichen der Maske, ergeben sich somit Werte um 0. Dagegen ergeben sich bei der Faltung der Maske mit dem Bereich einer Straßenmarkierung Werte von $2 \cdot w_m \cdot I_\Delta$, wobei I_Δ für die durchschnittliche Differenz zwischen den Intensitäten der Fahrspur (I_r) und der Markierung (I_m) steht. Das Ergebnis der Faltung kann somit als ein Wahrscheinlichkeitsmaß für eine detektierte Straßenmarkierung interpretiert werden. Sie liefert um so höhere Wahrscheinlichkeiten, je größer der Helligkeitskontrast I_Δ zwischen Fahrspurmarkierung und Fahrbahnbelag ist. Das Maximum der sich aus der Faltungen ergebenden Werte wird als Mittelpunkt der detektierten Fahrspurmarkierung interpretiert. Anhand eines Schwellwertes für I_Δ wird bestimmt, ob eine Markierung detektiert wurde.

Zur zeitlichen Fusion der Messungen wird ein Kalman-Filter analog zu [2] verwendet, der das über die Zeit mitgeführte Klothoidenmodell an die im Intensitätsbild gefundenen Messungen anpasst.

In den folgenden Abschnitten wird eine Erweiterung des o.g. Verfahrens vorgeschlagen, bei dem zusätzlich das Tiefenbild genutzt wird, um die Fahrspur zu schätzen und die Zuverlässigkeit der Fahrspurmarkierungsdetektion zu erhöhen.

4.1 Ausschluss ungültiger Messungen

Das Tiefenbild der PMD Kamera kann verwendet werden, um die detektierten Markierungen zu verifizieren und Fehlmessungen beispielsweise an vorausfahrenden Fahrzeugen, die offensichtlich aus der erwarteten Straßenebene ragen, zu verwerfen. Um die Entscheidung treffen zu können, ob sich ein Tiefenwert in der erwarteten Ebene befindet, muss die Ebene der Fahrspur modelliert werden. In dem Bereich des Systems, in dem die Markierungen der Fahrspur im Intensitätsbild sichtbar sind, ist die „flat earth hypothesis"gültig, d.h. es wird angenommen, dass die Fahrbahn in einer geraden Ebene liegt. Daher müssen nur die Orientierung der Kamera zur Straßenebene, sowie die Höhe der Kamera über dem Boden bekannt sein, um eine Ebene in das Tiefenbild zu projizieren.

Anhand dieses Modells lassen sich Annahmen über die erwarteten Tiefenmessungen ableiten. Diese können mit den tatsächlich gemessenen PMD-Tiefenwerten verglichen werden. Liegt die Differenz der beiden Werte außerhalb des Toleranzbereichs, deutet dies auf eine Fehlmessung z.B. an einem vorausfahrenden Fahrzeug hin. In einem solchen Fall wird die Messung verworfen, um die Schätzung der Fahrspurparameter nicht zu stören.

Abb. 4. Versuchsstrecke auf einem Gelände der Universität Karlsruhe (TH).

4.2 Nickwinkelschätzung

Die Differenz zwischen den gemessenen und den vom Modell vorausgesagten Distanzwerten kann auch verwendet werden, um den Nickwinkel des Fahrzeugs relativ zum Boden zu bestimmen. Nickbewegungen treten insbesondere bei Bodenwellen und Schlaglöchern auf und müssen für eine korrekte Projektion des Fahrspurmodells in das Sensorbild geschätzt werden. Durch die Stoßdämpfer des Fahrzeugs können sich sowohl die Höhe als auch die Orientierung der Kamera relativ zur Bodenebene ändern. Die Höhe wird als konstant approximiert, da die Höhenänderung im Vergleich zur Nickbewegung zu einem deutlich geringer sichtbaren Unterschied in den Abbildungseigenschaften führt. Der Winkel wird geschätzt, indem die Distanz jedes gemessenen Höhenwerts zum Ebenenmodell mittels eines Kalmanfilters minimiert wird. Messwerte mit einer zu großen Differenz von der aktuell geschätzten Straßenebene gehen nicht in die Schätzung ein. Dies soll zum einen verhindern, dass Ausreißer die Messung verfälschen, zum anderen kann man so auch Fehlmessungen an vorausfahrenden Fahrzeugen für die Ebenenschätzung ausschließen.

5 Ergebnisse

Anhand von Straßenmarkierungen auf einem Gelände der Universität Karlsruhe (TH) (Abbildung 4) konnte die Funktionstüchtigkeit der ersten Stufe des vorgestellten Systems gezeigt werden. In der gezeigten Sequenz wurde ausschließlich das Intensitätsbild des PMD-Sensors verwendet. Für diese Form von Trackingsystemen ist es sehr aufwendig, anhand von annotierten Sequenzen das Verfahren zu testen, da für jedes Einzelbild eine große Anzahl an Fahrspurmodellparametern vorgegeben werden müsste. Daher wird anhand einiger Beispielsequenzen eine qualitative Evaluierung durchgeführt.

In Abbildung 5 sieht man, wie die Fahrspur im Intensitätsbild verfolgt wird. Die Parameter der Fahrspur können im Allgemeinen zuverlässig geschätzt und verfolgt werden. Ab Frame 285 ist aufgrund der starken Krümmung der Fahrspur die linke Markierung nicht mehr im Intensitätsbild zu sehen, da sie außerhalb des vom Infrarotlicht beleuchteten Bereichs liegt. In Frame 375 ist die linke Fahrspurmarkierung wieder sichtbar. Aufgrund des Ausbleibens von Messwerten für die linke Fahrspurmarkierung ist in diesem Frame eine geringe laterale

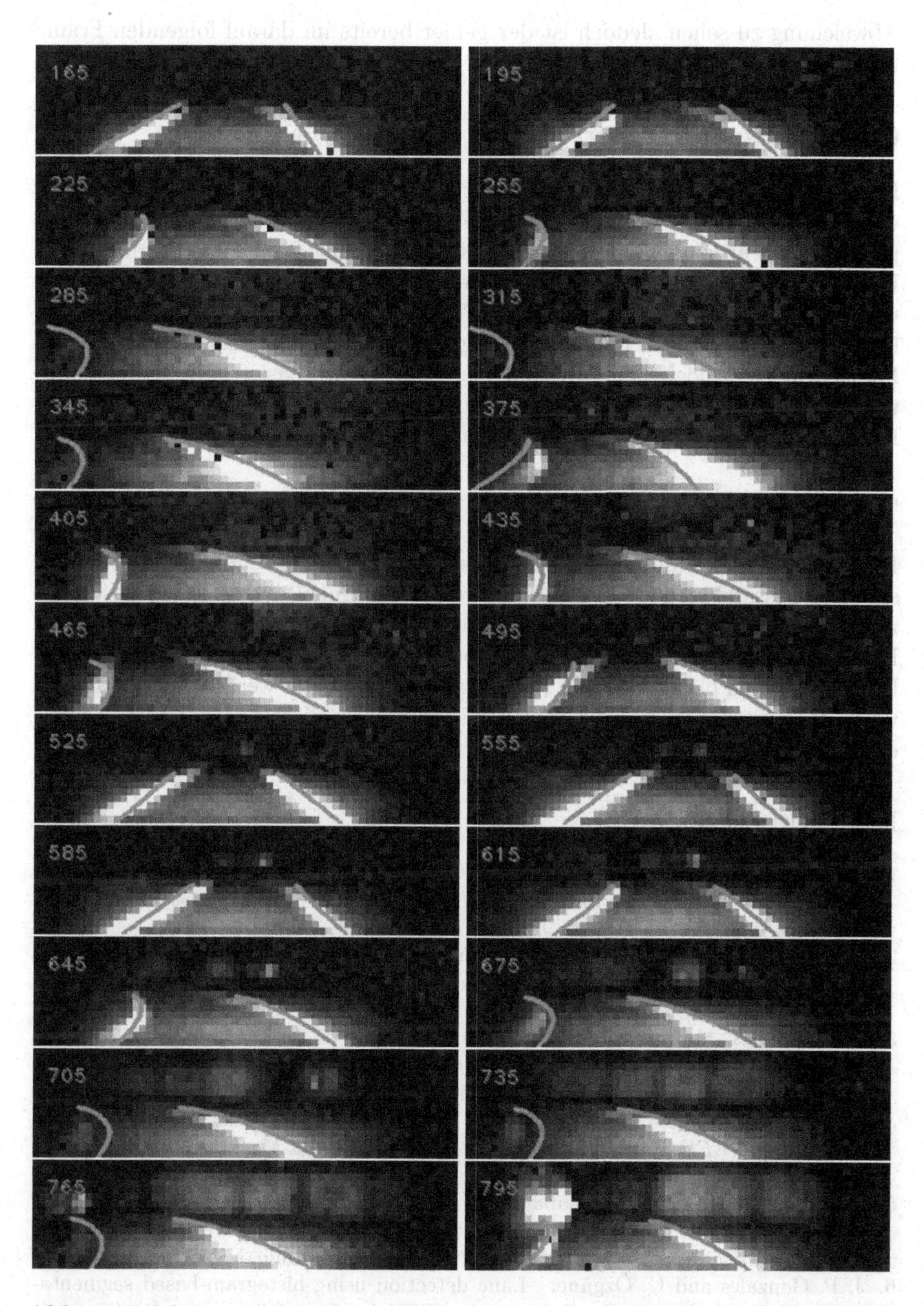

Abb. 5. Verfolgung von Fahrspurmarkierungen im Intensitätsbild einer PMD Kamera.

Abweichung zu sehen. Jedoch ist der Fehler bereits im darauf folgenden Frame korrigiert.

6 Zusammenfassung

In diesem Artikel wurde ein System zur Verfolgung von Fahrspuren unter Verwendung von aktiven PMD-Tiefenbildkameras vorgestellt. Neben den Fahrspurparametern wurde auch die Position und Orientierung des Fahrzeugs relativ zur Fahrspur geschätzt. Es wurden die Vorteile bei der Verwendung der Intensitäts- und Tiefenbilder des PMD-Sensors im Vergleich zu Farbkameras vorgestellt, die fremdlichtunabhängigen Fahrspurverfolgung unter direkter Verwendung von 3D Informationen ermöglichen. Mit Hilfe eines kalmanfilterbasierten Ansatzes konnte gezeigt werden, dass das ein klothoides Fahrspurmodell an die detektierten Fahrspurmarkierungen angepasst werden kann.

7 Ausblick

Das Verhalten der Fahrspurerkennung kann durch die Verwendung weiterer Sensoren verbessert werden. Um beispielsweise Gierwinkel und Position des Fahrzeugs prädizieren zu können, sind weitere Messgrößen wie Geschwindigkeit und Lenkwinkel des Fahrzeugs wichtige Informationen. Auch Messungen von Farbkameras können parallel zu den PMD-Daten ausgewertet werden, um die Reichweite des Systems zu steigern. Über zusätzliche Prädiktions- und Messschritte des Kalman-Filters können diese Sensormessungen in das System einfließen.

Literaturverzeichnis

1. C. R. Jung and C. R. Kelber. A lane departure warning system based on a linear-parabolic lane model. In *Proc. of the IEEE Intelligent Vehicles Symposium (IV'04)*, pages 891–895, Parma, Italien, June 14-17 2004.
2. R. Risack, P. Klausmann, W. Krüger, and W. Enkelmann. Robust lane recognition embedded in a real-time driver assistance system. In *Proceedings of the IEEE Intelligent Vehicles Symposium '98*, pages 35–40, Stuttgart, Germany, October 1998.
3. Y. Otsuka, S. Muramatsu, and T. Monji. Multitype Lane Markers Recognition Using Local Edge Direction. In *Proc. of the IEEE Intelligent Vehicles Symposium (IV'02)*, pages 604–609, Versailles, Frankreich, June 17-21 2002.
4. E. D. Dickmanns and B. D. Mysliwetz. Recursive 3-d road and relative ego-state recognition. *IEEE Transactions on Pattern Analysis and Machine Intelligence*, 14, 1992.
5. S.-S. Ieng and J.-P. T. R. Labayrade. On the design of a single lane-markings detector regardless the on-board camera's position. In *Proc. of the IEEE Intelligent Vehicles Symposium (IV'03)*, pages 564–569, Columbus, Ohio, USA, June 9-11 2003.
6. J. P. Gonzales and U. Özgüner. Lane detection using histogram-based segmentation and decision trees. In *Proc. of the IEEE Intelligent Transportation Systems Conference*, pages 346–351, 2000.
7. H. Heinol and R. Schwarte. Photomischdetektor erfasst 3d-bilder. *Elektronik*, 12, 1999.

Ein Organic Computing Ansatz zur Steuerung einer sechsbeinigen Laufmaschine

Adam El Sayed Auf, Svetlana Larionova, Florian Mösch, Marek Litza, Bojan Jakimovski und Erik Maehle

Universität Lübeck, Institut für Technische Informatik, Ratzeburger Allee 160, 23538 Lübeck

Zusammenfassung. Obwohl die Rechengeschwindigkeit von Computern und die Komplexität unserer Systeme ständig zunimmt, sind die heutigen Laufmaschinen nicht in der Lage, sich mit den Fähigkeiten von Landtieren wie zum Beispiel Insekten zu messen. Das Verständnis biologischer Konzepte und das Lernen von der Natur könnten zur Verbesserung der heutigen Maschinen beitragen und sie ein wenig "lebensähnlicher" machen. Dieser Artikel stellt einen Kontrollarchitekturansatz basierend auf "Organic Computing"-Prinzipien vor, der die Nutzung von Dezentralisierung und Selbstorganisation an einer sechsbeinigen Laufmaschine demonstriert. Die vorliegende Arbeit erklärt die elementaren Mechanismen für das gerade Laufen, das Kurvenlaufen sowie das Drehen auf der Stelle und den Umgang mit strukturellen körperlichen Änderungen wie einer Beinamputation und stellt die Ergebnisse experimenteller Versuche vor.

1 Einleitung

Die Fortbewegung mit Beinen stellt verschiedene Herausforderungen dar. Angefangen bei der Steuerung eines Beins, das verschiedene Bewegungsphasen mit unterschiedlichen Aufgaben meistern muss, über die Koordination aller Beine zur Generierung effektiver Laufmuster, bis hin zur Anpassung der eingesetzten Gangart an die Umweltbedingungen und an eine zu erfüllende Aufgabe. Im Tierreich meistert jedes Landlebewesen diese Aufgaben. Bei Landtieren ist ein fließender Übergang zwischen unterscheidbaren Laufmustern zu beobachten. Auch bei Insekten ist dieses Verhalten zu beobachten und führt zu der Annahme, dass die Laufsteuerung nicht auf vordefinierten Laufmustern, sondern auf allgemeinen Regeln basiert, die eine entsprechende Anpassungsfähigkeit bieten. Die vorliegende Arbeit stellt einen Organic Computing Ansatz vor, der auf einer sechsbeinigen Roboterplattform getestet wird.

2 Die Roboter-Plattform

OSCAR (Organic Self-Configuring and Adaptive Robot) ist eine sechsbeinige Laufmaschine mit 19 Freiheitsgraden. OSCAR ist ein symmetrischer Roboter mit einem runden Körper und sechs, in einem Winkel von 60° zueinander stehenden, Beinen. Mit ausgestreckten Beinen erreicht die Maschine eine

Spannweite von 74,5 cm. Jedes Bein besitzt drei Freiheitsgrade und ist mit einem binären Kontaktsensor ausgestattet. Die binären Kontaktsensoren signalisieren einem Bein, ob es den Boden berührt. OSCARs mit einem Servomotor horizontal beweglicher Kopf besteht aus einer drahtlosen Kamera und einem Wärmesensor. Während die Kamera in der Mitte des Kopfes ein Farbbild an einen PC sendet, erkennt der Wärmesensor rechts von der Kamera Wärmequellen wie zum Beispiel Menschen. Die eingesetzte Hardware auf dem Roboter besteht aus einem SD21-Servotreibermodul und einem in Java programmierbaren JControl/SmartDisplay. Die Hardwareeinheiten sind mit einem I^2C-Bus verbunden.

3 Software-Architektur

Die Organic Robot Control Architecture - ORCA - wurde als modulares und hierarchisches System entworfen, um eine einfache Handhabung zu gewähren und auf einer ebenfalls modular und hierarchisch organisierten sowie verhaltensbasierten Roboterarchitektur einsetzbar zu sein [1,2].

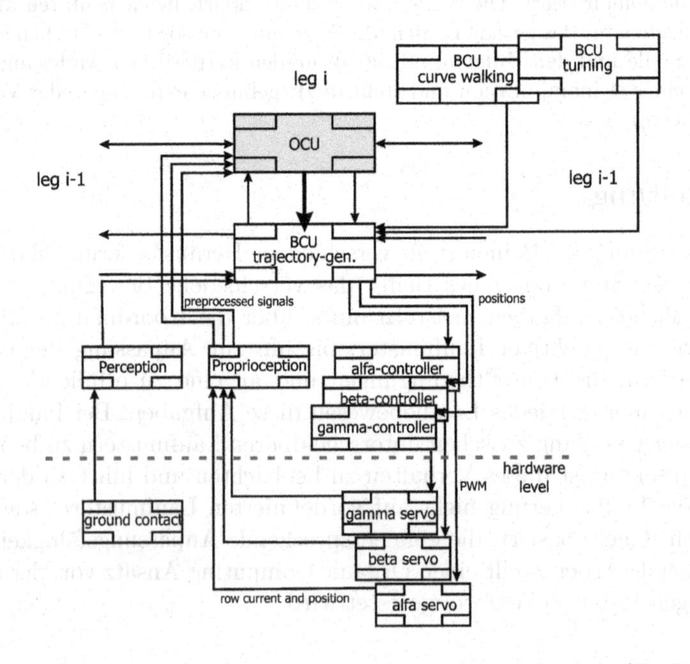

Abb. 1. Ausschnitt aus der Organische Roboterkontrollarchitektur(ORCA) für ein Bein

Ein auf ORCA basierendes System wurde entwickelt, dass durch die Nutzung von Basic Control Units (BCUs) die angestrebte Funktionalität erreicht.

Jede BCU kapselt eine spezifische Funktionalität, wie zum Beispiel die Implementierung generischer Signalfiltermodule oder PID-Steuerungen. Organic Control Units (OCUs) ergänzen die BCUs. Eine OCU nutzt die gleiche einheitliche Schnittstelle wie die BCUs, um Daten auszutauschen oder Aktivitäten auszulösen. Im Gegensatz zu BCUs realisieren OCUs keine vordefinierten, maßgeschneiderten Funktionen für den Roboter, sondern beobachten und überwachen die von BCUs generierten Signale. Ist in den überwachten Signalen eine signifikante Veränderung zu beobachten, kann die OCU durch Parameteranpassung der betroffenen BCU reagieren. Durch Definition von Normalbereichen für die von BCUs generierten Signale kann eine OCU entscheiden, wann eine Parameteranpassung zur Systemnormalisierung durchgeführt werden muss. Zusätzlich sollen die BCUs unter Ausnutzung eines Kurzzeitgedächtnisses in der Lage sein zu lernen, um ihre eigenen Reaktionen in ähnlichen Situationen in der Zukunft zu verbessern. Das hier beschriebene BCU-Konzept weist Ähnlichkeiten zu dem der Modularen Kontrollarchitektur Version 2 (MCA2) auf, das unter anderem im Roboter LauronIII genutzt wird. Neben der Lernfähigkeit einer BCU liegt der Hauptunterschied zur MCA2 im OCU-Konzept und der Möglichkeit eine oder mehrere BCUs auf ihre normale Funktion hin zu überwachen. Auf dem ORCA-Ansatz basierend und durch biologische Experimente und Steuerungen wie das Walknet [3] inspiriert, wird hier eine dezentrale Steuerung zur organischen Laufmustererzeugung eingesetzt.

4 Selbstorganisierende Laufmuster

Jedes der sechs Beine setzt sich aus drei Gelenken zusammen und nutzt seine eigene Steuerung, die durch eine separate BCU zur Trajektoriengenerierung implementiert ist (Abb. 1). Diese BCUs erzeugen Positionsvorgaben für die drei Gelenk-BCUs (Alfa, Beta, Gamma), die wiederum PWM (Pulsweiten modulierte) Signale an die entsprechenden Servomotoren senden. Um eine alternierende Stemm-Schwingbewegung zu erreichen, nutzt die Trajektorien-BCU die Informationen des Bodenkontaktsensors und zweier Extrempositionen: der posterioren Extremposition (PEP) und der anterioren Extremposition (AEP). Jede der sechs Trajektorien-BCUs nutzt die gleiche Koordinationsregel, um ihre Bewegungen mit den benachbarten Steuerungen zu harmonisieren. Die Bodenkontaktsignale werden durch Wahrnehmungs-BCUs aufgenommen und zu den Trajektorien-BCUs gesendet, die die Signale an die Trajektorien-BCUs der benachbarten Beine weiterleiten. Empfängt die Trajektorien-BCU eines Beins nicht von beiden Nachbarbeinen ein Bodenkontaktsignal, unterdrückt diese einen Wechsel in die Schwingphase. Diese Koordinationsregel sichert mit einer maximalen Anzahl von drei gleichzeitig schwingenden Beinen einen stabilen Stand. Die Kombination aus lokaler, alternierender Beinbewegung und der beschriebenen lokalen Koordinationsregel führt zu einem globalen und organischen Laufverhalten. Änderungen der Stemmdauer ergeben fließend ineinander übergehende Laufmuster durch die selbstorganisierenden Eigenschaften des Systems, ohne auf vordefinierte Gangarten zurückzugreifen.

Einer der Vorteile von OSCARs symmetrischem Körper besteht in der Fähigkeit sich um sich selbst zu drehen, ohne mehr Platz in Anspruch zu nehmen als in stehender Position. Ein Drehverhalten des Roboters wird durch eine BCU erreicht, die die AEP und PEP jedes Beins auf dieselben Werte setzt. So kann durch Beibehaltung der Koordinationsregeln und gleichzeitige Veränderung weniger Parameter ein völlig anderes Verhalten erzeugt werden. Der Kurvenlauf stellt neue Herausforderungen dar, da hier unterschiedliche Bewegungen verschiedener Beine gefordert sind. Ein einfacher Ansatz für das Kurvenlaufen besteht darin, die Stemmbewegung der drei innen liegenden Beine durch Zusammenführen von AEP und PEP zu verkürzen. Werden die Extrempositionen eines Beins soweit zusammen geführt, dass sie die gleiche Position beschreiben, tritt das Bein auf der Stelle. Wird diese Verschiebung bei den inneren Beinen weiter fortgesetzt und die Extrempositionen entfernen sich wieder von einander, führt das zu dem oben beschriebenen Drehverhalten des Roboters. Ein fließender Übergang von geradem Laufen über eine immer steiler werdende Kurve bis hin zum Drehen auf der Stelle wird durch kontinuierliche Verschiebung der Extrempositionen erreicht.

Biologische Studien mit der Stabheuschrecke *Carausius morosus* haben gezeigt, dass die Trajektorien jedes Beins individuell verändert werden [4]. Weitere biologische Experimente und Computersimulationen konnten zeigen, dass mit einer dezentralen Steuerung in Kombination mit lokalen Regeln Kurvenlaufen erreicht wurde, das auf individuellen Stemmbewegungen basiert [5]. Im ORCA-Projekt wird ein Ansatz zum Kurvenlaufen evaluiert, bei dem eine Verschiebung von AEP und PEP in den Vorderbeinen durch eine BCU erzeugt wird, die sich durch lokale Regeln auf die posterioren Beine auswirkt. Wird die Veränderung der AEP und PEP eines Vorderbeins durch das ipsilaterale Mittelbein detektiert, passt dieses ebenfalls seine Extrempositionen an. Detektiert das ipsilaterale Hinterbein eine Veränderung der Mittelbeinextrempositionen, passt auch dieses seine Stemmbewegung an. Die Modifikation der Extrempositionen in den Vorderbeinen beeinflusst somit durch lokale Regeln alle anderen Beine.

Ein Beispiel für eine einfache OCU-Funktion zeigt eine simulierte Beinamputation. Eine OCU, die ein nicht funktionsfähiges Bein erkennt, modifiziert die verantwortliche Trajektorien-BCU so, dass sie die Bodenkontaktsignale ihrer rechten Nachbar-BCU an die linke Nachbar-BCU weiterleitet und umgekehrt. Dadurch bleibt die selbstorganisierende Koordination bestehen und das Laufmuster passt sich an die neue physische Struktur des Systems an [6].

5 Experimente und Ergebnisse

Der Roboter kann sich auf einer 230 cm langen und 160 cm breiten ebenen Lauffläche frei bewegen. 310 cm über der Lauffläche befindet sich eine Kamera, die die verschiedenen Testläufe aufzeichnet. In dem aufgezeichneten Szenario ist der Roboter durch zwei Marker, und eine Wärmequelle durch einen weiteren Marker gekennzeichnet. Zur Positionsbestimmung ist der Roboter mit einem mittigen Marker und zur Auswertung seiner Körperorientierung mit einem Marker zwischen den beiden Vorderbeinen versehen. Der Abstand vom mittigen Marker zum Aufsatzpunkt eines Beins kann je nach Beinstellung zwischen 18 und 26 cm variieren. Es wurden neun verschiedene Roboter-Wärmequelle-Konfigurationen aufgezeichnet, um den Laufweg des Roboters zu analysieren: Geradeauslaufen, Linkskurvenlauf, Rechtskurvenlauf und diese drei jeweils ein weiteres Mal mit einer rechten Mittelbeinamputation und einer linken Mittelbeinamputation. Durch aktives Schwenken seines Kopfs nimmt der Roboter abhängig von der Entfernung das Wärmequellenziel wahr. In Abb. 2 sind sechs Koordinatensysteme zu sehen,

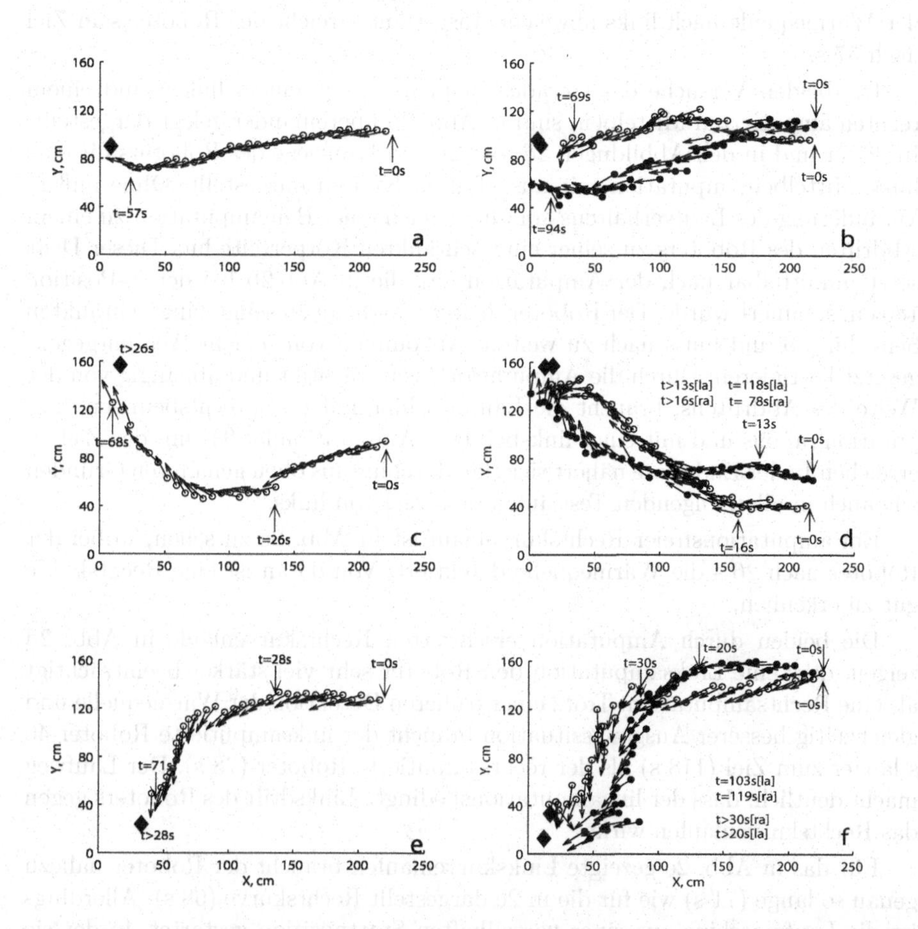

Abb. 2. Roboterpositionsangaben(XY). Mittelpunkt des Roboters ist als Kreis dargestellt, Orientierung als Pfeil. Rauten kennzeichnen Wärmequellenziel. b,d und f zeigen zwei Amputationsläufe. Ausgefüllte Kreise zeigen linksamputation[la]. Start- und Zielzeiten sowie t für Zielerkennung Kurven sind angegeben.

auf deren X- und Y-Achsen die Position des Roboters in cm abgelesen werden kann. Der Mittelpunkt des Roboters ist durch einen Kreis symbolisiert, von dem aus ein Pfeil in die Orientierungsrichting der Maschine zeigt. Eine Raute zeigt die Position der Wärmequelle an. Die über die Zeit aufgenommenen Positionen des Roboters ergeben den Laufweg des Sechsbeiners und sind mit zusätzlichen Zeitenangaben versehen. Der Zeitpunkt t=0 und die verstrichene Zeit am Ziel ist für jede Abbildung angegeben. Die Kurvenläufe sind zusätzlich mit dem Zeitpunkt der Wärmequellenwahrnehmung gekennzeichnet.

In Abb. 2a ist der gerade Lauf des Roboters dargestellt. Durch die bereits erwähnte Installation des Wärmesensors rechts von der mittigen Kamera (4,5 cm) ist gut zu erkennen, dass die Maschine mit abnehmender Entfernung von der Wärmequelle nach links abweicht. Insgesamt erreicht der Roboter sein Ziel nach 57 s.

Die beiden Versuche des Geradeauslaufens mit je einem linken und einem rechten amputierten Mittelbein sind in Abb. 2b übereinander gelegt dargestellt. In dieser und in den Abbildugen 2d und 2f sind Laufwege des Roboters für eine linke Mittelbeinamputation mit ausgefüllten Kreisen dargestellt. Ohne äußere Veränderung des Laufverhaltens kommt es nach einer Beinamputation zu einem Abdriften des Roboters zu seiner eingeschränkten Körperseite hin. Dieser Drift setzt unmittelbar nach der Amputation ein, die in Abb.2b bei der X-Position 180 cm simuliert wurde. Der Roboter driftet von da an zu seiner eingeschränkten Seite hin ab und muss nach zu weitem Abkommen von seinem Weg entgegengesetzt korrigieren. Durch die Amputation beeinträchtigt und abhängig von der Weite des Abdriftens, braucht die Laufmaschine mit einer rechtsbeinigen Amputation[ra] 69s und mit einer linksbeinigen Amputation[la] 94s um das Ziel zu erreichen.In der Endphase nähert sich die Maschine aus oben genannten Gründen wie auch in allen folgenden Testläufen dem Ziel von links.

Ein amputationsfreier Rechtskurvenlauf ist in Abb. 2c zu sehen, wobei der Roboter nach 26 s die Wärmequelle detektiert. Von da an ist eine Rechtskurve gut zu erkennen.

Die beiden durch Amputation erschwerten Rechtskurvenläufe in Abb. 2d zeigen, dass eine Linksamputation den Roboter sehr viel stärker beeinträchtigt als eine Rechtsamputation. Trotz einer früheren Detektion der Wärmequelle und gleichzeitig besserer Ausgangssituation braucht der linksamputierte Roboter 40 s länger zum Ziel (118 s) als der rechtsamputierte Roboter (78 s). Der Laufweg macht deutlich, dass der linkamputationsbedingte Linksdrift des Roboters gegen das Rechtskurvenlaufen wirkt.

Für das in Abb. 2e gezeigte Linkskurvenlaufen braucht der Roboter nahezu genau so lange (71 s) wie für die in 2c dargestellt Rechtskurve (68 s). Allerdings ist die Laufmaschine aus einer vorteilhaften Startposition gestartet, in der sie bereits leicht zum Ziel hin orientiert stand.

Die Rechts- und Linksamputationen für den Rechtskurvenlauf in Abb. 2f werfen die Frage auf, warum der Roboter mit einer Linksamputation, die durch den Linksdrift in die gleiche Richtung wirkt wie das Linkskurvenlaufen, länger braucht als bei dem Rechtskurvenlaufen mit einer Rechtsamputation. Ein Erklärungsansatz für dieses Ergebnis könnte auf der oben beschriebenen Installationsposition des Wärmesensors liegen, der den Roboter zusätzlich zu dem Linksdrift und dem Linkskurvenlaufen in der Endphase vom Ziel zu weit nach links ablenkt. Der Laufweg des rechtsseitig eingeschränkten Roboters weist ein ähnliches Muster zu dem in Abb. 2d gezeigten linksseitig beeinträchtigten Rechtslauf. Der Rechtsdrift wirkt hier dem Linkskurvenlauf entgegen und führt zu einer späteren Zielankunft (119 s). In diesem Lauf wird die Wärmequelle erst nach 30 s erkannt.

Der hier vorgestellte Ansatz zur Steuerung der sechsbeinigen Laufmaschine OSCAR zeigt, dass komplex wirkendes Kurvenlaufen mit sechs Beinen mittels einer dezentralen Steuerung mit einfachen lokalen Regeln und durch die Veränderungen weniger Parameter erzeugt werden können. Darüber hinaus kann durch kontinuierliche Veränderung von Parametern ein fließender Übergang zwischen verschiedenen Laufverhalten erreicht werden. Die hier dargestellten Experimente zeigen, dass ohne zusätzliche Modifikation der Laufmuster auch bei starken Einschränkungen wie Beinamputationen das System eine akzeptable Anpassungsfähigkeit aufweist. Durch die hier aufgetretenen Probleme, wie zum Beispiel der durch die Installation des Wärmesensors bedingte Linksdrift des Roboters und das Entgegenwirken von Kurvenlaufen und Amputationseinflüssen drängen sich die Fragen auf, in wieweit durch zusätzliche Modifikation der Laufmuster diese signifikant optimiert werden können. Des Weiteren stellt sich die Frage, wie das System kleinere Defekte, wie zum Beispiel fehlende Schrauben oder versteifte Gelenke, kompensieren kann.

Literaturverzeichnis

1. Brockmann W, Großpietsch K.-E, Maehle E, Mösch F: ORCA - Eine Organic Computing-Architektur für Fehlertoleranz in autonomen mobilen Robotern. Mitteilungen der GI/ITG-Fachgruppe Fehlertolerierende Rechensys., Nr.33, 3-27 St. Augustin 2006
2. Brockmann, W, Maehle E, Mösch F: Organic Fault-Tolerant Control Architecture for Robotic Applications. 4th IARP/IEEE-RAS/EURON Workshop on Dependable Robots in Human Environments, Nagoya University/Japan 2005
3. Dürr V, Schmitz J, Cruse H: Behaviourbased modelling of hexapod locomotion: Linking biology and technical application. Arthropod Structure and Development, 33 (3),237-250, 2004
4. Dürr V, Ebeling W: The behavioural transition from straight to curve walking: kinetics of leg movement parameters and the initiation of turning. The Journal of Experimental Biology 208, 2237-2252, 2005
5. Rosano H, Webb B: The control of turning in real and simulated stick insects. Proceedings of the IX SAB, Lecture Notes in Artif. Intelligence, Volume 4095, Rome 2006
6. El Sayed Auf A, Mösch F, Litza M: How the Six-legged Walking Machine OSCAR Handles Leg Amputations. Proceedings of the Workshop on Bio-Inspired Cooperative and Adaptive Behav. in Robots at the SAB IX, Rome 2006

Bionic Tactile Sensor for Near-Range Search, Localisation and Material Classification

Volker Dürr[1,2], André F. Krause[1], Matthias Neitzel[3], Oliver Lange[3], Bert Reimann[3]

[1] Abt. Biol. Kybernetik, Universität Bielefeld, Postfach 100131, D-33501 Bielefeld
[2] Present address: Zoologisches Institut, Universität Köln, Weyertal 119, D-50923 Köln
[3] Fraunhofer IFF, Abteilung Robotersysteme, Sandtorstr. 22, D-39106 Magdeburg

Abstract. Insects use their antennae (feelers) as near range sensors for orientation, object localisation and communication. Here, we use the stick insect antenna as a paragon for an actively moved tactile sensor. Our bionic sensor uses vibration signals from contact events for obstacle localisation and classification of material properties. It is shown how distance is coded by salient peaks in the frequency spectrum, and how the damping time constants can be exploited to distinguish between eight objects made of a range of materials. Thus, we demonstrate application of bionic principles for non-visual, reliable, near-range object localisation and material classification that is suitable for autonomous exploratory robots.

1 Introduction

Walking animals are autonomous mobile systems of prime performance, partly due to their highly adaptive locomotor behaviour, partly due to their sensory abilities that allow for rapid and parallel object recognition and scene analysis. In animal near-range sensing, the active tactile sense is often of central importance: many insects actively move their antennae (feelers) and use them for orientation, obstacle localisation, pattern recognition and even communication [1]; mammals like cats or rats use active whisker movements to detect and scan objects in the vicinity of the body. Here we use the antenna of the stick insect *Carausius morosus* [2] as the biological model for a bionic sensor for reasons summarised by Dürr and Krause [3]. Insect-like tactile sensors have been pioneered by Kaneko and co-workers, who used either vibration signals [4] or bending forces [5], both measured at the base of a flexible beam, to determine contact distance. In contrast, we use a single acceleration sensor located at the tip of the probe [6]. Contact distance is determined using the peak frequency of the damped oscillations of the free end [7].

2 Bionic Implementation of an Insect-like Feeler

The robotic feeler was based on major morphological characteristics of the stick insect antenna, such as two rotary joints that are slanted against the vertical plane and the presence of a vibration sensor. The scale is approx. 10:1 to match that of the Bielefeld insectoid walking robot TARRY (Fig. 1). The actuator platform consists of two orthogonal axes. Two 6V DC motors (Faulhaber 1331T 006SR) were used rather than servo

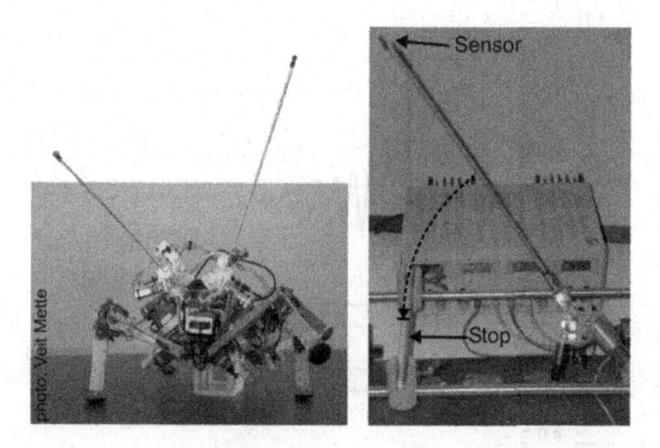

Fig. 1. Left: The Bielefeld insectoid robot TARRY, equipped with bionic feelers of prototype 1 as described by Lange et al. [6]. Right: Experimental setup for distance measurements with prototype 2, as described below. Horizontal rods of two materials were used as obstacles, and their distance relative to the feeler was varied. After a downward swoop (broken arrow) the feeler hits the stop, resulting in vibration of the free end that could be measured by a distal motion sensor.

motors to minimise self-stimulation of the probe due to discrete acceleration steps. The linkage was designed to mimic the action range of the stick insect, amounting to 90° vertical range, centred 10° above the horizon, and to 80° horizontal range centred 40° to the side. Two rotary position sensors (muRata SV01A potentiometers) monitor orientation of the probe. Positioning is limited by slack in the motors and amounts to approx. 5 mm at the tip of a 40 cm probe (approx. 7°). An adapter allows exchange of different probe types. The present probe prototype consists of a 33 cm polyacrylic tube that carries a distal two-axis acceleration sensor (Analog Devices ADXL210E). Total probe length is 41.3 cm. Total weight of the feeler prototype 2 shown in Fig. 1 is 175 g.

3 Contact Localisation

As a first test of sensor performance in contact localisation and material classification, we constrained the movement to the vertical axis and analysed sensor readings upon contact with a horizontal stop made of either aluminium (Ø = 11.8 mm) or wood (Ø = 9.6 mm). The start angle of the probe was 75° and speed at contact was about 80°/s. Upon contact with the stop, a pressing phase occurred until the motor current reached the current limitation of 50 mA. The duration of this pressing phase was 52 ms (grey shading in Fig. 2). Sensor readings and motor voltage were sampled at a rate of 1 kHz and 2.5 mV resolution (CED power 1401, with Spike2 software). The contact could always be detected easily and reliably by means of a simple threshold for the vertical acceleration. Non-zero horizontal acceleration indicated small sideward slip along the contacted rod. Only the vertical sensor reading was used for further analysis. For all materials tested, vertical acceleration showed damped harmonic oscillations with two main frequency components, the high frequency component having a shorter time constant than the low frequency component.

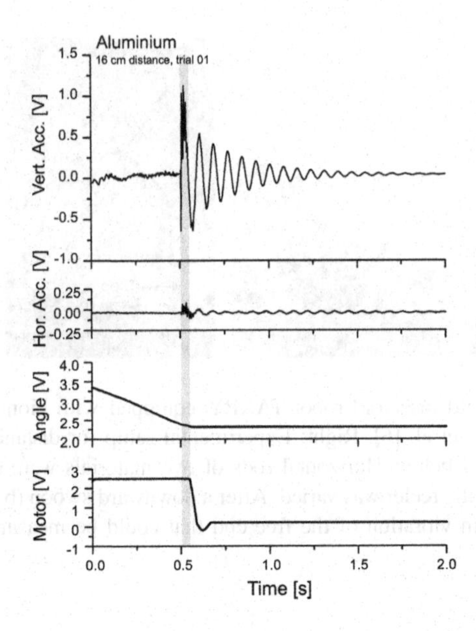

Fig. 2. Sample contact measurement, where the sensor swooped down to touch an aluminium rod at 16 cm distance. The 50 mA current limitation of the motor ensures a brief pressing event (grey shading). Vertical acceleration exhibits two superimposed damped harmonic oscillations.

The frequency spectra of the recorded oscillations always showed a salient low frequency peak, followed by one or more high frequency modes (Fig. 3, left). In order to limit further analysis to two modes only, the spectra were divided into a low frequency range and a high frequency range. Then, the frequency, F, of the largest peak was determined (filled symbols in Fig. 3). Frequencies of both peaks increased exponentially with contact distance (Fig. 3, right), the low frequency peaks having approximately three times lower standard deviation (S.D.) than the high frequency peaks. Judged by the S.D. of low frequency peaks, the linear fits to log(F) allows an average precision of 6.2 mm for distance measurements based on a single contact measurement.

4 Classification of Material Properties

Besides distance measurement, the feeler is capable of classification of obstacle properties such as compliance. Tactual classification can be based on differences in energy dissipation in the material, resulting in different damping time constants of the contact-induced vibrations. In a series of experiments, eight objects were tested with material densities ranging from 0.04 g/cm^2 (sponge) to 2.77 g/cm^2 (aluminium). Seven objects were cylindrical in shape, mostly with diameters close to 10 mm, the eighth object was box-shaped (sponge). Contact signals from materials with strongly different stiffness, like a sponge and a PVC rod were easily classified by eye, owing to marked differences in initial peak amplitude and number of oscillations (data not shown). In the following

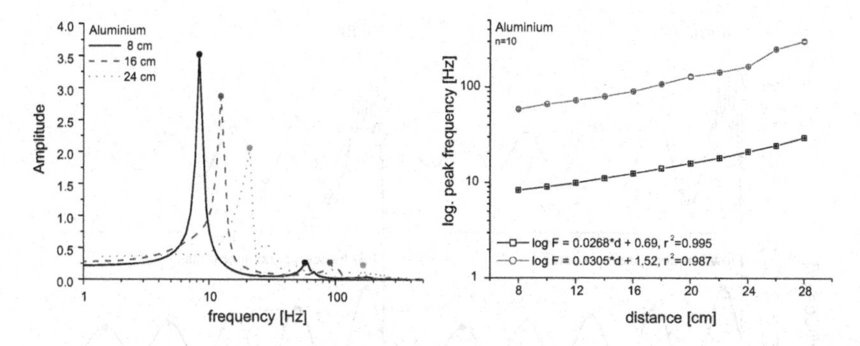

Fig. 3. Contact distance is encoded by oscillation frequencies. Left: FFT amplitude spectra of three single contacts with an aluminium rod, taken at 8, 16 and 24 cm distance. As contact distance increases, the low frequency peak decreases in amplitude and shifts to higher frequencies. Multiple high frequency modes may occur. The largest mode beyond 55 Hz was analysed further. Right: Peak frequencies increase exponentially with distance (n=10, means +- S.D., equations give S.D.-weighted linear regression fits and coefficients of determination).

we demonstrate the ability to distinguish a wooden rod from a metal rod, i.e. two stiff materials that can not easily be discriminated by optical surface features.

At first sight, differences between the two representative response time courses shown in Fig. 4 appear rather subtle. Even after decomposition of the signal into the frequency bands that were previously used for FFT peak extraction, both high and low frequency components look very similar because frequency content depends on contact distance rather than material property.

However, extraction and rectification of the local extremata revealed robust differences in decay time constants that could be measured reliably by curve fitting of a 1st order exponential decay function (Fig. 5). For both frequency components, amplitude and time constant of the fit functions were statistically significantly different for the two materials (t-test; τ_{low}: $t = 3.140$, $p = 0.0057$; τ_{high}: $t = 7.736$, $p < 0.001$; A_{low}: $t = -3.683, p = 0.0017; A_{high}$: $t = -5.934, p < 0.001$).

As an alternative, potentially faster analysis algorithm, response time courses were simply low-pass-filtered by a Gaussian kernel of 38 ms width, and rectified extremata were fitted by a 2nd order exponential decay function to account for the two decay time constants. As in the FFT-based decomposition algorithm, both time constants revealed highly significant differences (t-test; τ_{low}: $t = -6.720$; τ_{high}: $t = -5.536$, $p < 0.001$).

In the examples shown in Figs 3 to 5, the original data were not filtered and the split frequency that divided the FFT spectrum into a low and a high frequency band varied among situations. For robot applications, this somewhat arbitrary data processing is unacceptable. Rather, it was our goal to apply a single algorithm for object classification in all measurements, irrespective of contact distance and object material. The most satisfying results were obtained with the following algorithm: 1. splitting the FFT spectrum into a low frequency band below 55 Hz and a high frequency band between 55 and 250 Hz); 2. reconstructing low and high frequency components by inverse FFT; 3. extraction of local extremata with a minimum interval of 3 ms and minimum absolute

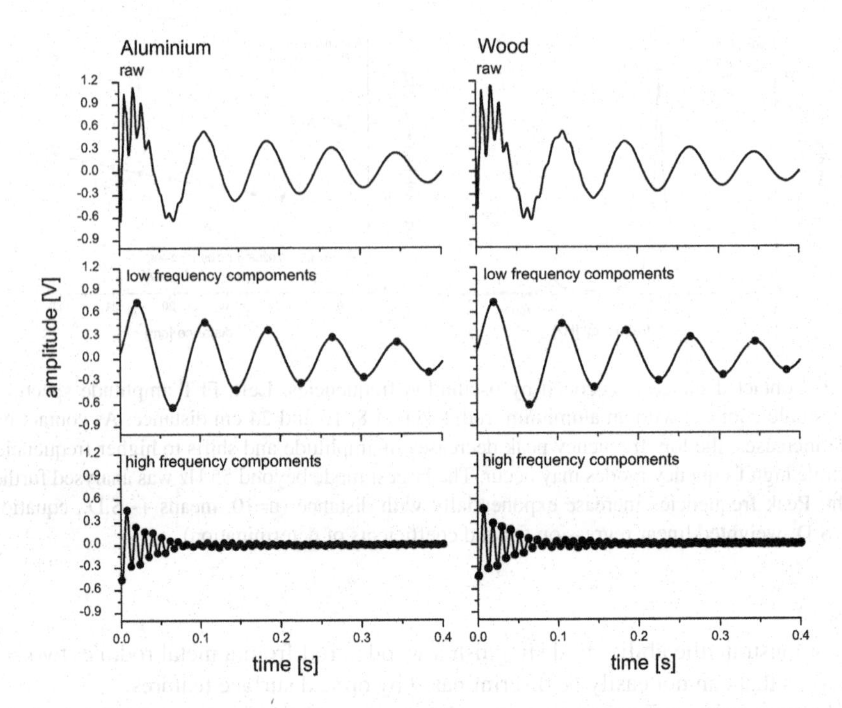

Fig. 4. When touching different objects or materials, sensor readings hardly differ in frequency content (top), and even after decomposition, both low (mid panels) and high frequency components (bottom) look very much alike for both materials.

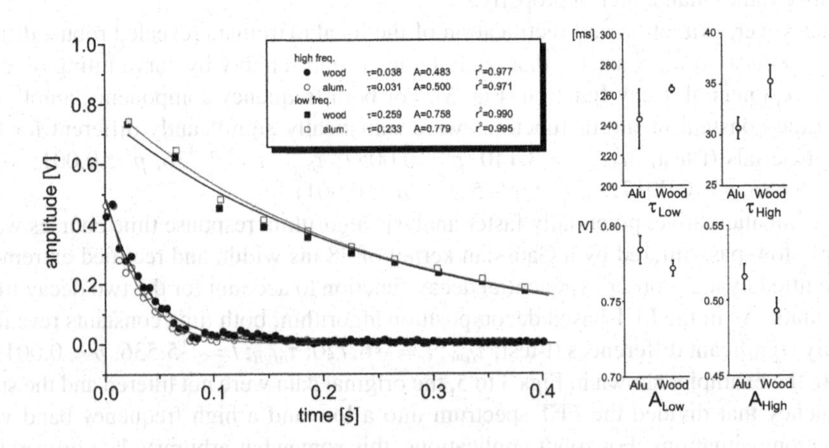

Fig. 5. Analysis of decay time constants allows material classification, as shown here for an aluminium rod and a wooden rod (same objects as in Fig.4). Extraction and rectification of local extremata of sensor reading reveals different time courses of the decay. Fitting first order exponential decay functions to single trial data (left) results in significantly different time constants, τ, and amplitudes, A, for both frequency components (right, n=10). Fits were calculated using the Levenberg-Marquardt algorithm of Origin (Microcal).

amplitude of 15 mV; 4. rectification and logarithmic transformation of measured voltages; 5. linear regression, resulting in amplitude and time constant of the exponential damping function.

One remarkable feature of this algorithm is the low variability of the results. For all materials except the sponge, standard deviations of decay time constants, τ, were always 2 ms or less. In case of low frequency components, the coefficient of variation was particularly small ($< 1\%$). Due to the small variability, measurements from different materials could be distinguished with great reliability. Paired t-tests for each combination of materials and each one of the four decay parameters gave statistically significant differences in 95 of 112 cases (85%). Assuming that statistical significance is equivalent to reliable material assignment during classification, each pair of objects could be distinguished based on at least one parameter, and all but two pairs could be distinguished based on three parameters. The decay time constants of low frequency components could always be distinguished with very high reliability because the standard deviations of τ_{low} never overlapped for any pair of objects.

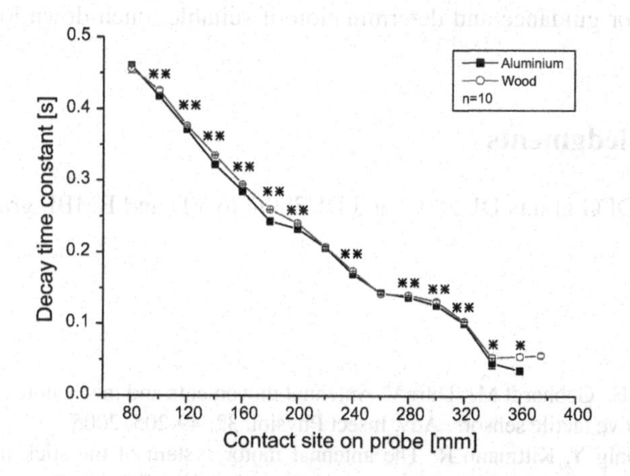

Fig. 6. Dependence of decay time constants on contact site. Two materials were compared, a soft wood rod (open circles) and an aluminium rod (solid squares). Time constants were calculated from slopes of linear fits to log-transformed peaks of low frequency components. Error bars depict the S.D., asterisks label statistically significant differences (n=10; ** $p < 0.0001$; *$p < 0.05$).

Potential problems of classification based on decay parameters could occur as decay time constants change with the frequency and, thus, contact distance. To test whether it is possible to distinguish time constants at any contact location, we compared contact signals of a soft wood rod and an aluminium rod at contact locations along the entire length of the probe (80 mm to 375 mm). For both objects, decay time constants decreased with contact distance in a similar, quasi-linear manner. Time constants of the two materials were statistically different at all but four contact sites, revealing that object and material classification is possible along 75% of the probe length, where one half of the problematic range contains the most proximal and most distal sites.

5 Conclusions

Insect antennae can serve as useful paragons for the engineering of artificial tactile feelers for near-range sensing. Non-visual distance measurement and object or material classification can be based on the analysis of damped harmonic oscillations of the free end. We have shown that even single contacts allow fairly accurate object localisation, using simple, robust and fast FFT peak extraction, rather than computationally expensive stereovision or motion parallax algorithms used in visual systems. In addition, we describe an algorithm for reliable distinction of eight different objects made of metal, wood and various plastics with different density and compliance.

So far, we have demonstrated reliable measurements in a stationary setup. Given its small weight and the possibility to implement the suggested algorithms on a digital signal processor (DSP), the feeler can be mounted to autonomous exploratory robots for near-range sensing. In combination with continuous active searching movements [1, 2], tactual localisation and material classification allows sequential probing of edges and surfaces for near-range scene analysis. On a walking robot like TARRY (Fig. 1), feelers may be used for guidance and determination of suitable touch-down locations of the front legs.

6 Acknowledgments

Supported by DFG grants DU380/3 and DU380/4 to VD and BMBF grant 0313766 to VD and OL.

References

1. Staudacher E., Gebhardt MJ, Dürr V: Antennal movements and mechanoreception: neurobiology of active tactile sensors. Adv. Insect Physiol. 32: 49-205, 2005.
2. Dürr V, König Y, Kittmann R: The antennal motor system of the stick insect *Carausius morosus*: anatomy and antennal movement pattern during walking. J. Comp. Physiol. A 187: 31-144, 2001.
3. Dürr V, Krause A: The stick insect antenna as a biological paragon for an actively moved tactile probe for obstacle detection. In: Berns K, Dillmann R (eds.) Climbing and Walking Robots - From Biology to Industrial Applications. Proc. 4th Int. Conf. Climbing and Walking Robots (CLAWAR 2001), Professional Engineering Publishing, Bury St. Edmunds, London: 87-96, 2001.
4. Ueno N, Svinin MM, Kaneko M: Dynamic contact sensing by flexible beam. IEEE-ASME Trans. Mechatronics 3: 254-264, 1998.
5. Kaneko M, Kanayma N, Tsuji T: Active antenna for contact sensing. IEEE Trans. Robot. Autom. 14: 278-291, 1998.
6. Lange O, Reimann B, Saenz J, Dürr V, Elkmann N: Insectoid obstacle detection based on an active tactile approach. In: Witte H (ed.) Proceedings of the 3rd Int. Symposium on Adaptive Motion in Animals and Machines (AMAM 2005), 2005.
7. Lange O, Reimann B: Vorrichtung und Verfahren zur Erfassung von Hindernissen. German Patent 102005005230, 2005.

Motion Planning Based on Realistic Sensor Data for Six-Legged Robots

Thomas Ihme and Uli Ruffler

Mannheim University of Applied Sciences, Windeckstr. 110, 68163 Mannheim, Germany. t.ihme@hs-mannheim.de

Abstract. Walking robots often use gait pattern to stride over the erth surface. In rough terrain this concept reaches its limitations, therefore reactive control mechanisms were introduced. In heavily unstructured terrain the robot is more reacting than actually moving. Motion planning based on gathered terrain information can help to reduce the necessary reflexes.
This article adresses the problem of real-time motion planning for walking robots. Therefore motion planning is regarded as optimization problem which is solved using a heuristical local search algorithm. It is described how we model the optimization problem how to solve it using random sampling.
Because realistic sensor data is less reliable the farther away the object is from the sensor we show how to break down the planning distance to small parts. Further more we show how to modify the algorithm to compose movements seamlessly so we can stop the actual movement and plan the next steps in case the robot encounters an obstacle the sensor has missed.
Experiments have shown the capabilities of the actual implementation but the tests have also schown the restrictions. The algorithm needs to be improved to find more good solutions in the given time, otherwise the locomotion gets interupted.

1 Introduction

Legged vehicles can help to get access to many parts of earth surface which wheeled vehicles can not cope. Different concepts are used to control legged locomotion in unstructured environment. Simple control concepts use gait pattern, which define a fixed sequence of footholds. Many investigations on gait pattern were carried out regarding stability and velocity [1] and they are used either directly [2–4] or indirectly [5, 6]. They are suitable for quite flat terrain. Reactive control components like the elevator reflex [7] are added to improve walking capabilities and terrain adaptation. But problems arise if the exception handling dominates the normal walking process. Gait planning can help to minimize exception handling occurring. To plan movements, a sensor is needed which provides information about places that are reached in the future. Therefore, a sensor for at least the near-fields is needed [8, 9]. This sensor should provide information about the relief in robots surrounding. The information may obtained with help of a stereo vision system. This paper adresses the planning for the near-field area.

2 Related Work

There exist many control systems for walking robots. Gait pattern as used in [1,3] are stable but not reliable on uneven ground. Even reactive control components like used in [7] have the mentioned drawbacks. Motion planning in [10] is only used to control gait parameters like stroke height. Planning as described in [11] switches between proper gait pattern, but these are limited. In [12] the whole motion of the robot is planned. Genetic algorithms and backtracking is used for this. But there are no real-time assertions. The ordinal optimization approach used in [13] cannot guarantee that a solution is found.

3 Motion Planning as Optimization Problem

In [14] and [15] various heuristical local search algorithms for motion planning are investigated regarding efficiency and usability. Motion planning is regarded as optimization problem. As a result random sampling is suggested as a suitable method and a test version is implemented in an simulation environment. In that simulation environment the terrain information is provided as height map.

By the claim for a *good* solution the problems may be treated as an optimization problem: Find a valid solution (movement) from the solution space (all possible movements) that is optimal regarding given objectives. To solve the optimization problem, a formal definition and an algorithm for solving it are needed.

4 Moddelling the Optimization Problem

A formal optimization problem is a triple (U, S, ϕ). The input U parameterizes the set of valid solutions $S(U)$. The weighting function ϕ defines some value by mapping every elements to a real number:

$$\phi : S(U) \mapsto \mathbb{R} \tag{1}$$

This triple has to be defined for our given problem. The input consists of the source and destination position and the environment information generated from the sensor data. The positions are defined by two-dimensional world coordinates. The environment information is given by a height map which defines the height of a point every 100 mm.

The solution space represents all valid movements. It should include *every* possible solution. Otherwise a good one could already be excluded by the definition. The whole movement is composed by the motion of the individual legs and the robot body. Each of them is described by a reference point. For the legs this is the foot, for the body the center of gravity. Their movement is described by a list of *events*. An event defines a linear movement between two points in a given time. By concatenation it can be used for linear approximation with arbitrary precision. So seven lists of such events are needed for describing the movement of the robot.

The weighting function assigns a value to reflect the quality of a movement, the maximum reflects the best. Several criteria for this are considered. They are combined to define the final value. The most important criterion is the speed, which is defined by the distance to the destination divided by the time. The faster, the better the movement is. Another criterion is the stability of the robot. This is affected by the ground and the arrangement of the legs. For the latter case the stability margin (as described in [16]) gives a good measurement. The minimal value for the whole movement is calculated. The bigger, the lower is the risk to tip over. To incorporate ground stability, slope areas are defined. The robot can loose it's grip on this (outside the friction cone). Within this simulation, the ground inclination is used. The lower it is, the better the movement. An additional criterion may define forbidden areas for places where the surface is out of reach (e.g. a hole) or the ground is defined as unsure. All these conditions can be incorporated into a weighting function

$$\psi_i : S(U) \mapsto \mathbb{R}. \tag{2}$$

These terms are linearly combined to the final value:

$$\phi(s) = \sum_i \lambda_i \psi_i(s). \tag{3}$$

The λ_i allow to adjust the influence of the criteria.

5 Actual State

Due to the complexity of the problem no exact solving algorithm is known. So a way is the use of a good heuristics. In [14] several heuristics are discussed and *Random Sampling* shown to be appropriate.

A way of generating random valid movements is needed for the heuristics. This appears to be a nontrivial task. No efficient algorithm is known for only determining, if a valid movement exists [12]. So the requirement is lowered to an algorithm which generates random movements that are valid in most cases.

The algorithm first determines a path to the destination. Therefore a random number of random robot positions is generated. Then the body movement range regarding the actual feet placement is calculated. Then one foot is choosen to be lifted or set down respectively. If the foot shold be set down, a valid foot position is calculated. Afterwards a new valid body position is choosen within the previously computed body movement range.

These steps are repeated until the destination is reached or threashold of number of movements is reached. If the threashold is exeeded, the hole motion is discarded.

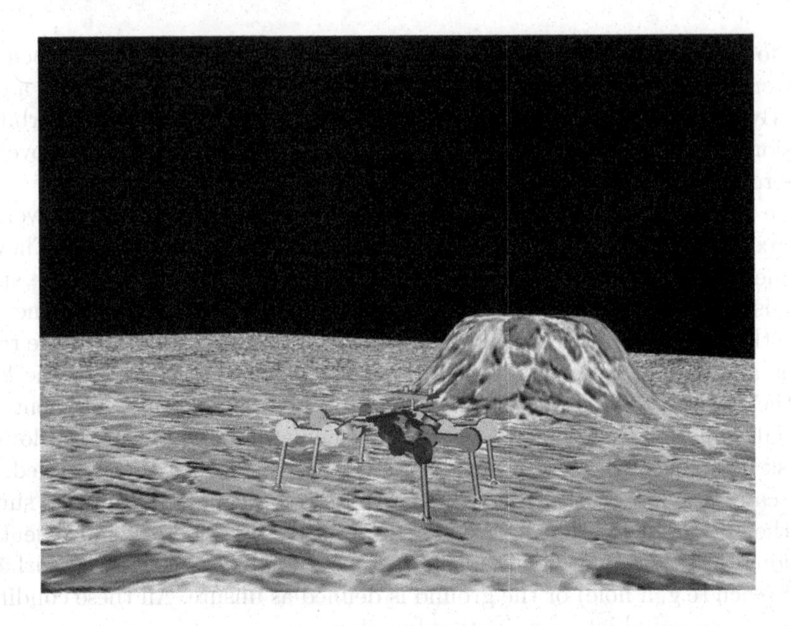

Fig. 1. Robot visiualization

For proper handling of invalid solutions a penalty value is used. They are treated as valid but really bad. So they should never occur as optimum.

The world model is represented by a raster image where the green channel of a pixel corresponds to the height. The real robot has to gather this information with its stereo vision system. A combination of a block matching and a graph cut algorithm is currently in development. This allows to create various scenarios. The movement of the robot is planned regarding the given terrain. To verify the results a visualization was developed (see figure 1).

6 Continuous Motion Planning

The above described way of motion planning bears several problems. On the one hand a real robot cannot plan the whole way at once; because the sensors can probably not provide enough information with the needed accuracy for the whole distance. On the other hand, the sensor information may not be reliable, so the planed motion could not be executed. Therefore we have to modify the actual method to handle these problems.

This leads us to plan only short distances and compose the motions. The routing for the whole path is not considered for the short-distance motion planning.The benefit of this incremental plannig is that the next movement can be improved while the robot is walking. And in case the actual movement gets interrupted, the next steps starting from the actual robot position can seamlessly be planned starting from the actual position.

The distance and the number of allowed foot steps are reduced for the short-distance motion planning. Step by step of the actual best movement is performed until a better movement is found. Then the new movements can be joined to the actual movement which leads to continuous motion. But because of the assumption in the given algorithen that the robot touches the ground with all feet, simply joining movements causes jerky motion because every partial movement starts with all feet down. Therefore we need to give up this assumption. This raises internel problems because of the internal representation of movements. The algorithm holds the movement as a sequence of stable robot configurations – i. e. which feet are in the stemming phase. Each robot configuration in the movement is guaranteed to be stable. But due to the synchronous movement of the legs, it's not safe to say if the robot is in a stable situation between two successive configurations. To be more precise, in some situations the legs are forced to move to not accessible positions near the robot body. Therefore for the time being the range of the legs will be restrict to avoid these critical situations. This restricts the search space which means we possibly lose good solutions.

Now that the algorithm can plan the gait while the robot is walking, the next step is to get the world model data via the stereo vision system. Figure 2 shows a sample disparity map produced with a graph cut algorithm [17].

7 Experimental Results

Implementation and tests have shown, that the modified motion planning algorithm is able to solve various terrains. But the tests have also shown the restrictions. The original algorithm solved a flat land terrain with one big obstacle which the modified algorithm isn't able to solve anymore. The reason is, because continuous planning in small distances does not do routing anymore. The robot walks strait to the obstacle until the next destination isn't reachable.

Furthermore the quality of the solution found depends on the running time of the algorithm. Figure 3 shows the experimental results on various terrains. As one can see, the number of solutions found depends on the given terrain. The more dents and wrinkles an area shows, the less movements are computed. As the number of improvements depends on the number of computed movements the quality of the movement is restricted by computation time and terrain complexity.

As the experiments have shown, the time between two successive movements is not enough to find a good solution in time. Therefore the algorithm needs to be improved to get a smooth motion.

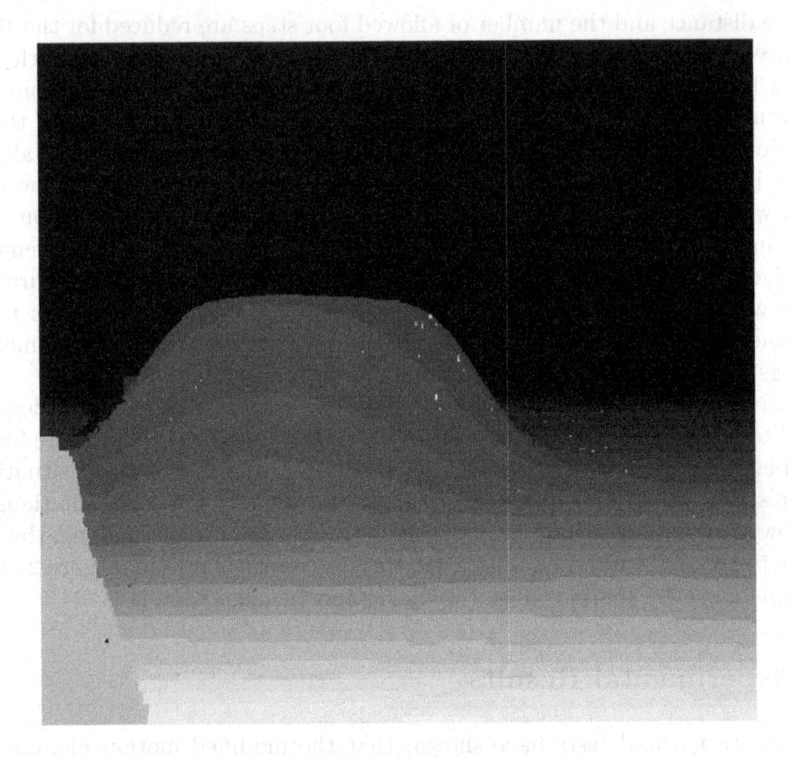

Fig. 2. Disparity map produced from scene in figure 1

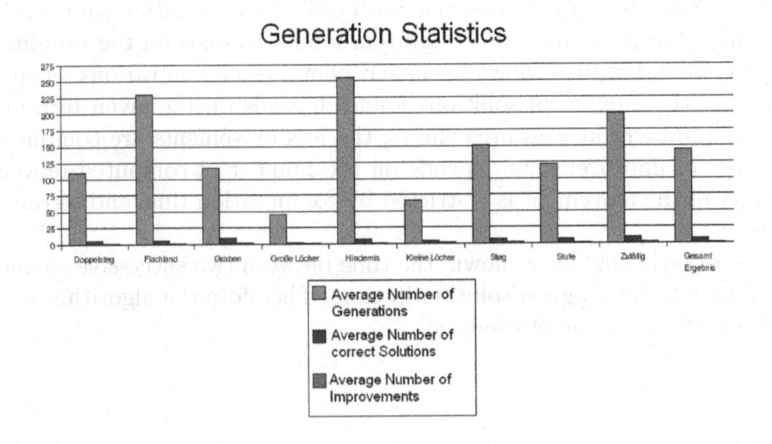

Fig. 3. Generation distribution on various terrains

References

1. Shin-Min Song and Kenneth J. Waldron. An anaytical approach for gait study and its applications on wave gaits. *The International Journal Of Robotics Research*, 6(2):60–71, Summer 1987.
2. T. Ihme. Posture control and distributed force sensing for technical applications of walking robots. In *Proceedings of the 11th International Conference on Advanced Robots*, volume 2, pages 1032–1037. University of Coimbra, June 30 – Jule 3 2003. Coimbra, Portugal.
3. Cynthia Ferrell. A comparison of three insect-inspired locomotion controllers. *Robotics and Autonomous Systems*, 16:135–159, 1995.
4. F. Pfeiffer, J. Eltze, and H.-J. Weidemann. Six-legged technical walking considering biological principles. *Robotics and Autonomous Systems*, 14:223–232, 1995.
5. Holk Cruse et al. Walking: A complex behaviour controlled by simple networks. *Adaptive Behaviour*, 3(4):385–418, 1995.
6. T. M. Kubow and R. J. Full. The role of the mechanical system in control: a hypothesis of self-stabilization in hexapedal runners. *Royal Society London*, 354:849–861, 1999.
7. B. Gaßmann, K.-U. Scholl, and K. Berns. Locomotion of LAURON III in rough terrain. In *International Conference on Advanced Intelligent Mechatronics*, volume 2, pages 959–964, Como, Italy, July 2001.
8. R. C. Luo and M. G. Kay. Multisensor integration and fusion in intelligent systems. *IEEE Transactions on Systems, Man, and Cybernetics*, 19(5):901–931, September/October 1989.
9. T. Ihme. *Steuerung sechsbeiniger Laufroboter unter dem Aspekt techischer Anwendungen.* Dissertation, Universität Magdeburg, März 2002.
10. M. A. Jiménez and P. González de Santo. Terrain-adaptive gait for walking machines. *The International Journal of Robotics Research*, 16(3), June 1997.
11. D. Wettergreen. *Robot walking in natural terrain.* PhD thesis, Carnegie Mellon University, 1995.
12. C. Eldershaw. *Heuristic algorithms for motion planing.* D.Phil. Thesis, University of Oxford, 2001.
13. C.-H. Chen, V. Kumar, and Y.-C. Luo. Motion planning of walking robots in environments with uncertainty. In *Journal for Robotic Systems*, volume 16, pages 527–545. 1999.
14. R. Bade, A. Herms, and T. Ihme. Motion planning for a legged vehicle based on optical sensor information. *Armada, M.; González de Santos, P. (Eds.): Climbing and Walking Robots. Proceedings of the 7th International Conference CLAWAR 2004.*, 2005. Madrid, Spain; Springer-Verlag.
15. T. Ihme. Motion planning for a legged vehicle based on optical sensor information. *Scharff, P. (Publ.):: 3rd International Symposium on Adaptive Motion in Animals and Machines (AMAM 2005)*, 2005. TU Ilmenau.
16. E. Papadopoulos and D. Rey. A new measure of tipover stability margin for mobile manipulators. In *IEEE International Conference On Robotics and Automation*, 1996.
17. Claude Heischbourg. Gewinnung eines Geländeprofils mittels Sensordaten und Bewegungsplanung. Bachelor Thesis. Hochschule Mannheim., März 2007.

A New, Open and Modular Platform for Research in Autonomous Four-Legged Robots

Martin Friedmann[1], Sebastian Petters[1], Max Risler[1], Hajime Sakamoto[2], Oskar von Stryk[1] and Dirk Thomas[1]

[1] Simulation, Systems Optimization and Robotics Group,
Technische Universität Darmstadt, Hochschulstr. 10, D-64289 Darmstadt, Germany
www.sim.tu-darmstadt.de

[2] Hajime Research Institue, Ltd., Osaka, Japan

Abstract. In this paper the design goals for a new, open and modular, four-legged robot platform are described that was developed in reaction to the open call for a standard platform issued by the RoboCup Federation in 2006. The new robot should have similar motion and sensing capabilities like the previously used Sony AIBO plus several new ones. The hardware and software should be open, modular and reconfigurable. The robot should be resonably priced and allow annually upgrades.

1 Introduction

Between 1999 when Sony released the first of in total three robot generations and January 2006 when Sony announced the discontinuation of its production the AIBO robot [1] had found remarkable acceptance. It was, however, not only used for its original determination as a home entertainment robot but also found widespread use as an affordable standard platform for many research and teaching projects in robotic agents at universities. This was a result of Sony's publication of a programmable interface based on OPEN-R [2] which allowed to read the sensors and to send commands to the actuators.

One of the many applications and presumable the most popular is the use and investigation of the robot as a standard platform for autonomous robot soccer teams in the Four-Legged Robot League [3] of the RoboCup [4] since 1999. One of the main features of this league is the fact that all teams use the same standard robot platform and, besides of wear and tear, only the software differs which allows to evaluate different approaches, e.g., for vision, behavior and motion, in a challenging benchmark scenario.

As a reaction to the discontinuation of the AIBO a call for tenders for a standard robot platform for robot soccer was announced by the RoboCup Federation in November 2006 [4] with the following characteristics:

- A standard platform: No hardware development should be required (or allowed) by the teams during competitions. The robot must have an operating system and software development environment allowing full control of sensors and actuators. The platform should be modular, permitting upgrades and modifications from year to year.

- Many degrees of freedom: Quadruped robots allow for a large variety of gaits and kicks. The new platform need not be a quadruped but it should have a sufficient number of degrees of freedom that teams can create interesting new behaviours and modes of locomotion.
- Directed perception: The robot is required to have onboard colour vision but not an omnidirectional camera since it is wished that teams develop methods for active perception.
- Full Autonomy: The robots are required to be fully autonomous. That is, they must have on-board computing resources sufficient to meet all processing requirements. No off-board computation is allowed. The robots must operate with no intervention by team members and minimal intervention by referees. Games typically consist of two half parts, each of them lasting for around 15 min, with a 10 mn break.
- Wireless communication: The robots must be capable of wireless 802.11 communications permitting the exchange of information between robots on the field.
- Physical characteristics: Ideally, the robot should be relatively small such that several can fit comfortably on one of the current RoboCup fields. Robots that are visually appealing will be looked upon favourably.
- (optional) Compatibility with some available robot development software.

Among the eight submitted proposals four tenderers including the robot presented in this paper were invited to demonstrate their robots during RoboCup 2007 in July in Atlanta. This paper describes the design issues and selections undertaken to meet the above mentioned requirements in mechanics and kinematics, sensing and computing abilities for the proposed four-legged robot including a comparison with the currently used Sony AIBO ERS-7 robot in the four-legged robot league.

2 Design of the Four Legged Robot

The call for tenders would in principle also allow a humanoid robot. However, the authors which already have developed a powerful humanoid robot [5] refrained from this variant as the cost for such a single, powerful humanoid robot would result in an overall cost comparable to that for a whole team of four or five four-legged robots. This is due because of the larger number of motors with much higher performance and cost needed for a powerful humanoid robot compared with a four-legged robot.

The proposed new four-legged robot not only features a modular, kit style design which facilitates the extension by further actuators or sensors but also facilitates repair and maintenance and, thus, reduces cost for purchase and operation of the robot. Furthermore, the new robot has similar motion and sensing capabilities as the Sony AIBO plus several additional ones.

2.1 Mechanical Design

Various kinematical designs were considered and tested in a 3D kinematic motion and camera simulation (see Fig. 1). Each leg consists of three rotational joints. Special attention was also given to the design of the robot's head and neck joints which features three degrees of freedom allowing to look in any direction including backwards (through the legs) as well as a wide range of motions for ball manipulation. The final kinematic design allows a wide range of motion capabilities which include the well established low stance walking on the forearms currently common in the Four-Legged Robot League. This walking gait has the advantage that a lower height of the center of gravity above ground is more stable with respect to shocks. Also the robot can see a ball directly in front of it and can still see parts of the environment. This is has not been possible for an upright gait with the AIBO. The new robot therefore is designed to being able to position the head for looking forward at high and also low height above the ground. Furthermore, the robot can look underneath its torso to the back and see the world behind upside down. It can now also kick the ball with the head underneath the torso to the back.

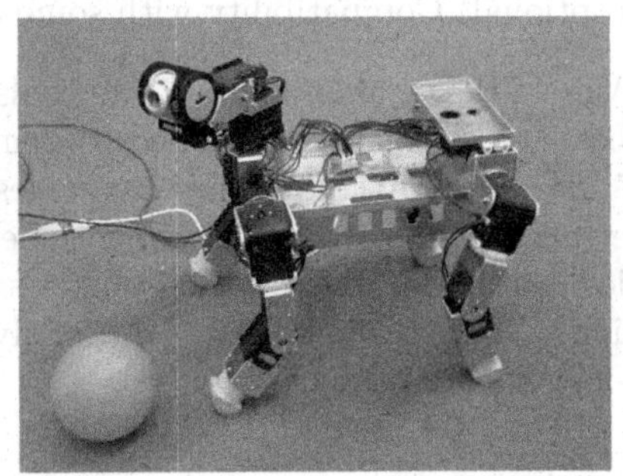

Fig. 1. Left: Simulation of the locomotion of the proposed four-legged robot and images captured from its simulated camera. Right: Robot model for the mechanical motion apparatus.

A servo motor module has been selected which provides a torque of $16.5 kgf cm$ at 10 V operation voltage and speed of 0.196/60 degs which is high enough to expect about the same speed of locomotion as can be achieved with a Sony AIBO in RoboCup. The servos are connected by a serial bus with the main controller, allowing high control rates (125 Hz and higher). As the servos are linked by a daisy-chain bus, more servos can be added easily for research projects beyond the RoboCup. To provide constant conditions for the servos over the whole time of operation a switching voltage regulator is used. It provides a constant voltage independent from the charge status of the batteries. Furthermore, at the disposal of the robot programmer now are not only motor position but also temperature, load, input voltage and speed of the motors.

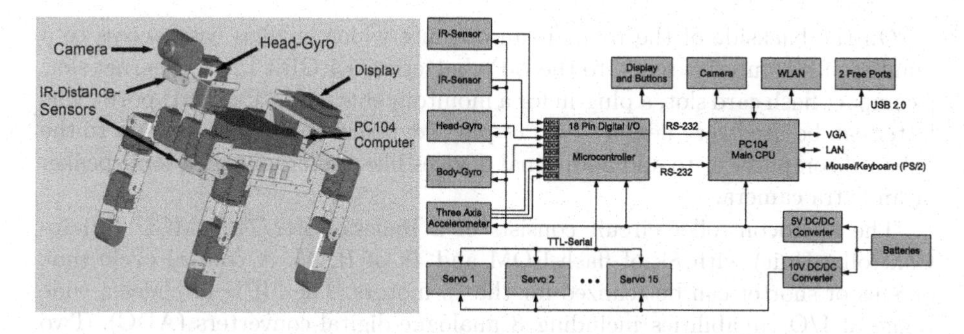

Fig. 2. Left: CAD-Drawing of the robot. Right: Structure of the robot's components.

2.2 Sensing

The main sensor of the robot is a Philips SNC900 webcam in the head. This camera provides a high resolution of 640x480 and frame rate of up to 90 fps. The horizontal aperture angle is 45 degrees. Drivers are available for current windows plattforms as well as for Linux. A driver for Windows CE as been developed as well.

Two infrared distance sensors in the chest and in the head, allow detection of objects independent of the motion of the robot's body. The selected sensor provides a measuring range of 10 to 80 cm. In the torso of the robot, a 3D accelerometer is mounted to measure if the robot has fallen over and to which side. A 1D gyroscope measures the angular velocity around the vertical axis and can be used for improved odometry calculations. The use of an additional gyroscop in the head enables research in the field of inertial stabilization of the camera's field of view during walking. Further sensing capabilies are provided by the selected servo motors as mentioned earlier.

2.3 Computing Capabilities

The robot is equipped with an onboard PC and an additional microcontroller circuit for interfacing with the servos and sensors (see Fig. 2).

For the onboard PC a PC 104 standard platform with 500 MHz was chosen, allowing easy exchange/upgrade of the CPU for projects with higher computational demands. The numerical coprocessor facilitates the development of algorithms with intensive floating-point arithmetics where as on the AIBO only fixed-point arithmetics was available. The selected computer has low battery requirements and does not need an external cooler. It includes USB 2.0, onboard graphics, sound interfaces and 100/1000 MBit Lan. Up to 1024MB of RAM may be installed. For wireless comunication an USB WLAN adapter will be included. On the robot's back a display (with two lines of 16 characters each) is provided enabling some online monitoring and debugging as well as 4 push buttons for programmable commands like start or stop. Both are accessed by RS232.

On the backside of the robot is an opening which enables easy access to a number of I/O interfaces and to the LiPo batteries: a 1 GBit LAN Ethernet slot, a compact flash card slot, a plug-in for a monitor cable, and 2 free USB ports. The latter can be used very flexibly, e.g., to plug keyboard and mouse directly to the onboard computer or to add additional devices like a microphone, a loudspeaker or an extra camera.

The microcontroller circuit consists of a Renesas SH2/7125 MCU (Micro-Controller-Unit) with 8k of flash-ROM and 4k of RAM. A control cycle time of 8 ms or shorter can be realized for the 15 motors. The MPU provides a wide range of I/O capabilities including 8 analogue-digital-converters (ADC). Two ADCs are hard-wired to the most relevant directions of the acceleration sensor, the other six ADCs may be accessed freely by pin headers. In the circuit 18 digital I/O pins and may be accessed by pin headers. The firmware of the micro-controller will be open and a flash development kit is available which enables the robot programmer to modify the firmware as needed, e.g., for inverse kinematics calculations.

Fig. 3. The new four-legged robot on the right together with the robot previously used in the RoboCup Four-Legged Robot League (© Katrin Binner/TU Darmstadt).

2.4 Comparison with the Sony AIBO ERS-7

The basic kinematics of the robot is roughly comparable to that of an AIBO with three degrees of freedom in each leg and in the head. The robot is expected being able to reach a similar fast walking speed. A similiar variety of gaits can be realized. Additionally, fast upright gaits can be implemented, which were not useful for the AIBO because of the design of its point-like feet-ground contact which provides only low friction foot contact in upright positions and leads to slipping of the feet when the legs propell the robot forward in upright walking position. The foot design of this robot provides enough friction at ground contact to develop fast upright walking gaits. Furthermore, the wider stance of the robot provides more robustness against collisions from the side and allows new ways of ball manipulation, e.g., kicking the ball behind the robot underneath its torso.

The camera resolution and image quality of 640 x 480 pixels is significantly larger than of the 208 x 160 pixels camera of the AIBO ERS-7. The new camera offers a significantly higher framerate of 90 instead of 30fps. The robot can reach about the same camera positions as the AIBO. But also additional positions are possible like looking to the front in high or low neck position above ground or looking back underneath the robot to see the world behind upside down.

As inertial sensors, the AIBO had one three-axis accelerometer in the torso whereas the new robot has in addition a 1D gyroscope in the head (to enable research in inertial stabilization of the field of view) as well as in the torso to measure angular rotation around the vertical axis (to be used for improved odometry calculations). Unlike AIBO the robot's servos offer the possibility to directly access temperature, load and torque values.

The proposed four-legged robot has a modular, kit style design. The robot programmers will have the possibility to select their preferred real-time operating system, e.g., Windows CE or RT-Linux or to reprogram the microcontroller. Both operating system will come with a basic software development kit and demo programs for basic robot operation. Despite the fact, that the robot is a verstaile platform for research in autonomous four-legged robots, most parts of the robot can easily be reused or reconfigured for other robot applications like the motors, the microcontroller, the camera, the main computer or the sensors.

3 Conclusions and Outlook

Design considerations and specifications for a new standard four-legged robot platform for research and education have been presented which offers many new research opportunities compared to the robot previously used in the Four-Legged Robot League of the RoboCup. Also careful considerations have been made to provide a platform useful for research beyond the field of robot soccer.

So far the motion capabilities of a first demonstrator robot have been tested and the complete computing and sensing hardware has been integrated into the robot. Also an outer design for the new four-legged robot has been developed in cooperation with Gotha Design, Germany (Fig. 3). Furthermore a first omnidirectional walking motion for remote control using a joystick has been implemented based on the the robot framework `RoboFrame` [6]. A demonstration to the international scientific public has been carried out successfully on July 7 during RoboCup 2007.

The described robot provides an open, modular and reconfigurable platform for research in legged autonomous systems. As the system uses standard busses, it can be extended easily, e.g. by adding PC104 components. The main CPU board can be exchanged for other, stronger CPUs. Additional analogue and digital sensors may be added to the controller's spare ADC and digital I/O pins. Due to the serial bus additional servos can be added without changes to the hardware. The proposed new robot enables a large variety of motion and sensing capabilities and an open, modular and reconfigurable hardware and software design at a moderate price. The modular design also facilitates repair and maintenance. It is therefore well suited as a autonomous legged robot platform for university research and education.

More information about the robot including videos and photos is available from the website www.thenewrobot.com.

References

1. M. Fujita and H. Kitano. Development of an autonomous quadruped robot for robot entertainment. *Autonomous Robots*, 5(1):7–18, 1998.
2. M. Fujita and K. Kageyama. An open architecture for robot entertainment. In *Proc. 1st Intl. Conf. on Autonomous Agents*, pages 435 – 442, Marina del Rey, CA, USA, 1997.
3. M. Veloso, W. Uther, M. Fijita, M. Asada, and H. Kitano. Playing soccer with legged robots. In *Proc. IEEE/RSJ Intl. Conf. on Intelligent Robots and Systems*, pages 437–442, Victoria, BC, CAN, Oct. 13-17 1998.
4. RoboCup. www.robocup.org. webpage, RoboCup Federation.
5. M. Friedmann, J. Kiener, S. Petters, H. Sakamoto, D. Thomas, and O. von Stryk. Versatile, high-quality motions and behavior control of humanoid soccer robots. In *Proc. Workshop on Humanoid Soccer Robots of the 2006 IEEE-RAS Int. Conf. on Humanoid Robots*, pages 9–16, Genoa, Italy, Dec. 4-6 2006.
6. M. Friedmann, J. Kiener, S. Petters, D. Thomas, and O. von Stryk. Modular software architecture for teams of cooperating, heterogeneous robots. In *Proc. IEEE Intl. Conf. on Robotics & Biomimetics*, pages 613–618, Kunming, China, Dec. 17-20 2006.

Entwurf und Simulation eines Laufalgorithmus für einen zweibeinigen Laufroboter

Jörg Fellmann, Thomas Ihme und Kai Wetzelsberger

Hochschule Mannheim, Windeckstr. 110, 68163 Mannheim, Germany.
t.ihme@hs-mannheim.de

Zusammenfassung. Laufroboter eröffnen die Möglichkeit, höchstmögliche maschinelle Mobilität in der von Menschen geschaffenen Umwelt zu zu realisieren, die von radgetriebenen Robotern nicht zu erbringen ist. Humanoide Laufroboter bieten insbesondere die Möglichkeit, Bewegungsabläufe des Menschen experimentell zu untersuchen. Zur Untersuchung von Laufmustern und Bewegungsabläufen besteht das Ziel, den an der Hochschule Mannheim entwickelten Laufroboter realitätsnah mittels einer Physics Engine zu simulieren. Erste Ergebnisse zur Simulation des Roboters und eines statisch stabilen Laufmusters werden in diesem Artikel vorgestellt.

1 Einleitung

Die zweibeinige Fortbewegung bietet im Gegensatz zur radgetriebenen höchstmögliche Mobilität in der heutigen von Menschen geschaffenen Umwelt. Während beispielsweise sechsbeinige Laufroboter für eine sehr große statische Stabilität ausgelegt sind, um in sehr schwierigem Gelände zu operieren, bieten zweibeinige humanoide Roboter die Möglichkeit, Laufbewegungen und Bewegungsabläufe in für den Menschen geschaffenen Umgebungen zu untersuchen. Die Realisierung eines solchen Roboters erfordert die Lösung etlicher Probleme auf unterschiedlichen Gebieten. Der kinematische Aufbau beeinflusst beispielsweise die Beweglichkeit des Roboters und die dafür notwendigen Berechnungen, die nur auf Basis einer geeigneten Rechnerarchitektur realisierbar sind. Mit Hilfe von Sensoren können Informationen über die Stabilität des Roboters und dessen Umgebung gewonnen werden. Um mögliche Probleme vor der Realisierung des Roboters zu erkennen und die systematische Untersuchung von Bewegungsalgorithmen durchführen zu können, ist eine realitätsnahe Simulation sehr hilfreich. Diese sollte die real verfügbaren Sensorinformationen in möglichst gleicher Weise beretstellen können. Für einen zweibeinigen Roboter sind Sensorinformationen für die Stabilität des Roboters von besonderem Interesse. Aktuelle Entwicklungen von Physics Engines versprechen hierfür entsprechende Unterstützung. Ziel ist, zunächst ein statisch stabiles Laufmuster für den an der Hochschule Mannheim konstruierten zweibeinigen Laufroboter (Abbildung 1 und 3) zu entwerfen und zu testen und aufbauend auf den Erfahrungen später Probleme zur dynamischen Stabilität zu untersuchen. In den folgenden Abschnitten wird zunächst

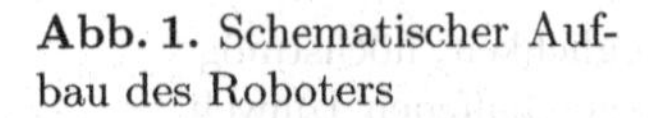

Abb. 1. Schematischer Aufbau des Roboters

Abb. 2. Modell in der Simulationsumgebung

Abb. 3. Mechanik des Roboters

auf Stabilitätskriterien eingegangen und dann die Simulation mittels Physics Engine näher betrachtet. Im letzten Teil das auf den aktuellen Möglichkeiten abgestimmte statisch stabile Laufmuster vorgestellt.

2 Stabilitätskriterien

Ein Stabilitätskriterium ist der wichtigste Bestandteil eines Laufalgorithmus. Insbesondere bei zweibeinigen Laufrobotern, da diese einen relativ hoch gelegenen Schwerpunkt auf einer verhältnismäßig kleinen Standfläche haben und somit schon konstruktionsbedingt sehr instabil sind.

Stabilitätskriterien können in zwei Kategorien aufgeteilt werden: statische und dynamische. Bei einem statischen Stabilitätskriterium werden nur statische Kräfte in die Analyse mit einbezogen. Dies erlaubt allerdings nur geringe Geschwindigkeiten, da der Einfluss dynamischer Kräfte mit steigender Geschwindigkeit schnell zu groß wird.

Im Gegensatz dazu erlauben dynamische Stabilitätskriterien auch höhere Geschwindigkeiten, da hierbei auch dynamische Kräfte beachtet werden. Bei zweibeinigen Laufrobotern häufig verwendet wird hierfür der ZMP (Zero Moment Point) [1]. Der ZMP entspricht dem Punkt in der Standfläche, an dem die Kraft senkrecht wirkt, und keine Momente entstehen. Zur Planung und Steuerung von Laufmustern bietet sich der ZMP gut an. Häufig wird er dazu entlang einer vorgegebenen Trajektorie innerhalb der Standfläche bewegt. Sollte der Roboter allerdings bereits instabil sein, kann mit dem ZMP kein weiterer nutzen mehr gewonnen werden. Um auch in solchen Fällen noch geeignet reagieren zu können, bietet sich die Verwendung des FRI (Foot Rotation Indicator) an [2]. Hiermit können auch die Momente bestimmt werden, die den Roboter zum kippen bringen.

Um die neu entwickelte Konstruktion und die dafür hergeleiteten kinematischen Berechnungen zu prüfen, wurde zuerst ein statisches Stabilitätskriterium verwendet. Aufbauend darauf soll später der Laufalgorithmus um ein dynamisches Stabilitätskriterium erweitert werden.

3 Simulationsumgebung

In der heutigen Zeit bieten Computerspiele ein Höchstmaß an Realitätsnähe, was sich vor allem in den physikalischen Effekten eines solchen Titels zeigt. Computerspiele bestehen im Wesentlichen aus zwei Komponenten. Zum einen der Grafik Komponente, welche für die Visualisierung der Szene zuständig ist, sowie der Physik Komponente die auf Grundlage Newtonscher Gesetze das physikalische Verhalten der Objekte realisiert. Die Entwicklung der dafür eingesetzten Physik–Engines ist sehr komplex und Zeitaufwendig. Da Physik Engines eine immer größere Bedeutung erlangen und die Komplexität der physikalischen Möglichkeiten sowie die Genauigkeit der Berechnungen ein Indikator für eine leistungsfähige Engine sind, haben sich diverse Softwarefirmen rein auf die Entwicklung von Physik Engines spezialisiert. Heutige Physik Engines sind so leistungsfähig, das sie nicht nur Einsatz im Entertainmentbereich finden, ferner können sie auch für wissenschaftliche Projekte einsetzt werden. Zu diesem Zweck untersucht die Hochschule Mannheim die Eignung einer Physik Engine als Simulationsumgebung für den konstruierten zweibeinigen Roboter. Hierzu wird eine Simulationsumgebung entwickelt, die im wesentlichen aus zwei Komponenten besteht: Die Physikkomponente die das realistische Verhalten des Roboters gewährleistet, sowie der Grafikkomponente die zur Visualisierung der simulierten Szene eingesetzt wird. Die schwierigkeit besteht darin, eine möglichst realistische Nachbildung der realen Gegebenheiten sicher zu stellen. Als problematisch stellt sich die realistische Nachbildung der Gelenkmotoren, sowie des dazu entwickelten Reglungssystems dar. Erstes Ziel der Simulationsumgebung ist es, den in der Theorie entwickelten statisch stabilen Laufalgorithmus in der Simulation zu testen um damit Rückschlüsse auf die Qualität und Eignung des entwickelten Laufmusters zu sammeln. Ferner soll evaluiert werden, ob die Simulationsumgebung geeignet ist, dynamische Laufalgorithmen zu prüfen. Weiterhin wird untersucht, ob alle notwendigen Sensorinformationen die für eine dynamische Stabilität wie ZMP erforderlich ist simuliert werden können.

Die Vorteile einer solchen Simulationsumgebung sind vielfältig. Zum einen können jegliche Bewegungsalgorithmen zuerst simuliert und evaluiert werden, um eventuell enthaltene Fehler vorzeitig zu erkennen. Weiterhin ist es möglich, ein Geländeprofil zu simulieren um das Verhalten des Laufalgorithmus zu erforschen, ohne das Material des Roboters zu belasten.

Um eine Szene möglichst realistisch darzustellen ist es notwendig, die Newtonschen Gesetze auf die Simulierte Szene anzuwenden. Eine Physik Engine erfüllt im Wesentlichen drei Aufgaben:

1. Kollisionserkennung
2. Solve Constraints
3. Update System

Die Kollisionserkennung beschäftigt sich mit der Erkennung auftretender Kollisionen zwischen den simulierten Objekten. Wird eine Kollision festgestellt, kommen Constraints zum Einsatz, welche für die Anwendung der Newtonschen Gesetze auf die involvierten Objekte sorge tragen. Das *Update System* übernimmt drei Teilaufgaben. Zum einen werden die Ergebnisse des *Constraint Solvers* übernommen und somit der neue Status der Objekte bestimmt. Da es sich bei einer Simulation um einen kontinuierlichen zeitlichen Ablauf handelt, in der sich Objekte bewegen, kollidieren und auf andere äußere Einflüsse reagieren, verwendet das *Update System* Zeitschritte zur Bestimmung des neuen Zustandes der Objekte [3,4]. Zur Simulation wurde die AGEIA PhysX Engine genutzt.

Zur Evaluierung der entwickelten Simulationsumgebung kommt ein auf die notwendigen Grundformen reduziertes Modell des konstruierten Zweibeiners zum Einsatz. Die hierzu herangezogenen Daten wurden aus der ProEnginner CAD Konstruktionszeichnung (Abbildung 1) extrahiert, um ein realistisches Abbild des realen Roboters innerhalb der Simulation zu erhalten. Um das statisch stabile Laufmuster zu testen, ist es vorerst ausreichend die Beine des Roboters zu simulieren. Der Oberkörper wird zunächst nur als statisches Objekt ohne Bewegungsfunktion modelliert .

Um den zweibeinigen Laufroboter adäquat zu simulieren wurden die Masseneigenschaften, Objektmaße sowie die realen Trägheiten aus dem CAD Konstruktionsmodell auf das Simulationsmodell übertragen. Die simulierten Motoren werden über eine Kaskadenregelung gesteuert. Hierbei wird ein zweischleifiger Regelkreis, bestehend aus einem P–Führungsregler zu Regelung der Winkelposition, sowie ein PI–Folgeregler zur Ausregelung der Geschwindigkeit der Motoren verwendet. Abbildung 2 zeigt das Modell des Roboters in der Simulationsumgebung.

Schwierigkeiten bei der Nutzung der PhysX SDK ergeben sich bei der Modellierung komplexer kinematischer Ketten. Hierbei ist zu beobachten, dass bei steigender Anzahl an Gelenkcontraints Ungenauigkeiten durch Fließkommarberechnungen sowie durch den numerischen Integrator zur Bestimmung der Zeitschritte auftreten. Diese Ungenauigkeiten summieren sich mit steigender Anzahl an Gelenkconstraints in dem Maße, dass Gelenkverbindungen gelöst und somit die Verbindungsstellen der Gelenke nicht mehr 100% eingehalten werden.

Weiterhin ergeben sich Beschränkungen in der benötigten Abtastrate des Reglungsystems dadurch, dass die maximale Abtastrate durch die aktuelle Framerate bzw. durch die diskreten Zeitschritte der Physiksimulation begrenzt wird. In einer realen Umgebung sind für die Regelung konstante Abtastraten im Bereich von wenigen Millisekunden erforderlich. In der Simulation hingegen handelt es sich um variable Abtastzeiten, die im Bereich von 20–40ms je nach aktueller Framerate liegen. Hierdurch können Instabilitäten der simulierten Regler auftreten. Durch diese Instabilitäten wird der beobachtete Fehler der oben erwähnten Gelenkconstraints zusätzlich verstärkt, was zur Instabilität des gesamten Systems führen kann.

Die Ergebnisse der Simulation haben gezeigt, dass die realistische Simulation der realen Laufmaschinen mittels aktueller Physik Engines prinzipiell möglich ist. Eine Verbesserung kann dahingehend erzielt werden, dass die Simulation zweistufig durchgeführt wird. Folglich sollte eine Trennung des Interaktionsmodells des Roboters und der Simulation der Aktoren durchgeführt werden. Somit sind Echtzeitregelungen der Aktoren realisierbar. Die Ergebnisse der Regelung

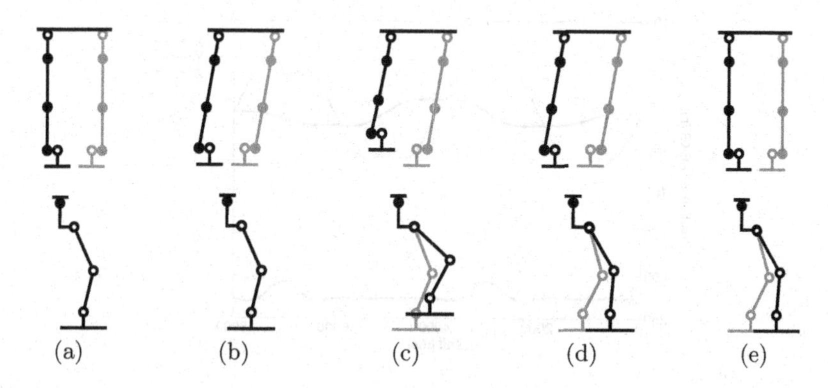

Abb. 4. Laufmuster

werden dann auf das Simulationsmodell übertragen. Weiterhin sollte eine Verbesserung der Algorithmen der Gelenkconstraints des SDK's auf die speziellen Anforderungen durchgeführt werden.

4 Statisch stabiles Laufmuster

Um praktische Versuche zu vereinfachen, wurde ein parametrisiertes Laufmuster entwickelt. Hierdurch kann mit wenig Aufwand das Laufmuster mit verschiedenen Eigenschaften in der Praxis untersucht werden. Das entwickelte Laufmuster kann mit insgesamt fünf Parametern angepasst werden: Schritthöhe, Schrittweite, Gewichtsverlagerung, Absenkung des Oberkörpers und Dauer eines Schritts. Das Laufmuster wird interpoliert, um eine flüssige Bewegung der Beine zu erhalten. Als besonders geeignet hierfür hat sich die Spline–Interpolation herausgestellt. Das Laufmuster kann wahlweise mit kubischen Polynomsplines und B–Splines interpoliert werden. Beide Verfahren bieten Vor- und Nachteile.

In Abbildung 4 sind die wichtigsten Phasen des Laufmusters zu erkennen. Das Laufmuster kann in insgesamt vier Phasen unterteilt werden:

1. (a) → (b): Gewichtsverlagerung auf ein Bein
2. (b) → (c): das andere Bein anheben und nach vorne Bewegen
3. (c) → (d): das Bein wieder absetzen
4. (d) → (e): Gewicht wieder in Mitte verlagern

5 Simulation des Laufmusters

Bevor mit praktischen Versuchen begonnen wurde, wurde der Laufalgorithmus entsprechend simuliert und die gewonnen Daten überprüft, insbesondere im Hinblick auf die Stabilität. Abbildung 5 zeigt den Verlauf der Beintrajektorien des linken Beins im kartesischen Raum für insgesamt vier Schritte. An der Y Kurve

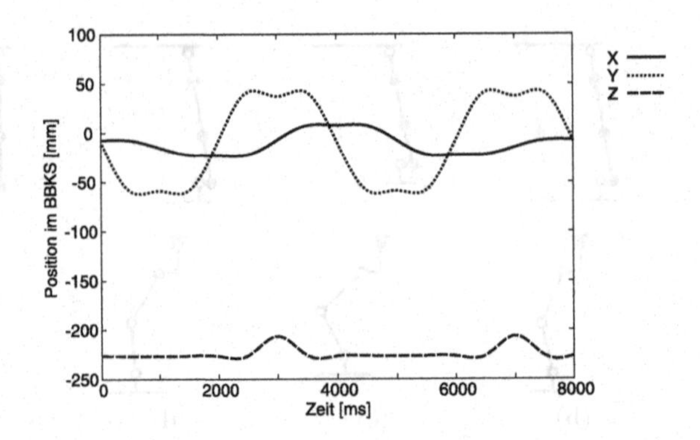

Abb. 5. Beintrajektorie linkes Bein interpoliert mit kubischen Polynomsplines

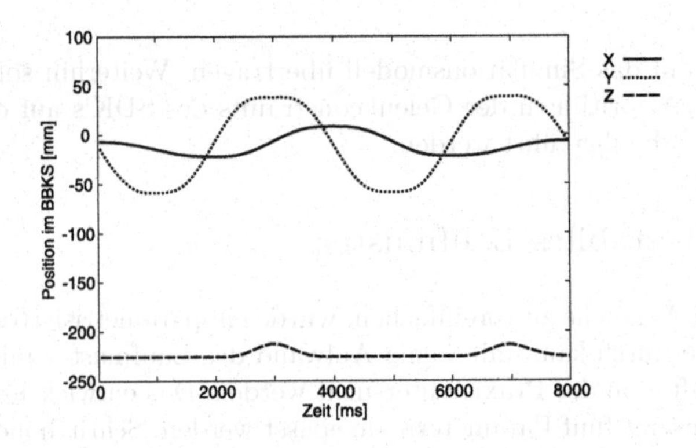

Abb. 6. Beintrajektorie linkes Bein interpoliert mit B-Splines

ist deutlich die seitliche Gewichtsverlagerung zu erkennen. Die Z Kurve zeigt hingegen das Anheben des Beins.

Die Abbildung 5 zeigt die Trajektorien bei Interpolation mit Polynomsplines. Im Vergleich hierzu sind in Abbildung 6 die Trajektorien bei Interpolation mit B–Splines zu sehen. Wie zu erkennen ist, bieten diese deutlich flachere Kurven und weniger Oszillationen als die Polynomsplines. Dies wird vermutlich auch bei praktischen Versuchen zu einem besseren Ergebnis führen.

Abbildung 7 zeigt den Verlauf der Stabilität. Die Kurven X und Y zeigen die Position des Massenschwerpunktes relativ zur Standfläche entlang der entsprechenden Achsen. 0 bedeutet hierbei, dass der Massenschwerpunkt direkt im Mittelpunkt der Standfläche liegt. ± 1 bedeutet, dass der Punkt auf einer Kante der Standfläche liegt. In den Phasen, in denen nur ein Bein Bodenkontakt hat - die also am kritischsten sind für die Stabilität, da die Standfläche minimal ist – liegt der Massenschwerpunkt entlang der Y Achse nahe am Mittelpunkt der Standfläche und bietet somit optimale Stabilität. Im gesamten Verlauf der beiden Kurven liegen die maximalen Ausschläge in etwa im Bereich von $\pm 0,5$. Somit ist zu jedem Zeitpunkt eine Stabilitätsreserve gegeben.

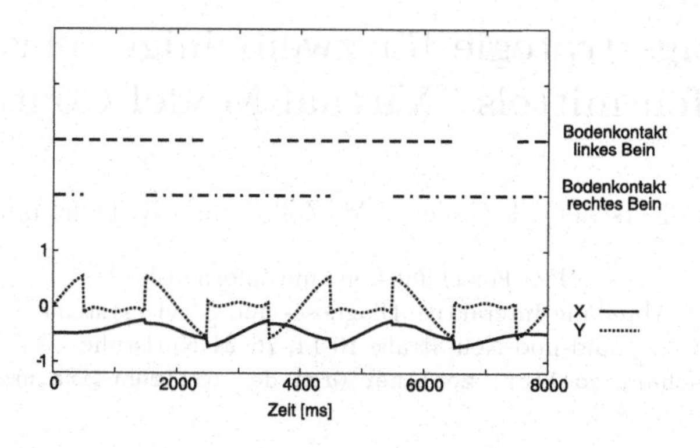

Abb. 7. Verlauf des Stabilität

6 Fazit

Auf Grund der aufgeführten Beschränkungen der Physik-Engine erscheint es zur Zeit nur sinnvoll, statisch stabile Laufmuster zu testen. Auf Grund der Rechenleistung des Roboters wurde ein Parameter–variables Laufmuster entwickelt. Die Simulation des Laufmusters zeigt, dass prinzipiell die geforderten Stabilitätskriterien erfüllt werden. Dies lasst sich durch die Simulationsumgebung validieren. Ein dynamisch stabiles Laufmuster wird erst nach Einführung der vorgestellten Erweiterungen der Simulationsumgebung adäquat testbar.

7 Danksagung

Die Autoren danken der Karl-Völker-Stiftung an der Hochschule Mannheim für die Unterstützung des Projektes.

Literaturverzeichnis

1. Miomir Vukobratović and Branislav Borovac. Zero-moment-point - thirty five years of its life. In *International Journal of Humanoid Robotics*, volume 1, pages 157–173, 2004.
2. Ambarish Goswami. Foot rotation indicator (fri) point: A new gait planning tool to evaluate postural stability of biped robots. In *IEEE International Conference on Robotics and Automation*, pages 47–52. Detroit, MI, USA, Mai 1999.
3. Johan Göransson. Agentphysics: software design for pluggable real time physics middleware. Master's thesis, Lulea University of Technology, 2005.
4. Henrik Hansson. Craft physics interface. Master's thesis, Linköping University, Department of Electrical Engineering, 2007.

Regelungsstrategie für zweibeiniges elastisches Laufen mittels "Virtual Model Control"

T. Kerscher, M. Göller, J.M. Zöllner und R. Dillmann

FZI Forschungszentrum Informatik
Abteilung Interaktive Diagnose- und Servicesysteme
Haid-und-Neu-Straße 10-14, 76131 Karlsruhe
{kerscher, goeller, zoellner}@fzi.de, dillmann@ira.uka.de

Zusammenfassung. Ziel dieses Vorhabens ist die technische Umsetzung des "elastischen Laufens" durch die Realisierung biomechanisch motivierter Regelungsstrategien. Als dafür nötigen elastischen Antrieb wird ein künstlicher Muskel nach dem McKibben-Prinzip verwendet. Dieser Muskel zeigt trotz einiger Nachteile sehr ähnliches statisches und dynamisches Verhalten wie der biologische Muskel und hat sich daher für dieses Vorhaben als idealer Antrieb herausgestellt. Mit Hilfe des "Virtual Model Control" wird eine Regelung für elastisches Gehen entworfen, welche direkt und indirekt die Eigenschaften der Muskeln für eine flüssige, energieeffiziente Bewegung verwendet.

1 Einleitung

Zur Steuerung von zweibeinigen Laufrobotern werden weltweit in erster Linie Regelungsstrategien wie z.B. die Zero-Moment-Point (ZMP) [1] oder die Center-of-Pressure (CoP) Methode [2] eingesetzt. Diese Regelungsverfahren benötigen sehr genaue Modelle des Roboters und der Umwelt, daraus resultieren hohe Anforderungen an die Recheneinheit sowie für die integrierten Sensorsysteme, die teilweise nicht befriedigt werden können [3]. Als Antriebe solcher Systeme werden hauptsächlich steife Antriebe verwendet [3,4]. Elastizitäten findet man wenn überhaupt nur als passive, stoßabsobierender Element. Die Elastizität, die zur anpassungsfähigen Lokomotion notwendig ist, wird durch eine aktive Regelung der Motoren künstlich erzeugt [5].

Erkenntnisse aus der Biomechanik zum menschlichen Rennen und Gehen zeigen allerdings, dass der Mensch bei der Fortbewegung starken Gebrauch der Feder-Dämpfer-Eigenschaften der Muskeln macht [6,7]. Die Muskulatur und das mechanische System werden dabei so konfiguriert, dass sich ein selbststabilisierender Zyklus einstellt. Von Seiten der Biomechanik stehen Modelle für das Rennen und das Gehen zur Verfügung, die die Vorgänge im Bein durch ein Feder-Masse-System und einem Satz von Regeln zur Einstellung der Federkonstanten abhängig von Geschwindigkeit, Auftreffwinkel und Schwerpunkthöhe beschreiben [8,9].

Ziel dieses Vorhabens ist die technische Umsetzung des elastischen Laufens durch die Realisierung biomechanisch motivierter Regelungsstrategien. Als dafür nötigen elastischen Antrieb wird ein künstlicher Muskel nach dem McKibben-Prinzip verwendet [10,11]. Dieser Muskel zeigt trotz einiger Nachteile sehr ähnliches statisches und dynamisches Verhalten wie der biologische Muskel und hat sich daher für diese Vorhaben als idealer Antrieb herausgestellt. Mit Hilfe des "Virtual Model Control" nach [12] wird eine Regelung für elastisches Gehen entworfen, welche direkt und indirekt die Eigenschaften der Muskel für eine flüssige, energieeffiziente Bewegung verwendet.

2 Der fluidische Muskel als elastischer Antrieb

Die Verwendung künstlicher Muskeln nach dem McKibben-Prinzip in der Robotik ermöglicht es ähnliche Bewegungssysteme wie die der Natur aufzubauen und dadurch die Analogie zum biologischen Antrieb für die Entwicklung neuer Regelungsstrategien für Lokomotion und Manipulation zu entwickeln. Neben den vielen Vorteilen solcher Muskeln wie z.B. die passive Dämpfung, die inherente Elatizität, das gute Kraft-Gewicht-Verhältnis sowie die Möglichkeit solche Muskeln trotz schädlichen Umwelteinflüssen zu verwenden, existieren auch Nachteile der Muskeln wie z.B. das nichtlineare Verhalten. Daher ist es für die Verwendung dieser Muskeln notwendig eine genaue Modellierung des Muskels durch zu führen.

Die Berechnung der Muskelkraft für den in dieses Vorhaben verwendete fluidische Muskel MAS der Firma FESTO kann aufgrund seiner Feder-Dämpfer-Eigenschaft aus einem Term zur Berechnung des Federkraftanteils und einem für die Berechnung des Dämpferanteils zusammengesetzt werden [13]:

$$F_{Muskel}(\kappa, \dot{\kappa}, p) = F_{Feder}(\kappa, p) + F_{Dämpfer}(\dot{\kappa}, p) \tag{1}$$

Dabei hängt die Muskelkraft sowohl von den Muskelparametern ab wie von dem Relativdruck p, der Kontraktion κ sowie der Kontraktionsgeschwindigkeit $\dot{\kappa}$ des Muskels ab. Die Herleitung sowie die genauen Formeln für den Federkraft-, Dämpferanteil sowie die Differentialgleichung für den Muskeldruck sind in [13] dargestellt.

Zur Evaluierung des Muskelmodells einerseits und Vergleich des Muskelverhaltens mit dem des biologischen Muskelverhalten andererseits wurde für den fluidischen Muskel ein Quickrelease Versuchsaufbau angelegt an [7] entworfen. In [13] wird dieser Testaufbau genauer beschrieben und gezeigt, dass mit Hilfe des entwickelten Muskelmodells das statische sowie das dynamische Verhalten des Muskels nachgebildet werden kann. Weiterhin haben die Untersuchungen am Quickrelease-Teststand gezeigt, dass der fluidische Muskel ein sehr ähnliches Verhalten wie der biologische Muskel zeigt [13]. Zusätzlich konnte gezeigt werden, dass es möglich ist die Steifigkeit des fluidischen Muskels zu variieren.

Die allgemeine Eignung eines antagonistisch arbeitenden Muskelpaares als elastischer Antrieb wurde mit Hilfe eines Eindimensionalen Versuchstands (EDV) durchgeführt. Der Versuchstand besteht aus ein Körper der angetrieben durch

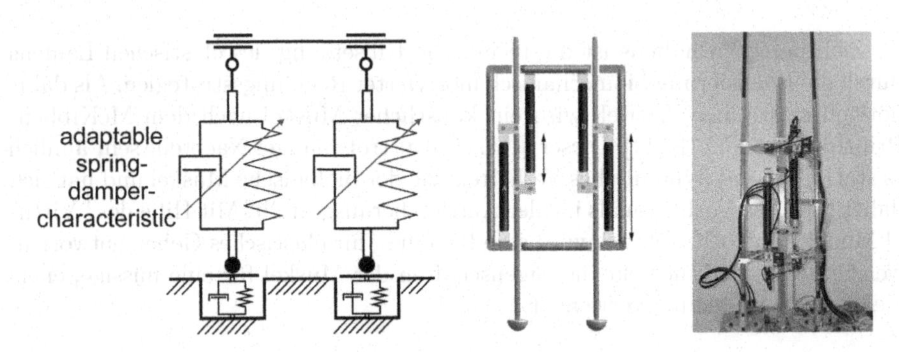

Abb. 1. (links) Grundidee des Eindimensionaler Versuchsstandes (EDV) (Mitte) Schematische Darstellung des EDVs (rechts) Eindimensionaler Versuchsstand

zwei antagonistisch angetrieben Schubgelenke entlang seines einzigen Bewegungsfreiheitsgrad in vertikaler Richtung in eine stabile Schwingung versetzt wird (Abbildung 1). Hierbei wird ein antagonistisches Muskelpaar als einstellbares Feder-Dämpfer-System verwendet. Durch die Variation der Muskelparameter kann die Resonanzfrequenz des Gesamtsystem beeinflusst werden [13].

3 Beschreibung des Robotermodells

Zur Evaluierung der Regelungsstrategien für elastisches Laufen wurde ein vereinfachtes Modell für das Zweibeinsystem verwendet. Die Anzahl der Freiheitsgrade pro Bein wurde auf fünf festgelegt. Die zugehörigen Gelenkpositionen und Achsen sind in Abbildung 2 zu sehen.

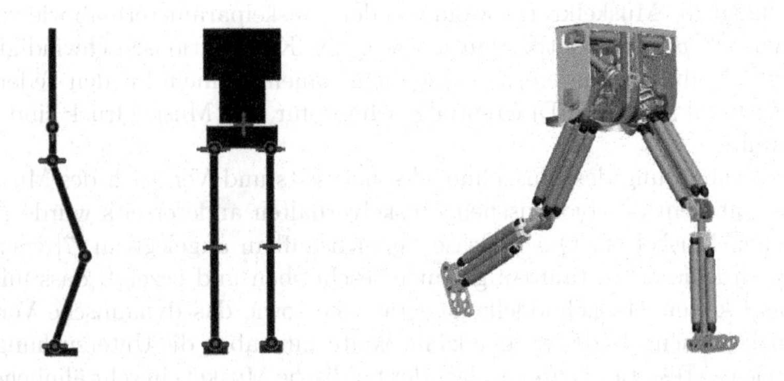

Abb. 2. (links) Gelenkachsen: Die 12 Gelenkachsen des Robotermodells (rechts) CAD-Modell des Roboters

Die Bewegungsfreiheitsgrade dieses vereinfachte Model reichen aus um eine gerade Bewegung zu Erzeugen. Es ist allerdings notwendig ein Verdrehung der Hüfte um die Vertikale zu verhindern, da ohne diese Einschränkung die Bewegungsfreiheitsgrade des hier verwendet Beines nicht ausreichen würden.

4 Die "Virtual Model Control"-Methode

Mit dem Konzept des "Virtual Model Control" (VMC) nach [12] ist es möglich eine Regelung zu erzeugen, die ohne die explizite Berechnung der inversen Kinematik auskommt. Die Kontrolle des Roboters wird nach einem einfachen, intuitiven Prinzip durchgeführt. Sie erfolgt ausschließlich durch das Anlegen externer Kräfte. Die Erzeugung dieser Kräfte durch virtuelle Federn ermöglicht die Generierung sehr natürlich wirkende Bewegungen. Dabei werden diese äußere Kraft zwischen einen Punkt auf dem Roboter und dem gewünschten Zielpunkt gelegt. Durch geschickten Einsatz der Jakobi Matrix für eine kinematische Kette (z.B. ein Roboterbein) werden aus der virtuellen äußeren Kraft diejenigen Gelenkmomente berechnet, welche die äußere Kraft kompensieren würden. Tauscht man das Vorzeichen der errechneten Kraft, kann man das Robotersegment an einer Feder, ähnlich einer virtuellen Impedanzregelung, durch den Raum führen.

Von entscheidender Bedeutung ist die Wahl der beiden Angriffspunkte einer 'Virtual Component'. Die VC rechnet eine Kraft, die zwischen zwei Robotersegmenten wirken soll auf die dafür benötigten Gelenkmomente um. Eines dieser Segmente bezeichnet man als 'Aktionframe' (AF), das andere als 'Reactionframe' (RF). Als Aktionframe wählt man das Segment, das die, durch die Kraft erzeugte, Aktion ausführen soll. Ansonsten ist die Kraft aufgrund des Prinzips von 'Kraft gleich Gegenkraft' auf beide Segmente identisch, wenn auch mit umgekehrtem Vorzeichen.

5 Regelung für elastisches Gehen mittels der VMC-Methode

Der Aufbau des erforderlichen Netz aus solchen virtuellen Kräften für die Erzeugung von elastischen Gehens wir in drei Schritten durchgeführt. Als erstes wird eine zunächst einfache Regelung generiert, die dem Modell das Stehen ermöglicht. Aufbauend darauf werden die virtuellen Kräfte für die Bewegung der Hüfte und der Kniee hinzugeführt. Basierend auf diesen virtuellen Kraftkomponenten kann dann die vollständige Gangkontrolle für dynamisches Gehen entwerfen werden.

Für den Schwerkraftausgleich wird pro Bein eine VC benötigt, die eine virtuelle Federkraft nach oben erzeugt. Um ein stabiles Stehen, das Fixieren der beiden rotatorischen Freiheitsgraden der Hüfte, der Absicherung gegen seitliche Verschiebungen sowie der Haltung des Oberkörperssind weiter VCs notwendig.

Für ein sicheres Gehen sind 23 "Virtual Components" notwendig, die ständig neu parametrisiert, aktiviert oder deaktiviert werden müssen. Um hierbei die Federeigenschaft der künstlichen Muskeln möglichst gut nutzen zu können, werden die Knie- und Fußgelenke, soweit möglich, passiv gelassen. Das heißt es wird eine Spannung für das Gelenk, bzw. ein Druck für die Muskeln eingestellt, so dass das Gelenk seine Position beibehält. Danach werden die Ventile geschlossen, und stehen auch für die Regelung nicht mehr zur Verfügung.

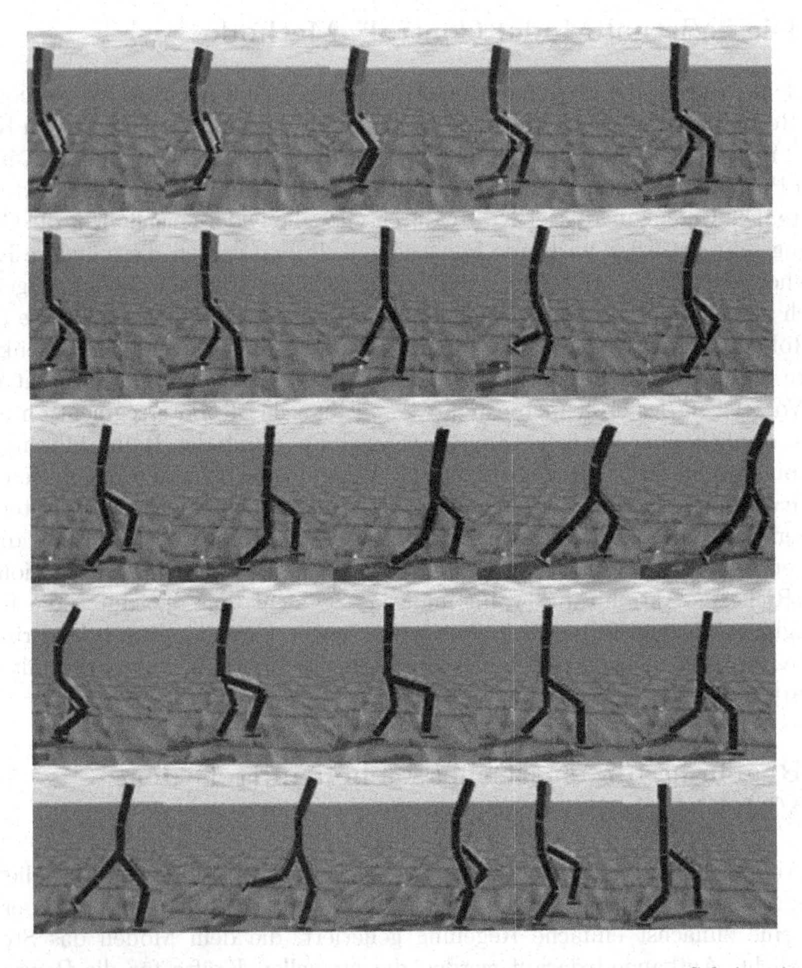

Abb. 3. Dynamisches Gehen: Der Roboter steht, leitet den ersten Schritt ein und geht dann zwei Gangzyklen. Die Bilder wurden in Abständen von jeweils 1er Sekunde aufgenommen.

Der Algorithmus für das dynamische Gehen ist anfänglich in Form eines Automaten, mit einem Zustand für die jeweiligen Gangphasen, realisiert. Sein Verhalten basiert auf Ereignissen und die daraufhin stattfinden Aktionen werden als motorisches Verhalten erzeugt. Ein typischer Gangzyklus sieht wie folgt aus. Der Algorithmus schwingt ein Bein nach vorne. Hierbei bedient er sich einer dynamischen Schrittweite, die entsprechend zur höchsten Geschwindigkeit der Hüfte in der vorangegangen Stemmphase gewählt wird. Ist das Schwungziel des Fußes erreicht, wird, falls nötig, die Krümmung im Knie korrigiert und das Bein versteift. Ist dies geschehen, wird das Bein abgesenkt und gleichzeitig werden die Muskeln des Oberschenkels passiv geschaltet, d.h. die Ventile geschlossen und aus der Regelung der VCs entfernt. Nach dem Aufsetzen des Fußes wird in die Double-Support-Phase übergegangen. Hier wird, sollte die Geschwindigkeit der Hüfte zu gering sein, Kraft in Oberschenkeln und Waden generiert, um den Roboter nach vorne zu stemmen. Ist die Hüfte am Standbein angekommen werden die Beinschwinger-VCs aktiv und die Hacke wird kurz angezogen, um den Fuß vom Boden zu lösen. Der Fuß schwingt dann zunächst zu einer gehobenen Position, die von der aktuellen Hüfthöhe abhängig ist. Sobald er den Standfuß überschreitet, senkt er sich wieder leicht zu seinem endgültigen Schwungziel ab. Die Ergebnisse der Simulation des entwickelten Algorithmus für das dynamische Gehen sind in Abbildung 3 dargestellt.

6 Zusammenfassung und Ausblick

Mit Hilfe des "Virtual Model Control" wurde eine Regelung für elastisches Gehen entworfen, welche direkt und indirekt die Eigenschaften der fluidischen Muskel für eine flüssige, energieeffiziente Bewegung verwendet. Dafür wurde ein Modellregler entworfen, der dem Robotermodell einen stabilen Stand und erste einfache Bewegungen ermöglicht. Hierbei wird durch makroskopische, externe Kräfte das gewünschte Gesamtverhalten des Modells beschrieben. Die externen Kräfte werden dann auf die einzelnen, dafür benötigten, Gelenkmomente umgerechnet. Der implementierte Gangzyklus zeigt, dass es möglich ist mit intuitiven Methoden, ohne Verwendung komplizierter Mechanismen wie einer "Zero Moment Point" Regelung oder einer inversen Kinematik, einen sicheren Gang zu erzeugen, der nicht an die Kriterien der statischen oder dynamischen Stabilität gebunden ist. Er durchläuft sowohl statisch , dynamisch stabile, als auch instabile Phasen. Der Algorithmus erinnert dabei an ein verhaltenbasiertes System. Zu bestimmten Ereignissen, die während des Ganges auftreten, werden verschiedene Aufgaben erzeugt. Diese werden daraufhin von unabhängig voneinander, oder sogar konkurrierend zueinander, wirkenden "Virtual Components" erfüllt. Der Effekt auf das Modell ist hierbei die Summe der Einzeleffekte der einzelnen VCs.

Des Weiteren konnte gezeigt werden, dass es im Zuge eines solchen Gangzyklus mit künstlichen Muskeln von elastischer Bauart möglich ist, in speziellen Phasen des Ganges Energie zu speichern, und diese selbstständig wieder abzugeben. Hierzu wurden die Beine in einen passiven Modus versetzt, in dem die Muskeln in einem vorher eingestellten Spannungszustand verharren. Sie bilden somit ein Feder-Dämpfer System. Im folgenden werde diese bis jetzt nur in einer Simulation getesteten Verfahren auf einem realen Robotersystem implementiert und evaluiert.

Literaturverzeichnis

1. M. Vukobratovic, Yu. Stepanenko, *On the stability of anthropomorphic systems*, Mathematical Biosciences 15, 1-37, 1972.
2. Sardain P., Bessonnet G. (2004). Force acting on a Biped Robot. Center of Pressure – Zero moment point. *IEEE Transactions on Systems, Man and Cybernetics*, Part A, Vol. 34.
3. K. Loeffler, M. Gienger, F. Pfeiffer, *Sensors and Control Concept of Walking "Johnnie"*, The Int. Journal of Robotics Research, vol. 22, pp. 229 - 239, 2003.
4. Yu Ogura, H. Aikawa, L. Hun-ok, A. Takanishi, *Development of a human-like walking robot having two 7-DOF legs and a 2-DOF waist*, Proceedings of the International Conference on Robotics and Automation, 2004.
5. T. Nagasaki, S. Kajita, K. Yokoi, K. Kaneko, K. Tanie, *Running pattern generation and its evaluation using a realistic humanoid model*, Proceedings of the International Conference on Robotics and Automation, pp. 1336 - 1342, 2003.
6. R. Blickhan, *The spring-mass model for running and hopping*, Journal of Biomechanics, Vol. 22, No 11/12, 1217-1227, 1989.
7. T. McMahon, *Muscles, Reflexes, and Locomotion*, Princeton Univ. Press, Princeton, NJ, 1984.
8. A. Seyfarth, H. Geyer, M. Günther, R. Blickhan, *A movement criterion for running*, Journal of Biomechanics, Vol. 35, Issue 5, 649-655, 2002.
9. H. Geyer, *Simple models of legged locomotion based on compliant limb behaviour*, PhD Thesis, University of Jena, Germany, 2005
10. Daerden F., Lefeber D., *Pneumatic artificial muscles: actuators for robotics and automation*, European Journal of Mechanical and Environmental Engineering, 47(1):10-21, 2002.
11. Produktkatalog 2004 – Antriebe *http://www.festo.com*
12. J.E. Pratt. *Virtual Model Control of a Biped Walking Robot.*, Diplomarbeit, MIT, 1995
13. T. Kerscher, J. Albiez, J.M. Zöllner, R. Dillmann, *Biomechanical inspired control for elastic legs* 9th Int. Conf. on Climbing and Walking Robots (CLAWAR), 2006.

Predictive Behavior Generation – A Sensor-Based Walking and Reaching Architecture for Humanoid Robots

Michael Gienger, Bram Bolder, Mark Dunn, Hisashi Sugiura, Herbert Janssen and Christian Goerick

Honda Research Institute Europe,Carl-Legien-Straße 30, D-63073 Offenbach am Main, Germany

Abstract. This paper presents a sensor-based walking and reaching architecture for humanoid robots. It enables the robot to interact with its environment using a smooth whole body motion control driven by stabilized visual targets. Interactive selection mechanisms are used to switch between behavior alternatives for searching or tracking objects as well as different whole body motion strategies for reaching. The decision between different motion strategies is made based on internal predictions that are evaluated by parallel running instances of virtual whole-body controllers. The results show robust object tracking and a smooth interaction behavior that includes a large variety of whole-body postures.

1 Introduction

Research on humanoid robots is increasingly focusing on interaction in complex environments, including autonomous decision making and complex coordinated behavior. Several interactive robot systems were already introduced. A complete architecture for a small humanoid (Sony QRIO) that uses a central action selection driven by so called *behavior values* provided by the individual behaviors is described in [1] [2]. Kismet [3] also realizes a variety of interaction abilities and contains both a powerful vision and attention system and behavior selection. The main focus of this system is child-like interaction and developmental learning.

In this paper, we will present a system that enables a humanoid robot to interact with a human. The perception is based on a so called proto-object representation. Proto-objects are a concept originating from psychophysical modeling [4] [5] [6]. They can be thought of as coherent regions or groups of features in the field of view that are trackable and can be pointed or referred to without identification. Novel in the context of humanoid robots are the following key points:

- The use of proto objects to form stable hypothesis for behavior generation, e. g. for tracking or reaching for objects.
- Decision mechanisms that evaluate behavioral alternatives based on sensory information and internal prediction.

- A motion control system that can be driven by a wide range of possible target descriptions and that ensures smooth well coordinated whole body movements.

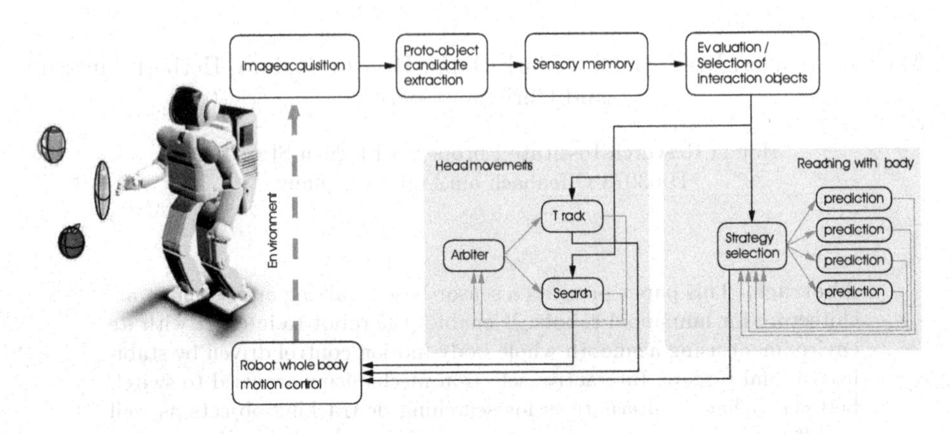

Fig. 1. Overview of the system design.

The general design of the system is depicted in Fig. 1. The perception system uses visual features and stereo based 3d information to detect relevant visual stimuli. It keeps this information as proto-objects in a short-term sensory memory. This sensory memory is then used to derive targets for visual tracking and to form stable object hypotheses from which movement targets for reaching movements can be derived. A prediction based decision system selects the best movement strategy and executes it in real time. The internal prediction as well as the executed movements exploit an integrated control system that uses a flexible target description in task space in addition to cost-functions in null space to achieve well coordinated and smooth whole body movements.

2 Proto-object Based Perception

In the following, the characteristics of the perception are explained in more detail.

Proto-object Candidate Extraction: To generate proto-objects, the image processing has to find entities in the environment that are dynamically stable in position and extent. Efficient methods to find such entities are color and texture segmentation algorithms, or feature extractors for unique salient points. To obtain 3d information, stereo disparity calculations or other stereo algorithms can be used. We extract 3d ellipsoids from the visual input based on a color segmentation and a disparity algorithm. The extracted blobs encode the position, metric size, and orientation of significant visual stimuli.

Proto-objects in Sensory Memory: To form stable object hypotheses, the sensory information is buffered and organized consistently. This is done in form of proto-objects in sensory memory. The incoming blobs are mapped to proto-objects in sensory memory. If the memory is empty, a proto-object is generated from blob data. If the sensory memory already contains one or more proto-objects, a prediction for each proto-object is generated. The prediction is compared to the new measurement. According to the result, either a new proto-object is generated, or the prediction is employed to update an existing proto-object.

Evaluation / Selection of Interaction Objects: The output from the sensory memory is evaluated with respect to the object criteria (in this case distance, size, and minimum elongation). The results are categorized into

- **Found:** The object is found in the visual field.
- **Memorized:** The object is not found in the visual field, but has been found recently.
- **Inaccurate:** The object is found, but close to the image boundary. Since it is only partially visible, the estimation results are likely to be inaccurate.

The 3-d data and the above evaluation result is sent to the behaviors (search, track, reach). Each behavior can then extract the relevant information.

3 Behavior Generation

3.1 Tracking and Searching

The output of the sensory memory is used to drive two different head behaviors: 1) searching for objects and 2) gazing at or tracking objects. Separate from these behaviors is a decision instance or *arbiter* [7] that decides which behavior should be active at any time. The decision of the arbiter is solely based on a scalar value that the behaviors provide, which we call a *fitness value*. This fitness value describes how well a behavior can be executed at any time. In this concrete case, tracking needs at least an inaccurate proto object position to look at. Thus the tracking behavior will output a fitness of 1 if any proto object is present and a 0 otherwise. The search behavior has no prerequisites at all and thus its fitness is fixed to 1.

The search behavior is realized by means of a very low resolution inhibition of return map with a simple relaxation dynamics. If the search behavior is active and new vision data is available it will increase the value of the current gaze direction in the map and select the lowest value in the map as the new gaze target. The tracking behavior is realized as a multi-tracking of 3-dimensional points. The behavior takes all relevant proto-objects and object hypotheses into account and calculates the pan/tilt angles for centering them in the field of view. The two visual interaction behaviors together with the arbiter switching mechanism show very short reaction times and have proven efficient to quickly find and track objects.

3.2 Reaching

Similarly to the search and track behaviors, the reaching behavior is driven by the sensory memory. It is composed of a set of internal predictors and a strategy selection instance. Each predictor includes a whole body motion controller and a cost function evaluation. The underlying whole body motion control is based on the scheme by Liégeois [8][9][10] for redundant systems. The trajectories to reach towards the proto objects are generated interactively using a dynamical systems approach. The trajectories are projected into joint space using a weighted generalized pseudo-inverse of the task Jacobian. Redundancies are resolved by mapping the gradient of an optimization criterion into the null space of the motion. In this work a joint limit avoidance criterion is used. Details on the whole body control algorithm are given in [11][12]. The whole body controller is coupled with a walking and balancing controller, which stabilizes the motion. This scheme allows to perform even fast dynamic whole body motions in a stable way.

Strategy Selection

The idea is to evaluate a set of different behavior alternatives ("strategies") that solve the task in different ways. In the following, the task of reaching towards an object and aligning the robot's palm with the objects longitudinal axis will be regarded. In a first step, the visual target is split up into different motion commands, with which the task can be achieved. Four commands are chosen: Reaching towards the target with the left and right hand, both while standing and walking. While the strategies that reach while standing assume the robot model to be fixed, the strategies involving walking are based on on a kinematic "floating base" description of the robot model (Fig. 2 [11]). This way, the heel position of the control model is permanently updated according to the given target and the null space criteria that are incorporated within the whole body motion controller. This leads to a very interesting property of the control scheme: the control algorithm will automatically compute the optimal stance position and orientation with respect to a given target and the chosen null space criteria. If a walking strategy is selected, the floating frame is set as the target for a step pattern generator, which generates appropriate steps to reach the computed heel position and orientation. Now each strategy computes the motion and an associated cost according to its specific command. The cost describes the suitability of the strategy in the current context. It is based on the evaluation of a multi-criteria cost function that is composed of the following measures:

- **Reachability:** Penalizes if the target cannot be reached with the respective strategy.
- **Postural discomfort:** Penalizes the proximity to the joint limits when reaching towards the target.
- **"Laziness":** Penalizes the strategies that make steps. This way, the robot prefers standing over walking.

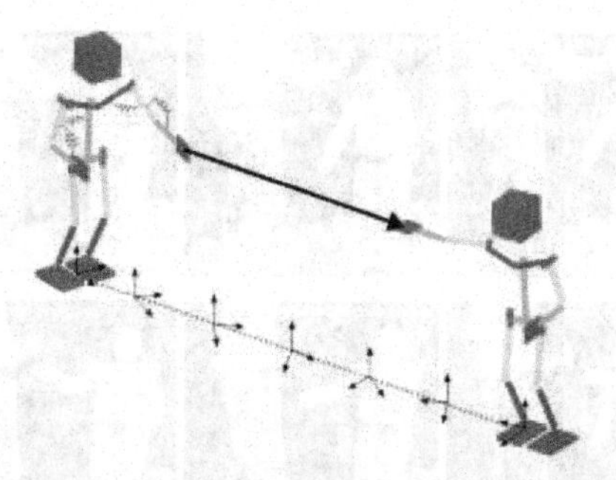

Fig. 2. "Floating" heel frame: The stance position of the feet is the result of the null space motion. It is a local optimum with regard to the given task.

- **Time to target:** Penalizes the approximate number of steps that are required to reach the target. This makes the robot dynamically change the reaching hand also during walking.

The costs are evaluated by the strategy selection process, and the strategy with the lowest cost is identified. The corresponding command is given to the physical robot. The robot is controlled with the identical whole body motion controller that is employed for the internal simulations. An interesting characteristic of the system is the temporal decoupling of real robot control and simulation. The strategies are sped up by a factor of 10 with respect to the real-time control, so that each strategy has converged to the target while the physical robot still moves. Therefore, the strategies can be regarded as prediction instances, since they look some time ahead of the real robot. Nevertheless, the control algorithms running within the strategies and on the robot are identical. From a classical point of view, the predictions could be seen as alternative results of a planning algorithm. A major difference is their incremental character. We use a set of predictors as continuously acting robots that each execute the task in a different way. The most appropriately acting virtual robot is mapped to the physical instance.

4 Results

The system as described above was tested many times with different people interacting with ASIMO with a variety of target objects. The scenario was always to have a human interaction partner who has an elongated object that was shown or hidden in various ways to ASIMO. The system is not restricted to only one object. If a number of objects are close to each other, the system will try to keep all objects in the field of view. If they are further apart, the objects leaving the field of view will be neglected after a short while and the system will track the remaining object(s). Objects are quickly found and reliably tracked even when moved quickly. The robot will reach for any elongated object of appropriate size that is presented within a certain distance — from 20cm to about 3m.

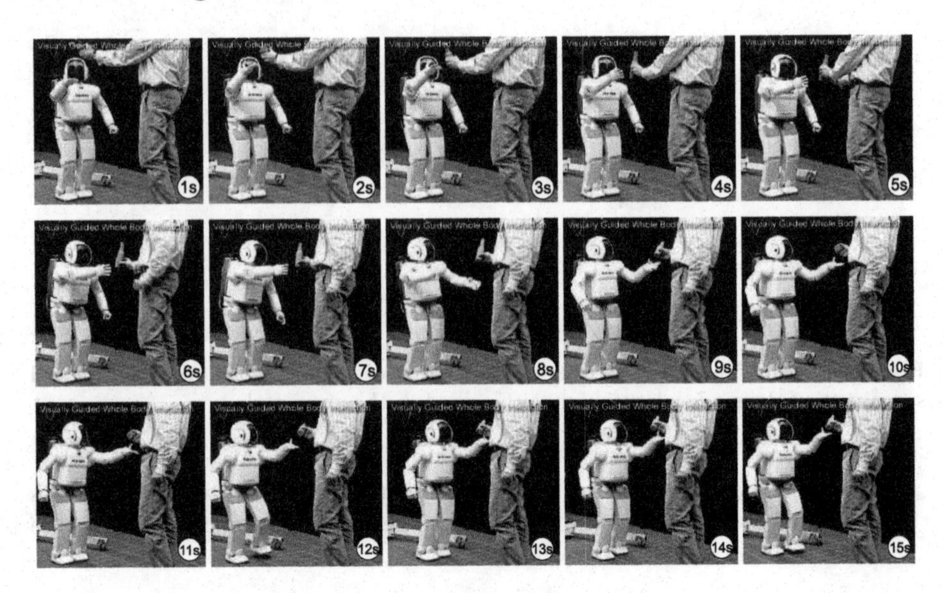

Fig. 3. Snapshot series from an experiment.

ASIMO switches between reaching with the right and left hand according to the relative object position with some hysteresis. It makes steps only when necessary. Fig. 3 shows a series of snapshots taken from an experiment. From second 1-7, ASIMO is reaching for the green bottle with its right hand. This corresponds to the first phase in Fig. 4. At second 8, the object gets out of reach of the right hand, and the strategy selection mechanism selects the left hand reaching strategy, still while the robot is standing (Second phase in Fig. 4). At second 12, the object can neither be reached with the left hand while standing. The strategy selection mechanism now selects to reach for the object with the left hand while walking towards it (Third phase in Fig. 4). The whole body motion control generates smooth motions and is able to handle even extreme postures which gives a very natural and human-like impression even to the casual observer.

5 Conclusions

We presented an architecture that interactively generates robot behaviors to interact with a human partner. The scheme employs internal predictions of behavioral alternatives in order to select the most suitable behavior in a given situation. The presented methods work in real-time and have successfully been tested on the humanoid robot ASIMO. Future work will go in the direction of interactivity, planning and real-time simulation, and providing efficient tools for decision making processes and learning.

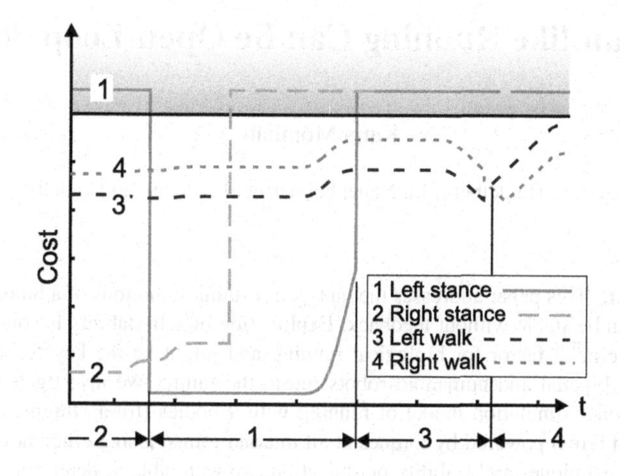

Fig. 4. Progression of fitness values over time.

References

1. Fujita, Takagi, and Hasegawa. Ethological modeling and architecture for an entertainment robot. In *ICRA*, 2001.
2. Fujita, Takagi, and Hasegawa. An ethological and emotional basis for human-robot interaction. *Robotics and Autonomous Systems*, (3-4), 2003.
3. Cynthia Breazeal and Brian Scassellati. How to build robots that make friends and influence people. In *IROS*, 1999.
4. Ronald A. Rensink. Seeing, sensing, and scrutinizing. *Vision Research*, 40:1469–1487, 2000.
5. Austen Clark. Feature-placing and proto-objects. *Philosophical Psychology*, (4):443–469, December 2004.
6. Zenon W. Pylyshyn. Visual indexes, preconceptual objects, and situated vision. *Cognition*, (1):127–158, June 2001.
7. Thomas Bergener, Carsten Bruckhoff, Percy Dahm, Herbert Janssen, Frank Joublin, Rainer Menzner, Axel Steinhage, and Werner von Seelen. Complex behavior by means of dynamical systems for an anthropomorphic robot. *Neural Networks*, 1999.
8. A. Liégeois. Automatic supervisory control of the configuration and behavior of multibody mechanisms. *IEEE Transactions on Systems, Man, and Cybernetics*, (12), December 1977.
9. James. D. English and Anthony. A. Maciejewski. On the implementation of velocity control for kinematically redundant manipulators. *IEEE Transactions on Systems, Man, and Cybernetics*, pages 233–237, May 2000.
10. Yoshihiko Nakamura. *Advanced Robotics: Redundancy and Optimization*. Addison-Wesley Publishing, 1991.
11. Michael Gienger, Herbert Janssen, and Christian Goerick. Task oriented whole body motion for humanoid robots. In *Proceedings of the IEEE-RAS/RSJ International Conference on Humanoid Robots*, 2005.
12. Michael Gienger, Herbert Janssen, and Christian Goerick. Exploiting task intervals for whole body robot control. In *IEEE/RSJ*, 2006.

Human-like Running Can Be Open-Loop Stable

Katja Mombaur

IWR, University of Heidelberg, Im Neuenheimer Feld 368, 69120 Heidelberg, Germany

Abstract. This paper addresses the question if running motions of a human-like robot can be stable without feedback. Exploitation of self-stability is considered to be a crucial factor for biological running and might be the key for success to make bipedal and humanoid robots run in the future, We investigate a two-dimensional simulation model of running with 9 bodies (trunk, thighs, shanks, feet, and arms) powered by torques at all internal joints. Using efficient optimal control techniques and stability optimization, we were able to determine torque inputs and spring-damper parameters that lead to fully open-loop stable running motions.

1 Introduction

The past few decades have seen a remarkable development in the field of humanoid robots, producing robots that can walk, climb stairs, avoid obstacles and even lift off the ground for very short periods of time [8]. But despite all this technological progress there is still a big difference between humanoid robots and their biological counterparts in terms of speed ($6km/h$ vs. $36km/h$) and efficiency, and it will take many more years, until we will see a robot running as fast and as elegantly as a human. Stability control of fast motions still is a big technological issue, even though technical signal processing can be faster than neural signal transmission. But the problem is that most humanoid robots are based on conventional robotics control concepts using rigid components and high gain controllers which are very suitable for accurate path following, but seem to be less adequate to bring speeds motion speeds up to a biological level since the online computational effort is too high.

Running in nature is in particular characterized by a high level of self-stability. During the biological learning process, motions evolve in such a way that they harmonically fit to the kinematic and dynamic properties of the walking systems and that the natural stability properties of the system are exploited such that systems tend to stabilized themselves. Small perturbations of the original gait cycle are thus - at least to some extent - automatically coped with, and do not have to be actively dealt with by the online control system. It is this property that allows animals and humans to run at very high speeds. And addressing this issue also seems to be the key of success for making humanoid and other bipedal robots faster.

In order to enhance the stability of humanoid robots as much intelligence and knowledge as possible should be put into the choice of design parameters and open-loop input controls of a robot in order to enhance the exploitation of self-stability. This approach is taken by many researchers of the passive-dynamic walking community now also shifting to actuated mechanisms with some feedback control (e. [2]). Martijn Wisse an co-workers in Delft have assembled a remarkable series of robots of increasing complexity and with a high level of self-stability [10], the tuning of which was mainly based on years of practical robot building and experience.

We take an alternative approach and aim at increasing natural robot stability by applying model-based optimization. Based on rigid-body system models of robot motions and efficient optimal control techniques, we were able to produce fully open-loop stable motions for a series of robot configurations and motions, such as walking, running and somersaults e.g. [5, 6, 7].

The present paper builds on [9], the focus of which was to use optimal control methods to produce bipedal running motions for human-like geometries and mass distributions and joint torque inputs. However, stability issues have not been considered in this context, assuming the availability of a feedback control system capable to stabilize the motion. In this paper we show that it is even possible to generate, for human-like masses, mass distributions and geometries to generate running motions that are open-loop stable just by modifying spring-damper parameters and input torques.

2 Formulation and Solution of Optimal Control Problems Involving Stability

Models of periodic running gaits involve multiple phases, each with its own set of governing equations, and we assume that the order but not the duration of phases is known. The number of degrees of freedom as well as the number of free control variables $u(t)$ (i.e. actuator inputs in physical terms) can be different in each phase. Each phase is described by a set of highly nonlinear differential equations (ODEs or DAEs, depending on the choice of coordinates). Between phases, there may be discontinuities in the state variables. For a detailed description on the model of the biped robot, we refer to [9].

The problem of generating an optimal periodic gait based leads to the formulation of a multi-phase optimal control problem of the following form:

$$\min_{x,X,u,p,T} \quad \int_0^T \phi(x(t),u(t),p)\,dt + \Phi(T,x(T),X(T),p) \tag{1}$$

$$\text{s. t.} \quad \dot{x}(t) = f_j(t,x(t),u(t),p) \quad \text{for} \quad t \in [\tau_{j-1},\tau_j], \quad j = 1,\dots,n_{ph},\ \tau_0 = 0, \tau_{n_{ph}} = T \tag{2}$$

$$x(\tau_j^+) = x(\tau_j^-)) + J(\tau_j^-) \quad \text{for} \quad j = 1,\dots,n_{ph} \tag{3}$$

$$\dot{X}(t) = \frac{\partial f_j}{\partial x}(t,x(t),u(t),p)X(t) \quad \text{for} \quad t \in [\tau_{j-1},\tau_j] \quad \text{with} \quad X(0) = I \tag{4}$$

$$X(\tau_j^+) = \Big(\Big(f_{j+1}(\tau_j^+) - f_j(\tau_j^-) - J_t - J_x f_j(\tau_j^-)\Big) \cdot \frac{1}{\dot{s}} s_x^T + I + J_x\Big) X(\tau_j^-) \quad \text{for} \quad j = 1,\dots,n_{ph} \tag{5}$$

$$g_j(t,x(t),u(t),p) \geq 0 \quad \text{for} \quad t \in [\tau_{j-1},\tau_j] \tag{6}$$

$$r_{eq}(x(0),..,x(T),p) = 0 \quad (7)$$

$$r_{ineq}(x(0),..,x(T),p) \geq 0 \quad (8)$$

In these equations, x are the state variables, u the controls, p the parameters, and T the overall cycle time, with τ_j being the phase separation times. The dynamics and discontinuities of the rigid body system model are considered as constraint of the optimization model (2), (3).

The objective function of interest is given in very general form; very often it is related to energy consumption or efficiency of a motion. Here, we are in particular interested in objective functions related to the stability of gaits. Stability can be formulated by several criteria, most of which are related to the monodromy matrix of the periodic solution $X(T)$ which describes the sensitivity of the trajectory end values with respect to initial values. For the computation of stability we therefore have augmented the system dynamics by the corresponding variational differential equation (4) and discontinuity update equations (5). Here, we use the most common criterion for stability, which is the spectral radius of the monodromy matrix, which, according to Lyapunov's first method, has to be smaller than one ($\rho(X(T) < 1$) to induce stability.

For the solution of the above problem we built upon the optimal control methods based on the direct boundary value problem approach developed by Bock and co-workers ([1],[3],[4]) and adapted them to handle index-3 DAEs and higher order derivatives of the dynamics. We use a direct method for the optimal control problem discretization and a multiple shooting state parameterization which transforms the original boundary value problem into a set of initial value problems with corresponding continuity and boundary conditions. The resulting structured non-linear programming problem is solved by an efficient tailored SQP algorithm.

3 Results of Stability Optimization

We briefly present results for a stability optimization run for the bipedal model. We have used human data for segment lengths, masses and moments of inertia of bodies. This data has been fixed for the computations presented here, but we also have preformed computations leaving all these parameters free which for sake of brevity will however not be presented in this paper. We have varied input torque histories and parameters of spring-damper elements that act at all interior joints. The computations revealed that it is in fact possible to produce open-loop stable running for human-like data using adequate torque inputs and spring-damper elements.

In figures 1 and 2 we show this stable solution which is characterized by a spectral radius of 0.5 and a cycle time of 0.194 s.

4 Conclusions

The results of this paper show that it is possible to produce bipedal human-like running motions that are stable without feedback. These results are very encouraging for the design of humanoid robots. If correctly applied, these methods might support the design phase and the choice of actuator inputs of robots and simplify the complex task of stability control by enhancing the exploitation of self-stability of the dynamical system.

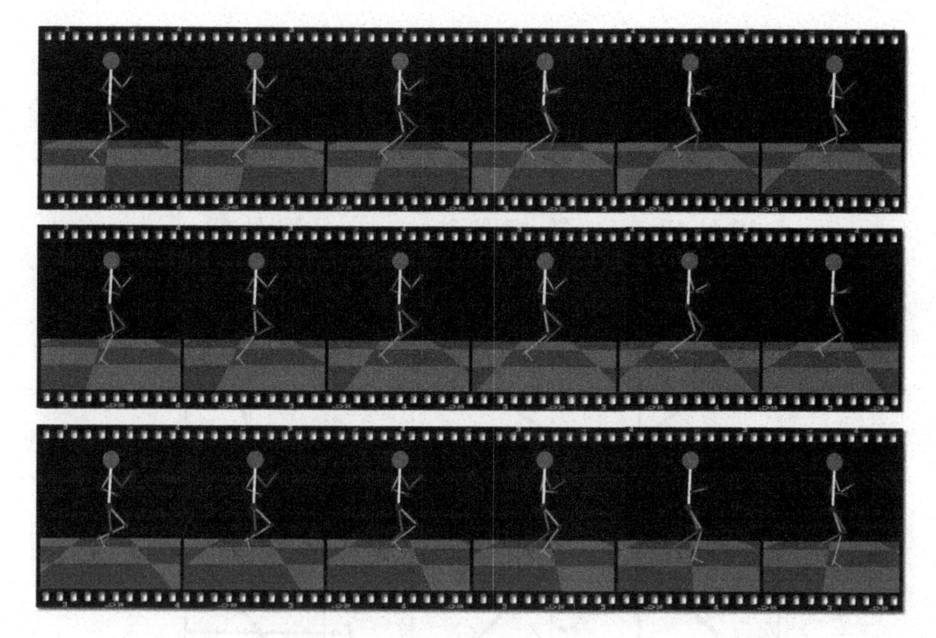

Fig. 1. 2D running motion resulting from stability optimization

5 Acknowledgments

The research project has been supported by the German Ministry of Education and Research (BMBF) within the framework *"Bionik – Innovationen aus der Natur"*. The work of Gerrit Schultz, who established the model equations of the bipedal robot, is gratefully acknowledged.

References

1. H. G. Bock and K.-J. Plitt, A multiple shooting algorithm for direct solution of optimal control problems, in *Proceedings of the 9th IFAC World Congress, Budapest*, 1984.
2. S. H. Collins and A. L. Ruina and R. Tedrake and M. Wisse, Efficient bipedal robots based on passive-dynamic Walkers, in *Science*, **307**, (2005)
3. D. B. Leineweber, I. Bauer, H. G. Bock and J. P. Schlöder, *Comput. Chem. Engng* **27**, 157 (2003).
4. D. B. Leineweber, A. Schäfer, H. G. Bock and J. P. Schlöder, *Comput. Chem. Engng* **27**, 167 (2003).
5. K. D. Mombaur, R. W. Longman, H. G. Bock and J. P. Schlöder, Open-loop stable running, on *Robotica*, **23**, 01 (2005
6. K. D. Mombaur, H. G. Bock, J. P. Schlöder and R. W. Longman, Self-stabilizing somersaults, in *IEEE Transactions on Robotics*, **21**, 6, (2005)

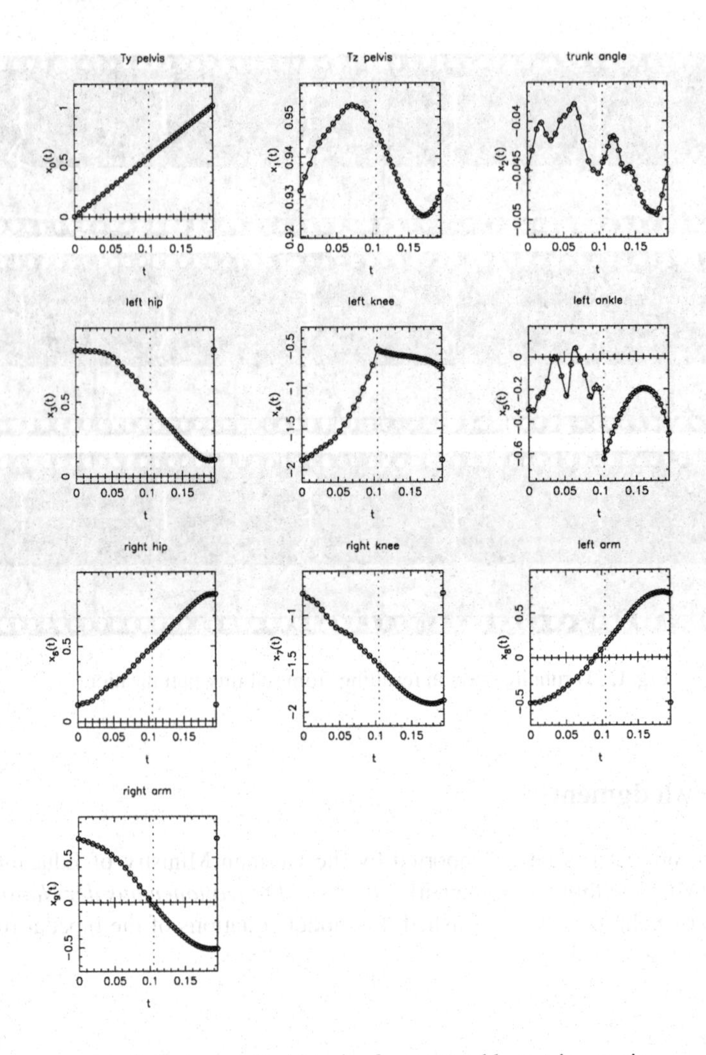

Fig. 2. State variable histories for most stable running motion

7. K. Mombaur, H. Bock, J. Schlöder and R. Longman, Open-loop stable solution of periodic optimal control problems, in *ZAMM*, 2005.
8. Proceedings 2006 IEEE-RAS International Conference on Humanoid Robots (HUMANOIDS 06), Genova, Italy, Dec. 2006
9. Gerrit Schultz, Katja Mombaur, Optimal control of human-like running, submitted, 2007
10. Martijn Wisse, Presentation at *Dynamic Walking Conference*, Ann Arbor, Mai 2006, www.dynamicwalking.org/downloads/DW2006Abstracts.pdf

Exploring Toe Walking in a Bipedal Robot

James Andrew Smith and Andre Seyfarth

Lauflabor, Institute for Sports Science, Friedrich-Schiller University,
Dornburger Strasse 23, 07743 Jena

Abstract. The design and development of locomotory subsystems such as legs is a key issue in the broader topic of autonomous mobile systems. Simplification of substructures, sensing, actuation and control can aid to better understand the dynamics of legged locomotion and will make the implementation of legs in engineered systems more effective. This paper examines recent results in the development of toe walking on the JenaWalker II robot. The robot is shown, while supported on a treadmill, to be capable of accelerating from 0 to over 0.6 m/s without adjustment of control parameters such as hip actuator sweep frequency or amplitude. The resulting stable motion is due to the adaptability of the passive structures incorporated into the legs. The roles of the individual muscle-tendon groups are examined and a potential configuration for future heel-toe trials is suggested.

1 Introduction

The design and development of locomotory subsystems is a key issue in the broader topic of autonomous mobile systems. While wheels and tracks are often the subsystems of choice for use in ground-based systems, legged and even hybrid wheeled-leg subsystems may be also be appropriate, depending on the given task and work environment. Unfortunately, all engineered legged systems developed to date are still outperformed by the multitude of efficient and effective examples found in nature. For this reason, many researchers are re-examining biological systems for inspiration and insight in the development of the next generations of legged systems.

Simplification of substructures, sensing, actuation and control can aid to better understand the dynamics of legged locomotion. The RHex biped [1] is an effective running system with a control strategy that requires leg recirculation to achieve toe-clearance during leg protraction. While the underactuated JenaWalker [2] also houses compliant limbs, judicious selection and distribution of mono- and biarticular compliant elements negates the requirement for recirculation and results in more human-like walking. The JenaWalker II presented here is a continuation of this previous work and serves as a testbed to study the effect of individual substructures in the leg on the resulting gait.

The spring-like properties of muscle-tendon complexes are well known and have been the topic of many biomechanics studies [3] [4]. The insights provided by biomechanicists have inspired engineers to develop robots with comparable

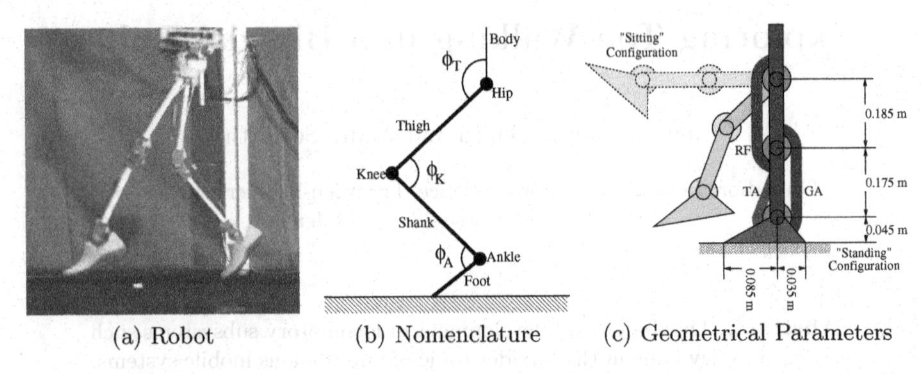

(a) Robot (b) Nomenclature (c) Geometrical Parameters

Fig. 1. The JenaWalker II robot on a treadmill (left), the leg link and joint nomenclature (middle), and the geometrical parameters and layout (right) of the gastrocnemius (GA), tibialis anterior (TA) and rectus femoris (RF) elements.

characteristics to walking and running animals [5]. While there has been a tendency to model bipedal walking as stiff (i.e. the inverted pendulum) [3] [6] and modeling bipedal running as compliant (i.e. the spring-loaded inverted pendulum) [7], it has become increasingly evident that *both* gaits utilize compliant elements [8] [9].

While it is the objective of the authors' ongoing work to study both walking and running, the former is the focus of this paper. Of the walking gaits, the heel-toe walking mode is standard for most humans but is sometimes replaced by the "primitive" [10] toe walking gait in small children, in ballet dancers and in people with certain neuromuscular diseases [11]. It is often caused by a shortening of the Achilles tendon, resulting in an *equinus* ankle configuration. The current configuration of the JenaWalker II, shown in Fig. 1a., is relatively simple and it follows that the resulting gaits will also be relatively simple, making the study of toe-walking appropriate at this early stage.

One of the strong motivating factors behind the study of toe-walking was to reduce the effect of impact at touchdown found during heel-toe or flat-footed ambulation. In flat-footed walking both the heel and toe of the foot contact the ground at approximately the same time, while in heel-toe walking the heel contacts first, followed by a shift to the ball of the foot. In both cases the impact phase is characterized by the leg's effective configuration as a two-segment system, thus requiring that the knee flex during stance for the leg to display any compliance. Toe walking, on the other hand, allows the leg to operate as a three segment system from the moment of impact, allowing either knee or ankle flexure to result in compliant leg activity. As the control and leg parameters used in the trials presented here (as well as in preliminary trials) generally resulted in straight-knee stance phases, the availability of ankle flexure guarantees that the leg will demonstrate at least some overall compliance.

2 Methods

The Jena Walker II, a bipedal robot, shown in Fig. 1a., consists of two modular legs. Each leg consists of rigid segments, joint modules and easily replaceable springs spanning hip, knee and ankle joints. The robot has a 0.45 m hip height and weighs about 1.78 kg, of which approximately two-thirds are suspended by an elastic rope; other geometrical and mass parameters are listed in Table 1. The foot consists of a prosthetic foot (SACH child foot, Otto Bock; slightly modified to fit the robot ankle joint and mechanical cabling). While four major leg muscle-tendon groups are usually represented in the robot by compliant structures: tibialis anterior (TA), gastrocnemius (GA), rectus femoris (RF) and biceps femoris (BF), only three (TA, GA and RF) are used in the results presented here, shown in Fig. 1c. Except for the TA, all muscle-tendon groups span two joints leading to an inter-joint coupling within the leg. Spring constant and spring length values are given in Table 2. The robot is constrained to the sagittal plane on a treadmill (Schmidt Sportsworld) via an overhead boom. In the standing configuration (see Fig. 1c.) the pivot of the overhead boom is about 1 m from the bottom of the robot's foot. Actuation is provided by two Maxon RE-Max 29 motors with 128:1 GP-26 B gearheads. Control is provided by a custom-programmed robot control unit. Motor power is also supplied to the robot by the robot control unit and is limited to a maximum of 24 Volts DC and about 2.5 Amperes.

The robot's hip actuators were set to oscillate out-of-phase with a peak-to-peak amplitude of 49°, an inclination bias of 7° and a period of 0.66 s. The length of the gastrocnemius foot extensor cable of each leg was shortened to give the ankle an approximate 130° extension value. The RF and TA muscle-tendon groups are represented by linear metal extension springs (Associated Spring SPEC 0E0360-0411500M and 0E0120-0181370S, respectively). The spring constants and rest lengths, as well as the spring lengths in two different leg configurations are given in Table 2. The two leg configurations are shown in Fig. 1c.

Table 1. Robot and Simulation Model Geometry and Mass Parameters

Parameter	JenaWalker II Robot
Total Mass (free)	1.780 kg
Total Mass (suspended)	0.590 kg
Joint Mass	0.060 kg
Thigh Link Mass	0.010 kg
Shank Link Mass	0.010 kg
Foot Mass	0.090 kg
Thigh Link Length	0.185 m
Shank Link Length	0.175 m
Foot Height	0.045 m
Foot Length	0.120 m

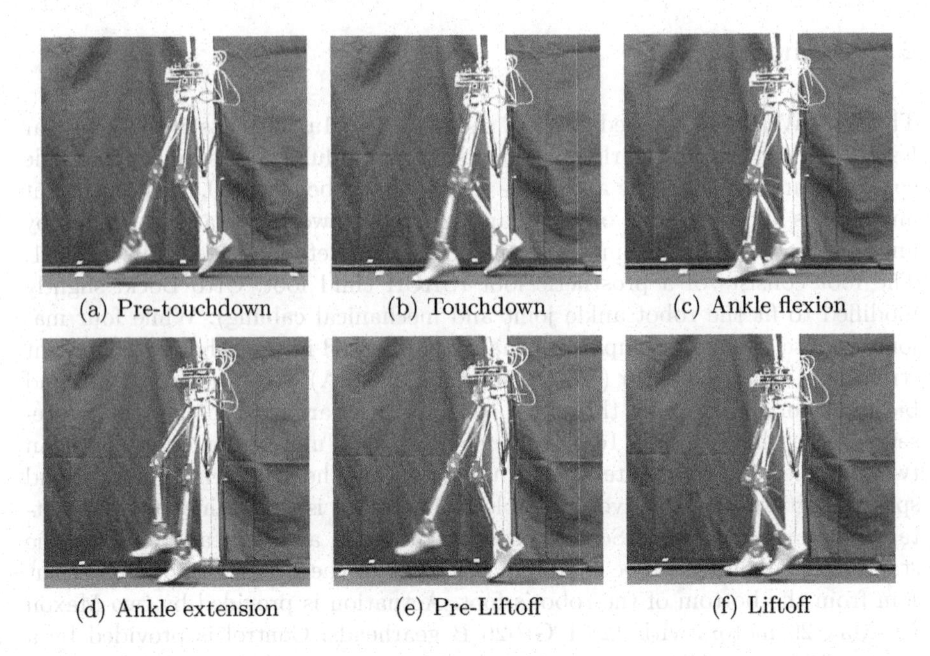

(a) Pre-touchdown (b) Touchdown (c) Ankle flexion

(d) Ankle extension (e) Pre-Liftoff (f) Liftoff

Fig. 2. Still frames from video taken while the robot walked at 0.682 m/s.

Table 2. Robot leg spring parameters. Refer to Fig. 1c for an illustration of the "sit" and "stand" leg configurations.

Muscle	Type	Spring Constant [N/m]	Rest Length [m]	Sit Length [m]	Stand Length [m]
Rectus Femoris (RF)	Metal Ext. Spring	1030	0.040	0.040	0.050
Tibialis Anterior (TA)	Metal Ext. Spring	320	0.038	0.065	0.065
Gastrocnemius (GA)	Tensioned Cable	n/a	n/a	n/a	n/a

3 Results

The robot was made to toe walk at various treadmill-induced speeds (0.243, 0.366, 0.489 and 0.682 m/s) using fixed hip control and leg compliance characteristics (i.e. a hip frequency of 1.5 Hz and compliance values listed in Table 2). At all speeds induced by the treadmill, there is a match between the hip oscillation frequency and the resulting stride frequency. The stance phase was also found to be over 50% of the gait cycle in all four trials, matching an intuitive, but not formal, definition for walking.

The three individual three leg joints (hip, knee and ankle) demonstrate the following noteworthy characteristics. The hip angle tracings of Fig. 3 illustrate that thigh retraction and protraction occur in both the leg stance and leg flight stages of walking. In fact, the thigh begins its protraction during the middle of

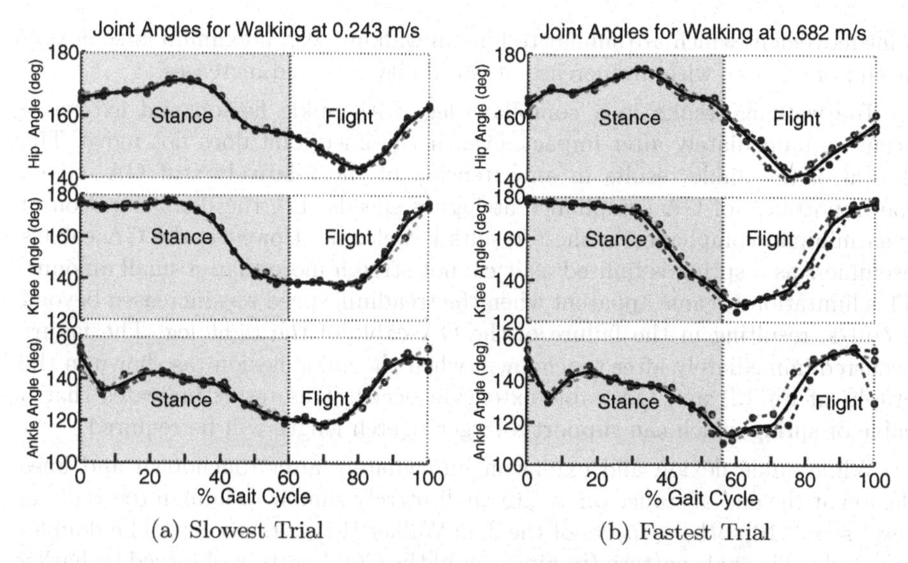

(a) Slowest Trial (b) Fastest Trial

Fig. 3. Leg joint angles for walking at lowest and highest speeds reported. Positive slopes refer to joint extension, and negative slopes to flexion. Retraction occurs with positive hip joint slope and protraction with negative hip joint slope.

the stance phase, as seen by its negative slope. The knee also shows a change in behaviour at the midpoint of stance, where it changes to flexion from its original extended (i.e. straight) joint configuration. Maximum knee flexion occurs at, or slightly after, the leg liftoff condition. Maximum knee extension, which leads to the straight knee behaviour, begins approximately halfway through the flight phase. The ankle joint exhibits a combined flexion-extension movement during the first portion of stance as a response to the impact between the foot and the treadmill belt. In addition, some flexion continues until the foot liftoff condition.

Since the hip frequency remains fixed, the only possible strategy for the biped to match the treadmill speed is by increasing its step length. This is made possible by passive increases in hip, knee and ankle amplitudes, as is apparent in a comparison of Figs. 3a and 3b. This is due to the inclusion of compliant elements in the leg, such as a plastic coupler between the hip gearhead motor and the hip joint, as well as the explicit mechanical springs distributed throughout the leg.

4 Discussion

Steady toe walking was found to be achievable from 0 m/s to almost 0.7 m/s. The resulting gaits maintained a stride frequency of 1.5 Hz at all speeds. While neither the characteristics of the extension springs, nor the control action of the hip motors changed during the trials, the differences in the tracings of the joint angles illustrate the presence of passive dynamic adaptation of the legs to increases in treadmill speed. The results are speed-dependent knee and ankle joint movement which are similar to human walking (e.g. maximum knee flexion at end of stance), with an increase in variability as speed increases.

Toe walking results in a compliant leg, with ankle flexion and extension occuring immediately after impact, even if the knee joint does not move. The flexion of the ankle results in an extension of the relatively stiff GA. Given the importance of GA compliance at higher speeds [12], the demonstration of even minimal compliance in these results is welcome. However, the GA cable's usefulness as a spring is limited as it cannot stretch more than a small amount. This limitation became apparent when the treadmill speed was increased beyond 0.7 m/s, resulting in the failure of the GA cable of the right leg. The failure occurred immediately after touchdown, when the ankle flexion (as shown in the graphs of Fig. 3) and GA cable extension occur. This result indicates that a cable or spring which can support a larger stretch length will be required.

While ankle flexion and extension immediately after touchdown and knee flexion at the end of stance phase are qualitatively similar to human toe walking results [13] [10], other aspects of the JenaWalker II results are not. The double-humped ankle angle pattern (reminiscent of the COM pattern observed by Farley during walking [14]) found by both Perry [10] and Jaeger [13] to occur after the impact management phase is essentially absent in the robot results. This is perhaps a further indication of the potential importance for compliance in structures such as the GA and soleus (SOL) muscle-tendon groups.

Interestingly, Perry's toe walking trials showed reduction in knee flexion as compared to heel-toe walking in the late stance and swing phases. While the JenaWalker II also shows limited knee flexion, it is most evident in the *first half of the stance phase* of the JenaWalker II trials, see Figs. 2a - 2d, as well as Fig. 3, making the leg look particularly stiff. In addition, this gait seems to rely on the mechanical joint limit built into the knee. Future work will examine configurations of the robot which do not rely on these mechanical limits to develop stable walking or running.

The toe-walking trials have allowed an examination of the roles of the three muscle-tendon groups included in the JenaWalker II. The GA is shown to absorb a portion of the impact at touchdown. However, there isn't a rapid extension of the ankle joint that one would associate with unloading of the GA. The GA is, thus, essentially limited to synchronization of the flexion and extension of the knee and ankle joints, as observed in human running results [9]; therefore negating the possibility of out-of-phase joint action usually seen in human walking. The TA, given that it contracts at the moment of foot impact, acts simply as an antagonist to the GA. The role of the RF, as seen here, is to prepare the leg for landing. It is loaded during the late stance phase when both the hip and knee flex and contracts during mid to late flight. Because it is unopposed by an antagonist (e.g. the biceps femoris) the knee, and therefore the leg, is placed in a straight configuration. The introduction of a BF mechanism would seem appropriate to develop a slightly flexed (crouched) knee configuration prior to stance. This would enable the knee to act in a compliant fashion, making heel-toe walking more feasible.

5 Conclusions

The introduction of toe walking to the robot enables it to walk with a compliant gait even though the knee does not participate in overall leg compliance. The leg compliance is due to the compliant action about the ankle joint, in spite of the fact that the gastrocnemius cable is relatively stiff. This toe walking leg configuration is shown to enable the biped to walk at over 0.6 m/s while also reducing the effect of impacts previously seen in flat-footed or heel-toe walking. While overall leg compliance is demonstrated it is not identical to results observed in human trials, most probably due to the minimal number of muscle-tendon group structures, as well as the lack of sufficient gastrocnemius compliance. The rectus femoris would seem to be responsible for the straight-knee stance, making the future use of an opposing biceps femoris a possibility for the development of a compliant configuration suited to the more common heel-toe walking.

Acknowledgments

The authors are supported by the Thuringian HWP and the German DFG.

References

1. N. Neville, M. Buehler, and I. Sharf. A bipedal running robot with one actuator per leg. In *IEEE Int. Conf. Robotics and Automation*, Orlando, USA, May 2006.
2. F. Iida, Y. Minekawa, J. Rummel, and A. Seyfarth. *Intelligent Autonomous Systems*, chapter Toward a Human-Like Biped Robot with Compliant Legs, pages 820–827. Number 9. IOS Press, 2006.
3. R. McNeill Alexander. Three uses for springs in legged locomotion. *International Journal of Robotics Research*, 9(2), 1990.
4. T. A. McMahon. *Muscles, reflexes, and locomotion.* Princeton University Press, Princeton, N.J., USA, 1984.
5. M. Raibert. *Legged Robots That Balance.* The MIT Press, Cambridge, USA, 1986.
6. T. McGeer. Passive bipedal running. Technical report, Simon Fraser University, Centre For Systems Science, Burnaby, B.C., Canada, 1989.
7. R. Blickhan. The spring-mass model for running and hopping. *J. Biomech.*, 22:1217–1227, 1989.
8. H. Geyer, A. Seyfarth, and R. Blickhan. Compliant leg behaviour explains basic dynamics of walking and running. *Proc. R. Soc. B*, 273(1603):2861 – 2867, 2006.
9. S. Lipfert and A. Seyfarth. Elastic legs in human walking. *J. Biomech.*, 40(S2):S385, 2007.
10. J. Perry, J. M. Burnfield, J. K. Gronley, and Mulroy S. J. Toe walking: muscular demands at the ankle and knee. *Arch Phys Med Rehabil*, 84(1):7–16, Jan. 2003.
11. E. P. Schwentker. Toe walking. Online publication, eMedicine.com, July 2004.
12. M. Ishikawa, P. V. Komi, M. J. Grey, V. Lepola, and G.-P. Bruggemann. Muscle-tendon interaction and elastic energy usage in human walking. *J. Appl. Physiol*, 99:603 – 608, 2005.
13. C. Jaeger. Einfluss der Fusshaltung und Laufgeschwindigkeit auf die Biomechanik des Gehens. Diploma thesis, FSU-Jena, Jena, Germany, October 2006.
14. C. T. Farley. Determinants of the center of mass trajectory in human walking and running. *The Journal of Experimental Biology*, 201:2935 – 2944, 1998.

Simulating Muscle-Reflex Dynamics in a Simple Hopping Robot

Andre Seyfarth[1], Karl Theodor Kalveram[1,2] and Hartmut Geyer[1,3]

[1] Locomotion Laboratory, University of Jena, Germany
[2] Institute of Experimental Psychology, University of Duesseldorf, Germany
[3] Media Lab, Massachusetts Institute of Technology, Cambridge, USA
andre.seyfarth@uni-jena.de,
www.lauflabor.de

Abstract. In legged systems, springy legs facilitate gaits with subsequent contact and flight phases. Here, we test whether electrical motors can generate leg behaviors suitable for stable hopping. We built a vertically operating sledge actuated by a motor-driven leg. The motor torque simulates either a linear leg spring or a muscle-reflex system. For stable hopping significant energy supply was required after midstance. This was achieved by enhancing leg stiffness or by continuously applying positive force feedback to the simulated muscle. The muscle properties combined with positive force feedback result in spring-like behavior which enables stable hopping with adjustable hopping height.

1 Introduction

Design and construction of legged robots are constrained by the properties of actuators, for instance by the specific torque-current and speed-torque relationships of motors, or the gear induced friction. In order to improve the efficiency and stability of the gait patterns (e.g. walking, running, hopping), often spring-like structures are introduced in walking machines. Thereby it is assumed that mainly the tendons in the biological muscle-tendon-joint system contribute to the observed elastic behavior of legs. When simulating muscle-reflex dynamics [1], however, we found that the reflex-driven muscle itself can behave spring-like even if the tendons are completely stiff. Hence, quasi-elastic limb behavior does not necessarily require passive elastic-compliant structures within the body.

The present paper is concerned with one-legged hopping on place with subsequent contact and flight phases. Can such a hopping pattern also be considered to emerge from pure muscle-reflex activity?

To test this hypothesis we built a simple hopping device called Marco hopper. Marco consists of a body and a motor-driven leg moveable in the vertical direction.

The question is, what types of force generation laws produce force patterns which move the body during stance such that alternating flight and stance phases occur. The advantage of Marco is that different types of force generation laws can easily be selected and applied via the motor. Explicitely, we do not intend to get hopping by control, that is to say, by prescribing a desired trajectory to the sledge and/or rod and enforcing the Marco to keep that trajectory using negative feedback and/or feedforward control. We rather aim at self-stabilizing oscillations which only use intrinsically given and peripherally measurable states of sledge and rod to shape ground reaction forces resulting in stable hopping.

The purpose of the paper, therefore, is to demonstrate conditions and requirements which provoke or impede stable bouncing of a hardware hopper, without using a pattern-based movement controller.

2 Methods

2.1 The Marco Hopper

Fig. 1(a) shows the technical realization of the Marco hopper. A sledge representing the body slides through ball bearings on a vertical rail. A rod representing the leg is attached to the sledge and is allowed to move up and down relative to the sledge. On the sledge, a motor is mounted. It drives the rod via a toothed wheel fixed on the motor shaft, which in turn scrolls a toothed belt attached to the rod. If the rod's foot has ground contact (stance phase), the sledge can be accelerated upward by an appropriate current through the motor. Without ground contact (flight phase), the common centre of mass of sledge and rod follow the laws of free fall. Below the rod's foot point a ball consisting of Adiprene (a highly damping material) is attached. This shock absorber attenuates impacts on the ground plate which could damage the device. A Maxon DC motor ADS50/5 with a build in gear box (gear ratio 1:14) actuates the rod. The weight of the sledge is 1.3 kg, the weight of the rod is 0.5 kg. The gear enhances the inertia of the rod by 1.9 kg, and the friction force by 6 N. That means that the gear makes the rod with respect to the sledge a very inert and stiff device, as indicated by the fact that the rod sticks on the sledge and is not pulled down by gravitation if the sledge is lifted up.

The motor is driven by a Mattke MAR24/6Z power amplifier adapted to current control. Here, the current through the motor is strictly proportional to the input voltage of the amplifier, regardless of the motor speed. Because the amplifier automatically counterbalances the electro-dynamical back EMV of the motor, the force exerted by the motor can be read from the input voltage into the amplifier.

Three sensors capture the state of Marco: A POSIMAG system measures the y-position y_S of the sledge, a tachometer coupled to the gear's drive side measures the y-velocity $\mathrm{d}y_L/\mathrm{d}t$ of the rod, and a strain gauge on the ground plate beneath the rod measures the contact force. The length y_L of the rod is computed by numerical integration of the tachometer signal. The scaling is chosen such that y_S agrees with y_L during stance, and that at the deepest position of the sledge both y_S and y_L reach zero.

Data conversion is managed by the Meilhaus AD/DA computer interface card ME2600i. The data are processed by Matlab/Simulink and RealTime Workshop.

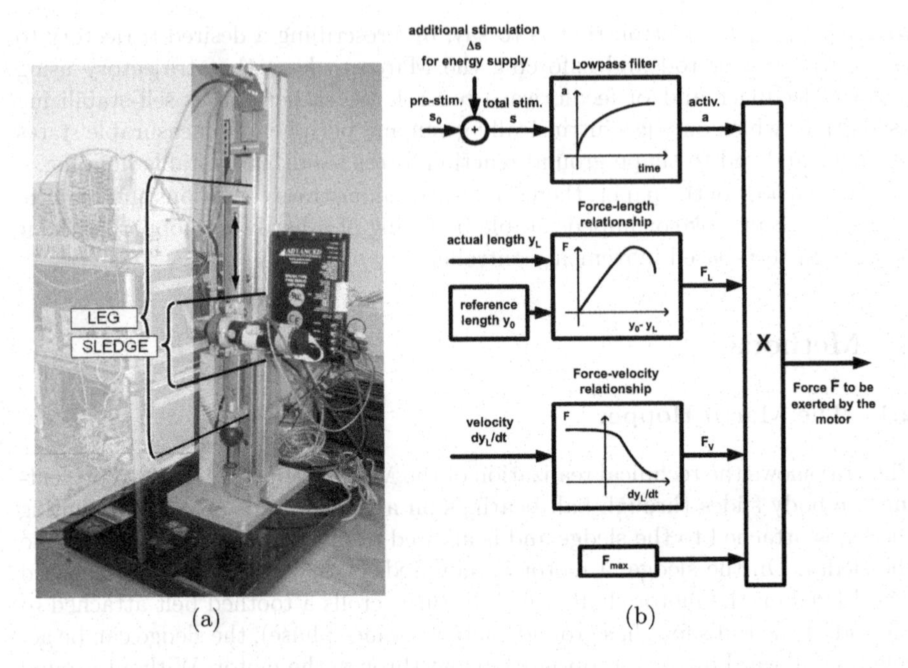

Fig. 1. (a) The Marco hopper consists of a sledge with a motor driven telescopic leg. (b) Basic muscle-like force generator used in Marco. The model merges lowpass filtered stimulation s, the force-length dependency $F_L(y_L - y_0)$ and the force-velocity dependency $F_V(\mathrm{d}y_L/\mathrm{d}t)$ by multiplication. The product F represents the force to be applied to the DC motor. To supply energy, an additional input is provided by which an extra stimulation Δs can be superimposed to the constant stimulation bias s_0.

All values - inside and outside of Simulink - are calibrated and checked to correspond to the international system (SI) of units. Notice that the amplifier limits the current to 6.3 A. This limit was carefully avoided in the control program in Matlab/Simulink.

2.2 How to Make Marco Hopping

Principally, stable hopping is achievable only if the energy losses of the bouncing system can be compensated. The question is, whether the energy supply is scaleable in such a manner that overcompensation or undercompensation can be avoided, or at least balanced out on average over several hopping periods.

Regarding a hopping mechanical systems, energy can be enhanced only in the ground contact phase (stance phase). Midstance, that is the point of time at which the rod reaches the minimum length respectively the sledge the deepest position, sections the stance phase into two parts, stance1 before and stance2 after midstance. Obviously, (positive) energy supplied in stance1 cannot refill the energy reservoir, because the additional energy is consumed by braking the sledge, and only prevents the sledge to fall as deep as it would have fallen without

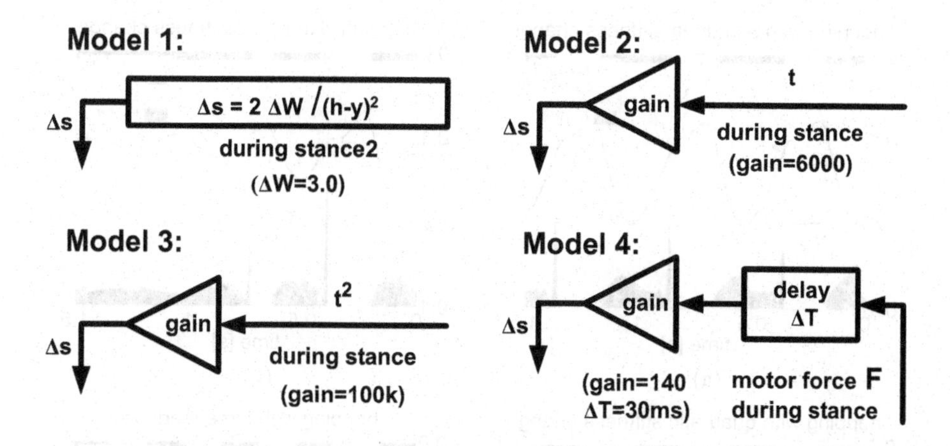

Fig. 2. Models of energy supply in Marco. The explicit numerical values of the selected parameters refer to Fig. 3.

that energy supply. In contrast, energy supplied in stance2 can contribute to upwards acceleration of the sledge, such that the kinetic energy at the end of the contact phase can be managed to reach or exceed the kinetic energy at the beginning of the contact phase. Therefore, energy feeding should be asymmetrical with respect to midstance: During stance2, the energy fed into the system should be greater than during stance1.

2.3 The Force Generating Laws

The force generating law of the leg during gound contact is, according to the Hill-type muscle model, modeled as a product of basically three variables (Fig. 1(b)): The lowpass filtered stimulation s which results in the activation a of the driving system, the force-length relationship F_L which describes the force as dependent on the deviation of the rod's actual length y_L from a reference length y_0, and the force-velocity relationship F_V which maps the force as dependent on the velocity dy_L/dt by which the length of the rod changes [1]. Usually, these variables are on hand in a normalized fashion. Therefore, a fourth factor representing the maximum isometric force F_{max} is then needed for the overall adjustment. Here, F_{max} was set to 1 because we didn't apply any normalizations. It should be mentioned that in an elastic object the notation "reference length" refers to the rest length, that is the length the object would attain without being exposed to external forces. In Marco, the reference length y_0 of the rod is arbitrarily chosen to $y_0 = 0.11$ m. Notice that the real muscle is stretched in the ground contact phase, whereas the rod exerts force in the compressed mode, so the sign in the x-axis of the force-length curve is inverted for usage in Marco. For energy supply, an additional input called Δs is provided by which an extra stimulation can be added upon the basic pre-stimlation s_0.

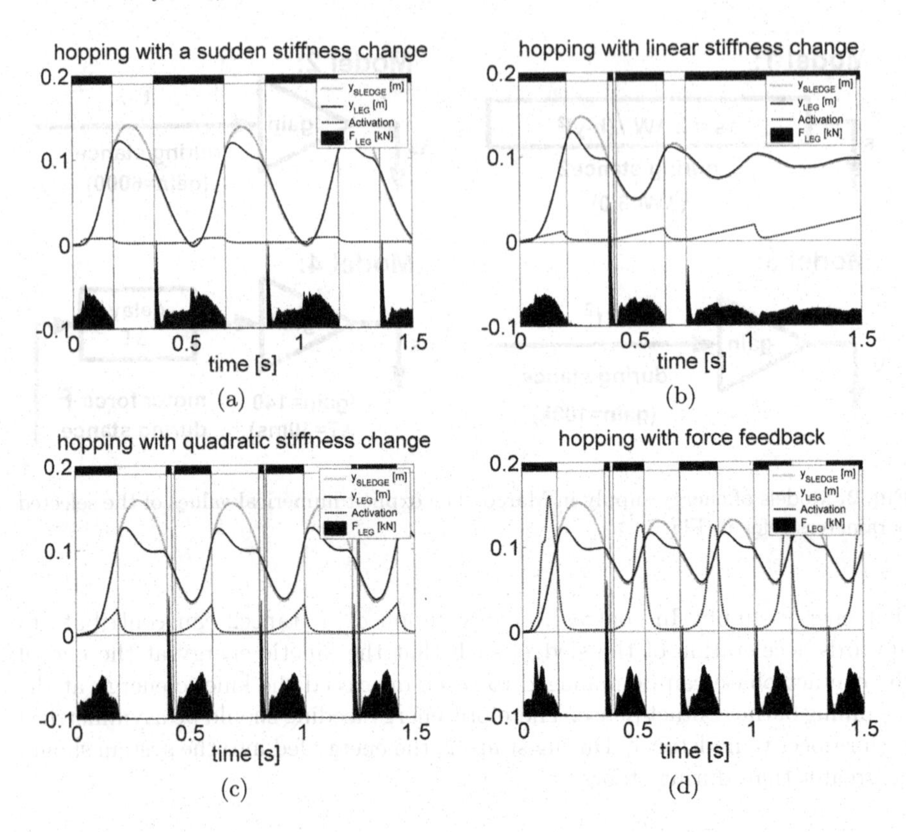

Fig. 3. Four hopping experiments: (a-c) Simulated leg stiffness during contact and (d) simulated muscle-reflex system. Leg stiffness is increased with time: (a) at midstance or continuously in a linear (b) or quadratic fashion (c). Shortly before ground contact the leg was somewhat shortened to attenuate the landing impact.

3 Four Models for Energy Supply and Results

We derived from the basic model of Fig. 1(b) four submodels which differ with respect to the manner by which the energy admitted in stance2 is made exceeding the energy supplied in stance1. The models are sketched in Fig. 2. In all models, the same force-length relationship was applied using

$$F_L = \begin{cases} y_0 - y_L & \text{if } y_0 - y_L \geq 0 \\ 0 & \text{else} \end{cases} \quad (1)$$

.

The force-velocity dependency was set to 1, hence, it had no influence. In model 4, however, a second curve with a nonlinear decay was selected.

Model 1: Here, the behavior of a mechanical spring, which is essentially given by Hooke's law, was the force generating law. The stimulation s can therefore be interpreted as the stiffness of this spring. If the basic stimulation is held constant, the maximum potential energy of this spring is given by

$$W + \Delta W = (s_0 + \Delta s)/2 \cdot (h - y)^2, \tag{2}$$

where h denotes the deepest position of the sledge attained in midstance, y the position the sledge will attain when the ground contact is lost and the flight phase starts, and ΔW the increase of energy if the stimulation is enhanced by Δs during stance2. The value of h is measured and held back by a Simulink unit when the sledge velocity goes, coming from negative values, through zero. In our system, y is expected to reach at least the reference length y_0 which is 0.11 m. So we determined the 'stiffness' enhancement during stance2 by

$$\Delta s = 2\,\Delta W/(h - y)^2, \tag{3}$$

where ΔW is the amount of energy we wished to inject into the system. Model 1 was operated with $s = 180\,\text{N/m}$ and ΔW ranging from 3.0 to 2.4 Nm. These parameter values induced stable hopping, whereby the apex heights decreased from 0.15 to 0.14 m. At $\Delta W = 2.2\,\text{Nm}$, however, hopping ceased after two jumps. Fig. 3(a) shows the result for $\Delta W = 3.0\,\text{Nm}$.

Model 2: In this version, we increased linearly the stimulation Δs to be added to the basic stimulation s_0 during the complete stance phase, starting with zero at the beginning of ground contact. We applied gains ranging between 4000 and 6000 N/m, but we did not succeed in achieving stable hopping. In Fig. 3(b) the result for a gain of 6000 N/m is sketched.

Model 3: Here we increased the stimulation Δs quadratically with respect to time (model 3 in Fig. 2). With gains between 60 kN/m and 125 kN/m stable hopping could be achieved. Fig. 3(c) visualizes the result with a gain of 100 kN/m.

Model 4: In this approach we implemented a muscle-reflex mechanism, namely, a positive force feedback. The feedback signal was delayed with times between 20 and 50 ms during the complete ground contact phase of the rod. The force-length relationship was the same as in the models 1-3 The force-velocity relationship was either given the value 1 during stance as in the other models or an exponential dependency on velocity after midstance:

$$F_V = \begin{cases} \mathrm{e}^{-2\,\mathrm{d}y_L/\mathrm{d}t} & \text{if } \mathrm{d}y_L/\mathrm{d}t \geq 0 \\ 1 & \text{else} \end{cases} \tag{4}$$

Both versions of the force-velocity dependency resulted in stable hopping patterns, as expected from previous simulations. For the exponentially dropping force-velocity relationship, a force-feedback delay of 30 ms and a gain of 140 N/m the result is given in Fig. 3(d). For $F_V = \text{const} = 1$, however, the slope in stance2 was steeper and produced a more asymmetrical positional trajectory of the sledge with a slightly higher apex (not shown).

4 Discussion

The purpose of this study was to demonstrate how stable hopping can be generated in a robot leg: It demands to replace the lost energy. This can be performed in different ways. The common feature of the tested models was that the energy supply after midstance exceeded the energy supply before midstance.

Model 1 generated stable hopping pattern with the lowest activation difference between the two stance phases. The apex height was clearly dependent on Δs, the stimulation added upon the basic stimulation s_0 during stance2. Supply models 3 and 4, too, produced stable hopping with apex heights scaleable through gain changes. Supply model 3, applying quadratic stiffness change, achieved the highest apices. Model 4, governed by positive force feedback, achieved higher hopping frequencies than model 3, hence, the apex height was smaller in model 4.

The advantages of models 3 and 4 compared to model 1 are, that no measurements are necessary to determine the instant of midstance and the minimum height of the sledge. The hopping oscillations are completely selfpreserving. The movement patterns are simply determined by the gain in the feedback loop. The disadvantage of models 3 and 4 is that in stable hopping considerably higher activation values occur than in model 1, which may overdrive the amplifier respectively the muscle.

The outstanding feature of model 4 is that its built-in muscle-reflex mechanism, the positive force feedback, is capable of generating stable and scaleable hopping patterns even in a robot.

At last it should be noted that the limited ranges in gain parameters and hopping heights are likely due to the very high energy losses caused by the extremely high friction in the gear, and also due to the necessity to avoid overdriving the power amplifier.

Acknowledgments

This study was supported by grants SE1042/2 and KA417/24 of the German Research Foundation (DFG).

References

1. Geyer H, Seyfarth A, Blickhan R: Positive force feedback in bouncing gaits? Proc Roy Soc B **270**: 2173-2183, 2003

Advanced Swing Leg Control for Stable Locomotion

Yvonne Blum, Juergen Rummel and Andre Seyfarth

Locomotion Laboratory, University of Jena, Germany,
yvonne.blum@uni-jena.de,
www.lauflabor.de

Abstract. Locomotion can be described as a subsequent series of stance and flight phases. In both phases the leg properties can be adapted. Here we consider spring-mass running with a linear adaptation of two leg parameters, leg angle and leg stiffness, during swing phase. The region of stability is characterized by the basin of attraction with sufficient reduction of a given perturbation within one step.
The proposed swing-leg control predicts a substantial region of alternative swing leg adjustment rates. The resulting control redundancy includes different foot placement strategies which could be used to manage landing impacts and running stability in one consistent approach.

1 Introduction

Due to its simplicity and its explanatory power, the spring-mass model is an adequate mechanical template to describe bouncing gaits like running, jumping or hopping. Here, the complex structure of a human leg is simplified by a linear spring attached to a point mass representing the body's center of mass [1].

For given system energy steady state locomotion can be described based on three leg parameters: the angle of attack, the leg stiffness and the rest length of the leg. For proper adjustments of these parameters and speeds higher than 3.5 m/s self-stable locomotion is found [2]. Here we ask, to what extent the region of stable running can be enlarged (e.g. to include lower speeds) by adapting the leg parameters during swing phase. It has been previously shown that running at low speeds can be stabilized by employing leg retraction prior to contact [3].

In human and animal locomotion leg stiffness can be adjusted by the neuromuscular system. Similar adjustments of elastic properties have already been implemented in technical legs [4]. In the present study we propose a linear stiffness change of the leg during swing phase in addition to swing-leg retraction. For periodic running (satisfying constant apex heights of two subsequent flight phases) we consider combinations of constant leg stiffness and leg angle rates that guarantee stable locomotion over a large range of speeds. The identified combintions of both swing-leg control strategies can be used in legged robots based on compliant leg behavior.

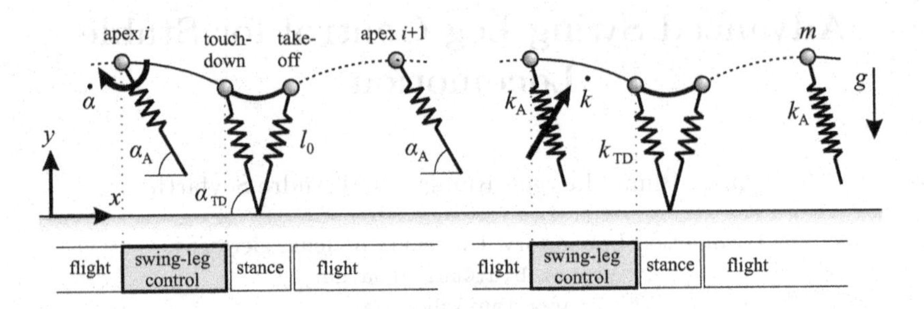

Fig. 1. The spring-mass model for running with two swing-leg control strategies: leg rotation (left) and stiffness adaptation of the leg spring (right).

2 Methods

Model: The planar spring-mass model is characterized by alternating flight and stance phases (Fig. 1). The body is represented as a point mass which is, during stance, influenced by gravity $\boldsymbol{g}$ and a force exerted by the leg spring (stiffness k_{TD}, rest length l_0) attached. The equation of motion is

$$m\ddot{\boldsymbol{r}} = k_{\mathrm{TD}} \left(\frac{l_0}{|\boldsymbol{r}|} - 1 \right) \boldsymbol{r} - m\boldsymbol{g}, \tag{1}$$

where $\boldsymbol{r} = (x, y)$ is the position of the center of mass. If the length of the massless spring reaches its rest length, the system changes into flight phase and describes a ballistic curve. Touch-down occurs if the landing condition $y \leq l_0 \sin(\alpha_{\mathrm{TD}})$ is satisfied. Since the system is conservative and the ground is even the systems state during flight can be fully described by the horizontal velocity v_{X} and the apex height y_{A}, which is the upper point where the vertical velocity v_{Y} equals zero. In this paper, we define the system energy $E = m\,g\,y_{\mathrm{A}} + m/2\; v_{\mathrm{X}}^2$ by choosing a reference velocity $v_{\mathrm{X,REF}}$ and an apex height of $y_{\mathrm{A}} = l_0$. The model parameters are mass $m = 80\,\mathrm{kg}$, leg length $l_0 = 1\,\mathrm{m}$, and gravitational acceleration $g = 9.81\,\mathrm{m/s^2}$.

System analysis: The running system can be analyzed using a return map of the state vector. A one-dimensional return map of two subsequent apex heights $y_{\mathrm{i+1}}(y_{\mathrm{i}})$ can be used to describe the system's stability. Periodic running requires a solution where $y_{\mathrm{i+1}} = y_{\mathrm{i}}$, indicating a fixed point y^* in the apex return map. Stability of the periodic movement can be identified using the slope s in the neighborhood of the fixed point

$$s = \left. \frac{dy_{\mathrm{i+1}}}{dy_{\mathrm{i}}} \right|_{y^*}, \tag{2}$$

where the condition $|s| < 1$ must be fulfilled. A zero slope indicates superstable running where small perturbations will be completely compensated after one step. A stable fixed point has a basin of attraction which is limited (i) by an apex-height y_{i+1} lower than the landing condition $l_0 \sin(\alpha)$, (ii) by potential energy $m\,g\,y_{\mathrm{i}}$ higher than the system energy E, and (iii) by a second fixed point.

To characterize how fast the system returns to the stable solution after perturation, we start the simulation at the perturbed apex $y_{\mathrm{i}} = y^* + y_{\mathrm{P}}$ (apex condition: $v_{\mathrm{Y}} = 0$), where y_{P} is a small deviation of magnitude 0.001 m and 0.05 m. The horizontal velocity v_{X} is adapted such that the system energy remains constant. Now the slope can be calculated approximately as the difference quotient $s = \left(y_{\mathrm{i+1}} - y^*\right)/y_{\mathrm{P}}$.

Control strategy: The swing-leg control, proposed here, intends to adapt the leg parameters leg angle α and leg stiffness k during the second half of flight phase, starting at the instant of apex t_{A}. The parameters will be adapted using constant rates of change $\dot{\alpha}$ and $\dot{k}$

$$\alpha(t) = \alpha_{\mathrm{A}} + \dot{\alpha} \cdot (t - t_{\mathrm{A}}) \tag{3}$$

$$k(t) = k_{\mathrm{A}} + \dot{k} \cdot (t - t_{\mathrm{A}}). \tag{4}$$

The parameters at apex α_{A} and k_{A} are chosen such that for given rates the touch-down values α_{TD} and k_{TD} equal the constant parameters of a previously found periodic solution $\alpha_{\mathrm{A}} = \alpha_{\mathrm{TD}} - \dot{\alpha} \cdot t_{\mathrm{F}}/2$ and $k_{\mathrm{A}} = k_{\mathrm{TD}} - \dot{k} \cdot t_{\mathrm{F}}/2$, respectively. The time $t_{\mathrm{F}}/2$ corresponds to the duration remaining from apex to touch-down obtained from the apex height y_{A} of the periodic solution $(t_{\mathrm{F}}/2)^2 = 2/g\,(y_{\mathrm{A}} - l_0 \sin\alpha_{\mathrm{TD}})$. The swing-leg control ends at touch-down and during stance the leg stiffness is constant k_{TD}.

3 Results

We first have to find steady state running for a given parameter set. The apex heights of periodic running are mapped for a constant leg stiffness k and a number of system energies E in Fig. 2(a), and for varying stiffness at one energy level in Fig. 2(b). Many solutions for cyclic running result for given energies or given leg stiffness. In both cases an adequate angle of attack can be found to achieve equal apex heights of two subsequent steps. With increasing leg angles a lower system energy (Fig. 2(a)) or a higher leg stiffness (Fig. 2(b)) is needed to achieve a periodic solution at the same apex height. It also becomes clear that, aiming at constant apex height, the duration of the flight phase lenghtens with leg softening (Fig. 2(b)).

To demonstrate results for the proposed swing-leg strategies, one solution of periodic running has been selected. We choose a reference velocity of 2.5 m/s and a leg stiffness of 20 kN/m, typically observed in human running [3]. Then we calculate the apex height and angle of attack such that the time $t_{\mathrm{F}}/2$ remaining from apex to touch-down is 50 ms (see Table 1). This solution is found to be unstable without control, with a slope s greater than one ($s = 1.69$).

Fig. 3 shows not only one but many combinations of stiffness change and retraction leading to superstable running ($s = 0$)) for small perturbations. Moreover, a linear relationship between both parameters is found. The control strategies $\dot{k}$ and $\dot{\alpha}$, are replaceable since a rate of stiffness change exists for zero leg

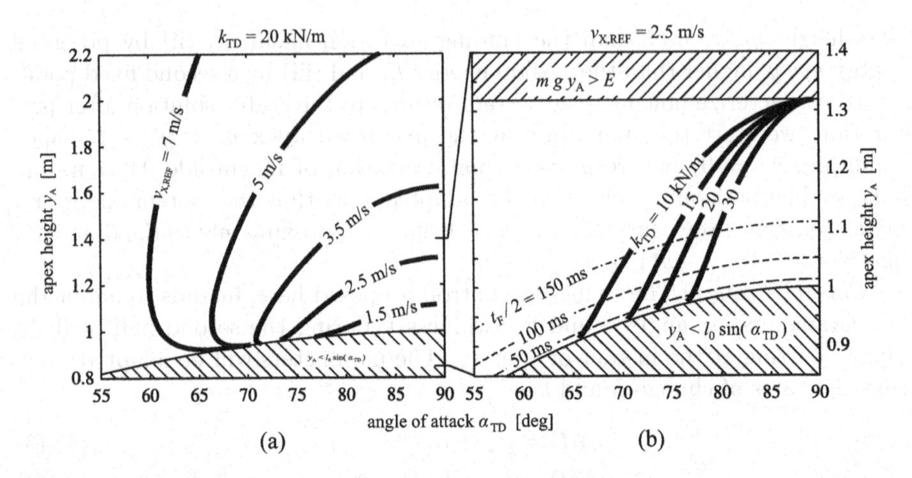

Fig. 2. Apex heights of steady state running solutions in the spring-mass model: (a) for constant leg stiffness k_{TD} and various system energies E (represented by reference velocities $v_{X,REF}$), and (b) for constant system energy E. Each point on the thick lines represents a fixed point in the apex return map. The thin lines in (b) show the apex height corresponding to the time $t_F/2$ remaining from apex to touch-down. During this time the advanced swing-leg control is applied.

rotation ($\dot{\alpha} = 0$) resulting in a superstable running pattern and vice versa. We call these values the optimal rate of stiffness change $\dot{k}_{OPT}$, respectively optimal speed of leg rotation $\dot{\alpha}_{OPT}$ (see Table 1 for numerical values).

Beside the optimal control, it is important to know how accurately the swing-leg control has to be tuned for adequate stabilization. Herefore, we demand the resultant slope to lie within $s = (-0.5, 0.5)$. Thus, a small perturbation will be at the worst bisected after one running step. Fig. 3 shows the resultant region of moderate control settings which lies left and right along the line for superstable control. This region linearly widens with increasing change of stiffness and increasing leg retraction speed. The width of the mentioned $s = (-0.5, 0.5)$ region is found to be relatively large (e.g. for $\dot{k} = \dot{k}_{OPT}/2$ the leg should retract with a speed $\dot{\alpha}$ between 19 and 79 deg/s). Hence, the swing-leg controller does not need to be specifically adjusted for stable running.

The swing-leg control is also tested for larger perturbations, $y_P = 0.05$ m (Fig. 3, dashed lines). For swing-leg retraction ($\dot{\alpha} > 0$) similar results compared to smaller perturbations can be observed, whereas for a protracting leg the regions of stabilization differ from each other. We examine this difference using the apex return maps shown in Fig. 4. The solutions (b), (c), and (d) are selected from the $s = 0$ line in Fig. 3 and generate a dead-beat control for small perturbations. The mappings (b) and (d) have a positive slope for higher apices and longe distance from the diagonal, originating from control settings with leg retraction. The mentioned properties of the return map are good to stabilize large dirsturbances as exemplary shown in the mapping (d) where a perturba-

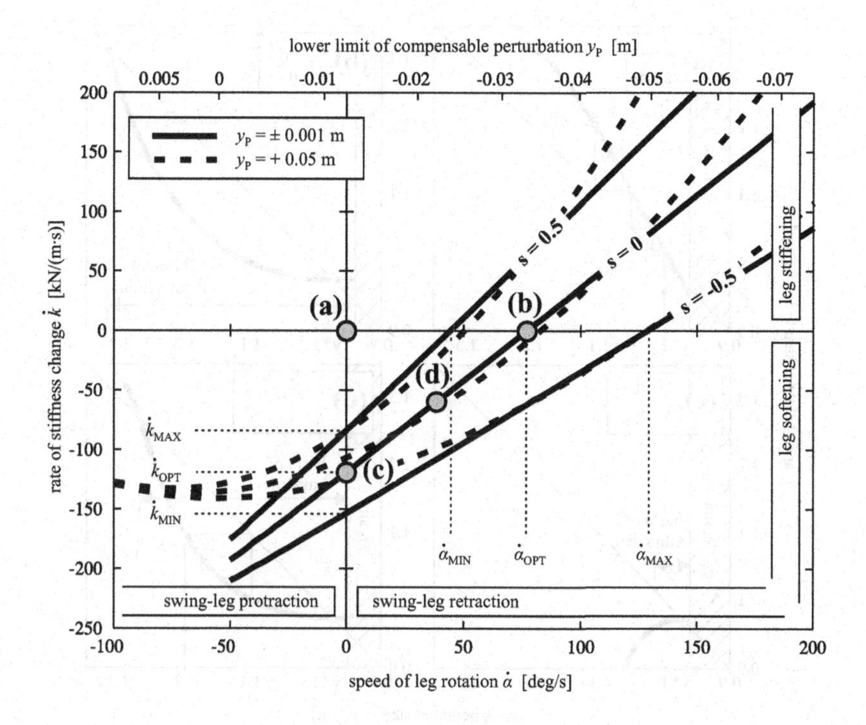

Fig. 3. Stability of one periodic running solution (first row in Table 1) dependent on swing-leg control $\dot{\alpha}$ and $\dot{k}$. The quality of stabilization is illustrated by the slope s near the fixed point in the apex return map for small perturbations (thick solid lines) and one larger disturbance (thick dashed lines). The top axis shows how large a negative perturbation can be, dependent on leg rotation $\dot{\alpha}$, such that the runner doesn't stumble.

tion of $y_P = 0.227$ m ($y_i = 1.2$ m) is compensated after three running steps. The control for optimal change of stiffness ($\dot{k} = \dot{k}_{OPT}$ and $\dot{\alpha} = 0$) generates a negative slope for larger perturbations and the system could stumble after one step. As shown in Fig. 4(c), the basin of attraction for compensating pertubations is very restricted compared to the solutions with leg retraction. Hence, for stabilizing larger perturbations the single swing-leg strategies are not exchangeable but a combination of both (d) produces advantageous stability in running. Furthermore, the basin of attraction shifts to greater negative values of perturbations with increasing retraction speed (see top axis in Fig. 3). Since the faster retraction starts with a smaller leg angle α_A the ground clearance increases and the stumble limit decreases to lower apices.

4 Discussion

In this paper, we proposed a conceptual method for stabilizing running and tested it with the spring-mass model. The method is divided into two parts,

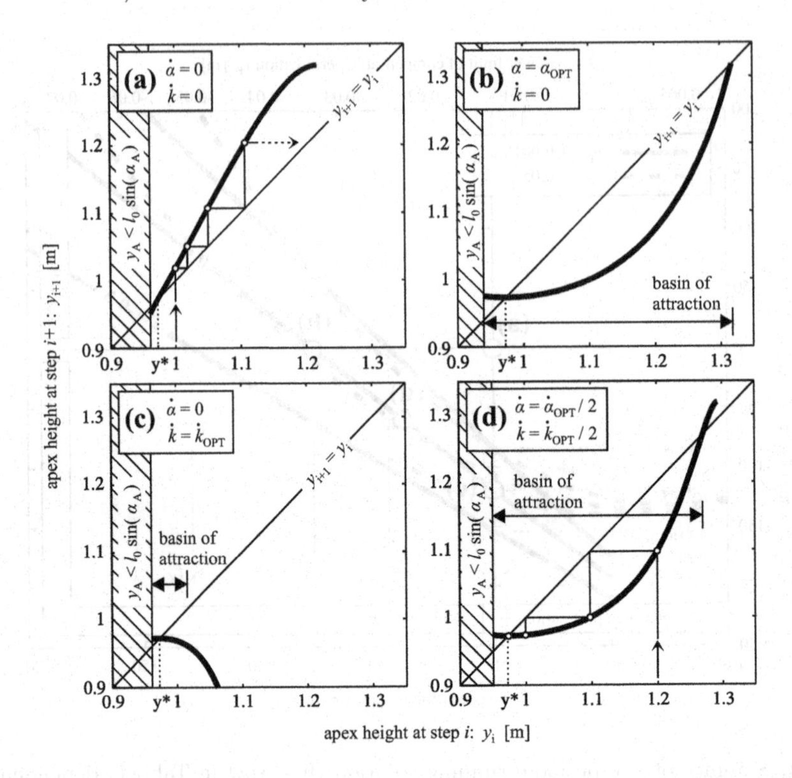

Fig. 4. Return maps of the apex height $y_{i+1}(y_i)$ for the same periodic running solution (first row in Table 1) and some swing-leg strategies. The graphs correspond to the parameter combinations selected in Fig. 3.

the swing-leg retraction and the stiffness adaptation, which are both suffient for stabilization of existing periodic running solutions. We have shown that the leg retraction is not a unique method while it seems to be essential for successful legged locomotion [6]. However, in experiments on human running [5] a mean retraction speed of $\dot{\alpha} = 44\,\text{deg/s}$ has been measured which is much lower than the model predicted values for optimal stabilization ($\dot{\alpha}_{OPT} = 77 - 104\,\text{deg/s}$) at related conditions. This let us assume that further control strategies are used to improve locomotion. The change of leg stiffness during flight could be one of them where a dead-beat control can be observed for small perturbations. Although, the stiffness adaptation alone is largely limited in compensating disturbances, in a combined control it might help to reduce the required rotational speed (Fig. 3). Assuming a non-massless leg, the running system could then be stabilized with a lower amount of forces and probably higher energy efficiency.

The proposed control strategy intends to adapt the leg stiffness during flight with the leg becoming softer with increasing flight time. However, the stiffness adaptation, respectively the leg softening, could also be done during stance phase. This possibility was discovered in segmented legs as passive built-in mechanism resulting in improved stability compared to the spring-mass model [7].

Table 1. Selected periodic running solutions and parameters for optimal swing-leg control and limitations. The last row contains human data [5].

properties of the periodic solution					swing-leg control					
$v_{X,REF}$ [m/s]	$t_F/2$ [ms]	y_A [m]	k_{TD} [kN/m]	α_{TD} [deg]	$\dot{\alpha}_{MIN}$	$\dot{\alpha}_{OPT}$ [deg/s]	$\dot{\alpha}_{MAX}$	$\dot{k}_{MIN}$	$\dot{k}_{OPT}$ [kN/(m·s)]	$\dot{k}_{MAX}$
2.5	50	0.973	20	73.8	44	77	129	-154	-119	-84
2.5	100	1.015	20	75.1	62	104	159	-249	-191	-132
5.0	50	0.940	20	68.1	-24	-9	22	-17	11	39
5.0	100	0.968	20	66.8	2	27	60	-67	-35	-3
2.7	23	1.017	25	73.7	9	44	79		n/a	

The here investigated model is limited in compensating negative perturbations, respectively running a step upward (Fig. 4). If a running system has to deal with very uneven ground it could choose a periodic solution with a higher apex enhancing the ground clearance. However, since the rate of changes of the leg parameters need to be higher (Table 1), this option might be disadvantagous. Another possibility for successful running on largely uneven ground was experimentally observed as the adaption of leg length [8,9]. Taken into account that the nominal length of a segmented leg is an easy changeable parameter, a length adjustment of the leg could also enhance running stability. Investigations on this topic remain for future studies to further advance the swing-leg control.

Acknowledgements

This study is supported by the German Research Foundation (DFG, SE1042).

References

1. Blickhan R: The Spring-mass Model for Running and Hopping. J Biomech 22: 1217-1227, 1989
2. Seyfarth A, Geyer H, Guenther M, Blickhan R: A Movement Criterion for Running. J Biomech, 35: 649-655, 2002
3. Seyfarth A, Geyer H, Herr H: Swing-leg Retraction: a Simple Control Model for Stable Running. J Exp Biol 206: 2547-2555, 2003
4. Van Ham R, Vanderborght B, Van Damme M, et al.: MACCEPA: The Actuator with Adaptable Compliance for Dynamic Walking Bipeds. CLAWAR, 2005
5. Lipfert S, Seyfarth A: How similar are walking and running? (in prep.)
6. Herr HM, McMahon TA: A Galloping Horse Model. Int J Robot Res 20: 26-37, 2001
7. Rummel J, Seyfarth A: Stable Running with Segmented Legs. Int J Robot Res (submitted)
8. Blickhan R, Seyfarth A, Geyer H, et al.: Intelligence by Mechanics. Phil Trans R Soc A 365: 199-220, 2007
9. Daley MA, Felix G, Biewener AA: Running Stability Is Enhanced by a Proximo-distal Gradient in Joint Neuromechanical Control. J Exp Biol 210: 383-394, 2007

Learning the Inverse Model of the Dynamics of a Robot Leg by Auto-imitation

Karl Theodor Kalveram[1,2] and Andre Seyfarth[1]

[1] Locomotion Laboratory, University of Jena, Germany
[2] Institute of Experimental Psychology, University of Duesseldorf, Germany
kalveram@uni-duesseldorf.de,
www.lauflabor.de

Abstract. Walking, running and hopping are based on self-stabilizing oscillatory activity. In contrast, aiming movements serve to direct a limb to a desired location and demand a quite different manner of control which also includes learning the physical parameters of that limb. The paper is concerned with the question how reaching a goal can be integrated into locomotion. A prerequisite of piecing together both types of control is the acquisition of a model of the limb's inverse dynamics. To test whether auto-imitation, a biologically inspired learning algorithm, can solve this problem, we build a motor driven device with a two-segmented arm. A preliminary study revealed that at least the forearm - with the upper arm fixed - can be made controllable by this method we called "auto-imitatively adaptable inverse control".

1 Introduction

Walking, running and hopping can be traced back to self-stability [1] and thus do not require a sophisticated online controller, that is to say, do not demand to prescribe desired trajectories to the joints and to enforce the organism or the machine to keep these trajectories using negative feedback and/or feedforward control. Rather, locomotion movements emerge from the physical design of the respective limbs, especially from the geometry of the limb segments aided by spring-like properties of muscles, from rhythmic ground contacts and from simple muscular incitements, all together making the leg a self-stabilizing oscillator [2].

In contrast, a goal oriented movement directs a limb to an intention-determined location where a contact with the environment shall happen in the near future. As illustrated in Fig. 1 also such goal directed movements can be applied to legged locomotion, for instance to place the foot only on those locations where a ground contact is appropriate or safe. Like a freely swinging arm, a leg must also perform a goal directed movement in the swing phase.

This suggests that findings related, for instance, to the control of aiming in arm movements are also relevant for the control of legs. It is likely that in contrast to pure locomotion, aiming requires on-line control: There exists experimental evidence that humans control goal directed forearm movements in a feedforward

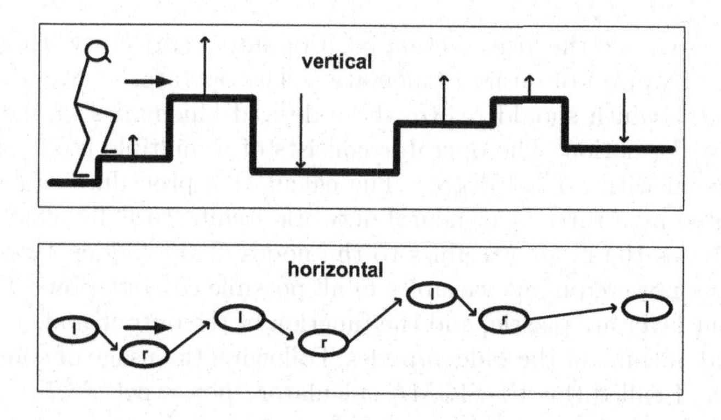

Fig. 1. Targets to be hit by a foot during walking or running.

manner through an inverse model of the arm's dynamics, assisted by low gain negative feedback seemingly exerted by a mechanical spring [3].

In the following, it will be illustrated what is meant by these two basic types of control, how we modeled them in Simulink, how we implemented auto-imitation, a learning algorithm to acquire the inverse model, how we extended the auto-imitation approach to achieve online learning, and how we tested the concept by hardware. The direction for future research will also be given. The reader, however, should take in mind that we are not interested in building running and walking robots, rather, that we engage in using robots to reveal principles of human movement control.

2 Theory

Fig. 2 illustrates the problem to be solved in goal directed movements using a one-segmented arm, and referring to the engineer's notations of inverse control [4] and/or computed torque [5]. A known torque Q applied about the joint predictably moves the arm by an angle φ. Regarding the feedforward control of movement, however, the concern is inversely oriented: Now an angular goal φ is given first. To reach this goal, a desired angular trajectory leading from the actual angular position to the desired goal position has to be planned.

From this trajectory the torque trajectory has to be computed which, when applied, realizes the desired angular trajectory and, finally, also the desired goal position [6]. Obviously, the torque computation includes the arm's inertia, the gravitational torque which varies sinusoidally with the angle φ, as well as damping and friction. To diminish the effects of unforeseen external perturbations, negative positional feedback control can be added. The template for Simulink is given in Fig. 3 which merges several points of view into one drawing.

To begin with: the system to be controlled is given by the arm's tool transformation which includes the dynamics and kinematics of the arm. Feedforward control is exerted by the arm's inverse model, referred to as operator. The input of the operator is provided by the pattern generator which turns the distance between the goal and the arm's actual position into a trajectory (that is, a temporal series of values) of desired kinematics. The operator's output is a torque trajectory Q_{ff} which should realize these desired kinematics at the output of the tool transformation. The operator consists of a multiple input/ single output polynomial with a fixed degree. The calculation procedure can graphically be represented by a three layer neural network architecture, by which the input layer distributes the input variables to the nodes of the hidden layer, which in turn multiply powered input variables in all possible combinations. The weights of the output layer are plastic, and the function of the output node is to sum up the weighted outputs of the hidden nodes. Following the usage of computational neuroscience, I called this PI/SIGMA calculator "power net" [6,7].

The training of the operator power net, that is, the determination of its weights in such a manner that the network's output meets the target values to the best possible degree, is performed online in the auto-imitation loop, where a copy of the power net, called the learner, is located. Here, the learner power net correlates the actual kinematics, measured peripherally and entering the regular inputs, with the torques actually exerted to the arm and entering the teaching input. This results in weights which can immediately be "mirrored" to the operator. So the operator, which does not actively participate in the learning process, can continuously be updated by its twin which is capable of learning, but unable to operate the arm [8]. Thus, the operator-learner design overcomes the serious drawbacks of a temporal disjunction between learning and operating, and the necessity of greatly rewiring the network after completion of learning, both inherent in the approach of "direct inverse modeling" [9]. Assistive negative feedback control is assumed to be realized exclusively mechanically [3], that is, without a temporal delay, a further difference to currently propagated controllers

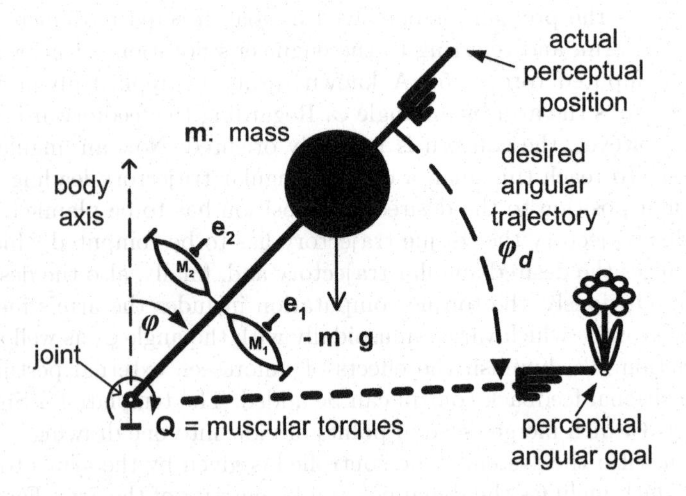

Fig. 2. A one-segmented arm performing a goal directed movement, driven by an antagonistic pair of muscles M1 and M2. See text for more information.

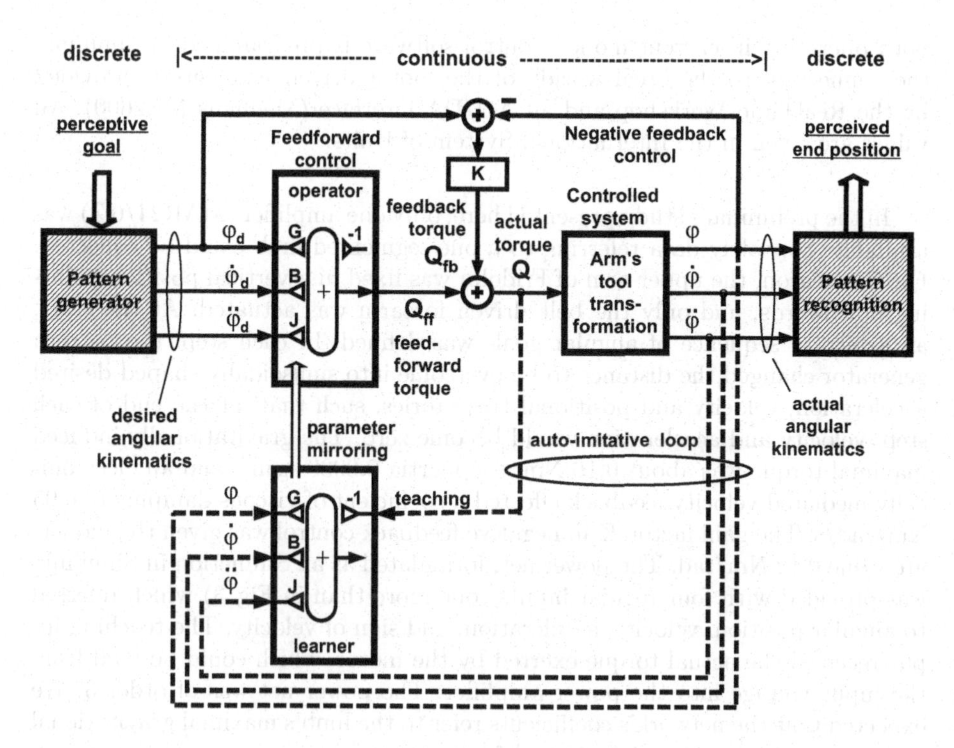

Fig. 3. Auto-imitatively adapting inverse control, assisted by negative feedback control, and provided with separated operating and learning. The structures lined in the operator and learner indicate artificial neural networks of the same architecture. See text for more information.

[10,11,12]. This allows the application of high loop gains K without loss of stability. If well adapted, the proposed control scheme allows the reaching of desired angular positions precisely, and to react to unforeseen external perturbations in a highly elastic and stable fashion. The concept, auto-imitation included, has been verified using a simulated arm with one and two segments [6,13].

3 Experiment

The purpose of the present paper is to demonstrate that the concept of auto-imitative adaptive inverse control is applicable also to a hardware robot limb. The device constructed for this purpose is called Fridolin and is sketched in Fig. 4: Two flat brushed ironless DC motors (Mattke GDM 12 Z) are mounted opposite of one another. One motor drives the "upper arm" directly, the other the "forearm" via a belt. Each motor bears a tachometer (Mattke T 50) fixed on its shaft. Angular position is computed by integration, and angular acceleration is calculated by taking the derivative of the tachometer's output. The motors are operated by analogue power amplifiers (Mattke MAR24/6 Z and MAR24/12 ZE) both operating in current mode. Control software is programmed in Simulink, the connection to the "real world" of the motor driven segments is provided by the RealTime Workshop and an AD/DA interface (Meilhaus ME2600). All values are given in the International System of Units.

In the preliminary study presented here, only one amplifier (MAR24/6 Z) was available. So, solely data referring to a one-segmented limb could be collected. For this reason, the upper arm of Fridolin was fixed in a vertical position pointing downwards, and only the belt driven forearm was actuated. At the start, an arbitrary sequence of angular goals was defined. In each step, the pattern generator changed the distance to be overcome into sinusoidally shaped desired acceleration, velocity and positional trajectories, such that, at the end of each step, velocity and acceleration would become zero. The gravitationally induced maximal torque was about 0.16 Nm, the inertia 0.0039 kg m^2, and an electronically mediated velocity feedback effected a coefficient of viscous damping of 0.05 Nm/rad/s. The gain factor K in negative feedback control was given the moderate value 0.12 Nm/rad. The power net, formulated as an S-function in Simulink, was provided with four regular inputs (one more than in Fig. 3) which referred to angular position, velocity, acceleration, and sign of velocity. The teaching input received the actual torque exerted by the motor, which could be read from the input voltage into the power amplifier. The power net was of order 3. We expected that the network's coefficients refer to the limb's maximal gravitational torque, viscous damping, inertia and friction.

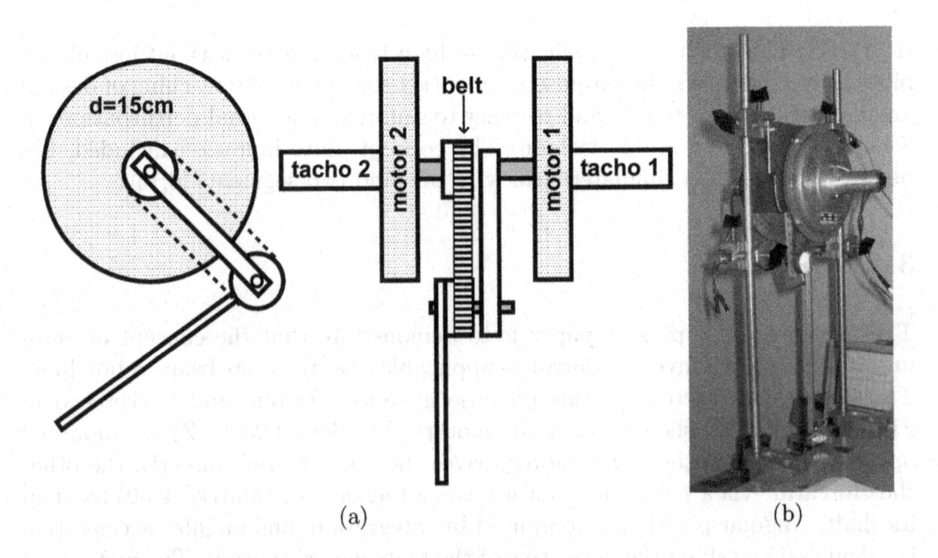

Fig. 4. (a) schematic and (b) photograph of the Fridolin Reacher.

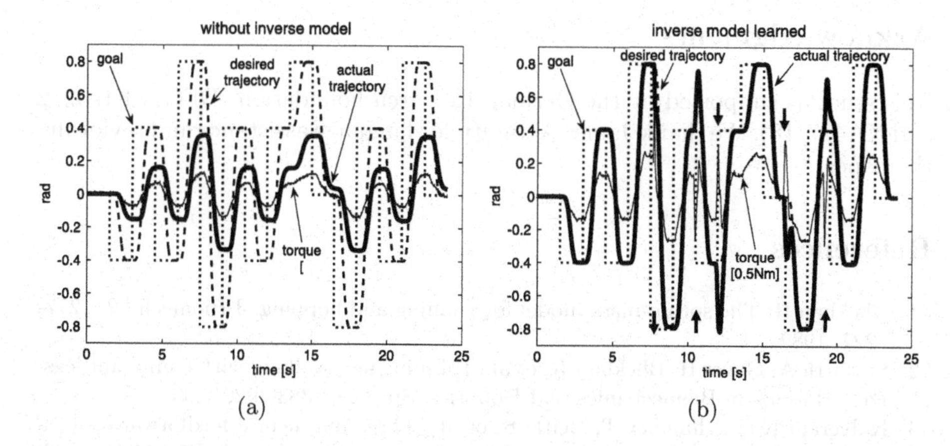

Fig. 5. Auto-imitative learning of the inverse model of the dynamics of a swinging robot leg. (a) Prior to learning, with negative feedback control only. (b) After 50 steps with auto-imitation. The arrows indicate short perturbation impulses. See text for more information.

4 Results

Before auto-imitation was switched on, the actual angular trajectory tracked the desired trajectory poorly (Fig. 5(a)). After auto-imitation was enabled, tracking performance quickly improved. A nearly perfect congruence of both trajectories was achieved after presenting a sequence of 50 goals to the controller (Fig. 5(b)). Now the power net had reached a set of coefficients which enabled the controller to quickly iron out even heavy disturbing impulses (marked by the vertical arrows).

5 Discussion

Hypotheses about how organisms control their actions are difficult to test. At first, an approach should be subject to a simulation test, which will uncover logical and conceptual faults. Next the hypothesis should undergo the hardware test, the only way to recognize whether real world conditions have been overlooked which are important for an effective functioning of the system under consideration. At last the so called behavioral matching test should be applied. In this test, the effects of perturbations administered to the simulated and the organismic system are compared. The more these effects resemble each other, the higher is the probability that the conceived manner of control is applied in the organism. The Jena Walker [2], the Marco Hopper [14] and the Fridolin Reacher (introduced this paper) are the hardware stages in this verifying process.

Obviously, reaching a goal and rhythmic locomotion are quite differently controlled. Further research is necessary to gain insight into how both types of control can co-operate to achieve locomotion behavior which is also capable of reaching goals.

Acknowledgments

This study is supported by the German Research Foundation (DFG, SE1042/2 and KA417/18). We thank James A. Smith for language assistance and reviewing the paper.

References

1. Blickhan R: The spring-mass model for running and hopping. J Biomech 22: 1217-1227, 1989
2. Seyfarth A, Geyer H, Blickhan R, et al.: Running and walking with compliant legs. Fast Motions in Biomechanics and Robotics, Springer: 383-402, 2006
3. Kalveram KT, Schinauer T, Beirle S, et al.: Threading neural feedforward into a mechanical spring: How biology exploits physics in limb control. Biol Cybern 92: 229-240, 2005
4. Widrow B, Walach E: Adaptive inverse control. Prentice-Hall: 1996
5. Sciavicco L, Siciliano B: Modelling and control of robot manipulators. Springer: 1996
6. Kalveram KT: A neural network model rapidly learning gains of reflexes necessary to adapt to an arm's dynamics. Biol Cybern 68: 183-191, 1992
7. Kalveram KT: Power series and neural-net computing. Neurocomputation 5: 165-174, 1993
8. Kalveram KT: The Inverse Problem in Cognitive, Perceptual and Proprioceptive Control of Sensorimotor Behaviour (Towards a Biologically Plausible Model of the Control of Aiming Movements). Int J Sport Exercise Psychol 2: 255-273, 2004
9. Jordan L: Supervised learning and systems with excess degrees of freedom. COINS Technical Report 88-27: 1-41, 1988
10. Wolpert DM, Ghahramani Z, Jordan MI: An internal model for sensorimotor integration. Science 269: 1880-1882, 1995
11. Miall RC, Wolpert DM: Forward models for physiological motor control. Neural Netw 9: 1265-1279, 1996
12. Sabes PN: The planning and control of reaching movements. Curr Opin Neurobiol 10: 740-746, 2000
13. Kalveram KT: Sensorimotor sequential learning by a neural network based on redefined Hebbian Learning. Artificial Neural Networks in Medicine and Biology, Springer: 271-276, 2000
14. Seyfarth A, Kalveram KT, Geyer H: Simulating Muscle-Reflex Dynamics in a simple Hopping Robot. this issue

A Mobile Service Robot for Life Science Laboratories

Erik Schulenburg, Norbert Elkmann, Markus Fritzsche and Christian Teutsch

Fraunhofer Institute for Factory Operation and Automation,
Sandtorstrasse 22, 39106 Magdeburg, Germany,
<firstname>.<lastname>@iff.fraunhofer.de

Abstract. In this paper we presents a project that is developing a mobile service robot to assist users in biological and pharmaceutical laboratories by executing routine jobs such as filling and transporting microplates. A preliminary overview of the design of the mobile platform with a robotic arm is provided. Safety aspects are one focus of the project since the robot and humans will share a common environment. Hence, several safety sensors such as laser scanners, thermographic components and artificial skin are employed. These are described along with the approaches to object recognition.

1 Motivation

Biological and pharmaceutical research entails a great deal of repetitive manual work, e.g. when preparing experiments or loading equipment such as drying chambers and centrifuges. Classical automation interconnects such units with band conveyors or indexing tables. The basic idea behind the Life Science Assistant (LiSA) is to interconnect equipment with a mobile service robot, thus making automated experiment cycles flexible, while allowing stations to be used simultaneously for other purposes. In addition, the robot will help lab technicians prepare experiments, e.g. by collaboratively executing transportation tasks or filling microplates. The LiSA project is constructing a demonstrator that executes the aforementioned tasks.

Safety aspects, only treated marginally in similar projects [1], are one focus of the project. Since robots and humans share a common environment, safety is an important issue in service robotics. It assumes even greater importance in the life sciences because a robot may handle toxic or hazardous substances.

Figure 1 presents a design study of the particular robot currently under development. The development work will converge in the construction and testing of the final service robot by March 2009.

2 Project Overview

Development of the LiSA robot incorporates different objectives. First of all, a mobile platform with a custom-build robotic arm has been designed (see Fig-

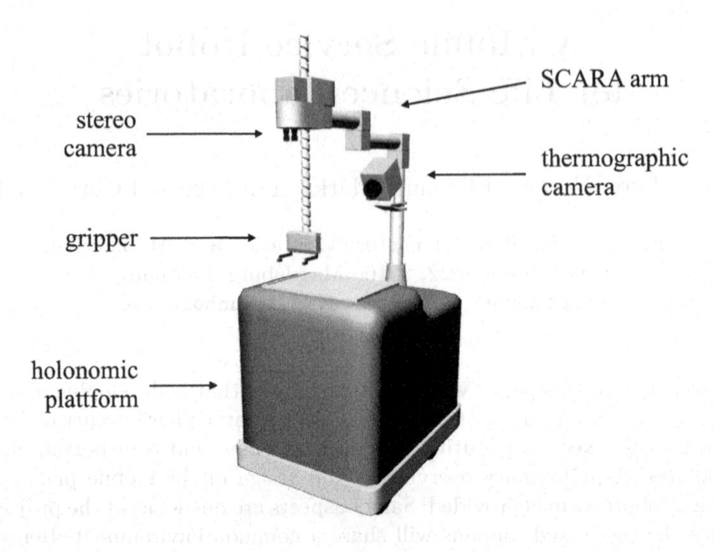

Fig. 1. LiSA platform design study.

ure 1). The platform is equipped with a holonomic drive to provide the high maneuverability needed to navigate in a cramped laboratory environment. Two SICK s300 laser scanners are mounted at opposite corners of the platform. The scanners' 270° field of view generates a 360° field of permanent 2-D view. This is used together with a gyroscope and wheel encoders for Markov localization in an a-priori map.

Since the robotic arm basically performs pick-and-place operations, a classical SCARA design with a two-finger gripper was selected. The robotic arm is able to operate to the left or right of the mobile platform. It is equipped with a stereo camera system for object recognition and camera-guided movement, the approaches to which are described in section 4. Additionally, a combined camera device delivers images in the visible as well as the infrared spectrum. It is mounted on a rotating stage at the base of the robotic arm and moves in concert with the arm. This camera is utilized to roughly localize objects and to detect human interaction in front of the gripper. This is just one of many components that assure interaction with the LiSA service robot is safe. Further safety aspects are described in section 3.

Intuitive multimodal interaction is another objective of the LiSA project. To this end, a commercial dialog engine is employed, which supports mixed-initiative, natural language dialogs and conversation in full sentences. It has been upgraded for simultaneous input through a touch-sensitive graphical user interface. This permits combining touchpad input and speech signals in a single statement, e.g. by combining the sentence "Take the sample from this point to that point" with two touchpad input events on the map of the laboratory.

3 Safety

Since robots and humans share a common environment and actually cooperate, safety is an important aspect of service robotics. Current standards, e.g. EN ISO 13849 (Safety of machinery), primarily target the industrial sector and are inappropriate for mobile robot assistants. A first approach to provide general principles for the design of human-machine interaction systems has been done with EN ISO 10218-1. The ensuring basic requirements are:

- Maximum speed of tool center point (TCP) of 250 mm/s,
- Maximum effective force of 150 N,
- Reduced power of 80 W,
- Survey of the TCP position, ensuring safe distance to humans and
- Immediate stop if humans enter the robot's workspace.

Approaches to safety conformable design of robot assistants include passively compliant systems and actively monitoring sensors [2].

The LiSA project has employed several safeguards to protect humans and the environment. Along with the safety scanners (SICK s300) and classical bumpers around its bottom edges, the platform is equipped with four additional laser scanners (Hokuyo URG-04LX). These scanners are mounted at the bottom of each of the robots' sides and angled upward, creating a protective funnel utilzed for 3-D obstacle avoidance. A violation of a scanner's protective field will cause the platform to slow down or stop immediatety.

The slow moving robotic arm is also equipped with multiple safety features. Torque measurement and contouring error control are integrated in the joints for collision detection and the manipulator is covered by a pressure-sensitive artificial skin that also provides information on the location of a collision. The manipulator itself is padded to prevent injuries.

The gripper ist additionally monitored by a thermographic camera to detect humans through their body heat. Figure 2(a) presents a sample image from the thermographic camera.

4 Object Recognition

Optical sensors identify and recognize the exchange positions and the microplates. To reliably position the gripper vis-à-vis objects being picked up, two digital cameras sample the immediate environment. Their lenses enable capturing an area of about $400 \times 300\, mm$. By using subpixel interpolations, a resolution of ca. $9\, pixels/mm^2$ is produced, which is sufficient to determine the necessary positions with the accuracy required.

The detection of the microplates at the exchange positions is based on a fast and adaptive segmentation approach. In the first step, a histogram is computed. As proposed by Rosin [3], the histogram value at the half between the minimum and the maximum is taken as the binarization threshold. The segmented result represents the area of the microplates. In subsequent steps, the border is calculated in an 8-neighborhood. The rotating calipers method is used to obtain the smallest bounding rectangle from the extracted contour. This rectangle's orientation defines the orientation of the microplate's orientation (see Figure 2(b)).

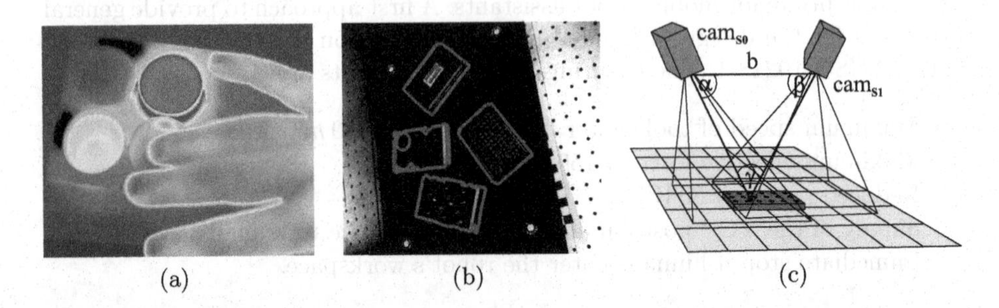

Fig. 2. Components of LiSA's optical system. A thermographic component for detecting human interaction (a), a camera component for 2-D position tracking (b) and a stereoscopic sensor for 3-D sampling (c).

The determination of exact 3-D position and orientation is based on a photogrammetric approach and uses both digital cameras. Their positions and orientations are predetermined in a prior calibration step [4]. The triangulation principle serves as the basis for calculating the relative 3-D coordinates of objects visible to both cameras (see Figure 2(c)). Corresponding pixel pairs are identified by a statistical correlation between image segments on the epipolar lines [5]. The small base distance b of 150 mm necessitates aligning the camera's perspective to attain sufficiently high precision ($< 0.5\,mm$) in the stereo-vision approach based on triangulation. When the robotic arm moves, the algorithms not only track the 2-D position of microplates but also take 3-D samples of an object's surface. The resultant height data supports algorithms that detect plates on top of one another.

References

1. Scherer T., Poggendorf I., Schneider A., et al.: A service robot for automating the sample management in biotechnological cell cultivations. Proc. Emerging Technologies and Factory Automation (ETFA'03), Vol. 2: 383–390, 2003
2. Hägele M., Schaaf W., Helms E.: Robot assistants at manual workplaces: Effective co-operation and safety aspects. Proc. of the 33rd International Symposium on Robotics 2002 / CD-ROM: Proceedings (ISR 2002), Stockholm, Schweden, 2002
3. Rosin P.L.: Unimodal thresholding. Pattern Recognition 34(11): 2083–2096, 2001
4. Zhang Z.: A flexible new technique for camera calibration. IEEE Transactions on Pattern Analysis and Machine Intelligence, 22(11):1330–1334, 2000
5. Shi J., Tomasi, C.: Good features to track. Proc. Computer Vision and Pattern Recognition (CVPR'94): 593–600, 1994

Sensorsonden für Sicherheits- und Bewachungsroboter
Eine experimentelle Untersuchung

Kai Pfeiffer, Gernot Gebhard und Susanne Oberer

Fraunhofer IPA, Abteilung Robotersysteme, Nobelstr. 12, 70565 Stuttgart
kai.pfeiffer@ipa.fraunhofer.de

1 Einleitung

Die mobile Robotik hält immer mehr Einzug in Aufgabengebiete, die bisher aufgrund von räumlichen oder bewegungstechnischen Aspekten ausschließlich menschlichem Personal vorbehalten waren. Der klassische Objekt- oder Anlagenschutz ist eines dieser Aufgabengebiete. In diesem Bereich ist man aber bisher nicht alleine auf den Menschen angewiesen. Es wird vielmehr ein hybrides Konzept aus flexiblem Wachpersonal und statischen Sensoren wie Kameras oder Rauchmeldern eingesetzt. Durch die Festinstallation von Kameras und anderen Sensoren wird eine zeitgleiche und zuverlässige Überwachung eines großen Areals ermöglicht. Das Wachpersonal übernimmt mit Rundgängen nicht nur die Überwachung des verbleibenden Areals, sondern bringt durch seine Sinne auch zusätzliche Sensoren ein und überprüft Meldungen des Überwachungssystems. Momentan erhältliche Überwachungsroboter können nur die beschriebenen Funktionen des Wachpersonals übernehmen. Eine dauerhafte, flächendeckende Überwachung wie bei einem fest installierten System ist die nächste Stufe, die mit mobilen Sicherheitsrobotern erreicht werden soll. Bei Erreichen dieser Stufe könnten unter anderem autonome Sensorsonden, welche in [1] ausführlich beschrieben werden, zum Einsatz kommen. Im Folgenden werden zunächst die Anforderungen für die Verwendung von Sensorsonden skizziert und anschließend eine erste Integration von Sonden in die Hardware eines mobilen Sicherheitsroboters vorgestellt. Anschließend werden die Anforderungen an Strategien zur optimalen Ausbringung von Sonden je nach Aufgabenstellung aufgezeigt. Abschließend werden im Ausblick mögliche Ansätze für Ausbringstrategien angeführt.

2 Anforderungen und erste Integration

2.1 Anforderungen

Aus der Sicht der Anwender von mobilen Sicherheitsrobotern stellen sich gewisse Anforderungen an den Einsatz von Sensorsonden, die sich wie folgt darstellen:

– *Plug&Play:* Die mechanischen wie elektrischen Komponenten, die zur Verwendung von Sensorsonden benötigt werden, sollen sich möglichst einfach in bestehende Sicherheitsroboter integrieren lassen.

- *Beliebig Konfigurierbar:* Es sollen sich die Sonden mit beliebigen Sensoren bestücken und der Roboter mit beliebigen Sonden ausrüsten lassen.
- *Kreuzweise Verwendung:* Es soll möglich sein, dass Sonden, die ein Roboter ausgebracht hat, von einem anderen wieder aufgesammelt werden. Dies kann soweit gehen, dass ein Roboter sich Sonden von einem Ort holt, um sie an anderer, wichtigerer Stelle wieder auszubringen.
- *Einfach Skalierbar:* Der Roboter soll in die Lage versetzt werden, auf eine beliebige Anzahl von Sonden zurückgreifen zu können.
- *Robust:* Sensorsonden die bei der kleinsten Vibration ausfallen stellen keinen Mehrwert dar. Die Sonden müssen in ihrem Einsatz verlässlich sein.
- *Outdoortauglich:* Da sich Überwachungsaufgaben auch auf den Außenbereich erstrecken, sollen Sensorsonden für diesen Einsatz geeignet sein. Es muß zumindest auch outdoortaugliche Sonden geben.

Um Sensorsonden einzusetzen, muss ein Sicherheitsroboter über eine Ausbringeinheit verfügen, die die Sonden transportiert und für den Einsatz bereithält.

2.2 Umsetzung

Auf Grundlage von identifizierten Anforderungen wurde eine erste Magazineinheit konstruiert, die in Abb.1 dargestellt ist. Diese Magazineinheit ist in der Lage sechs Sensorsonden in einzelnen Magazinplätzen eines drehbaren Magazins zu verwahren, diese einzeln auszubringen und wieder aufzunehmen. Damit die einzelnen Sonden voneinander unterscheidbar sind, verfügt die Magazineinheit über eine Leseeinheit mit der RFID-Markierungen der einzelnen Sonden beim Drehen des Magazins gelesen werden können. Zur korrekten Ausrichtung der Sonde nach dem Wiederaufnehmen bzw. vor dem Auslegen interagieren in der vorliegenden Magazineinheit die Zentriereinheit der Sonde, der Federrahmen in jedem Magazinplatz und das drehbare Magazin.

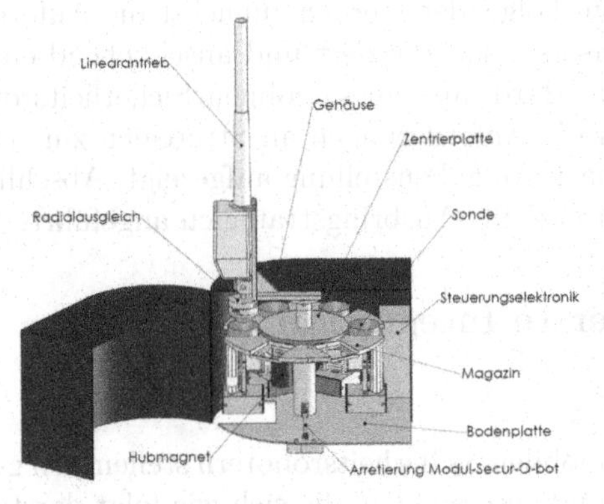

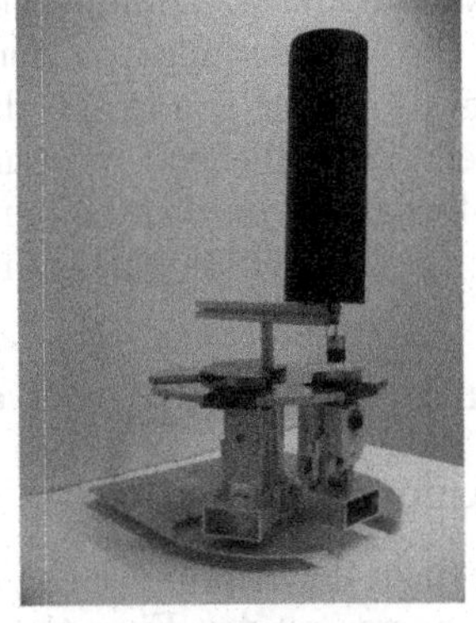

Abb. 1. Prototyp einer Magazineinheit für Sensorsonden

Eine weitere identifizierte Forderung an eine Magazineinheit ist die leichte Nachrüst- und Austauschbarkeit. In vorliegendem Fall wurde die Einheit derart gestaltet, dass sie auf der Oberseite des vorhandenen Roboters über eine Kombination aus mechanischer und elektrischer Steckverbindung angebracht werden und durch einen Schnellverschluss leicht wieder demontiert werden kann. Die elektrische Schnittstelle beschränkt sich auf die Energieversorgung und eine Ethernet Verbindung zur Ansteuerung des Magazins durch den mobilen Roboter.

3 Ausbringstrategien

Wie bei der Installation von statischen Überwachungssensoren ist bei der Ausbringung von Sonden die Auswahl der Sensoren und die Sondenpositionierung von entscheidender Bedeutung. So können für sensiblere Bereiche höherwertige Sensoren zum Einsatz kommen als für Bereiche die unkritischer sind. Darüber hinaus hat die Sensorauswahl wieder Einfluss auf die Positionierung. Wenn nur wenige hochwertige Sensoren zur Verfügung stehen, so müssen diese derart positioniert werden, dass sie den besten Wirkungsgrad erreichen. Dies betrifft häufig die Flächen- beziehungsweise Raumdeckung.
Grundsätzlich hängt eine Ausbringstrategie vom Einsatzszenario ab. Da autonome Sensorsonden nach [1] grundsätzlich zwei Funktionen erfüllen können, nämlich die Vergrößerung des zeitgleich überwachten Areals und die Vergrößerung des Kommunikationsnetzes, müssen die Einsatzszenarien auch gemäß dieser beider Funktionen unterteilt werden. Folgende Hauptszenarien lassen sich für die Vergrößerung des Überwachungsareals unterscheiden:

- *100-prozentige Abdeckung:* Der zu überwachende Bereich soll zu 100 Prozent durch eine ausreichende Anzahl verfügbarer Sonden abgedeckt werden.
- *X-prozentige Abdeckung:* Ein definierter Anteil des Bereiches soll mit einer ausreichende Anzahl an Sonden überwacht werden.
- *Maximale Abdeckung bei n Sonden:* Eine festgelegte Anzahl von Sonden soll beliebig zur maximalen Abdeckung eingesetzt werden.
- *Bestes Sonden- / Deckungsverhältnis:* Es soll die beste Nutzung der Sonden zur Überwachung eines Bereiches ermittelt werden. Es kann sinnvoll sein, wenn man mit 5 Prozent weniger Abdeckung eine Sonde für andere Aufgaben einsparen kann.

Für die drei letzten Hauptszenarien sind folgende Erweiterungen denkbar:

- *Priorisierung von Bereichen:* Einigen besonders empfindlichen Bereichen, wie zum Beispiel Eingängen oder Flurkreuzungen, sollte eine höhere Überwachungspriorität zuteilbar sein.
- *Feste Sondenpositionen:* Es sollten fest vorgegebene Sondenpositionen in die Strategie integrierbar sein. Somit können einige Bereiche fest vorgegeben und andere variabel gehalten werden.
- *Sperrbereiche:* Im Überwachungsareal sollen Sperrbereiche eingetragen werden können, die aus der Überwachung ausgeklammert werden.

Zusätzlich sollen für alle Einsatzszenarien noch folgende Punkte erfüllt werden:

- *Flexibilität:* Die Ausbringstrategien sollen sich an jede beliebige Umgebung anpassen können. Gerade im Außenbereich sollten müssen 3D Informationen der Umgebung mit in die Berechnung einfließen.
- *Schnelle Berechnung:* Die Ablagepunkte für die Sonden müssen für eine zuverlässige Überwachung zeitnah berechnet werden können.
- *Einfache Skalierbarkeit:* Eine Ausbringstrategie soll bei jeder beliebigen Größe oder Form des zu überwachenden oder mit einem Kommunikationsnetzwerk zu versehenden Bereiches anwendbar sein. Angestrebt ist ein linearer Zusammenhang zwischen der Größe des Areals und dem Aufwand der Berechnung.
- *Interoperabilität:* Die Strategien sollen Schnittstellen zu anderen Robotern vorsehen. Wenn mehr als ein Roboter ein Gelände überwachen oder mit einem Kommunikationsnetzwerk versehen soll, ist es notwendig die Ausbringstrategien aller Roboter im Verbund arbeiten zu lassen.

4 Ausblick

Es sind bereits Arbeiten durchgeführt worden, die sich mit der Berechnung der optimalen Anbringpositionen von fest installierten Kameras in Gebäuden befasst haben, wie z.B. in [2]. In [2] definiert sich die optimale Auslegung hauptsächlich durch die Kosten der Kameras und deren Installation. Des Weiteren wurden die möglichen Positionen der Kameras durch ein Raster diskretisiert. Die Vielzahl der Parameter der einzelnen Sonden, der Umgebung und der Anwendungsszenarien führt dabei aber zu einer hohen Komplexität.
Besser geeignet als klassische mathematische Ansätze scheinen daher evolutionärer Algorithmen. Da diese Verfahren jedoch mehrere Iterationen benötigen, um der optimalen Lösung nahe zu kommen, ist es durch die Forderung nach Schnelligkeit der Berechnung wichtig, dass die Gütefunktion des evolutionären Algorithmus, in vorliegendem Fall die Berechnung der Flächendeckung durch die Sensoren, möglichst einfach ist. [3] und [2] beschreiben beide die Berechnung sichtbarer Polygone von einzelnen Punkten aus, wobei in [3] das Ziel eine Verbesserung der Berechnungszeit bei mehreren Zugriffszyklen ist, was für die Verwendung als Gütefunktion eines evolutionären Ansatzes von Vorteil ist.

Literaturverzeichnis

1. Pfeiffer, K.: *Probes for security and surveillance robots.* In: SSRR 2004 Conference, Bonn, 2004.
2. Erdem, U. M., Sclaroff, S.: *Automated camera layout to satisfy task-specific and floorplan-specific coverage requirements.* In: technical report of Department of Computer Science, Boston, MA, 2004.
3. Ghodsi, M., Zarei, A. R.: *Efficient Computation of Query Point Visibility in Polygons with Holes.* In: 21st Annual ACM Symposium on Computational Geometry, Pisa, Italien, Juni 6-8 2005.

Ein Framework für automatisierte Betriebshöfe mit intelligenten Nutzfahrzeugen

Philipp Wojke

Universität Koblenz-Landau, Institut für Softwaretechnik,
Universitätsstraße 1, 56070 Koblenz

Zusammenfassung. Dieser Artikel stellt ein flexibles Framework zur Erstellung von Leitsteuerung für automatisierte Betriebshöfe vor. Das Framework ergänzende Komponenten erlauben die Anpassung an unterschiedliche Anforderungen. Erreicht wird dies durch eine gezielte Abstraktion der durchzuführenden Abläufe und der verwendeten Daten. Die Anwendbarkeit des Frameworks wird exemplarisch anhand der Simulation eines Betriebshofs gezeigt.

1 Einleitung

Bisher wird im Bereich des automatisierten Fahrens vorrangig Grundlagenforschung betrieben, Schwerpunkte sind beispielsweise das automatische Aufsatteln einer Wechselbrücke, die optimale Wegfindung oder die Disposition der autonomen Fahrzeuge. Nun muss untersucht werden, wie die gewonnen Ergebnisse gemeinsam in Anwendungen genutzt werden können.

Ein Anwendungsgebiet ist der automatisierte Betriebshof, auf dem Fahrzeuge autonom Tätigkeiten ausführen (siehe [1]), z.B. Andocken an Laderampen, Umsetzen von Wechselbrücken oder Tanken. Unfälle durch fehlende Aufmerksamkeit oder mangelnde Fähigkeiten der Fahrer werden vermieden und die Effizienz der Abläufe durch eine bessere Koordination der Fahrzeuge gesteigert. Eine zentrale Leitsteuerung koordiniert alle Tätigkeiten und bindet weitere logistische Systeme des Betriebshofs an, die insbesondere die Aufträge für die Leitsteuerung generieren. (siehe [2]).

Die Entwicklung spezieller Leitsteuerungen kann durch den Einsatz eines Frameworks vereinfacht werden, das eine Architektur, grundlegende Funktionalitäten sowie abstrakte Abläufe und Datenstrukturen definiert. Dieses Framework kann dann durch speziell implementierte Komponenten zu vollständigen Leitsteuerungen ergänzt werden.

2 Strukturelle Architektur

Bei der Entwicklung des Frameworks wurde insbesondere auf die Flexibilität des Frameworks und der damit entwickelten Leitsteuerungen Wert gelegt. Daher wurde eine serviceorientierte Architektur (SOA) gewählt (siehe Abb. 1 sowie [3]). Im Folgenden werden die Bestandteile der Architektur genauer beschrieben.

Grundlegend für die Aktivitäten der Leitsteuerung sind die Daten, welche die aktuellen und geplanten Zustände und Tätigkeiten aller Fahrzeuge und Gegenstände auf dem Hof beschreiben. Im Stil einer Repository-Architektur stellen Verwaltungskomponenten die Konsistenz der Datenbestände sicher und bieten über Schnittstellen anderen Komponenten Dienste zum Abfragen und Manipulieren der Daten an.

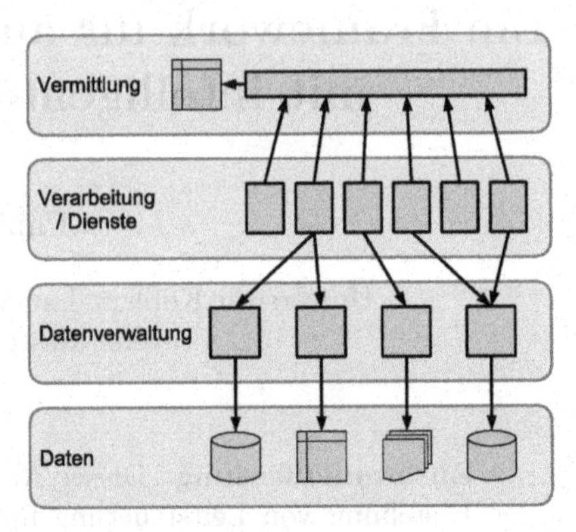

Abb. 1. Architektur des Frameworks mit Benutzungsbeziehungen

Diese Datendienste werden durch verschiedene verarbeitende Komponenten genutzt, welche ihrerseits Dienste anbieten, z.B. die Bestimmung eines Fahrwegs oder die Zerlegung einer Aufgabe in Teilaufgaben. Über ein Nachrichtensystem werden Kontroll- und Statusdaten mit den Diensten ausgetauscht, ansonsten wird das Datenrepository genutzt. Komplexere Dienste werden durch funktionale Zerlegung auf einfachere Dienste zurückgeführt.

Alle verfügbaren Dienste werden in einem Verzeichnis vermerkt. Nach dem Vermittler-Muster werden die Nachrichten an die dafür registrierten Komponenten weitergeleitet, d.h. der Anbieter eines Dienstes muss einem Nutzer nicht bekannt sein. Bei geeigneter Ausprägung des Nachrichtensystems sowie der Datenverwaltung ist auch die Umsetzung der Leitsteuerung als verteilte Anwendung möglich. Für die verarbeitenden Komponenten ist dies transparent, d.h. an diesen muss keine Veränderung vorgenommen werden.

3 Funktionale Architektur

Bei der zentralen Koordination des Betriebshofes übernimmt die Leitsteuerung insbesondere vier grundlegende Aktivitäten (siehe Abb. 2):

- Die Verwaltung der benötigten Informationen.
- Die Planung der Ausführung von Aufträgen.
- Die Ausführung geplanter Tätigkeiten.
- Die Überwachung der Ausführung.

Zur Verkürzung der Bearbeitungszeit von Aufträgen werden Aufträge schrittweise in Aufgaben und letztendlich in einzelne elementare Tätigkeiten zerlegt, die dann, soweit möglich, parallel verarbeitet werden (Pipelining). Die Aufgaben eines Auftrags werden auf Konsistenz und Ausführbarkeit geprüft und, wenn notwendig, in einzelne Teilaufgaben zerlegt. Hierzu wird auf Dienste zurückgegriffen, die auf einen Aufgabentyp, z.B. Fahraufgaben, spezialisiert sind.

Sind alle notwendigen Daten vorhanden, dann wird die Aufgabe zur Disposition an die Ausführung übergeben. Hier werden die enthaltenen elementaren Tätigkeiten entsprechend ihrer Abhängigkeiten geordnet und, sofern alle notwendigen Bedingen erfüllt sind, ausgeführt. Dabei werden Befehle an die ausführende Einheit übermittelt und Statusmeldungen ausgewertet.

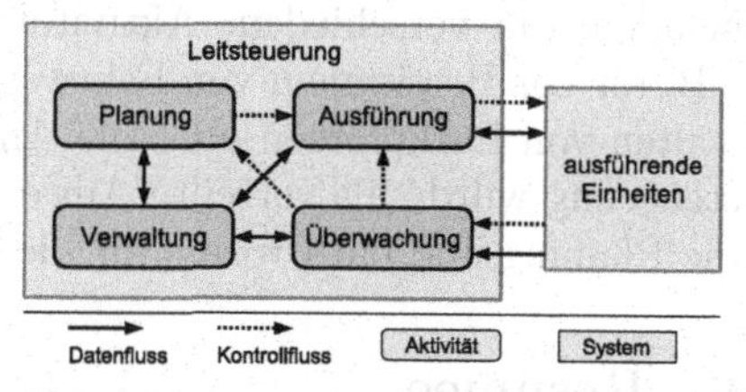

Abb. 2. Grundlegende Aktiviäten einer Leitsteuerung

Die Überwachung vergleicht den Zustand der ausführenden Einheit mit dem geplanten Zielen und berechnet die Abweichungen. Kleinere Abweichungen, die noch innerhalb des Plans liegen, werden an die Ausführung gemeldet, welche korrigierend eingreift. Bei größeren Abweichungen, die außerhalb des Plans liegen, wird die aktuelle Ausführung unterbrochen. Der Auftrag muss dann zurückgewiesen oder neu geplant werden.

4 Entwicklung spezieller Leitsteuerungen

Das Framework definiert verschiedene Datenstrukturen, Aktivitäten, Dienste und Protokolle und stellt Implementierungen durch Bibliotheken zur Verfügung. Zum Erreichen einer hohen Flexibilität und Anwendbarkeit ist das Framework abstrakt gehalten. An definierten Erweiterungspunkten ist es zu einer speziellen Leitsteuerung zu ergänzen. Dies kann durch Konfiguration oder Spezialisierung vorhandener Komponenten oder durch Hinzufügen neuer Bestandteile geschehen. Zur Konfiguration der Komponenten und Dienste verwendet das Framework generative Mechanismen. Für den einfachen Austausch von Daten werden offene Formate wie XML verwendet.

Mit Hilfe des Frameworks können einerseits in sich geschlossene Komponenten für Familien von Leitsteuerungen entwickelt werden, andererseits ist es möglich Datenstrukturen und Algorithmen verschiedener Komponenten einer Leitsteuerung aufeinander abzustimmen und so auch spezielle Anforderungen zu erfüllen.

5 Anwendungsbeispiel fahrerlose Rollende Landstraße

Zur Überprüfung der Anwendbarkeit des Frameworks wurde eine spezielle Leitsteuerung für einen automatisierten Umschlagbahnhof der Rollenden Landstraße (RoLa) realisiert. Am Bahnhof übergeben oder übernehmen Fahrer Auflieger oder Gespanne. Auf dem Gelände werden autonom die Züge be- oder entladen. Da entsprechende Fahrzeuge und Infrastruktur nicht real zur Verfügung stehen wurden diese simuliert (siehe Abb. 3).

Mit Hilfe des Frameworks wurde eine prototypische Leitsteuerung mit einem Aufbau nach [2] und [4] entwickelt. Als Datenrepository werden objektorientierte Datenstrukturen verwendet, statische Beschreibungen werden aus XML-Dateien geladen. Für verschiedene Aktivitäten wurden spezielle Dienste implementiert, z.B. für das Bestimmen von Fahrwegen mit Hilfe eines Wegenetzwerks, das Verwalten von Parkplätzen oder die Anbindung einer 3D-Visualisierung. Die Leitsteuerung wurde als verteilte Anwendung implementiert, wobei ein Prozess für die Planung und ein Prozess für die Ausführung zuständig ist.

6 Resümee

Mit Hilfe des Frameworks konnte ein funktionierender Leitstand für einen Betriebshof realisiert werden. Die Kapselung und die geringen direkten Abhängigkeiten der einzelnen Komponenten ermöglichten eine einfache Entwicklung und erlauben das Austauschen der prototypischen Komponenten gegen alternative Implementierungen. Viele der verwendeten Dienste abstrahieren von der speziellen Anwendung fahrerlose RoLa. Allerdings schränkt die konkrete Implementierung eines Dienstes die Wiederverwendung ein, da sie ein Konzept oder Verfahren fixiert, z.B. die Wegfindung mit Hilfe eines vorgegebenen Wegenetzes. Dennoch konnten viele Komponenten der RoLa-Leitsteuerung für eine weitere Leitsteuerung, die eines intelligenten Speditionshofs, verwendet werden.

Abb. 3. Simulation des RoLa-Bahnhofs Regensburg

Auch die Implementierung einer Leitsteuerung als verteilte Anwendung war mit Hilfe des Frameworks möglich. Durch Einsatz eines speziellen Nachrichtenvermittlers und eines replizierten Datenbestandes konnte dies ohne Anpassung der verarbeitenden Komponenten erreicht werden.

Insgesamt wurde die angestrebte Flexibilität des Frameworks und der damit erstellten Leitsteuerungen erreicht und die Anwendbarkeit nachgewiesen. Zur weiteren Bewertung des Frameworks soll die Leistungsfähigkeit der erstellten Leitsteuerungen durch verschiedene Simulationen ermittelt werden.

Literaturverzeichnis

1. Richard Bishop (2000): Intelligent vehicle applications worldwide, IEEE Intelligent Systems 15(1), S. 78-81, IEEE, Piscataway, NJ
2. Verein Deutscher Ingenieure (2005): VDI 4451 Blatt 7 - Kompatibilität von Fahrerlosen Transportsystemen (FTS) - Leitsteuerung für FTS, Beuth, Berlin
3. Douglas K. Barry (2003): Web Services and Service-oriented Architecture: The Savvy Manager's Guide, Morgan Kaufman, San Francisco, CA
4. Dieter Zöbel, Christian Weyand, Philipp Wojke (2005): A Versatile Software Architecture for Maneuvering many Articulated Vehicles, Proceedings of the 2nd International Workshop on Intelligent Transportation (WIT'2005), S. 131-136, IEEE, Hamburg, Germany

Sensor Proccessing and Behaviour Control of a Small AUV

Jan Albiez, Jochen Kerdels, Sascha Fechner and Frank Kirchner

DFKI Robotics Lab, Robert-Hooke-Strasse 5, 28259 Bremen, Germany
jan.albiez@dfki.de

Abstract. This paper presents the design of the electronics, the sensor data processing scheme and the implementation of the behaviour based control for a small autonomous underwater vehicle (AUV). The robot has a volume of 12dm^3 and is used as a demonstration vehicle for underwater ai-technologies. The thruster configuration allows the μAUV to hover and its active light sensors enable obstacle detection abilities. The control features several behaviours like obstacle detection and depth sensor calibration and is completely autonomous. An ATMega128 functions as onboard CPU and due to the limited computing power we use a special scheduling algorithm which also acts as the behaviour arbiter.

1 Introduction

To present the possible applications of artificial intelligence in underwater robotics and offshore technology on the 2007 CeBIT fair in Hannover/Germany, we used an aquarium (lwh 3x1x0.8m) with a mockup of a future underwater production facility. To enhance the attraction of this demontration to the fairs audience we wanted to use two completly autonomous underwater vehicles (AUV), which are small enough to navigate inside the aquarium. Because of the required small size of these vehicles we named them μAUV, and they are at the moment the smalles full autonomous AUVs worldwide.

For the μAUV the traditional approaches for controlling small scale AUVs like the Serafina [2] can't be used. The pressured space in the μAUV is to small for the hardware components needed to apply higher behaviours and sensor systems. Therefore we had to develop a high integrated sensor-actor-proccessing scheme to control the μAUV.

During the mechanical construction of this vehicles we encountered several problems which only arrise when building small scale underewater vehicles. First of all is the surface tension. For bigger vehicles (e.g. [1]) surface tension is not a problem, but on the size of the μAUV the buoyancy of several gramms, generated by the surface tension, is a serious problemfor the actuators. We had to keep the area exposed to the surface as small as possible to prohibit the μAUV from "glueing" at the surface. A second problem we encountered is the accumulation of gas bubles at the surface of the vehicle. This normal physical phnomena causes the same problem as the surface tension be increasing the buoyancy.

Fig. 1. The vehicle has a cylindrical body with 55 mm in diameter, 125 mm long and has five thruster to hover.

In the following we present the electronics, the sensor system and the internal programming of the μAUV (s. fig. 1) as well as the resolts from the tests on this years CeBIT fair and the conclusions we made from these results.

2 Electronics

The design of the μAUV electronics was a challenging task. In a cylindrical space of just 40mm in diameter and 67mm in height a microcontroller, the power electronics, a pressure sensor, 12 light sensors, 8 ultra bright LEDs and the interconnections of all these components had to be placed (s. fig. 2). Two detachable tubes on either side of the vehicle's main hull contain the electricity supply. Inside these tubes are four AA batteries with 2.7Ah providing electricity for up to 2.5h.

The used microcontroller is an 8-bit ATMega128 with 128KB flash memory and 4KB SRAM (s. [3] for technical specification and datasheet). With the chip running at 14.7456MHz it has to generate the PWM signals for motor control, measure the 12 light sensors and the pressure sensor and control the movements of the vehicle via a behaviour based approach. As all these different tasks have particular requirements with respect to CPU time and periodicity, a very lightweight non-preemptive scheduler was implemented.

The main sensor used is the TCS230 on the sensor-boards. It is a RGB light-to-frequency sensor which generates an output frequency between 1Hz and 600kHz proportional to the measured light intensity of the selected channel (red, green, blue or clear). The frequency is measured by the microcontroller via an externally triggered counter unit. Between one and four light sensors are placed on each sensor board together with an ultrabright green LED (6000mcd). There are two sensor boards on the left, right and bottom side of the vehicle and one sensor board in the front and back respectively.

In addition to the light sensors a pressure sensor is integrated into the hull of the vehicle. The MPX5100DP is used to meter the depth of the vehicle by measuring the differential pressure between the inside and outside of the μAUV. The sensor has a measuring range of 0 – 100kPa, thus covering depths between 0cm and 1000cm. Besides determining the depth the sensor can also be used to detect leaks since the differential pressure drops in such a case and the vehicle will dive to a higher depth than expected.

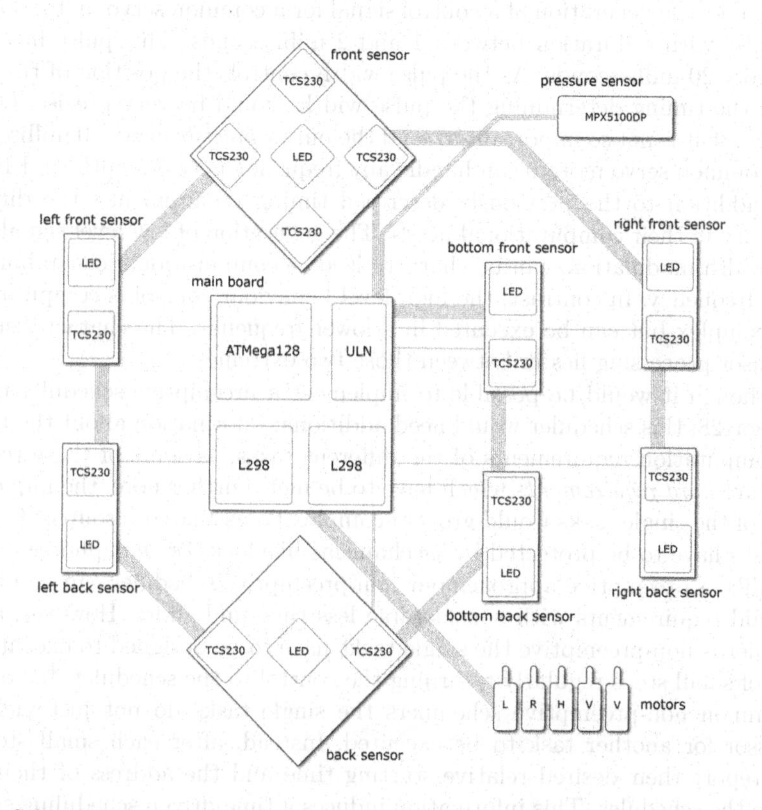

Fig. 2. Schematical overview of the electronic components and their interconnection being packed into a cylindrical space of 40mm in diameter and 67mm in height.

3 Software

The software running on the microcontroller of the μAUV can be divded into three major parts. First, the generation of low level signals, e.g. PWM, to control the power electronics of the vehicle. Second, the measurement of the light and pressure sensors and third, the high level control of the vehicle. Each of these tasks has quite different requirements with respect to computational time and periodicity. Thus we developed a small lightweight non-preemptive scheduler dealing with those requirements.

3.1 Scheduling

To implement a scheduler on a small system with limited capabilities, such as the ATMega128, a number of interdependent aspects have to be balanced. Most of the tasks running on a microcontroller have certain time constrains. Some tasks need an absolute precise timing, where others tolerate some variance. As an example, the generation of a control signal for a common servo motor consists of a pulse with a duration between 1 and 2 milliseconds. This pulse has to be sent every 20 milliseconds. As the pulse width controls the position of the servo motor, the timing determining the pulse width should be very precise. On the other hand, it is not so important to send the pulses *precisly* every 20 millisecond. Most common servo motors can handle any frequency between 50Hz and 100Hz.

In addition to the previously described timing requirements, the different tasks vary in their computational needs. The generation of low level signals, e.g. pulse width modulation, can be characterized as computational cheap but with a high frequency. In contrast, the high level behaviour control is computational more complex but can be executed in a lower frequency. The characteristics of the sensor processing lies in between those two extremes.

Although it would be possible to implement a preemptive scheduler on the ATMega128, this scheduler would need additional information about the timing and computation requirements of the different tasks, as some of these requirements are *hard requirements* which have to be met. Furthermore, the implementation of the single tasks would grow in complexity, as shared resources between the tasks have to be protected by mechanisms like locks or semaphores.

Unlike a preemptive approach our non-preemptive scheduler can handle the aforesaid requirements with considerable less time and effort. However, as the scheduler is non-preemptive the single tasks have to be designed to execute as a series of small steps regularly returning the control to the scheduler. In contrast to common non-preemptive schedulers the single tasks do not just yield the processor for another task to be executed. Instead, after each small step the tasks report their desired relative starting time and the address of their next step to the scheduler. This information induces a time-driven scheduling scheme which specifies the execution sequence of the different tasks implicitly (s. Fig. 3). The scheduler itself has just to keep the list of next steps in order and has to execute these steps at their desired execution times. If a collision with respect to the execution times of two or more steps occurs, a "‘first come first serve"’ approach is choosen. For this reason the timing between two steps of a task can diverge from the desired timing. If absolute presice timing must be guaranteed it has to be generated inside a single step of a task as each step is a atomic function which is never interrupted.

Furthermore, due to the fact that the tasks do not only report the desired relative starting time of their next step but also the address of their next step, the internal structure of a task consisting of a interconnected set of steps resembles the structure of a state machine. As many applications, e.g. behaviour control or the generation of control signals, can be modelled as state machines their implementation easily fits in this programming scheme.

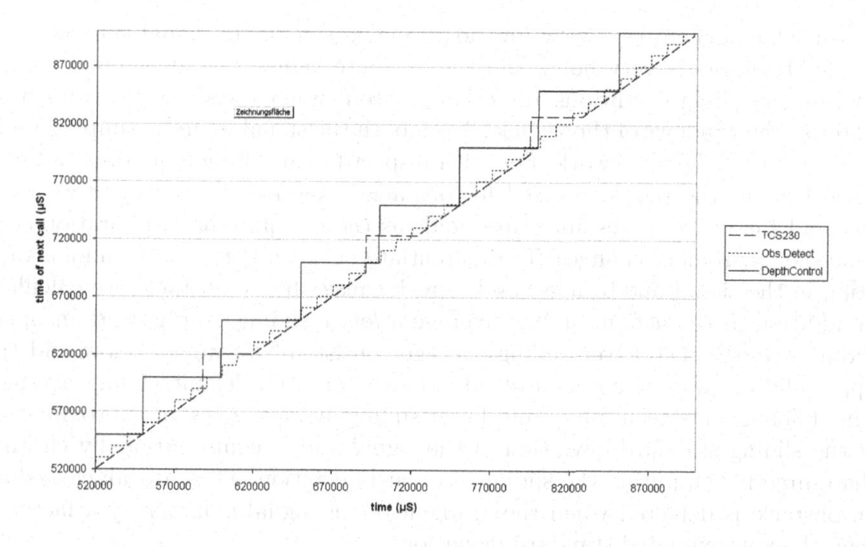

Fig. 3. Example for the automatic interleaving of the single steps of 3 tasks running in parallel on the ATMega128.

3.2 Sensor Processing

The μAUV relies on two types of sensors. A pressure sensor which measures the differential pressure between the inside and outside of the vehicle and eight RGB light-to-frequency sensors which measure the intensity of red, green and blue light at different locations on the vehicle (s. Fig. 2).

The differential pressure between inside and outside of the vehicle is used to estimate the depth of the vehicle. For every centimeter in depth the pressure rises by 1 hectopascal. The pressure outside of the vehicle is not only affected by the pressure originated by the water column above the vehicle, it is also affected by the atmospheric pressure at water level. As the pressure inside the vehicle is constant after it is sealed, pressure changes in the atmosphere influence the estimation of the vehicle's depth. The difference between a high-pressure area and a low-pressure area is around 30 hectopascal or about 30 centimeter in terms of the depth estimation. For this reason the μAUV periodically recalibrates the minimum and maximum sensor values by surfacing to water level for the minimum pressure value and descending to the ground for the maximum pressure value.

The eight RGB light-to-frequency sensors which are distributed over different locations on the vehicle measure the light intensity of red, green and blue light at their particular positions. The sensors generate a square wave whose frequency is proportional to the intensity of light measured. One of the sensors main purposes is obstacle detection. To detect an obstacle, the green light intensity is measured before and during a green LED pointing outwards is turned on (s. Fig. 1). If an obstacle is near it reflects the green light and a significant increase in the green light intensity can be detected. In contrast to the pressure sensor which generates a very low-noise analog signal, the signal generated by the light sensors is very noisy and the absolute values vary depending on the enviromental light conditions and other enviromental causes, e.g. the condensed water at the windows of the vehicle. To smooth the signal we use a simple sliding average filter. The filter works fine with respect to cancellation of noise, but also smoothes out the peaks we need for obstacle detection. Furthermore we want to avoid the usage of absolute thresholds as these require new calibration each time the enviroment changes. To differentiate between between a common variation in the signal due to noise and a peak caused by an obstacle, we calculate in addition to the default sliding average a *lower* sliding average and an *upper* sliding average. The lower sliding average consists of all values below and the upper sliding average consists of all values above the default sliding average. The difference between upper and lower sliding average gives an approximation of the sliding standard deviation of the signal and is computationally cheaper than directly computing the sliding standard deviation. Thus a peak caused by an obstacle is detected when the gradient of the signal is larger by a factor α then the approximated standard deviation.

3.3 Behaviour Control

As described in section 3.1 the structure of each single task running on the μAUV resembles a state machine. Therefor the behaviour is organized as a set of small interacting state machines where each state machine is responsible for a specific task. This means that the complete behaviour arbitration is done directly by the scheduler-behaviour interaction. Basic tasks include depth control, sensor reading and filtering, obstacle detection, motor control and higher behaviour, e.g. responsible for long-time periodic tasks like recalibration of the depth sensor. The different modules communicate simply via shared variables. This can be done without any protective mechanisms, e.g. locks, as the single steps of the tasks are atomic functions which are never interrupted by another task or the scheduler.

As an example, if the obstacle detector module registers an obstacle it reports this by writing an accordant intensity value in an obstacle-detected variable. As long as the intensity of the obstacle stays quite small and the obstacle position is not directly in the way of the vehicle, the obstacle information is only used by the motor control module wich will slightly adjust the motor values to extend the distance to the assumed obstacle. Instead, if the intensity value of the obstacle is high and/or the obstacle is directly in the way of the vehicle, the higher behavior control will trigger an evasive movement.

The whole behaviour system is inspired by the behaviour network architecture presented in [4], scaled down to the resources available on a small microcontroller system.

4 Evaluation

The μAUV have been successfully used as demonstrators over the complete duration of this years CeBIT fair in Hannover/Germany. We used four different systems with two systems in the water and two systems being recharged. The hardware of the system worked reliable and all systems were still running after one week of daily eight hours of demonstration. At the end of the week we noticed a certain amount of corrosion in the motors and around the power connectors as a direct result of electrolysis. The runtime of a battery charge was around two and a half hours.

The clear glass of the aquarium posed a problem for the μAUV's obstacle avoidance algorithm. The amount of light reflected by the glass was neglectable as long as the the front sensor of the μAUV was not positioned rectangular to the glass, which resulted in a lot of collisions or "hanging around the glass"-positions. As negatively as this looks in the first place as much it was approved by the audience, since it was possible to get a reaction from the μAUV by placing a hand directly at the glass, enhancing the reflective properties of the glass and triggering the obstacle avoidance behaviour, giving the whole demonstration an interactive components.

By running the "sleep" and the "sensor callibration" behaviours with a very short frequency (3min and 2min), there was always enough action inside the aquarium to hold the visitors at the booth. This, from an engineering point ridiculous, short frequency is the statistically proofed maximum time of an visitor observing a demonstration at a fair.

5 Conclusion

Using micro-scale underwater vehicles as a demonstrator for new underwater technologies and as attraction for a fair-booth proofed to be a highly successful project. The actual design flaws of the current μAUV are mainly its limited computing capabilities and the major corrosion problem at the motors and the power connectors. We are currently making a redesign of the μAUV. This μAUV^2 incorporates a better computer architecture based on a DSP/FPGA combination, uses a sensor suite enhanced by a small CCD camera, has a better thruster system and will also apply a diving cell to adjust buoyancy. The μAUV^2 will then not only used as a demonstration vehicle but also as basis-system for master and bachelor student projects.

References

1. Clarke, H. et al.: Design and Development of the AUV Harp. 3rd Annual International Autonomous Underwater Vehicle Competition, Orlando, (2000).
2. Navinda Kottege and Uwe R. Zimmer: Relative Localization for AUV swarms. Proceedings of the International Symposium on Underwater Technology, Tokyo, Japan, 2007
3. ATMega128: Technical specification and datasheet. http://www.atmel.com/dyn/resources/prod_documents/doc2467.pdf
4. Jan Albiez: Verhaltensnetwerke zur adaptiven Steuerung biologisch motivierter Laufmaschinen Dissertationsschrift, GCA Verlag, Februar 2007

The MiCRoN Robot Project

Ramon Estaña and Heinz Woern

Institute for Process Control and Robotics (IPR), Build. 40.28,
Universitaet Karlsruhe (TH), 76128 Karlsruhe, Germany
{estana, woern}@ira.uka.de

Abstract. The MiCRoN project aimed at the development of a new micro-robot system based on flexible mobile, 1 cm^3 sized robots acting autonomously. The eight European project partners started in March 2002 with the development of a system based on the results from the EU-Miniman Project. As a result, several fully independend and untethered working micro-robots have been developed that are handling parts with the size of about 60 μm under a local, robot-based microscope. Using a completely new, high resolution navigation system, the robots can be navigated within 5 μm. The minimal step width of the platform is 2 to 4 nanometer. The robot can be equipped with several tools for micro- and nano-handling as well as for biological cell handling. The energy support is realised with a power floor by using magnetic fields, while the communication is done via infra red. The robot itself is currently one of the highest integrated micro tools.

1 Introduction

The MiCRoN project's outcome is a major contribution in the field of micro mechatronic components. Five cm^3-sized robots have been developed using low voltage piezo actuators and hybrid on-board electronics. Several micro tools were developed:

- Millimetre-sized grippers for the 3D assembly of meso-scale objects,
- A robot-mounted micro syringe chip for the injection of substances into living cells
- Atomic Force Microscope (AFM) tools for standard AFM imaging and using functionalised nano tips for biological experiments

The robot actuators have been built by using a novel rapid prototyping process for multilayer piezoceramics; the robot hardware consists of a less than 1 cm^2 onboard electronics module. Other major contributions of the project are methods for wireless micro-robot operation. A power floor has been built as a working prototype, which transmits electrical energy to mobile units operating on a 220 × 200 mm^2 area. Infrared communication schemes have been developed for controlling a small group of robots. An advanced control system has been realised including an implementation of the progressive Kalman Filtering Theorem. This software package includes all software needed for robot control, navigation, planning, simulation and user interfacing. For the integrated onboard vision system, a camera, which can be mounted on mobile micro-robots, has been developed into a working prototype. This system can generate 3D data of micro manipulation scenarios. The computer vision system developed offers a broad range of stable recognition algorithms for micro handling applications. In the field of object localisation, the global localisation system represents a major achievement. This system has reached final prototype state with a position resolution of about $4\mu m$ over the complete size of the workspace. By using phase shifting algorithms the resolution of the system is about $1\mu m$.

2 Robot Design

The platform consists of a locomotion system allowing a velocity of about 0.5 millimetres per second comÂbined with a large working area ($220 \times 200\ mm^2$) and nanometer resolution. The robots navigate on a flat, horizontal surface using holonomic movements. The main tasks of the locomotion system are to bring the handling-tools (e.g. grippers) to the region of interest or to transport micro objects. The hardware platform incorporates advanced, beyond state-of-the-art technological solutions. The system design enhances the performance achievable by each individual micro-robot by suitably distributing various mechanical degrees of freedom (DOF) among the micro-robots to enable complex object handling and manipulation. Piezo actuators have been incorporated due to their excellent resolution. An onboard IR module assures the communication with a host computer. The onboard electronics controls the robot motion, generates and amplifies the driving signals for all actuators and tools and pre-processes the signals from the on-board sensors. Power management was a critical issue to ensure autonomous operation of the robot for the longest time possible. A power consumption of significantly less than 1 W per robot was aspired. In particular, heat management was important from both an energy saving point of view and to avoid detrimental effects resulting from overheated system components or manipulated objects.

2.1 Wireless Power Supply

The wireless power transfer is implemented by an external magnetic field generator, the so-called Power Floor. It provides a travelling magnetic field throughout the working area, powering the robot via a miniaturised robot coil. The operating frequency is defined as 500 kHz. The coil power pack with resonant, rectifying and filtering circuit is designed in a volume of $11,5 \times 11,5 \times 4mm^3$. In order to reduce the skin effect, the coil is wound with 200 turns of Litz-wire, which is composed of 30 twisted Ø 0,03 mm enamel copper wires. The output voltage depends directly on the intensity of the external magnetic field, which is tuned to transfer a power output of 330 mW / 3.3 V from the coil power pack.

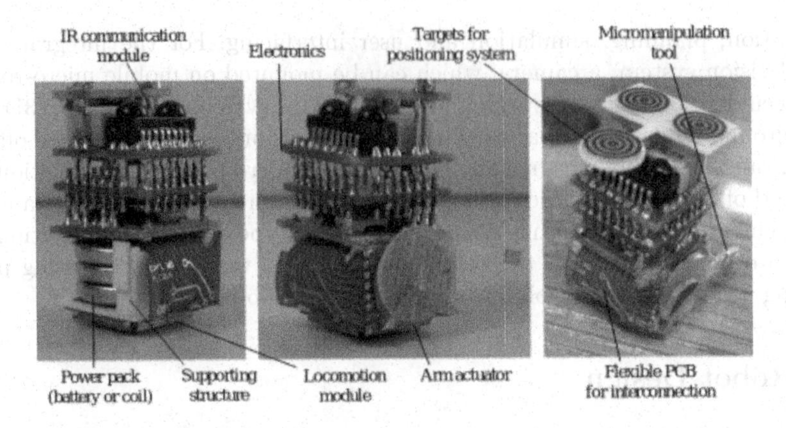

Fig. 1. Different modules of the final robot.

3 Integrated Micro Manipulation Actuators

3.1 Atomic Force Microscope Tool

The local position sensor is based on an AFM scanner mounted on a rotor high motion positioning actuator. The AFM sensor consists of one position scanner and one cantilever. The scanner is made of 4 PZT stack actuators that permits movements with 3 DOF (x,y,z) and the cantilever contains a force sensor based on a piezoresistance (see Fig. 2).

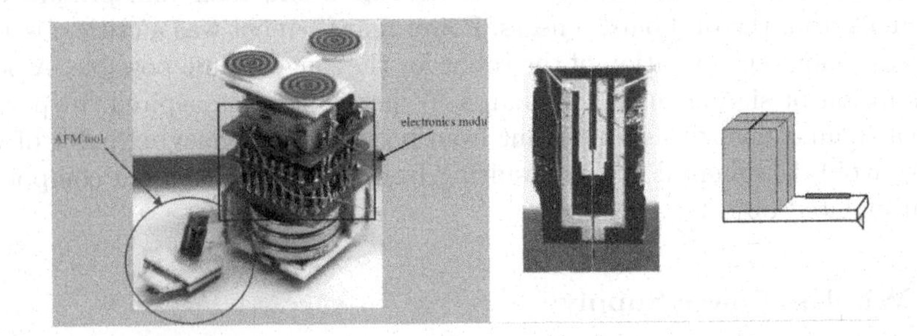

Fig. 2. XYZ-Positioning Sensor for the AFM-tool

The AFM tool consists of three main components: 1.) the AFM probe with the integrated piezoresistance, 2.) an AFM holder for easy probe exchange and 3.) the XYZ scan stage.

3.2 The Rotatorial Micro Actuator

A rotational drive has been developed, evaluated and redesigned to be a suitable interface between robot and tool. Five rotational drives with specific rotors for each tool have been built (see Fig. 3). Furthermore, the rapid prototyping technique for making multilayer piezoceramics, developed in the beginning of the project, has been utilised to make the drivers for the grippers.

The maximum torque of the motor is 80μN at a drive voltage of 50 V and a spring force of 1.2 N. The rotational actuator has extremely good motion resolution ($0,1\mu$rad) for driving frequencies up to about 80 Hz (0.1 rpm). Fast transport can be achieved in the frequency range 3–6 kHz (4 rpm). The power consumption is about 1 mW and 80 mW respectively.

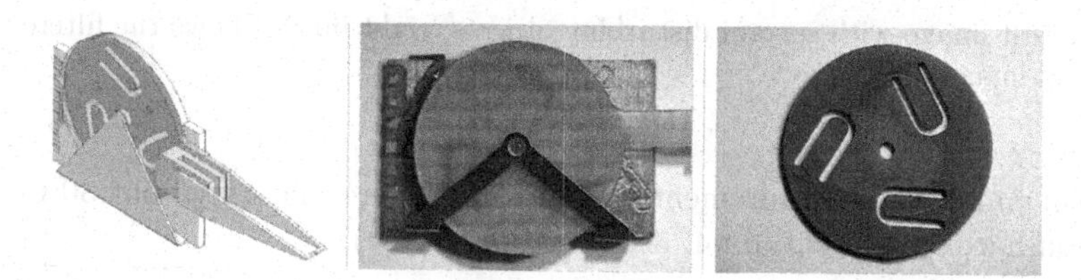

Fig. 3. Micromanipulation module with rotational actuator (Ø 9.2 mm) mounted on a printed circuit board with a tool (gripper) integrated directly onto the rotor (left). Micromanipulation module without tool (centre). The rotational actuator (right).

A micro gripper was developed which consisting of a piezo-electric actuator with gripper arms of stainless steel machined by Electro Discharge Machining (EDM). Although in this work, U-shaped actuators were used for the steel grippers, in theory bar shaped actuators could also be used. The stainless steel gripper tips are machined using wire EDM. The total gripper length is approximately 12 mm and the tip thickness of the gripper is approximately 60μm.

4 Position Sensing System

One project goal was the development of a position sensing system with a resolution of about 5 μm. This has been successfully realised and works now in a stable prototype status. A partly-virtual Moiré-based interferometer was developed to reach this demand. This measurement tool is needed to get the precise positions of the micro-robots. The software communicates via TCP/IP with the robot control software and sends the coordinates of the Moiré-marks.

One test setup for the measurement system in a real environment that contains optical obstacles is shown in Figure 4 (left). There are several objects in this image: a.) micro-robots with equipped Moiré-marks, b.) chessboard-like distortions on the working floor, and c.) other black objects which are not a aprt of a micro-robot. These objects have to be distinguished from the Moiré-marks, so that a successful measurement cycle is guaranteed (see result in Fig. 4, right).

A good practice for increasing the measurement quality is the usage of phase shifting. A common phase shifting method using four 90° phase shifts has been used. The result is an error surface, which shows a statistical measurement error

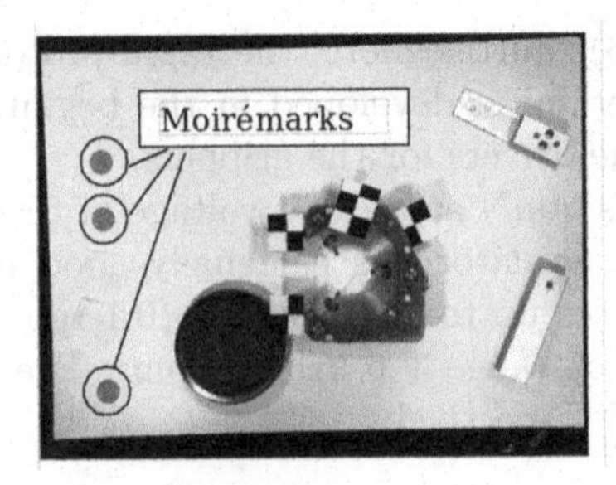

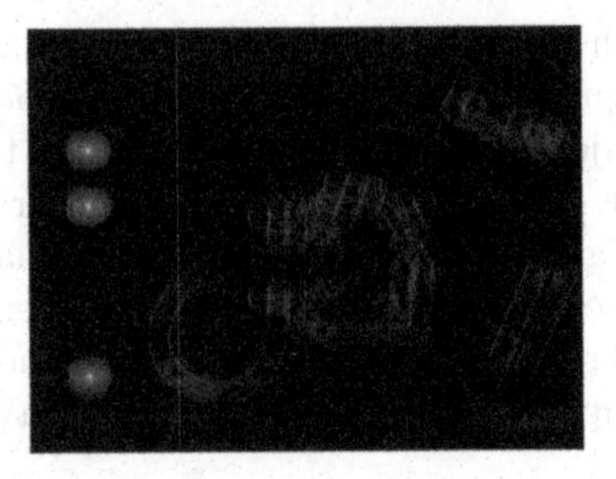

Fig. 4. Test image with several disturbing objects; right image shows the filtered measurement image

of about 5μm. The measurement time for one Moiré-mark is about 30 ms with common hardware (Pentium 4, 3 GHz, 1 GB RAM).

4.1 Test-Bed for the Untethered Robot System

The evaluation system that has been set up provides a platform to integrate the whole MiCRoN system including powering, communication, controlling, vision and so on.

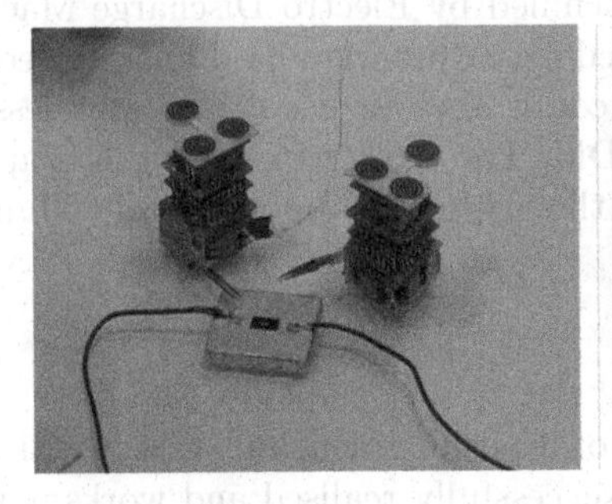

Fig. 5. The test bed for the untethered robots; left robot tethered because of additional energy supply for solering experiment

A two-staged approach has been developed for the position control system. It consists of a driver that operates in an open loop and a controller that is in charge of planning and closed-loop control, the Autonomous Execution Module. The controller uses the feedback of the vision system. The driver is based on a mathematical model that represents the inverse actuation of the robot. The model is calibrated offline. Different optimising techniques have been tested, including genetic programming.

5 Different Experiments with the MiCRoN-Robots

Two main experiment setups have been planned and tested to prove the robot functionalities: a) 3D assembling tasks with the micro gripper and b) AFM experiments. For more informations an the cell mannipulation with the syringe chip, please refer to the reference list at the end of this paper.

5.1 Experiments with the Micro Gripper

The micro component was finally chosen as an SMT resistor of size $150 \times 300\mu$m, developed and supplied by Taiyo Yuden, to our knowledge the smallest SMT component available in the world at that time. Other components were tested such as a square capacitor of size $175 \times 175\mu$m.

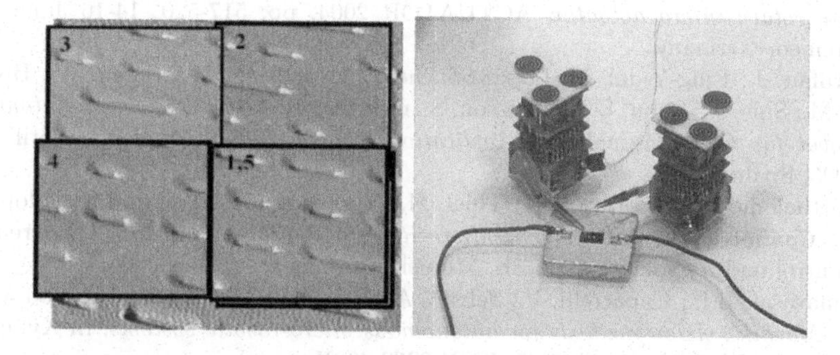

Fig. 6. AFM scan example (left) and the assembling experiment setup (right).

5.2 Experiments with the Onboard AFM

Fig. 6, left shows a scan of the pits in the polycarbonate surface of a CD-ROM realised with the AFM scanner integrated on the tethered micro-robot. The total image size is about 11μm $\times 11\mu$m. The distance between the lines of pits is about 1.6 μm. The line frequency for all tests was between 0.5 and 5 Hz, depending on the scan size. It is difficult to control the tip deflection if the scanning velocity is increased.

6 Future Work

The next steps based on the results of the MiCRoN project can be divided into two parts: state of the micro mechatronic components and outlook on the MiCRoN system.

Regarding the integration of all subsystems some additional efforts will make the full realisation of the proposed scenarios possible.

The main idea behind the project, the development of an intelligent micro-robot cluster to solve tasks that cannot be solved with a single robot, is continued and even intensified in the context of the I-SWARM project.

In terms of commercialisation potential of a micro-robotic system like the MiCRoN system, the same boundary conditions apply as for the Miniman project: such a micro-robotic system can be considered as a laboratory tool, given further system development and refinement of the man-machine interface (both in terms of software and the robotic hardware).

References

1. Snis, N.; Simu, U. and Johansson, S.: *A Piezoelectric Disc-shaped Motor using a Quasi-static Walking Mechanism*; J. Micromech. Microeng. 15 (2005) 2230-2234
2. Varidel, T.; Driesen, W.; Bergander, A. and Breguet J.-M.: *High precision miniature rotary micro actuator*, ACTUATOR 2004, pp. 517-520, 14-16 June, 2004, Bremen, Germany.
3. Brufau, J.; Puig-Vidal, M; López-Sánchez, J.; Samitier, J.; Driesen, W.; Breguet, J.-M.; Snis, N.; Simu, U.; Johansson, S; and Gao, J.: *MICRON: Small Autonomous Robot for Cell Manipulation Applications*, ICRA 2005, Barcelona, April 18-22, 2005, Spain.
4. Vartholomeos, P.; Loizou S.G.; Thiel, M.; Kyriakopoulos, K.J. and Papadopoulos, E.: *Control of the Multi Agent Micro-Robotic Platform MiCRoN*, Conference on Control and Applications, IEEE, Munich, Germany, October 2006.
5. Amavasai, B.P.; Caparrelli, F.; Selvan, A.; Boissenin M.; Travis, J.R. and Meikle, S.: *Machine vision methods for autonomous micro-robotic systems.* In Kybernetes Journal, Vol. 34 no. 9/10 2005, ISSN 0368-492X.
6. Estaña, R. and Woern, H.: *Moiré-based positioning system for small micro manipulation units.* In Optical and Microtechnology Products Conference, volume 1, OMP OPTO MICRO PRODUCTS, pages 75 - 81. AMA Service GmbH, AMA Service GmbH, May 2004.
7. Otero, J.; Saiz, A.; Brufau, J.; Colomer, J.; Ruíz, R.; López, J.; Miribel, J.; Puig, M. and Samitier, J.: *Reduced Dimensions Autonomous AFM System for working in Microbiorobotics* BioRob 2006. The first IEEE / RAS-EMBS International Conference on Biomedical Robotics and Biomechatronics. Pisa, Tuscany, Italy. February 20-22, 2006
8. Tagliareni, F.; Nierlich, M.; Steinmetz, O.; Velten, T.; Brufau, J.; López-Sánchez, J.; Puig-Vidal, M. and Samitier, J.: *Manipulating biological cells with a micro-robot cluster*; International Conference on Intelligent robots and systems IROS 2005: ISBN 0-7803-8912-3, pp. 426-431; Alberta, Canada

Mobile Robot Navigation Support in Living Environments

Christopher Armbrust, Jan Koch, Ulf Stocker and Karsten Berns

The Robotics Research Lab, University of Kaiserslautern
P.O. Box 3049, D-67653 Kaiserslautern, Germany
{c_armbru, koch, u_stocke, berns}@informatik.uni-kl.de

Abstract. Navigation and application functionality of mobile robots rely on their collision-avoiding capabilities, also known as local navigation. We present the mobile robot ARTOS (Autonomous Robot for Transport and Service) that is particularly designed to operate in living environments and therefore faces the problem of fuzzy and unstructured obstacles. The local navigation architecture is motivated regarding decisions on sensor hardware setup as well as the software layers that support and influence navigation control.

1 Introduction

The mobile robot ARTOS is a base platform for mobile services in assisted living environments. Beneath simple transport tasks, the system is envisioned to facilitate multiple multimedia applications such as remote human interaction or emergency monitoring. ARTOS shall act and react as mobile sensor and actor agent for the intelligent living environment. Systems like laser range finder and ultrasonic sensors have been used for some time now[1]. Unlike many robots, the range finding sensors on ARTOS cover the whole motion area. The system concept for obstacle avoidance regarding hardware and software setup is the main topic of this work. The combination of sensor systems with overlapping detection areas supports high detection safety. The sensor abstraction, which uses so-called sector maps, offers additional possibilities for sensor fusion. We motivate our approach according to state of the art systems and show the advantages of our setup. Beginning with a motivation of the various sensor hardware, we lead over to the sensor data abstraction that is done within a sector map representation.

2 System Design

The physical shape of ARTOS has been designed for application in living environments, see Tab. 1. The chassis was kept as small as possible so ARTOS can easily pass doors and find its way through small passages between pieces of furniture.

2.1 Mechatronic Components

ARTOS possesses a tilting mechanism which ensures that the drive wheels and at least one coaster wheel are always on the ground. This mechanism consists of a pivot-mounted plate to which the centered components are attached.

Size	length: 55cm, width: 33cm, height: 26cm
Weight	self: 25kg, payload: 50kg
Kinematics	differential drive
Wheels	2 active on centered axis, 2 passive at front and rear
Motors	2 Faulhaber 2657WO24CR
Dynamics	max. speed: 50 cm/s, max acc.: 25 cm/s^2
Power	2 12V lead batteries with 10Ah
Operation Time	approx. 4h

Table 1. Mechatronic Overview of ARTOS.

The system uses a low-power PC for task management, and high-level control, see Tab. 2. This has been implemented using the Modular Controller Architecture (MCA), a framework for robot control systems, which is closer described in [2] and [3]. Drive instructions are passed over CAN-Bus to the signal processors that control the motor speed.

Computer	VIA Epia C7, CAN Interface
DSP Boards	developed at the Robotics Research Lab
Motor Control	Motorola DSP 56F803
Operating System	Gentoo Linux, Kernel 2.6.16
Multimedia	Speakers, microphone, serial display, TTS
Camera	Philips USB PWC Webcam

Table 2. Control Hardware and Multimedia on ARTOS.

In Fig. 1 one can see ARTOS in an environment, populated with real-life obstacles. The following artefacts have to be considered critical for mobile robot navigation and thus have to be detected accurately.

- **static obstacles** like walls
- **quasi-static obstacles** like heavy furniture which stays in the same place for a long period of time
- **dynamic obstacles** like doors, small objects, humans and pets

2.2 The Range Finding Hardware

The different detection areas of the sensors are shown in Fig. 2 while some characteristics of the sensors are shown in Tab. 3. For planar view in forward direction we use the Hokuyo URG-04LX. Especially its small size but also low weight, low energy consumption and reasonable precision make it perfectly suitable for our

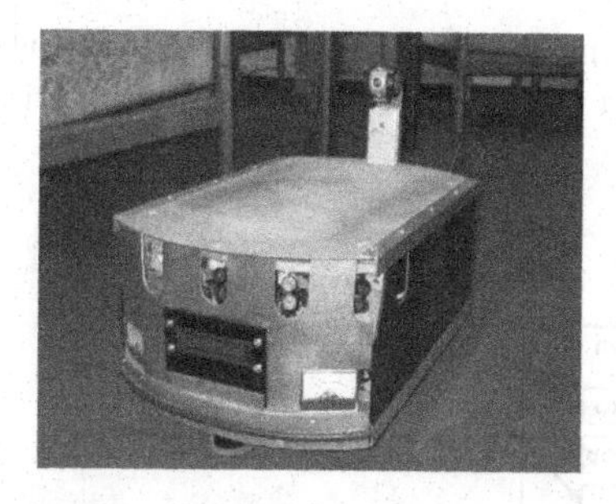

Fig. 1. ARTOS in the BelAmI Lab. Visible are the laser range finder, the front bumper and the ultrasonic sensors.

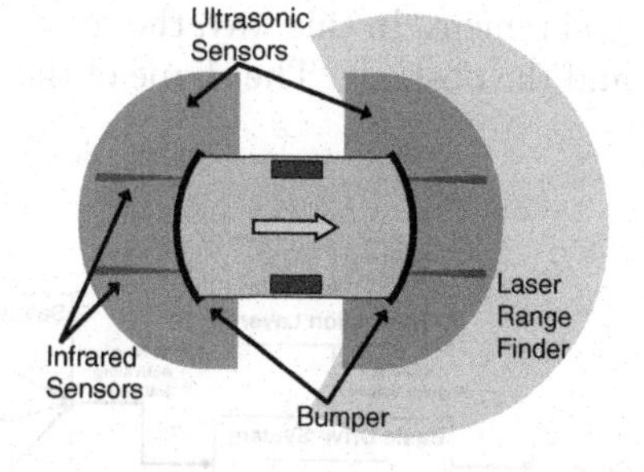

Fig. 2. The sensors of ARTOS and the regions they monitor.

cause. Best measurement results are returned with light reflecting objects. Two belts of seven ultrasonic sensors each are mounted under the cover, in front and rear direction. Especially for higher obstacles in close proximity, the ultrasonic system provides suitable detection quality, especially with solid objects with good reflecting characteristics. Problems occur with objects that dampen sound waves like pillows and curtains. For detecting negative obstacles like stairheads, four infrared sensors (Sharp GP2D12) are attached to the bottom of ARTOS. Two tactile sensors are placed at front and back to detect collisions.

sensor	shape	range	response time	precision
laser	plane	4m, 240°, 0.36° resolution	100ms	1cm
ultrasonic	cone	approx. 80cm, cone angle 60°	400ms	2cm
infrared	beam	approx. 80cm	25ms	1cm
bumper	tactile	digital	1ms	

Table 3. Overview of the sensor systems mounted on ARTOS.

3 Control Software for Local Navigation

Distances measured by the sensor hardware are stored in data structures called sector maps. These sector maps are accessed by software behaviors that influence the robot's trajectory by slowing down or changing direction (see Fig. 3).

3.1 The Sector Map Representation

Each sector map can be seen as a virtual sensor. A sector is a part of the detection area of this virtual sensor. Each virtual sensor can be described and configured in a configuration file. Hence, the pose and the number of sectors and their attributes are generic. In case of the laser range finder the virtual sensor subtracts the distance between the sensor and the shape of the robot from the real measurement. In this way, the sector distances are the distances between the robot and the obstacle. The shape of the robot is also stored in the configuration file.

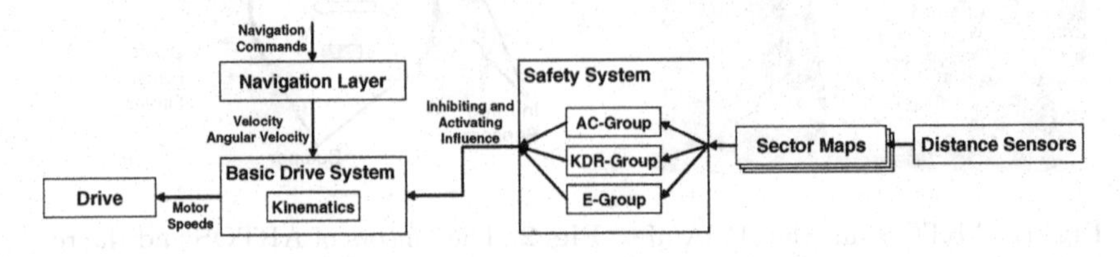

Fig. 3. Overview of the software architecture of ARTOS' control system.

Both groups of ultrasonic sensors are merged to one virtual sensor each. Each ultrasonic sensor contributes to a single sector of the ultrasonic sector map. Also the position and range information of the sectors is explicitly stored in the map. The angular detection area of the laser range finder is split into sectors of approx. 20°. One significant distance per sector is chosen as a representative of the nearest detected obstacle in this sector as there are more scan points than sectors. In case of the robot ARTOS, the laser range finder is defined as a virtual sensor with eleven equidistant sectors.

3.2 The Behaviour-Based Anti-Collision System

The next level of robot control uses the data in the sector map as primary sensor input. The collision avoidance system that follows a behaviour-based approach is explained in the next section. So it is possible to combine a group of ultrasonic sensors to one virtual distance sensor.

Following the approach of [4], a net of hierarchically organised behaviours influences the robot's trajectory whenever it comes too close to an obstacles[5]. The system consists of three types of safety behaviours which monitor different parts of the sector maps described in the previous section.

- *Anti-Collision* (AC)
- *Keep Distance Rotatory* (KDR)
- *Evasion* (E)

Anti-Collision monitors the sectors in front of the robot and reduces speed depending on the distance to the nearest obstacle.

Keep Distance Rotatory considers lateral sectors and avoids collisions between obstacles and the sides of the robot. Driving a curve or turning in place near an obstacle could also lead to a collision, as the robot has an oblong shape. The behavior inhibits the rotational movement towards the obstacle and initiates a rotation in the opposite direction.

Evasion turns the robot away from obstacles right in front of it. This is necessary as *Anti-Collision* would keep the robot from moving ahead and *Keep Distance Rotatory* would not turn as there is nothing in one of its monitored sectors.

Emergency Stop is another safety behaviour, but far simpler than the three main safety behaviours. It monitors the two bumpers and the four IR-sensors and exerts an inhibitory influence on the motion of the robot if sensor values enter a critical range.

Table 4 shows the distance values at which the main safety behaviours are fully activated or not activated at all, respectively. These values build the thresholds for the calculation of the strength of a safety behaviour's response to an obstacle at a distance d. Different kinds of functions are used therefor. One of them is given exemplarily in equation (1).

Behaviour	not activated at ($d_{\text{min act}}$)	fully activated at ($d_{\text{max act}}$)
Anti-Collision	500 mm	200 mm
Keep Distance Rot	300 mm	50 mm

Behaviour	activation at	deactivation at
Evasion	600 mm	750 mm

Table 4. Distance values for full and no activation of the main safety behaviours.

$$f_{\text{distance reaction}}(d) = \begin{cases} 1 & \text{if } d \leq d_{\text{max act}}, \\ 0 & \text{if } d \geq d_{\text{min act}}, \\ \frac{1}{2} - \frac{1}{2} \cdot \sin\left(\left(\frac{d - d_{\text{max act}}}{d_{\text{min act}} - d_{\text{max act}}} - \frac{1}{2}\right) \cdot \pi\right) & \text{else} \end{cases} \tag{1}$$

To make the anti-collision system easily extendable, a group of safety behaviours monitors only one sector map. For a new sensor system, which is represented by its sector map, one has to create a new instance of a safety behaviour and add it to the correct group. Additionally, different instances of the behaviours are created for different areas (front, back, left, right) around the robot. For example, there are two instances of *Keep Distance Rotatory* monitoring the left and right lateral areas of the sector map of the laser scanner.

4 Tests and Results

In this work we presented an architectural approach that starts at the well-selected set of sensor systems. We described the robot ARTOS and its hierarchical setup with data abstraction and behaviour-based collision prevention. Fig. 4 shows the activation of several safety behaviours while the robot comes close to an obstacle. The laser scanner that shows in forward direction influences the behaviour-based collision-avoidance to induce safe sidestepping. If obstacles come too close to the front or the sides of the system, speed is reduced to a reasonable amount according to the metric distance. Special behaviours for ambiguous situations are implemented that force a decision, for example when an obstacle is right in front of the robot. Our sector map is a powerful instrument for generic data abstraction of distance information. On one side the complexity of data is reduced, which allows clear decisions, on the other hand the important data regarding obstacle representatives in key areas is kept so that no information remains unconsidered.

Future work will consider the need for high-level navigational behaviours and action-selection components. The sensor systems will be extended for applications where the robot carries high-profile structures or goods.

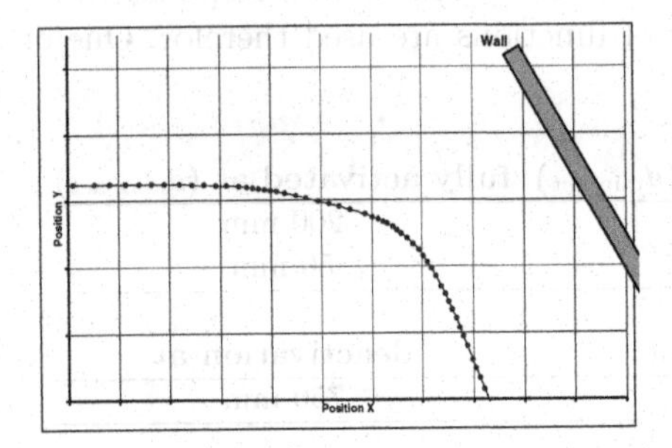

Fig. 4. The motion of the robot when approaching a wall at an angle of 60° (AC, KDR and E activated).

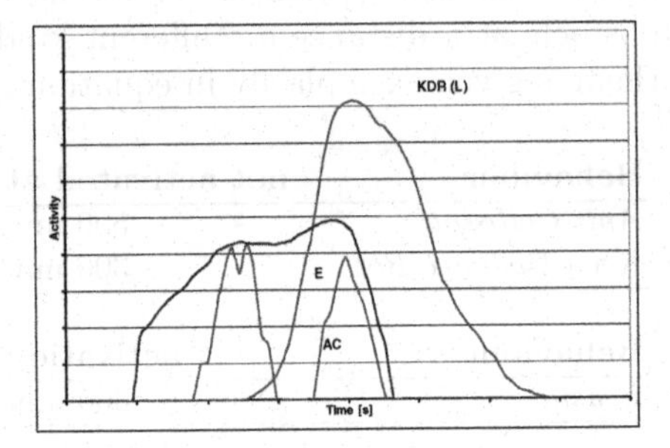

Fig. 5. The activities of AC, left KDR and E when approaching a wall at an angle of 60°.

5 Acknowledgements

We gratefully acknowledge the funding of the BelAmI project by the State Ministry of Science, Education, Research and Culture of Rhineland-Palatinate, by the Fraunhofer-Society and by the German Federal Ministry of Education and Research.

References

1. D. Fox, W. Burgard, and S. Thrun, "A hybrid collision avoidance method for mobile robots," in *IEEE International Conference of Robotics and Automation*, Leuven, Belgium, 1998.
2. K.-U. Scholl, J. Albiez, B. Gassmann, and J. Zöllner, "Mca - modular controller architecture," in *Robotik 2002, VDI-Bericht 1679*, 2002.
3. J. Koch, M. Anastasopoulos, and K. Berns, "Using the modular controller architecture (mca) in ambient assisted living," in *3rd IET International Conference on Intelligent Environments (IE07)*, Ulm, Germany, September 24-25 2007.
4. R. Arkin, *Behaviour-Based Robotics.* MIT Press, 1998.
5. C. Armbrust, "A behaviour-based drive and anti-collision system for an autonomous mobile robot," Project Thesis, University of Kaiserslautern, 2007, unpublished.

Autorenverzeichnis

Printing: Mercedes-Druck, Berlin
Binding: Stein+Lehmann, Berlin